ETHNOGRAPHIC INSIGHTS ON LATIN AMERICA AND THE CARIBBEAN

ETHNOGRAPHIC INSIGHTS *on* LATIN AMERICA *and the* CARIBBEAN

Edited by Melanie A. Medeiros and Jennifer R. Guzmán

UNIVERSITY OF TORONTO PRESS
Toronto Buffalo London

© University of Toronto Press 2023
Toronto Buffalo London
utorontopress.com
Printed in the USA

ISBN 978-1-4875-4798-1 (cloth)   ISBN 978-1-4875-5559-7 (EPUB)
ISBN 978-1-4875-5150-6 (paper)   ISBN 978-1-4875-5336-4 (PDF)

All rights reserved. The use of any part of this publication reproduced, transmitted in any form or by any means, electronic, mechanical, photocopying, recording, or otherwise, or stored in a retrieval system, without prior written consent of the publisher – or in the case of photocopying, a license from Access Copyright, the Canadian Copyright Licensing Agency – is an infringement of the copyright law.

Library and Archives Canada Cataloguing in Publication

Title: Ethnographic insights on Latin America and the Caribbean / edited by Melanie A. Medeiros and Jennifer R. Guzmán.
Names: Medeiros, Melanie A., editor. | Guzmán, Jennifer R., editor.
Description: Includes bibliographical references and index.
Identifiers: Canadiana (print) 20220480133 | Canadiana (ebook) 20220480206 | ISBN 9781487547981 (cloth) | ISBN 9781487551506 (paper) | ISBN 9781487553364 (PDF) | ISBN 9781487555597 (EPUB)
Subjects: LCSH: Ethnology – Latin America – Case studies. | LCSH: Ethnology – Caribbean Area – Case studies. | LCSH: Latin America – Social conditions – Case studies. | LCSH: Caribbean Area – Social conditions – Case studies. | LCGFT: Case studies.
Classification: LCC GN564.L29 E84 2023 | DDC 305.80098 – dc23

We welcome comments and suggestions regarding any aspect of our publications – please feel free to contact us at news@utorontopress.com or visit us at utorontopress.com.

Every effort has been made to contact copyright holders; in the event of an error or omission, please notify the publisher.

We wish to acknowledge the land on which the University of Toronto Press operates. This land is the traditional territory of the Wendat, the Anishnaabeg, the Haudenosaunee, the Métis, and the Mississaugas of the Credit First Nation.

University of Toronto Press acknowledges the financial support of the Government of Canada and the Ontario Arts Council, an agency of the Government of Ontario, for its publishing activities.

Contents

Introduction and Maps   1

Section One: An Introduction to Latin America and the Caribbean   11

1 Using Ethnography to Learn about Latin America and the Caribbean   15
   MELANIE A. MEDEIROS AND JENNIFER R. GUZMÁN

2 Old New World: An Archaeological Introduction to Latin America and the Caribbean   27
   JAMES J. AIMERS

3 Check Your Narratives: Essentials for Understanding Latin American and Caribbean History, 1400–Present   42
   RYAN M. JONES

Section Two: Race, Racialization, and Racism   67

4 Raciality and Belonging in Cuban Tourism   71
   L. KAIFA ROLAND

5 Protecting White Comfort and White Supremacy in Rio de Janeiro, Brazil   84
   JENNIFER ROTH-GORDON

6 The "Paradoxical" Persistence of Haitian Vodou after the Cholera Epidemic   95
   GUILBERLY LOUISSAINT

Section Three: Ethnicity, Citizenship, and Belonging   107

7   Language and the Emplacement of Indigenous Citizenship in Peru   111
    SANDHYA KRITTIKA NARAYANAN

8   Post-Multicultural Anxieties? Trajectories of Indigenous Citizenship in La Guajira, Colombia   123
    PABLO JARAMILLO

9   A Panamanian of West Indian Descent: An Autoethnographic Study of Citizenship and Belonging   134
    LAVERNE M. SEALES SOLEY

Section Four: Gender and Intersectionality   145

10 The Racial Politics of Queer, Urban, Second-Generation Indigenous Lima Locals   149
    DIEGO ARISPE-BAZÁN

11 Racialized Geographies and the "War on Drugs": Gender Violence, Militarization, and the Criminalization of Indigenous Women in Mexico   161
    ROSALVA AÍDA HERNÁNDEZ CASTILLO

12 After the Mosquito: Caring for Children with Congenital Zika Syndrome in Bahia, Brazil   173
    K. ELIZA WILLIAMSON

Section Five: Language in Society   185

13 Rap *Originario* and Language Revitalization in Southern Mexico: The ADN Maya Collective   189
    JOSEP CRU

14 Kreyòl in Cuba: Writing Resistance, Affirming Haitian Heritage   200
    MARIANA F. PAST

15 Linguistic Bias or a Chance to Get Ahead: Linguistic Repertoires in Aruban and Curaçaoan Schools   213
    KEISHA WIEL

Section Six: Politics and Power   225
KARLEEN JONES WEST

16 Congressional Candidates and Political Campaigns in Clientelist Systems: Condoms and Concrete in Oaxaca, Mexico   229
KARLEEN JONES WEST

17 NGOs as "Necessary Evils": Challenges of Doing Good in Urban Northeast Brazil   241
LUMINIȚA-ANDA MANDACHE

18 The Role of Masculinity in Connecting Knowledge and Politics: Pension Experts in Chile   252
MARIA J. AZOCAR

19 Indigenous Governance and Legal Pluralism: Constitutional Reform and Political Conflict in Bolivia   265
MATTHEW DOYLE

Section Seven: Political Violence and Its Legacies   279

20 Violence and the Ethnographic Turn in Contemporary Colombian Art   283
ANA GUGLIELMUCCI AND ESTEBAN ROZO

21 Film Reception and Audience Ethnography: Charting Local Imaginaries of Violence in Contemporary Argentina and Colombia   297
NICK MORGAN, PHILIPPA PAGE, AND CECILIA SOSA

22 Cementerio XXX: The *Desaparecidos* of "Post-Conflict" Guatemala   309
SARAH MAYA ROSEN

23 A Crack in the Wall: Ethnography as Solidarity with Indigenous Political Prisoners in Oaxaca, Mexico   320
BRUNO RENERO-HANNAN

Section Eight: Poverty, Precarity, and Resilience   333

24 Flipping the City: Space and Subjectivity in São Paulo, Brazil's Zona Sul Periphery   337
CHARLES H. KLEIN

25 Ties that Bind in the Dominican Republic: Buying Food on Credit in Corner Stores   349
CHRISTINE HIPPERT

26 "If It Wasn't for COVID, I Wouldn't Be Married": Disruption, Agency, and Making a Living in Chiapas, Mexico   360
KATIE NELSON

27 Music, Movements, and Maria: Narratives of Music in Post–Hurricane Maria Puerto Rico   371
MELISSA CAMBERO SCOTT

Section Nine: Development and Sustainability   383

28 Conceptions of Risk and Resettlement in Belenino River Communities in Peru   387
SHARON GORENSTEIN RIVERA

29 Forced Displacement and Indigenous Resettlement Planning in Colombia's Coal Region   399
EMMA BANKS

30 "*No a La Mina*": Indigenous Organizations' Rejection of Toxic Mega-Mining in Mexico's Isthmus of Tehuantepec   411
ALESSANDRO MOROSIN

Section Ten: Tourism and Its Effects   425

31 Structural Racism and Occupational Segregation in the Ecotourism Industry of Northeast Brazil   429
MELANIE A. MEDEIROS AND TIFFANY HENRIKSEN

32 Between the Edible and the Inedible: Cultural Tourism and Culinary Meaning in the Ecuadorian Amazon   441
SARAH RACHELLE RENKERT

33 Of Cash and Candy: The Complex Effects of Tourism on the Growth of Maya Children from Yucatán, Mexico   452
KRISTI J. KRUMRINE

Section Eleven: Migration and Kinship   465

34   Digital Solidarities, Transnational Families, and the Nicaraguan Refugee Crisis in Costa Rica   469
CAITLIN E. FOURATT

35   Love, Money, and a Secret Divorce: Patriarchy and Senior Women's Caregiving in Mexican Migration   483
NORA HAENN

36   "I Am Going without Knowing the History of My People": Young People's Engagement with the Past, Present, and Future in the Guatemalan Diaspora in Southern Mexico   496
MALTE GEMBUS

Conclusion   509

Text Credits   511

Index   513

Introduction and Maps

Learning about a region like Latin America and the Caribbean can be a daunting task. Where do you start? And how can you get a real sense of what life is like? Studying maps or reading news coming out of the region can help, but these bird's-eye views do not capture the life experiences, aspirations, difficulties, values, circumstances, or perspectives of the people who live there. To understand a region in that degree of detail, it is necessary to narrow your focus to see the specifics of what is going on in a particular place with particular people facing a particular issue. Studying a series of specific case studies together has the benefit of providing a broad view that takes in the scope and range of diverse realities that make up and characterize that region.

As ethnographers who have conducted research and taught about Latin America and the Caribbean, we hope that this volume will provide a resource for learning about the region following just such an approach. The chapters in this volume provide a collection of zoomed in and zoomed out views that show some of the many similarities and unifying features of the region as well as highlighting the incredible diversity of human experience that characterizes life across the many nations that make up Latin America and the Caribbean. This book brings together a collection of research that illustrates the dynamic ways people across these nations are confronting and responding to the most pressing contemporary problems facing the world today. It is our hope that these case studies resonate, inform, and inspire readers to learn more about – and more from – the people who make up this globally important region.

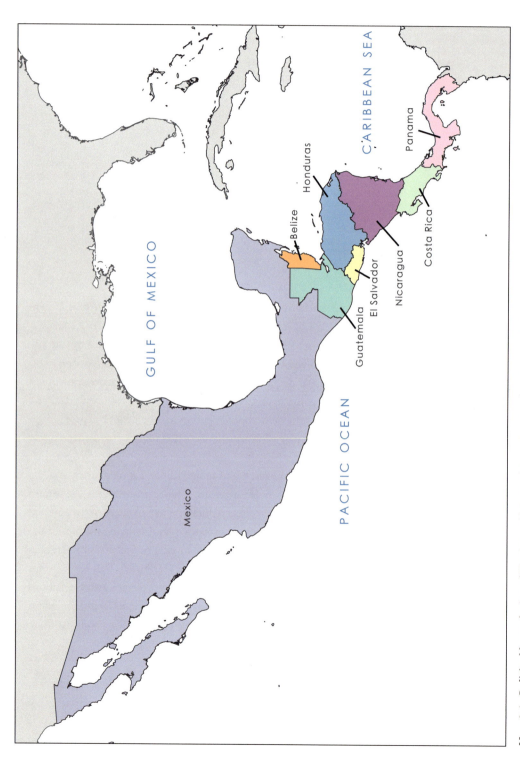

Map 0.1. **Political boundaries of Mexico and Central America.** Cartographer: Nykole E. Nevol.

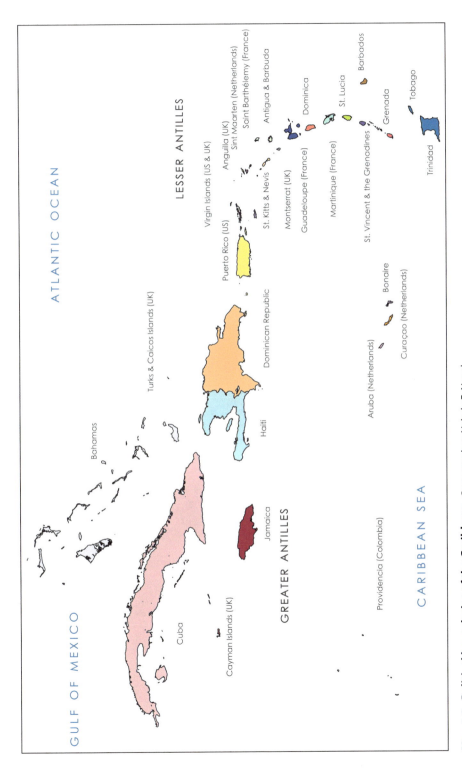

Map 0.2. Political boundaries of the Caribbean. Cartographer: Nykole E. Nevol.

Map 0.3. Political boundaries of South America. Cartographer: Nykole E. Nevol.

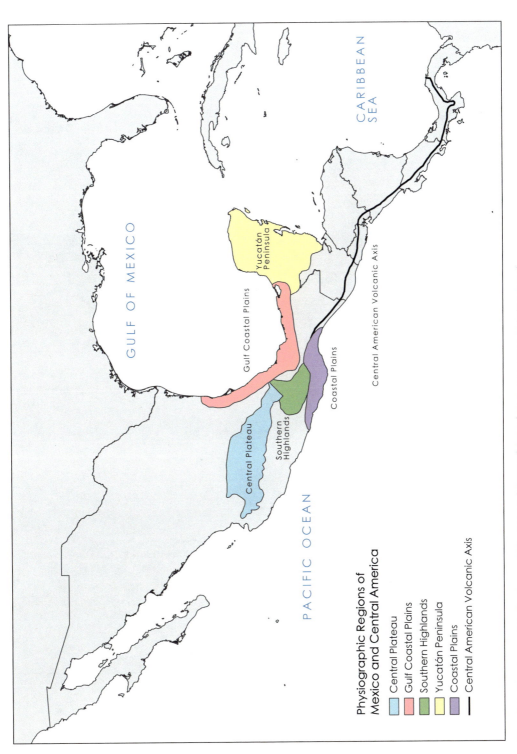

Map 0.4. **Physiographic Regions of Mexico and Central America.** Cartographer: Nykole E. Nevol.

Map 0.5. Physiographic Regions of South America. Cartographer: Nykole E. Nevol.

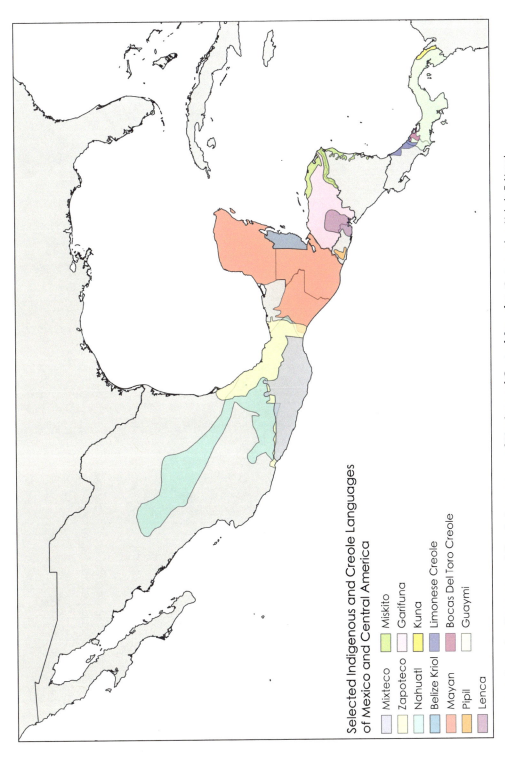

Map 0.6. Selected Indigenous and Creole Languages of Mexico and Central America. Cartographer: Nykole E. Nevol.

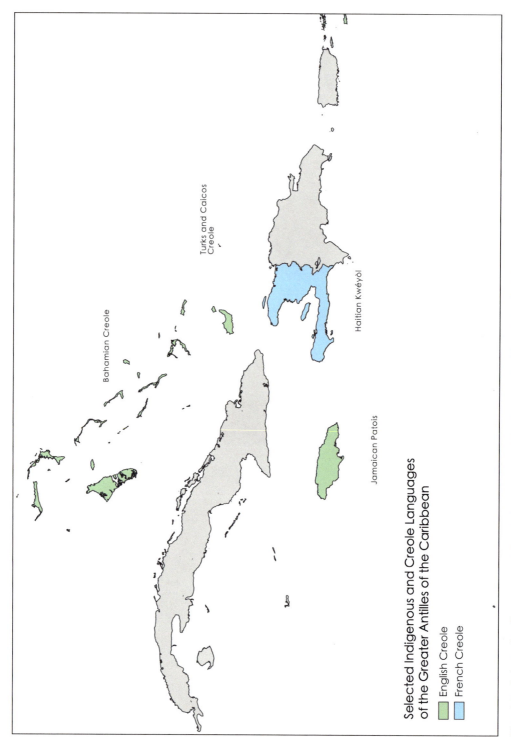

Map 0.7. Selected Indigenous and Creole Languages of the Greater Antilles of the Caribbean. Cartographer: Nykole E. Nevol.

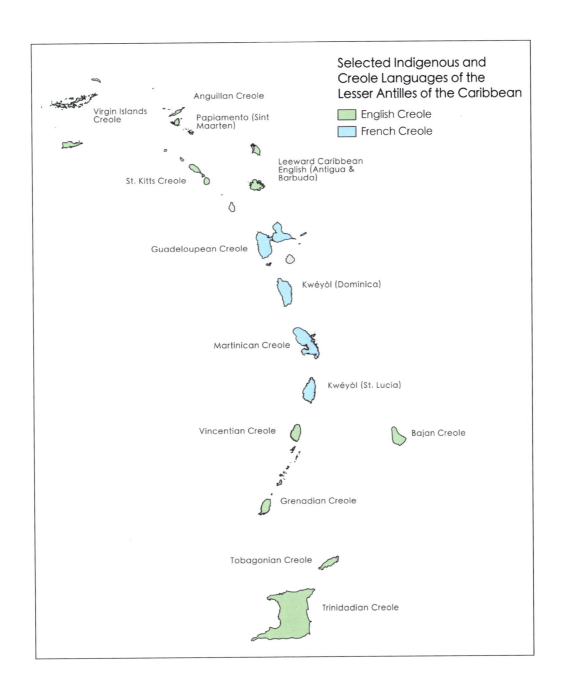

Map 0.8. Selected Indigenous and Creole Languages of the Lesser Antilles of the Caribbean.
Cartographer: Nykole E. Nevol.

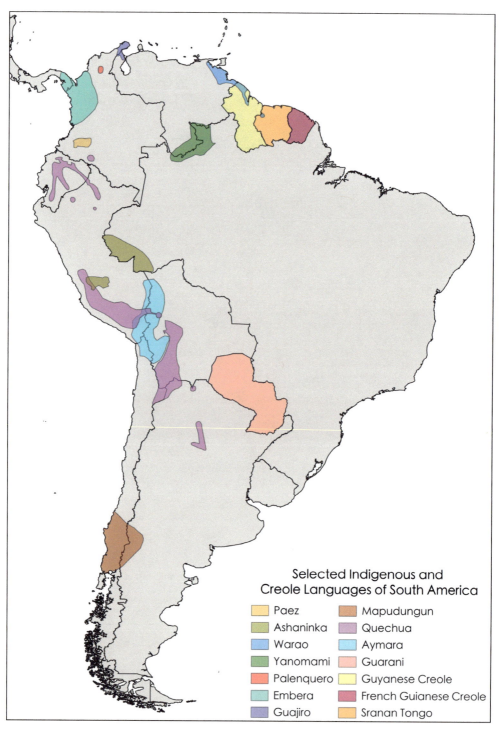

Map 0.9. Selected Indigenous and Creole Languages of South America. Cartographer: Nykole E. Nevol.

SECTION ONE

An Introduction to Latin America and the Caribbean

Comprising much of the Western Hemisphere, the countries of Latin America and the Caribbean span almost a half million square miles (CIESIN 2013) and have a combined population of close to 650 million people (United Nations 2019). People living throughout Latin America and the Caribbean reflect the region's immense geographic, environmental, linguistic, and cultural diversity. At the same time there are several shared historical processes that have shaped the region and that underpin the most pressing contemporary issues that people in the region are facing. Today, two decades into the twenty-first century, people living in Latin America and the Caribbean are confronting a host of social, economic, political, and ecological challenges and are doing so with ingenuity, drawing on deep cultural legacies and building new cultural innovations to problem solve. Some of the dynamic phenomena that are at play across the region include the following:

- *Identity and belonging*: Enduring and new ideas about citizenship, nationality, and ethnicity are under debate as people reconsider what group membership means and how privileges are differentially distributed according to hierarchies. Material consequences of these debates are significant, with some people framed as deserving and others as undeserving of rights, access, and resources.
- *Racialization*: The assignment of people to racialized identities continues to shore up, reinforce, and reinvent systems of privilege and oppression that have a long history in the region. Indigenous peoples, descendants of European settlers, descendants of enslaved Africans, and later waves of labor immigrants from Asia and the Middle East are viewed through the lenses of those historical legacies and are unequally affected by them.
- *Climate change and extractivism*: Accelerating pressures to capitalize on natural resources and grow national economies have led to wide-ranging development projects that include clear-cutting forests, the construction and operation of hydroelectric dams and

transportation infrastructure, mining, and fossil fuel extraction. As these initiatives damage the ecological systems on which people depend for their health and livelihoods, these projects have led to high-stakes confrontations and debates about sustainability and the unequal distribution of benefits and harms from the exploitation of natural and national resources.
- *Gender and sexuality*: Changing norms, laws, and practices surrounding gender and sexuality are opening new possibilities of human expression and relationships in some places, even while patterns of violence and repression continue to disproportionately affect women and those who identify as LGBTQ+.
- *Urbanization*: Residents of rapidly growing cities face increasing needs for housing, clean water, food, healthcare, and education. Along with these needs come associated problems of urbanization and industrialization: pollution, waste management, and risk of infectious diseases that policymakers and community members must grapple with.
- *Political economy*: The foundation of political economic systems across the region were laid during the periods of colonization and imperialism and more recently and radically altered by Cold War relations and the globalization of the economy, unleashing the mobility of capital and simultaneously regulating and constraining the mobility of people.
- *Art*: An abundance of artistic production in areas of music, dance, television, film, and theater depicts and critiques broken systems, on the one hand, and celebrates resiliency and creativity on the other. New emergent genres build on local traditions and global artistic phenomena.
- *Migration*: Both within and across national borders, increasing numbers of people are migrating in response to complex push and pull factors, including economic and labor pressures, political instability, violence, and climate change, much of which is attributable to the complex exploitative relations between the Global North and the Global South.

The three chapters in this section provide a foundation for reading chapters throughout the rest of the book. In Chapter 1, we introduce ethnography, the research method and written genre that is used by anthropologists and other social scientists who study social and cultural phenomena through long-term commitment, observation, and involvement in a particular place. In Chapter 2, Aimers lays out the contours of the long history of human residence across Latin America and the Caribbean, using evidence from the archaeological record to provide a description and timeline. In Chapter 3, Jones picks up the history of the region at the point of European invasion and extends it to the present. He challenges readers to consider how the history of Latin America and the Caribbean has been narrativized and often minimized and misrepresented in popular perception.

REFERENCES

Center for International Earth Science Information Network (CIESIN)/Columbia University. 2013. *Urban-Rural Population and Land Area Estimates Version 2*. Palisades, NY: NASA Socioeconomic Data and Applications Center (SEDAC).

United Nations Population Division. 2019. *World Population Prospects: 2019 Revision*.

CHAPTER ONE

Using Ethnography to Learn about Latin America and the Caribbean

Melanie A. Medeiros and Jennifer R. Guzmán

This book introduces contemporary life in Latin America and the Caribbean and is organized as a collection of ethnographic case studies. An ethnographic case study is a richly descriptive account that highlights a specific community; provides contextualization concerning history and power structures; and features the stories, actions, and perspectives of that group to illustrate how they make sense of and respond to their circumstances. This kind of writing has the advantage of showing in detail how specific people living in a particular place experience, interpret, reproduce, resist, and respond to macro-scale phenomena like displacement, poverty, racism, or climate change and the associated challenges that these issues pose in their everyday lives. A key advantage of case studies is that they aim for specificity rather than generalization, focusing on events that happened, what people did, and what they had to say about them considering the values, resources, traditions, and relationships that shape how matters play out. By looking at a case in detail, we can learn more about how power and change play out in the day-to-day lives of individuals while also examining how they are constitutive of phenomena in the larger scales of community, organization, neighborhood, city, district, state, nation, region, and world.

Ethnographic case studies are shaped by the research tradition of **ethnography**, a methodology that originated in anthropology but is now used by scholars across many social sciences. In this chapter we explain what ethnography is, what sorts of knowledge it can produce, and how ethnographers work when they are in the field and when they are writing. Ethnographic research includes both a means for studying a phenomenon or community – *fieldwork* – and a means for presenting the findings from that fieldwork – *ethnography*. We start this chapter with a discussion of fieldwork followed by a discussion of style in ethnographic writing. The last part of the chapter provides helpful tips for how to read and interpret the ethnographic case studies in this collection and how to look for connections across them. Drawing connections across cases is critical to understanding the contemporary struggles and innovative responses

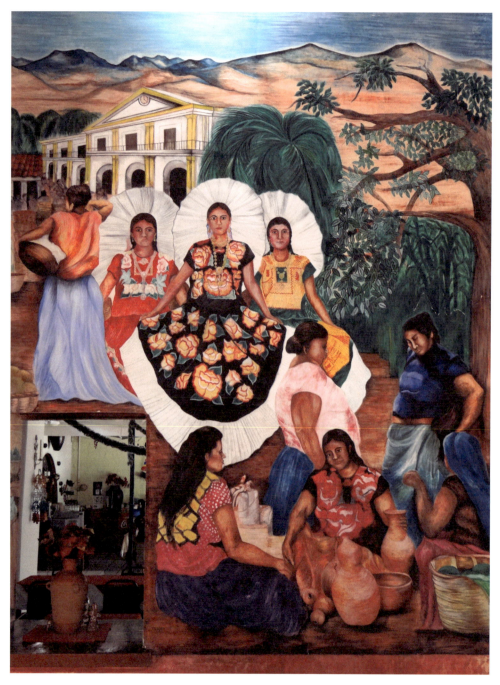

Figure 1.1. Mural of Zapotec Women in Scaru Bar-Restaurant, Tehuantepec, Isthmus Region, Oaxaca, Mexico. Photo by Adam Jones (CC BY 2.0).

that people are employing across Latin America and the Caribbean today, as well as the ways that these processes influence and are influenced by global events.

DOING ETHNOGRAPHY: AN INTRODUCTION TO ETHNOGRAPHIC RESEARCH

Ethnographic research is a form of descriptive, longitudinal research in which the researcher – called the ethnographer – involves themself in a community to gain first-hand insights on people's perspectives and experiences. Conventionally this has meant a year or more of fieldwork and dedicated language learning for ethnographers who are not members of the communities they study. However, these practices are changing, owing to both challenges and innovations in the twenty-first century. Some ethnographers today are crafting fieldwork arrangements that minimize travel, to reduce COVID-19 transmission risk and environmental harm, and that foreground collaborative work across distances, efforts that have been enabled by advances in communicative technologies.

Ethnographic fieldwork is driven by *research objectives*, a set of clearly defined goals – often framed as questions – that guide a researcher's investigation. Research objectives are informed by both theory and practical considerations. For example, a researcher who wants to understand how a new cross-cultural healthcare policy shapes people's health and well-being will create a set of research objectives that considers what other research has found about similar programs in other places and the particular history, public health profile, social structure, and concerns of the community where the program is being implemented. These considerations can ensure that the fieldwork to study the implementation is well informed and planned effectively.

Part of the fieldworker's goal is to gain an **emic** perspective – an understanding of issues that reflects how people in the community view those issues. The ethnographer subsequently analyzes what they learned, identifying specific occurrences, experiences, and events and unpacking the meanings that people give to them. In this step of the process, the ethnographer often seeks to craft a more **etic** interpretation of local issues, one that is shaped by social scientific theory and by the ethnographer's own interpretations from having participated in the community. In this sense, ethnographic research is a process of knowledge construction, where the ethnographer is the research instrument, and the ethnographer's learning process and interpretation is critical to drawing meaning out of the messiness of real life (Blommaert and Jie 2010).

Ethnographic research is longitudinal, meaning that it involves a long-term engagement by the ethnographer with the community and the issues they are interested in. Even prior to beginning fieldwork, ethnographers prepare by studying the historical, political, economic, social, cultural, and environmental context of the place and the issues where they will work. **Ethnographic fieldwork** involves living among and interacting with people at a field site, the place where an ethnographer conducts their research. An ethnographer's field site can be as small as an urban garden, a neighborhood graffiti-art collective, or a Bible study group or as large as the mega-city of Rio de Janeiro or the South American trade bloc organization Mercosur. For example, some ethnographers do research on how organizations function, and they do this by spending a lot of time within that organization, talking to and spending time with the people who work or volunteer there. Ethnographers who have a larger field site, like Quito, Ecuador, for example, will choose to focus on one group of people or one specific community living in that city. So, in other words, two key components of ethnographic fieldwork involve a clear sense of place – the *where* of fieldwork – and the *who* – the community of people who are in focus. Ethnographers who want to learn about communities that are mobile or that span geographical sites may opt to conduct **multi-sited ethnography**. Given the accelerating rates of migration that are occurring today, a multi-sited approach is increasingly common. You will see examples of this approach in Chapters 34 and 36. Finally, field sites can also include virtual worlds, such as interactive gaming communities or Facebook breast cancer support groups, where the ethnographer immerses themself in an online community.

The focus of research objectives has also changed over time. Ethnographic fieldwork approaches were originally developed in the first decades of the twentieth century by Western European and North American anthropologists. Most often these anthropologists were interested in documenting the cultures of Indigenous people in the Global South or in colonial or post-colonial settings. At the time, anthropological research objectives ostensibly focused on the documentation of **culture**. Contemporary ethnographers have moved away from studying culture as a static entity, in large part because this focus often aligned with and supported colonial objectives and projects. Early studies of culture frequently objectified "local" people and practices, construed them as exotic, and reified cultural hierarchies that implicitly rationalized colonialism and slavery. By contrast, ethnographers today most often focus their research questions and objectives on problems or issues facing a group of people in a certain setting to better understand these real issues. For example, rather than studying the diet and food customs of Mayan people in Mexico as isolated cultural traditions, contemporary ethnographers might study the ways that historical and social processes, including colonialism, political violence, and globalization, impact Mayan families' food security and food consumption. Another thing that has changed significantly is that it is no longer just Western Europeans and North Americans taking on the roles of ethnographer. There are ethnographers from all over the world studying people in their own countries or from other countries. Some ethnographers choose to study communities of which they themselves are members, an approach that allows them to use their lived expertise to gain insights. This approach, called **autoethnography**, moves away from early models of the ethnographer as a "professional stranger" (Agar 2008). Instead, autoethnographers draw on personal experiences to inform their understanding of a topic or issue (see Chapter 9 for an example).

Another recent emergence in ethnographic research is that it is more collaborative than in the past. Today many ethnographers work in partnership with community organizations to develop their research questions and objectives and to collect data, ensuring that the research conducted is of interest to the community and, when possible, helps to address community concerns or needs. This collaboration is often referred to as **engaged ethnography**. As a result of these collaborations, ethnographic research is moving away from a model in which research objectives are determined by the ethnographer alone and instead focuses on matters that the ethnographer *and* the community they are collaborating with find relevant and important. Several of the chapters in this volume put into practice the principles of engaged ethnography (see Chapters 11, 23, 29, and 36).

Methods

The methods used in ethnographic fieldwork can vary greatly depending on an ethnographer's *where*, *who*, and *what*. However, there are several qualities that are characteristic of most fieldwork. These include that fieldwork is personal, collaborative, hermeneutic (i.e., interpretive), and creative (Campbell and Lassiter 2014). Ethnographers spend extensive time with and talking to people in a community, getting involved in what goes on in daily life, and often helping in specific endeavors. These sorts of activities constitute the core of fieldwork and are referred to as participant observation. **Participant observation** involves participating in the day-to-day living of the people the ethnographer is studying, making observations, and asking questions when appropriate about what the ethnographer is observing. For example, an ethnographer studying language plurality in a Peruvian town might accompany research participants during a workday at the market, observing their conversations with customers and with other market vendors in several different languages (see Chapter 7). A key component of participant observation is the writing of **field notes**. Field notes document what happens – what the ethnographer is seeing, hearing, thinking, feeling, and even tasting and smelling in the process of participant observation.

Another method ethnographers use to gain an emic understanding of a group of people and the challenges they face is interviews. Ethnographers often use **key informant interviews** when they are embarking on a new study and need important introductory information. They may continue to contact their key informants throughout their research to ask further questions and clarify things they have observed. Another common form of interview used in ethnographic research is the **life history interview**. The life history interview method invites participants to recount the major events constituting the arc of their life and encourages participants to elaborate on their responses in great detail.

Photography, audio-recording, and videography are other important tools used in fieldwork. With these methods, ethnographers use technology both to document what they are seeing and hearing and as a means of engaging with their research participants. For example, some ethnographic studies employ the method of **photovoice**, providing research participants with cameras so they can document and reflect on their own lives in conversation with the ethnographer. Other ethnographers may use images in ethnographic interviews. For example, in Medeiros and colleagues' (2021) study on satirical political memes in Brazil, college students from three Brazilian cities were invited to view a selection of memes and explain their meaning and sociopolitical significance. In these interviews, the memes served as a useful resource for learning about these college students' perspectives on Brazilian politics.

Because ethnographic fieldwork requires intimate and long-term engagement with community members at a field site, it is a time-consuming and personally demanding approach that can require several years to complete. In addition, some research objectives cannot be answered with ethnographic approaches. For example, ethnographic fieldwork is not an effective way to gather "big number" data about phenomena like demographic patterns (e.g., the number of people in Belize who consider themselves to be of one ethnic background versus another). And because ethnographic methods focus on obtaining a deep understanding of issues in one place, findings are generally not amenable to identifying statistical correlations (e.g., a percentage increase or decrease of a given disease over time in a particular country). Because different research approaches are suited to providing different kinds of information, ethnographers sometimes cite statistics and other research findings from quantitative studies in their case studies. This background information serves to contextualize and complement the findings from their ethnographic fieldwork.

The Ethics of Ethnography

There are several ethical principles that guide ethnographers as they conduct their fieldwork, present their research to various audiences, and write up their findings. The specific definitions and understandings of these principles are dynamic and reflective of ongoing discussions among scholars. For example, the American Anthropological Association maintains a blog about ethics and periodically updates their statement on the principles guiding professional responsibility. The three most enduring and important ethical principles can be summarized as the ethnographer's commitments to do no harm, gain informed consent, and maintain anonymity and confidentiality.

Whenever an ethnographer seeks to obtain access at a field site and wishes to recruit people to participate in their research, they must obtain permission from institutional leaders and **informed consent** from potential participants. This ethical tenet requires that the ethnographer be frank and forthcoming about who they are, what their research interests and objectives are, and the methods they plan to use in the study. This process ensures that people are fully informed about the research, including understanding any benefits or risks that could result from participating, before they choose to be involved, for example by allowing an ethnographer to interview them or shadow them as they go about their day. Informed consent is an ongoing process, meaning that ethnographers must be communicative and available over the course of a study and respect a participant's wishes if they change their mind about participating.

Another significant ethical principle is to **do no harm**. This principle is especially important considering the historical legacy of early ethnographic research that rationalized colonial domination and bolstered inaccurate and harmful racial theories. Since the early decades of the twentieth century, ethnographers have criticized research that has the potential to harm the people who collaborate or participate in ethnographic research. The injunction to do no harm extends to research that could cause harm to an entire community, for example studies during the nineteenth century that provided a rationale for colonial control over local populations. And it includes research that might bring harm to individuals; for example, a study of people's opinions about a violent, authoritarian regime could potentially put research participants at risk of retribution from that government. Ethnographers must ensure that the communities with whom they conduct fieldwork will not be harmed during the research process or after the results are made public.

The ethical principle to do no harm is closely tied to the principle of maintaining the **anonymity** of the research participants. This includes ensuring that names or other identifying traits are not documented in the ethnographic writing that is a product of the research. Often ethnographers will assign a pseudonym to each research participant so that they can quote people or write about things that happened during fieldwork without revealing the participants' identities. Ensuring anonymity helps protect research participants and reduces the risk of harm that could come from people sharing their experiences and opinions with the researcher. Confidentiality entails protecting the safety of a researcher's data as an additional means for mitigating potential harm. In some cases, participants may prefer to have their real names used in publications because they want to be recognized as the source of important information (Campbell and Lassiter 2014; see also Chapter 19). In these cases, ethnographers must weigh the benefits and risks of disclosing identities alongside participants' preferences to reach the most ethical decision possible.

ETHNOGRAPHIC STYLE AND READING ETHNOGRAPHY

Ethnographic Style

Up until now we have been discussing ethnography as a field research approach; however, the term *ethnography* is also used to refer to the medium through which ethnographers share their research results. Most commonly, ethnographers publish their findings as a book, an article in an academic journal, or a chapter in a book like this one. These sorts of publications are

ethnographies or, when they are shorter, ethnographic case studies. The results of ethnographic research can also be presented in other forms, including ethnographic films.

Ultimately, ethnography is *interpretive* – it is not a mere statement of facts or a straightforward report of what happened, as this would not illuminate much. It would fail to convey the meaning and importance of the particular incidents that are written about or of a specific quote from an interview. Part of the ethnographer's responsibility is to help the reader understand the context of the events and people they write about and to convey how and why reported events and stories from people's lives matter. Ethnographers do so by drawing on the knowledge they gain from the experience of "being there" in the field – spending time and initially finding everything confusing and then getting involved, progressively noticing things and understanding more, asking questions, hearing stories, building relationships, taking and sharing pictures, making maps, documenting all the information they can find, collecting documents, filming, and continuously writing about the process of their own learning.

Some of the stylistic features that characterize ethnographic writing include the following. Watch for these features as you read the ethnographic case studies presented in this book:

- **Cultural relativism** is a practice of nonjudgment that comes from the ethnographer's understanding that any group or community's values, beliefs, and behavioral norms are a product of culture, history, environment, and political economic conditions, and these should not be measured in comparison to the values, beliefs, and norms of a different group. Recently, there has been a movement in ethnographic research toward **critical cultural relativism**, which is an approach that seeks to identify the ways that certain cultural beliefs and practices work alongside systems of privilege and oppression, benefiting some people and harming others. Critical cultural relativism works to identify power differentials that negatively affect some members of a community. Such power differentials, rather than the cultures themselves, are issues that ethnographers can ethically critique. For example, an ethnographer practicing critical cultural relativism might acknowledge that gender-based violence in a particular setting is a product of specific historical and political economic phenomena in that place while also presenting an evidence-based critique of the practice as harmful to women.
- **Thick description** is the use of vivid and detailed writing to portray the setting of the ethnographer's field site; specific events that occurred; and the knowledge, actions, and words of the people who were involved. This type of writing aims to show rather than tell readers what something is like. Because thick description presents a phenomenon in detail, it can help to reveal how apparently simple things often involve a lot of complexity.
- **Polyvocality** (poly = many, vocal = relating to the human voice) is the practice of having many different research participants' voices represented in ethnographic writing. This includes the use of direct quotes from a wide variety of research participants, many of whom may express directly opposing views. The goal of polyvocality is to allow the reader to

hear directly from community members themselves and, as a result, understand the plurality of perspectives that exist about a given issue. Importantly, the practice of polyvocality is also a corrective to the totalizing white male Western voice and gaze that characterized early ethnographic writing.

- **Reflexivity** describes the writing convention in which the ethnographer selectively discloses aspects of who they are as a person and a researcher to convey to readers the ways the ethnographer's various identities impacted their fieldwork experience, the questions they asked, people's responses, and even the ethnographer's analysis and interpretation of data. By writing reflexively, the ethnographer documents their own positionality with respect to the community and the phenomena they study. This practice acknowledges the impossibility of an objective perspective and instead leverages the knowledge-building potential of subjectivity; in every case, what the ethnographer sees, hears, writes about, and understands is necessarily influenced by who they are.

How to Read the Ethnographic Case Studies in This Book

If this is your first time reading ethnography, then you may feel uncertain about the best approach to take when reading the ethnographic case studies in this book. As for any other academic text, active reading is important. Taking notes, underlining or highlighting important stretches of text, writing down questions that arise as you read, and documenting observations that stood out to you are all strategies to help you read actively, understand what you have read, and retain the ideas from each chapter. Students often ask us, what should I underline or what should I take notes on? Here are some specific things to pay attention to when reading an ethnographic case study; after you finish reading, take the time to write down the answers to these questions in your notes:

- Who is the author (ethnographer)?
    - What do they tell you about themselves (nationality, gender, field of study, etc.)?
    - How have different aspects of the ethnographer's identity affected their fieldwork experience and their research results?
- Where was the ethnographer's field site? What place is highlighted in the chapter?
    - What are the most important things to know about this place, based on how the ethnographer described it? Consider geography/environment, social structures, and features of history, language, and culture.
- What were the research objectives that guided the ethnographer's fieldwork?
    - What phenomenon, problem, or process does the research illuminate?
    - What did you learn about this issue that is particular to this place? And how do the findings from research in this place potentially illuminate how this issue works on a broader scale or in comparison to other places?

- With whom did the ethnographer conduct their research? What is the community that is in focus?
    - Why did the ethnographer choose this community for their research?
    - What are some of the characteristics of the people they interviewed or with whom they conducted participant observation? For example, did the ethnographer focus on people of a particular gender, age, or profession? Why did they select that group of participants?
- What did the ethnographer discover? What were their main findings?
    - Try to write a one paragraph summary in your own words that synthesizes what the ethnographer learned through their research.
- What are the key concepts from the chapter, and what are their definitions?
    - Look at the list of key concepts at the conclusion of the chapter; make sure you understand the definition of each. Try to identify an example from the chapter that illustrates each concept.

Preceding the ethnographic case studies that make up most of this book, the next two chapters in the Section 1 provide critical historical information that will help you better understand the contemporary phenomena explored in later chapters. As you read Chapters 2 and 3, consider this question: How does learning about geography, archaeology, myths, and narratives of the past help us understand the present?

REFLECTION AND DISCUSSION QUESTIONS

- What characteristics make ethnographic research different from other types of research?
- What are some of the strengths of using ethnographic research to study contemporary life in Latin America and the Caribbean?
- What ethical principles must ethnographers follow when conducting fieldwork and when writing ethnography?
- What are the defining features of ethnographic writing?

KEY CONCEPTS

- **anonymity**: An ethical principle that ensures that participants' names or other identifying traits are not documented in the ethnographic writing that is a product of the research.
- **autoethnography**: An approach that draws on personal experiences to inform the ethnographer's understanding of a topic or issue.

- **critical cultural relativism**: An approach that seeks to identify the ways that certain cultural beliefs and practices work alongside systems of privilege and oppression, benefiting some people and harming others.
- **cultural relativism**: A practice of nonjudgment that comes from the ethnographer's understanding that any group or community's values, beliefs, and behavioral norms are a product of culture, history, environment, and political economic conditions, and these should not be measured in comparison to the values, beliefs, and norms of a different group.
- **culture**: The beliefs, values, norms, traditions, and institutions of a group of people.
- **do no harm**: An ethical tenet in which ethnographers must ensure that the communities they conduct fieldwork with will not be harmed during the research process or after the results are made public.
- **emic**: An understanding of issues that reflects how people in the community view those issues.
- **engaged ethnography**: A research approach that prioritizes working in partnership with community organizations to develop research questions and objectives and to collect data. This approach ensures that the research that is conducted is of interest to the community and, when possible, helps to address community concerns or needs.
- **ethnographic fieldwork**: Living among and interacting with people at a field site, the place where an ethnographer conducts their research.
- **ethnographic research**: A form of descriptive, longitudinal research in which the researcher – called the ethnographer – involves themself in a community to gain firsthand insights into people's perspectives and experiences.
- **ethnography**: The medium through which ethnographers share their research results; most commonly books, an article in an academic journal, or a chapter in a book.
- **etic**: An interpretation of local issues that is shaped by social scientific theory and by the ethnographer's own interpretations from having participated in the community.
- **field notes**: The ethnographer's detailed daily notes on what they are observing and doing during fieldwork.
- **informed consent**: An ethical tenet requiring that the ethnographer be frank and forthcoming about who they are, what their research interests and objectives are, and the methods they plan to use in the study.
- **key informant interviews**: Interviews conducted with community leaders or people with advanced understanding of the issues facing the community.
- **life history interviews**: Interviews in which the ethnographer asks open-ended questions that encourage research participants to narrate their life experiences from early childhood to the present day and to elaborate on key events and memories in detail.
- **multi-sited ethnography**: An approach that involves doing fieldwork in more than one location to document life across the places where members of a given community reside or migrate.

- **participant observation**: Participating in the daily lives of the people the ethnographer is studying, making observations, and asking questions when appropriate about what the ethnographer is observing.
- **photovoice**: A method in which research participants are given cameras to record significant places, people, or moments in their lives and asked to write about or discuss their photos with the ethnographer.
- **polyvocality**: The practice of having many different research participants' voices represented in ethnographic writing.
- **reflexivity**: The writing convention in which the ethnographer selectively discloses aspects of who they are as a person and a researcher to convey to readers the ways the ethnographer's various identities impacted their fieldwork experience, the questions they asked, people's responses, and even the ethnographer's analysis and interpretation of data.
- **thick description**: The use of vivid and detailed writing to portray the setting of the ethnographer's field site; specific events that occurred; and the knowledge, actions, and words of the people who were involved.

EXPLORE FURTHER

- American Anthropological Association. "Statement on Ethics: Principles of Professional Responsibility." https://ethics.americananthro.org/category/statement.
- Bejarano, Carolina Alonso, Lucia López Juárez, Mirian A. Mijangos García, and Daniel M. Goldstein. 2019. *Decolonizing Ethnography: Undocumented Immigrants and New Directions in Social Science*. Durham, NC: Duke University Press.
- Mannik, Lynda, and Karen McGarry. 2017. *Practicing Ethnography: A Student Guide to Method and Methodology*. Toronto: University of Toronto Press.

REFERENCES

Agar, Michael. 2008. *The Professional Stranger: An Informal Introduction to Ethnography*, 2nd ed. Bingley, UK: Emerald Publishing.

Blommaert, Jan, and Dong Jie. 2010. *Ethnographic Fieldwork: A Beginner's Guide*. Bristol, UK: Multilingual Matters.

Campbell, Elizabeth, and Luke Eric Lassiter. 2014. *Doing Ethnography Today: Theories, Methods, Exercises*. New York: Wiley-Blackwell.

Medeiros, Melanie A., Patrick McCormick, Erika Schmitt, and James Kale. 2021. "*Barbie e Ken Cidadãos de Bem*: Memes and Political Participation among College Students in Brazil." In *Precarious Democracy: Ethnographies of Hope, Despair, and Resistance in Brazil*, edited by Benjamin Junge, Alvaro Jarrin, Lucia Cantero, and Sean T. Mitchell, 218–31. New Brunswick, NJ: Rutgers University Press.

CHAPTER TWO

Old New World: An Archaeological Introduction to Latin America and the Caribbean

James J. Aimers

The past is never dead. It's not even past.

William Faulkner (1951)

This chapter is a brief overview of the archaeology of Latin America and the Caribbean from the initial peopling of the Americas to the start of the colonial period. Although there is no doubt that colonial powers fundamentally transformed Latin America and the Caribbean, it is also true that a basic familiarity with the region's Indigenous cultures is valuable for a fuller understanding of the people there today. Throughout this short review I provide suggestions for more detailed sources, and I suggest some general ones at the end.

NOTES ON TERMINOLOGY

In archaeology, dates are written in several ways. The abbreviation BC ("Before Christ") or BCE ("Before Common Era") refers to the number of years before the birth of Christ. In the discussion below, you will also see BP ("Before Present"). This term was coined in the 1950s, so "present" is taken to be 1950. Thus, 4000 years BP is about 2052 BC (or BCE), although most archaeologists just add 2000 years to BC dates since 50-year increments are rarely important (or even detectable) in archaeology. AD is an abbreviation for "Anno Domini." In this case, years are counted forward from the birth of Christ. In archaeology, AD is often replaced by the term CE, which refers to "Common Era." Periods are sometimes used in these terms (i.e., AD or A.D.). In this discussion I follow the format of the source I'm using (e.g., BC versus BP).

I also use the terms *prehistory* and *prehistoric* in this chapter. These terms are generally used to describe periods of human history without written records. The history/prehistory distinction also distinguishes the work of historians from that of archaeologists, but the distinction has less meaning in cultures that are studied archaeologically but have writing systems (e.g., the ancient Maya). The term *prehistory* is not meant to imply that people without writing did not have histories. Prehistoric cultures are those whose histories were not written or that are studied using predominantly archaeological techniques (i.e., interpretations rely mostly on artifacts and other forms of **material culture**, such as pottery and stone tools).

Finally, *New World* is often used to describe the Western Hemisphere (North, Central, and South America and neighboring islands). The term was coined by Europeans in the sixteenth century but is still used in part because, as I describe below, human presence in the Western Hemisphere occurred much later than in the *Old World*. A glossary of other archaeological terms can be found at https://tinyurl.com/Archaeology-Glossary.

GEOGRAPHICAL AND ENVIRONMENTAL VARIATION

Latin America includes the area between northern Mexico and the southernmost tip of South America (Tierra del Fuego, split between Chile and Argentina). The Caribbean includes the islands and coasts in and around the Caribbean Sea, extending about 4,000 kilometers (1,860 miles) from the mouth of the Orinoco River in Venezuela to Florida and the Yucatán. The eastern edge of the Caribbean is defined by three major island groupings: the Lesser Antilles, the Greater Antilles, and the Bahamas (Ross et al. 2020). Considered together, Latin America and the Caribbean encompass spectacular geographical and environmental variability, including some of the world's highest mountains, richest coastal environments, largest rivers, driest deserts, and most expansive tropical forests. South America has all 28 types of climates used in the Köppen-Geiger climate classification system, and the tropical Andes alone "are the most biodiverse region on earth" (Moore 2014, 37).

Archaeologists have divided up this giant area in a variety of ways and have given three areas unique archaeological names that differ from geographical ones like "Central America" (Map 2.1). Mesoamerica is the archaeological term for an area defined by prehistoric cultures that shared several pre-contact cultural characteristics, including maize agriculture, a shared calendrical system, and urbanism (Creamer 1987). Mesoamerica includes most of present-day Mexico, Guatemala, Belize, and parts of El Salvador, Nicaragua, and Costa Rica. The Central Andes is defined archaeologically as the area occupied by the Inca (or Inka) empire at its peak, including Peru and parts of Ecuador, Bolivia, Argentina, Chile, and Colombia. Archaeologists call the area between Mesoamerica and the Central Andes the Intermediate Area. This somewhat poorly defined and relatively understudied area includes parts of Honduras and most of the territory of Nicaragua, Costa Rica, Panama, Colombia, Venezuela, and Ecuador. Standard geographical terms are used for other areas (e.g., the Amazon basin, the Caribbean).

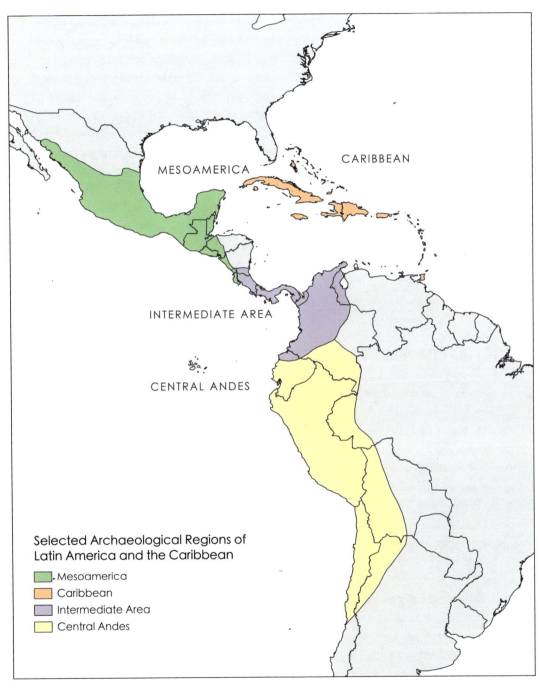

Map 2.1. A map of the archaeological regions of Latin America and the Caribbean that are discussed in this chapter. Cartographer: Nykole E. Nevol.

As is the case elsewhere, the natural environment presents both challenges and opportunities for human occupation. Coastal areas offer abundant aquatic resources while tropical forests support copious animal and plant life. A variety of cultural adaptations, like irrigation and terracing, allowed humans to live in all but the driest deserts and highest mountains. A notable pattern is that many of the most complex cultures in the New World were not associated with the most optimal environments. Complexity is measured archaeologically by things like site hierarchies (e.g., villages, towns, and cities), **social stratification** indicated in variation in burial goods and architecture, and economic specialization in the production and exchange of goods. Some of the earliest settlements in the New World are in the rich environment of coastal Ecuador, but these societies never developed the complexity that societies in less favorable locations did. For example, Maya civilization developed in tropical forests that were deficient in key resources like salt and obsidian. The archaeological explanation is that a lack of specific resources in a given area encouraged trade and interaction, and this is correlated with increased social complexity (e.g., to build and maintain irrigation projects in areas with inadequate rainfall). Interaction and increasing complexity are correlated with a range of phenomena, including the growth of population centers from small hamlets to cities and increased social stratification.

THE FIRST PEOPLES OF LATIN AMERICA AND THE CARIBBEAN

In 1589, the Jesuit missionary José de Acosta speculated that Latin America's earliest Indigenous peoples were hunters from Asia (Siberia) – an idea that now has near universal support among scholars (Fagan 1991, 56). The details, however, are still unclear. Did these settlers move across the Bering Strait (a strait across the Pacific and Arctic oceans from the Chukchi Peninsula of Russia to Alaska's Seward Peninsula) on foot, in boats along the coasts, or both? Did they come in one wave, or many? The most animated debates have been about when exactly they arrived in the **Pleistocene** (aka the Ice Age, ca. 2,580,000 to 11,700 BP). For decades researchers believed that movement south from Alaska could have only happened when there was an ice-free corridor around 13,000 years ago (this is part of what is called the "Clovis hypothesis," a name derived from a type of stone point used for big game hunting), but we now have a number of much earlier dates: "Archaeological excavations in Chiquihuite Cave in northern Mexico by Ardelean and colleagues provide evidence of human occupation about 26,500 years ago. This Mexican site now joins half a dozen other documented archaeological sites in northeast and central Brazil that have yielded evidence suggesting dates for human occupation between 20,000 and 30,000 years ago" (Gruhn 2020, 47). The rapid spread of people from North to South America suggests that boats were involved in at least some of this movement.

The islands of the Caribbean were settled gradually and significantly later than the Latin American mainland, but the dating of Caribbean settlement and the geographical source of the settlers has been debated. Fortunately, new genetic research is helping to answer these questions.

Two recent studies (Fernandes, Sirak, and Ringbauer 2020; Nägele et al. 2020) suggest that **foraging** people arrived in canoes from coastal Central or South America in the so-called Lithic Age, as early as 8000 BP, probably settling first in Cuba. Similarities in stone tools in Belize and Cuba also suggest that their origin included Central America. During the subsequent Archaic Age people spread to other Caribbean islands. Much later, around 2500 BP, a second group of pottery-making farmers related to the Arawak speakers of northeast South America arrived, probably from coastal Venezuela. These people settled in what is now Puerto Rico and then moved westward through the islands of the Caribbean where their remains are considered evidence of what is called a Ceramic Age.

This new genetic evidence has other interesting implications. For example, Ceramic Age people appear to have almost completely replaced original populations, suggesting that violence or the spread of disease may have been involved. Another finding of Fernandes, Sirak, and Ringbauer (2020) is that different pottery styles of the Ceramic Age – often used by Caribbean archaeologists as evidence of the arrival of new groups of people over time – are now likely to have been stylistic innovations by the same people. Finally, their study suggests that the contact-era population of two of the Caribbean's largest islands (Hispaniola and Puerto Rico) may have numbered as few as 10,000 to 50,000 people – much fewer than the million described by Columbus or the 250,000 to 1 million suggested in some recent scholarship (Gershon 2020).

VARIATION IN PREHISTORIC LIFEWAYS THROUGH SPACE AND TIME

Issues of timing and origins aside, we have good evidence of how early New World peoples made a living. For decades, archaeologists believed that Pleistocene people were focused on hunting megafauna (large game), but we now see a broader range of opportunistic foraging strategies adapted to varied local environments (Roosevelt et al. 1999; Moore 2014, 79). After the Pleistocene, the **Holocene** (ca. 11,700 BP to present) climate got warmer and wetter and big game declined (at least in part because of human hunting), so people concentrated more on plants. Shellfish middens (middens are garbage deposits) found at coastal sites and other evidence shows that early people used marine resources as well. Increased use of plants led gradually to domestication, which allowed people to settle seasonally or permanently in various places. **Domestication** was a gradual and not necessarily intentional process (Moore 2014, 102–6), and its appearance varied in time, from about 11,000 BP in South America (Quilter 2014, 92; Moore 2014, 137, 150) to 9000 BP in Mesoamerica (Coe, Urcid, and Koontz 2019, 26–30), to about 2500 BP in the Caribbean (Pagán-Jiménez 2013, 392) with the arrival of South American people and their domesticates.

Important domesticated food plants in Latin America and the Caribbean include squash, manioc, a variety of beans and chilies, and, above all, maize and potatoes (for reviews of pre-Columbian foods, see Staller 2021; Staller and Carrasco 2010). The increased yields provided by

horticulture and later **agriculture** led to larger populations in ever-larger settlements. Villages emerged in the Andes by 6000–4000 BC (Quilter 2014, 73), by about 1900 BC in Mesoamerica (Evans 2013, 100), and as early as the end of the Archaic Age in the Caribbean (ca. 800–200 BC) (Keegan and Hofman 2017, 49, 59).

Compared to the Old World, in ancient Latin America there were few wild animals that could be easily domesticated, so relatively few were. In Mesoamerica, these included dogs (which were used in hunting, as pets, and as an important food source), turkeys, and the Muscovy duck. In South America, important domesticated animals include the llama, alpaca, and guinea pig (still a ritually important food). The most important Caribbean domesticated animals were brought by settlers from Central and South America (see LeFebvre and DeFrance 2018).

Settled people with surplus resources could engage in trade, which is in turn linked to social stratification. In some areas, elites came to convince others that their power was divinely ordained. Although it is tempting to think of a tidy narrative in which relatively egalitarian hunter-gatherers developed over time into agriculturalists in ever-more complex and stratified societies, this was not the case everywhere in Latin America and the Caribbean. Varied **adaptive strategies** related to gathering, hunting, fishing, herding, and horticulture/agriculture were, and still are, found across Latin America and the Caribbean. For example, people on Caribbean islands have a long history of combining crop production with hunting, fishing, and shellfish collecting. Foragers were most common in marginal environments, such as the driest parts of northeastern Mexico (Taylor 1972) and in the high Andes of Chile (Cornejo and Sanhueza 2011), but foragers were also present in the more comfortable environment of western Cuba until about AD 900 (Lawler 2020). Further complicating the picture, some of the first groups that Europeans encountered in the New World were semisedentary societies in the Caribbean, and foragers and sedentary people also coexisted in various regions (e.g., in highland Chile around AD 1000). As ever, people adapt to the opportunities and limitations of their local environment.

The presence of pottery is generally associated with settled life and was probably developed independently in several regions. Currently, the earliest known pottery is from an Amazonian fishing village dating to 8000–7000 BP (Moore 2014, 203). Prior to these finds, the earliest known pottery was dated to about 5000 BC at the well-studied Valdivia culture on the Pacific coast of Ecuador (Moore 2014, 183–7). Early pottery in Mesoamerica dates to about 3600 BP, with most archaeologists comfortable with origins to the south (Coe, Urcid, and Koontz 2019, 34). The appearance of pottery in the Caribbean dates to about 2600 BC (Keegan and Hofman 2017, 44).

Other important technologies include textiles and metallurgy. Textiles are known as early as 12,800 BP in the Andes (Jolie et al. 2011), but poor preservation makes it difficult to determine when textiles appeared in Amazonia, Mesoamerica, or the Caribbean. Metalwork emerges in the Andes around 4000 BP (Quilter 2014, 107) but is not particularly common until after 800 AD in western Mexico and after 1200 AD in the Caribbean (Martinón-Torres et al. 2012).

WHAT'S IN A NAME?

Archaeologists sometimes know what prehistoric groups called themselves (e.g., the Zapotecs of Mexico), but we often lack written records or descendants who identify with archaeological remains. In these cases, archaeologists create new names for groups of artifacts (especially pottery and lithics) that are distinctive to a particular time and place and are thought to express distinct ancient cultural identities. So, archaeologists recognize that the Moche of Peru had a recognizable art style and distinctive cultural and religious traditions, but we don't actually know what these people called themselves.

That naming is not a trivial issue is most clear in the Caribbean, where a variety of names have been used for various "archaeological cultures," but the degree of independence or interrelatedness of these groups is not entirely clear. Older studies tend to refer to just three major groups in the prehistoric Caribbean (the Ciboney, Arawaks, and Caribs), but more recent archaeology is challenging and refining this simplistic view by adding new cultural names based on artifacts (Reid and Gilmore 2014, xvii). For example, the name "Taino" is traditionally used to describe Arawak speakers at the time of European contact, but the name "is currently under heavy scrutiny because the term often masks the diversity of peoples and cultures that inhabited the islands at the time of contact" (Reid et al. 2014, 8). Further complicating things is that new excavations often reveal that these archaeologically designated cultures began earlier or persisted longer than thought, or they overlapped. My point here is that names we use to designate prehistoric peoples are under near constant re-evaluation, and thus the archaeological literature can be confusing as it is (hopefully) refined over time.

The archaeology of the Caribbean is particularly complex because of the diversity of cultures in the area, frequent movements of people, and the variety of names that have been used in the classification of those peoples and the periods in which they lived. In their excellent book *The Caribbean before Columbus*, Keegan and Hofman (2017, 21) admit that the situation is "chaotic" but with an underlying order provided by groupings of material culture that are thought to be the stylistic expressions of different Caribbean cultures across space and through time. What is clear is that the Caribbean was settled by people from South America and probably Central America, and that after settlement there was plenty of contact among people of the coasts and islands of the Caribbean. As with the rest of Latin America, we must recognize that cultural diversity, interaction, and change long preceded European contact.

SOCIOPOLITICAL ORGANIZATION

In terms of sociopolitical organization, Latin American and Caribbean societies at the time of the first European incursions can be characterized as bands, tribes, chiefdoms, or states. This typology was developed by Elman Service in 1962 and has since been criticized as overly simplistic (e.g., Kang 2005), but it is still used because, like all typologies, it provides a useful starting point for comparison.

Bands are small (rarely larger than about 100 people), mobile, relatively egalitarian groups that were characteristic of human life everywhere before the advent of domestication. For example, early occupants of the Amazon basin had "a broad-spectrum economy of humid tropical forest and riverine foraging" (Roosevelt et al. 1999, 373). In the prehistoric New World, foraging bands are best known from what is called the Desert tradition (ca. 75,000 BC to 2000 BC). Mobile bands are characteristic of the earliest people in the New World, and few groups who made their living exclusively through hunting-gathering existed in Latin America and the Caribbean in later prehistory. Today, these groups have been absorbed into modern Latin American nation-states.

Tribes can comprise up to a few thousand people and are typically associated with horticulture or pastoralism (herding), but opportunistic foraging and fishing are also common. Members of tribes identify beyond their kin (e.g., with their village), and because these groups are larger, they have clear leaders. Nevertheless, power structures are still relatively egalitarian, consensus based, and not inherited. Leaders are often chosen based on personal qualities like charisma, and leadership changes frequently. Tribal politics and religion are often closely related, for example in the institution of the shaman, a part-time religious specialist who also has important leadership roles. The prehistoric horticultural Saladoid people of the Caribbean and the contact-era Island-Carib societies of the Windward Islands are examples (Reid et al. 2014, 5, 9). The Yanomamo of the Amazon region of Brazil and Venezuela are probably the best-known recent tribal people of Latin America.

Chiefdoms are a sort of middle category between tribe and state. These socially stratified societies could include thousands of people. Subsistence strategies varied, but agriculture was typical of chiefdoms. Chieftainship was hereditary and institutionalized, and the chief of one village had some measure of control over other villages in the chiefdom. Paramount leaders could be women or men and were often in charge of both ritual and the redistribution of food and other resources (Torres and Reid 2014, 101). The Intermediate Area is perhaps best known for several "highly developed chiefdom societies" (Frost and Quilter 2012, 231), as is the Caribbean (e.g., Taíno), but chiefdoms were also found across South America and varied greatly in terms of size and degree of centralization of power (Villamarin and Villamarin 1999).

State-level societies are those with clearly defined boundaries and a central government that controls a legal system and monopolizes the use of physical force. States typically have official religions and recognizable state art styles. Bureaucratic roles in states exist separate from the individuals who hold them at any given time (e.g., the office of the paramount ruler outlives the people who occupied it at any given time). States often coexist with bands, tribes, and chiefdoms (Villamarin and Villamarin 1999, 583). I discuss some prominent states below.

Many state-level societies are referred to as *civilizations*. Civilization is "not one of the basic societal types … but rather, is a set of features that accompany the more complex types, the ranked chiefdom and especially the stratified state" (Evans 2013, 140). Characteristics of civilizations include food surpluses, three-tiered settlement patterns (e.g., villages, towns, and cities), differential access to resources, occupational specialization, formal political institutions, writing/math, monumentality, calendrics, state religions, and state art styles. Cities and writing are often considered key elements of civilizations, but not all civilizations have them. For example, the Inca built one of the largest empires in history without writing (although they could record things using a now poorly understood recording system of knots on strings called the *quipu*), and the dispersed nature of Maya "garden cities" is quite different from the denser urbanism of many other parts of the world. Because the term *civilization* is vague and variably defined, and there is frequently debate about which states are appropriately described with this term (e.g., the Olmec in Mesoamerica and the Moche in the Andes), I simply refer to *states* in this chapter.

PRE-EUROPEAN STATES OF LATIN AMERICA

There were two core areas for the development of states in Latin America and the Caribbean before European invasion: Mesoamerica and the Central Andes. By the time of European contact, both regions had long histories of sociopolitical and economic complexity, including numerous state-level societies. This degree of complexity was not found in the Intermediate Area nor the Caribbean beyond the Caribbean coast of Mesoamerica, although both areas were home to complex chiefdoms.

The Olmec of the Gulf Coast region of Mexico are generally considered the earliest state in Mesoamerica, although there is some debate about whether they may have been an advanced chiefdom or "incipient" state. Whatever one calls the Olmec, they were no doubt highly complex by at least 1200 BC when the major site of La Venta had large pyramids around monumental courtyards, large residential structures usually called palaces, stone ball courts, and monumental stone art (including their famous carved heads weighing up to 50 tons). Perhaps more indicative of a state is the extent of Olmec influence across Mesoamerica at this early time, as indicated by Olmec objects and iconography found hundreds of kilometers away (e.g., in El Salvador).

Mesoamerica after the Olmec was home to diverse state-level cultures, including the Maya, Teotihuacan (a city-state), Zapotecs, Mixtecs, Toltecs, Tarascans, and Aztecs (the best current review is Evans 2013). Although they all shared some general Mesoamerican characteristics, such as maize agriculture and a distinctively Mesoamerican calendrical system, each also had their own languages, political systems, and religious beliefs. When the Spanish arrived in Mesoamerica, the two most important state-level societies were the Aztecs and the Maya.

Maya settlements were evident by about 1000 BC, but the Maya Classic Period peak is normally dated to about 300–900 AD, after which many sites in their central area were abandoned. Although this is often called a collapse, many sites were not abandoned (Aimers 2007), and when the Spanish made contact with a Maya trading canoe in 1502 the Maya lived in villages, towns, and small cities run by hereditary elites. Although the Maya fought the Spanish at times (most famously in the Caste War of Yucatán, AD 1847–1901) one of their main strategies was avoidance. As for the Spanish, their immediate interest in the early colonial period was not the Maya region but the area occupied by the Aztecs to the west and, somewhat later, the Inca and other groups in South America.

The Aztecs rose from one of many immigrant groups in Central Mexico in the 1200s AD to a massive, militaristic empire. Aztec state religion demanded blood sacrifice from virtually everyone and provided a useful rationale for the capture of adjacent people and territory. The other motivation for Aztec imperialism is the same as other empires: resources from conquered peoples. Even now there are groups of people who speak versions of the Aztec language (Nahautl) as far away as El Salvador, showing the reach of Aztec trade and migration. Aztec imperialism meant that when the Spanish arrived the Aztecs were surrounded by people who resented them, and the Spanish effectively exploited this in their alliances with Indigenous groups in Central Mexico. This, along with European weapons and diseases like smallpox, helps explain the downfall of this mighty empire in about two years (1519–1521 AD).

In the Andes, the site and culture known as Chavin emerged around 900 BC and is usually taken to indicate the first complex sociopolitical formation with extensive regional influence in the Andes. Military imagery is absent from Chavin, but religious imagery abounds, and the site is usually considered a pilgrimage site with widespread influence.

Other major Andean cultures include the Moche, Sican, Nazca, Huari, and Tiahuanaco (for reviews, see Moore 2014; Quilter 2014). The Inca empire was the last of the Andean states before European contact, and there are significant parallels to the Aztec case. The Inca also rose rapidly from one of several competing local groups to create an empire extending 5,500 kilometers (3,400 miles) north to south, including parts of ancient Colombia, Ecuador, Peru, Chile, Bolivia, and Argentina. The empire included about 10 million people who spoke more than 30 languages (Cartwright 2014). As with the Aztecs, Indigenous enemies and introduced diseases played key roles in their defeat by the Spanish in 1532.

ETHNOCENTRIC AND PRESENTIST VIEWS OF THE PAST

As Restall and Lane (2011, 3) note, in the colonial era, "the overwhelming European tendency was to view natives as a single, inferior people," and this ethnocentric view has not changed all that much in popular views of the archaeology of Latin America and the Caribbean. For example, there is a tendency to assume that pre-Columbian cultures were more violent than cultures today (particularly because of the dark appeal of human sacrifice to contemporary eyes). Archaeology and ethnohistory are challenging this view, showing, for example, that the use of violence in cultures like the Aztecs and Inca was culturally modulated and highly controlled. So, the famously violent Aztecs were disgusted by the indiscriminate use of violence by the Spanish on the battlefield and elsewhere because the Aztecs themselves closely defined when, how, and by whom violence could be used (e.g., through rules of war and a legal system arguably more advanced than contemporaneous European ones). Death by sacrifice was honorable to many pre-Columbian peoples, just as death in war is honorable to many contemporary people, but random violence was probably rare in these highly organized systems.

Similarly, it is easy to take a "presentist" view of the past, in which we assume things that are normal to us would be normal to pre-Columbian people. This can be dangerous when their past is used to justify our present. For example, we may try to normalize the extreme economic inequality of contemporary capitalism with a discussion of the phenomenal wealth of the Inca emperor versus his subjects, but we know that the success of the empire rested in part on a system of roads and storehouses that allowed leaders to feed distant members of the empire in times of need. We can also attempt to lend historical credibility to contemporary war and invasion with well-documented examples of Inca imperial cruelty. If we force the Inca into categories we recognize, we can portray them as benevolent socialists or brutal fascists when in fact the archaeology suggests something in between, or both (Quilter 2014, 273).

The most striking set of presentist attitudes center on social issues like hierarchy, gender, and sexuality. **Gender complementarity** is the idea that men and women fulfill separate but important roles in society; gender complementarity in archaeology is seen as an alternative to gender hierarchy, in which men's activities are valued more than women's. The out-of-date image of the earliest settlers as megafauna-focused hunters foregrounds the role of hunting (associated with men), downplays the role of gathering (associated with women), and the idea of "man the hunter" is routinely evoked in popular discussions of male aggression and violence (see Sussman 1999). Taken-for-granted assumptions about the naturalness of male power and dominance are challenged by warrior women among the Moche and Maya and the importance of gender complementarity in the Andes. A supposedly natural gender dichotomy is challenged by third-gender people among pre-Columbian cultures and the dual-gendered nature of many pre-Columbian gods. The assumption that same-sex sexual behavior was despised in the past (an idea most clearly tied to colonial attitudes) is belied by the institutionalized role of *xochichua*, male assistants and sexual partners to Aztec warriors (for more pre-Columbian examples, see Aimers 2020).

CONCLUSION

As I have indicated above, the archaeological diversity of the pre-contact cultures of Latin American and the Caribbean make it difficult to draw general conclusions. This contrasts with popular views, which tend to underestimate the sophistication of pre-Columbian cultures while assuming they were all similar. Rigorous archaeological research in this huge area is less than 200 years old and has been unevenly focused on some areas (e.g., the Maya, Aztec, and

Inca regions) while others are much less known (e.g., the Amazon basin). Similarly, we understand the period just before European contact much better than earlier periods. Nevertheless, the slow but steady work of archaeologists, art historians, and others is gradually adding depth and texture to what we know about this giant region in the past.

REFLECTION AND DISCUSSION QUESTIONS

- The band/tribe/chiefdom/state typology classifies and defines levels of sociopolitical complexity. How does it help us to understand why or how complexity develops?
- Consider various aspects of human life, like social structure, economics, religion, gender/sexuality, politics, kinship, art, and so on. Which aspects of Indigenous life do you think changed the most after the European invasion? Which do you think changed the least?
- Discuss examples of presentism you have encountered in the media or in your personal life. Why are presentist arguments so common?

KEY CONCEPTS

- **adaptive strategies**: The ways that humans adapt to the natural environment, especially how food is acquired.
- **agriculture**: Intensive domesticated plant production that may include draft animals, irrigation, terracing, fertilizers, and so on.
- **domestication**: "The process by which changes in the morphology or genetics of plants and animals occur as a result of human interventions, often by artificially selecting species that have certain qualities" (Moore 2014, 132).
- **foraging**: Hunting and gathering; foragers acquire most of their food from the natural environment rather than through plant and animal domestication.
- **gender complementarity**: The idea that men and women fulfill separate but important roles in society. Transgender and nonbinary people participated in these systems.
- **Holocene**: A period dating from 11,700 BP to the present and represents a warmer period than the preceding Pleistocene or "Ice Age" (Quilter 2014, 56).
- **horticulture**: Sometimes called gardening, refers to domesticated plant production that is less intensive than agriculture (e.g., uses simple tools).
- **material culture**: Any physical thing made or used by humans.
- **Pleistocene**: Also called the Ice Age, the era from 2,580,000 to 11,700 BP.
- **social stratification**: The organization of human society into hierarchically ranked groups (e.g., castes, classes).

EXPLORE FURTHER

- BBC. 2002. *The Lost Pyramids of Caral*.
- Evans, Susan Toby. 2013. *Ancient Mexico and Central America: Archaeology and Culture History*. 3rd ed. New York: Thames and Hudson.
- Keegan, William F., and Corinne L. Hofman. 2017. *The Caribbean before Columbus*. New York: Oxford University Press.
- Moore, Jerry D. 2014. *A Prehistory of South America: Ancient Cultural Diversity on the Least Known Continent*. Boulder: University Press of Colorado.

ABOUT THE AUTHOR

James J. Aimers is an archaeologist and a professor of anthropology at the State University of New York at Geneseo. His research has focused on the ancient Maya, especially pottery, architecture, and the Maya "collapse" era. Aimers's other research interests include the study of art and gender/sexuality from prehistory to the present.

REFERENCES

Aimers, James J. 2007. "What Maya Collapse? Terminal Classic Variation in the Maya Lowlands." *Journal of Archaeological Research* 15: 329–77. https://doi.org/10.1007/s10814-007-9015-x.

———. 2020. "Queer New World: Challenging Heteronormativity in Archaeology." In *An Open Invitation to LGBTQ Studies*, edited by Deborah Amory and Sean Massey. Geneseo, NY: State University of New York OER Services. https://courses.lumenlearning.com/suny-lgbtq-studies/chapter/introduction-3.

Cartwright, Mark. 2014. "Inca Civilization." In *World History Encyclopedia*. https://www.worldhistory.org/Inca_Civilization.

Coe, Michael D., Javier Urcid, and Rex Koontz. 2019. *Mexico: From the Olmecs to the Aztecs*. 8th ed. New York: Thames and Hudson.

Cornejo B., Luis E., and Lorena Sanhueza R. 2011. "North and South: Hunter-Gatherer Communities in the Andes Mountains and Central Chile." *Latin American Antiquity* 22 (4): 487–504. https://doi.org/10.7183/1045-6635.22.4.487.

Creamer, Winifred. 1987. "Mesoamerica as a Concept: An Archaeological View from Central America." *Latin American Research Review* 22 (1): 35–62.

Evans, Susan Toby. 2013. *Ancient Mexico and Central America: Archaeology and Culture History*. 3rd ed. New York: Thames and Hudson.

Fagan, Brian M. 1991. *Kingdoms of Gold, Kingdoms of Jade: The Americas before Columbus*. London: Thames and Hudson.

Fernandes, D.M., K.A. Sirak, and H. Ringbauer. 2020. "A Genetic History of the Pre-contact Caribbean." *Nature* 590: 103–10. https://doi.org/10.1038/s41586-020-03053-2.

Frost, R. Jeffrey, and Jeffrey Quilter. 2012. "Monumental Architecture and Social Complexity in the Intermediate Area." In *Early New World Monumentality*, edited by Richard L. Burger and Robert M. Rosenswig, 231–52. Tallahassee: University Press of Florida.

Gershon, Livia. 2020. "What Ancient DNA Reveals about the First People to Populate the Caribbean." *Smithsonian Magazine*. https://www.smithsonianmag.com/smart-news/dna-study-shows-caribbean-was-populated-two-waves-180976646.

Gruhn, Ruth. 2020. "Evidence Grows for Early Peopling of the Americas." *Nature* 584: 47–8. https://doi.org/10.1038/d41586-020-02137-3..

Jolie, Edward A., Thomas F. Lynch, Phil R. Geib, and J. M. Adovasio. 2011. "Cordage, Textiles, and the Late Pleistocene Peopling of the Andes." *Current Anthropology* 52 (2): 285. https://doi.org/10.1086/659336.

Kang, Bong Won. 2005. "An Examination of an Intermediate Sociopolitical Evolutionary Type between Chiefdom and State." *Arctic Anthropology* 42 (2): 22–35. https://doi.org/10.1353/arc.2011.0004.

Keegan, William F., and Corinne L. Hofman. 2017. *The Caribbean before Columbus*. New York: Oxford University Press.

Lawler, Andrew. 2020. "Invaders Nearly Wiped Out Caribbean's First People Long before Spanish Came, DNA Reveals." *National Geographic*. https://www.nationalgeographic.com/history/article/invaders-nearly-wiped-out-caribbeans-first-people-long-before-spanish-came-dna-reveals.

LeFebvre, Michelle J., and Susan D. DeFrance. 2018. "Animal Management and Domestication in the Realm of Ceramic Age Farming." In *The Archaeology of Caribbean and Circum-Caribbean Farmers (6000 BC–AD 1500)*, edited by Basil A. Reid, 149–70. New York: Routledge.

Martinón-Torres, Marcos, Roberto Valcárcel Rojas, Juanita Sáenz Samper, and María Filomena Guerra. 2012. "Metallic Encounters in Cuba: The Technology, Exchange and Meaning of Metals before and after Columbus." *Journal of Anthropological Archaeology* 31 (4): 439–54. https://doi.org/10.1016/j.jaa.2012.03.006.

Moore, Jerry D. 2014. *A Prehistory of South America: Ancient Cultural Diversity on the Least Known Continent*. Boulder: University Press of Colorado.

Nägele, Kathrin, Cosimo Posth, Miren Iraeta Orbegozo, Yadira Chinique de Armas, Silvia Teresita Hernández Godoy, Ulises M. González Herrera, Maria A. Nieves-Colón, et al. 2020. "Genomic Insights into the Early Peopling of the Caribbean." *Science* 369 (6502): 456–60. https://doi.org/10.1126/science.aba8697.

Pagán-Jiménez, Jaime R. 2013. "Human–Plant Dynamics in the Precolonial Antilles: A Synthetic Update." In *The Oxford Handbook of Caribbean Archaeology*, edited by William F. Keegan, Corinne L. Hofman, and Reniel Rodriguez Ramos, 391–406. New York: Oxford University Press.

Quilter, Jeffrey. 2014. *The Ancient Central Andes*. New York: Routledge.

Reid, Basil A., and R. Grant Gilmore, eds. 2014. *Encyclopedia of Caribbean Archaeology*. Gainesville: University Press of Florida.

Reid, Basil A., Corinne L. Hofman, R. Grant Gilmore III, and Douglas V. Armstrong. 2014. "Introduction: Caribbean Prehistoric and Historical Archaeology." In *Encyclopedia of Caribbean Archaeology*, edited by Basil A. Reid and R. Grant Gilmore III, 1–30. Gainesville: University Press of Florida.

Restall, Matthew, and Kris Lane. 2011. *Latin American in Colonial Times*. New York: Cambridge University Press.

Roosevelt, Anna Curtenius, M. Lima da Costa, C. Lopes Machado, N. Mercier, M. Michab, H. Valladas, J. Feathers, et al. 1999. "Paleoindian Cave Dwellers in the Amazon: The Peopling of the Americas." *Science* 272 (5260): 373–84. https://doi.org/10.1126/science.272.5260.373.

Ross, Ann H., William F. Keegan, Michael P. Pateman, and Colleen B. Young. 2020. "Faces Divulge the Origins of Caribbean Prehistoric Inhabitants." *Scientific Reports* 10 (147). https://doi.org/10.1038/s41598-019-56929-3.

Staller, John E., ed. 2021. *Andean Foodways: Pre-Columbian, Colonial, and Contemporary Food and Culture.* New York: Springer.

Staller, John E., and Michael D. Carrasco. 2010. "Pre-Columbian Foodways in Mesoamerica." In *Pre-Columbian Foodways in Mesoamerica: Interdisciplinary Approaches to Food, Culture, and Markets in Ancient Mesoamerica*, edited by John E. Staller and Michael Carrasco, 1–20. New York: Springer.

Sussman, Robert W. 1999. "The Myth of Man the Hunter, Man the Killer and the Evolution of Human Morality." *Zygon: Journal of Religion and Science* 34 (3): 453–71. https://doi.org/10.1111/0591-2385.00226.

Taylor, Walter W. 1972. "The Hunter-Gatherer Nomads of Northern Mexico: A Comparison of the Archival and Archaeological Records." *World Archaeology* 4 (2): 167–78. https://doi.org/10.1080/00438243.1972.9979530.

Torres, Joshua M., and Basil A. Reid. 2014. "Chiefdoms (Cacicazgos)." In *Encyclopedia of Caribbean Archaeology*, edited by Basil A. Reid, 100–2. Gainesville: University Press of Florida.

Villamarin, Juan, and Judith Villamarin. 1999. "Chiefdoms: The Prevalence and Persistence of 'Senores Naturales' 1400 to European Conquest." In *The Cambridge History of the Native Peoples of the Americas*, edited by Frank Salomon and Stuart B. Schwartz, 577–667. Cambridge: Cambridge University Press.

CHAPTER THREE

Check Your Narratives: Essentials for Understanding Latin American and Caribbean History, 1400–Present

Ryan M. Jones

Some of the most consequential events in history have occurred in Latin America and the Caribbean.¹ Yet many may be surprised to hear this, because world historical narratives often minimize the region (Seigel 2004). Beyond certain moments – Columbus's arrival in 1492, the Conquest, the Mexican Revolution, the Cuban Missile Crisis – "history" supposedly happened elsewhere. As US diplomat Henry Kissinger told Gabriel Valdés, Chile's foreign minister in 1969:

HK: "History has never been produced in the South."
GV: "Mr. Kissinger, you know nothing of the South."
HK: "No, and I don't care." (Hersh 1982)

Similarly, in 1971 President Richard Nixon quipped, "Latin America doesn't matter … people don't give one damn about Latin America" (Fukuyama 2007, 177). Were they right? It may not be immediately obvious, but what these men offered was an *interpretation* of history. They provided a *narrative* that said some places matter – where "real" history happens – and some places do not. Their viewpoint was a product of five centuries in which the "West" (Western Europe, the United States) and the "North" (the United States, Western Europe, Japan, China, Russia) came to dominate the world. In that view, the "South" – the developing world, including Africa, much of Asia, Latin America, and the Caribbean – mattered less.

But narratives can be checked – that is, questioned, challenged, investigated, and reconsidered. Doing so is important because while Latin America and the Caribbean have been long recognized for having valuable commodities, their peoples have been regarded as lacking

---

1 Thanks to Anne MacPherson, Justin Behrend, Ryan Bean, David Tamarin, the editors, and the reviewers for incisive comments that improved this chapter.

historical agency – that is, their actions are not seen as consequential. Yet looking at historical evidence, a better argument is that the region's essential roles have been "silenced" or made "unthinkable," as historian Michel-Rolph Trouillot (1995) put it. Some histories are distorted by how people want to remember the past, while others are perceived as dangerous because they challenge preferred narratives and politics. Consider the Haitian Revolution (1791–1804). Responding to nearly two centuries of brutal colonialism based on enslaving Africans and influenced by ideas of liberty and equality also present in the American and French Revolutions, this revolution overturned French imperial rule. More importantly, it was the first slave rebellion that resulted in an independent nation. Because it dramatically changed the socioeconomic and political order that enshrined white power over enslaved Africans, it was more radical than the American Revolution, which left slavery intact (Knight 2000, 103). Yet the idea that enslaved Africans could assert power and rule effectively – and that Europeans were not inherently superior – was unthinkable to the era's powers. Europe and the United States embargoed Haiti. Then, in exchange for recognizing Haiti's independence, France demanded payment for its loss of "property" (including the slaves). This indemnity – comparable to billions in today's US dollars – left Haiti economically devastated, indebted to foreign banks, and poor ever since. Haiti mattered so much that it was purposefully ruined and its critical history silenced. It has since been unfairly seen as an exemplary case of how Latin American and Caribbean nations are incapable of prospering or ruling themselves. Even so, Haiti's example, if unacknowledged, proved influential. Within years, Britain and France abolished their slave trade, and in subsequent decades, abolition gradually won across the Americas (Knight 2000, 114–15).

Latin American and Caribbean history is replete with similar cases. This chapter aims to help you think about and through that history critically. It explores examples useful for understanding this volume's other chapters. It argues that the region, like Haiti, matters – historically and to our present world. I invite you to think like a historian, not simply view "History" as a static repository of facts free from human interpretation. Because we can do an online search at will, it is tempting to believe that all knowledge is accessible. Yet no archive, library, or database is complete; humans (and algorithms) choose what to remember, silence, and emphasize. Thus, it is essential to understand that every historical narrative or claim is someone's interpretation. But as new evidence is found and ideas are debated, historians revise and reinterpret the past – they "check their narratives," questioning what they know as "true," what subjects need attention or to be emphasized, and whose voices have been silenced. I invite you to do the same as you unpack the challenging issues raised below.

While it is impossible to cover the region's history comprehensively in a single chapter, and generalizations are unavoidable, I examine several important historical arguments about Latin America and the Caribbean, as well as how they have been "checked" or revised with alternatives. I limit my focus to nations sharing histories of Spanish, Portuguese, and French (aka "Latin") colonialization. As such, "Latin America" below includes mainland countries, the Spanish Caribbean, and Haiti. Throughout, I have italicized important terms.

CHECKING NARRATIVES: PERIODIZATIONS AND INTERPRETATIONS

Historians study *change* and *continuity over time*; we organize history into *periods* that are relational and that reflect interpretations of which changes matter. For Latin America, traditional periods include pre-Columbian (before 1492), the Colonial/Early Modern Era (ca. 1453/1492–1821), and the Modern Era (1821–present). Historians further divide these into the Conquest (of major Indigenous civilizations, 1492–1536) and Habsburg (1516–1700) and Bourbon (1700s–1821) eras, named for ruling imperial families; the National Period (nineteenth century) when Latin Americans forged independent nations; the twentieth century (including the World Wars and Cold War era); and the Contemporary Period (since the 1990s). There are also thematic periods: the Baroque era, Ages of Discovery and Liberty, and the Enlightenment.

Periods are useful, even necessary, but they are interpretations, not facts. Those above prioritize traditional forms of power (e.g., governments) as significant and universalize European experiences as global experiences rather than reflecting the perspectives of most people in the region. Consider that in 1492, the Mexica (Aztecs), Inca empire, and post-classic Mayan cities were *contemporaries* of Tudor England, Ming China, the Ottoman Empire, the Holy Roman Empire, and the Golden Horde. Their societies straddled a period of worldwide change: the end of the Reconquista; Constantinople's fall; the Mali Empire's decline; the rise of Russia; Japan's warlord period; and the founding of global, seaborne empires by Castille and Portugal. This means that these were not ancient civilizations. Nor were they primitive. Tenochtitlán, the Mexica capital, was one of the world's largest cities (just as Mexico City, its sequel, is now). Conquistador Hernán Cortés and his men marveled at the grand city built on islands in Lake Texcoco and ringed by floating gardens. As one remarked: "These great towns and temples and buildings rising from the water, all made of stone, seemed like an enchanted vision …" (Díaz 1963, 214–15). To the south, the Inca built an enormous empire with monumental architecture and extensive roads – all without money, wheels, or writing, supposed requirements for "civilization." Highly organized rulers demanded labor (the *mit'a*) but provided security and food during crises and recorded information through an ingenious system of knotted cords, the *quipu*. But this sophistication is silenced in traditional periodization. Because they lacked large-scale animal domestication, guns, disease resistance, and steel, Indigenous civilizations have been seen as inferior to their contemporary civilizations. This is a narrative we can check – it suggests the Conquest was inevitable. Opposing views suggest the Conquest was a contested, incomplete process. So which was it? How would we know?

Historian Camilla Townsend argues there are two ways of understanding the past: (1) It is either fundamentally different and "unknowably remote" because we remain trapped in our presentist worldviews; or (2) it is different, but some fundamental human experiences are shared and similar to our own (Townsend 2019, 212). "History" is not static: What we know, value, or emphasize changes over time. Thus historians collect evidence, then make interpretations (i.e., *historiography*) of what mattered. Histories are *arguments* based on evidence, not straightforward, encyclopedic accounts of incontestable facts, wars, dates, and "great men." The best histories offer clear evidence from many sources. In sum: How do historians check a narrative or an interpretation? We look at evidence and historiography. We consider alternatives.

This may not be how you learned "History" – and it can be unnerving to think that our understanding of the past is interpretive rather than factual. That's because interpreting the past is a way of deriving meaning from it. Understandably, people regard certain interpretations as "true." Here's an example: One of the world's most influential maps has been Flemish cartographer Gerardus Mercator's 1569 world map. Often found in classrooms even today, it presents an interpretation so familiar that it is assumed to depict the world *as it is*: The North is "up," the South is "down." The map made navigating oceans easier but distorted the world through a Eurocentric lens: Europe (and Mercator's home in Flanders) is centered, while the Northern Hemisphere looms over everything else. Europe dwarfs South America, which is in fact nearly twice its size. Mexico appears smaller than Alaska, when it is larger. Northerners have grown accustomed to seeing themselves as "above," and perhaps more significant than, "others" abroad. Yet there is no "up" or "down" on a sphere or in celestial space. As such, Uruguayan artist Joaquín Torres García's *América Invertida* (1943) offered an alternative interpretation: South America is "inverted" and "up"; Uruguay, not Flanders, is centered (Figure 3.1). Torres reminds us that maps are interpretative representations of what matters; by "inverting" the world, he asks us to rethink what we believe to be true.

"LATIN" AMERICA

Like these maps, the term "Latin America" is an interpretation. Who is part of it? Does it begin at the Rio Grande? Chicago's Pilsen neighborhood? Patagonia? Does it include the Caribbean? Historically, "Latin America" as a concept has multiple definitions: geographic, cultural, ideological. South Americans used the phrase first; later, the French used it to justify their nineteenth-century interventions in Latin America and to emphasize ideas of order, tradition, and local autonomy. Embracing "Latin" identity was relational. Proponents laid claim to certain foundations of Western civilization – Ancient Rome, democracy, and Christianity – and emphasized "Latin" similarities in social and spiritual cultures, shared hierarchies, paternalism, patriarchy, Catholicism, and Romance languages. As such, Latin America was defined against the "America" led by the United States and its "Anglo-Saxon," Protestant, individualist culture and belief in rationalism (Tenorio-Trillo 2020).

Another part of defining "Latin America" is through historical interpretation. Here's one of the most pervasive narratives describing the region: *Latin America has been trapped in a cycle for 500 years in which they've done civilization "wrong."* This cycle began with the Conquest, after which the Spanish created an empire in which social inequality, underdevelopment, economic exploitation, and cultural superstition (rather than rational thought)

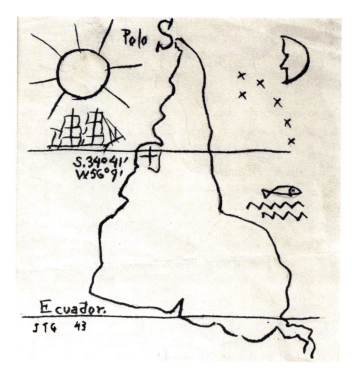

Figure 3.1. *América Invertida* [*America Inverted*] (1943), by Uruguayan painter Joaquín Torres García (1874–1949).
Source: Wikimedia Commons.

reigned. Eventually in the nineteenth century, spurred on by new ideas and revolutions, Latin Americans achieved independence. But then, instead of building successful republics, many nations fell under the control of *caudillos* (charismatic military and political strongmen) and remained dependent economically on foreign powers and culturally on the Catholic Church – "proving" that they could not rule themselves. Modern attempts to forge democracy, while sometimes successful, often failed, and the cycle continued. Elected governments fell to dictators; foreign companies and countries leveraged advantages with local elites who profited while common people suffered. By the 1950s, state violence, civil wars, drug conflicts, and immigration crises erupted in many nations, each with legacies that continue today.

Certainly, this master narrative references real events, but it too easily suggests little has changed over time, and at its extreme, that Latin Americans are incapable of effective self-rule, poor, and backwards. It reduces, and even denies, historical agency, casting Latin Americans monolithically through stereotypes as passive, inept, and corrupt. Offering a version of this narrative, Marie Arana (2020) contends that Latin America's "essence" has been shaped by three crucibles: extractive economics, strongman rule and violence, and crushing religiosity, the traumatic experiences of which inscribed failure and violence directly into Latin

Americans' genes. In addition, the argument goes, corruption and impunity have prevented the region from changing since the colonial era. This reductive, deterministic narrative needs to be checked: Versions have helped bolster justifications for colonial-era conquest, neocolonialism, and US domination during the nineteenth and twentieth centuries, and later "shocks" forcing significant economic changes.

That colonialism left indelible effects is not in doubt. Historian John Charles Chasteen (2016) argued that violence, inequality, and subjugation marked Latin American history. Each country, though distinct, shares a colonial birth "in blood and fire, in conquest and slavery" (1). Descendants of Europeans tend to be wealthy and powerful, while those of subjugated Africans and Indigenous peoples remain poor. Mexican writer Octavio Paz (1992) viewed colonial trauma – and resulting racial mixing where Mexicans descended from conquerors and victims alike – as defining characteristics of Mexican identity. Uruguayan Eduardo Galeano (1997) argued that for centuries, foreigners – particularly from Spain, Portugal, and the United States – slashed open Latin America's "veins" for exploitation, leading to the region's persistent problems of inequality and underdevelopment. For him, Latin America's problems, rather than being inherent, instead directly stem from such foreign interventions.

The danger of "doing it wrong" master narratives is that they generalize genealogies of current inequalities and overemphasize trauma and violence, thereby silencing important historical differences between places and peoples. The region's history, Mexican historian Enrique Krauze (2020) reminds us, is not monolithic. Real, if unequal, progress has also occurred: For all their problems, Latin America and the Caribbean have produced the world's largest collection of functioning democracies.

DISCOVERIES

So what is gained by thinking in terms of master narratives – and what is silenced? Who has historical agency in them? Take, for instance, the classic, misleading "Age of Discovery" narrative that includes such feats as Columbus's voyages and Magellan's crew circumnavigating the world. Swashbuckling adventures can be compelling, and certainly the world changed dramatically after 1492. But who discovered what? The "New World" was new to Europeans, not its inhabitants. Calling the period the "Age of Discovery" privileges European experience, obscuring the actual discovery of the Americas millennia earlier by people crossing between Asia and Alaska, whether using coastal sea routes or the Beringia land bridge. Yet this flawed narrative is common. In Ridley Scott's 1992 film *1492: Conquest of Paradise*, Columbus, played by Gerard Depardieu, peels an orange and tells his son the world is round, as if he were the first to realize that by sailing west he would arrive in Asia. Yet people since the Ancient Greeks had grasped the world's spherical shape, whereas Columbus thought it was pear shaped. While he did not arrive in Asia, he nevertheless, according to the narrative, "discovered" America.

Scholars have long known that the Norse people were the first Europeans to arrive. Columbus himself disputed his "discovery," boasting he had found parts of the Indies (Japan, India, China, Spice Islands) that Marco Polo missed. Others, like explorer Amerigo Vespucci, for whom the region is now named, recognized the Americas as "new."

Columbus's arrival was significant. It led directly to Spain's global empire. But accurate narratives are more complicated than heroic tales. Who narrated his exploits mattered: He boasted of riches, but peers and the Spanish crown learned he lied. His contemporary critics regarded him not as some far-thinking genius but as a brutal man who supported slavery, child sex trafficking, and horrific violence against the initially welcoming Indigenous population, who, if they did not produce the required gold or goods, were maimed. If they tried to escape, they were killed. Their only alternative was being worked to death. Within a generation, the Spanish decimated them.

So why does the United States, which Columbus did not visit, honor him? In 1907, facing hostility from nativist Anglo-Americans, Italian immigrants in Denver sought an Italian hero who could be universalized. So they celebrated Columbus, and the familiar narrative of Columbus's heroism soon spread. Today many people challenge this holiday because of his brutality and instead commemorate Indigenous Peoples' Day to recognize those harmed by European colonialism. When Columbus's supporters say that this "revises" history, they are right. But such critiques started in his own time, not in today's politics.

LEGENDS

After Columbus, Spain built the world's first global empire. Envying Spain's wealth and power, imperial competitors sought to undermine its reputation – while deflecting from their own brutal colonialism. They portrayed Spaniards as superior to Indigenous peoples but also as "bad guys" forcibly colonizing and converting them, committing genocide, and wasting natural resources in their quest for gold and glory. In contrast, Indigenous peoples were "good guys": innocent, passive, peaceful, child-like victims who did not use resources well but lived harmoniously with nature (aka, *Noble Savages*). Over time, this criticism became the "Black Legend," the "accumulated tradition of propaganda and Hispanophobia according to which the Spanish empire is regarded as cruel, bigoted, degenerate, exploitative and self-righteous in excess of reality" (Gibson 1958, 13). Conversely, the so-called White or Pink Legend promoted by Hispanophiles offered a more favorable view: Spain brought "civilization" to the Americas, which Indigenous peoples needed because they were weak, backwards, non-Christian savages, some of whom practiced human sacrifice. In both legends, Spaniards were superior historical agents who dominated, civilized, or exploited Indigenous peoples.

The Black Legend helped justify opposition to Spanish power while ensuring Indigenous peoples remained seen as incapable of self-determination. What began as colonial-era propaganda has influenced historical narratives since, laying the blame for Latin America's woes at the feet of an allegedly feudal, corrupt, and brutal Spanish civilization. Many Latin Americans after independence believed this. As a young liberal in 1844, Chilean Francisco Bilbao railed "Spain is our past." To him, Spain had inflicted political, religious, and family hierarchies that made "slaves" of everyone except for a handful of powerful men (Bilbao 1844).

The Black Legend was also foundational for regarding Latin Americans as inferior geopolitically. Having long expelled Indigenous peoples from east of the Mississippi River, the nineteenth-century United States turned greedily toward Mexico. The resulting Mexican–American War (1846–1848) was fought because of slavery and racism, much like its sequel, the US Civil War. To many US Americans, mixed-race Mexicans inherited Spanish civilization and were unfit to rule their vast territory. War proponents believed that "Anglo-Saxon energy" would overwhelm Mexicans, just like Indigenous peoples, because they were allegedly lazy, passive imbeciles. Proponents also lusted for Californian ports and lucrative Asian trade. Yet some, including John Quincy Adams, Abraham Lincoln, and Ulysses S. Grant, warned that the unjust war would beget more war – which is precisely what occurred. The irony is that the United States fought to expand slavery, rather than promoting its stated ideals of liberty, whereas Mexico had ended slavery years earlier. Which country was, therefore, truly barbaric?

How this war has been remembered in patriotic terms illustrates how history is made of interpretations. In the United States, it is typically misremembered through phrases like "Remember the Alamo!" and alleged Mexican aggression, which legitimated US intervention. That Norteamericano immigrants, who elected to die instead of complying with Mexican laws they derided, lost that battle *10 years before* the Mexican War matters little. Afterward, US Americans claimed they spread civilization south and west, camouflaging imperialist expansion with claims of "Manifest Destiny." For Mexico, the disastrous war cost half its territory but kindled nationalism. Several military cadets, the Niños Heroes, refused to surrender as US forces entered Mexico City; their deaths helped Mexicans reframe defeat as honorable (Henderson 2007). Left out of both interpretations is the Comanche's key role: Their Comanchería, covering much of what is now Texas and the Plains states, spent years destabilizing Mexico's frontier, encouraged in part by the United States. Thus Mexico's loss was as much due to the Comanche as it was to US American superiority or military might (Delay 2007).

Over time, the Black Legend shifted from viewing Spain as powerful, if barbaric, to Spain as a failed, despotic civilization. This is the Spain lampooned in 1890s political cartoons calling for Uncle Sam to liberate its colonies, portrayed as victimized Latin American "damsels" (Pérez 2008). Once again, the US intervened: The Spanish–American War (1898) launched decades of US "civilizing" interventions. Afterward, one 1899 *Puck* cartoon portrayed Cuba and Puerto Rico as unruly children needing education – that is, unfit for self-rule. Such interventions often supported corporate interests or propped up dictators; Puerto Rico remains a US colony today. But the paternalist interventions also helped forge Latin American identity: Bilbao, who faced prosecution and exile to France for his ideas, helped originate the concept of "Latin America" following the Mexican–American War (Tenorio-Trillo 2020). Years later, Jose Martí, Cuba's most famous patriot who died fighting for independence from Spain in 1895, urged that Latin Americans should be ruled by their own ideas – and peoples – not by foreigners (Martí 1891). He inspired others thereafter, including revolutionaries like Fidel Castro, whose movement overthrew Cuba's US-backed dictatorship in 1959.

ENCOUNTERS, NEGOTIATIONS, AND EMPIRE

Because Spain and the United States acted upon Latin America and the Caribbean, they were seen as historical agents – both in their own time and since – in contrast to the region's "passive" inhabitants. Better interpretations avoid this binary by recognizing the region's history as comprising mutually constitutive, rather than one-sided, interactions (Seigel 2004, 440). For instance, reframing the "Discovery" as "Encounter(s)" acknowledges that the New World was a site of significant, if not neutral nor equal, encounters between Europeans, Indigenous peoples, Africans, and Asians in one place for the first time. Each group "discovered" other peoples and places beyond their previous knowledge, and these encounters profoundly reshaped the world in political-economic, environmental, and cultural terms. Perhaps more importantly, the Encounters began the "Columbian Exchange": a still ongoing exchange of biology and cultures between Old and New Worlds (Crosby 2003). For example, Europeans brought diseases – including influenza and smallpox that decimated Indigenous populations – and livestock, such as cows, pigs, and sheep, that damaged the environment but provided new foods. New World plants and animals, in turn, spread to Europe and beyond (some becoming destructive there, too). We associate potatoes with Ireland, tomatoes with Italy, chilies with Thailand, and papaya with tropical Asia, but all originated in the Americas, whereas crops famous in tropical America – coffee, sugar cane, and bananas – are Old World species.

The Spanish and Portuguese arrived in the Americas following the nearly 800-year "Reconquista" to remove Muslims from the Iberian Peninsula. The Conquest was the Reconquista's sequel, whose legacies influenced empire building in important ways. Three of these included (1) setting precedents for Spanish identity, colonial expansion, and "gold, glory, and God" (i.e., seeking wealth, glory, and Catholic converts); (2) setting patterns of colonization, which focused on founding towns that legitimated conquest, using display violence to force enemies' surrender, and cultivating local allies to assist in governing territory; and conversely, (3) modeling openness to living in a multi-ethnic society, such as had existed in Medieval Iberia during periods of *convivencia* (living together). Even so, the Conquest was incomplete. Maps showing continuous empires suggest uniform control where it did not exist. Early conquistadors were not exclusively white but a motley crew of different ethnicities, including Indigenous peoples and Africans seeking gold and glory, rather than a formal army led by exceptional white men (Restall 2004).

Moreover, the Conquest did not occur identically everywhere. In the Caribbean, Spain destroyed Indigenous peoples. Many regard this as genocide, making the Black Legend particularly accurate there. On the mainland, events played out differently, even as colonialism remained violent and destructive. Familiar narratives, broadly under the "guns, germs, and steel" rubric (Diamond 1997), suggest that disease and Spanish technological superiority doomed Indigenous communities and enabled the Conquest. Historians have challenged this view with better interpretations: Indigenous peoples were not uniformly desolated by conquest, nor simply victims of invasion or imperialism. While disease certainly destabilized Indigenous communities – contributing to Tenochtitlán's defeat (1521) and the Incan civil war (1530s) – attributing the Conquest primarily to disease flirts with biological determinism (i.e., that it was inevitable) and silences Indigenous agency. And more important than technology were Indigenous allies; for instance, the city-state of Tlaxcala – Tenochtitlán's mortal enemy – allied with Cortés, providing the army (thousands strong) and resources necessary for victory. While glorifying themselves, the Spanish nevertheless acknowledged this debt, rewarding the Tlaxcalans with high status in the empire when compared to other Indigenous peoples (Restall 2004). Historian Laura Matthew (2007) has questioned how "Spanish" the Conquest in Mesoamerica actually was, since most of those involved were Indigenous. Spanish-led attacks sped up in-progress wars among Indigenous groups, who used the attacks as opportunities. Rather than viewing themselves as simply Spanish subjects, many, like the Tlaxcalans, imagined the Conquest as building *their* power and fulfilling their long-held ambitions.

Violence continued on imperial frontiers, such as against Mapuche people in modern-day Chile, who never surrendered, and New Mexico's Pueblo people, whose 1680 revolt established autonomy until a brutal reconquest (1692–1700). But in cities where the Mexica, Inca, and others once ruled, the Spanish built upon Indigenous institutions and surviving peoples who, like the Tlaxcalans, were incorporated into the empire. In this sense, the Spanish empire was not as uniformly oppressive as the Black Legend alleged. Instead, by the mid-1500s it was a multicultural empire offering opportunities for many, if not all, people therein (Kamen 2004). As such, *negotiation within domination* should be a primary framework for understanding this empire, not just *exploitation* (Ruiz Medrano and Kellogg 2010). Negotiation between rulers and subjects delivered unequal benefits and justice; nevertheless, Indigenous peoples and Africans negotiated within the system that dominated them. This ensured that colonialism endured: Rather than being only victims, many understood the imperial apparatus as potentially responsive to modification. Of course, success rested on being able to manipulate the system; not all achieved Tlaxcala's status. Many were enslaved or forced to work in mines and plantations. Even so, their negotiations and acts of resistance – oftentimes by women – also ensured Indigenous and African cultural survival (Cope 1994).

Reinterpreting history does not mean dismissing how Spanish colonialism and conquistadors, including Columbus, Cortés, and the Pizarros, were violent. Catastrophic Indigenous population decline occurred until the early 1600s with significant consequences. In the first

100 years following 1492, millions of Indigenous peoples died from disease, warfare, and famine in "The Great Dying." So many people died it may have affected Earth's climate (Koch et al. 2019). Yet these deaths, as well as the cruel working conditions and forced religious conversion foisted on surviving Indigenous peoples, also horrified some Spaniards who became advocates, at least in part, for Indigenous rights. Queen Isabela la Católica forbade Indigenous slavery and reformed the forced-labor *encomienda* system; her grandson Carlos I's "New Laws" (1542) abolished it entirely. Nevertheless, exploitation continued, triggering Spaniards to wrestle with its moral and legal implications. Bartolomé de las Casas, an influential thinker radicalized after seeing Columbus's brutality and the *encomiendas* up close, argued against forced conversion and violence in the Valladolid Debate (1550–1551) with Juan Ginés de Sepúlveda, who viewed Indigenous peoples as "natural slaves." De las Casas's position would prove more influential, and Indigenous peoples gained certain protections.

Nevertheless, the empire required labor. So Spain turned to African slavery; while imports of enslaved Africans began soon after the Spanish arrived in the Americas, they increased dramatically by 1600. Spain was a key actor in a significant historical shift: redefining slavery from an economic status – treating slaves as "others" based on religion, language, culture, or caste – to an economic status organized by race-based othering. Defining categorical *race* – seeing Europeans as "white" and Africans as "black" based on physical characteristics – had already begun with mid-1400s Portuguese colonization of Atlantic islands (Blackburn 2010). Iberian colonization in the Americas accelerated this process, meaning race-based slavery was readily available for Spaniards looking to justify protecting (if still subordinating) Indigenous peoples, while also dehumanizing Africans as "natural" slaves. Millions of enslaved Africans suffered the Middle Passage; most went to the Caribbean and Brazil, rather than to North America.

Indigenous population decline also enabled the *Pristine Myth* – the idea that the New World was an Eden waiting for European exploitation. This view was only possible because there were "empty" spaces where Indigenous peoples had been destroyed or displaced and because Europeans did not believe they properly used the land. This myth was featured in Enlightenment texts, including those by John Locke, whose views influenced English colonialism, the American and French Revolutions, and National Period thinking on government, liberalism, and the "Indian question" (whether Indigenous peoples should be integrated into or segregated from Latin American nations). More recently, some Western environmentalists have incorporated this myth, assuming the natural world is separate from humans rather than acknowledging that places like the Amazon rainforest were built environments in which humans intervened. Setting aside "pristine" spaces can also be a form of colonialism; thus this myth influences current debates on who can use rainforest resources.

Economically, colonial-era Latin America was central to the first global economic system in which Spain traded vast quantities of American silver to Asia – particularly to Ming China, which used silver as currency and possessed valuable trade goods (Flynn and Giráldez 2002). Mined by Indigenous slaves, then fashioned by mints, the Spanish dollar – known as a *peso* ("weight") for its uniform silver content – became the world's first global currency. Spanish, and subsequently Mexican, pesos remained legal tender globally into the nineteenth century and inspired the US dollar. While colonial Latin America – and Spain – have been seen as peripheral to the capitalist world system, they literally bankrolled the modern world's emergence, capitalism's expansion, and industrialization with wealth derived from exploiting silver, slavery, and sugar. Other powers – England, France, and Holland – benefited as silver flowed to merchants and banks across Europe, ultimately enabling the "*Great Divergence*," the socioeconomic shift in which capitalist, industrial Western European nations became dominant, global political-economic powers by the nineteenth century. Only with the Americas' wealth could Europe overtake Middle Eastern and Asian peers (Pommeranz 2000). Ironically, the surplus wealth also produced negative conditions that ultimately undermined both Ming China and Spain, thereby enabling the rise of competing European empires.

Eighteenth-century Bourbon reforms stabilized the Spanish empire's finances and bureaucracy but also greatly expanded African slavery and stripped *criollos* – American-born people of European descent – of political-economic status. This kindled a new "American" identity among criollos, many of whom read Enlightenment ideas of liberty and representative government in coffee houses and questioned Spanish rule. The reforms also stoked political-cultural consciousness among Indigenous and mixed-race peoples. Andeans rejected being treated as *subalterns* – that is, as exploited, lower-status people excluded from power – and instead began glorifying Inca imagery in Cuzco, the former capital (Serulnikov 2005). Túpac Amaru II's rebellion (1780–1782) combined Incan revivalism – he claimed to descend from the last Inca emperor – with emerging political consciousness. While Amaru still honored the Spanish king, his rebellion seriously challenged bureaucrats. Recalling how officials butchered Inca leaders, he was forced to watch his family die, then was executed by being drawn and quartered. Afterward, officials tried to suppress Inca culture and the Quechua language.

For centuries, most imperial subjects believed they had direct personal relationships with the king, despite him being thousands of miles away. Pageantry displaying royal effigies in the Americas reinforced this bond and fostered the imperial system's success and durability (Osorio 2004). But, like Amaru, people did not always feel this affinity with royal officials. As such, Amaru's revolt was a harbinger: In just 40 years, the empire disintegrated as Americans rejected submission to Spanish control.

NATIONS AND CHALLENGES

It is far easier to tell unified narratives about the colonial era than about nineteenth- and twentieth-century Latin America and the Caribbean. What follows is more generalized than you would receive in a detailed course. Nevertheless, historians agree that significant changes occurred when the region shifted from colonialism to independent nations. Revolutionary events in the late eighteenth and early nineteenth centuries undermined Spanish and Portuguese control. First the American, French, and Haitian Revolutions inspired Latin Americans with their political-economic ideas and proved people could overturn monarchies. Then when Napoleon's forces invaded Iberia (1807–1808) a *crisis of legitimacy* erupted: If the king no longer ruled Spain, why should his colonies remain loyal? Within two years Americans across the continent rebelled. In 1810 Mexicans, led first by priest Miguel Hidalgo, challenged Spanish authorities, carrying images of the *Virgen de Guadalupe* (a name given to Jesus's mother Mary in Catholicism) into battle as early nationalist symbols. In South America, Simon Bolívar (1783–1830), known as the Liberator, first fought to free Venezuela, then was forced into Caribbean exile in 1814. There he earned Haiti's funding and support – provided he abolish slavery in liberated territories – and then led forces to free "Gran Colombia." From the south, José San Martín's forces liberated Argentina and Chile; together, they liberated Peru.

By the 1820s, except for Cuba and Puerto Rico, most of Latin America was precariously independent. Aside from Mexico's brief empire and Brazil's durable one until 1889, most nations were constitutional republics. Independence, though, came at a cost: It meant destroying the flexible, responsive imperial system with a "vast and responsive social, political, and economic system that had functioned relatively well, despite its many imperfections" (Rodriguez 2000, 151). Thus, in contrast to the United States, Latin America started at a disadvantage; while Bolívar and others imagined a unified hemispheric power, this did not come to be. Instead, facing unstable political-economic situations; inheriting legacies of racism, inequality, and patriarchy; and lacking infrastructure (due to colonialism prioritizing exports), most nations faltered. Gran Colombia fragmented into Ecuador, Colombia, and Venezuela by 1831. The Federal Republic of Central America achieved independence twice – from Spain (1821) and Mexico (1823) – then disintegrated into Guatemala, Nicaragua, Honduras, El Salvador, and Costa Rica by 1840. Independent Argentina descended into decades-long civil war. In the post-independence power vacuum, local control trumped centralized national control. Across the region, two political factions – liberals and conservatives – contested power. *Caudillos* – epitomized by Antonio López de Santa Anna (Mexico) and Juan Manuel de Rosas (Argentina) – seized power, but by mid-century, republican governments, often headed by liberals, reasserted power.

Thus, since independence, the region has been where advocates of different political-economic policies have fought. The central question is this: Who belongs – and who does not – as part of each nation? Among the ideologies used to answer it have been **liberalism**, *conservativism*, and *nationalism*. In many ways, Latin America has been a laboratory for classical liberalism, an Enlightenment-era political-economic ideology that called for laissez-faire economics; limited, representative governments; and individual rights. Liberals supported progress, "reason" over religion, universal values over local traditions, free markets, and global capitalism. Liberalism influenced revolutions, overturning established orders, and enshrined, to varying degrees, liberty, equality, and individual rights, though these were sometimes limited to those deemed "civilized," thereby marginalizing people of color and women. Nonetheless, liberalism shaped constitutions, citizenship, and societies. Meanwhile, conservatives generally favored maintaining unequal, colonial-era social, racial, and gendered hierarchies that enshrined white male dominance, land ownership, political power, and religious authority.

Both liberals and conservatives in the new Latin American republics faced a daunting task: building nationhood from disparate populations separated by distance and both geographical and cultural divisions. Each attempted to create what Benedict Anderson called an **imagined community**, a socially constructed idea of nationalism, sovereign and limited, to which both rulers and those they governed could imagine they belonged (Anderson 1998). What made Mexicans distinct from Peruvians, Argentinians, or Brazilians? Using symbols, flags, rituals, and print media, nations defined themselves with stories about their origins, identity, and cultural authenticity. Nineteenth-century liberals generally envisioned more inclusive, modern republics than conservatives, who favored limiting social mobility. Between 1850 and 1890, liberals abolished slavery where it still existed, wrote constitutions affording significant rights (including freedom of the press, separation of church and state, and rights to privacy), and modernized nations (by building railroads and reforming institutions). Although limited at times by racism and patriarchal norms, liberals progressively expanded their imagined communities.

In the twentieth century, liberals and conservatives continued contesting power; in some places, like Colombia, this led to civil war (1948–1958). At the same time, new political groups emerged. Some were led by *populists* – charismatic, paternalistic leaders similar to *caudillos* – who combined ideas from across the political spectrum and rode waves of nationalism to power by incorporating additional people previously left out of politics. Those like Lázaro Cárdenas (Mexico), Getúlio Vargas (Brazil), and Juan Perón (Argentina) consciously positioned themselves as "fathers" to the poor and friends of the middle class. In response, conservatives frequently allied with regimes deploying extreme nationalism through anti-democratic *authoritarianism*. These included dictatorships under Trujillo (Dominican Republic), the Duvaliers (Haiti), Batista (Cuba), and the Somozas (Nicaragua); murderous right-wing military governments in Guatemala, Argentina, Brazil, and Chile; and one-party rule in Mexico. These authoritarian regimes, often acting with international approval or indifference, used *state violence* against their own people to harshly limit who belonged in their nation's imagined community; they launched "dirty wars" during the Cold War that targeted, tortured, and "disappeared" trade unionists, political dissidents, socialists, and students. The United States often supported neocolonialism and state violence for its own interests. Since 1846, Latin America has been the "empire's workshop," where the United States has experimented with economic, political, and military interventions later used elsewhere, such as in Vietnam and the Middle East (Grandin 2021).

Young people emerged as a significant political force by the mid-twentieth century. They had benefited from expanding economic opportunities, literacy, family-oriented social programs, and increased standards of living. Both working-class and middle-class youths agitated for equitable politics and wealth distribution, as well as the right to dress as they pleased and listen to rock 'n' roll. Many challenged patriarchal norms of gender and sexuality; most identified as local reformers and as part of global youth cultures. Many participated in protests; in 1968, when events like the Prague Spring, May '68 riots (Paris), intensification of the Vietnam War, and political assassinations (e.g., Martin Luther King, Jr.) roiled the world, students in Mexico and Brazil protested dictatorships and marched in solidarity with peers abroad, then faced brutal crackdowns. In Mexico, the one-party state murdered peaceful students at Tlatelolco two weeks before hosting the Olympics, thereby cannibalizing Mexico's future to preserve "order" (Pensado 2013). Other regimes, like Brazil, similarly targeted youths, stoking a "moral panic" linking sexual minorities with communists (Cowan 2016). Nevertheless, many students, radicalized by activism and countercultural movements, went on to lead nations after the dictatorships fell. Overall, Latin America has mattered as a key battleground, not just between Cold War ideas of political liberalism and socialist or communist alternatives, but between two visions of homegrown democracy: one expansive, egalitarian, and vibrant, the other unequal and limited (Grandin 2011).

In economic terms, nineteenth-century Latin Americans won political freedom but struggled with colonial legacies of unequal wealth distribution. Countries then became ensnared within *neocolonial* relationships with the United States and European powers that left them vulnerable to boom and bust economic cycles based on exports like bananas, rubber, guano, minerals, and nitrates. Foreign companies also exerted significant influence: the United Fruit Company (now Chiquita) turned Central America into "banana republics" focused on fruit exports rather than local development. Scholars have called this economic relationship **dependency**: an economic system where resources flow from poorer "peripheral" countries to enrich wealthier nations. Because Latin America produced mostly raw materials (i.e., less-valuable commodities), over time its wealth diminished when purchasing manufactured goods and other higher-value commodities it needed from developed countries. This relationship underdeveloped the region (Prebisch 1962). Whereas dominant narratives claimed Latin America did modernization "wrong," dependency theorists have argued that the system was in fact designed to extract wealth and channel capital away from the region and into the coffers of corporations centered in the "core" nations of Europe and North America.

Challenging dependency, US imperialism, and violent regimes, Latin Americans throughout the twentieth century experimented with nationalist and leftist policies (i.e., politically left of liberals). Many questioned capitalism as the universal developmental model, particularly given persistent inequalities. From the late 1800s, Leftists used trade unions, anarcho-syndicalist movements, political parties, social protests, and revolutions to effect changes. Some countries deployed redistributive socioeconomic policies. Following their revolution (1910–1920) – a multifaceted civil war marked by agrarian, popular uprisings – Mexicans implemented in part a radical constitution (1917) with provisions for workers' rights, protections for women and children, land redistribution, and the separation of church and state. Other countries tried *socialism* – advocating social/collective rather than private ownership of the economy. Most important was Cuba: Its revolution (1953–1959) toppled US-backed dictator

Fulgencio Batista; afterward, a revolutionary government successfully expanded social programs, education, and healthcare. However, inequalities persisted, and as Cuba turned toward authoritarian communism in the 1960s and 1970s, it targeted opponents and labeled them as "anti-social" and unfit to be Cuban citizens. As such, Catholics, dissidents, and gay men were sent to "re-education" camps to "learn" to be "real" men, revolutionaries, and even heterosexual. Many opponents fled or were exiled. Leftist ideas also influenced Nicaragua's Sandinista movement (1970s–1980s), which toppled the Somozas; Peru's left-wing military dictatorship (1968–1975); and *liberation theology*, a Catholic revivalist movement that challenged social inequality, church hierarchies (associated with conservative power), and state violence in the second half of the twentieth century.

Many countries adopted *import substitution industrialization* (ISI), where domestic industries produced goods for local consumption and export. ISI limited foreign imports with protectionist tariffs, diversified economies, and fostered prosperity in industrializing, urbanizing countries like Mexico, Argentina, and Brazil. Leftists advocated going further by nationalizing resources and industries. In 1938, Mexico's Cárdenas nationalized petroleum, implementing constitutional provisions requiring resources to be owned by Mexicans. Decades later, Chilean Salvador Allende's socialist government (1970–1973) nationalized copper. Such actions sought to reclaim resource benefits for the people. But some Chileans thought Allende moved too cautiously; thus, workers seized factories to forge a revolution "from below" (Winn 1989). Simultaneously, conservatives conspired to thwart Allende's administration. Protests erupted into the streets, and soon a violent military coup occurred, leading to Augusto Pinochet's brutal dictatorship (1973–1990).

Liberals by this time had split into two camps: those supporting political progress (and programs like ISI) and neoliberals, who abhorred socialism and promoted privatization, austerity, "universal" free markets rather than protectionism, and dismantling social welfare programs. Gaining power by the 1970s, neoliberals often worked for right-wing, socially conservative regimes and used political or economic "shocks" (crises) to advance their policies. For instance, following Pinochet's coup overthrowing Allende, the Chicago Boys – Chilean economists trained at the University of Chicago – pushed through such changes (Klein 2007). By allying with violent regimes, neoliberals undercut claims that liberalism equaled political freedom. While neoliberalism remains influential and neoliberals have won elections since the 1980s, they have faced resistance from liberal and left-wing parties, as well as from other groups, such as Mexico's Zapatistas, an Indigenous-led movement that emerged in protest against the North American Free Trade Agreement (1994), and the region-wide Pink Tide (late 1990s–2000s) in which Leftists, including Bolivia's first Indigenous president Evo Morales, gained power by rejecting neoliberalism as another form of colonialism. Today, student and other activism in Puerto Rico, Chile, Mexico, and Argentina, among other places, remains influential against neoliberalism, corruption, and US interventionism – and in defining democracy itself.

RACE

Historians recently have explored *histories from below*, giving voice to everyday experiences, and *intersectionality*, in which issues of race, class, gender, and sexuality are seen as interconnected rather than discrete. These methods are essential for understanding Latin America and the Caribbean, perhaps more of a "melting pot" than the United States, which boast a highly mixed-race population derived from settlement patterns, colonialism, and immigration to three regions: the Highlands, Lowlands, and Temperate South. The Highlands in Mexico and the Andes fostered Indigenous empires upon which Spain built its own. Since early colonialism involved men moving without families, this ensured most of the population remained either Indigenous or became *mestizos* – people of mixed European/Indigenous descent. In contrast, tropical Lowlands in the Caribbean, Atlantic Brazil, and coastal areas had smaller Indigenous populations, which further declined after 1492. There, African slavery predominated, producing cash crops like sugar, coffee, and cotton. These regions today have large Afro-descendant or mixed-race populations. In both regions, a sizable European-descendant minority exists. Compared to the Highlands and Lowlands, the Temperate South was a colonial backwater lacking exploitable resources, urban Indigenous populations, and numerous enslaved Africans – despite Montevideo and Buenos Aires being major Bourbon-era slave ports. Local leaders thus imagined this region as a place where a "pure," "white," "civilized" society could exist. Argentina, Chile, southern Brazil, and Uruguay attracted millions of immigrants (particularly Italians and Spaniards) in the nineteenth century through promises of farmland and economic opportunities. Five "revolutions" – agricultural, demographic, industrial, liberal, and transportation – produced a surplus European population that drove this mass migration (Moya 1998). New immigrants often struggled to assimilate; nevertheless, they reshaped nations through labor, political activism, language use, and culture.

Understanding these trends tells us only so much. Histories of race are too complicated to fully explore here. But, speaking generally, racial hierarchies (*castas*) developed in the colonial era that ranked people of European descent as most "civilized," with mixed-race, Indigenous, and African peoples below. These categories were not static; in some cases, people had social mobility, depending on their education, occupation, or location (Cope 1994). Many enslaved Africans temporarily freed themselves and formed new communities in the continent's interior – such as Brazil's *quilombos* – demonstrating their own claims to being civilized. By the nineteenth century, a central question was whether Latin America was civilized *because* of its mixed-race heritage or despite it. Was it the epitome of Western ideals of equality, or inferior because those ideals were intended only for white people? Independence overlapped with the "Age of Liberty." But to be "free" was to not be enslaved – and to be *able to own others*. Europeans could claim to be free precisely because they enslaved others (Grandin 2015). While most Latin American nations abolished slavery over time following independence, it persisted in Brazil (until Princess Isabel ended it in 1888) and in Spain's remaining colonies, Puerto Rico (until 1873) and Cuba (until 1886). Racism continued. Some worried Indigenous peoples prevented modernization. To solve this "Indian question," Mexican liberals turned to education and forced integration; Argentine liberals preferred *whitening*: exterminating and dislocating Indigenous peoples while encouraging European immigration.

But by the 1900s, many nations emphasized racial mixing as foundational to national identity. Mexico's José Vasconcelos advocated for the "Cosmic Race"; Brazil's Gilberto Freyre called for "Racial Democracy." Such perspectives simultaneously defined Latin America's mixed-race population as valuable while minimizing racial inequalities and expressing preferences toward whiteness (and European ideas of civilization), thus still marginalizing people of color. Proponents of *indigenismo* in Mexico and Peru celebrated past Indigenous cultures as uniquely "national" in museums to locals and tourists, but offered limited support to living Indigenous communities (Knight 1990). Guatemalan neoliberals co-opted multiculturalism, often touted as an opposing ideology, by recognizing certain Indigenous rights and opposing others (Hale 2002). Cuba boasted that it vanquished racism – then criticized US racial strife – but stifled Afro-Cuban critics. Issues of race, therefore, remain unresolved throughout the region; people of color continue to advocate for policy changes, land reforms, and cultural autonomy (Wade 2010). Enduring questions include the following: Do equality and national identities require homogenizing racial identities? Does erasing difference reinscribe hierarchies of inequality? And can affirming race help overturn injustice? (Appelbaum, Macpherson, and Rosenblatt 2003).

WOMEN, GENDER, AND SEXUALITY

Classic narratives paint Latin America as rife with *machismo*, a heteronormative gender ideology of male superiority. This narrative asserts that Latin Americans do gender "wrong," as machos are irrational brutes. While machismo does exist, it cannot be reduced to stereotypes of men dominating women. Historically, Latin American and Caribbean women have played significant roles as agents and symbols. During the Encounters, formerly enslaved Nahua noblewoman Malintzín helped Cortés ally with Tlaxcala and translated between him and Moctezuma. These actions undermined the Mexica. As such, Malintzín, known today as Malinche, is remembered by many as a traitor; *malinchista* in Mexico and Central America is a pejorative term for someone preferring foreign cultures while disdaining their own. Yet Malinche also has been regarded as Mexico's symbolic (racial) mother: She had a *mestizo* child with Cortés. Most Mexicans have similarly mixed heritage. Thus, competing narratives are at work: Malinche as victim – of the Mexica, Cortés, and colonialism – and as a deceptive woman. Instead, her life, remarkable linguistic aptitude, and key historical role should be understood as showcasing women's survival (Restall 2004; Townsend 2019).

Other women have served as positive symbols. Perhaps the first authentic American voice was Mexican nun Sor Juana Inés de la Cruz (1648–1695). Highly intelligent, she faced a difficult choice to either marry the Church or a husband. She chose the convent and for a time thrived, because convents offered women significant opportunities for learning and enterprise. Many had libraries, ran schools, put on cultural performances, and created the foods, such as Mexico's *mole poblano*, for which their areas would become famous. While the Church tried to silence her, Sor Juana's written work survived; today, she is a Mexican hero. An earlier nun, Catalina de Erauso (the "Lt. Nun," 1585/92–1650) rejected the limiting choice of marriage or church life entirely; instead, Erauso famously lived as a man and conquistador, thereby enjoying numerous opportunities open only to men (De Erauso 2011). Scholars debate if Erauso was a lesbian, a trans person, or simply performing masculinity. What is clear is that gender and sexuality operated differently in colonial America than stereotypes – that is, of conservative Catholicism, rigid gender binaries, and heteronormativity – might suggest. Her swashbuckling memoir has long been a favorite among my students.

Women's experiences point to how history is not simply a linear narrative of progress. One of liberalism's central claims was that it promoted "civilization." But independence for women meant "one step forward, two steps back" (Dore 2000). Deemed inferior and outside the body politic, they lost status in the early nineteenth century and were denied basic citizenship. This is ironic, given women's roles in the independence era from fighters such as Micaela Bastidas Puyucahua, Túpac Amaru II's wife, to strategic players like Josefa Ortiz de Domínguez, who hosted meetings where Mexicans plotted their rebellion. Nevertheless, even elite women were expected to conform to the domestic sphere and occupations; politics and public life were men's domains. Of course many, particularly women of color, had to work in public, their labors exploited until their activism pushed through reforms.

Women gradually won suffrage and greater political power. Nineteenth-century first-wave feminists fought against family laws, which had become more patriarchal after independence, and for access to higher education (particularly in law, medicine, and dentistry). Women played key roles in expanding education through normal schools and literacy campaigns. As they themselves became better educated and more prosperous, they pushed for women's suffrage, though nations frequently stalled their access. Puerto Rico and Ecuador granted voting rights first (1929), but it took Mexico until 1953, despite women's essential roles in promoting revolutionary programs. The rights Argentine women won influenced its most famous woman, Eva Perón. During Peronist Argentina (1946–1955), she helped integrate poor *descamisados* (shirtless ones) and the working class into her populist husband Juan Perón's political base. Her charisma bolstered his success and inspired others long after her death – memorialized in Andrew Lloyd Weber's musical *Evita*. Decades later, few figures had the political capital necessary to openly resist Argentina's El Proceso dictatorship (1976–1983), which "disappeared" students, leftists, and religious figures. But women successfully protested in Buenos Aires's Plaza de Mayo. Wearing cloth diapers around their heads as symbols of motherhood, they helped topple the dictatorship. Similar efforts challenged authoritarianism elsewhere. Latin Americans have since shown themselves comfortable with electing female presidents, such as Michelle Bachelet (Chile), Cristina Fernández de Kirchner (Argentina), and Dilma Rousseff (Brazil).

These examples were not sidebars to "main" historical narratives but constitutive of them. The same is true for what scholars call "queer" history, which helps illuminate the limits of imagined communities. Take Mexico's Famous 41 Scandal (1901). Police raided a party where men, half of them in drag, danced. The press discussed the event for days; the number 41 signified being queer for decades thereafter (Irwin 2003). From one perspective, the scandal might seem to reveal a homophobic state and press punishing queer men, thereby fitting stereotypes of machismo. Mexico, like other Latin American nations, did at times arrest, imprison, and exile queer people as "anti-social" individuals while deploying disciplines like criminology, sexology, and anthropology for nationalist aims to reform and punish those deemed abnormal (Jones 2017). Yet this history is more complex than straightforward repression. Many nations, including Mexico in 1871, decriminalized non-procreative sex well before the United States, thereby limiting, at least officially, state interference in private lives. Working-class Mexicans did use the Famous 41 to criticize the Porfirian dictatorship's (1876–1910) excesses; they labeled sumptuous parties and cross-dressing as emblematic of negative foreign influences because they imagined Mexican nationalism and masculinity differently. Nevertheless, the *ambiente* – the queer social world – actually flourished visibly in working-class neighborhoods until the 1950s. Thereafter, queer people rejected marginalization. Queer Mexicans marched in solidarity with workers, students, and leftists in 1978, 10 years after Tlatelolco, and held their first Pride parade the following year. That same decade, queer Brazilians challenged that nation's dictatorship. In both, political coalitions involving queer people emerged that redefined national identities (De la Dehesa 2010).

TRANSCULTURATION

Today, negative stories abound about drug wars, immigration crises, coups, and corruption. While these serious problems exist, it is also true that the media has bought into master narratives of Latin America and the Caribbean "doing it wrong." Regarding the region as inherently or uniquely dangerous belies important historical facts (Krauze 2020). Tens of millions died in European-based world wars; countless others did in the previous millennia. Imagine if we talked about European civilization with the same negative stereotypes used for Latin America and the Caribbean. Too many narratives focus on trauma as the defining characteristic of being Latin American. Recognizing trauma is important. But what if we discussed resilience, joy, and 500 years of cultural production not as historical footnotes but as evidence of the *limits* of trauma as an all-encompassing narrative frame? Where we might expect people to lose hope, we find resilience. From Havana to Rio, joy is common – and not just among the wealthy.

Studying culture with histories from below offers a useful model for understanding the region. One of the most significant, unintended consequences of the Encounters and Columbian Exchange is what Cuban thinker Fernando Ortiz (1995) called **transculturation**: the fusing of distinct cultural elements into new cultures. Latin American and Caribbean cultures have blended European, Indigenous, and African cultures, as evident in the music, food, art, dialects, architecture, and other cultural forms that come from the region. Even Catholicism – used as a tool of conquest – became transculturated in the Americas, with saints acquiring traits from previous Indigenous and African beliefs. Argentine tango, Brazilian samba, and Cuban son are forms of transculturated music and dance. Numerous Chinese, Japanese, Korean, and Syrio-Lebanese immigrants settled in Brazil, Peru, Mexico, and Cuba. Each has contributed to transculturation, particularly in terms of food. Mexico City's most famous dish, *tacos pastor*, is a variation of shawarma.

Latin Americans have also used transculturation as a form of *soft power* – that is, influencing through culture or ideology rather than force. State-funded muralism by painters including Diego Rivera and José Orozco visually defined Mexican nationalism, but also influenced Depression-era art worldwide, Mexican–American identity, and Latin America's global reputation. Mexican cuisine's popularity is another example – who doesn't like Taco Tuesdays? Today, Mexico's mezcal is regarded as a globally prestigious artisanal spirit. Soft power is found in films, telenovelas (*Ugly Betty*, for instance), literature, martial arts (Brazilian capoeira), and music, from the styles already mentioned to bossa nova, mariachi, and reggaetón, a product of the Puerto Rican diaspora blending Caribbean music and hip hop. And it is found in sports: The region produces some of the world's best soccer players. Latin America and the Caribbean's cultural influence cannot be denied.

CONCLUSION: LISTENING TO THE PAST

This chapter has argued that history is made of interpretations – dominant and alternative narratives. Here is a concluding example: Latin Americans have deployed political soft power in international forums by calling for human rights, peace, and national sovereignty rather than perpetual violence and dependency. The *testimonio*, a style of historical writing, exemplifies this form of soft power. Rigoberta Menchú's 1984 *testimonio* brought international attention to atrocities committed during Guatemala's civil war, earning her the 1992 Nobel Peace Prize. Critics like anthropologist David Stoll (1999) challenged her claims, stating that a younger brother who supposedly died of starvation never existed and that she was better educated than stated. Menchú dismissed these critiques: "I'd like to stress that it's not only *my* life, it's also the testimony of my people" (1984, 1). Her *testimonio* – factual for the community, not necessarily individually – challenged power structures by calling attention to silenced histories. The controversy thus rested on who got to narrate Guatemala's history – an Indigenous activist or an "objective" Western scholar – and what constituted "real" facts. It was all about interpretation.

Latin America *does* have complex histories that have mattered. In this chapter, I have necessarily made generalizations and offered just a beginning for understanding the "vast universe that for convenience we call Latin America" (Krauze 2020). Understanding the region's history requires nuanced interpretations – and listening to voices that have often been silenced. The other chapters in this volume will allow you to continue learning beyond misleading, totalizing, negative narratives – and to question what stories are told, who gets to tell them, and what has been silenced.

REFLECTION AND DISCUSSION QUESTIONS

- How do we "check our narratives"? That is, how is "history" made of interpretations, rather than simply a repository of facts? Why do interpretations matter? What do they reveal or hide? Who is qualified to make these interpretations?
- How does the concept of "historical agency" help us understand and rethink Latin American and Caribbean history, and the narratives, assumptions, and stereotypes we might have?
- What important similarities can be seen in Latin America and the Caribbean in the colonial and post-independence eras? What has changed over time?
- Why has Latin America and the Caribbean mattered in history, despite what people like Kissinger and Nixon argued?

KEY CONCEPTS

- **dependency**: The theory that resources flow from a poor periphery to a wealthy core, impoverishing the former and enriching the latter, leading to underdevelopment and economic, political, or cultural subordination within world systems. This theory was used to challenge models of modernization and assertions of Latin America and the Caribbean being "backwards."
- **historical agency**: The ability of individuals, groups, or entities to make choices and take actions that impacted the past – and shaped the present – even if in small ways. Whereas older historical narratives championed "great men" as agents, more recent scholarship asserts that people's everyday actions are forms of agency.
- **imagined community (nationalism)**: Conceives of the nation as a social construct in which the population and those that govern it imagine themselves to belong to the same community, using symbols, media, and other means to generate their shared belonging and identity. It is sovereign, limited in scope (not everyone belongs), and imagined because most people within a nation will never know each other.
- **liberalism**: A political, social, and economic philosophy that has promoted, to varying degrees, individual rights, free markets, civil liberties, representative government by consent, and equality before the law.

- **transculturation:** The merging of cultures into a new cultural phenomenon, which shares attributes with but is distinct from the original cultures. Such merging is not necessarily equal, and transculturation is often an unintended consequence of colonialism.

EXPLORE FURTHER

- Galeano, Eduardo. 1997. *Open Veins of Latin America: Five Centuries of the Pillage of a Continent.* New York: Monthly Review Press.
- Grandin, Greg. 2015. *Empire of Necessity: Slavery, Freedom, and Deception in the New World.* New York: Picador.
- Restall, Matthew. 2004. *Seven Myths of the Spanish Conquest.* New York: Oxford University Press.
- Tenorio-Trillo, Mauricio. 2020. *Latin America: The Allure and Power of an Idea.* Chicago: University of Chicago Press.
- Townsend, Camilla. 2019. *Fifth Sun: A New History of the Aztecs.* New York: Oxford University Press.

ABOUT THE AUTHOR

Ryan M. Jones is an associate professor of history at SUNY Geneseo, specializing in modern Latin American, Mexican, and gender and sexuality histories. He is co-editor with Veronika Fuechtner and Douglas Haynes of *A Global History of Sexology* (University of California Press, 2017). His current book project, *Erotic Revolutions*, is a history of Mexico City's *ambiente*, or queer social world, 1871–1960.

REFERENCES

Anderson, Benedict. 1998. *Imagined Communities: Reflections on the Origins and Spread of Nationalism.* New York: Verso.

Appelbaum, Nancy, Anne Macpherson, and Karin Alejandra Rosenblatt. 2003. *Race and Nation in Modern Latin America.* Chapel Hill: University of North Carolina Press.

Arana, Marie. 2019. *Silver, Sword & Stone: Three Crucibles in the Latin American Story.* New York: Simon & Schuster.

Bilbao, Francisco. 2019 (1844). "Chilean Sociability." Translated by James A. Wood. In *Problems in Modern Latin American History*, 5th ed., edited by James A. Woods and Anna Rose Alexander. Lanham, MD: Rowman & Littlefield.

Blackburn, Robin. 2010. *The Making of New World Slavery.* New York: Verso.

Chasteen, John Charles. 2016. *Born in Blood and Fire*, 4th ed. New York: Norton.

Cope, R. Douglas. 1994. *The Limits of Racial Domination: Plebian Society in Colonial Mexico City, 1660–1720.* Madison: University of Wisconsin Press.

Cowan, Ben. 2016. *Securing Sex: Morality and Repression in the Making of Cold War Brazil.* Chapel Hill: University of North Carolina Press.

Crosby, Alfred. 2003. *The Columbian Exchange: Biological and Cultural Consequences of 1492.* Westport, CT: Prager.

De Erauso, Catalina. 2011. *Lieutenant Nun.* Translated by Michele Stepto and Gabriel Stepto. Boston: Beacon Press.

De la Dehesa, Rafael. 2010. *Queering the Public Sphere in Mexico and Brazil: Sexual Rights Movements and Emerging Democracies.* Durham, NC: Duke University Press.

Delay, Brian. 2007. "Independent Indians and the U.S.-Mexican War." *American Historical Review* 112 (1): 35–68. https://doi.org/10.1086/ahr.112.1.35.

Diamond, Jared. 1997. *Guns, Germs, and Steel.* New York: Norton.

Díaz, Bernal. 1963. *The Conquest of New Spain.* Translated by J. M. Cohen. Harmondsworth, UK: Penguin.

Dore, Elizabeth. 2000. "One Step Forward, Two Steps Back: Gender and the State in the Long Nineteenth Century." In *Hidden Histories of Gender and the State in Latin America*, edited by Elizabeth Dore and Maxine Molyneux, 3–32. Durham, NC: Duke University Press.

Flynn, Dennis O., and Arturo Giráldez. 2002. "Cycles of Silver: Global Economic Unity through the Mid-Eighteenth Century." *Journal of World History* 13 (2): 391–427. https://doi.org/10.1353/jwh.2002.0035.

Fukuyama, Francis. 2007. "A Quiet Revolution: Latin America's Unheralded Progress." *Foreign Affairs* 86 (6): 177–82.

Galeano, Eduardo. 1997. *Open Veins of Latin America: Five Centuries of the Pillage of a Continent.* New York: Monthly Review Press.

Gibson, Charles. 1958. *The Colonial Period in Latin American History.* Washington: Service Center for Teachers of History.

Grandin, Greg. 2011. *The Last Colonial Massacre: Latin America and the Cold War.* Chicago: University of Chicago Press.

———. 2015. *Empire of Necessity: Slavery, Freedom, and Deception in the New World.* New York: Picador.

———. 2021. *Empire's Workshop: Latin America, the United States, and the Making of an Imperial Republic.* New York: Picador.

Hale, Charles R. 2002. "Does Multiculturalism Menace? Governance, Cultural Rights, and the Politics of Identity in Guatemala." *Journal of Latin American Studies* 34 (3): 485–524. https://doi.org/10.1017/S0022216X02006521.

Henderson, Timothy. 2007. *A Glorious Defeat: Mexico and Its War with the United States.* New York: Hill and Wang.

Hersh, Seymour. 1982. "The Price of Power: Kissinger, Nixon, and Chile." *The Atlantic*, December 1982.

Irwin, Robert McKee. 2003. *Mexican Masculinities.* Minneapolis: University of Minnesota Press.

Jones, Ryan M. 2017. "Mexican Sexology and Male Homosexuality: Genealogies and Global Contexts, 1860–1957." In *A Global History of Sexual Science*, edited by Veronika Fuechtner, Douglas Haynes, and Ryan M. Jones, 232–57. Berkeley: University of California Press.

Kamen, Henry. 2004. *Empire: How Spain Became a World Power, 1492–1763.* New York: Harper Collins.

Klein, Naomi. 2007. *The Shock Doctrine: The Rise of Disaster Capitalism.* New York: Metropolitan Books.

Knight, Alan. 1990. "Racism, Revolution, and Indigenismo." In *The Idea of Race in Latin America 1870–1940*, edited by Richard Graham. Austin: University of Texas Press.

Knight, Franklin W. 2000. "The Haitian Revolution." *American Historical Review* 105 (1): 103–15. https://doi.org/10.2307/2652438.

Koch, Alexander, Chris Brierley, Mark M. Maslin, and Simon L. Lewis. 2019. "Earth System Impacts of the European Arrival and Great Dying in the Americas after 1492." *Quarternary Science Reviews* 207 (1): 13–36. https://doi.org/10.1016/j.quascirev.2018.12.004.

Krauze, Enrique. 2020. "The History of Latin America Is Not a Monolithic Story." *Literary Hub*. https://lithub.com/the-history-of-latin-america-is-not-a-monolithic-story.

Martí, José. 1891. "Nuestra América." *La Revista Ilustrada de Nueva York*, January 10.

Matthew, Laura E. 2007. "Whose Conquest: Nahua, Zapoteca, and Mixteca Allies in the Conquest of Central America." In *Indian Conquistadors: Indigenous Allies in the Conquest of Mesoamerica*, edited by Laura Matthews and Michael R. Ouidjk. Norman: University of Oklahoma Press.

Menchú, Rigoberta. 2010 (1984). *I, Rigoberta Menchú*, 2nd ed. Translated by Ann Wright. New York: Verso.

Moya, Jose. 1998. *Cousins and Strangers: Spanish Immigrants in Buenos Aires, 1850–1930*. Berkeley: University of California Press.

Ortiz, Fernando. 1995. *Cuban Counterpoint: Tobacco and Sugar*. Translated by Harriet de Onís. Durham, NC: Duke University Press.

Osorio, Alejandra. 2004. "The King in Lima: Simulacra, Ritual, and Rule in Seventeenth-Century Peru." *Hispanic American Historical Review* 84 (3): 447–74. https://doi.org/10.1215/00182168-84-3-447.

Paz, Octavio. 1992 [1950]. *El Laberinto de la Soledad*. Mexico: Fondo de Cultura Económica.

Pensado, Jaime M. 2013. *Rebel Mexico: Student Unrest and Authoritarian Political Culture during the Long Sixties*. Stanford, CA: Stanford University Press.

Pérez, Louis A. 2008. *Cuba in the American Imagination: Metaphor and the Imperial Ethos*. Chapel Hill: University of North Carolina Press.

Pommeranz, Ken. 2000. *The Great Divergence: China, Europe, and the Making of the Modern World Economy*. Princeton, NJ: Princeton University Press.

Prebisch, Raúl. 1962. "The Economic Development of Latin America and Its Principal Problems." *Economic Bulletin for Latin America* 7 (1): 1–23.

Restall, Matthew. 2004. *Seven Myths of the Spanish Conquest*. New York: Oxford University Press.

Rodriguez, Jaime O. 2000. "The Emancipation of America." *American Historical Review* 105 (1): 131–52. https://doi.org/10.2307/2652440.

Ruiz Medrano, Ethelia, and Susan Kellogg. 2010. *Negotiation within Domination: New Spain's Indian Pueblos Confront the State*. Boulder: University of Colorado Press.

Seigel, Micole. 2004. "World History's Narrative Problem." *Hispanic American Historical Review* 84 (3): 431–46. https://doi.org/10.1215/00182168-84-3-431.

Serulnikov, Sergio. 2005. "Andean Political Imagination in the Late Eighteenth Century." In *Political Cultures in the Andes, 1750–1950*, edited by Nils Jacobsen and Cristóbal Aljovín de Losada, 257–77. Durham, NC: Duke University Press.

Stoll, David. 1999. *Rigoberta Menchú and the Story of All Poor Guatemalans*. New York: Westview Press.

Tenorio-Trillo, Mauricio. 2020. *Latin America: The Allure and Power of an Idea*. Chicago: University of Chicago Press.

Townsend, Camilla. 2019. *Fifth Sun: A New History of the Aztecs*. New York: Oxford University Press.

Trouillot, Michel-Rolph. 1995. *Silencing the Past: Power and the Production of History*. Boston: Beacon Press.

Wade, Peter. 2010. *Race and Ethnicity in Latin America*. London: Pluto Press.

Winn, Peter. 1989. *Weavers of Revolution*. New York: Oxford University Press.

SECTION TWO

Race, Racialization, and Racism

Race is a social identity category that was created during the colonial period as a technology of power that enabled Europeans to categorize themselves as superior to the people they enslaved and colonized. Precursors to ideas about racial difference can be traced to the published accounts of early European explorers who wrote about their travels to the Americas and other parts of the world. These publications, which circulated widely across Europe, depicted non-Europeans as exotic and characterized them by their unfamiliar forms of political organization, dress, and religious practices, as well as phenotypically different in their skin pigmentation, hair, and body composition. By the late seventeenth century, observations about human variation had become a European fascination. Theorists posited competing classification systems for homo sapiens, some asserting that humans could be split into subspecies or races – with some more evolved than others. These erroneous ideas served capitalist ventures and empire building in Latin America and the Caribbean. They lent a veneer of science to arguments in favor of slavery, the exploitation of Indigenous peoples, and the occupation of Indigenous land. These arguments posited that Afro-descendant and Indigenous peoples were biologically different from Euro-descendant people and thus benefited from European domination.

Even well into the twentieth century, pseudoscientists, among them some anthropologists, claimed there were genetic differences between groups of people with differing physical traits. According to these theories, racialized groups, including Black, white, Indigenous, and Asian people, had different innate abilities, intelligence, and value as human beings.[1] Since the 1970s, an abundance of reliable research has debunked the idea that race is biological, demonstrating that there are no significant genetic differences between human beings, who have approximately

---

1 Note that, as a sign of respect for Afro-descendant and Indigenous peoples and identities, we have elected to capitalize the terms "Black" and "Indigenous" whenever we refer to people or their identities, experiences, and history.

99.9 per cent identical DNA. Thus, rather than a biological fact, race is actually a social and cultural construction. Despite these findings, **racialization** – the process of assigning racial meaning to people, things, places, and behaviors and categorizing people according to ideas about race – continues today. And people often view themselves and others through the lens of racial identity.

Racialization differs depending on historical context. For example, in the United States, the legacy of *hypodescent* (the "one drop rule") shapes the way racial groups are conceptualized. Beginning in the seventeenth century, laws dictated that children born to parents with any African ancestry would be categorized as Black. Although hypodescent is no longer invoked legally, it continues to inform everyday constructions of race. People who have an ancestor of African descent are often racialized or identify themselves as Black, even if other ancestors were not. Conversely, American Indian identification is legally based on an assessment of a person's "blood quantum," limiting who can claim Native identity.

In Latin America and the Caribbean, race continues to be an important social identity category that shapes people's life chances, though the ways in which racial identity works in the region differ significantly from the United States. Across the region, contemporary racial classification is closely tied to historical and contemporary practices and ideas about ***mestizaje*** (miscegenation; *mestiçagem* in Portuguese) – the mixing, through marriage, cohabitation, or sexual reproduction, of people classified in different racial groups. Acceptance of *mestizaje* and assumptions about its effects have resulted in conceptions of race that are based not only on physical features but also on considerations of class, education, occupation, language, clothing and hair style, geographic location, and other factors. For example, in Brazil two people may exhibit similar physical traits but have different racial identities as a result of their differing incomes, musical tastes, and clothing styles. Racial identities are also relational, dynamic, and may shift as people move from one racializing context to another. For example, many people in the Dominican Republic, irrespective of their ancestry, identify as *Indio*, a label that erases African ancestry and celebrates colonial links to Spain (not to the Indigenous Taíno community of pre-contact Hispaniola). However, in the United States, Dominicans are likely to be categorized as Black and may begin to identify themselves this way.

Throughout much of Latin America and the Caribbean, *mestizaje* has been viewed as a pathway to whitening national populations. Building on notions of race as modifiable, countries, including Brazil, Argentina, and Chile, offered generous incentives for Europeans to settle in their newly formed nation-states, often on land that had been seized from Indigenous communities (see Chapter 3). The underlying assumption of these policies was that whiteness (and its association with Europe) was a marker of modernity, and that the combination of Indigenous displacement, settler colonialism, and racial mixing would ensure a whiter, more modern nation.

Throughout much of the twentieth century, arguments were made that the acceptance of *mestizaje* was a sign of racial tolerance and signaled the absence of racism in parts of Latin America and the Caribbean. These arguments were often raised with explicit comparisons to overt racial discrimination and segregation in the United States. In Brazil, a widespread conviction that racism and racial discrimination could not exist in a racially mixed society was described as **racial democracy**. Black scholars and activists have since exposed the myth of racial democracy and demonstrated that **racism** – a power system that grants some people resources, opportunities, privilege, and power while limiting access for others – persists in Latin America and the Caribbean, both interpersonally and structurally.

The pervasiveness of racial ideologies and racism in Latin America and the Caribbean is visible in a widespread preference for whiteness. **Whiteness**, associated with wealth, privilege, power, and modernity, is a social and cultural construction that works to define who exhibits characteristics associated with being "white" in a given society. The construction of whiteness limits who can reap the social benefits of the racial hierarchy – that is, who has access to **white privilege**. For example, in Brazil employers often advertise that they are looking for employees with *boa aparência* (good appearance), a euphemism for European physical features. This hiring criteria functionally excludes Afro-descendant people from labor opportunities.

The chapters in this section focus on the construction of blackness and the ways anti-Black racism persists, despite local and global efforts to combat racism. In Chapter 4, Roland examines how racial ideology influences notions of belonging in Cuba's tourist spaces. In Chapter 5, Roth-Gordon studies white, middle-class Brazilians to show how racism manifests itself in both obvious and discreet ways to protect white privilege and white comfort. In Chapter 6, Louissaint shows how Haitian Vodou is stigmatized as anti-modern because of its categorization as a Black Atlantic tradition, yet, despite the stigma, Vodou perseveres.

KEY CONCEPTS

- *mestizaje* (miscegenation; *mestiçagem* in Portuguese): The mixing, through marriage, cohabitation, or sexual reproduction, of people classified in different racial groups.
- **race**: An invented system that divides human beings into purportedly distinct groups based on certain phenotypic traits. This system was created under the incorrect presumption that there are biological subgroups among humans.
- **racial democracy**: A widespread conviction that racism and racial discrimination could not exist in a racially mixed society.
- **racialization**: The process of assigning racial meaning to people, things, places, and behaviors and categorizing people according to ideas about race.
- **racism**: A power system that grants some people resources, opportunities, privilege, and power while limiting access for others.
- **whiteness**: A social and cultural construction that works to define who exhibits characteristics associated with being "white" in a given society.
- **white privilege**: The social benefits of the racial hierarchy afforded to people categorized as "white."

EXPLORE FURTHER

- To learn more about race, racialization, and racism, read **Section 4** and **Chapters 24** and **31**.
- Bacelar Da Silva, Antonio José. 2022. *Between Brown and Black: Anti-Racist Activism in Brazil*. New Brunswick, NJ: Rutgers University Press.
- Dawson, Allan Charles. 2014. *In Light of Africa: Globalizing Blackness in Northeast Brazil*. Toronto: University of Toronto Press.
- Goodman, Alan H., Yolanda T. Moses, and Joseph L. Jones. 2012. *Race: Are We So Different?* New York: Wiley-Blackwell.
- Hayes, Robin J., dir. 2015. *Black and Cuba*.
- Kenny, Mary Lorena. 2018. *Deeply Rooted in the Present: Heritage, Memory, and Identity in Brazilian Quilombos*. Toronto: University of Toronto Press.
- Loewe, Ronald. 2010. *Maya or Mestizo: Nationalism, Modernity and Its Discontents*. Toronto: University of Toronto Press.
- Padilha, José, and Felipe Lacerda, dirs. 2002. *Ônibus* 174 (Bus 174). [Brazil]
- PBS. 2011. *Black in Latin America*.
- Wade, Peter. 2017. *Degrees of Mixture, Degrees of Freedom: Genomics, Multiculturalism, and Race in Latin America*. Durham, NC: Duke University Press.

CHAPTER FOUR

Raciality and Belonging in Cuban Tourism

L. Kaifa Roland

On a hot day in late July 2001, I tagged along as Yeshua escorted a group of five white Canadian women to the beach from the Playa del Este hotel in which he worked. We arrived in Santa María by taxi and, after paying the beach attendant, began setting up our things on the beach chairs we had rented under a large shady tree. Within minutes, a police officer approached and asked Yeshua and me for our *carnets identidades* – our ID cards. As a dark-complexioned African American woman, I was growing accustomed to such interactions, but opted to exercise my tourist persona by pretending not to understand Spanish; Yeshua, on the other hand, had no choice. He surrendered his ID while explaining to the police officer that he was not a hustler who surreptitiously associates with foreigners for financial gain but a legally employed tourism worker who had brought the Canadians and me – a US American – for a day at the beach. In the month that I had been conducting research in Cuba, I was already accustomed to being stopped when in the presence of white-skinned tourists; however, when the officer left, the women wanted to know what had just happened. As I had observed him respond on previous occasions, Yeshua shrugged his shoulders and explained that the police officer "must have been confused."

What Yeshua left unsaid was whether the source of the officer's "confusion" was the well-worn assumption in post-emancipation societies like Cuba that darker skin suggests some form of criminality, or whether something else was also at play in this touristic context, given that my own skin color was eventually overlooked in favor of my foreign status. In this chapter, I attend to such questions of racialized belonging. Who belongs where? Who should be in the company of whom? What are the criteria by which belonging is determined? Are there categories of intermediate belonging? I draw from my ethnographic research in the context of Cuban tourism to analyze how beliefs about place of origin, status, classed behavior, and appearance are defined by and help define the concept of "race."

CUBA'S COLOR COMPLEX

Many foreign visitors today are struck by how frequently Cubans invoke terms that refer to phenotypical distinctions during ordinary conversation, especially given the oft-cited racially democratic conviction that in Cuba (as opposed to the United States, for example) "race doesn't matter." My 80-year-old neighbor Saida explained, "*Aquí, no hay nada de raza*. We're all the same. I've got a little bit of everything in me. *Llevo negro esclavo, español, Indio – llevo todo!* Just like my grandchildren – you see these here, but I've also got a nephew who is *prieto, prieto, prieto*! But how adorable he is!" In Saida's declaration that "race is a non-issue" in Cuba, she cites her own racial composite of "Black slave, Spanish, and Indian" as an example. Still, as she contrasted the lighter-complexioned *trigueño* (olive-skinned) offspring with whom she lived to her nephew who is "very, very dark!" one can glean the back hand of Cuban raciality in the exceptionality of his being both "dark" and "adorable," based on the conjunction "but" Saida used to link the two adjectives. Upon closer analysis of Cuban racial terminology, the same pattern evident elsewhere in Latin America and the Caribbean becomes clear: In general, Blackness and Black identifying features are denigrated in comparison to whiteness or features identified as "whitened."

There is a broad range of racialized color terms used today in Cuba (and elsewhere in Latin America). The *blanco* or "white" category almost exclusively links racial designation to hair color, with the significant exceptions of "olive-skinned" *trigueños*, who have straight black hair, and *lechosos*, who have a complexion described as "milky white." The different gradations of *negro* (Black) and *mulato* (mixed/brown) – featuring dark and light skin color variants and also considering hair texture and facial features – address the extent of discernible African ancestry. For example, standing behind someone with straight black hair and naturally tanned arms, a Cuban may identify them as a *trigueña*. However, when that same person turns around and their full lips or nose are visible, that same person might be called a *mulata clara* (light-skinned *mulata*).

Phenotypic traits are not the only markers of race; classed behaviors also influence people's perceptions of race (see Chapter 31). For example, Yeshua once explained to me that he considers himself *negro*, though due to both his soft hair texture and his mild manners, people generally refer to him alternately as a *negro adelantado* (Black person advancing toward whiteness) or a *mulato oscuro* (dark-skinned *mulato*). While race in Cuba is flexible, performed, and tied to class and other such traits as much as to skin color, it is also organized around a categorical contrast between white and Black, with the former valued and the latter devalued. In other words, while individuals can move up and down the racial hierarchy – **whitening** themselves, for instance, by behaving in certain (white) ways, or darkening themselves by behaving in other (Black) ways – they nevertheless enact these performances within a system that remains defined by long-standing meanings associated with skin color. An interaction I had in Trinidad-de-Cuba in which a heavyset *trigueño* musician endearingly referred to me as a *mulata* reflects this preference for whiteness. His bandmate told me I should say "thank you," presumably for the "compliment" of whitening me because of my classed (and gendered) status and behaviors, despite my dark skin and coarsely textured hair.

APPROACHING "RACE"

I am deliberate in the terms I use to describe racial-ness. If historical notions of "race" as a biological category have now been scientifically discredited, I am interested in unearthing beliefs about race that remain to this day. Because the social legacy of assumptions about biological "race" remains powerful, many scholars hesitate to discard the "race" concept altogether (see, for example, Hartigan 2005). In this chapter I speak to the slippage between historical conceptions of biological "race" and the social legacy of "race" through my choice of terminology. Rather than validate long-standing notions of scientifically grounded biological differences between peoples of varied phenotypes (i.e., "race"), I emphasize the ways those various phenotypes retain lived meanings in the real world as a result of the legacy of these notions (Harrison 1998). Throughout the chapter, I use the grammatically descriptive term **racial** to mean of or having to do with loaded conceptions of difference based on physical appearance (which terms like "race" and "ethnicity" frequently code). Likewise, I use **raciality** to describe how "race" operates in day-to-day practice, such as who is presumed to live in certain neighborhoods, listen to certain music, or have the means to eat in a particular restaurant. The Cuban context regularly reiterates the need to shift the scholarly focus from "race is how race looks" to "race is as race does." In other words, how people are raced in Cuba attends to a complicated matrix that includes both physical appearance and behaviors associated with particular racial groups.

Though it was not my intention, I inadvertently stumbled into noticing raciality in Cuba as I studied the implications of tourism for that country's socialist ideology. Before I could even talk to the tourists, I was constantly barred access to tourist sites until I had proven my foreignness, and thus my "belonging" in those sites. Whether I acted like I did not understand Spanish (as in the opening narrative) or displayed the copy of my passport I had learned to keep with me at all times, I was being asked to demonstrate on which side of the tourism divide I belonged: Because of my phenotypic traits hotel security guards, restaurant hosts, and police regularly classified me among their fellow marginalized Cubans, but my performances of foreignness often led those same gatekeepers to shift the focus from my Cuban-looking skin to the Otherness of my behaviors. In addition to security staff, my many observers (mostly Cubans, but occasionally tourists) measured my success or failure at performing the multiple identities I was interpreted to hold by categorizing me as a Cuban, a tourist, or a student from a developing country benefiting from Cuba's policy of socialist outreach that provides free training in medicine or dentistry (see also Allen 2009). Until I introduced myself, no one ever imagined I was an anthropologist.

Between 1999 and 2012, I conducted approximately 22 months of ethnographic research in various sites of Cuban tourism, including hundreds of structured and unstructured interviews among a diverse and random sampling of both Cubans and tourists. Moreover, through participant observation as I resided among each group, I gained a much more textured understanding of each group's motives and thought processes regarding the Other. Finally, though I fit neither group technically, as an anthropologist of color I had to analyze my own positionality at the intersection of both Cubans and foreign tourists. In the following sections, I strive to balance my own reflexivity with the voices of the tourists and Cubans from whom I gained an understanding of the shades of belonging.

REVITALIZED RACIALITY IN THE REVOLUTION

As a left-leaning African American, I entered the Cuban research site with an expectation that the socialist revolution had leveled class differences and made the multiplicity of skin color variations featured in Cuba nearly insignificant (see Allen 2009). Cuba's socialist ideology has certainly impacted the complexion of Cuba's class structure. Prior to the revolution's triumph in 1959, US political and business interests were paramount and catered to by Cuba's white(r) elite classes. Revolutionary Cuba has eliminated those two sources of severely imbalanced political, social, and economic power by implementing policies that improved access to education and healthcare for all Cubans while aspiring to equalize income distribution (Sawyer 2005). However, for the half century since that time, power has been concentrated exclusively in the hands of the Communist Party, whose members are largely men of European descent. To be sure, their class-leveling policies have significantly improved the life chances of Cubans of color in comparison to the pre-revolutionary period, but they have not been able to legislate old racial prejudices away completely (Allen 2009; Fernández 2010; de la Fuente 2001). Despite the systemic restructuring of education, hiring, and (to a lesser degree) housing policies early in the revolution, the legacy of nineteenth-century emancipation era beliefs about the meanings of skin color and belonging remain.

When the Soviet Union fell in 1989, the Cuban economy was devastated because it relied so heavily on trade with and investment from the Soviet Union because of the US embargo. The economy would likely have collapsed entirely except that, counter to revolutionary ideals, state officials opted to revive the tourism industry. Tourism quickly overtook sugar as the primary engine of Cuba's economy. The Cuban state insisted on maintaining a socialist economy for the general populace, even as it encouraged the growth of a restricted capitalist sector related to tourism. From the early 1990s until 2021, foreign currencies like dollars or euros were converted to the Cuban convertible peso (CUC), which had much more value than the domestic Cuban peso (CUP or MN). One result of this increasing proximity of the global economy in Cuba is increasing inequality fostered between those who have access to foreign currency through tourism or remittances (money sent to Cubans by family living outside of Cuba) and those who do not (Allen 2009; Roland 2011). For example, a family that is able to make their home amenable to foreign tourists has the capacity to rent out rooms in their *casa particular* (private accommodation) as a bed and breakfast for CUC$15 to $30 per night, in contrast to the average (converted) worker salary of CUC$20 per month that is standardized by the state. The housing scenario, in which white(r)-skinned families tend to live in nicer homes in tourist-friendly areas reflects historic racialized residential patterns. Moreover, because the majority of those who have fled into exile since the rise of the revolution were white, their (largely) white family members who remained in Cuba are the greatest beneficiaries of foreign remittances that can assist them in upgrading their homes for rental by tourists. Based on such structural inequalities, Cubans of African descent are less likely to have legal access to the money tourists bring to the country. Instead, Cubans of color have been compelled to rely on "creative home economics" (Allen 2009) that I describe elsewhere as *la lucha* – the struggle to survive (Roland 2011). Still, while these inequalities are raced, this form of racialization extends beyond skin color (Allen 2007).

RACIALIZED TOURISM

I met Grace, Marta, and Rodrigo – three tourists from Barcelona – during my first visit to Santiago-de-Cuba. We hired a driver in Céspedes Park in the center of town to take us to the shrine of Cuba's patron saint, La Virgen de la Caridad del Cobre (The Virgin of the Copper Mines Charity). Because of the dictates against Cubans associating with foreigners, the driver told me to sit in the front seat, but not to speak if the police approached since I looked Cuban enough. We were, indeed, stopped four times en route because of the obvious foreigners in the backseat of our illegal taxi, though with no repercussions. Each time, the driver explained that I was his cousin who lived abroad, and the Spaniards were my friends. Apparently, this cover story of my partial belonging satisfactorily provided the bridge that explained to authorities why white foreigners might be safe in a privately owned Cuban car.

The driver later deposited us at Siboney Beach, where our multi-hued group attracted a great deal of attention from the largely Cuban beachgoers. Aside from a few vendors, Jorge and Lenyn were the only ones who dared to come and talk with us. A conversation ensued about what Grace called the "tourist ghettos" that are endemic to Cuban tourism, where tourists have access to the most desirable recreational spaces while Cubans are generally excluded. Like many young people who seek a more "authentic" travel experience involving high levels of integration with local residents, the Spaniards were offended by the enforced nature of tourist-only spaces. Indeed, Jorge and Lenyn showed Grace and me one such

Figure 4.1. Comandante Ché Guevara contemplates the state of Cuba's revolution from artwork in the lobby of Havana's luxurious Meliá Cohiba hotel. Photo by L. Kaifa Roland.

"tourist ghetto" later that night when we encountered the crowd of Cubans hoping to get into Casa de la Trova – a popular dance locale notorious for arbitrarily limiting the numbers of Cubans permitted inside at the national currency price.

The physical separation of Cubans from tourists is fostered by Cubans' long-standing bias toward whiteness, as well as the class chasm created by Cuba's post-Soviet dual monetary system that gives convertible currency holders significantly more buying power than those who only have national currency, as described above. One of the greatest ironies in today's tourism is that these inequalities are mobilized in the name of a revolution that purportedly sought to create an egalitarian society (see Figure 4.1). To make sense of this apparent contradiction it is necessary to unpack the nature of the relationship between raciality, tourism, and belonging in today's Cuba.

A key consideration is that the Cuba experienced by tourists is markedly different from the Cuba of Cubans. Mass international tourism (the form that predominates in Cuba and is preferred by the government) is a capitalist business that requires prompt smiling service and systemic efficiency. Cuba is a socialist country in which efficiency is rare due to the centralized system of economic organization, and in which one might hope for "promptness," "smiles," or "service" but seldom all three at once. Contrasted with their Cuban hosts who live constrained by the scarcities of the socialist system during the post-Soviet era, tourists in Cuba generally exist in a leisure world of excesses – too much food, too much drink, too much time – though, by Cuban standards, they are charged exorbitant prices for such capitalistic indulgences. My research found that (1) the Cuba of tourists is one of leisure and privilege and (2) interactions between tourists and Cubans revolve around questions of power and belonging. I contend that each of these attributes are influenced by Cuban understandings about the status and place of white people, Black people, and other non-white people.

The Yuma "Race"

In the word *yuma*, Cuban popular parlance has captured the racial meanings behind both the social status measures and the visual cues involved in Cuban tourism. The term originated in the early 1990s when many Cubans watched the film *3:10 to Yuma* (Yuma, Arizona) on television, and it referred specifically to US Americans (then rarely seen in Cuba). By the time I conducted my research later in the decade, *yuma* had come to refer to a broader sector of non-Cuban "Others" whom my interviewees repeatedly told me were easily recognizable by their clothes (especially their shoes), their hairstyles or facial hair (for men), their skin colors (especially obvious attempts at tanning), and their entire *forma de ser* (their way of being). Because most tourists visited from Canada and Europe – especially Spain, France, Germany, and Italy – *yuma*s were presumed to be white.

As is the case in many tourist destinations around the world, in Cuba "Their" (tourist) skin color has been associated with global wealth, while "Our" (local/Cuban) complexion is associated with the dependence of global poverty. Therefore, non-white *yumas* who travel to Cuba from elsewhere in the Americas often have their foreignness scrutinized through a performative lens that closely considers such cultural markers as clothes, hair, skin color, and comportment (Johnson 2003). Only after those behavioral cues have been accurately interpreted are those Black and brown tourists recognized and treated as *yumas* who belong in tourist spaces rather than Cubans who are assumed not to have the means to partake in tourist spaces. This conceptual movement between color and class categories replicates the kind of cultural whitening described earlier that "advanced" my status from Blackness to mulata-ness.

Also tellingly, Cubans distinguished between this wealthier racialized group of *yumas* from other foreigners from developing countries who were in Cuba to benefit from its international socialist outreach programs in medicine and education. Russian teens, for example, though often phenotypically *rubios* (blondes), were quickly dismissed as potential clients by the hustlers

I interviewed who targeted tourists with such comments as "they're just Chernobyl victims here for medical treatment." Visibly outsiders, but also easily recognized as non-monied, this intermediate group might be racialized as *mulato* because of their lack of wealth, irrespective of their phenotypic traits. For their part, Cuban nationals of all complexions were treated by tourism's gatekeepers as criminally as well as culturally suspect, paralleling what I have described as Cuban understandings of *negros* as suspicious, loud, and otherwise inappropriate in spaces of leisure. In other words, in tourism spaces Cubans are racialized as non-white and therefore not belonging irrespective of what they actually look like, which mirrors the treatment of Black Cubans who historically have been treated by elite, white(r) Cubans as not belonging.

Returning Cubans who live abroad complicate tourism's racialized schema perhaps more than any other category of visitor. They are Cuban, but they no longer belong to the Cuban nation by virtue of their departure – and, I would add, by virtue of the foreign capital to which they now have access. I rarely encountered visiting exiles in tourist spaces, likely because the purpose of their visit was to reunite with family more than to "tour" per se (i.e., sightseeing, conspicuous consumption). Aside from the airport departure terminal, the only noteworthy occasions I have seen returning Cubans in tourist spaces were in nightclubs and swimming pools where they were generally allowed to "pass" among the *yuma* population. At a nightclub in Santiago, for example, a white-skinned visiting Cuban seemed to be authenticating his Cuban-ness for the benefit of the growing crowd of onlookers by displaying his skill at dancing the rumba. His elite whiteness (read: outsiderness) is what made his proficiency at rumba – a music and dance form based in African and Spanish music (read: insiderness) – so remarkable. Structurally, such Cubans are "mulaticized" by their liminal insider/outsider position in both tourism and the Cuban nation.

Of Bracelets and Belonging

From the tourist's point of view, I found it useful to conceive of the resort as a multi-ethnic/lingual/national village that generally remained segregated along in-group lines. As I observed the phenomenon, only children under 13 dared to traverse those boundaries. From the hotel's point of view, however, the only national distinction that mattered was whether the guest was Cuban or not, a distinction embodied in the plastic hospital-style bracelets issued to all tourists staying in all-inclusive hotels throughout the country – most notably the beach areas of Havana's Playas del Este, Varadero, Trinidad, Cayo Largo, and Cayo Coco. Such bracelets are used in hotels and nightclubs around the world, but their meaning is magnified in the socialist yet racialized context of today's Cuba: They indicate who belongs in tourist spaces, who does not, and how much access they should have to "the good life."

Upon checking in, each guest at an all-inclusive hotel is given one of these brightly colored bracelets and told that they should wear it at all times to use the hotel's amenities. Most guests keep their bracelets on far beyond the confines of the resort, but I met several who resented having their tourist status labeled and refused to wear them at all, keeping them, instead, in pockets or purses. One francophone Swiss woman was so bold as to discard hers altogether on the first day: "I put it in the garbage the moment I got in my room because I refuse to be tagged like a dog!" This woman recognized that the wristbands identified her as part of a privileged group, but she did not recognize that these bracelets might mean something different for a person who "looked Cuban" and may need them as a signifier of belonging. Still, not all of these rebellious tourists were white; I met a 70-something brown-skinned Canadian woman of Egyptian descent who grinned as she flashed her wristband to me from her beach bag. After a few days in the hotel, one is generally known to security and staff and would rarely be barred from the hotel's facilities, even without a bracelet. Nonetheless, I witnessed a few incidents in which security officers asked to see guests' bracelets. If the bracelets were not produced, a key or valid room number would suffice. On very rare occasions, I observed security actively pursuing foreign white men who were using their color advantage to enjoy the hotel's amenities, though they were not actually guests. Especially among repeat travelers, there is an increasing recognition of the power of white skin and foreign-ness (see Roland 2011).

Until the expansions offered since Raúl Castro inherited the presidential reins from his brother Fidel in 2008, among the few Cuban nationals who could hope to partake in the luxuries of the new tourist industry were honeymooners and vanguard workers – the top-producing, hardest-working exemplars of the revolution's socialist ideals of humility, sacrifice, and service toward the greater good. Because the convertible currency prices of the hotels are generally far beyond what any Cuban who works for the state can afford, their visits are highly subsidized, and – before Raúl's expansions at least – they were allowed to pay the same amount in national currency. That is, if the hotel room normally cost CUC$50 per night, a subsidized Cuban national would pay MN$50 per night (CUC$2.27). To signify what their peso rate allowed them – the same all-inclusive meals as tourists but limited alcoholic beverages – Cuban tourists would wear differently colored bracelets. During my fieldwork, I never heard any Cubans complain about their differential tagging. Indeed, those with whom I spoke were grateful for the opportunity to partake in resort tourism at all and acknowledged the arrangement as completely fair. In Cuba's racial scheme, these admissible Cubans might be conceived as mulaticized through the nature of their partial belonging in tourism spaces.

Cubans who are neither vanguard workers nor honeymooners are rarely permitted beyond the lobbies of hotels without paying a day fare (or having it paid by a guest). The pass they receive for the CUC$5–$10 fare allows them to eat, drink, and swim, but visiting Cuban nationals are seldom allowed into guest rooms at all due to concerns about sexual services or theft that might occur beyond the watchful eyes of hotel staff. The high price of entry precludes harassment by hustlers, and if the gatekeeper is at all suspicious they can always refuse service. Indeed, the very presence of security guards at the door serves to intimidate and remind the majority of bracelet-free Cubans that they must remain outside hotels altogether.

Power and Belonging

"I used to sit out on the Malecón with my friends and we'd look up at the nightclub in the Habana Libre [hotel] and watch the lights flash. We'd just imagine what a good time people must be having …" – Yeshua, age 24

"People from other countries can come here [to Cuba] but Cubans can neither enter their hotel nor visit the other countries." – Niyelis, age 19

If Cubans racialized tourists as *yumas* for whom the nation's scarce material resources are reserved, where does that leave everyday Cubans? While they have been promised the fruits of tourism's economic earnings in the form of continued socialist benefits, Cubans largely remain outsiders to the capitalist lifestyle in their midst. I recorded countless examples of such exclusions during my research (see also Allen 2009). One particularly notable occasion involved 32-year-old Javier.

As a light-complexioned *mulato* with hazel eyes and dreadlocked hair, Javier explained: "My mother is *blanca*, my father was a *mulato oscuro* (dark-skinned *mulato*), so in this country they call me *jaba'o*. But I am Rasta, so I consider myself to be *negro*. *Yo soy negro* (I am Black)." After a month of providing me with a wealth of information about his native country during my first sojourn in fieldwork, I offered Javier some of my clothes and shoes to give to his teenage daughter. Knowing the edicts against Cubans in hotel rooms, I invited Javier to wait for me in the lobby while I went to retrieve the items. He opted instead to wait outside, across the street from the hotel. By the time I returned some 5 to 10 minutes later, Javier had been detained by the police. I rushed over and explained that Javier had been waiting for me – an American staying in the hotel. The police officer disregarded me and continued calling Javier's information into his walkie-talkie. Finding no hustling record of note, Javier was eventually given back his ID with the admonition that he "stay away from tourists." After the officer departed, I tried to calm Javier, who paced back and forth angrily shaking his head. In his frustration and humiliation, tears filled his eyes as he exclaimed: "This happens to me every day, and it's just because of the way I look!" If white(r)-skinned Cubans in tourist spaces were mulaticized when they participated in the tourist industry because of the assumption that they had the means to belong, here Javier's Rastafarian appearance signified the unkemptness of an impoverished and criminalized person. In the Cuban context, Javier's Black(ened) self-identification served to clarify his place as an outsider for tourism's gatekeepers.

CONCLUSION

One night, three Cuban men were walking down Havana's popular Malecón boardwalk: Marco and Dario were dark-complexioned men of obvious African descent, while Tony had large blond curls and white-complexioned skin. As the three walked, they were greeted by a young (white) man they used to know from California. Without addressing Tony or the Californian at all, a police officer approached and asked for Marco and Dario's ID cards. The Californian tried to explain that they were all his friends, prompting the officer to ask Tony if he was also Cuban. When Tony did not lie, his ID card was also collected, and all the Cubans were taken to the police station. While both Marco and Dario had been arrested for tourist-related incidents before, this was Tony's first such encounter with the police.

This chapter began with Yeshua declaring that the police officer who asked for his ID card was "confused." At many points in this chapter it has become clear that the police (and other tourism gatekeepers) readily interpret Blackness as a sign of undesirable criminality. The confusion comes because while not all Black people are criminals, they are structurally defined by their general undesirability. The unprovoked arrest of Tony and his friends invites the question, what constitutes a Black person? Who is racialized as inside the sphere of belonging, and who is racialized as an outsider? With Tony's and my own experiences in mind, I ask, how stable are these categories? These are questions of belonging. I have illustrated that in Cuba's Latin American and Caribbean context, early notions of "race" emphasized origins and behaviors linked to income and status as much as they attended to physical differences among groups. At its core, then, "race" is not about skin color; it is about the hierarchized valuation of difference. Racialization is about determining who should have access to certain privileges in contrast to who should be deemed marginal to privilege and power. I have proposed here that the key to understanding the racialized nature of tourism is to clarify embedded social assumptions about perceived Blackness, whiteness, and mixedness. If raciality is not only about appearances, but also about questions of belonging as place of origin, status, and classed behavior, then it becomes clear how studying tourism provides a means for better understanding how assumptions about "race" operate in the real world.

Deconstructing what "race" means and how "race" acts in Cuba's multi-hued revolutionary society supports an understanding of how raciality plays out in a highly lucrative form of popular culture that brings people of different complexions, nationalities, and global class status into proximity – tourism. Do similar questions of belonging reveal themselves in other places, or with other global forms of popular culture like salsa, reggae, or hip-hop music? Sports phenomena like basketball, baseball, or soccer? How about spiritual practices like Santería or yoga? What role does the participants' (assumed) place of origin, culturally based behaviors, status, or appearance play in either the successful production or consumption of these practices? If race scholarship has long failed to effectively communicate how a cultural construction like "race" can still hold meaning even when it has been scientifically disproved, then a key recommendation evolving from this study is that we must increasingly deconstruct how raciality operates in myriad popular practices like tourism to clarify for the non-academic public that "race" today is not just about skin color – if it was ever about skin color at all.

REFLECTION AND DISCUSSION QUESTIONS

- What is the utility of thinking about the differences between humans as "racial" rather than in terms of "race"?
- Based on what you have learned in this chapter, what are some ways that raciality is constructed differently in Cuba from what you know of the United States? How are Blackness, whiteness, and mixedness understood differently in each place? How are they similar?
- How is tourism in Cuba a racialized space? Can you think of an instance from your own travel experiences where tourism involved racialization?
- How have you observed "belonging" to be at play in the contemporary racial arena of your home country?
- How do you understand the relationship between what is generally called "race" and your understanding of "culture"? How are they interrelated, and in what ways are they distinct?

KEY CONCEPTS

- **racial**: As an adjective, racial is a descriptive term that speaks to issues involving differences that appear to be based on physical appearance but are more likely based in perceptions of cultural beliefs or behaviors.
- **raciality**: If racial is an adjective, raciality is a noun that describes how the artificial concept of "race" operates in the real world. Though race isn't real, raciality is.
- **whitening**: The concept of cultural "whitening" assumes a categorical contrast between white and Black, with the former valued and the latter devalued; individuals can move up and down the racial hierarchy – "whitening" themselves, for instance, by behaving in certain (white) ways, or darkening themselves by behaving in other (Black) ways.

EXPLORE FURTHER

- To learn more about challenges surrounding tourism in Latin America and the Caribbean, read the chapters in **Section 10** and **Chapter 26**.
- Bastian, Hope. 2018. *Everyday Adjustments in Havana: Economic Reforms, Mobility, and Emerging Inequalities.* Lanham, MD: Lexington Books.
- Spence Benson, Devyn. 2017. "Conflicting Legacies of Antiracism in Cuba." *NACLA Report on the Americas* 49 (1): 48–55.

ABOUT THE AUTHOR

L. Kaifa Roland is an associate professor of anthropology and director of the Global Black Studies program at Clemson University. Her research interests include tourism, entrepreneurship, racial and gender constructions, popular cultural practices, and critiques of capitalism. With a regional focus on the Caribbean and the broader African diaspora, she has conducted extensive field research in Cuba for more than 20 years.

REFERENCES

Allen, Jafari Sinclaire. 2007. "Means of Desire's Production: Male Sex Labor in Cuba." *Identities: Global Studies in Culture and Power* 14 (1–2): 183–202. https://doi.org/10.1080/10702890601102647.

———. 2009. "Looking B[l]ack at Revolutionary Cuba." *Latin American Perspectives* 36 (1): 53–62. https://doi.org/10.1177/0094582X08329425.

de la Fuente, Alejandro. 2001. *A Nation for All: Race, Inequality, and Politics in Twentieth Century Cuba*. Chapel Hill: University of North Carolina Press.

Fernández, Nadine. 2010. *Revolutionizing Romance: Interracial Couples in Contemporary Cuba*. New Brunswick, NJ: Rutgers University Press.

Harrison, Faye. 1998. "Introduction: Expanding the Discourse of Race." *American Anthropologist* 100 (3): 609–31. https://doi.org/10.1525/aa.1998.100.3.609.

Hartigan, John. 2005. "Culture against Race: Reworking the Basis of Racial Analysis." *South Atlantic Quarterly* 104 (3): 543–60. https://doi.org/10.1215/00382876-104-3-543.

Johnson, E. Patrick. 2003. *Appropriating Blackness: Performance and the Politics of Authenticity*. Durham, NC: Duke University Press.

Roland, L. Kaifa. 2011. *Cuban Color in Tourism and La Lucha: An Ethnography of Racial Meanings*. New York: Oxford University Press.

Sawyer, Mark. 2005. *Racial Politics in Post-Revolutionary Cuba*. Cambridge: Cambridge University Press.

CHAPTER FIVE

Protecting White Comfort and White Supremacy in Rio de Janeiro, Brazil

Jennifer Roth-Gordon

One day after visiting the Piraquê social club in Rio de Janeiro with a few local friends, I walked through the guardhouse, past the turnstiles, and out onto the busy city street that led to the public parking lot and formed part of the pedestrian/bike path that circled the city's lagoon. Sofia's teenage son was, as usual, on his iPhone and probably absorbed in a YouTube video or video game. As he walked out onto the street with us, Sofia turned and immediately cried out (in Portuguese), "Bruno! Where do you think you are? Paris? Lisbon? Put your phone away!" Her sarcasm belied her frustration and concern that he was not paying attention to his surroundings, as we had crossed over the threshold beyond the guarded gates of the private club and onto unprotected city streets. But her comment was layered with meaning, both personal and racial. Her choice of cities was not random: The day before our outing, her family had returned from a winter break trip to France and Portugal. While the Brazilian currency had devalued, making trips to the United States (and the popular destination of Disney World, see O'Dougherty 2002) very expensive, this year she had been able to take her family on a multi-week vacation to Europe. Her sharp words to her son, then, did not mean to suggest that he did not belong in those places. Instead, she offered a subtle critique of their own city and country – places that had failed to control street crime and drug violence and were unable to offer her family the level of protection they had enjoyed while in Europe.

The social club they belong to, the international travel they had just taken, and her son's iPhone all reveal the Brazilian family's middle-class status. The significance of iPhones and other Apple devices is hard to overstate. While they remain expensive prestige items in the United States as well, they are hard to come by even in Rio, which boasted the first Apple store in all of Latin America. Computers and phones are heavily marked up with import taxes, and many middle-class Brazilians try to buy new technology when they are able to travel abroad to the United States and Europe. They also often trade on a network of friends and family that travel when they cannot afford to, to bring US status goods to them. Access to the latest models of phones, ear buds, and laptops therefore points not only to higher levels of disposable income but also to global mobility. Given the high price on many of these items, they often remain beyond the reach of the majority of Brazil's residents and are the most common object of theft. But travel and the latest technology are not just signs of wealth; they are also signs that connect Brazilians, who worry about their country's (lack of) whiteness, to whiter "First World" places.

In this chapter, I show how an analysis of mundane interactions – such as Sofia's chastizing of her son – can reveal hidden **racial logics** that explain not only how people think about race, but also how they make sense of the racially unequal world they live in. Researching **racial inequality** generally involves investigating how nonwhite people are denied resources and rights due to their race (see Chapters 12 and 31). In this case, a white mother spoke to her white son surrounded mostly by people identifying as white, and they do not appear to be talking about race at all. I will argue, however, that this interaction works to uphold **white supremacy** and what I call "white comfort." I approach racial inequality by "studying up" – examining the lives of people in positions of relative racial and class privilege – to explain how and why white middle-class Brazilians like Sofia justify inequality and allow state violence against people of color to continue.

"COMPULSORY CLOSENESS" AND DAILY LIFE IN RIO DE JANEIRO

Visiting the Piraquê social club is a little like visiting Las Vegas or the Epcot Center in Disney World. The buildings are all designed to look like one is walking down the streets of a small village in the Alps, with small white structures decorated with external wood beams outlining their A-framed roofs (Figure 5.1). While the architecture is decidedly European, the scenery is breathtakingly Rio: Instead of snow-capped mountains, one looks up at the iconic Cristo on Rio's rainforest-covered hills. Though there is no view of the beach (located only a 5-minute drive away), the club occupies a tiny peninsula filled with palm trees that juts out into a scenic lagoon and thus allows for relaxing water-side dining. Once you have crossed over into the club, there is no contact with Rio's busy city streets. Re-creating their own private version of public city spaces (down to the famous black-and-white tiled sidewalks typical of Rio and other Portuguese colonial cities), there are small plazas with park benches, a news stand selling magazines and children's toys, and even a popcorn vendor with the usual options of salty or sweet caramelized popcorn sold in small paper bags to be consumed as "street food." On the club grounds there is a beauty salon, a library, a reading room, a large playroom with separate sections for children of different ages, a movie theater, a brightly colored children's playground, several restaurants offering everything from drinks and ice cream popsicles to fine dining, and sports facilities of all types, including swimming pools, a gymnastics studio, and large soccer fields. The club thus folds public into private in a sheltered car- and crowd-free space. Rio

Figure 5.1. The Piraquê social club in Rio de Janeiro, Brazil. Photo by Marcelo Costa Braga.

residents of all backgrounds will tell you that what's great about Brazil is that everyone can go to the beach, since it is free and open to all, but social clubs offer the Brazilian middle class and the wealthy (who have not fled to gated communities) carefully guarded outdoor spaces. Here they can let their children run free, unattended, without worrying about crime, violence, or what they perceive to be dangerous social mixture. Rio's stores and restaurants may offer semi-private spaces that are also guarded by private security, but social clubs are entirely private spaces open only to members, their guests, and pre-screened employees.

I had returned to Rio de Janeiro in January 2019 for another phase of my research, in which I studied white middle-class families through a large private school where I had enrolled my own children for the academic year in 2014. Though we were very well received, my multi-racial family stood out in the school: We were one of few non-Brazilian families, and while my husband, biological son, and I blended in with the lighter-skinned population of the school, my adopted son and daughter were far darker than the majority of the students and teachers. Most of the school would identify as white or *moreno* (brown), while two of my children were readily identified as *negro* (Black). By the time of this visit to the social club, I had interviewed dozens of mothers and other teachers and caregivers (including some fathers), and I had spent many hours joining them for everyday activities that ranged from dropping kids off at school, attending school functions, sitting on the sidelines while our children participated in after-school activities, to taking them to birthday parties and social gatherings on weekends and over school holidays. Like us, the families that I befriended had children ranging in age from 3 to 16, and they all lived in the middle-class and upper-middle-class neighborhoods of Copacabana, Ipanema, and Leblon. Many of them owned three-bedroom condos in gated buildings with doormen that were often in close proximity to *favelas* (shantytowns). While these condominium dwellers were generally white and relatively wealthy (though not the uber rich or the Brazilian elite), their well-maintained buildings were adjacent to poor, mostly nonwhite favelas that climbed the hills separating the wealthier neighborhoods. Characterized by self-constructed homes and precarious infrastructure, favelas are now euphemistically called *comunidades* (or communities) in an attempt to erase the stigma of associations with poverty, Blackness, criminality, and drug-related violence. Sometimes condominium dwellers were so physically close to favela residents that they could see each other's homes from their windows, and they frequently shared the same city streets.

Rio residents thus experience a "compulsory closeness" with one another (Veloso 2010) that is unusual given the fact that most of the world's cities offer more physical distance between the "haves" and the "have nots." In Rio, as in much of Latin America, the whiter wealthier middle class has retreated from many shared public spaces and what are often poor-quality public services. They rely on private doctors and healthcare rather than free but overburdened and under-resourced public clinics, and they send their children to private schools and private after-school activities. In addition to seeking higher-quality services, they are also fleeing from the high levels of crime and violence that are part of the daily experience of living in a city like Rio. This means that they seek to avoid public transportation like buses, though the middle class will ride on the metro in certain parts of the city. In densely packed neighborhoods like Copacabana, Ipanema, and Leblon, members of the middle class will walk through city streets that poor nonwhite residents also use to access grocery stores, local bakeries, and banks; these services are often unavailable in their own favela neighborhoods. Families like Sofia's are surrounded by evidence of the city's stark inequality: Barefoot and shirtless children and families sit on strips of cardboard on sidewalks outside trendy air-conditioned restaurants and boutique stores that sell expensive perfumes, chocolates, and clothing.

Daily interactions with people who are hired (often at or slightly above minimum wage) to protect, assist, or provide care for one's family serve as additional reminders that members of the middle class reside in a city characterized by high levels of poverty and stark social and racial inequality. In all spaces they frequent, members of the white middle class are used to having mostly poor people of color present in manual or service-level positions. This includes in their homes, as their condominium buildings all have doormen, and they frequently have domestic workers who either live with them (though this is less common these days) or come to cook, clean, and care for children several days a week. These interactions belie a kind of uncomfortable intimacy for everyone involved: Domestic workers and nannies have to navigate the high levels of access they have to their employer's private lives and personal possessions. While their job requirements entail responsibility for washing the family's clothes and straightening up rooms, they also interact in relatively tight spaces that require explicit and implicit negotiation. Are they allowed to sit on the living room sofa? Which bathrooms can they use? If the child they care for normally sleeps in a parent's bed and they require someone to lie with them before they fall asleep, the caregiver might be asked to perform this nightly ritual in the parent's stead. This kind of contact across race and class lines is deeply embedded into everyday life for many Rio residents.

While the social clubs that white middle-class families frequent offer refuge in the form of guarded, less crowded private space, they do not completely shelter members from the city's social mixture. White and wealthy patrons are surrounded by members of the working class, who are often darker skinned, who either accompany them to the club as babysitters or nannies or are employed by the club to serve at the restaurants, clean, and maintain the facilities. These are decidedly not white-only spaces, but they are spaces designed for white people who make up the vast majority of the clientele. Members often have large social circles who gather at these clubs, and children feel at home there, running off to meet friends and ordering snacks on their family's tab. Many middle-class children learn to swim at these clubs, as there are few public pools in the city. Along with visiting shopping malls, movie theaters, restaurants, and the beach (one of the less guarded spaces they visit), social clubs were a common space of leisure for the middle-class families I knew. The day after Sofia's return from Europe (and my family's arrival to Rio), we had gathered at the club to catch up while the children ran around and played.

"WHERE DO YOU THINK YOU ARE?"

After returning from trips to Europe or the United States, my white middle-class friends almost always commented on how safe they felt walking around while abroad. Rio suffers from high levels of police violence (up to five people a day were killed in 2019) and an incredibly high rate of homicides (three times the level of the United States). This violence also threatens children: At least one died per month from a stray bullet in gunfire exchanged between drug gangs or with the police (Harris 2021). Even though the deadly combination of militarized police, armed drug traffickers, and perpetual "urban warfare" most heavily impacted poor Black families living in favelas, white middle-class families felt the daily effects of living in a city with high levels of crime and violence. I did not meet a family that had not personally experienced muggings or theft, which could include being robbed at gunpoint or having money or cell phones taken out of the hands of children. These not uncommon and frequently discussed experiences led to ubiquitous parental fear and the never-ending management of risk.

It is often hard to explain to those who haven't experienced it directly how much living in a dangerous city changes a person and influences their thinking, their daily choices, and their relationship to their own body. In English we have the phrase "street smarts," but this underestimates the sheer amount of time and energy that goes into navigating public spaces in Rio. Perhaps a relatable example would be living life during the COVID-19 pandemic, where every outing seemed filled with potential risk (of an unknowable magnitude) and every action had to be strategically calculated in relation to this sense of risk. Middle-class parents like Sofia worried about how their kids traveled through city spaces, what they were carrying, when they were old enough to travel alone, what they should be looking out for, how parents could follow their movements from afar, and what could be done to enhance safety.

A vast array of defensive measures to reduce risk were taken up by all Rio residents. Though I describe practices among the white middle class, residents of marginalized communities were subject to far greater risk, exposed to higher levels of crime and violence, and could not always engage in the measures middle-class families took up to try to minimize their exposure to dangerous situations. Middle-class children were carefully warned never to answer their cell phone on a public street. They were to duck into a store or restaurant, behind security guards, before making or answering a call. They sometimes were given a second, older cell phone that they could offer up if they were mugged. And they were warned to be especially careful around the entrances to their private schools, which were seen as prime spots for targeting youth with expensive technology. When and if they were allowed to travel alone, they often had strict instructions to call their parents before heading out and upon arrival at their destination. Almost all parents tracked their children's phones and some used apps that would let them know if their children's batteries were low, which might explain why they weren't picking up their phones. Parents often tracked their children's Uber rides and either upgraded to more expensive cars and rides or looked carefully at the safety profile of the driver they had been assigned. Sometimes they sent messages to the drivers ahead of time so that the driver would know a parent was watching over the child on their ride.

These concerns over the physical well-being of their families sometimes translated into support for state violence. It is well-established that **anti-Black state violence** continues unchecked in Brazil, where the number of people killed by the police annually is nearly eight times the number of people killed by the police in the United States, despite a smaller national population. Politicians have been successfully elected based on campaigns that explicitly endorsed police killings through slogans such as "*Bandido bom é bandido morto*" (A good criminal is a dead criminal). This expression offers an excellent example of how racial inequality happens and why it is tolerated by many in Brazil, as it advocates for patterns of racial violence that entail killing "criminals" and protecting "upstanding" Brazilian citizens without unpacking how those categories are racially loaded. Thus, one can support this idea (that criminals who threaten others deserve to die) without acknowledging or critically analyzing how this benefits white people (who are treated as if they are the only "upstanding" citizens) and how it terrorizes Black neighborhoods and communities (which are overpoliced and readily associated with criminality). All of these many daily experiences with inequality, crime, and violence feed into and help explain the significance of Sofia's remarks.

PROTECTING WHITE COMFORT

Brazil's claim to be a "racial democracy" in which all people are treated equally – regardless of race – has been repeatedly challenged (Sheriff 2001), and Rio residents today will mostly all agree that racism does exist in Brazil. Black activists began using the slogan "*Vidas Negras Importam*" (Black Lives Matter) even before the 2020 worldwide protests in response to George Floyd's brutal murder in the United States. Several months later, on the eve of Black Consciousness Day (a relatively new day of national recognition), a Black man named João Alberto Silveira Freitas was beaten to death in a supermarket in the south of Brazil by two security guards. Like George Floyd, Beto (João Alberto's nickname) also died of asphyxiation, and his brutal killing (over a minor altercation after which he refused to leave the store) was also filmed and broadcast to the world. Activists have described the number of Black lives cut short by police and drug gang violence as an ongoing "Black genocide." Though many members of Brazil's white middle class would not agree with this description, they are aware of the frequent police brutality that impacts largely poor Black male youth.

Within this context, Sofia's critique of the insecurity of daily life in Rio de Janeiro points to assumptions that white people, first and foremost, should be protected. She has just left a private club that affords families like hers a high level of security. We could describe her comment as a call to uphold white privilege, including her family's rights to acquire and display wealth, consume imported goods, and move freely and safely through public city spaces. But I have begun using the term **white comfort** to not just talk about privileges that white people "have" in relation to people of color, but also to highlight the naturalization of expectations about how white people should live in the world. With the term white comfort, I highlight a widespread belief that white people's lives should be protected and made more comfortable and an awareness that this sense of safety and security will come at the expense of nonwhite Others. This includes the increased access to the labor of Black Brazilians – who are paid low wages to tend to white middle-class children, clean white middle-class homes, and guard their buildings and the spaces they frequent – often at the expense of their own families. Through the term white comfort, I suggest that white people engage in a hyper-valuation of white life and well-being as they justify the ways that their own protection should come first (see also Mills 1997).

In this incident, in which Sofia does not directly mention whiteness, white life, or white comfort, she also implies – but does not say – who her son needs to protect himself from. iPhones do not steal themselves, and the target of her fear are "criminals" who are assumed to be poor Black male youth. Here her awareness of the brutality (and corruption) of the Brazilian police cannot match or override her concern for her family and their need for protection – even as she knows it makes Black mothers' own sons less safe (Smith 2016). Within a context in which the descendants of the enslaved continue to be controlled through their employment in service positions and through state violence, in what has been called the "afterlife of slavery" (Hartman 2007; Sharpe 2016), a defense of whiteness entails a certain level of support for the suppression and control of Black Brazilians. Here, understandable concerns for her family's well-being are grounded in the conviction that a functioning society should prioritize white comfort and control Black male criminality.

CONCLUSION

As an ethnographer, I watch and describe how racial inequality happens in everyday life. This may seem like a strange thing to say: Racial inequality is more often *measured* or *tracked*. Social scientists who study structural racism, such as police violence or health disparities, often turn to quantitative research methods to document broad societal patterns in which people wind up with unequal life chances and experiences (of being protected/killed by the police or gaining/not gaining access to healthcare) based solely on their race. It might seem more intuitive to say that I watch *racism* happen in real life, on a daily basis, but, as in Sofia's example, that's rarely what I see. In talking about racism, both Brazilians and North Americans most often mean active racism – individual acts in which people obviously intend to harm someone due to their perceived racial difference. I'm less interested in these more overt and obvious encounters because the enormous differences in life chances and how people live can't be explained by these relatively rare intentional acts.

The mother–son interaction that I have described did not involve active racism, and it isn't best described as a *microaggression* – an act that is more common but less obviously racist (a form of passive racism that is harder to see). Microaggressions still cause harm to people of color; they include instances where white people touch or even "pet" a Black person's hair, thus emphasizing their difference from a white beauty norm and making them feel less human. Studies of inequality often ask important questions about dehumanization: How does a society demean certain groups of people and justify their unequal treatment? How do whole groups of people come to be seen as undeserving? This chapter illustrates the flip side of this question by asking how select groups of people come to be seen as *more* human and *more* deserving. Sofia's comment to her son is better described as an example of upholding white supremacy, through the racial logic of white comfort. Over hundreds of years, transatlantic enslavement created the conditions for white supremacy and anti-Black racial violence, suggesting that only people racialized as white were worthy of protection, in particular from Black people who were deemed racially inferior and often controlled through state violence. My attention to white comfort – as a hidden but fundamental racial logic – has been profoundly influenced by Black theorists who have carefully laid out the ongoing stakes of anti-Blackness and white supremacy (Hartman 2007; Sharpe 2016).

In the interaction analyzed here, a mother criticizes her son for his inattentiveness and lack of caution. She has explicitly taught him to be careful on city streets. But what she is also teaching him, more covertly, is that as a member of the white middle class, he deserves protection from the Black "criminals" who might seek to harm him or gain access to his prized possessions. This might be viewed as an act of motherly protection, but it cannot be separated from a worldview in which upstanding white citizens are taught to fear imagined Black criminals. Under this racial logic, racial inequality and racial violence are unfortunate, but they are also justified and necessary, particularly in a notoriously dangerous place where neither the city, the state, nor the federal government has been able to control drug-related crime and violence. In this moment, a teenager is reminded that he is valuable and worthy because of his whiteness and his ability to temporarily reside in the more "civilized" and whiter European capital cities of Paris and Lisbon – places where white citizens are understood to be better protected. The critique he has learned is not that a government should serve and provide for all of the people residing within its borders, but rather that evidence for Brazil's national failure lies in its inability to protect hardworking white citizens who can display their connections to whiteness.

As I exit the carefully guarded space of a private social club and return to the social mixture of Rio's city streets, I watch as racial inequality is naturalized and explained in real time – and not through acts of active racism, microaggressions, or even more passive, unconscious acts of racial bias. Indeed, no one has mentioned race at all, and no one present has been mistreated or maligned. And yet a racial hierarchy has been preserved, and the Brazilian government has been critiqued for its inability to protect its white citizens. Daily interactions like this one, in which white supremacy goes unchallenged and is passed down to the next generation, show how racial inequality is upheld not only by acts we would describe as "racist" but also through more hidden racial logics – in which the superiority of white people and the need for their protection circulate and shape people's understanding of themselves and the world around them, allowing for the dehumanization of Black people and the perpetuation of centuries of anti-Black state violence.

REFLECTION AND DISCUSSION QUESTIONS

- How is inequality naturalized through everyday encounters? What specific examples can you offer of how we are surrounded by messages on the news, in advertisements, and on social media that make inequality seem normal and acceptable?
- How is inequality lived and naturalized every day through the organization of (urban) space? What examples can you give of ways that race and class segregation continue, even when no laws allow for exclusion or limitations on how and where people can move?
- Why is inequality so hard to challenge? What might convince those who continue to benefit from race, class, and other hierarchies to engage in the struggle for racial and social justice?

- Why is it sometimes easier to think about examples such as the one presented in terms of socioeconomic class inequality (the "haves" versus the "have nots") rather than about race? How and why is racial inequality harder for some people to see and talk about?
- What are some of the challenges and possibilities offered by "studying up"? What can it tell us about inequality? Why might it be difficult to study?

KEY CONCEPTS

- **anti-Black state violence**: Patterns of violence against Black people that are either directly or indirectly supported by the government and often justified through fears that Black people are inherently violent and need to be controlled.
- **racial inequality**: The differential treatment of groups of people based on ideas of racial difference. These ideas are often used to justify inequitable access to rights and resources, including (but not limited to) wealth.
- **racial logics**: Beliefs in the innate racial superiority of white people and the inferiority of people of color that uphold our understanding of our society and influence how we interpret the world we live in.
- **white comfort**: The ways that a society is structured to secure white safety and well-being through the labor and enforced vulnerability of racialized Others.
- **white supremacy**: An overall climate, racial order, and way of organizing society in which white people are given preferential treatment over people of color, though this does not need to be encoded into law. The term *white supremacist* is generally reserved for people or groups that outwardly support this arrangement and may advocate for racial violence to protect this racial order.

EXPLORE FURTHER

- To learn more about racial inequality and racism in Brazil, read **Chapters 12**, **24**, and **31**.
- Alves, Jaime Amparo. 2018. *The Anti-Black City: Police Terror and Black Urban Life in Brazil*. Minneapolis: University of Minnesota Press.
- Harris, Bryan. 2021. "Militias, Corruption, and COVID: Rio de Janeiro's Deepening Crisis." *Financial Times*, March 6. https://www.ft.com/content/6dfd75c9-579e-445c-82af-2e7c3cb16f9a.
- Roth-Gordon, Jennifer. 2017. *Race and the Brazilian Body: Blackness, Whiteness, and Everyday Language in Rio de Janeiro*. Oakland: University of California Press.
- Vox. 2020. "What It Means to Be Black in Brazil." *YouTube*, September 23. https://tinyurl.com/Black-in-Brazil.

ABOUT THE AUTHOR

Jennifer Roth-Gordon is a cultural and linguistic anthropologist and associate professor in the School of Anthropology at the University of Arizona. She has been conducting research in Rio de Janeiro, Brazil, on race, whiteness, and racial inequality since 1995. She is the white mother of a biological white son and two adopted Black children, all three of whom serve as honorary co-researchers when she conducts research on parenting and family life in Rio and also as research participants who allow her to make comparisons to daily family life in the United States.

REFERENCES

Harris, Bryan. 2021. "Militias, Corruption, and COVID: Rio de Janeiro's Deepening Crisis." *Financial Times*, March 6. https://www.ft.com/content/6dfd75c9-579e-445c-82af-2e7c3cb16f9a.

Hartman, Saidiya V. 2007. *Lose Your Mother: A Journey along the Atlantic Slave Route*. New York: Farrar, Straus, and Giroux.

Mills, Charles W. 1997. *The Racial Contract*. Ithaca, NY: Cornell University Press.

O'Dougherty, Maureen. 2002. *Consumption Intensified: The Politics of Middle-Class Daily Life in Brazil*. Durham, NC: Duke University Press.

Sharpe, Christina. 2016. *In the Wake: On Blackness and Being*. Durham, NC: Duke University Press.

Sheriff, Robin E. 2001. *Dreaming Equality: Color, Race, and Racism in Urban Brazil*. New Brunswick, NJ: Rutgers University Press.

Smith, Christen A. 2016. "Facing the Dragon: Black Mothering, Sequelae, and Gendered Necropolitics in the Americas." *Transforming Anthropology* 24 (1): 31–48. https://doi.org/10.1111/traa.12055.

Veloso, Leticia. 2010. "Governing Heterogeneity in the Context of Compulsory Closeness: The 'Pacification' of Favelas in Rio de Janeiro." In *Suburbanization in Global Society*, edited by Mark Clapson and Ray Hutchison, 253–72. Bingley, UK: JAI Press.

CHAPTER SIX

The "Paradoxical" Persistence of Haitian Vodou after the Cholera Epidemic

Guilberly Louissaint

A *GEN DE LWA*

We arrived on a motorcycle taxi in front of a small tin-roofed temple in a rural neighborhood on the outskirts of the port city of Saint-Marc, Haiti, about a half-hour north of downtown (*la ville*). I was accompanied by Max, an herbalist and an educated businessman who owned a small boutique in the city. Max was an active Vodouisant, or follower of **Haitian Vodou**, a syncretic faith drawing on both West and Central African religions and Catholicism, but also a spiritual belief system unto itself. Although he had taken up residence in the downtown area, Max often traveled to the rural communities on the outskirts of Saint-Marc, not too far from where his mother and some of his extended family lived, to participate in local religious gatherings. It was Max who invited me to this event, known as a *Gen de Lwa*, a religious gathering that includes prayer, ritual dancing, and drumming where the faithful seek answers regarding health or financial burdens and hope to receive messages regarding personal tribulations from deceased loved ones or ancestral spirits. The terms *Gen de Lwa* and *Gens* are used interchangeably, but often the term *Gen* refers more specifically to Catholic prayer masses, while *Gen de Lwa* are the syncretic Vodou gatherings occurring weekly around many *Lakous* (shared communal spaces) throughout Haiti. *Gen de Lwa* include different practices ranging from prayers, songs, and dances to ritual possessions in which *lwa* (Vodou spirits) possess the body of a Vodou practitioner or follower to give guidance regarding sickness or personal tribulations.

When Max and I entered the temple (a large tent with a living, decorated tree as the center pole), there was already a group of about 20 people holding hands and praying in a large circle, dressed in bright clothes of white, red, blue, green, and yellow hues. The group was multigenerational, made up mostly of women and feminine-presenting bodies, some seemingly disabled, seated on a large plastic tarp spread on the bare floor and inscribed with the mysterious,

Figure 6.1. The Artibonite River, Haiti. Photo by Kendra Helmer (CC0).

evocative word "UNSAID." Because we had trouble finding the event and were late, Max and I stood outside the circle with a few others, men with whom Max was joking about politics, work, and women. We observed the prayer led by an energetic *Houngan* (high priest), identifiable by a ceremonial shirt and who moved around the outside of the circle of participants.

By the time we sat down, the group was ending their prayers with a cry of "*Ayibobo!*" The circle dispersed, and the attendees, including Max and myself, started drinking tea. After some extended small talk, Max and I traveled to a second location along with a small group. We located and joined a larger outdoor gathering, also made up of people who lived nearby. Many of the women who had attended the earlier prayers were dressed now not in their colorful clothing but all in white, as were some of the observers. The gathering was on a grassy rise, a small hill overlooking the Artibonite River (Figure 6.1). Near the drummers, a table had been beautifully arranged by a group of women who had worked together to prepare for the event and was laden with cassava, cooked rice, popcorn, and drinks and protected by a white canopy. On the ground were *vève*, graphic ritual symbols of Haitian Vodou spirits drawn in straight and curved lines, in this instance using charcoal; materials from soot to flour can also be used to create *vève*.

Just as the ceremony started, an older Haitian man standing near the ritual table of food interrupted the proceedings with an announcement. He seemed to be known to the group, and I gathered he was from the area. He loudly asserted that this was a satanic gathering and forcefully claimed "*Bondey pap kontan!*" (God would not be happy!) and, further, told the attendees that what they were doing here *"Ap sevi djab!"* (was serving demons). The followers and head Houngan immediately and fiercely defended the space by scolding the man until finally, after about 10 minutes, he physically removed himself, clearly outvoted by over 80 participants and observers who stood and waited for the ceremony to commence. An older woman next to me scoffed at the man, questioning his sanity and marveling at his audacity in interrupting a spiritual gathering. Not too long after the man was escorted from the area and everyone had taken a moment to process this one-person protest, the drumming, dancing, and singing began. It soon became clear to me why we were so near the water. Close to where I was standing, a young woman who looked to be in her early thirties suddenly fell to the ground and started to roll down the gentle hill into the river; she was not the only one.

I took out my phone to film, and I had captured a few shots when I heard a resounding "*Non! Non! Non!*" I turned to see a woman who told me to stop and went on to press me about whether I was planning to put these videos on Facebook. When I assured her that I was not, she gave me a skeptical, worried look but let me be. I had no intention of uploading the videos but, feeling the sting of embarrassment, I put my phone away. I was by no means the only one filming and for a moment felt unfairly targeted. But a part of me did understand why I had been singled out: Mine was an unfamiliar face, and the gathering was somehow as intimate as it was public.

I begin this chapter with a description of the *Gen De Lwa* ceremony precisely because it did not have to be found or uncovered. Although in an outlying area, it was not hidden or shrouded in mystery, as many imagine Vodou practices and rituals to be. It was quotidian, a product of the humble spiritual labor of people in the Haitian countryside who drew strength from and found community in the practice of Vodou. It was an example of the collectivity that has sustained Haitian spiritual practices for so long, even in the wake of evangelical assaults, gangs, and paramilitary violence sanctioned by the state, which have interrupted ceremonies, destroyed ritual spaces, and impeded the ability to gather. This ceremony near the Artibonite River had traversed the communal, the sacred – and, almost a decade earlier, the tragic. In 2010, the Artibonite became a conduit for the waterborne spread of cholera, producing the largest cholera epidemic to happen to a single country in modern times. The epidemic decimated the communities in and around Saint-Marc that had already been ravaged, along with the rest of Haiti, by a 7.0 magnitude earthquake. The cholera epidemic entangled Haiti in an international political coverup that centered on Haitian Vodou and witchcraft.

Because the Artibonite river valley is a stronghold of Vodou, and there is widespread stigma surrounding Vodou practice, the Haitian government and United Nations officials were quick to attribute the widespread outbreak of cholera to Vodou. Additionally, in rural areas, many believed that cholera was caused by witchcraft and black magic, leading to attacks on Vodou practitioners and those who adhere to the spiritual tradition (Frerichs 2017). This assignment of culpability is profoundly revealing of the ways Vodou, a cultural form that some people consider regressive, is stigmatized and scapegoated as the source of Haiti's social ills.

As anti-Vodou sentiment continued to gain momentum in 2010, an intensive investigation by leading French epidemiologist Renaud Piarroux identified the specific strain of cholera present in the Artibonite. He discovered that, in fact, United Nations (UN) peacekeeping troops had brought the microorganism with them when they traveled to Haiti from a mission in Nepal, where they had contracted cholera (Frerichs 2017). The revelation that the true source of the contagion was UN troops and not practitioners of Vodou led to mass protests in the affected areas, the already exhausted and distrustful populace joining together in displays of grief and anger to demand answers (Mallon Andrews 2015). In 2016, building on his previous work demonstrating that the spread of cholera is often blamed on those in a society who are considered different or "other," American professor of epidemiology Ralph Frerichs cited Vodou's paradoxically marginal status in Haitian society (i.e., it is stigmatized but perseveres) as what made it vulnerable to scapegoating in the case of this outbreak. Piarroux's investigation proved definitively that the outbreak was not a recurrence of a disease endemic to Haiti, as had been claimed, and that it had no link to Vodou. According to the National Cholera Surveillance System, the Centers for Disease Control, and the Pan American Health Organization, the Artibonite region was hit the hardest during the cholera outbreak, with over 17,000 cases and 3,069 total deaths in the region (Barzilay et al. 2013). As anthropologist Jemima Pierre (2022) describes it, "The cholera epidemic is an extension of a totality of violence – material, political, and ecological – enacted by the UN peacekeeping mission" (2). While the focus of this chapter is on understanding the stigma surrounding Vodou and its perseverance in light of the cholera epidemic, other studies highlight the political, social, and ecological effects of the cholera epidemic in Haiti and the complexity of the broader consequences of international disaster relief efforts (Frerichs 2017; Mallon Andrews 2015).

In this chapter, through ethnographic sketches of public religious gatherings held in Saint-Marc during 2018–2021, I will explore the paradoxical status of contemporary Haitian Vodou and its role as a complex social system with multiple functions. The paradox lies in the ways in which Vodou is depicted as a regressive cult and dangerous cultural form at the heart of the nation's ills, and yet is ubiquitous in the day-to-day lives of Haitians and has far-reaching, positive influence as a spiritual practice. This ethnography sheds light on the critiques of Vodou in the wake of the political, natural, and epidemiological disasters that are the hallmarks of Haitian history.

A STOP ON THE BLACK ATLANTIC

The small port city of Saint-Marc is a growing regional hub that is positioned between the island's major urban centers and surrounded by mountains, traversing rurality and urbanity and defying spatial classification as either a town or city. Saint-Marc, like many developing centers, is multifaceted. It is a popular Haitian commercial port of entry, a site of major political resistance from the 1791 Revolution through the Duvalier dynasty in the twentieth century (Scott and Rediker 2020, 18), and the birthplace of some of the country's most prominent historical figures, from Jean Baptist Point du Sable, the founder of the American City of Chicago, to Hector Hippolyte, Haitian Vodou priest and the father of Haitian spiritual art. According to historical records, during the pre-Columbian period (1000 BCE–1000 CE), the area was a Taíno town called Amani. The founding date of the city of Saint-Marc is thought to be either 1695 or 1716.

After the displacement of Indigenous peoples, many wealthy French families from the port cities of Nantes, Bordeaux, La Havre, and La Rochelle came to Saint-Marc to establish trading houses and slave ship-building services, turning the town into a small commercial hub during the French plantation period (Destin 2011). Historians have traced a direct line between the development of the port of Saint-Marc to the infusion of capital from Nantes (Destin 2011). Saint-Marc was more than just a dot on the oceanic map showing the spread of African cultural forms throughout what is known as the "Black Atlantic," or the Afro-diaspora formed by the colonization and establishment of plantation economies throughout North and South America and the Caribbean (Gilroy 1994). To give a sense of the scale and brutality of the slave regime on the more than 7,000 plantations of Saint-Domingue (as colonial Haiti was called) consider this: So many enslaved Africans died due to corporal punishment, hazardous living conditions, and the rationing of food by masters that "as a consequence, the colony was forced to import Africans at a rate which, by the time of the Haitian revolution, had grown to at least 40,000 each year" (Robinson [1983] 2021, 146). Saint-Marc was also the site of a major anti-colonial movement in the 1790s, led by white/Creole/mixed-race elites who were invested in preserving slavery and were almost successful at wresting control of Haiti from the French government (Destin 2011). Had they been successful in negotiating independence from France, the Black Republic of Haiti might never have been born.

When the Republic of Haiti was founded in 1804 after the success of the Revolution and the declaration of independence from France, it was also the first society in the history of the world to be created by formerly enslaved people (Robinson [1983] 2021), the first Black Republic. After the Revolution, Saint-Marc became a site of intense resistance to the centralization of state power in the capital city, along with many other provincial ports. In the early twentieth century, Saint-Marc's status as an important hub of commerce was elevated by the construction of the Compagnie Nationale railroad system. This rail network was used by American corporate entities to infiltrate markets, with the help of Haitian elites, and establish the Haitian American Sugar Company (HASCO) and Société Haïtiano-Américaine de Développement Agricole (SHADA), and to transport passengers, flour, cement, bananas, and sisal from plantations in the Saint-Marc area (Destin 2011).

By the latter part of the last century, however, Saint-Marc began a prolonged economic decline. It was a site of pro-democracy political resistance against the paramilitarized authoritarianism of the Duvalierist state (Long 1986), which used the paramilitary force of the Tonton Macoute to centralize power and weaken the smaller municipalities. It did so by sabotaging the railroad lines into Saint-Marc, leading to disruption of the import/export trade, scarcity of provisions, the eventual closure of the railroad system, and an even sharper decline in Saint-Marc's economy. Today the port city of Saint-Marc continues to grow, increasing in both size and population because of internal displacements caused by disasters and growing gang influence in the rural areas of Haiti.

A RACIALIZED CRITIQUE OF VODOU

It was 8:00 p.m. on a wide soccer field full of people – or should I say full of the evangelical faithful? It was not my first time at a *kwazad* – "crusade" – an open-air event usually hosted by a group of evangelical Christian pastors and churches in the downtown area, in parks, or in other recreational spaces. I had last witnessed a *kwazad* the previous summer, in 2018, when I first started my preliminary fieldwork in Saint-Marc, accidentally coming across one while in *la ville* near a market. As I waited for my late-night egg sandwich to be prepared, I became curious about the event itself, its purpose, and the people in the audience. I was mesmerized by the anti-Vodou, anti-same-sex coupling, and pro-American statements that were met with "amens" and cheerful affirmations from the crowd. After hearing about a *kwazad* taking place near where I was lodging, I made it my mission to find a spot in the back of the field, near the entrance – not amid the large, shoulder-to-shoulder crowd, but close enough to listen to the pastor's sermon. I attended with Maria, a mother of three and a distant family friend; Maria had been the one to tell me about the event. She had quickly become one of my go-to people when I sought to deepen my understanding of local goings-on. This *kwazad* was held toward the edge of town, though it still drew a large crowd. I decided to film the event. One piece of the pastor's rhetoric caught my attention:

> *Lèzòm sevi avec entèlijans pou yo fe, le choix extrodinairee*
> *Lèzòm fè elicopte*
> *avion*
> *Lèzòm fè bilding*
> *Lèzòm fè pon*
> *Ayisyen vire chen*
> *Gade sa nou fè!*
> *Ayisyen tounen chen*
> *Ayisyen tounen kochon*
> *Ayisyen tounen chat*
> *Haitains pran lòt Ayisyen ak vire yo pou zomibes.*

Man works with intelligence, to make extraordinary choices
Man made helicopter
airplane
Man made building
Man made bridge
Haitians turn into dog
Look at what we do!
Haitians turn into dog
Haitians turn into pig
Haitians turn into cat
Haitians take other Haitians and turn them into zombies.

In the preacher's rhetoric he invoked the myth of the "shapeshifter," which plays a critical role in Haitian folkloric traditions of resistance. The ability to transcend human form and "turn into" a dog, a cat, or a pig re-emerged as a critical mystical ability to elude colonizers during the war for independence (Derby 2015). The pastor's sermon made a pointed and striking distinction between a "man" and a "Haitian" – referring to "man" as *lèzòm* while clearly distinguishing between what "man" does versus what Haitians do, and denouncing the belief in spiritual traditions and "cult"-like practices. As the sermon continued, the pastor started naming important *lwa* (Vodou spirits) and saints who were venerated in the Haitian Vodou pantheon, such as Ezili, Ogou, St. James, and St. Anne. He positioned these figures as representative of the anti-modern animality of Haitians and juxtaposed them with the image of "man's" greatness.

The clergyman's denunciation of Haitian Vodou felt reminiscent of the passionate condemnation of Vodou by Haitian doctor Justin Chrysostome Dorsainvil, who was a prolific writer on Haitian history and social identity during the mid-twentieth century. The broader demonization of Haitian Vodou can be traced to Dorsainvil's influential body of work, including *Manuel d'histoire d'Haïti* (the *Haitian History Textbook*), *Vaudou et Névrose* (*Voodoo and Neurosis*), and *Vaudou et Magie* (*Voodoo and Magic*) (Magloire 1999). Dorsainvil equated Vodou, as a cult brought to Haiti by enslaved people, with neurosis and an evolutionary cultural deficiency, calling it parasitic and characterizing it as backward (Dorsainvil ([1931] 1975, 14). For Dorsainvil, who valorized the "French" colonial aspects of the Haitian identity, features of Haitian Vodou such as spirit possession were a form of inherited racialized psycho-neurosis that were uniquely Haitian and even evidence of Black inferiority. Simultaneously, in North America, Vodou was demonized, appropriated, and commodified – transmogrified within North American popular culture into "Voodoo," with all its attendant stereotypes and quintessential mark as "Other" (Richman 2005). According to historian Sibylle Fischer (2005), the demonization of Haitian culture was a critical part of the making of North American **modernity** by framing North America as "modern" in comparison to "unmodern" Haiti. The marked rise in visual, literary, and ethnographic "othering" and demonization of Vodou – and of Haiti as a whole – in North American cultures, and its misappropriation and misrepresentation as "black magic" throughout the nineteenth and twentieth centuries, were tied to assaults against Haitian sovereignty (Richman 2005).

To Dorsainvil, Haitian Vodou was itself a reason for the nation's lack of social progress and a form of illness or neurosis that was enabled by the Houngan (Dorsainvil [1931] 1975), as well as evidence of a weakness specific to the Black people – as were, he believed, other cultural forms arising in the Caribbean and the Atlantic African diaspora. But as the work of West Indian psychiatrist Frantz Fanon illuminates, Black cultural and religious forms are not only individually misjudged and maligned as pathogenic, but are tied to a larger racial order where Blackness (whether people or forms) is construed as a "parasite in the world" (Fanon 1967, 78). Today, the historical demonization of Vodou and of Blackness continues through new means, such as placing blame during an infectious disease outbreak and the rhetoric of Christian fundamentalism.

A PARADOX

Maria would habitually attend *kwazad*, but she did not consider herself an evangelical Christian. In the same way, although she attended and had taken me along to *Gen de Lwa*, Maria was not an active Vodouisant. For Maria and for many Haitian women, both kinds of gatherings provided a therapeutic and spiritual space where desires could be manifested. But when the discourse turned, Maria was quick to leave; "*Mwen prale Pastor commence pale politik* (I am leaving; the pastor has started to talk about politics)" was Maria's way of signaling to me that it was time to leave the *kwazad*. After we had left the soccer field, we were in an isolated enough space where Maria felt comfortable venting to me. Maria questioned the faith of some of those in attendance, asserting that some were only pretending to believe and would in fact go see a Hougan if they were sick or wanted to, say, seek revenge on others. I knew she was right: Although many of the believers were agreeing with what the pastor was preaching, for a good number of them the question of faith versus practice was a lot more complicated – and their allegiances were mixed, even though the pastor's rhetoric seemed intolerant of dissent.

While Maria interpreted the actions of those at the *kwazad* as religious hypocrisy, for me her statements invoked an interesting question: What is it about Vodou and its unique status as both a syncretism and a form of **cultural survival** that makes it almost impossible to eliminate from the social fabric of Haitian society even though it is demonized by evangelicals, the media, missionaries, and authoritarian regimes, and even after decades of suppression? How has it endured, and why?

In 2021, in the wake of the assassination of President Jovenel Moïse, Maria and I were walking to a *Gen de Lwa* when she insistently showed me her phone. Playing on her screen was a series of videos of Haitian Vodou rituals – from prayers to dances – taking place in Lakous throughout Haiti in the name of "Justice for Jovenel Moïse." Although Maria was not a fan of the president and his policies, his untimely death and the acts of the assassins – sponsored by Haitian elites abroad as well as in concert with Colombian ex-military – did not sit well with her. She was also impressed by the collaborative and collective responses of the Vodou temples. These feelings, shared by many Haitians, served to galvanize opposition. Maria and I arrived at a *Gen de Lwa* that was taking place near downtown Saint-Marc, in the temple of a *Mambo Na* (high priestess), an older woman in her late fifties who was dressed very casually. Unlike my planned excursion to a *Gen de Lwa* with Max, my attendance with Maria was impromptu: In distress over financial pressures and her children's educational future, Maria felt that she urgently needed to speak to a higher power – in her words, "*Sam pa we yo* (Those I don't see)" – referring to her ancestral spirits. It seemed that this was the opportunity Maria was waiting for. After giving me instructions on what to do with my candle, Maria turned her face to her own and poured out her soul, cataloging problems, some of which she had related to me in the past, but now it was clear that she was giving an accounting to the departed, especially her deceased mother. Although less dramatic than the rituals at the first *Gen* I attended, these prayers were personal and called for relief from disease, for love, and for answers and solutions from the *lwa* and saints.

Despite the anti-Black historical representation of Haitian Vodou, Maria's earnest prayers demonstrate how Vodou occupies an enduring role in Haitian culture and identity, a shared worldview – indeed, the bedrock of Haitian society. Born out of the transatlantic slave trade, Vodou provides a spiritual way of being, the fluid spiritual pulse that served to empower an enslaved people in the age of revolution and continues to provide a spiritual means of facing hardship today.

From the late nineteenth century to the mid-twentieth century, some of the most renowned Haitian ethnographers from the anti-racist camp of Haitian ethnology, such as Jean Price-Mars and Anténor Firmin, pushed back against the characterization of Haitian Vodou as a feature of Haitian backwardness that can be seen in both Dorsainvil and in the contemporary pastor's *kwazad* sermon. Price-Mars and Firmin instead positioned Vodou within a complex heritage of African spiritual beliefs and practices that are rooted in African social thought and in Indigenous and European spiritual beliefs. Contemporary scholars, such as Afro-Caribbean scholar of spirituality Jacqui Alexander (2016) position Black Atlantic religions like Haitian Vodou as important ways of being and knowing in the world. Linguist and historian of Vodou Claudine Michel (2005) describes Haitian Vodou as built on survival, taking on multiple functions in Haitian society, and centered on the pillars of community and collectivity. This scholarship and my ethnographic data reveal the powerful function Vodou has across the social domains of Haitian life and the reasons it endures despite its stigmatization.

CONCLUSION: INDISPENSABILITY

The paradox of how Haitian Vodou, stigmatized as regressive and dangerous, endures within Haitian society may best be understood through an understanding of its social indispensability (Serres and Schehr 2007). Although according to some Vodou is the cause of the nation's maldevelopment, it also has a powerful function across the social domains of Haitian life. When Vodou practitioners and practices were scapegoated as the cause of the 2010 cholera epidemic that killed thousands, it was profoundly descriptive of a complex ecology of racialized oppression that illuminates paradoxes in Haitian society. However, through my own repeated encounters with Vodou's dual social positioning, I have seen that, despite earthquakes, a devastating cholera epidemic, and political upheaval, the social life of Vodou shows remarkable persistence, driven by what Alexander (2016) calls "spiritual work" (322) – the unassuming, constant devotion of the faithful.

REFLECTION AND DISCUSSION QUESTIONS

- Why was Haitian Vodou blamed for the 2010 cholera epidemic? How does this reflect broader ideas of Vodou as "backward" and "anti-modern"?
- What is the relationship between the stigmatization of Vodou and anti-Blackness?
- Why does Haitian Vodou endure despite its stigmatization?
- What factors might contribute to the resurgence of religion in Haiti and elsewhere in times of upheaval, such as after an earthquake or the assassination of a leader?

KEY CONCEPTS

- **cultural survival**: Cultural forms that have endured despite adversity or the advent of new forms.
- **Haitian Vodou**: A syncretic Black Atlantic spiritual epistemology based in ancestral worship.
- **modernity**: An era associated with the advancement of science and technology, including industrial and communication technologies; beliefs, ideologies, values, and norms related to capitalism, including individualism and productivity; a decline in religiosity; and rapid urbanization. Modernity presupposes and is based on the existence of what is not "modern" – or, in other words, that which is thought to be outmoded, backward, and benighted.

EXPLORE FURTHER

- To learn more about the relationship between racialization and modernity, read **Chapter 10**.
- To learn more about diasporic Haitians living in Cuba and the Dominican Republic, read **Chapters 14** and **25**.
- Giroux, Henry A. 2010. "Zombie Politics and Other Late Modern Monstrosities in the Age of Disposability." *Policy Futures in Education* 8 (1): 1–7.
- Ramsey, Kate. 2015. *The Spirits and the Law: Vodou and Power in Haiti*. Chicago: University of Chicago Press.
- Strongman, Roberto. 2008. "Transcorporeality in Vodou." *Journal of Haitian Studies* 14 (2): 4–29.

ABOUT THE AUTHOR

Guilberly Louissaint is an instructor and Ph.D. candidate in cultural anthropology at the University of California, Irvine. His specific areas of expertise are Caribbean, medical, and political anthropology. He researches biomedical and Haitian Vodou healing practices and post-disaster politics.

REFERENCES

Alexander, M. Jacqui. 2016. *Pedagogies of Crossing: Meditations on Feminism, Sexual Politics, Memory, and the Sacred*. Durham, NC: Duke University Press.

Barzilay, Ezra J., Nicolas Schaad, Roc Magloire, Kam S. Mung, Jacques Boncy, Georges A. Dahourou, Eric D. Mintz, Maria W. Steenland, John F. Vertefeuille, and Jordan W. Tappero. 2013. "Cholera Surveillance during the Haiti Epidemic – The First 2 Years." *New England Journal of Medicine* 368 (7): 599–609. https://doi.org/10.1056/NEJMoa1204927.

Derby, Lauren. 2015. "Imperial Idols: French and United States Revenants in Haitian Vodou." *History of Religions* 54 (4): 394–422. https://doi.org/10.1086/680175.

Destin, Lemarec. 2011. *La ville de Saint-Marc: Histoire, Économie, Politique et Société: Des Origines à 1971*. Montréal: Éditions DAMI.

Dorsainvil, J. C. (1931) 1975. *Vodou Et Névrose: Médico-Sociologie*. Port-au-Prince, Haiti: Éditions Fardin.

Fanon, Frantz. 1967. *Black Skin, White Masks*. Translated by Charles Lam Markmann. New York: Grove Press.

Fischer, Sibylle. 2005. *Modernity Disavowed: Haiti and the Cultures of Slavery in the Age of Revolution*. Durham, NC: Duke University Press.

Frerichs, Ralph R. 2017. *Deadly River: Cholera and Cover-up in Post-Earthquake Haiti*. Ithaca, NY: ILR Press.

Gilroy, Paul. 1994. *The Black Atlantic: Modernity and Double Consciousness*. Cambridge, MA: Harvard University Press.

Long, William. 1986. "1,000 Join Anti-Duvalier Protest in Haiti Port City." *Los Angeles Times*, February 3.

Magloire, Gérarde. 1999. "Haitian-Ness, Frenchness and History." In *Pouvoirs dans la Caraïbe Revue du Centre de Recherche sur les Pouvoirs Locaux dans la Caraïbe*, 18–40.

Mallon Andrews, Kyrstin. 2015. "Protest in the Time of Cholera: Disease and the Metaphors of Health and Politics." *Canadian Journal of Latin American and Caribbean Studies / Revue Canadienne des Études Latino-Américaines et Caraïbes* 40 (1): 63–80. https://doi.org/10.1080/08263663.2015.1031493.

Michel, Claudine. 2005. "Vodou in Haiti: Way of Life and Mode of Survival." In *Vodou in Haitian Life and Culture*, edited by Claudine Michell and Patrick Bellegarde-Smith, 27–37. London: Palgrave Macmillan.

Pierre, Jemima. 2022. "Cholera, Colonization, and the UN's Militarized Humanitarianism in Haiti." *Fieldsights*, January 25. https://culanth.org/fieldsights/series/ecologies-of-war.

Richman, Karen E. 2005. *Migration and Vodou*. Gainesville: University Press of Florida.

Robinson, Cedric J. (1983) 2021. *Black Marxism: The Making of the Black Radical Tradition*. London: Penguin Books.

Scott, Julius Sherrard, and Marcus Rediker. 2020. *The Common Wind: Afro-American Currents in the Age of the Haitian Revolution*. London: Verso.

Serres, Michel, and Lawrence R. Schehr. 2007. *The Parasite*. Minneapolis: University of Minnesota Press.

SECTION THREE

Ethnicity, Citizenship, and Belonging

Ethnicity is one of the predominant ways that people across Latin America and the Caribbean perceive themselves and others. A key component of social identity, ethnicity refers to the shared historical, cultural, and sometimes genealogical connection within a particular group of people. It is the component of social identity that aligns with a sense of cultural heritage and is often reflected in the languages or dialects a person speaks, in their religion, and in their behavioral norms, values, beliefs, and traditions. Many of the most salient ethnic identities in the region are tied to a particular Indigenous identity, while others hearken back to European colonial heritage, and still others stem from later waves of migration to and within the region.

Perceptions about ethnic identity sometimes align with nationality. For example, many Chileans conceptualize their ethnic identity primarily as Chilean and in contrast to national neighbors in Peru, Bolivia, or Argentina. By contrast, Madrasi people are an ethnic group in Guyana whose identity is framed in terms of shared history and religious traditions. Descendants of South Indian indentured servants, Madrasi follow a branch of Hinduism that is characterized by shaktism and ritual practices that include trance. Importantly, the Madrasis' class position and phenotypic traits (darker pigmented skin and curly hair) played a role in their characterization as ethnic Others within the Guyanese population, illustrating how racialization and class often overlap in processes of ethnic differentiation.

While ethnic identity often aligns with other aspects of social identity (e.g., nationality, religion, race, and class), it is also interrelated with gender and sexuality, aspects of personal identity. For example, among Indigenous Isthmus Zapotec people of Mexico, individuals who are designated male at birth and whose expression is feminine are referred to as *muxe*, a third category of gender identity. Perhaps unsurprisingly, many of the ways people express ethnic identity in daily life are tightly aligned with gender expression, such that a person is readily recognizable to others as a Zapotec *muxe*, a Mayan woman, or a *mestizo* man in Mexico. This is because the expression of femininity, masculinity, or androgyny in dress and behavior is informed by the norms, values, and traditions of ethnic groups.

The social construction of ethnic categories and the reification of ethnic identities are important because they are consequential. Ethnicity is often leveraged in processes of oppression, marginalization, and conflict. For example, during the Guatemalan civil war (1960–1996) the Guatemalan government targeted Indigenous Maya people, using this ethnic community's presumed support for leftist rebels as a justification for mass murder. In contrast, ethnic identity can be powerfully instrumental in struggles for justice. For example, ethnic communities and organizations play pivotal roles in activism across Latin America and the Caribbean today, including leading efforts to resist polluting industries, reclaim Indigenous autonomy, and protect water, sacred land, and fragile ecosystems.

Multiculturalism, an approach to governance that arose together with neoliberalism at the close of the twentieth century, is common across Latin America and the Caribbean and typically involves an acknowledgment of ethnic plurality and the creation of targeted programming for minoritized ethnic groups, often those who have been harmed by historic injustices such as deterritorialization, forced migration, or genocide. As a result, much of contemporary policymaking and disputes over the use of resources fall along lines of ethnic solidarity and differentiation.

Citizenship, the status of individuals belonging to a nation (or "imagined community"; see Chapter 3), is most often framed in terms of nation-states (i.e., countries) and is associated with the conferral of certain rights and benefits by the state. **Indigenous citizenship**, by contrast, stems from Indigenous peoples' ancestral claims to membership in Indigenous nations and can be of great symbolic value. While it is uncommon for Latin American and Caribbean nation-states to recognize the sovereignty of Indigenous nations within their territorial boundaries, there are a few exceptions. Bolivia is a self-designated "plurinational state," and several Indigenous nations within Bolivia have officially recognized systems of self-government, following the passage of the 2010 Framework Law on Autonomies 031/10.

The chapters in this section demonstrate complexities between ethnic identity, citizenship, and belonging in nation-states and Indigenous nations. In Chapter 7, Narayanan explores a multilingual community where ideologies about language purity impact people's senses of themselves as citizens of Indigenous Quechua or Aymara nations. In Chapter 8, Jaramillo examines how multicultural policies in Colombia have obliged people in the department of La Guajira to reconceptualize their ethnic identities and frame themselves as Indigenous to access resources. Finally, in Chapter 9, Seales explores factors influencing notions of citizenship and belonging for ethnic West Indians in Panama during and following the US occupation of the Panama Canal Zone.

KEY CONCEPTS

- **citizenship**: The membership status of individuals belonging to a nation.
- **ethnicity**: The shared historical, cultural, and sometimes genealogical connection within a particular group of people.
- **Indigenous citizenship**: Membership in an Indigenous nation. This form of citizenship generally relies on an individual's ancestral ties to the community.
- **multiculturalism**: An approach to governance that typically involves an acknowledgment of ethnic plurality and the creation of targeted programming for minoritized ethnic groups, often those who have been harmed by historic injustices such as deterritorialization, forced migration, or genocide.

EXPLORE FURTHER

- To learn more about policies and practices aimed at recognizing Indigenous systems of governance and decision making, read **Chapters 19** and **29**.
- To learn more about ethnic solidarity and resilience, read **Chapters 13**, **14**, **23**, and **32**.
- Claveyrolas, Mathieu. 2021. "Guyanese Madrasis in New York City: 'It's All about Progress!'" In *Political Mobilisations of South Asian Migrants: Global Perspectives,* edited by Anne-Sophie Bentz and Lola Guyot, 49–77. *DESI* (5). Pessac: Presses Universitaires de Bordeaux.
- Da-Rin, Silvio, dir. 2012. *10th Parallel*. [Amazon/Brazil]
- Guerra, Elvis. 2019. "Being Muxhe in Juchitán, Mexico." *Cultural Survival Quarterly Magazine.* https://www.culturalsurvival.org/publications/cultural-survival-quarterly/being-muxhe-juchitan-mexico.

CHAPTER SEVEN

Language and the Emplacement of Indigenous Citizenship in Peru

Sandhya Krittika Narayanan

My neighbor Señora Florencia was an elderly Aymara-speaking woman in her late sixties. She was also trilingual in the three main languages of the Puno region: Quechua, Aymara, and Spanish. As her neighbor, I would spend many mornings and evenings helping her herd her flock of sheep or harvest various crops. During this time, she would tell me stories about her life. Some of them were personal, such as the day she married her husband. Other stories recounted the many ways that Puno had changed over the course of her lifetime. But every now and then she would tell me stories that gave me insight into how she came to be fluent in the three languages of the region. These stories included how she had to learn Spanish to sell the wool from her sheep in the central markets of Puno, or how she had to learn Quechua when she was sent to live with a Quechua-speaking family in another village as a young girl. Yet her linguistic knowledge was never explicitly mentioned in these stories. Instead, they were secondary details that served as background to the main experiences in her life. Given her linguistic background, I figured that Señora Florencia would have an easy time participating in a short sociolinguistic interview that was framed around two questions: What languages do you speak? And how do you self-identify?

Instead, I was surprised by how much difficulty Señora Florencia had in answering the first question about her linguistic knowledge. While she was able to say that she spoke Aymara, she was quick to point out that she did not speak "good" Aymara. Furthermore, she denied really knowing Quechua or Spanish, although many of our conversations took place in a mix of Spanish and Aymara. She had a similarly hard time figuring out how to self-identify, and after much deliberation she decided to be identified as *puneña* – a woman from Puno. But when I asked if she might also consider herself to be "Aymara," she seemed even more hesitant about self-identifying with this Indigenous, ethnic label. By the time we were ready to part ways, I felt confused as to why Señora Florencia not only denied her linguistic knowledge, but also had such a hard time with self-identifying as an Indigenous Aymara person.

Figure 7.1. The streets of Puno are normally divided between Quechua- and Aymara-speaking neighborhoods. During festivities, they are also the site of dances and parades where traditional Indigenous dances and songs from throughout the region are performed.
Photo by Sandhya Krittika Narayanan.

In this chapter, I address the ways the Indigenous Quechua and Aymara speakers in Puno and the Peruvian altiplano (high plains) negotiate their linguistic backgrounds and Indigenous ethnic identities and affiliations through focusing on how **language ideologies** and Indigenous **ethnolinguistic differences** play into larger discussions around Indigenous citizenship and the recognition of Quechua and Aymara Indigenous nations. In this case, ethnolinguistic differences are the ways in which different ethnic identities are formed around different languages, such as the formation of a Quechua or Aymara ethnicity around the differences between Quechua and Aymara as languages. The creation of these ethnolinguistic groups can lead to ideas about Indigenous citizenship, in which a person can identify as a legitimate individual or "citizen" of an Indigenous nation. Despite the ubiquity of multilingualism in the region, many Indigenous *puneños* devalue their own linguistic knowledge and ability to identify as Indigenous Quechua or Aymara because their linguistic and cultural practices differ from other places that are thought to be more authentically "Quechua" or "Aymara." As I will show, the ways that Indigenous Quechua- and Aymara-speaking *puneños* evaluate and downplay their linguistic knowledge and inclusion as Indigenous Quechuas and Aymaras are connected to

purist language ideologies that emphasize Indigenous linguistic purity as a way to legitimize Indigenous ethnolinguistic differences and Indigenous citizenship. But this chapter also presents an alternative story in which Indigenous *puneño* activists and media producers at a local Indigenous radio station challenged the dominance of purist language ideologies through the promotional materials they created for the 2017 national census. Multilingual areas like Puno and the altiplano therefore offer an ethnographic counterpoint to understand how Indigenous nationalism can be constructed and centered from places of linguistic and social diversity.

MULTILINGUALISM AND INDIGENOUS IDENTITY IN PUNO AND THE ALTIPLANO

SEÑORA PAULINA: *Señorita, porque viniste acá a Puno? Hay otros lugares, más bonitos que Puno, ves?* (Señorita, why did you come here to Puno? There are so many other places, much prettier, than here in Puno, right?)

SN: *Pero Señora, en Puno se habla Quechua y Aymara.* (But Señora, in Puno they speak Quechua and Aymara.)

SEÑORA PAULINA: *Aaaaa sí, eso sí ... aquí en Puno hay tres idiomas – el Quechua, el Aymara, y el Castellano. En otros lugares solamente hay el Quechua y Castellano, o el Aymara y Castellano. Así es pue.* (Aaaaaah yes, that is right ... there are three languages in Puno – Quechua, Aymara, and Spanish. In other places there is only Quechua and Spanish, or Aymara and Spanish. That's just how it is.)

Conversational exchanges like these were a constant throughout the duration of my ethnographic fieldwork in Puno, which spanned the course of three years. Many of my close interlocutors, like Señora Paulina, an elderly Quechua-speaking woman, were often confused about why I came to Puno and the Peruvian altiplano to do my research. The altiplano, which begins in the Department of Puno in Peru and extends into Bolivia, is a high-plains region in the Andes with elevations beginning at 3,800 meters above sea level and extending well above 5,000 meters. The high elevation brings with it many climatic extremes: intense sun during the middle of the day, intense cold at night, surprise hailstorms during the wet season, and strong winds from Lake Titicaca. In short, Puno was a hard place to live in.

Yet Puno had one thing that other regions in the Andes did not have. It was home to stable, long-term Indigenous multilingualism between Quechua and Aymara. As Señora Paulina corroborated, "in Puno there are three languages," with Spanish (*Castellano*) included in the multilingualism of the region. The persistence of Indigenous multilingualism in Puno separates the region from other places, where only one Indigenous language has been maintained. However, this multilingualism is by no means unique within the broader scope of the history of Puno and the altiplano. Contact and multilingualism between Quechua and Aymara speakers have been a feature of the altiplano for over five centuries, dating back to before the rise of the Inka empire (Adelaar and Muysken 2004). Today, you can hear this multilingualism anywhere you go throughout the altiplano. But it is most heard in the streets and villages surrounding the capital city of Puno.

To get a better understanding of what this multilingualism looks like, it is perhaps easiest to think about what it sounds like over the span of a single day of ethnographic fieldwork. I woke up early in the morning to the sound of Señora Florencia shouting commands in Aymara as she herded her sheep around my house. As I prepared my breakfast, I listened to the local Indigenous language radio station, Pachamama Radio. The local morning news was conducted mostly in Spanish, but sound bites for each individual news story would come from longer interviews, conducted in the "field" with individuals speaking in Quechua or Aymara. After finishing my coffee, I walked down to the main road to catch the local *combi* (collective transportation van), which took me into the main city of Puno about 30 minutes away. Often I rode with Señora Florencia's granddaughters, at that time both teenagers. Neither girl spoke much Aymara, but they both understood the language perfectly, translating for me what the other adults around us were saying. Most of the passengers, and the driver of the van, also conversed with each other in Aymara. But as we edged closer into the city, the passengers would change. As some Aymara-speaking passengers got off, other Quechua-speaking passengers would board the vehicle, chatting loudly in Quechua in seats that were once filled by Aymara conversations.

Once I was within the city's limits, I would get off the *combi* and walk through the city to get to the market where I conducted most of my fieldwork. As I walked through the various neighborhoods, I heard conversations move across different linguistic mediums. In one neighborhood, I passed by two older gentlemen discussing the news in a mixture of Aymara and Spanish. Then I walked through another neighborhood and passed by a *salteña* (empanada) stand, where an older gentleman flirted in Quechua with the woman who he has consistently purchased his breakfast *salteña* from for the past 15 years. After passing through these neighborhoods, I arrived at the market cooperative where I conducted the bulk of my fieldwork. The casual observer would only see rows of bright blue metal stalls covered with corrugated tin roofs, but for me each stall was like a little house, inhabited by an Indigenous Quechua- or Aymara-speaking woman. I would hop from stall to stall, practicing my Quechua or Aymara with each of these women, and over time developed close relationships with some, like Señora Paulina. I also noted how these ladies spoke with their clients and other co-vendors in the markets. Despite being dominant in one Indigenous language (either Quechua or Aymara), each vendor was able to switch across all three languages, incorporating some knowledge of the other Indigenous language when trying to sell goods to a client who spoke a different Indigenous language. Sometimes, these women made jokes with each other, in which a Quechua speaker might tease an Aymara speaker about her mispronunciation of words, and vice versa. As the sun began to set, I made my way to the radio station, Pachamama Radio. The station was always full of Quechua- and Aymara-speaking news correspondents and contributors coming and going through the halls of the building. While Indigenous news programs were often monolingual (i.e., only in Quechua, Aymara, or Spanish), each room was filled with speakers of different linguistic backgrounds and proficiencies. Even though the staff would claim fluency in one Indigenous language, their collective presence in the halls and recording rooms of Pachamama Radio made the radio station another multilingual world within Puno.

As I made my way back home, I took stock of the various kinds of multilingualisms that I encountered during the day. Some of it came from switching between Spanish and either Indigenous language in conversations. But there were also moments of borrowing, such as the ways that my market vendors and the younger news correspondents at Pachamama Radio borrowed and used words and phrases across the languages to make jokes and engage with speakers of different linguistic backgrounds. Sometimes speakers would comment on the words that were shared, like my market vendors who always loved that the word for the number three, *kimsa*, was the same in both Quechua and Aymara – a testament to the fact that borrowing and sharing across the languages has been a constant in this region. But it was not just these individual linguistic practices that made the region multilingual. Instead, it was how all these different ways of practicing multilingualism were maintained in this one region. Multilingualism in all its forms and practices did not just describe the region. It also described the daily linguistic and social practices embodied by all *puneños*.

THE CHALLENGES OF BEING MULTILINGUAL AND INDIGENOUS IN PUNO

The acoustic soundscape of Puno is characterized by this kind of complex, varied, and layered multilingualism between Quechua, Aymara, and Spanish. However, many of my interlocutors would devalue these complex fluencies, interpreting their linguistic practices as being signs of their own lack of fluency and preventing them from identifying themselves as "speakers" of any particular language. Most of my closest interlocutors, like Señora Paulina or Señora Florencia, would describe their linguistic knowledge as imperfect and incomplete – reflecting purist language ideologies that privilege using linguistic varieties that are free of any influence from other languages (Kroskrity 2000). Therefore, speaking "pure" Quechua means that speakers do not use linguistic elements from Spanish or Aymara. Similarly, speaking "pure" Aymara means that the speaker is only speaking words that have been deemed Aymara in origin. Therefore, *puneños'* partial hesitancy toward answering my question "What languages do you speak" reflects their own internalization of these purist language ideologies that mark their multilingual proficiencies as deviating from ideas of a preferred, purified linguistic variety.

Ideas around the existence of a purified Quechua or Aymara variety also come from speakers' increasing exposure to varieties that are recognized as more legitimate versions of their Indigenous language. For Quechua speakers, the Quechua variety that is spoken in Cusco has come to be ideologized as the "purest" and most original version of Quechua. For Aymara speakers, the most ideologically pure and authentic Aymara is the variety spoken in La Paz, Bolivia. The authenticity of the linguistic varieties from each area was so widely recognized that it was not uncommon for me to be told by my interlocutors, "Señorita, you should have gone to La Paz. They speak the best Aymara there," or "Señorita, you should have gone to Cusco. That is where the most authentic and original Quechua is spoken." For *puneños*, Cusco and La Paz were home to the most legitimate versions of their respective Indigenous languages. However, unlike Puno, Cusco and La Paz were both areas that were notably dominant in only one Indigenous language. Neither of these places had to negotiate the kinds of histories of multilingualism and inter-Indigenous interactions that have shaped the social and linguistic landscape in Puno.

The devaluation of multilingual practices extended to how Indigenous difference, citizenship, and nationhood were talked about in the region. As a result of increased visibility from Indigenous activism and mobilization over the past couple of decades, Quechua and Aymara have also become ideologized as two distinct Indigenous ethnolinguistic identities and nations (Narayanan 2018). These respective nations are imagined to contain a distinct set of Indigenous citizens who are bound through sharing a common language – a discourse that echoes Western European language ideologies that associate the legitimacy of a nation with a homogenous set of citizens who speak the same language (Bauman and Briggs 2003). Despite the non-Indigenous roots of such ideologies, such discourses are nevertheless recruited into projects around Indigenous sovereignty, where Indigenous nations are framed as being composed of socially, culturally, and linguistically homogeneous Indigenous citizens (Davis 2018; Shulist 2018). But in this process of linguistic and cultural homogenization, one variety and set of cultural practices is often selected as being the most authentic and emblematic of a particular Indigenous ethnic and national identity. When asked which variety or place is home to the most authentic version of their Indigenous language, most *puneños* agreed that Cusco was the center of the most original Quechua, and La Paz the most authentic Aymara. Furthermore, the most authentic Indigenous Quechua citizens also hailed from Cusco, just like the most authentic representations of Aymara Indigenous identity came from La Paz. Therefore, for *puneños,* the legitimacy of Quechua and Aymara identities tied to these places were derived from the perceived purity and authenticity of the Quechua and Aymara linguistic varieties that were spoken in each region.

Quechua- and Aymara-speaking *puneños*, therefore, find themselves at the margins of claiming this Indigenous citizenship, making it hard for them to answer my queries about how they self-identified ethnically. Many of my interlocutors could comfortably talk about their identity as being tied to their specific village, or being a *puneño*. But apart from those individuals who worked for organizations that were heavily involved in Indigenous activism and politics in the region, most of my interlocutors were not sure if they could, or even should, be identifying as "Quechua" or "Aymara."

COUNTING QUECHUAS AND AYMARAS

Given the hesitation toward answering my questions around linguistic knowledge and identity, I was curious about how the national census would fare locally during the fall of 2017. Taken every 10 years, the census is one kind of institutional record that documents the demographics of a nation. In Peru, this has often included statistics on the number of Indigenous language (referred to as *lengua materna*, or "mother tongue") speakers in the country. However, previous censuses did not document the diversity of Indigenous ethnic identities within the country, especially within the Andes. Thus, while previous censuses attempted to count the number of Quechua and Aymara speakers in the Puno region, they did not acknowledge the ways in which those speakers actively identified as Indigenous Quechua or Aymara. The 2017 census changed this by including for the first time categories that asked individuals to openly self-identity as either "Quechua" or "Aymara" (see also Chapter 10).

Such news was exciting for Indigenous activists and organizers, who were some of the few groups of individuals who actively identified and promoted the use of Indigenous ethnic identifiers like "Quechua" or "Aymara." But many of these activists and organizers were also keenly aware that the majority of *puneños* did not talk about themselves in the same way. Therefore, local Indigenous organizations, in partnership with the local census office in Puno, created promotional materials to encourage all *puneños* to take advantage of these new categories and see themselves as Indigenous "Quechuas" and "Aymaras."

One of the more active organizations in promoting this agenda came from Pachamama Radio, one of the two Indigenous activist radio stations in the region. Pachamama's producers, directors, and content creators knew that they needed to create promotional materials that would help Quechua- and Aymara-speaking *puneños* feel that they are Indigenous Quechua and Aymara citizens. Promotional materials therefore had to use Quechua and Aymara and feature themes that would resonate with speakers to help them see themselves as Indigenous, ethnic Quechuas and/or Aymaras. During my time at Pachamama, several of the directors and producers would describe their work as part of a larger process of *despertarse* ("to awaken") the political consciousness of *puneños* so that they take up the mantle of Indigenous citizenship and solidarity, which is necessary for these communities to fight for their political sovereignty and advocate for policies that address the abuses they have experienced from the state.

In the months that preceded the census, Pachamama Radio took the time to fill every open slot on their airwaves with a variety of advertisements meant to encourage *puneños* to openly identify as "Quechuas" and "Aymaras" on the census. Below are examples from an advertisement in each language.

Quechua Advertisement
1. *Jai! Hallp'amama!*
   "Oh great mother (earth)!"
2. *Awichakuna, awichukuna*
   "Grandmothers and grandfathers"
3. *Kayku kukallata haywayrikamuykichis*
   "With this small offering we present to you"

4. *nuqayku wayqikuna*
   "We (your) children"
5. *Vinuullawan insiensullawan*
   "with only this wine and incense"
6. *allin kawsaypi tiyakunaykupaq*
   "so that we can lead a good life"
7. *Ñañay-turaykuna,*
   "sisters and brothers"
8. *ñuqanchis quechuarunakunaqa,*
   "we, the Quechua peoples"
9. *sumaq kawsaypiraqmi tiyashkanchis kay pachanchiswan.*
   "we are still living well in this beautiful land and nature (of ours)"
10. *Ahinallatataq, kunan kay sensu nisqapi tapuriwasunchis hinaqa,*
    "in this way, for this census when we are called and asked therefore"
11. *ama mancharikuspa kutichikusunchis*
    "without fear we will all answer"
12. *quechuaruna(n) kayku nispa!*
    "telling them 'We are Quechua people!'"
13. (child's voice) *Qullasuyu chawpimanta(ta), Pachamama!*
    "From the center of Qullasuyu, Pachamama!"

Aymara Advertisement
14. (Music with a man shouting) *"Jallalla jilatanaka kullakanaka!"*
    "Cheers to all brothers and sisters!"
15. (man's voice) *Julian Apaza, Tupac Katari*
    "Julian Apaza, Tupac Katari"
16. *Aymaramarkasa, Abya Yala, América Latina*
    "The Aymara nation, Abya Yala, Latin America"
17. *Qhispayañtakiwa hispañiola janq'u janq'ianakakampiwa chaxwawaritayna*
    "They fought against the exploitative practices of the Spanish/white men"
18. (woman's voice) *Jichakamasa uñañchawipaxa jaqaskakiwa*
    "And through today we can see their fight endure"
19. *jiwasanakaru nayraru irpintañataki*
    "as it carries us forward into the future"
20. *Janiwa Aymara markaruxa chhaqtayapt'ichaniti*
    "Never will our Aymara nation disappear"
21. *Jicha jutiri censonxa ch'amampi saphjañani*
    "This coming census we will declare forcefully"
22. *Aymara jaqitwa sasina!*
    "(and say) I am Aymara!"

23. (child's voice) *Aymara markana arupa, Pachamama Radio*
    "The voice of Aymara nation, Pachamama Radio"

While both advertisements offer a lot to analyze in terms of Indigeneity and language use, I will focus on a few specific similarities that speak to issues of Indigenous language use and Quechua and Aymara ethnic identity in Puno. The first is that both advertisements placed their Indigenous languages and populations in relation to a deeper historical past. In the Quechua ad, Quechua is used to invoke not only mother earth, but also the grandparents or ancestors of the past (*awichakuna, awichukuna*), who represent the cultural and moral bedrock for Quechua speakers. The Aymara ad also created a similar kind of relationship between present-day Aymara populations and venerated ancestors of the past. However, instead of framing the invocation around all Aymara ancestors, the ad centered on two important historical Aymara leaders from the altiplano: Julian Apaza and Tupac Katari. Using Aymara to invoke these two figures not only signals the historical continuity of the Aymara people and identity in the region, but also establishes how that identity is based on a grander historical narrative of Aymara peoples rallying together and defending themselves against colonial (or Spanish) anti-Indigenous forces.

Both ads are also filled with various calls to action, encouraging their listeners to actively affirm their identity as either Quechua or Aymara. Such rhetorical devices create a sense of inclusivity that would allow *puneños* to identify as legitimate Quechua or Aymara citizens. Some of this was accomplished by using nouns that were either marked as plural or that denoted a larger plurality, indicating that being Quechua or Aymara was not simply an individual or personal choice, but rather a form of collective action that was necessary to build and strengthen the recognizability of each Indigenous nation. For instance, some of this plurality is explicitly mentioned through referring to Quechuas and Aymaras in terms of their larger populace, such as *wayqikuna* (children; Quechua, line 4), *ñañay-turaykuna* (sisters and brothers; Quechua, line 7), *quechuaruna(n)* (Quechua peoples; Quechua, line 12); *jilatanaka kullakanaka* (brothers and sisters; Aymara, line 14), and *Aymara jaqitwa* (Aymara person; Aymara, line 22). Inclusivity is also marked through using the inclusive *we*, which invites and includes the listener to be part of that same broader group. In Quechua, the inclusive *we* is marked by the pronoun ñuqanchis (i.e., *ñuqanchis quechuarunakuanaqa*; we (inclusive) the Quechua peoples; line 8). Similarly, in Aymara, this same kind of inclusivity is achieved by using the pronoun *jiwasanaka* (i.e., *jiwasanakaru*; us, line 19). Therefore, any speaker of Quechua or Aymara, regardless of their background, regional residence, or the specific variety of Quechua or Aymara they speak, was included within the broader collectivity of their Indigenous nation through the deployment of the inclusive *we*.

Despite using such linguistic devices, neither of these ads used linguistic varieties that mirrored the kinds of linguistic practices found in Puno. Both used little to no Spanish (with the exception of *vino* and *incienso* in the Quechua ad), and neither used words from the other Indigenous linguistic variety. Instead, as promotional materials created in an institutional setting, both advertisements used ideologically purified versions of both languages. Thus, these ads reproduced ideas around linguistic purism and its relationship with Indigenous ethnic authenticity and citizenship. However, from a different perspective, the use of these ideologically purified forms presented a different narrative of Puno and Quechua- and Aymara-speaking *puneños*. Because Puno has been defined by interactions between Quechua and Aymara speakers, *puneños* are often ideologically excluded from being considered ideal Indigenous speaker-citizens. Furthermore, Puno is also not perceived as a center of cultural and linguistic legitimacy in relation to Quechua and Aymara nationalism and identity because of the region's histories of inter-Indigenous interactions. Yet by using varieties that are more prevalent in the altiplano, the radio's choice to use a more ideologically pure and socially recognized version of Quechua and Aymara does not mark *puneños* as different than their more recognized Quechua and Aymara counterparts in Cusco and La Paz. Instead, the use of these ideologically purer varieties frames *puneños* as Indigenous citizens, whose Indigenous ethnic identities are as legitimate and authentic as those ethnic Quechuas and Aymaras from Cusco and La Paz. Thus, the active use of linguistic forms associated with more centralized places of recognizable Quechua and Aymara culture, language, and citizenship repositions Puno and the altiplano as another center of Quechua and Aymara linguistic, cultural, and political vitality and legitimacy.

CONCLUSION

Puno's status as a multilingual zone extends beyond the number of languages that are present in the region. Such multilingualism is infused into the day-to-day practices of speakers of different genders, linguistic backgrounds, and ages, who through their daily lives contribute to the vitality and stability of linguistic complexity in the region. Yet this linguistic and social complexity is not compatible with the ways that Indigenous nationalism and citizenship is talked about and recognized in the region, leaving many speakers to question their own linguistic knowledge, and legitimacy as Indigenous Quechua or Aymara citizens. However, other social actors, such as content producers and activists at Pachamama Radio, are working against such perceptions by creating media that not only includes the histories of Quechuas and Aymaras of Puno within their broader respective Indigenous nations, but also centers them as another capital of Indigenous ethnic and linguistic legitimacy in the region.

Most importantly, this chapter highlights the various challenges that Indigenous speakers from multilingual communities might have in identifying themselves and their linguistic varieties. The question "What languages do you speak?" could make speakers pause because they may have reservations about making claims about their linguistic knowledge, often reflecting some ideologized perception of the deficiencies they may observe between their speech practices and those of others. And the question "How do you ethnically self-identify?" might lead to moments of self-exclusion and separation away from other groups and collectivities. Yet it is also important to remember that the histories, practices, and societal changes that make answering such questions difficult or easy are also in flux, subject to new ideologies that shape the ways that individuals and groups come to identify themselves. Thus, for most of my research, the notion of being a citizen of an Indigenous nation, such as Quechua or Aymara, was still a contested way of self-identifying. Yet if the work done by activists and organizations like Pachamama Radio has shown anything, these modes of self-identification are fluid and dynamic as Indigenous communities and nations find new terms to define who they are and forge new relationships between those identities and the linguistic varieties they speak.

REFLECTION AND DISCUSSION QUESTIONS

- The multilingualism in Puno is both complex and the norm for most of the history of the region. But why is it that the various kinds of multilingual practices outlined in the chapter are devalued?
- How are issues around language purity and Indigenous nationhood for Quechua and Aymara speakers similar to "English-only" debates that take place in countries like the United States?
- After reading this chapter, how might you rephrase the two central interview questions to better capture the linguistic, social, and political complexity in Puno?

KEY CONCEPTS

- **ethnolinguistic differences**: The process by which ethnic groups are formed based on a shared linguistic variety.
- **language ideologies**: A set of ideas, perceptions, and attitudes about language use and their associations with a broader field of social differences.
- **purist language ideology**: A language ideology where a language must only use elements that are believed or perceived to come from within that language.

EXPLORE FURTHER

- To learn more about issues of ethnicity and identity in Peru, read **Chapter 10**.
- To learn more about the relationship between language and identity, read **Section 5**.
- Coronel-Molina, Serafín M. 2008. "Language Ideologies of the High Academy of the Quechua Language in Cuzco, Peru." *Latin American and Caribbean Ethnic Studies* 3 (3): 319–40.
- Swinehart, Karl F. 2012. "Metadiscursive Regime and Register Formation on Aymara Radio." *Language & Communication* 32 (2): 102–13.
- Zavala, Virginia. 2014. "An Ancestral Language to Speak with the 'Other': Closing Down Ideological Spaces of a Language Policy in the Peruvian Andes." *Language Policy* 13 (1): 1–20.

ABOUT THE AUTHOR

Sandhya Krittika Narayanan is an assistant professor of anthropology at the University of Nevada, Reno. She is a linguistic anthropologist whose work focuses on the consequences of language contact and multilingualism between Quechua and Aymara speakers in the Peruvian altiplano. As a first-generation immigrant and female scholar of color from a multilingual background, she is committed to using her background to promote linguistic diversity among Indigenous and marginalized languages and communities in the United States and abroad.

REFERENCES

Adelaar, Willem F. H., and Pieter Muysken. 2004. *The Languages of the Andes*. New York: Cambridge University Press.

Bauman, Richard, and Charles L. Briggs. 2003. *Voices of Modernity: Language Ideologies and the Politics of Inequality*. New York: Cambridge University Press.

Davis, Jenny L. 2018. *Talking Indian: Identity and Language Revitalization in the Chickasaw Renaissance*. Tucson: University of Arizona Press.

Kroskrity, Paul. 2000. "Language Ideologies in the Expression and Representation of Arizona Tewa Ethnic Identity." In *Regimes of Language: Ideologies, Polities, and Identities*, edited by Paul Kroskrity, 329–59. Santa Fe, NM: New School of American Research Press.

Narayanan, Sandhya Krittika. 2018. "Are We One? Quechua-Aymara Contact and the Challenges of Boundary Maintenance in Puno, Peru." *Language & Communication* 62 (September): 145–55.

Shulist, Sarah. 2018. *Transforming Indigeneity: Urbanization and Language Revitalization in the Brazilian Amazon*. Toronto: University of Toronto Press.

CHAPTER EIGHT

Post-Multicultural Anxieties? Trajectories of Indigenous Citizenship in La Guajira, Colombia

Pablo Jaramillo

When I first met Señora Helena she was living in a once-lustrous home in the Colombian border town of Maicao on the arid La Guajira peninsula. Not long after we met, she and what was left of her family decided to move to the old family *finca* (farm) a few miles from Maicao and turn it into a **ranchería** (traditional Indigenous hamlet) named Campamento. Soon Campamento became populated with related households living about 300 meters from one another. Household compounds composed of thatched roof and clay-walled houses also contained a detached kitchen structure, a toilet, a corral for the animals, and, occasionally, a well to access water. Cacti and shrubs dotted the landscape around the homes, and goats roamed freely.

Her family's decision to turn their *finca* into a *ranchería* seems to contradict the long and complex history of **mestizaje** (miscegenation), ethnic identity, and class in La Guajira. In Colombia, *fincas* symbolize the power of upper-class, *mestizo* landowners. Because Colombia's (like much of Latin America) social hierarchy values markers of whiteness and European "modernity," *rancherías* are less prestigious markers of social standing than *fincas* expressly because they are viewed as "traditional" Indigenous settlements. For Señora Helena's family, moving to the *ranchería* was a step toward a more Indigenous Wayúu ethnic identity, and thus a move that was contrary to the historical norm of some Indigenous people aspiring to become *mestizos* to move upward in the social hierarchy. What motivated Señora Helena and her family to seemingly put aside markers of their *mestizaje*, a status that previously granted them social privilege, and move toward Indigenous citizenship as Wayúu people?

To answer that question, in this chapter I describe the ways in which state attempts at multiculturalism through **social inclusion** policies, more specifically the Indigenous Families in Action program, intersected with the aftermath of armed conflict to create a new branding of "Indigenous citizenship" in Colombia. I explore the ways in which downward-mobilizing *mestizo* families, like that of Señora Helena, were compelled to renegotiate their identities and

Figure 8.1. From her kitchen, a Wayúu woman watches members of a humanitarian mission that is visiting her *ranchería*. Photo by Pablo Jaramillo.

lay claim to Indigenous citizenship to access the benefits of multicultural social inclusion policies. Finally, I discuss the ways in which state efforts at institutionalizing indigeneity created conflicts for communities already wrestling with what it means to be Indigenous in Colombia's emerging multicultural landscape.

MESTIZAJE AND SHIFTING ALLIANCES IN THE LA GUAJIRA PENINSULA

La Guajira peninsula constitutes the arid northernmost tip of South America. The location of the region has been a factor in both its marginality and its global interconnectedness (Guerra Curvelo 2007). Because of the region's lack of gold and its agricultural barrenness, Europeans overlooked it during the colonial period and in the early years of independence in the nineteenth century. At the same time, the cross-border smuggling of commodities, including hides, liquor, and pearls, in the Circum-Caribbean area was a source of power and wealth for

La Guajira's Indigenous inhabitants, the Wayúu. Elite Wayúu *apushis* (families) maintained power through their business enterprises, as well as through ritual bonds with Wayúu from subordinate family lineages. Although the Wayúu elites held formal government interventions at bay until the 1960s and 1970s, efforts at informal state control in the region prior to the late twentieth century took on the form of matrimonial and commercial alliances between Colombian state officials or private entrepreneurs (of European descent) and elite Indigenous Wayúu families. These alliances were mainly expressed through marriages of non-Indigenous men to Indigenous Wayúu women, which contributed to *mestizaje* and the emergence of a Guajiro ethnic identity that reflected the cultural mixture of these two groups.

Originally members of the Wayúu elite – her natal family actually founded the town of Maicao – Señora Helena's family was the product of such alliances. In her youth, Señora Helena was what was historically referred to in Colombia as a "Wayúu princess." The expression served to underscore the similarities in class and to downplay the ethnic differences involved in marriages between such "princesses" and the officers of the Colombian army they married. As *mestizo* Guajiro elites, her family was a key player in enabling the Colombian state to gain power within the region. They made way for the establishment of a police outpost and a local bureaucracy, and in exchange her family received advantages such as control over commercial routes and social status.

Guajiro elites retained territorial control of La Guajira's roads and ports, which were critical in the illegal trade of marijuana and cocaine during the 1970s and 1980s, increasing their economic and political power and challenging state efforts to govern the region and control illegal activity. The state's response to its lack of control over the territory, partly resulting from the empowerment of the Guajiro elites related to illegal smuggling, was twofold. First, the central government imposed strong policies to keep illegal trade at bay through the prosecution of people running these enterprises (Orsini Aaron 2007). The second strategy was for the state to politically engage with the Wayúu (a population regarded as "more Indigenous" than the *mestizo* Guajiros) through multicultural social policies, including the creation of *resguardos* (a type of reservation), thus undermining the power of the Guajiro families who had formerly acted as mediators between the Colombian state and the Wayúu people.

Additionally, in the late 1990s right-wing death squads made incursions into La Guajira as part of a nationwide phenomenon more generally called *paramilitarismo* – a scheme in which private armies (militias) divided into "blocks" (regional groups) worked in the service of large landowners and drug traffickers who were initially interested in repelling left-wing guerrillas from the region. Paramilitaries had been a constitutive part of Colombian reality since at least the 1950s (Taussig 2005), but they formalized in an unprecedented way during the 1980s (Medina Gallego 1990). When these organizations were outlawed by the government in the 1990s, a second wave of organizations emerged (Romero 2003); in 1997 these nascent groups set up an umbrella organization, *Autodefensas Unidas de Colombia* (United Self-Defense Forces of Colombia), and divided the national territory among its members. The Northern Block penetrated La Guajira in the late 1990s through alliances with some Guajiro families who welcomed the death squads as a means of tipping the balance of power in disputes with other local elite families.

Soon afterwards, the paramilitaries abandoned alliances with the Guajiros and took control of the region by killing whole families and securing strategic locations for smuggling. The Colombian army, motivated by a desire for greater control of the region, assisted the paramilitaries by providing information and contributing to ground operations that resulted in the deaths, forced displacement, and the disappearances of local community members (see Chapter 20). Some *mestizo* Guajiro families, including Señora Helena's family, collaborated with their Indigenous Wayúu allies to resist the supremacy of the paramilitaries, but they were soon defeated. This crisis, which lasted until 2006, led to the socioeconomic downfall of Guajiro families like Señora Helena's.

Responding to the armed conflict, the state, nongovernmental organizations (NGOs), and multilateral organizations conceived of ways to ameliorate the crisis. Government-administered reparations for human rights violations were at the forefront of efforts to address the effects of the armed conflict. As a result, almost overnight a vast part of the population of La Guajira became, in the state's eyes, not only "victims" but "Indigenous victims" of the armed conflict. The crisis also paved the way for other palliative, multicultural social inclusion policies, such as the Indigenous Families in Action program, that contributed to a reimagining of what it meant to be an Indigenous person in La Guajira. By the time the armed conflict had reached its most dramatic point in the early 2000s, Señora Helena's family's livelihood was considerably affected. The precarious position of *mestizo* Guajiro families compelled some of them to rethink their identities as Guajiros and reimagine themselves as Indigenous Wayúu citizens to gain inclusion in an awkward mélange of social policies and programs aimed at promoting multiculturalism.

MULTICULTURAL POLICIES AND STATE FRAMING OF INDIGENOUS CITIZENSHIP

Resguardos and *Reservas*

Multiculturalism is the name for a governmental policy approach involving the creation of programming specific to particular ethnic groups. In the late twentieth century, as *mestizo* Guajiro elites were consolidating their power, paving the way for state intervention in the region, and forming alliances with paramilitaries, Indigenous Wayúu people were targeted for government multicultural programs aimed at recognizing and including the oft-excluded Wayúu in the Colombian state. In the mid-1980s the government decreed nearly half of the Guajira peninsula a **resguardo** – a juridical arrangement intended to recognize and protect

Indigenous territory through the creation of reservations. The government declaration of the land as a *resguardo* gave Indigenous Wayúu residents the right to receive state resources, mainly in the form of government projects to improve their *rancherías*. However, these resources were not sent directly to the leaders of the *resguardo*'s *rancherías*, but rather to the municipal government to distribute them as they saw fit. To the Indigenous leaders of the *rancherías*, the distribution of resources via the municipal government was a problematic form of auditing and oversight.

Then, in the first decade of the twenty-first century, the government halted the declaration of *resguardos* and replaced them instead with *reservas* (reserves), another territorial construction that emerged from multicultural reforms (Decree 2164 of 1995). Like *reguardos*, **reservas** were territories recognized by the Colombian government as being inhabited by Indigenous peoples; however, *reservas* did not afford the same legal protection over territory (the land was alienable) and resources afforded *resguardos*. Although *reservas* did not entitle Wayúu communities to the inalienability of their land and funding like the *reguardos* did, residency on a *reserva* paved the way for a community's inclusion in other multicultural programs aimed at the social inclusion and welfare of Indigenous groups like the Wayúu. Thus, *reservas* were, in practice, a strategy for targeting certain people as Indigenous in social policy.

For Señora Helena and her family, reinhabiting Campamento as a *ranchería* rather than a *finca* meant refashioning alliances with "more Indigenous" Wayúu allies and laying claim to Indigenous citizenship. When families like Señora Helena's identified as *mestizo* Guajiros, former alliances with Wayúu allies turned into contractual arrangements for agricultural production and trade. In Campamento, the family started to refashion their relationships through ritual means common among the Wayúu, like the celebration of wakes and marriages, by helping allies in times of need, or by becoming leaders in the defense of the territory. This move away from a *mestizo* Guajiro identity toward a more Indigenous Wayúu one was risky; her family had enjoyed power and territorial autonomy precisely because, as Guajiros, they were outside of the scope of governmental recognition as Indigenous citizens.

In fact, when I suggested the possibility of declaring Campamento's land a *resguardo* so that she could receive more resources from the government, Señora Helena replied, "Resguardo no!" "Why not?" I asked, clearly confused. "I don't know, I don't like it," she finally replied. Over time I came to understand that since inclusion in a *resguardo* meant subjecting the *ranchería* to greater state control, Señora Helena was reluctant to claim Campamento's land as a *resguardo* or *reserva*. And yet, during visits from her neighbors and family, Señora Helena referred to a perceived lack of government resources for her *ranchería*, complaining, "Nothing for Campamento! Nothing!" Her frustration stemmed from the institutional obstacles surrounding accessing the benefits of multicultural programs as an Indigenous person who did not live on a *reserva*. Living in a *ranchería*, reactivating social relations with Wayúu families, and relying less on their *mestizo* relations was as far as she was able and willing to go to improve their circumstances while still avoiding governmental control.

In short, Señora Helena's dilemma could be put like this: The power and autonomy of the family before the paramilitary incursion had been partly guaranteed by its noninclusion in the Indigenous *resguardos* (and in other germane multicultural policies), but this meant they could not access national resources allocated to Indigenous peoples like the Wayúu. Before the paramilitary incursion, the family did not need such resources because they were sustained by their own businesses. After the paramilitary incursion, the family had lost control over trade routes and ports and, therefore, had started to depend on alternative sources of income. The family's challenge was figuring out how to access these resources while keeping a margin of autonomy and maneuverability to rebuild part of their power.

Post-Conflict Multiculturalism: Indigenous Families in Action

Because the armed conflict led to a full set of governmental policies and institutions that had the purpose of generating the social inclusion of Indigenous peoples in the nation-state (largely because they had been made vulnerable by indirect and direct state actions during the conflict) the benefits of identifying as Indigenous Wayúu increased. The first wave of these benefits included the Indigenous Families in Action program advanced by the National Institute of Rural Development (INCODER) and the Colombian Institute of Family Welfare (ICBF). Indigenous Families in Action, part of a Latin American experiment in governance and social welfare (IDB 2007), was an Indigenous version of a nationwide conditional cash transfer program that delivered subsidies to mothers (Latorre 2007).

Programs such as Indigenous Families in Action, which were intended to bring the benefits of full citizenship to marginalized populations, entailed membership in regulated multicultural organizations such as the Association of Traditional Authorities. Membership in these organizations were based, problematically, either in territorial fixity on a *resguardo* or *reserva* or on problematic notions of biological descent. Thus, people were subtly forced to emphasize the genealogical traits that defined them as Indigenous to access resources, even if they themselves, like the Wayúu, did not define indigeneity in terms of biological descent. Furthermore, for someone who did not live on a *reserva* to access the benefits of the Indigenous Families in Action program, such as the residents of Campamento, they had to become a holder of a *cédula de ciudadanía* (citizenship identity card, henceforth *cédula*) that listed them as Indigenous. To complicate matters, people could not apply as individuals for a *cédula*; Indigenous communities had to work through an intermediary who arranged the registration of entire communities. The state institution in charge (the National Registry of Civil Status) assigned individuals who were "Traditional Authorities" and Associations of Traditional Authorities with this task. In practice, this meant that an entire community would be represented by an officially recognized Traditional Authority and belong to an Association of Traditional Authorities.

Traditional Authorities were members of an Indigenous community who had a formalized – by local community standards – leadership role in the community. In Maicao, the registration of a person as a Traditional Authority took place in the municipal Bureau of Indigenous Affairs at the town hall, and the registered person would produce a list of people (supported by their signatures, fingerprints, and *cédula* numbers) confirming that this person was a local leader. The presence of a Traditional Authority did not entitle a community to receive the same resources destined for the populations of Indigenous *resguardos* or *reservas*. The advantage of a community leader becoming a Traditional Authority was access to the set of resources delivered to communities affiliated with Associations of Traditional Authorities (i.e., Indigenous Families in Action). However, participation in this system meant not only proving one's Indigenous citizenship through territory or genealogy and status as a Traditional Authority, but also submitting the community to the auditing techniques of the Association of Traditional Authorities. As a result, the use of state-sanctioned Associations of Traditional Authorities as the gateway to receiving the benefits promised to Indigenous peoples (as part of multicultural social inclusion processes) produced anxiety surrounding Indigenous citizenship. A paradoxical outcome of multiculturalism and social inclusion programs was the undermining of people's self-determination.

THE INSTITUTIONALIZATION OF INDIGENOUS CITIZENSHIP AND ITS EFFECTS

Back in Campamento, Señora Helena, having registered in the municipal Bureau of Indigenous Affairs of Maicao as a Traditional Authority, was able to access Indigenous Families in Action benefits for the community. To be included, the program asked every Traditional Authority to carry out a census in their communities. The Families in Action team gave every Traditional Authority a form to be photocopied and filled out with the information for every household in the *rancherías*. As an ethnographer, and concerned about possible outcomes from this census, I offered to lend a hand to my friend Daniela, a leader in the neighboring *ranchería*, to fill out the forms.

The form "requested" information about the members of each household, including the ID number of each individual. Additionally, the forms "asked" for information about Indigenous languages spoken by individuals, health coverage, and educational levels of members of the household. Having photocopied the forms, we visited the "households" of the *ranchería*; the community leader asked the questions, and I filled in the forms. Typically it was a woman in the household who replied to our questions and "managed" the identification documents, which they would remove from a folder hidden in the house. Inconveniences soon emerged. One resident, Carolina, said: "I am already registered with another leader." Daniela was visibly upset because, as she told me, "*tapush'sia* (she is our family)." Since kin relations and alliances are the bedrock of *rancherías* and Wayúu society, the registering of Carolina to a *ranchería* other than Daniela's destabilized these relations. In a swift response, Daniela looked for alternatives to balance her numbers and guided me along a pathway leading to Wawatamana, another *ranchería*.

In this way, among leaders who wanted to register as many people as possible to increase their leverage with state institutions, a race to fill out the forms emerged in and among *rancherías*.

One of the most remarkable outcomes of the census was the possessive language that people started to use about their own *ranchería* and its inhabitants, such as "Uniaka is Campamento's," "Campamento is my *ranchería*," and "the people of Campamento are mine." A leader from Campamento, Claudia, learning about my participation in the census of another *ranchería*, requested the forms from me "so [she] could have a look" – I assume this was based on the premise that ethnographers never say no. After I turned down her request, she left, upset, to continue her low-intensity war with a leader called Luis Angel, who was "registering people from Campamento as if they were from Uniaka." This complaint soon spread and was vocalized by other inhabitants of Campamento, such as Martha, who stated: "Uniaka does not even exist; this is a recent thing; that is their invention." I asked, "Whose invention?" Martha answered, "The leaders' inventions." This dispute raises a question: Is it the leader or the means (the censuses, workshops, and programs) that created these rifts?

More fundamentally, these and other issues carried with them increasing feelings of insecurity about kin relations and the implications of government-constructed notions of Indigenous citizenship and identity. People in the *rancherías* started to experience an increasing nervousness about the kinds of (dis)loyalty that could emerge from such a reconfiguration of "the family" along state-determined (read: household) lines. Campamento was not only "under siege" by outside leaders, such as Luis Angel, but also by people belonging to the same family. Helena's cousin, for instance, lived in a *ranchería* far from Campamento but had been visiting the latter quite often in the couple of weeks before the census. She was introduced to me warmly, but when it emerged that she had the intention of registering her household in her own census, rather than in Campamento's, people started calling her the unfriendly nickname of *La Rata* (the rat).

The most salient consequence of the census forms, as illustrated in the tensions between leaders obtaining households' records, was the new framing of the *ranchería* as a customizable entity to fit government intervention programs. A *ranchería* entails a complex notion of affinity and consanguine relations and is a spatial (through the location of houses and paths) and temporal (as represented in the family cemetery) representation of alliances in peace and war. Such an idea of interconnectivity is implicit in the idea of *apushi* (family) and its irreducibility to the set of households that integrate into it. Therefore, *rancherías* are not merely groups of households. However, because of the census, on a map the *rancherías* started to look less like territorial clusters resulting from consanguine relationships and alliances and more like a scattered set of households held together by their common inclusion in particular government social programs. To categorize a *ranchería* as a set of households, as the census successfully did, had important political uses. Each household unit now had a one-to-one relationship with state agencies that delivered benefits, and the interconnectivity of *apushi*, which historically had contributed to the resiliency and defense of families, could be diluted.

In the final stage of my fieldwork, I gathered with members of an Indigenous organization that had emerged because of legal and political concerns around the demand of reparations for Indigenous victims of the armed conflict. The purpose of our meeting was to analyze the challenge of creating "unity" in the organization. After hours of discussion among the leaders, Karmen, Señora Helena's niece, said, "we're selling ourselves off." Another leader, who did not belong to the organization, was cruder than that: "*el paisano* [a colloquial term for an Indigenous-looking person] is too interested; he goes wherever things are being given away." While the post-conflict context and state efforts at promoting multiculturalism offered ways to reimagine being an Indigenous person in Colombia, that reimagining existed within the parameters established by the government. Indigeneity began to mean entering negotiations with the state and bargaining with kin, allies, and other Wayúu families in unfamiliar ways. For some, like Karmen, this entailed the risk of transacting one's personhood and self-determination in exchange for social benefits.

CONCLUSION: MULTICULTURAL POLICIES AND THE EMERGENCE OF ANXIOUS ETHNIC SUBJECTS

The examples in this chapter serve to illustrate several ways in which multicultural policies and programs have contributed to what I call **anxious ethnic subjects** – people experiencing contradictory senses of performing certain versions of indigeneity that can garner them services, resources, or aid, but at the risk of commodifying key parts of Indigenous sociality and personhood, such as being part of a *ranchería*. Anxiety emerges both because of challenges to identity, in particular one's sense of self as Indigenous or not, and because of institutionalized and commodified forms of indigeneity that challenge local Indigenous understandings of family and community. These anxieties are linked to a sense of loss of the self and of community as a result of a trade-off between participation in social inclusion programs and objectified notions of Indigenous citizenship and identity.

In La Guajira, violence and multicultural policies, such as the establishment of *resguardos/reservas*, the Associations of Traditional Authorities, and the Indigenous Families in Action program, triggered transformations in identity. These transformations not only affected the Guajiros but influenced Wayúu understandings of what it meant to be Indigenous in terms of government multicultural programs aimed at social inclusion. State multicultural policies created ambiguous definitions of communities and families that contributed to the reimagination of indigeneity as an object that could be exchanged for the benefits of social inclusion.

There is an interesting – though sinister – cycle in operation here. First, the state's association of indigeneity with notions of vulnerability (i.e., notions that Indigenous peoples are poor) has emerged as a central trope to formulate a paternalistic relationship of care and protection between Indigenous peoples and the state. Second, multicultural policies created an experience of objectified indigeneity that was mediated through material objects (e.g., ID cards and survey forms, among other things) that stand for and authorize the Indigenous "identity" of the holder, and which can be exchanged for the benefits of social inclusion. Thus, persons framed as Indigenous by the state had to reimagine their indigeneity as "something" negotiable and in circulation, rather than self-determined. These two issues constitute the basis for the emergence of commodified identities as people wrestle with who they are in the eyes of the state and what that means for their access to resources. For Señora Helena and her family, the emergence of multicultural policies that distribute resources to communities identifying as Indigenous, combined with the effects of armed conflict on their livelihood, had a significant impact on their identities and their claims to Indigenous citizenship.

The bottom line is that the processes and programs described in this chapter, while aimed at encouraging multiculturalism and social inclusion, actively challenged self-determination and produced new notions of being and becoming Indigenous in Colombia. These programs, in turn, created relationships of dependency with the state, and threatened the interconnectedness of more traditional *apushi* alliances. In this case, the politics of recognition and the politics of the redistribution of resources had colluded to undermine self-determination rather than to produce greater justice, which is the elusive goal of multicultural policies.

REFLECTION AND DISCUSSION QUESTIONS

- What is *mestizaje* and how did it contribute to the formation of a Guajiro identity? How does this identity differ from an Indigenous Wayúu identity?
- What are the factors contributing to the emergence of anxious ethnic subjects in La Guajira, Colombia?
- In this case, communities must validate the indigeneity of its members – in other words prove their Indigenous citizenship – before they can access the multicultural programs aimed at extending the benefits of nation-state citizenship to all Indigenous Colombians. What is problematic about this approach to multiculturalism and "social inclusion"?

KEY CONCEPTS

- **anxious ethnic subjects**: People experiencing contradictory senses of performing certain versions of indigeneity that can garner them services, resources, or aid, but at the risk of commodifying key parts of Indigenous sociality and personhood.
- **mestizaje** (miscegenation): The mixing, through marriage, cohabitation, or sexual reproduction, of people classified in different racial groups.

- ***ranchería***: Traditional Indigenous hamlet composed of households connected through consanguine and other social bonds and that is based on traditional alliances.
- ***resguardo/reserva***: A government-sanctioned Indigenous reservation intended to recognize Indigenous territories.
- **social inclusion**: State efforts to include Indigenous peoples in the Colombian nation-state and the benefits of Colombian citizenship.

EXPLORE FURTHER

- To learn more about the complexities surrounding *mestizaje* and identity, read **Chapter 10**.
- To learn more about the legacy of armed conflict in Colombia, read **Chapters 20** and **21**.
- To learn about policies and practices aimed at recognizing Indigenous systems of governance and decision making, read **Chapters 19** and **29**.
- To learn more about how mining is affecting Wayúu communities, read **Chapter 29**.
- Gill, Lesley. 2009. "The Parastate in Colombia: Political Violence and the Restructuring in Barrancabermeja." *Anthropologica* 51: 313–25.
- Postero, Nancy Grey. 2007. *Now We Are Citizens: Indigenous Politics in Postmulticultural Bolivia*. Stanford, CA: Stanford University Press.

ABOUT THE AUTHOR

Pablo Jaramillo is an associate professor of anthropology at the Universidad de los Andes in Bogotá, Colombia. In addition to studying indigeneity in Colombia and Venezuela, his research also looks at the materiality and temporality of natural resources in Colombia.

REFERENCES

Guerra Curvelo, Weilder. 2007. *El Poblamiento del Territorio*. Bogotá: DMG.
IDB. 2007. *2007–2008 Report: Outsiders? The Changing Patterns of Exclusion in Latin America and the Caribbean*. Washington: Inter-American Development Bank.
Latorre, Maria. 2007. *Are Quasi-Experiments the Accurate Methodology for Evaluating the Impact of Conditional Cash Transfers in Colombia?* Master's diss., Social Policy, London School of Economics and Political Science.
Medina Gallego, Carlos. 1990. *Autodefensas, Paramilitares y Narcotráfico en Colombia. Origen, Desarrollo y Consolidación. El Caso "Puerto Boyacá."* Bogotá: Editorial Documentos Periodísticos.
Orsini Aaron, Giangina. 2007. *Poligamia y Contrabando: Nociones de Legalidad y Legitimidad en la Frontera Guajira*. Bogotá: Universidad de los Andes – CESO.
Romero, Mauricio. 2003. *Paramilitares y Autodefensas. 1982–2003*. Bogotá: IEPRI.
Taussig, Michael T. 2005. *Law in a Lawless Land: Diary of a "Limpieza" in Colombia*. Chicago: University of Chicago Press.

CHAPTER NINE

A Panamanian of West Indian Descent: An Autoethnographic Study of Citizenship and Belonging

LaVerne M. Seales Soley

Every morning my sister and I would wake up at 5 a.m., put on our school uniforms, have breakfast, and jump in the car for a 25-minute ride to the US-controlled Panama Canal Zone (CZ) to drop my father off at work. Before we could enter the zone, my father had to show his CZ identification card and an officer inspected our car; this could take as long as 15 minutes. Then, we would drive about one mile into the zone to drop him off and then turn around and drive to the school my sister and I attended outside the zone, and where my mother worked as an English-as-a-second-language teacher. At the end of the day, we would go back to the CZ area to pick up my father, but he had to walk out to meet us because we were not allowed to enter the zone without him.

The Canal Zone was administered, structured, and modeled after a large, southern US city. In addition to an appointed US governor who acted as administrator, the CZ had police officers and judges to uphold US laws. These laws governed daily life well into the 1980s, and there were strict rules regarding who could do what or go where in the zone. These rules discriminated against nonwhite, non-US citizens – in other words, people of West Indian descent, like me and my family (Corinealdi 2012). My uncles who worked for the canal lived with their families in the zone in a section designated for non-American workers, of which the vast majority were ethnic West Indians.

One of the most traumatic experiences of my childhood occurred while visiting my relatives in the zone. I was 9 years old, and I went to the grocery store in the CZ with my 20-year-old cousin to get some sugar for a cake my aunt was baking. As we were exiting the grocery store, an American police officer with a heavy southern drawl stopped us. The officer asked my cousin to show him her CZ identification card. Although I was bilingual, I didn't understand him at first and I asked him to repeat the question, which had been directed at my cousin. I didn't sound "American" like my cousin, who lived and went to school in the anglophone Canal

Figure 9.1. A West Indian man sprays larvicide into a ditch as part of a mosquito control program implemented during the construction of the Panama Canal (1910).
Photo by the Wellcome Collection (CC BY 4.0).

Zone, so he asked me for my ID card. Since I did not have an ID card the police officer separated us and asked me questions about why I was at the store. He detained my cousin, who was questioned for more than two hours and then taken to a judge who fined her and suspended her privileges in the CZ, all because I did not have a Canal Zone ID card. That experience left an imprint on me, and for many years I felt scared whenever I was in the zone.

This chapter, written as an **autoethnography**, uses a **narrative inquiry** approach to examine the realities of ethnicity, national belonging, and citizenship in the Republic of Panama through my experiences growing up as an ethnic West Indian in Panama during the US occupation of the Canal Zone. As one of the world's largest and longest human-made structures, the Panama Canal is one of the Seven Wonders of the Modern World. The Panama Canal was built primarily by people from the West Indies. In Panama, the term **West Indian** refers to people of African descent from the islands of Jamaica, Martinique, Barbados, and, to a lesser extent, Trinidad. Starting in the 1850s, many ethnic West Indians moved to Panama to work for the United Fruit Company and on the construction of the Panama Railroad and the Panama Canal, resulting in a West Indian ethnic identity that collapsed their nation-state affiliations (Senior 2014). These West Indians and their descendants were at the forefront of constructing, operating, and maintaining the engineering marvel that is the Panama Canal for more than a century. This chapter explores how shifts in Panama's political, economic, social, and cultural landscapes eventually contributed to national belonging and citizenship for ethnic West Indians – a community that was historically excluded from the Panamanian nation-state because of its complex association with the US-occupied Canal Zone.

DISCRIMINATION AND EXCLUSION DURING THE US OCCUPATION OF THE PANAMA CANAL ZONE

On November 3, 1903, 15 days after winning independence from Colombia, Panama's provisional government reluctantly signed the Hay-Bunau-Varilla Treaty, which allowed the United States to complete the construction of a canal that opened a maritime pathway between the Atlantic and Pacific Oceans (Major 1993). The treaty granted the United States the right to the perpetual use and occupation of the Canal Zone. From 1903 to 1979, the Panama Canal Zone was a self-governing US territory in Panama that consisted of the canal and the surrounding lands, waters, and airspace. The zone, which excluded the cities of Panama and Colón, had an area of 1,432 square kilometers and extended to approximately 8.1 kilometers on each side of the canal. The United States also frequently intervened in the political and economic affairs of the new Republic of Panama, and thus its rights over the Canal Zone created a hostile and imperialist political climate. This situation led to several protests and confrontations between Panamanians and Americans in the 1960s (Major 1993).

After a 1968 coup overthrew the elected president Arnulfo Arias, Colonel Omar Torrijos became the de facto military dictator. In 1977, he negotiated the Torrijos-Carter Treaty, which guaranteed that Panama would gain control of the Panama Canal after 1999, ending the 97-year US occupation (Major 1993). I was born in the 1960s, shortly after Torrijos took power, and it was a time of significant change in Panama. From my childhood to my late teens, our family lived in Colón, on the Atlantic side of the country, in what would be considered the suburbs. However, because my father worked for the Panama Canal and still had family living in the Canal Zone, I had some limited access to the CZ.

It was clear that my grandparents' and parents' experiences growing up in the US-occupied Canal Zone differed from my experiences growing up outside the Canal Zone under Torrijos's leadership. Born in the Canal Zone in the first half of the twentieth century, my grandparents and parents were not granted US citizenship, but because they grew up there and were educated, lived, and became employed in the zone, their Panamanian citizenship was constantly called into question (O'Reggio 2006). Within the zone, the United States employed a segregation system that – among other exclusionary practices, such as segregated housing, dining spaces, and schools – paid "silver," nonwhite, non-US citizens four times less than white, US citizen, "gold" workers. This system was called the gold and silver rolls system, and in 1948 it became the US Rate/Local Rate system (Corinealdi 2012). As a child, what I knew about the experiences of ethnic West Indians living in the Canal Zone was based on conversations I overheard, things I observed, or things people told me about life in the zone.

My father often shared stories about his experiences living and working on the Panama Canal. My father's grandparents migrated from Barbados to Panama for the employment opportunities there, and his family became part of the West Indian community working and living in the US Canal Zone. My father was born in the Canal Zone, attended Zone Colored Schools (c.f. Corinealdi 2012) with other West Indian students, and, after graduating in 1963, he was hired as a journeyman in the Panama Canal apprenticeship program as a shipfitter. Although it was considered an honor to be employed in any Panama Canal apprenticeship program, working for the Panama Canal gave my father first-hand experience with gold/silver disparities in the treatment of US American employees and ethnic West Indian employees.

The Industrial Division in which my father worked proved to be a microcosm of the racialized discrimination that existed in the Canal Zone. American employees were provided with bathrooms and lunchrooms that were separate and better than those used by ethnic West Indian employees, who were not US citizens and were racialized as nonwhite. The more prestigious, high-ranking jobs were assigned exclusively to Americans, regardless of their training. Although my father was among the best shipfitters in his division, time and time again he was denied promotions as a form of retaliation for being outspoken. Also, on several occasions, he was forced to train young Americans with no work experience who were then hired as managers. In addition, as a nonwhite, non-US citizen, my father – like many other ethnic West Indian workers – had to tolerate being humiliated by the Americans they were training. However, my father and many West Indian workers remained on the job because there were limited employment options outside of the Canal Zone for ethnic West Indian men in Panama.

My father would tell me about the ways that Panamanians also excluded West Indians and their descendants from Panamanian society and challenged their right to Panamanian citizenship. I remember being at a large family celebration in honor of my uncle receiving his first Panamanian passport. At first, I did not understand why we were celebrating something as mundane as a passport, so I discreetly asked my father about it. He explained that the full benefits of Panamanian citizenship, such as a passport, were not always available to ethnic West Indians. I asked how that could be possible since my uncle was born at Gorgas Hospital in the Canal Zone. My father said, "LaVerne, a couple of years ago, things were not what we have today. West Indians and their descendants were not welcome in Panama." He continued: "Initially, Panamanians tolerated West Indians, as they saw us as necessary to build the canal and they assumed that we would return to our islands once construction ended." According to my father, Panamanians expected that once West Indians completed the canal, jobs in the Canal Zone would go to Panamanians, and they resented the fact that West Indians remained in Panama (c.f. Senior 2014).

In 1928, the Panamanian government passed a law stating that children born in Panama to non-Panamanians after October 1928 would not be considered Panamanian nationals until they reached adulthood and announced their intent to claim Panamanian nationality, thus rendering them stateless until that point (Lasso de Paulis 2007). Later, the 1941 Constitution restricted citizenship even further and revoked the citizenship of ethnic West Indians (and other racialized groups) who had been born in Panama after 1928, as well as individuals who had been born in the US Canal Zone (Corinealdi 2012; O'Reggio 2006). Although the government eliminated the clauses excluding certain racial or ethnic groups and those born in the Canal Zone from becoming citizens in 1946, it did pass the Panamanian Nationality Law requiring that all children born to foreign parents demonstrate their "integration into the Republic" via Spanish-language skills and knowledge of Panamanian history (Constitución 1946, 4, cited in Corinealdi 2012, 92). While this law didn't invalidate the citizenship of ethnic West Indian children born in Panama, even those born in the US Canal Zone, it did prevent people who did not demonstrate "integration" from applying for and attaining identity cards and passports, thus limiting their employment opportunities in Panama and abroad (Corinealdi 2012).

Thus, throughout the first decades of the Panamanian Republic, my father and other ethnic West Indians were discriminated against in the US Canal Zone and excluded from US citizenship, and also rejected from belonging in the Panamanian nation-state. Considering Panama's exclusionary immigration and citizenship policies, my uncle's passport represented not only his ability to leave the country, but his full belonging in the Panamanian nation-state and the increased acceptance of ethnic West Indians, especially those who assimilated to Panamanian culture by learning Spanish.

INSTITUTIONALIZING BELONGING AND NATIONALISM TO END THE US OCCUPATION

Political and economic changes had significant ramifications for citizenship and belonging in Panama. As someone who grew up outside of the Canal Zone, and under the government of General Torrijos, there was a sense that ethnic West Indians were also Panamanians. General Torrijos actively fostered a sense of nation-state belonging. Time and time again he would appear on the radio and television to remind us that we were all together in this "*lucha*" (struggle) for "*soberanía total*" (total sovereignty) from US imperialism. Torrijos's discourse cultivated a sense of belonging for all Panamanians, irrespective of ancestry and ties to the Canal Zone. Exposed to these discourses, I remember feeling connected to my classmates and a sense of unconditional support and loyalty to my country, which was unequivocally Panama.

Ideologies surrounding nation-state belonging, citizenship, and nationalism were nurtured in Panamanian children through institutions such as education. Children would enjoy the country's most significant celebrations during "*Noviembre: Mes de la Patria*" (November: Month of the Homeland). November was characterized by celebrating independence and separation of the isthmus from Colombia and commemorating and honoring national symbols such as the flag, the coat of arms, and the national anthem. Every November 3rd, 4th, and 5th were special. When I was in primary and middle school, my family would drive to my uncle's house in the city before 7 a.m. to beat the traffic and get good parking. At exactly 7 a.m., after the pledge of allegiance and the singing of the national anthem in the main square, the celebration would begin – drumming and loud cheering on the streets indicated that the festivities had begun. By 8 a.m., we would see hundreds of people filling the main road. I was fascinated by the marching bands from each high school. The feeling of nationalism was contagious; it was hard not to feel proud of being Panamanian.

People who were not in the parade were walking, taking photos, and dancing. The most striking thing was that the Panamanian flag was everywhere. As Panamanians, we learned very early that these displays were not just a celebration of our independence. In school, teachers would reiterate that the red, white, and blue (the colors of the Panamanian flag) were to honor those heroes and martyrs who won battles and fought to return full sovereignty to the isthmus. Therefore, every house, car, shopping mall, building, and school had the Panamanian flag hanging for the entire month of November.

My pride in being Panamanian increased when my classmates and I learned about the *Día de los Mártires* (Martyrs' Day), which commemorated the January 9, 1964, protests and riots against US imperialism. Approximately 22 Panamanians, including students, were killed during a conflict with Canal Zone police officers. Although this event happened before most of us were born, it was recent enough that it directly impacted how we felt about the United States and our role in ensuring Panama's sovereignty. *Día de los Mártires* was one of our country's most solemn holidays because it reminded us of the ultimate patriotic sacrifice. Another institutional effort to instill nationalism in young people was the mandatory twelfth grade history class called "*Relaciones entre Panamá y Los Estados Unidos*" (Relations between Panama and the United States). In that class, we spent a full academic year learning about US imperialism in Latin America and specifically in Panama. We were told that we all had to unite as one nation against the United States for our *soberanía total*.

Strikingly, we never learned about Panama's treatment and exclusion of West Indians, and it was not covered in our history textbooks. My family's history in Panama was erased from formal historical accounts. Nevertheless, my classmates, friends, and I were still proud ethnic West Indians and Panamanians. We were genuinely bilingual and multicultural. Since our parents were from the anglophone West Indies, we spoke English at home and at the Protestant church frequented by other West Indians. We spoke Spanish socially and at school since it was and still is the official language of Panama. We ate West Indian food. Although Panamanians stigmatized these ethnic markers of West Indian identity during my parents' and grandparents' era, my classmates and I were able to embrace both these characteristics and a sense of pride in being Panamanian.

While I had heard anecdotally about Panamanian discrimination against ethnic West Indians and their exclusion by Panamanian society and the nation-state, I personally did not feel any resentment toward other Panamanians. Instead, my bitterness focused on the US's occupation of Panama – my country – and its exploitation of us Panamanians. In this way, Torrijos's efforts were successful – in his attempts to resist US imperialism he had convinced even those who had been excluded from the nation-state (i.e., West Indians) to embrace a Panamanian identity that would contribute to his vision of *soberanía total*. I remember watching the 1977 signing of the Torrijos-Carter Treaty on television, and I spoke with my high school classmates about how we would all work to ensure our country would be successful after the transfer of power. I decided I wanted to become a lawyer to help with the legal turnover. It was a time of celebration and hope. I saw Torrijos as a national hero, and my generation was inspired to do our part as others, like the student protesters in the 1960s, had before us.

FLEEING NORIEGA'S PANAMA

After Torrijos's death in 1981, Manuel Antonio Noriega, who was the chief of military intelligence in Torrijos's government, consolidated power and became Panama's de facto ruler. Under Noriega, life in Panama as I knew it changed for the worse. There were shortages of food and water, curfews were implemented, universities and schools struggled to keep their doors open, and there was political unrest. I remember when one of my mother's co-workers arrived at our house in tears. I could not quite hear the conversation, but I saw my mother grab her pocketbook, give her friend some money, and hug her. Later, I asked my mother what happened. My mother explained that Noriega had decided to pay teachers and government workers in food – literally rice and beans – so her friend had no money to buy milk for her children. Since my father worked for the Canal, we were not affected in the same way as other teachers and government employees. Noriega ruled by fear, and journalists soon began disappearing, mass incarceration was imposed, and violence erupted. Watching the news and reading the newspaper were stressful, and my parents did not allow us out of the house once the sun went down.

Because of the political unrest, my parents, like many ethnic West Indians, were fearful for our future. My father wanted to make sure we were safe and that we received a good education; at the time, the schools were constantly out on strike. There was also talk that Noriega was getting ready to close the borders so that no one could leave the country. As a result, many ethnic West Indians who had family ties in the United States decided to send their children to live with family or take early retirement and leave the country. By the end of the 1980s, many of my West Indian friends began to leave Panama.

I remember the afternoon when my father and mother informed my sister, brother, and I that we would be going to the United States to live with my maternal grandmother for a few years. They promised that we would return home to Panama once things stabilized. That was one of the most painful days of my life. We would have to leave our home, family, friends, and beloved country for – of all places – the United States. The plan was that my mother would take a leave of absence from work and travel with me and my siblings while my father would stay behind and continue working for the Panama Canal, where he was earning a relatively good income. So, in 1987, I reluctantly moved to the United States.

THE LIMITS OF PANAMANIAN NATIONAL BELONGING

By the 1990s, I was in my early twenties and there was political and economic stability in Panama, so I was able to return to visit several times. Noriega was no longer in power, and Panamanians' attention was on the handover of the canal and Canal Zone from the United States to Panama. From a political and economic perspective, Panama seemed to be quickly transforming for the better. However, from my perspective, the day-to-day life of Panamanians of West Indian descent seemed to have gotten worse.

One of the key mechanisms through which ethnic West Indians in Panama maintained our heritage was through speaking English and attending Protestant church services in English. The Protestant church was the backbone of the West Indian community since it was the place where our roots were celebrated. Most ethnic West Indians were Protestant, and the Protestant church in Panama had direct ties to the West Indies. To my surprise, when I was visiting Panama and decided to attend a church service, there were two services – one in Spanish, attended primarily by people my age and younger, and the other in English, attended mostly by people older than me. The Panamanian government had passed a law where half of the church services needed to be in Spanish. The Spanish service had three times as many people.

I attended both services and afterward invited my childhood friend, a minister in training, to have lunch with me. We decided to walk to the West Indian restaurant we ate at in high school. I could not believe my eyes. The small intimate restaurant was now four times bigger, and, to make matters worse, a tour bus had just arrived. My frustrations over the changes to the church services and what those changes meant for West Indian society were triggered over finding my favorite restaurant also transformed. I turned to my friend and asked, "What is going on?" Looking at me confused, he responded, "What do you mean?" I was speechless. Tears started rolling down my cheeks, and he said, "LaVerne, times have changed, and we have to change with the times. We were losing followers because of the language barrier and the lack of connection to the West Indian ways. The new generation of people of West Indian descent is not like ours that had balance. This generation is more interested in being part of Panamanian mainstream society." My friend spoke to the ways that ethnic West Indians had integrated into Panamanian society and were beginning to identify as part of a larger group of Spanish-speaking Afro-Panamanians, rather than as ethnic West Indians.

After that initial trip back, I was always happy to reunite with my friends and family in Panama but, little by little, I felt it was the end of life in Panama as I had known it. In 2001, I returned to Panama for the Christmas holidays, and the focus of the country at that time was on the operation of the canal and the upcoming celebration of the 100 years of independence from Colombia. Many ethnic West Indians of my parents' generation who had retired and relocated to the United States during the Noriega era were considering going back "home" to Panama, and eventually several of them did. But after 2001, I did not return to Panama for many years, as the transformation of the ethnic West Indian community, specifically my generation and younger, was just too painful for me to witness.

In 2008, I was working on a book project about Panama and needed to go back for a few weeks to conduct some research. What I did not anticipate was the racism I experienced while I was there. I made plans to meet two high school friends at a restaurant we had frequented during our late teen years. I was excited to see them, and I made reservations for a table at our favorite spot, overlooking the Pacific Ocean. When we arrived early and I requested the table, the waiter told us that the restaurant was full, and they had no availability. I politely said that I had reservations under Dr. Seales. The waiter responded, "You are Dr. Seales?" I confirmed this. From where we were standing, we could clearly see the table with my name on it. The waiter then said, "Then, unfortunately we do have your reservation, but your request for the table overlooking the Pacific Ocean can't be granted." Given my experiences with the way I was racialized as "Black" in the United States, I requested to speak to the manager. The manager also denied me the table I reserved.

We left the restaurant, and my friends were upset that I had made an "unnecessary scene." We took a walk on the beach as the sun set and spoke about what had happened. I explained that although some of my perceptions of Panama may have been informed by my experience and education in the United States, I was speaking from my viewpoint as a West Indian who grew up in Panama. I reminded them of our days back in high school, when we could still speak English among ourselves, when we were treated as equals, and when we were proud to be Panamanian. To prove my point, I walked them on the beach past that table I wanted. Sure enough, the tables were filled with either American tourists or Panamanians of Spanish descent. As the night progressed, we had deeper conversations about how much things had changed for ethnic West Indians in the last 40 years. I challenged my friends to reflect on our high school friends of West Indian descent and think about whether they still spoke English to their children. I pointed out the lack of representation of people of West Indian descent in the administration of the Panama Canal and the current government. Based on what I observed, I believe that West Indian assimilation into Panamanian society has raised challenges for ethnic West Indians – challenges that are hard for me to witness on my visits to the country.

CONCLUSION

My experiences and those of my family illustrate the ways one's sense of national belonging and identity may shift over time due to changes in the political, economic, social, and cultural context. I was born in the Canal Zone, and although I had access to it, I did not grow up there and so did not experience discrimination and exclusion in the same way that my parents and grandparents did. I navigated a different Panama. I was proud of my West Indian heritage but fully committed to the Panamanian ideal of *soberanía total*. My sense of self was also influenced by my emigration to the United States, where I continue to live and work, and my return trips to Panama. I have had to accept that many of my West Indian friends and family who have remained in Panama no longer view me as fully Panamanian because of my beliefs. I am not Panamanian enough for them, and I also no longer feel like an authentic Panamanian.

REFLECTION AND DISCUSSION QUESTIONS

- In what ways were ethnic West Indians in Panama discriminated against in the Canal Zone? How and why were they excluded from the Panamanian nation-state as well?
- How do history and ideas about race, ethnicity, language, and nationality shape identity in Panama?
- How did solidarity movements against US imperialism influence the identity of the author, a Panamanian of West Indian descent? How did moving away from Panama influence that identity?

KEY CONCEPTS

- **autoethnography**: A qualitative research method that uses an author's personal experience to describe the cultural, historical, political, and social realities of a larger community.
- **narrative inquiry**: A form of qualitative research that uses texts such as stories, autobiographies, journals, and family stories to give a voice to marginalized people and their lived experiences.
- **West Indian**: A term used to refer to people from the islands of Barbados, Grenada, Jamaica, Martinique, and Trinidad who went to work in Panama for the United Fruit Company and on the construction of the Panama Railroad and the Canal starting in the mid-nineteenth century.

EXPLORE FURTHER

- To learn more about the relationship between colonialism, language, and identity for West Indian communities, read **Chapter 15**.
- To learn more about other contemporary forms of US imperialism, read **Chapter 27**.
- Paulk, Julia. 2014. "Turning West Indian Memory into History and Redefining Panamanian National Identity in Melva Lowe de Goodin's *De/From Barbados a/to Panamá*." *Afro-Hispanic Review* 33 (2): 87–106.
- Seales Soley, LaVerne M. 2009. *Cultures and Customs of Panama*. Westport, CT: Greenwood Press.
- Talley, Steven R., and Richard Wortman, producers. 2019. *The Truth Behind the Panama Canal*. Spark. https://tinyurl.com/Behind-the-Panama-Canal.

ABOUT THE AUTHOR

LaVerne M. Seales Soley is an associate professor in the Languages and Cultures Department at California Lutheran University. Her research areas include Afro-Caribbean and Afro-Hispanic literature, education and culture, post-colonial theory, neocolonialism, race, and identity. She is the author of *Cultures and Customs of Panama*.

REFERENCES

Corinealdi, Kaysha. 2012. "Envisioning Multiple Citizenships: West Indian Panamanians and Creating Community in the Canal Zone Neocolony." *The Global South* 6 (2): 87–106. https://doi.org/10.2979/globalsouth.6.2.87.

Lasso de Paulis, Marixa. 2007. "Race and Ethnicity in the Formation of Panamanian National Identity: Panamanian Discrimination against Chinese and West Indians in the Thirties." *Revista Panameña de Política* 4: 61–92.

Major, John. 1993. *Prize Possession: The United States and the Panama Canal, 1903–1979*. Cambridge: Cambridge University Press.

O'Reggio, Trevor. 2006. *Between Alienation and Citizenship: The Evolution of Black West Indian Society in Panama 1914–1964*. Lanham, MD: University Press of America.

Senior, Olive. 2014. *Dying to Better Themselves: West Indians and the Building of the Panama Canal*. Kingston: University of the West Indies Press.

SECTION FOUR

Gender and Intersectionality

Like race and ethnicity, **gender** is an identity category shaped by historical, social, cultural, and political-economic processes. There is evidence that prior to encounters with Europeans, many societies across the Americas recognized a third gender category that was associated with specialized roles (see Chapter 2). However, with the expansion of European colonial projects came the imposition, often via powerful Catholic religious institutions, of Judeo-Christian ideas about sex and gender. These included binary distinctions for gender (woman/man) and sex (female/male), the presumption of correspondence between sex and gender, and associated **gender ideologies** – systems of beliefs and ideals about gender roles, gender-specific behavioral norms, and gender expression. In part because of these influences, research on gender in Latin America and the Caribbean historically focused on gender inequities in patriarchal societies. Two key theoretical observations from this research were about the widespread presence in the region of *marianismo* – a gender ideology named after the biblical figure of the Virgin Mary that frames women as chaste, submissive, and long suffering – and *machismo* – a gender ideology in which the performance of normative masculinity requires courage and a man's provision for his family but also normalizes male violence and sexual exploits (see Chapter 3).

Scholars have pointed out numerous shortcomings of the *marianismo/machismo* explanatory framework. First, it reinforces stereotypes about women and men, collapsing the dynamism of gender performance, ignoring the diversity of gender experience, and doing little to address the social and political-economic issues underlying gender inequities. For example, the *machismo* model suggests a certain universality among cis men's experiences. In reality, the performance of masculinity varies greatly across communities and individually. For example, Wentzell (2013) found that elderly Mexican men's performance of masculinity changed over time because of aging and shifting values and beliefs surrounding marriage. The *marianismo/machismo* dichotomy also ignores how the experience of gender is shaped by other social categories to which people belong. For example, *marian* ideals of femininity fail to account for the experiences of Afro-Peruvian women, who are often neglected in efforts to address intimate partner violence because they are stereotyped as aggressive and strong (opposites of *marian* qualities) and therefore presumed unlikely to be victims or in need of assistance.

Contemporary ethnographic studies have moved away from reductionist categories of "Latin American/Caribbean man" and "Latin American/Caribbean woman" to recognize the ways that gendered experience and gender inequities interact with race, ethnicity, sexuality, and class, as well as with sociocultural and political-economic processes. **Intersectionality**, a term coined by Black feminist legal scholar Kimberlé W. Crenshaw in the United States, refers to how the intersection of social categories creates converging systems of discrimination with compounding effects for people who are members of more than one marginalized group. A focus on intersectionality illustrates that early, universalizing claims about women's experiences erased the ways that Indigenous and Afro-descendant women experienced unique forms of oppression that stemmed from the intersection of their gender and racial positionalities and that were not comparable to the challenges faced by white/*mestiza* women. An intersectional framework can also shed light on how race and class influence both the performance of masculinity and men's relative positions in social hierarchies. Rural, working-class Black men in Brazil, for example, often struggle to satisfy normative gender expectations of being financial providers due to discriminatory employment practices that leave them underemployed.

Challenging the myths of sex and gender binaries, intersex, transgender, and sexually diverse people across Latin America and the Caribbean are increasingly organizing in struggles for equal rights, pointing out the array of gender and sexual diversity in communities across the region. Many Indigenous communities, including Isthmus Zapotec people in Oaxaca, Mexico, and Mapuche people in Chile and Argentina, have historically recognized third gender categories or more fluid gender experiences, for example. Yet acknowledgment and acceptance of gender and sexual diversity vary greatly, making different spaces and communities more or less safe for people whose gender or sexual identities or expressions are non-normative. For example, anti-LGBTQ+ policies and cultural norms in the English-speaking Caribbean spur many LGBTQ+ citizens to emigrate, creating a brain drain in these nations.

Importantly, social norms and legal policies are dynamic and can shift in response to concerted efforts to change laws and cultural values. Organizations and individuals leading pro-LGBTQ+ efforts have faced persecution in Venezuela, Cuba, and Nicaragua, but continual efforts have led to achievements in many parts of the region. In 2021, for example, cross-dressing was decriminalized in Guyana, Argentina added an option "X" as a third gender identity category for passports and other official documents, and Chile became the eighth country in the region to enact marriage equality.

Feminist movements have a long history in Latin America and the Caribbean, and the first decades of the twenty-first century were no exception. The period witnessed a renewal of feminist activism centered on reproductive rights, representation, and gender violence. Examples included protests against femicide in Mexico in 2009; the #NiUnaMenos movement that spread from Argentina to Chile, Mexico, and Peru in 2015; and the public, synchronized performance of a Las Tesis song denouncing victim blaming, "*Un violador en tu camino*" ("A rapist in your path"), recordings of which spread virally around the world in 2019.

The chapters in this section examine how gender intersects with other identities to impact people's perspectives and lived experiences. In Chapter 10, Arispe-Bazán explores the exclusion of Indigenous Peruvians from LGBTQ+ activism and ways that the performance of indigeneity has reinforced heteronormativity, leading urban queer people of Indigenous descent to grapple with their sense of self. In Chapter 11, Hernández Castillo documents how Indigenous women are criminalized and vulnerable to patriarchal violence at the hands of the state and paramilitaries as part of Mexico's "war on drugs." Finally, in Chapter 12, Williamson chronicles how working-class Black women in Brazil suffer the brunt of the Zika virus epidemic and subsequent state neglect as they care for children with microcephaly, often to the detriment of their own physical and mental health.

KEY CONCEPTS

- **gender**: The set of roles and expectations that a cultural group associates with different sexes.
- **gender ideologies**: Systems of beliefs and ideals about gender roles, gender-specific behavioral norms, and gender expression.
- **intersectionality**: How the intersection of social categories creates converging systems of discrimination with compounding effects for people who are members of more than one marginalized group.
- ***machismo***: A gender ideology in which the performance of normative masculinity requires courage and a man's provision for his family, but also normalizes male violence and sexual exploits.
- ***marianismo***: A gender ideology named after the biblical figure of the Virgin Mary that frames women as chaste, submissive, and long suffering.

EXPLORE FURTHER

- To learn more about gender ideology and masculinity, read **Chapter 18**.
- To learn more about LGBTQ+ activism, read **Chapter 24**.
- To learn more about the gendered experiences of cis women, read **Chapters 26** and **35**.
- Fernandez, Nadine T., and Katie Nelson, eds. 2022. *Gendered Lives, Global Issues*. Albany, NY: SUNY Press.

- Gutiérrez Alea, Tomás, and Juan Carlos Tabío, dirs. 1994. *Fresa y Chocolate (Strawberry and Chocolate)*. [Cuba]
- Lelio, Sebastián, dir. 2017. *Una Mujer Fantástica (A Fantastic Woman)*. [Chile]
- Maier, Elizabeth, and Natalie Lebon. 2010. *Women's Activism in Latin America and the Caribbean: Engendering Social Justice, Democratizing Citizenship*. New Brunswick, NJ: Rutgers University Press.
- Medeiros, Melanie A., and Keisha-Khan Y. Perry, eds. 2023. *Black Women in Latin America and the Caribbean: Critical Research and Perspectives*. New Brunswick, NJ: Rutgers University Press.
- Rondón, Mariana, dir. 2013. *Pelo Malo (Bad Hair)*. [Venezuela]

REFERENCE

Wentzell, Emily A. 2013. *Maturing Masculinities: Aging, Chronic Illness, and Viagra in Mexico*. Durham, NC: Duke University Press.

CHAPTER TEN

The Racial Politics of Queer, Urban, Second-Generation Indigenous Lima Locals

Diego Arispe-Bazán

In early December 2017, I returned to Lima, Peru, to follow up on my fieldwork and begin exploratory research in the city, gearing up for my next project. My first project had followed Iberian Spanish migrants to Lima in the 2010s and focused on history, race, gender, and post-colonialism. A month and a half before my 2017 visit, Peruvian mainstream news and social media accounts across multiple platforms erupted in a debate around the national census carried out in October of that year, due to the incorporation of a question on race. The last time there had been a similar question was in the 1961 census, and that question vaguely referred to cultural practices, dress, and spoken language. So why, reporters, pundits, and people in the capital city asked, was the census asking about race? Would anyone check whether people were properly sorting themselves as *indígena* (Indigenous), *negro* (Black), *blanco* (white), or **mestizo** (mixed race)?

Earlier that same year, the institution that conducts the census, the National Institute of Statistics and Information Technology (*Instituto Nacional de Estadística e Informática* – INEI), had created an online platform to carry out the very first survey (separate from the census) on LGBTQ+ populations in Peru (*Primera Encuesta para Personas LGBTI*) between May and August. For the first time in Peruvian history, sexual orientation and gender identity became visible, significant vectors of experience for the national government to incorporate into its official surveys; and, for the first time in the twenty-first century, there was a question on race.

In what follows, I identify the connections between queerness and race in contemporary Peru, specifically discussing how queer identities interact with diasporic Indigenous identities in a country that saw huge numbers of internal migrants leaving rural areas for the urban centers between the 1970s and late 1990s. While I employ insights gathered from my larger ethnographic engagement with the city of Lima between July 2015 and December 2016, this chapter will expand on what I learned from my friend and ethnographic interlocutor Angie, a lesbian woman in her mid-thirties, a Limeña (Lima resident, born in Lima), and daughter of farmworker migrants from the state of Huancavelica (Figure 10.1) in the Andean highlands. Focusing on a conversation between Angie and her close friend Mora about the census question on race and follow-up ethnographic interviews I conducted with her, I explain how a person's queer gender identity not only interacts with but partially defines racial belonging in the urban Andes. By embracing her queer identity, Angie, like many other diasporic Indigenous Peruvians, finds herself compelled to navigate complex identity formation processes, demonstrating that in the Andes – and perhaps Latin America writ large – race, class, gender, and sexuality are not only intersecting vectors but co-constitutive categories of belonging. This is because of the history and political economy of race in the region, which have resulted in the disenfranchisement of Black and Indigenous peoples, positioning them as anti-modern within a contemporary global context in which slowly changing sexual mores impact the rest of the world. Specifically, queer Lima locals aspire to connect with and approximate the gains of LGBTQ+ movements in cosmopolitan Europe and the United States, thus distancing themselves from "anti-modern," local Indigenous ways of life.

UNCOVERING RACIALIZATION IDEOLOGIES

My research in Lima started in Madrid, Spain. I was interested in the 2011 economic crisis caused by the collapse of the housing market, which led to extremely high unemployment rates in Spain for several years. Spanish nationals began to migrate to other countries, initially in Europe and then further and further away, including the former Spanish colonial domains in Latin America: Mexico, Argentina, and Chile as primary foci, with Peru and Ecuador as secondary arrival points. I began by reconnecting with Spanish citizens whom I had met in Madrid and Barcelona prior to their migration and expanded my group of interlocutors through their Iberian friends and colleagues. Next, I connected with Peruvians who spent time with the new arrivals, surveying the opinions of Lima locals on the topic of Spanish immigration. Having been born and having spent my childhood in Lima also meant reconnecting with family and old friends. I read the news and checked social media constantly to supplement my ethnographic data collection.

Spanish migrants' incursion into upwardly mobile, middle-class spaces in Lima triggered Peruvian anxieties about the colonial past and its relevance to the present. The migrants' increasingly successful entry into the Peruvian goods and services markets generated conflict with the local middle class. When I asked Peruvian neighbors and co-workers about the Spanish arrivals and what they thought about this new migration trajectory, many mentioned their frustration with the perceived ease with which the Iberians found jobs. More than one, including Peruvians who were so fair skinned I would have assumed they would check the *blanco* box of the census, complained about the Europeans' whiteness as an unfair advantage in the highly discriminatory Peruvian job market.

Figure 10.1. The Church of Saint Sebastian of Huancavelica, a city in the central Peruvian Andes, built in the 1600s. Photo by Daniel Chavez Castro (CC BY 3.0).

So I wondered: How did these Peruvian locals, written into colonial histories of race, understand their own identities? Toward the end of my time in Lima, I decided to inquire more about their personal biographies and understandings of race, which led me to my conversations with Angie and Mora.

RACIALIZATION: *MESTIZAJE* AS A WHITENING PROJECT

In metropoles like Lima, with its 10 million inhabitants, the great majority of them children or grandchildren of internal migrants displaced by economic hardship or escape from the violence of the 20-year internal armed conflict that began in 1981, becoming "deracinated" after a generation or two is often expected. Becoming untethered from their Indigenous roots regularly meant becoming *mestizo*, even without a change in physical, genealogic, or genetic features. As De la Cadena (2000) explains, racial mobility came along with upward mobility and vice versa in twentieth-century Peru. Indigeneity and modernity – expertise in technology, professionalization, cosmopolitan taste – were seen as opposites of one another.

The term *mestizo* only became common usage in the second half of the sixteenth century. *Mestizos* existed in a limbo space between the republics. Opting to give up one's Indigenous heritage meant giving up access to communal land, becoming displaced from the community whence they had been born. Yet the Indigenous population, the ethnic groups and communities who built societies in the Americas over centuries prior to Spanish colonization, were seen by the *conquistadores* as heretics, strange, dangerous, and inferior. Thus, during the colonial period, claiming *mestizo* identity allowed the possibility of marrying into a wealthier family, performing more lucrative labor, and becoming socially mobile in the colonial city (see also Chapter 8). By the time of independence (in 1821), the term referred to the ideology that the ostensibly genetic and cultural mix should inspire pride among Latin American nations. Mexican author José Vasconcelos (1925) famously described *mestizos* in his treatise on "The Cosmic Race" as the perfect fusion of European, Black, and Indigenous populations. Deeply racist notions undergirded this ideal, however: Vasconcelos assigned intellect, physical strength, and resilience in labor as the respective "positive" traits of each of the racial groups.

Peter Wade (2005) explains that "if one looks at mestizaje as a lived process, the relationship between inclusion and exclusion is not best conceived of as one of superficial mask and underlying reality. Rather it can be understood as the interweaving of two processes, both of which have symbolic and structural reality. These, in turn, constitute a mosaic" (240). Although Wade then problematically extrapolates lived experience to make a claim about the nation, his model of the racial mosaic illustrates my findings with second-generation internal migrants' processes of racial self-identification in Lima.

Mestizaje in the twentieth century has therefore more to do with acculturation for both Indigenous and white subjects – or more clearly, it is about "culture" (defined as customs/social practices) rather than physical features. Demonstrating a more *criollo* (hispanicized) identity had to do with success within a community, running a business where one would interact with urban elites, and of course wearing the proper fashions and keeping up with strict hygienic routines. Speech, more explicitly the prizing of monolingual Spanish identities and Spanish forms free of Indigenous pronunciation features, could mean everything from a promotion at work to safety on public transit (Babel 2018; Huayhua 2013). In anti-Indigenous discourse, performing *mestizo*-ness became a way to raise one's status, a purported "self-improvement" that incorporated the values and behaviors of "cultured" folk; in other words, white Europeans. Leaving behind indigeneity by moving to and acculturating into metropoles like Quito, Lima, Guayaquil, or La Paz became synonymous with "progress." The fact of racial inequality, the mapping of income and wealth inequality onto Black and Indigenous populations in Peru, points to a heavy disadvantage for these groups. Thus, instead of race as a set, inherent condition of the human body, we can think of **racialization**: the understanding of race as an effect of historical, political, and economic processes through social interactions between people and institutions.

QUEER RIGHTS IN LIMA

On April 12, 2014, a large group of demonstrators took over Plaza San Martín in Lima's historic district demanding that the Peruvian Congress take up a proposed bill to legalize same-sex civil unions. In addition, demonstrators showed support via social media platforms such as Facebook and Twitter using #UnionCivilYa, including pictures from the Plaza. However, prominent supporters of the Civil Union Bill have failed to account for intersections between racialized Indigenous identities and queerness. **Queerness** is the recognition of the inherently political nature of non-heterosexual, non-cisgender communities in the Western world and everywhere the West colonized, as they have fought and continue to fight for visibility and equal rights before their wider communities of origin and the states where they live and love.

One of the most highly publicized advertising campaigns backing the push for the Civil Union Bill was the "Imaginary Couples" ("*Parejas Imaginarias*") project. Inspired by a French photographer's series of portraits of heterosexual celebrities and public figures posing as imaginary same-sex couples, out Peruvian television personality reporter, talk show host, and game show host Beto Ortiz contacted a local photographer to produce a Peruvian iteration. In an op-ed describing the creative process for this version, Ortiz states that when he conceived of the idea, he acknowledged the danger of having the pieces be (in Ortiz's words) "*pacharaqueados*" (Ortiz, 2013). "*Pacharaco*" is a *limeño* term used to denote forms of unintentionally déclassé styles of music, fashion, or other forms of consumer expression and is directly associated with internal migrants from the Amazon and the Andean highlands, as well as coastal Black populations, all of which are assumed to be working class and thus lacking taste. All the celebrities in the photos were Lima locals, urban and white or very light skinned; not one Indigenous star appears among the cast. In his narrative, Ortiz names stars whom he reached out to but could not participate. Not a single star of the vast pop Andean folk nor Amazon tropical music scenes, whose massive audiences – primarily first- and second-generation internal migrants – is mentioned. Further, one of the celebrities included in the photographs is Aldo Mariátegui, former journalist, opinion contributor, and right-wing political pundit, who has more than once spoken against Indigenous peoples' rights to control their land, even employing racial slurs when writing about them. A well-circulated photo of the April 12 "March for Equality" features a large sign with a rainbow background that reads, in perfect English, "If god doesn't judge us why would you?" standing above the crowd at Plaza San Martin. US rapper Macklemore's pro-marriage equality track "Same Love" was a mainstay among posters on Peruvian Facebook groups and YouTube channels.

A competing "March for the Family" was organized by Christian and Catholic groups a few weeks after the #UnionCivilYa demonstration. Calling themselves a movement "in favor of the traditional family," the organizing members produced their own photo series, "Real Couples" ("*Parejas Reales*"). The shoot presents the heterosexual norm as conducive to positive, joyful affect. One particularly powerful image includes a man wearing highland Indigenous garb, with a wide smile holding a baby with a caption reading "#afamilyis a father in love with his daughter." In prominently portraying a highland Indigenous subject, the conservative group widened the scope of their campaign beyond the borders of the capital city. More significantly, the image makes an implicit connection between "family values" and the nation's roots, as if heterosexuality and indigeneity were synonymous. Not only does the image conjure general goodwill, but it also makes Indigenous subalterns visible (even if only as instruments of national pride), a feat yet to be accomplished by the other side.

Michael Horswell's (2006) groundbreaking work on the history of early Andean Indigenous gender and sexuality has demonstrated that prior to colonization there was not the same rigidity and perspective of enforced heterosexuality and cisgender identity in Indigenous communities. For example, he writes about third-gender priests called *Ipas*, who mediated between the masculine and feminine worlds in Incan rituals. The deity known as Chuqui Chinchay during the Inca empire, of which there is recorded history, was also a third-gender being, both masculine and feminine and neither. Mary Weismantel (2021) has used the record of Moche sexual pottery to show that this pre-Inca culture from the north coast of Peru had a rich, fluid understanding of sexuality that defies contemporary, Western boundaries. It is ironic, then, that post-colonization, indigeneity seems to be pitted against non-heterosexual, queer gender expressions and sexualities. There is a great deal of compelling evidence that non-heteronormative, non-cisgender subjects were recognized by pre-Columbian Indigenous groups in Peru, but these identities are only discussed by small groups of academics and activists, rather than hailed by most queer people in Lima as a major source of inspiration for their campaigns for recognition.

MESTIZA, BLANQUEADA, ANDINA, **AND EVERYTHING IN BETWEEN**

In December 2017, I asked Angie and Mora to meet me for dinner, to update them on my research and catch up. I could not expect the rich conversation we were about to have. What began as a casual conversation turned into an opportunity to condense several topics that had emerged as crucial to my research at the end of my time in Lima a year earlier. The ongoing nature of ethnographic research allowed me not only to reconnect with my interlocutors over time and learn more from them, but also to revise, specify, and delve deeper into key issues, including those surrounding race and queerness.

Mora asked me how my writing process was going. I told her I was writing a chapter on whiteness and race in Lima, and she and Angie told me they found the question of race fascinating, especially since it had been in the air ever since the national census. Both of them supported the inclusion of the question on race in the census, as (ideally) a means toward making visible and potentially granting benefits to marginalized Black and Indigenous populations in the country. But as we talked into the night at a local beer brewing company's restaurant, it became clear to us that the categories of race available were not only insufficient in capturing people's lived experience, but that other categories of experience – class, gender, and sexuality – had a direct impact on how *Limeños* saw themselves racially.

In the years I had known the two women, I had never inquired about how they identified racially; rather than allowing them to enlighten me about their own complex relationships with race I had simply assumed they were *mestizas* because of their urban, general middle-class appearance. Over the course of our conversation, the vector of class emerged as crucial in their racial self-understanding. Both Angie and Mora grew up in middle-class neighborhoods in Lima, and both were children of internal migrants. Mora's parents were from the southern coast and the Amazon jungle and Angie's were both from Huancavelica, a central highland *departamento* (akin to a US state).

Mora's strongest attachments were to her highland Aymara heritage, which she connected with through her paternal grandmother's stories of small towns in Puno in the southern highlands. Mora thus explained that in the census, she thought she checked the box for *mestiza*, even though she very much felt, because of her facial features, her hair, and her grandmothers' origins (one from Puno and one from the Amazonian *departamento* of Loreto) that she was Indigenous. Having been raised middle class and moving to a middle-class neighborhood seemed to distance Mora from this identity – Angie even joked that Mora had been "whitened" by having attended a prestigious, politically left-of-center private university. Angie, instead, rejected the label of *mestiza*, sharing that she identified most closely with the label *andina* (Andean) because of her parents' town of origin, declaring a general highland identity rather than a specific Indigenous one.

Our conversation intrigued me – it seemed that they were in effect theorizing about the nature of racialization processes in Peru using their own life experiences as data. I decided to follow up with Angie and conducted an ethnographic interview with her a few weeks later. She told me that while at dinner with Mora she remembered more clearly what she had checked on the census form. Since *andina* was not an option, she had chosen *Quechua*, a designation for Indigenous highland Andean populations who speak the Quechua language (known widely as the historic language of the Inca) and share syncretic religious practices (Indigenous and Catholic) as well as certain forms of collective social and economic organization around kinship and community ties.

However, like many internal migrants of the twentieth century, Angie's parents did not pass the language on to her. To this day, the Quechua language is stigmatized as "backwards" in the capital city, although some political headway has been made by artists, activists, and government representatives to revitalize it (Zavala 2019; see also Chapter 7). Angie did travel back to the town of Tullpa – her parents' hometown in Huancavelica – and recalled participating in religious celebrations, outdoor market openings, folk performances, and funerals. She still has family there she visits with some regularity. "I was born in Lima and that makes me a *Limeña*, but my whole family environment has deep roots in Tullpa, and so the general content of my life, when going to family reunions, for example, is very much marked by it."[1] Such rituals and celebrations in Tullpa included the *yunzas*, highland festivals that feature the communal chopping down of a tree decorated with gifts and colorful streamers, around which drinking, dancing, and performances are arranged.

Angie's parents had left Tullpa with her grandparents at different points in their early teens. They had met at the local Tullpa association meetings in Lima, married, and opened a small business in an informal (unofficial) open air market in the city, built up primarily by other migrant merchants.[2] Angie's parents sold clothes and fabric, and over the years they expanded their business many times over. By the time Angie was in her twenties, her parents moved out of the working-class neighborhood of La Victoria into the middle- and upper-middle-class area of Surco. To provide her with better living conditions and education, her parents acculturated themselves, and by extension Angie, into urban Lima as much as possible, sending her to a small, affordable private parochial school (where she met Mora), and attended the same private university as her friend. They did not plan for Angie to speak Quechua, just as they did not plan for her to herd livestock or help in the fields the way they once had. Acknowledging her life as that of an upwardly mobile urbanite, Angie understands herself as ethnically Quechua, but like Mora, would never make a claim to indigeneity per se or seek formal recognition as an Indigenous person. The economic and geographic distance from her parents' home and upbringing were significant. Her sense of self as Quechua or Andean relied on a sense of heritage, of extended kinship.

While Angie and Mora refer to their respective ethnic backgrounds, the larger issue of their identities is one of race. The distinction between Quechua and Aymara communities is an ethnic one, but not a racial one. In the colonial and post-colonial social hierarchy, whiteness was not legally disaggregated into, for example, "Frenchness" versus "Spanishness." Thus, the concept of *mestizaje* was never an ethnic one, but a racial one. The white–Black–Indigenous triad in the legal system was not an ethnic, but racial designation that subsumed multiple groups within. If race is a colonial category implemented to segregate, ethnicity has served instead to bind the community within. Mora and Angie's connections to their specific ethnicities is diffused because they were not brought up within an Indigenous community, but they are both certain they are not white, not only because of their kin relations but because of experiences of race and racism they have faced.

One such experience, Angie felt, had to do with her sexuality and her gender presentation, which distanced her from her highland Indigenous identity. Angie only wears long pants. She cuts her hair short with only some strands below the ears; she wears button-down shirts, suit

---

1 My translation from the original Spanish.
2 As part of "modernization efforts," the market, which had grown and spilled out of its area onto the streets of the district of La Victoria, was razed and the merchants' stands and goods demolished in 2012. By 2017, many of them returned to the streets around the location of the old market.

jackets, and fit trousers when attending a formal event. She has openly identified as a lesbian since college, and feels her style is in keeping with her sense of self as a queer woman. When she was a child, and into her teenage years, Angie felt limited in her ability to participate in the celebrations in Tullpa, although she enjoyed and continues to greatly enjoy them. One of the most important components of the *yunza* celebration is the performance of folk dances by community members, which include elaborate costumes, organized around multiple, gender-segregated dance troops. Angie was drawn to the dances from an early age, but realized that, to her dismay, she would not be able to learn the dances from the women in Tullpa and participate herself. Women wear dance costumes made up of brightly colored skirts, often with lace detailing, and collect their long hair in braids, decorated with colorful ribbons. The rules of the dance reinforce traditional masculine and feminine gender roles, both through the separation of the gender-specific group and the normativity of each group's attire and dance moves.

In college, Angie made the effort to go to a prominent folkloric music and dance school in Lima, where she thought she might be allowed some experimentation. She told school administrators she wished to participate in the *sikuri* troop. *Sikuri* troops are musicians, pan flute players, and drummers. They originate from Aymara culture, an ethnic group in the southern Peruvian highlands and Bolivia, over a thousand kilometers (and multiple steep peaks) away from Huancavelica. Because Angie was limited to the offerings of the school, she decided on that form because she had always enjoyed seeing the troops at festivals in Lima and elsewhere in the Peruvian Andes during her travels. The costumes include colorful hats and small capes, but also vests and long Black pants, traditionally meant for men. Even though she would not partake in the women's dances, Angie thought she could learn to be a *sikuri* as a means to engage in highland folklore. But when she inquired about joining *sikuri* classes, the teachers and administrators told her she could not, since at that school, the *sikuri* were exclusively male troops, and it would not make sense for her to participate. Because the *sikuri* were not traditional to her family's hometown, she thought it might allow her some mobility, some means to approach highland Indigenous folklore, but even then, she was turned away in this instance.[3]

Angie's queer gender expression seemed to make it more difficult for her to actively participate in highland community rituals. Vásquez Toral (2020) has described the highland *fiesta* as a traditionally patriarchal space. His work highlights the historical role of cross-dressing queer men and those otherwise assigned male at birth in the region of Jauja, a mere 200 kilometers north of Angie's parents' hometown. Ritual cross-dressing, he writes, exists in a space "between the masculine and the feminine – and in the process embodied patriarchalism – are repurposed by *cuir*[4] artists today in an effort to affect folklore … they have grown up with while facing

---

3 It must be noted that there are *sikuri* troops that do include women, Angie simply encountered an especially traditional one. Regardless, stout traditionalism and gender role policing remain linked in the space of the *fiesta*.
4 Political repurposing of *queer*, transliterated into Spanish as a means to remove Anglo-imperial intertextuality.

discrimination" (64). In my own search for sources, I have not come across much discussion on female performers wearing traditionally male attire or performing roles commonly performed by men in the fiestas. This blind spot in research further illustrates the barrier between Angie's search for a space within the fiesta. In January 2019, I saw two social media posts about women preparing to eventually participate in traditionally male dance of the *caporales* in the large fiesta of La Candelaria, in Puno, but none in Huancavelica, or really anywhere else in the Peruvian highlands. I argue that Angie's self-identification as *andina* comes in part from her non-normative gender presentation, tied to her expression of queer sexual identity. The diffusing of her ethnic identity as *Quechua* specifically, her approximation to becoming racially *mestiza*, is directly connected to standing between aspirations to foreign queerness presented as opposite to Indigenous localness.

CONCLUSION

The process of racialization, as expressed via self-identification (which the national census relies on), is bound up in social processes that emerge from experiences of gender and sexuality. One significant point of convergence for biologistic and constructivist approaches to race is that both prescribe limits to racial categorization – they set categories professed as immutable. Here, I have considered the complexities of racial and ethnic belonging demonstrated by Angie and Mora's reckoning of racial belonging as shaped by experiences of class, gender, and sexuality. Because of the social, political, and economic situation in Peru and other Andean countries, racialization processes replicate colonial forms of disenfranchisement and discrimination, even two centuries after independence. For queer Peruvians, especially those who can trace Indigenous heritage, including second- and third-generation internal migrants, their gender expressions and out and proud queer love align them with foreign civil rights projects.

Recent political and intellectual movements in the region are rethinking ways to make certain that those Indigenous communities with whom *mestizos* are able to find kinship can be recognized as a source of wisdom to imagine the future. The idea is not to claim indigeneity before the state, as this would distract and divert resources from communities in dire need of government recognition and assistance. Rather than appropriate these identities to reap the benefits of the few avenues of social and economic assistance available to Black and Indigenous peoples in Peru, the idea is to steer away from the assumption that proximity to Europeanness is akin to progress. Diasporic Andean identities like Angie and Mora's do not necessarily mean erasing the various rich Indigenous ethnic communities, but rather inviting communities to engage with their heritage otherwise. Conversely, this is also a key opportunity to think about the effects of colonization on ideas of gender and sexuality. Perhaps recognizing queerness in Indigenous Peruvians' past, be they Moche, Inca, or otherwise, might yield a more inclusive present and a more accurate image of the past.

REFLECTION AND DISCUSSION QUESTIONS

- What does Angie's story tell us about the way that gender identity influences ethnic or racial identity and vice versa?
- If there have always been queer people in the Andes, why is that in today's world queerness is considered antithetical to Peruvian culture, by some? What processes led to this ideology?
- What are some differences you see between how Angie and Mora define themselves racially and how cultural mores in the United States define race?
- How did you come to know what racial category you "belonged" in? What does this tell you about the process of racialization in your own community?

KEY CONCEPTS

- ***mestizo* (also *mestiza*, *mestizx*)**: A person with a mixed racial identity.
- **queerness**: The experience of non-heterosexual, non-cisgender identities as inherently political, having to constantly struggle against state and cultural institutions for equal rights and protections.
- **racialization**: The process of assigning racial meaning to people, things, places, and behaviors and categorizing people according to ideas about race.

EXPLORE FURTHER

- To learn more about issues of ethnicity and identity in Peru, read **Chapter 7**.
- To learn more about LGBTQ+ activism through performance art, read **Chapter 24**.
- García, María Elena. 2005. *Making Indigenous Citizens: Identities, Education, and Multicultural Development in Peru*. Stanford, CA: Stanford University Press.
- Wawzonek, Joseph J. 2017. "Sodomitical Butterflies: Male Homosexual Desire in Colonial Latin America." *Mount Royal Undergraduate Humanities Review (MRUHR)* 4.
- Weismantel, Mary. 2001. *Cholas and Pishtacos: Stories of Race and Sex in the Andes*. Chicago: University of Chicago Press.

ABOUT THE AUTHOR

Diego Arispe-Bazán is an assistant professor of instruction in anthropology at Northwestern University. His research moves between Lima, Peru, and Madrid, Spain, as well as other locales in the Andes, and focuses on how colonial history as a process both constitutes and is constituted by contemporary culture in Spain and the Andes. More recently, his work explores diasporic Andean Indigenous identities. He is also one of the organizers of the Thinking Andean Studies Conference (www.thinkingandeanstudies.com).

REFERENCES

Babel, Anna. 2018. *Between the Andes and the Amazon: Language and Social Meaning in Bolivia*. Tucson: University of Arizona Press.

De la Cadena, Marisol. 2000. *Indigenous Mestizos: The Politics of Race and Culture in Cuzco, Peru, 1919–1991*. Durham, NC: Duke University Press.

Horswell, Michael J. 2006. *Decolonizing the Sodomite: Queer Tropes of Sexuality in Colonial Andean Culture*. Austin: University of Texas Press.

Huayhua, Margarita. 2013. "Racism and Social Interaction in a Southern Peruvian Combi." *Ethnic and Racial Studies* 37 (13): 2399–417. https://doi.org/10.1080/01419870.2013.809129.

Ortiz, Beto. 2013. "Amar no es un Delito." *Peru21*. November 24. https://peru21.pe/opinion/amar-delito-133783-noticia.

Vasconcelos, José. 1966[1925]. *La Raza Cósmica: Misión de la Raza Iberoamericana*. Madrid, SP: Aguilar.

Vásquez Toral, Enzo E. 2020. "Complicating Hybridity: A View from/through the Andean Patron-Saint Fiesta." In *The Routledge Companion to Theatre and Performance Historiography*, edited by Tracy C. Davis and Peter W. Marx, 260–8. London: Routledge.

Wade, Peter. 2005. "Rethinking *Mestizaje*: Ideology and Lived Experience." *Journal of Latin American Studies* 37 (2): 239–57. https://doi.org/10.1017/S0022216X05008990.

Weismantel, Mary. 2021. *Playing with Things: Engaging the Moche Sex Pots*. Austin: University of Texas Press.

Zavala, Virginia. 2019. "Youth and the Repoliticization of Quechua." *Language, Culture and Society* 1 (1): 59–82. https://doi.org/10.1075/lcs.00004.zav.

CHAPTER ELEVEN

Racialized Geographies and the "War on Drugs": Gender Violence, Militarization, and the Criminalization of Indigenous Women in Mexico

Rosalva Aída Hernández Castillo

On January 16, 2018, 26-year-old Indigenous Purépecha activist Guadalupe Campanur Tapia was found raped and strangled to death in the northwestern Mexican state of Michoacán. Guadalupe was an active part of a social movement advocating for the autonomy of Indigenous peoples and self-governance in the Indigenous town of Cherán, where illegal logging at the hands of organized criminals and corrupt politicians threatened their communal lands. Since 2011, Guadalupe, along with other women and men from Cherán armed with rocks and sticks, had worked to expel organized criminals from their communal lands, including participating in local security patrols in defense of the forest. They had also undertaken a legal struggle for the defense of land and territory against the presence of corrupt political parties in the town, and for the legal authorization to employ their own Indigenous systems to elect authorities. Guadalupe's participation in these efforts was punished with death (Hernández Castillo 2018). Her murder was denounced as femicide, but also as a politically motivated homicide against Cherán's Indigenous autonomy movement. Her fellow activist and friend Carolina Lunuen took to social media to assert that Guadalupe's death "could be interpreted as a message to intimidate and silence those who are genuinely invested in valuing life through community actions that go beyond resistance. It is also a way to terrorize women, and in short, is an ethnocidal technique used to diminish the Purépecha community of Cherán's struggle for life" (Hernández Castillo 2018). Guadalupe's murder is just one example of how the Mexican army, police forces, and paramilitary groups have turned women's bodies into their battlefield in a counterinsurgency strategy that treats social movements as a potential danger to "social stability." Additionally, rather than just an act of repression, sexual violence is a message that promotes the demobilization of women and, ultimately, the displacement and dispossession of Indigenous peoples.

Illicit drug production and drug trafficking are a persistent problem in Mexico that is driven by ongoing demand for recreational drugs in the Global North. This situation has fostered an environment of extreme violence that is perpetrated by drug cartels and state authorities in a situation that is described as a "war on drugs." In this chapter, I discuss the analytical connection between racialization processes underlying the Mexican "war on drugs" and a feminist analysis of the gender violence that is committed by various armed groups in Mexico. Native American writers, such as Andrea Smith (2005), have documented how the construction of Indigenous women's bodies as territory has been part of colonization since its inception. In this onslaught of violence, women's bodies have become territories to be invaded and violated. Paraphrasing Segato (2008), the language of sexual violence uses women's bodies as a signifier to indicate the possession of that which can be sacrificed in the name of territorial control. In the case of women who participate in movements of resistance, sexual violence constitutes not only a form of punishment for challenging gender roles, but also a message conveyed through **patriarchal violence** – violence that creates or maintains male power and dominance over others or that avenges the loss of men's power. Simultaneously, destroying, mutilating, and disappearing women's bodies is another way of "writing on women's bodies a message of terror" that is aimed at everyone (Segato 2013).

This patriarchal violence is exercised on Indigenous bodies, which are constructed as disposable by a classist and racialized system that centers these extreme forms of violence in specific territories. Although the violence exerted by state security forces and organized crime is not explicitly racial in nature, and it does not affect Indigenous populations exclusively, it does have "racializing effects," since it disproportionately affects Indigenous populations, reproducing their marginality (Wade 2011, 17). Based on my long-term research with Indigenous Mexican women in prisons (Hernández Castillo 2016), and on my experience with expert witness reports on the impact of military violence against Indigenous women (Hernández Castillo and Ortiz Elizondo 2012), in this chapter I document how these racializing effects are also gendered. I examine the impact of sexual violence in militarized Indigenous territories. And I analyze the strategies of resistance that Indigenous women are developing to confront the "dreadful mosaic of violence" (Speed 2014) that is affecting their lives and their territories.

RACIALIZED GEOGRAPHIES IN THE "WAR ON DRUGS"

In Mexico, the national myth of *mestizaje* (miscegenation) has made it almost impossible to name and denounce the racism that structures social relations, institutions, and collective imaginaries (Moreno 2012). A commonsense notion has emerged in Mexico, claiming that "if all of us are partly Indigenous, we cannot be racist," an idea that obscures the ideology of whitening that prevails, even though post-revolutionary nationalism promoted *mestizofilia* – discourses that vindicate the historical "dead Indian" while excluding contemporary Indigenous peoples from the national project (see Castellanos et al. 2008). These perspectives demonstrate the centrality of racism in the **coloniality** of Latin American societies. The term *coloniality* designates a characteristic of the modern world relating to the inconclusive nature of decolonization. It describes the way colonialism continues to be present in the knowledge and bodies of Latin American modernity. In other words, while races do not exist as a genetic reality, they do exist as social constructs that emerged during colonization and continue to justify and structure inequality in our societies today.

Studies from the perspective of critical geography have analyzed **racialized geographies** – how the construction of territoriality and the distribution of space are influenced by racialization processes (Gilmore 2002). In other words, racial hierarchies locate certain bodies in certain spaces or unequally allocate resources and apply public policies to different territories, depending on the bodies that inhabit them. In contexts of extreme violence, such as currently experienced in Mexico, certain bodies – most often poor, racialized bodies – are dehumanized and are constructed as disposable and located in specific territories, as opposed to others, which are constructed as the *locus* of "valuable life" and are located in privileged geographical spaces (Mora 2016). As a result, in many of the Indigenous territories of Mexico, racialized illegality and the criminalization of those who are most vulnerable allows their human value to be rendered invisible, resulting in death. In this context of multiple violences, women's bodies in poor, racialized territories also become a signifier to mark control over those racialized geographies. In short, patriarchal violence against women becomes a marker of state control over racialized territories. In speaking of the existence of racialized geographies in the war on drugs, I refer to the specific ways in which the violence of militarization, paramilitarization, and organized crime has affected Indigenous territories.

Several authors have written about the impact of Mexican structural reforms of the last decade in terms of the harm done to the economy of Indigenous and peasant populations, contributing to migration and a market incursion of the production of natural drugs such as opium poppy and marijuana, as well as the recruitment of young Indigenous people by drug cartels (Emmerich 2013). The Indigenous regions of the states of Guerrero, Michoacán, Veracruz, Jalisco, Oaxaca, Chihuahua, Chiapas, Durango, and Sonora have been especially affected by militarization and the violence of the "*antinarco* war," in part because these economically marginalized regions have the characteristics of isolation that are necessary to produce illegal crops. Emmerich (2013) observes, "the production of illegal drugs is an activity that takes place in confined territories, with limited integration of the population, difficulties in land communication, an aggressive and exuberant geography, high levels of poverty, and limited state presence" (20), which is often the type of racialized geography that prevails in Indigenous territories.

The Felipe de Jesús Calderón Hinojosa presidential administration (2006–2012) marked the beginning of the Mexican armed forces' intrusion in security tasks that formerly corresponded to police work. During this period the country's militarization reached its peak across the states, where some 30,000 troops were mobilized, while army authorities were appointed to head the secretariats of public security. This was the beginning of the "war on drugs," an enforcement approach that focuses on military strategy in an attempt to recover public spaces and confront organized crime (Moloeznik and Suarez de Garay 2012). It is a strategy for territorial control that continued under the Enrique Peña Nieto administration (2012–2018). Rather than diminishing the influence of drug trafficking, this territorial occupation by the army has led to an increase in alcoholism, drug sales, and prostitution (Centro de Derechos Humanos Fray Bartolomé de las Casas 2015). The increase in military presence in Indigenous regions has limited women's mobility, and Indigenous women associate the military presence with the latent threat of sexual violence.

Although there is no reliable data regarding the identity of the victims of the "war on drugs," the context of racialization and structural poverty in which this strategy has been applied makes it likely that most of the 121,683 deaths reported by the National Institute of Statistics and Geography (INEGI) during the Felipe Calderón administration (2006–2012), the 156,000 deaths during the Enrique Peña Nieto administration (2012–2018), and the 105,000 deaths reported during the Andrés López Obrador administration (from December 2018 to January 2022) are of poor men and women with brown bodies. Similarly, these types of bodies constitute the bulk of the population imprisoned for *delitos contra la salud* (crimes against health), as drug-related crimes are typified.

Just as racial hierarchies affect the specific ways in which the war on drugs is experienced, gender hierarchies locate poor and racialized women and men in different contexts of criminalization and violence (Sieder 2017; Speed 2016). Women are murdered with greater violence or truculence, and using methods that produce greater pain, for a longer period of time, before causing death (INEGI 2015). The cruelty with which women's bodies are violated seems to be part of the strategy of terror used by the armed groups fighting each other in this unconventional war. Segato (2013) notes that violence against women is no longer a collateral effect of war, but a strategic objective in a new war scenario. Segato describes the existence of a "pedagogy of cruelty" that uses women's bodies as canvases to inscribe messages directed to enemy groups and to delimit territories. The following sections analyze how this patriarchal violence affects the bodies and lives of Indigenous women in poor racialized territories.

MILITARIZATION AND SEXUAL VIOLENCE AS COUNTERINSURGENCY TOOLS

The use of patriarchal violence as a counterinsurgency tool has for decades existed in many regions where Indigenous women have actively participated in the struggle for the defense of their lands and territories. The Indigenous women of the Regional Coordination of Communal Authorities (CRAC) in Guerrero, the women members of the Me'phaa Indigenous People's Organization (OPIM), and the peasant women from Atenco denounce the genocidal impact of neoliberal economic policies and these "security" policies on their peoples and, specifically, on women's lives. Their voices have reached international tribunals, constructing new self-representations that confront patriarchal violence and its implications. The presence of women organizers in a given community or region has almost become synonymous with political radicalism. In many Indigenous regions such women have become symbols of resistance and subversion and have therefore become the target of political violence. Among other cases, this violence is exemplified by the sexual violation of Valentina Rosendo Cantú and Inés Fernández Ortega.

On February 16, 2002, 17-year-old Valentina, an Indigenous Me'phaa woman and member of OPIM, was washing laundry in a stream close to her home in Guerrero when Mexican army officers began questioning her concerning the whereabouts of suspected criminals. The officers raped Valentina as they interrogated her. In the aftermath, Valentina was denied medical care for her injuries because the physician feared reprisal from the military (CEJIL 2016). Less than a month later, on March 22, Inés's home was raided by soldiers looking for her husband, who they accused of theft. When Inés, a non-Spanish speaker, was unable to answer the soldiers' questions they physically and sexually violated her. Inés walked for hours to file a complaint with a local prosecutor who refused to take on the case, citing that it was under the military's jurisdiction. The military promptly closed the case (CEJIL 2016).

In the face of the counterinsurgency strategy of patriarchal violence, Indigenous and peasant women activists like Valentina and Inés have responded with denunciations in national and international forums. Their voices have confronted the meaning behind patriarchal violence that intends to use the sexual violence inscribed on their bodies as a form of colonization. After eight years of witnessing impunity for the perpetrators of their attacks and the unresponsiveness of the Mexican legal system, Inés and Valentina decided to take their case to the international justice system. After two public hearings in 2010 at the Inter-American Court of Human Rights (IACHR), the Mexican state was found guilty of "institutional military violence," which meant that the IACHR acknowledged the army's responsibility in the violation of Inés and Valentina's human rights. In two public acts, Alejandro Poiré, the Minister of the Interior, apologized to Inés and Valentina in the name of the Mexican government. These acts of "Acknowledgement of Responsibilities" symbolized a political and moral triumph for the Indigenous women leaders. The apologies of the minister recognized the veracity of the women's claims, which were so often distorted by the operators of civil and military justice.

Inés and Valentina's testimonies speak of a decades-old continuum of violence, a main axis of which is the role of the army and paramilitary groups in the "dirty war" of the 1960s and 1970s. What we see today is a transformation from the counterinsurgency tactics of that time to those of the "war on drugs," which justify the intervention of the army in the everyday lives of hundreds of Indigenous and peasant communities. In seeking justice, Inés and Valentina highlighted the complicity of the army with municipal governments, organized crime, and paramilitary groups. Through their testimonies and denunciations, they developed a structural analysis of their experiences of violence, which points to the state's liability not only by omission, but also by commission. The women highlighted the existence of a policy of repression that transcended the violent acts of individual soldiers. Although the word *racism* was never used in their oral statements, the women's denunciation of a systematic use of military violence against Indigenous peoples and the disrespect shown to their human dignity by the justice officials was central to their testimonies. Because the institutional character of the violence they suffered was so clear to them, the women asserted that the imprisonment of the soldiers who raped them did not represent real justice and they demanded collective reparations. These communal reparations included the demilitarization of the region as a guarantee of nonrepetition. The "war on drugs" has implied new strategies of colonization and occupation of Indigenous territories. The struggle by Inés and Valentina has not been only for justice in their individual cases, but is a means to denounce the continuity of multiple violences affecting the lives of their people.

CRIMINALIZATION AND RESISTANCE STRATEGIES IN THE FACE OF VIOLENCE

The multiple acts of violence suffered by Indigenous women have been made possible not only by the impunity and ineffectiveness that characterize the security and justice systems, but also because violence often operates in the institutions that are supposed to protect us. Rather than the existence of a *parallel state* (Segato 2008) or a *shadow state* (Gledhill 2015), what we have is a narco-state in which the borders between organized crime and state officials have been erased. This was evident in the infamous Ayotzinapa case (Mora 2016), where collusion permitted the abduction and disappearance of 43 college students whose deaths have never been accounted for.

In this context, Indigenous women have found spaces of resistance in their communal security and justice systems, enabling them to confront the multiple acts of violence that affect their lives. The case of the CRAC of Guerrero, analyzed by Sierra (2009), is an example of the way Indigenous women have wagered on the transformation of their own justice institutions to gain greater space for participation while simultaneously developing practices of security and justice that the state has denied them. In the last 18 years, CRAC members have volunteered in the coastal and mountain regions of Guerrero, building an Indigenous justice and security system that has significantly reduced crime and promoted re-education processes to prevent organized crime from recruiting young people. Although the CRAC, locally known as the community police, is recognized under Law 701 for the Recognition, Rights and Culture of Indigenous Peoples of the state of Guerrero, and by Article 2 of the Mexican Constitution, many of its leaders are in prison, charged with "kidnapping" for detaining criminals and submitting them to re-education processes.

Among the CRAC members whose work has been criminalized is a commander from Olinalá, Guerrero, Nestora Salgado García, who was in jail for two years and eight months, charged with "kidnapping" for confronting networks of organized crime in the region. Although the community police of Olinalá had been recognized by the government of the state of Guerrero, which provided communication and transportation equipment, when CRAC went beyond solving minor local problems and started to confront the networks of organized crime that colluded with the municipal government, the group's actions were declared illegal. In the context of an expert witness report that I prepared for Nestora's defense, I collected testimonies from members of the CRAC in Olinalá and from people who had gone through the re-education system. These testimonies reveal that Nestora's gender had an influence on the virulence with which her leadership in the CRAC was criminalized (Hernández Castillo 2017). For a woman to denounce narco-state corruption and to refuse to sell out was taken as a personal offense by those who hold local power.

During the two years she was in prison, Nestora became a symbol of resistance for many women who struggle against patriarchal violence and in favor of Indigenous communities that defend their security and justice systems. Even though authorities attempted to isolate her in a high-security prison, Nestora did not stop denouncing the human rights violations committed against her, the CRAC, and several Indigenous resistance movements. Her freedom was obtained due to a combination of legal struggle, national and international solidarity, and the political pressure exerted by the United Nations Working Group on Arbitrary Detention. Now out of prison, Nestora has been leading a campaign to free political prisoners and to end the criminalization of Indigenous movements (Figure 11.1). In 2016, she was elected senator, the first Indigenous woman to occupy that position in the Mexican Congress.

Similarly, in 2011, a group of Purépecha women from Cherán, like Guadalupe, headed a resistance movement against dispossession and the destruction of their forests by loggers who had connections to organized crime and maintained a state of terror in the community, protected by the complicity of state and federal police (Velázquez Guerrero 2013). In a seminar on critical law, the Indigenous authorities (*keris*) spoke of the important role played by women from Cherán in heading the struggle against dispossession and for autonomy. In their testimonies they described how in April 2011, confronted with ongoing logging and the desecration of their sacred water springs, the Purépecha women grabbed sticks, hunting rifles, and machetes and went to confront the loggers. María, one of the participants in the uprising, said: "They destroyed all the forest, they are destroying our water sources; they took the men, they murdered them for doing their work. That's the reason for our rage, that's the reason we rose up" (García Martínez 2011, 1). The women and men from Cherán expelled organized crime from their communal lands, and also undertook a legal struggle for their autonomous rights, in litigation that included a demand for recognition of their own systems to elect authorities. On November 2, 2011, the Electoral Tribunal of the Federal Judiciary (TEPJF) ruled in favor of the recognition of the rights of Indigenous people living in Cherán to self-government and autonomy over their territory. On January 22, 2012, community members elected the High Council of Communal Government (*K'eri Jánaskakua*) using Indigenous Purépecha principles (Suprema Corte de Justicia de la Nacion 2014), and in 2018 Cherán held the inauguration of the members of its most recently elected 12-person council.

Figure 11.1. Nestora Salgado García, the former commander of the Coordinación Regional de Autoridades Comunales (CRAC; Regional Coordination of Communal Authorities) and the first Indigenous woman senator in the Mexican Congress. Photo by Rosalva Aída Hernández Castillo.

CONCLUSION

Although in Mexico military and paramilitary violence have not displaced as many people as in some other Latin American countries, such as Peru and Colombia (Global IDP 2004; Roldan 1998), the issue of forced displacement is becoming a political concern of social movements, as can be seen in communities of the mountain region of Guerrero, in San Juan Copala in Oaxaca, and in Acteal in Chiapas. In these racialized territories, women's bodies have become a battlefield and a means of sending patriarchal messages about the dispossession of territories and resources. In these cases, sexual violation and imprisonment tend to precede the violation and dispossession of Indigenous territories.

In this chapter, I have analyzed the connections among sexual violence, displacement, and dispossession in contexts of armed conflict and paramilitarization, where these strategies are part of what have been defined as "rape regimes," where the act of sexual aggression is connected to broader objectives of control and dispossession (Boesten 2010). Establishing analytical relationships among the multiple acts of violence experienced by displaced Indigenous and peasant women has been a challenge for women's human rights defenders who have set themselves the challenge of demonstrating that sexual violations on the part of paramilitary groups or state agents are neither the product of "uncontrolled sexual impulses" nor abuses by violent men, but are part of a broader strategy to promote displacement and dispossession (Céspedes-Baéz 2010). Human rights lawyers, such as Lina María Céspedes-Baéz in Colombia, have expressed that, given the difficulty in proving such interrelationships among multiple acts of violence under current legal terms, it is necessary to *create* legal tools to make visible the connections between these acts of violence. One such tool is what Céspedes-Baéz describes as "an irrefutable constitutional presumption that assumes the connection between the regime of sexual violence for the purpose of land and real estate dispossession, which would facilitate proving in a legal process not only the event of sexual violence, but the purposes behind it" (Céspedes-Baéz 2010, 300).

As argued here, violence against women that is experienced in the context of the war on drugs reproduces old war strategies that have taken on more violent forms in the context of "new informal wars" (Calveiro 2012); there have been racializing effects in Indigenous territories because of the increased conditions of vulnerability among these populations. From the perspective of patriarchal ideology, which continues to view women as sexual objects and as the keepers of family honor, rape, sexual torture, and bodily mutilations of Indigenous women also constitute an aggression against all the men in the enemy group: It is a way to colonize their territories, their goods, and their resources. However, it is important to remember that patriarchal violence and its symbolism work because the notions that give them meaning are shared by society as a whole and not only by those who defend the interests of large capital. The multiple strategies of resistance deployed by Indigenous women, and their voices in national and international forums, are confronting the patriarchal violence inscribed on their racialized bodies.

REFLECTION AND DISCUSSION QUESTIONS

- How and why are the Indigenous territories described in this case study examples of racialized geographies? What are some examples of racialized geographies in the country you live in or are from?
- How is the term *patriarchal violence* different from the concepts of political violence or sexual violence?
- Why are Indigenous women activists the targets of patriarchal violence in Mexico?
- What are Indigenous Mexican women doing to resist patriarchal violence?

KEY CONCEPTS

- **coloniality**: The way colonialism continues to be present in the knowledge and bodies of Latin American modernity.

- **patriarchal violence**: Violence that creates or maintains male power and dominance over others or that avenges the loss of men's power.
- **racialized geographies**: The ways in which the construction of territoriality and the distribution of space are influenced by racialization processes.

EXPLORE FURTHER

- To learn more about Indigenous activists in Mexico and the challenges they face, read **Chapters 23** and **30**.
- To learn more about political violence and its legacy, read **Section 7**.
- Colectiva#SOS Anti-racism, Gender and Justice. http://www.colectivasos.com/en.
- Hernández Castillo, Rosalva Aída. 2016. *Multiple InJustices. Indigenous Women, Law and Political Struggle*. Tucson: University of Arizona Press.

ABOUT THE AUTHOR

Rosalva Aída Hernández Castillo was born in Ensenada, Baja California, Mexico, and earned a Ph.D. in Anthropology from Stanford University in 1996. She is a professor and senior researcher at the Center for Research and Advanced Studies in Social Anthropology (CIESAS) in Mexico City. Her research and activism work to promote Indigenous and women's rights in Latin America. She has published 22 books, and her academic work has been translated into English, French, and Japanese. Her most recent book is titled *Multiple InJustices: Indigenous Women Law and Political Struggle in Latin America*. She is recipient of the Martin Diskin Oxfam Award for her activist research and of the Simon Bolivar Chair (2013–2014) granted by Cambridge University for her academic work.

REFERENCES

Boesten, Jelke. 2010. "Analyzing Rape Regimes at the Interface of War and Peace in Peru." *International Journal of Transitional Justice* 4: 119–32. https://doi.org/10.1093/ijtj/ijp029.

Calveiro, Pilar. 2012. *Violencias de Estado. La Guerra Antiterrorista y la Guerra Contra el Crímen como Medios de Control Global*. Mexico City: Editorial Siglo XXI.

Castellanos Guerrero, Alicia, Jorge Gómez Izquierdo, Guy Rozat, and Fernanda Núñez. 2008. *Los Caminos del Racismo en México*. México: Plaza y Valdez.

CEJIL. 2016. *Ines and Valentina*. Accessed November 29, 2021. https://cejil.org/en/case/ines-and-valentina.

Centro de Derechos Humanos Fray Bartolomé de las Casas. 2015. *La Iinsurgencia de los Derechos Humanos*. San Cristóbal de Las Casas: CDFBC.

Céspedes-Baéz, Lina-María. 2010. "La Violencia Sexual en Contra de las Mujeres como Estrategia de Despojo de Tierras en el Conflicto Armado Colombiano." *Revista Estudios Socio-Jurídicos* 12 (2): 273–304.

Emmerich, Norberto. 2013. *El Narcotráfico en los Territorios Indígenas de América Latina*. Accessed November 20, 2016. https://es.scribd.com/doc/194724881/El-narcotrafico-en-los-territorios-indigenas-de-America-Latina.

García Martínez, Anayeli. 2011. *Mujeres Encabezan la Resistencia en Cherán*. CIMAC México, July 19.

Gilmore, Ruth Wilson. 2002. "Fatal Couplings of Power and Difference: Notes on Racism and Geography." *Professional Geographer* 54 (1): 15–24. https://doi.org/10.1111/0033-0124.00310.

Gledhill, John. 2015. *The New Wars on the Poor: The Production of Insecurity in Latin America*. London: Zed Books.

Global IDP. 2004. *Profile of Internal Displacement in Peru*. Switzerland: Norwegian Refugee Council/Global IDP Project.

Hernández Castillo, Rosalva Aída. 2016. *Multiple InJustices. Indigenous Women, Law and Political Struggle*. Tucson: University of Arizona Press.

———. 2017. "Activismo Legal y las Paradojas de la Antropología Jurídica Feminista." In *Resistencias Penitenciarias: Investigación Activista en Espacios de Reclusión*, edited by Rosalva Aída Hernández Castillo, 51–83. Mexico: CIESAS/Juan Pablos Editores.

———. 2018. "Mujeres Indígenas: Violencias y Resistencias." *La Jornada*, January 24. https://www.jornada.com.mx/2018/01/24/opinion/020a1pol.

Hernández Castillo, Rosalva Aída, and Héctor Ortiz Elizondo. 2012. "Asunto: Violación de una Indígena Me'phaa por Miembros del Ejército Mexicano. Presentado ante la Corte Interamericana de Derechos Humanos." *Boletín Colegio de Etnólogos y Antropólogos Sociales* 2012: 67–81. https://www.scribd.com/doc/109260764/Boleti-n-Ceas-2012-Peritaje.

INEGI. 2015. "Estadísticas a Propósito del día Internacional de la Eliminación de la Violencia Contra la Mujer (25 de Noviembre)." http://www.inegi.org.mx/saladeprensa/aproposito/2015/violencia0.pdf.

Moloeznik, Marco, and María Eugenia Suárez Garay. 2012. "El Proceso de Militarización de la Seguridad Pública." *Frontera Norte* 24 (48): 121–44.

Mora, Mariana. 2016. "Ayotzinapa and the Criminalization of Racialized Poverty in La Montaña, Guerrero, Mexico." *POLAR* 40 (1): 67–85. https://doi.org/10.1111/plar.12208.

Moreno, Mónica. 2012. "Yo Nunca he Tenido la Necesidad de Nombrarme: Reconociendo el Racismo y el Mestizaje en México." In *Racismos y Otras Formas de Intolerancia: De norte a Sur en América Latina*, edited by A. Castellanos Guerrero and G. Landázuri Benítez, 15–48. Mexico: Universidad Autónoma Metropolitana.

Roldan, Mary. 1998. "Violencia, Colonización y la Geografía de la Diferencia Cultural en Colombia." *Análisis Político* 35: 3–22.

Segato, Rita Laura. 2008. *La Escritura en el Cuerpo de las Mujeres Asesinadas en Cd. Juárez*. Mexico: Tinta Limón.

———. 2013. *Las Nuevas Formas de la Guerra y el Cuerpo de las Mujeres*. Mexico City: Editorial Pez en el Árbol/Tinta Limón.

Sieder, Rachel, ed. 2017. *Demanding Justice and Security: Indigenous Women and Legal Pluralities in Latin America*. New Brunswick, NJ: Rutgers University Press.

Sierra, María Teresa. 2009. "Las Mujeres Indígenas ante la Justicia Comunitaria: Perspectivas desde la Interculturalidad y los Derechos." *Revista Desacatos* 31: 73–88.

Smith, Andrea. 2005. *Conquest: Sexual Violence and American Indian Genocide*. Boston: South End Press.

Speed, Shannon. 2014. "A Dreadful Mosaic: Rethinking Gender Violence Through the Lives of Indigenous Women Migrants." *Gendered Perspectives on International Development, Special Issue: Anthropological Approaches to Gender-based Violence and Human Rights* 304: 78–94.

———. 2016. "States of Violence: Indigenous Women Migrants in the Era of Neoliberal Multicriminalism." *Critique of Anthropology* 36 (3): 280–301. https://doi.org/10.1177/0308275X16646834.

Suprema Corte de Justicia de la Nación. 2014. *Cherán Case: Right to Consultation of the Indigenous Peoples in Legislative Processes*. Accessed November 29, 2021, https://www.scjn.gob.mx/derechos-humanos/sites/default/files/sentencias-emblematicas/summary/2020-12/Summary%20CC32-2014%20HRO.pdf.

Velázquez Guerrero, Verónica. 2013. *Reconstitución del Territorio Comunal: El Movimiento Étnico Autonómico de San Francisco, Cherán, Michoacán*. Ph.D. diss., CIESAS-Mexico.

Wade, Peter. 2011. "Multiculturalismo y Racismo." *Revista Colombiana de Antropología* 47: 15–35. https://doi.org/10.22380/2539472X.956.

CHAPTER TWELVE

After the Mosquito: Caring for Children with Congenital Zika Syndrome in Bahia, Brazil

K. Eliza Williamson

In October 2015, I was doing participant observation in the offices of the State Health Secretariat in Bahia, Brazil, when the news of the **Zika virus** and its link to congenital malformations began to make headlines. I was spending my days at the secretariat studying the work of government bureaucrats in maternal and infant health policy implementation – part of a research project I had planned long before I (and many around the world) even knew that Zika existed. Only a couple of months into this research, however, things began to shift dramatically. In hushed conversations in the halls of the secretariat I heard the words "Zika" and "microcephaly." People looked apprehensive. Closed meetings were called, most of which I was not invited to participate in. Those at the helm of the agency were called for local television interviews and quoted in local newspapers. The monthly public forum on maternal and infant health issues put Zika at the top of its agenda.

At home, I watched evening news reporters talk seemingly nonstop about Zika and **microcephaly**, a congenital condition in which the fetal brain stops developing, leading to babies born with smaller-than-typical heads and cognitive impairments (see Figure 12.1). They showed footage of newborn babies with these characteristic small heads in the arms of their distraught mothers, apprehensively gathered in hospital waiting areas. These images were often followed with graphs illustrating the sharp rise in the number of children born with microcephaly in just the last couple of months. The number of these births had increased exponentially in just a short period, and no one yet understood why. This spike in cases of microcephaly seemed to be concentrated in the northeastern region of Brazil, where Bahia is located.

I did not originally intend to study the social impacts of Zika. Before late 2015, the virus itself barely appeared in Brazil's national news, much less the international media. This is in part because, when Bahian scientists first identified the virus earlier that year, the symptoms of infection being reported – skin rash, body aches, fever – were comparatively mild in relation to

Figure 12.1. *Hold Me Mother* **(2018). A Brazilian mother embraces her child born with congenital Zika syndrome.** Photo by Felipe Fittipaldi (CC 4.0).

other mosquito-transmitted illnesses also present in the country, such as dengue fever, which can kill. Zika was even commonly referred to as "dengue lite," attesting to how harmless it was thought to be – that is, until the increase in microcephaly cases. It wasn't long before doctors in the neighboring state of Pernambuco discovered the link between Zika infection in pregnant people and fetal malformations – malformations that lead to a range of motor, sensory, and cognitive impairments collectively known as **congenital Zika syndrome (CZS)**.

While I had a view of the Zika outbreak from inside a government health agency at the epicenter of the public health crisis, I kept thinking about those mothers and babies on TV. How were they, the most directly impacted, experiencing the Zika virus outbreak? What would their lives be like when the outbreak was over, when public health agencies turned their attention back to other matters? How would they care for children with multiple disabilities over the long term? This led me to my ethnographic research with families raising children impacted by Zika. In this chapter, I examine how mothers navigate a shifting terrain of social assistance programs and therapeutic resources as they care for their disabled children. I argue that mothers' caregiving debilitates them in ways that cast in relief the noxious embodied effects of gendered and racialized inequities in contemporary Brazil.

TIMELINE OF AN OUTBREAK

Zika is transmitted primarily by the *Aedes aegypti* and *Aedes albopictus* mosquitoes as well as by sexual contact. The virus was first discovered in Uganda in 1947, in monkeys. The first human cases appeared in the early 1950s, and between the 1960s and 1980s it spread via human-to-human contact to parts of Asia. At that time, the total number of cases didn't amount to more than 14. It was still a very rare disease. The first large outbreaks of Zika were in the Pacific Islands, first in 2007 and then again in 2013/2014, when thousands of suspected cases were documented. Still, this news failed to reach international headlines. In March 2015, Brazilian health authorities reported to the World Health Organization (WHO) thousands of infections characterized by skin rashes, primarily in the Northeast. This turned out to be Zika.

The virus is believed to have arrived in Brazil around 2014, when Brazil was preparing to host the FIFA World Cup of soccer. This time it caused the largest outbreak seen yet: Hundreds of thousands of suspected cases were reported (Diniz 2017). Zika eventually spread to 86 other countries, including much of Latin America (World Health Organization n.d.). Brazil, however, remained the global epicenter of the outbreak. It was also the country with the highest number of congenital Zika syndrome cases. As of the latest publicly available data, there are over 3,500 confirmed cases of CZS nationwide (Ministério da Saúde do Brasil 2021). While the state of Pernambuco was spotlighted throughout the epidemic as the national epicenter within Brazil, the state of Bahia has long since surpassed it in numbers of children born with CZS: There are 585 children living with this condition (Secretaria da Saúda do Estado da Bahia 2021).

After doctors in Pernambuco linked Zika to congenital malformations, things escalated quickly. In November 2015, largely due to Zika's reproductive effects, the Brazilian government declared a public health emergency. In February 2016, the WHO elevated Zika to the status of a public health emergency of international concern (PHEIC) – a health event that may constitute an international risk (World Health Organization 2005, 9) – and health authorities across national borders were alerted to the potential impacts of Zika and concerted efforts were made to stop its spread and care for those affected.

While microcephaly is undoubtedly the most widely recognizable and publicized of Zika's effects, it is only one of the features of congenital Zika syndrome. Others include brain calcifications, enlarged brain ventricles due to an accumulation of cerebrospinal fluid, eye abnormalities leading to impaired vision, muscle contractures that restrict movement, and excess muscle tone that can make limbs stiff and difficult to move. Many of the children also have frequent epileptic seizures and other complications. All of this means that affected children have multiple disabilities and will need specialized care for the rest of their lives.

Zika's international emergency status lasted only until November 2016. A significant decline in the number of new cases, a slowing of the virus's global spread, and a marked decrease in the numbers of reported congenital malformations all contributed to the WHO's decision to shift from emergency to long-term approach. Zika has not disappeared: The virus still circulates, and it remains a haunting presence in the lives of thousands of families across Brazil. Zika therefore continues to deeply impact the lives of thousands of Brazilian children and their families.

STRUCTURAL VULNERABILITY AND ZIKA

Zika's impacts highlight Brazil's regional, racial, gender, and class inequalities. Parents raising children with CZS are primarily Black or Brown, poor, and live in neglected urban areas and the interior of the country. Mothers are usually children's primary or sole caregivers. While the *Aedes aegypti* mosquito can breed practically anywhere there is standing water, certain environmental and infrastructural conditions commonly found in impoverished areas – such as open sewers and uncollected trash piles – provide an especially favorable setting for mosquito proliferation. Combined with a lack of access to comprehensive reproductive healthcare, including safe and legal abortion, this meant that Brazil's most marginalized were also the most exposed to Zika and its long-term consequences (Diniz 2017). In other words, poor Black and Brown women were already **structurally vulnerable** – vulnerable to poor health and inadequate healthcare produced by unequal structural conditions (Quesada, Hart, and Bourgois 2011). Their structural vulnerability increased the likelihood that they would contract Zika, and this vulnerability was also exacerbated by raising children whose specialized needs mothers have little social support to provide (Williamson 2018).

The population of Bahia's state capital, Salvador, is majority Afro-descendant and well known for its diasporic Black culture. But like other Brazilian cities, Salvador is also home to pronounced racialized social inequality, clearly visible in the spatial organization and everyday life of the city: Whereas gated condominium complexes are home to largely white and light-skinned Bahians, the low-income neighborhoods (*periferias*) are overwhelmingly Black. Both Salvador's Afro-Brazilian culture and its racialized inequality are remnants of the city's colonial past: This city was one of Brazil's primary ports during the Atlantic slave trade. Of all the Africans who were captured and brought to the Americas, about 40 per cent went to Brazil (Costa 2000). Its sprawling districts of informal housing with precarious sewage and water infrastructure make Salvador a prime location for mosquito proliferation and, in turn, for the spread of mosquito-borne illnesses like Zika.

FIELDWORK

In 2016, some initial contacts via social media led me to a local organization called Abraço a Microcefalia (I Embrace Microcephaly), which was founded earlier that year by mothers of children diagnosed with CZS. Abraço is a space of mutual support for families in similar situations. Abraço has now grown to a full-fledged nongovernmental organization with a membership of over 300 families. It hosts bi-weekly gatherings for parents and kids (online during the COVID-19 pandemic); offers physical, speech, and occupational therapy services; and organizes regular donations of food and other basic necessities. Most of the families the organization serves are Afro-descendant, poor, and headed by mothers. In August 2016 I became a volunteer at Abraço, which involved assisting therapists with children's therapy sessions; helping organize regular gatherings; playing with children while parents were participating in workshops; stocking donated diapers, foodstuffs, and toys; among many other activities. I thus began a long-term relationship with the organization and especially with a core group of mothers and children who participated.

Since then, I have conducted informal and formal interviews with parents, observed children's early intervention therapy sessions, observed health worker training for caring for children with CZS in low-income households, joined parents in protest marches, and participated in mothers' WhatsApp message groups. Social media has also been a core part of our relationship and my research. During my time in Bahia, and since I left in mid-2019, I've kept in touch with my interlocutors, especially via WhatsApp, Facebook, and Instagram, where many of the mothers frequently post about their daily lives.

Because congenital Zika syndrome is a novel condition, much uncertainty still surrounds it. Doctors and scientists now have some idea of the developmental difficulties the children will likely face, based on their impairments, but there are no past cases to indicate what the future holds. In fact, some doctors told parents their children would not live past one year, and that if they did, they would be "vegetables" without meaningful lives. Thanks to mothers' fierce love and intensive caregiving, the children have consistently proved these doctors wrong. Many moms embrace the saying "*diagnóstico não é destino*" (diagnosis is not destiny). They actively keep space open for hope, and they do all they can to ensure the best possible developmental outcomes. But maintaining hope and providing care can be exhausting, especially under the weight of the structural inequalities that already constrain these families' lives.

MARIA AND BRUNO

I first visited Maria and her small son, Bruno, when they were living with her sister's family in one of Salvador's *periferia* neighborhoods. The two had just returned from one of Bruno's many weekly therapy appointments, and the little boy was resting in the living room next to us, in a specially designed chair that supported his head and neck, falling asleep in front of a children's show on the television set.

Maria identifies as Black (*Negra*) and her family belongs to what some call Brazil's "new middle class": those who were previously counted as "poor" but gained consumer purchasing power through the social programs of the Workers' Party governments between 2003 and

2016 (Klein, Mitchell, and Junge 2018).[1] Maria is her son's primary caregiver, and Bruno is her only child. Bruno's father abandoned them early on. During her pregnancy, Maria experienced several complications that forced her to leave the job she had at a shipping logistics company. After Bruno was born, her primary source of income was the small government stipend for disabled people or their caregivers living below the poverty line. So, like many of the mothers and kids, the two have lived precariously ever since, relying on help from Abraço and family to make ends meet.

Most of what little money Maria has goes toward Bruno. While Brazil's universal public health system provides free care, there are often long waitlists for appointments and equipment such as mobility aids and corrective orthoses for malformed limbs. Maria therefore scrapes together money to pay for a private health plan, which gives Bruno access to a wider range of therapy options and quicker access to services. And, like many of the other moms, she uses crowdfunding to gather donations from friends and family to help her pay for equipment and medications the public health system doesn't provide and Bruno's health plan doesn't cover. Nutritional supplements are also in high demand, especially those said to help with brain function.

But cultivating children's potential involves laborious efforts; investments of time, energy, and already-stretched financial resources to achieve; and this labor is potentially never-ending. Maria explained how she thought about Bruno's future in the following way:

> I don't have anything to hope for [*eu não tenho o que esperar*]. I don't hope … Well, I work so that he's able to do things. If he's going to do them, I don't know. I have no idea what might happen because, even though nothing [in the world] is for certain, with them [these children] it's even worse. Things can happen at any time, so I don't know. But I work, I work, I make an effort [*corro atrás*] so that he might do things.

In general, caring for a child with CZS is a *correria*; it involves a lot of "running around" and staying very busy. Mothers traverse the city, "up and down" (*pra cima e pra baixo*) – quite literally, due to Salvador's hilly geography – as children are shuttled to clinical appointments, diagnostic exams, and pharmacies to pick up medications, usually via public buses. The rhythm of life can be frenetic.

From birth until three years of age, the Brazilian Ministry of Health recommends that children born with disabilities be placed in early intervention programs to encourage children's "best possible development" (Ministério da Saúde do Brasil 2016, 9–10). This intensive care directed at cultivating disabled children's development is an example of what Mattingly, Grøn, and Meinert (2011) refer to as "chronic homework": the diverse kinds of work family members do at home to treat and manage children's chronic illnesses. For my research participants,

---

1   The term "new middle class" is contentious. For a discussion, see Klein, Mitchell, and Junge (2018).

chronic homework involves things like administering medications, performing prescribed sensory stimulation exercises, fixing specially prepared meals, cleaning and replacing parts of gastric feeding tubes when children have them, and researching unfamiliar symptoms that may emerge. Even "basic" tasks like feeding require much more time and effort, since children's difficulties chewing and swallowing can make mealtimes dangerous without the right technique and supervision. The bulk of this intensive caregiving falls to mothers (Mauldin 2016) and is layered on top of other domestic duties, like keeping the house clean and organized, doing the shopping, and cooking meals for other family members.

Maria finds pleasure and fulfillment in caring for Bruno, watching as he responds to therapy and seeing his developmental progress over time, knowing that all her efforts are paying off. But she also admits how exhausting this intensive caregiving can be: *Cansaço* (exhaustion) is a word mothers use frequently to describe their daily routines.

LILIANA AND DIEGO: COVID-19, LOCKDOWN, AND "LEARNING TO LIVE WITH PAINS"

Liliana is no stranger to exhaustion. Like Maria, Liliana was in her late twenties when I met her, mother to a little boy named Diego. Unlike Maria, though, she lived with her husband, Diego's father. Like most of the families, they lived in an auto-constructed home in an urban *periferia*. Liliana worked in her father-in-law's small grocery store in the neighborhood until she became pregnant with Diego, and her husband, Danilo, was unemployed but picked up work here and there fixing air conditioning units. Liliana identifies as *parda* (Brown or mixed race). Diego is the couple's only child, but he requires near-constant care.

In late 2020 I spoke with Liliana via WhatsApp. I wanted to know how she and her family were faring during some of the worst months of the COVID-19 pandemic, which hit Brazil particularly hard (Kerr et al. 2021). Lockdown measures implemented that year meant that, like parents around the world, moms of kids with CZS had to adjust to the reality of being at home with their children all day, all the time. Whereas therapy appointments and Abraço meetings had them out of the house during most days, now they were stuck in place. Also, like many places around the world, Brazilian hospitals were overwhelmed with COVID-19 patients, not least because of the federal government's denialism and grave mishandling of the public health crisis (Ortega and Orsini 2020). This meant that it was now risky even to take children to emergency rooms, which mothers do for treatment of acute (non-COVID-related) respiratory infections and other health complications. With diminished access to vital healthcare resources, parents in my research felt growing anxiety, fearing for their children's well-being as well as their own (c.f. Matos and Silva 2020).

The COVID-19 pandemic and its collateral effects exposed the structural vulnerability of those like Maria and Liliana who were already living with the effects of intersecting forms of social inequities. Liliana expressed this eloquently in our WhatsApp conversation. She spoke of the difficulties imposed by the pandemic and its mishandling, but also of continuing problems brought on by government neglect and faulty social policy. She told me that she was angry at her country and its leaders

> not just because of the children's lives but also in terms of my life and [other] moms' lives, with everything we go through, we feel as if our lives were paralyzed [*paralisado*] … We haven't had any attention/care [*atenção*]. [Liliana, November 2020][2]

Liliana referred specifically to a recent concession made by the federal government to award children with microcephaly a lifetime monthly pension (*pensão vitalícia*). While this may sound like a major victory, the details of the pension made it a disappointment for many. Liliana referred to it as "six for half a dozen … the same thing" as before, because it concedes an identical minimum monthly amount to another government disability and caregiving benefit that most of the families were already receiving – the BPC (UNELAC n.d.). Since families must choose one or the other, the pension ultimately "makes no difference," as Liliana told me. She still cannot afford to pay for outside help with Diego's care, which would alleviate her burden. Once the COVID-19 pandemic eventually ends, paid care might also allow her to study for a post-secondary degree, which would make her more competitive in Brazil's dismal job market and have a chance of making more than minimum wage. With these possibilities unavailable, Liliana felt her plans for a better life were foreclosed.[3]

Of course, unlike Maria and Bruno, who live alone, Liliana and Diego live with Danilo. Where was he in this picture? Liliana summed it up with an example:

> I can't even go to the grocery store alone because I don't have anyone to leave Diego with. The other day I asked his father to watch him while I went to the mall; it was hell! He was calling me every five minutes to come back home. The boy only had lunch [late] in the afternoon because [his father] didn't want to feed the boy because of his eating difficulties.

Our conversation took place when the little boy was about to turn five years old, meaning that in five years Danilo had not learned how to properly feed his own son. Liliana resented this. Added to all the other restrictions, her husband's failure to shoulder childcare responsibilities made it so that Liliana "felt like a slave without her own life, a prisoner in my house." Liliana expressed many of these grievances through idioms of embodied suffering, like being "paralyzed." She continued:

---

2 My translation; edited for clarity.
3 In February 2019, the federal government issued an executive order giving children born with microcephaly a lifelong monthly pension equal to one minimum monthly salary (R$1,045 as of this writing, or about US$188 under the exchange rate at the time).

> This routine is exhausting [*esgotante*] for me … these last months were really difficult. I didn't go totally crazy [*surtar de vez*] because God didn't let me, [but] I almost went mad!

During lockdown, Liliana contracted chikungunya, another mosquito-borne disease, and had to endure its characteristic fevers, rashes, headaches, and joint pain while keeping up Diego's care routine at home. "I ended up self-medicating because I didn't have anyone to leave Diego with to go to the doctor," she told me. Caring for her own physical and mental well-being had become extremely difficult, and this added to her feeling of hopelessness. Problems just seemed to keep stacking up with no reprieve on the horizon. When she did attempt to leave the house for a dental consultation regarding a broken tooth, she injured her knee and ankle in a fall. "I'm learning to live with pains," Liliana said. "Now I understand how people get depression or even go crazy!"

Liliana's narrative points to multiple sources of suffering, entangled in multiple systems of power. She felt her life was "paralyzed" because the Brazilian government refused to offer her and other parents raising children with CZS the proper material conditions for a dignified life, one in which they might have the means to pay for the care their children needed – and which they needed, to have a break at least occasionally – and a chance at getting ahead financially, at least partially a product of structural racism (see Chapter 31). Her story of how even a simple trip to the grocery store was hindered by Danilo's failure to partake in a significant way in Diego's care indicates how patriarchal values shape the lives of women like Liliana: Childcare, especially care of disabled children, is women's responsibility; very little of it is shared by men. Consequently, Liliana felt like a "slave" and a "prisoner" in her own home. She was also exposed to chikungunya likely because of where she lives – in a poor, urban *periferia* – and this negatively impacted her health, not least because a lack of reliable childcare prevented her from leaving the house to see a doctor. When we spoke, she said she was still feeling the collateral effects of that infection in her body. The injury to her ankle and knee from the fall she took further debilitated her.[4] These physical complaints were joined by mental health issues, as she confessed to "almost [going] mad." All of this together made her feel resigned to, as she told me, "learning to live with pains" (*aprendendo a viver com dores*). Liliana experienced both acute and chronic health issues because of the conditions under which she labored to make sure her son was well cared for. Her caregiving under conditions of duress – of economic crisis and chronic poverty, of oppressive gender relations, of exposure to infectious disease – debilitated her. Her body (and mind), which she uses to sustain her son's well-being, bears the marks of the wearing down that these multiple, intersecting conditions produce.

---

4 My use of the term *debilitated* here draws on the work of Jasbir K. Puar (2017), who defines debilitation as "the slow wearing down of populations" as opposed to "the event of becoming disabled" (xiii–xiv). I contend that debilitation captures the embodied experiences of the mothers in my research, who largely would not identify themselves as "disabled" but nevertheless are worn down by the conditions under which they care for their children.

CONCLUSION

The Zika virus, like many other infectious diseases, had – and has – unequal impacts on different people. This is true not just of the epidemic's outbreak, but also its "afterlife." Because poor, racialized women like Maria and Liliana are structurally vulnerable, they were the ones most exposed to Zika infection in the first place *and* the ones whose health is most heavily impacted by the effects of caregiving under wearying conditions. As parents of children with congenital Zika syndrome, they provide intensive, specialized care to protect their children's well-being and, they hope, increase the chances of better developmental outcomes. Constrictive gender roles make it so that this care labor falls primarily or solely on mothers, regardless of whether women are partnered or not. The relative lack of social support for this intensive caregiving compounds its difficulty, making it a constant struggle for these women to give their children the attention they need while also taking care of themselves. Without the financial means to hire professional caregivers, and thus without much hope of gaining employment in the formal labor market, mothers raising children with CZS can be stuck in a cycle of poverty that reinforces both their and their children's vulnerability. Care work under these conditions of chronic scarcity and crisis debilitates mothers by requiring Herculean efforts to provide care that could and should be shared by others. The effects of this tiring and largely solitary work show up on and in mothers' bodies, in the form of pain, exhaustion, mental illness, and chronic conditions.

The impacts of infectious disease outbreaks can have long-lasting and unequal effects on people. In Brazil, the Zika virus epidemic most impacted low-income Black and Brown women who were infected with the virus during pregnancy and gave birth to children with congenital Zika syndrome. Anthropologists concerned with the impacts of infectious disease should pay attention to the afterlives of epidemics and pandemics, listening to those whose lives have been most affected by them to better understand how such diseases "live on" even after outbreaks are officially declared to have ended. We should also understand these experiences of infectious disease aftermaths as situated in specific times and places. Brazil's multiple crises, including the economic recession that has led to austerity policies that further weaken vital public support infrastructure, as well as COVID-19, which has compounded the chronic overcrowding of the underfunded public health system due to the government's grave mishandling of the pandemic, has deeply shaped what resources are available (or not) to mothers like Maria and Liliana and, therefore, their embodied experiences of caring for their disabled children.

REFLECTION AND DISCUSSION QUESTIONS

- In what ways do structural inequalities impact how different people experience infectious disease outbreaks? Why is it important to consider these inequalities in anthropology?

- How does scientific uncertainty about Zika and congenital Zika syndrome influence the way parents see their children's disabilities? Thinking about other pandemics, such as COVID-19, what other effects of scientific uncertainty can you think of?
- Who are the caregivers in your life? How do you think caring impacts them, perhaps in both positive and negative ways? If you are a caregiver yourself, how does caring impact you?

KEY CONCEPTS

- **congenital Zika syndrome (CZS)**: A condition in which the Zika virus attacks the developing child's central nervous system in its mother's uterus so that it is born with microcephaly, brain calcifications, enlarged brain ventricles, eye abnormalities, muscle contractures, and/or excess muscle tone.
- **microcephaly**: A congenital condition in which the head is smaller than average due to incomplete fetal brain development.
- **structural vulnerability**: Vulnerability to poor health and inadequate healthcare that is produced by unequal social conditions.
- **Zika virus**: A virus transmitted by mosquitoes and sexual contact that causes symptoms similar to those of dengue and can also cause congenital malformations in the fetuses of pregnant people.

EXPLORE FURTHER

- To learn more about racial inequality in Brazil, read **Chapters 5**, **24**, and **31**.
- To learn more about the social and economic effects of the COVID-19 pandemic, read **Chapters 26** and **33**.
- Diniz, Debora. 2016. *Zika, the Film*. Anis Instituto de Bioética. https://tinyurl.com/Zika-the-Film.
- Human Rights Watch. 2017. "Neglected and Unprotected: The Impact of the Zika Outbreak on Women and Girls in Northeastern Brazil." https://tinyurl.com/Neglected-and-Unprotected.
- Kremer, William. 2018. "Zika Love Stories." *BBC News*. https://tinyurl.com/Zika-Love-Stories.

ABOUT THE AUTHOR

Eliza Williamson is a cultural medical anthropologist who researches maternal and infant health policy and caregiving among families impacted by the Zika virus in Bahia, Brazil. She is a lecturer in the Latin American Studies Program and the Department of Romance Languages and Literatures at Washington University in St. Louis.

REFERENCES

Costa, Emília Viotti da. 2000. *The Brazilian Empire: Myths & Histories*. Chapel Hill: University of North Carolina Press.

Diniz, Debora. 2017. *Zika: From the Brazilian Backlands to Global Threat*. London: Zed Books.

Kerr, Ligia Regina Franco Sansigolo, Carl Kendall, Rosa Lívia Freitas de Almeida, Maria Yury Ichihara, Estela Maria L. Aquino, Antônio Augusto Moura da Silva, Ricardo Arraes de Alencar Ximenes, et al. 2021. "COVID-19 in Northeast Brazil: First Year of the Pandemic and Uncertainties to Come." *Revista de Saúde Pública* 55: 35. https://doi.org/10.11606/s1518-8787.2021055003728.

Klein, Charles H., Sean T. Mitchell, and Benjamin Junge. 2018. "Naming Brazil's Previously Poor: 'New Middle Class' as an Economic, Political, and Experiential Category." *Economic Anthropology* 5 (1): 83–95. https://doi.org/10.1002/sea2.12104.

Matos, Silvana Sobreira de, and Ana Cláudia Rodrigues da Silva. 2020. "Quando Duas Epidemias se Encontram: A Vida das Mulheres Que Têm Filhos com a Síndrome Congênita do Zika Vírus na Pandemia da COVID-19." *Cadernos de Campo (São Paulo – 1991)* 29 (supl): 329–40. https://doi.org/10.11606/issn.2316-9133.v29isuplp329-340.

Mattingly, Cheryl, Lone Grøn, and Lotte Meinert. 2011. "Chronic Homework in Emerging Borderlands of Healthcare." *Culture, Medicine, and Psychiatry* 35 (3): 347–75. https://doi.org/10.1007/s11013-011-9225-z.

Mauldin, Laura. 2016. *Made to Hear: Cochlear Implants and Raising Deaf Children*. Minneapolis: University of Minnesota Press.

Ministério da Saúde do Brasil. 2016. "Diretrizes de Estimulação Precoce: Crianças de Zero a 3 anos com Atraso no Desenvolvimento Nuropsicomotor Decorrente de Microcefalia." https://pesquisa.bvsalud.org/portal/resource/pt/lis-35448.

———. 2021. "Situação Epidemiológica da Síndrome Congênita Associada à Infecção pelo Virus Zika, 2015 a 2020." *Epidemiological Bulletin* 52. http://plataforma.saude.gov.br/anomalias-congenitas/boletim-epidemiologico-SVS-04-2021.pdf.

Ortega, Francisco, and Michael Orsini. 2020. "Governing COVID-19 without Government in Brazil: Ignorance, Neoliberal Authoritarianism, and the Collapse of Public Health Leadership." *Global Public Health* 15 (9): 1257–77. https://doi.org/10.1080/17441692.2020.1795223.

Puar, Jasbir K. 2017. *The Right to Maim: Deability, Capacity, Disability*. Durham, NC: Duke University Press.

Quesada, James, Laurie Kain Hart, and Philippe Bourgois. 2011. "Structural Vulnerability and Health: Latino Migrant Laborers in the United States." *Medical Anthropology* 30 (4): 339–62. https://doi.org/10.1080/01459740.2011.576725.

Secretaria da Saúde do Estado da Bahia. 2021. "Boletím Epidemiológico: Síndrome Congênita Associada Ao Zika Vírus e/Ou Outras Etiologias (SCZV)." *Epidemiological Bulletin*. Salvador, Brazil: Secretaria da Saúde do Estado da Bahia. http://www.saude.ba.gov.br/wp-content/uploads/2017/11/boletimMicrocefaliaAbril2021.pdf.

UNELAC. n.d. Beneficio de Prestação Continuada (Continuous Benefit Programme). https://dds.cepal.org/bpsnc/programme?id=43.

Williamson, K. Eliza, Cíntia Engel, and Helena Fietz. "The Chronification of Home-Making in Brazil: Women Caregivers in Dis/abling Spaces." *Space & Culture*, accepted.

World Health Organization. n.d. "Zika Virus Disease." Accessed January 15, 2022. https://www.who.int/westernpacific/health-topics/zika-virus-disease.

———. 2005. *International Health Regulations,* 3rd ed. Geneva: World Health Organization. Accessed July 7, 2022. https://www.who.int/publications-detail-redirect/9789241580496.

SECTION FIVE

Language in Society

Because people are socialized into their native languages from infancy and come to associate language varieties with family, community, and heritage, language is one of the most psychologically profound ways that people perceive themselves and others. As a result, language is much more than a medium of communication. It is among the most important human inventions, a critical marker of identity, and a means of individual and collective expression.[1]

In Latin America and the Caribbean, which has some of the most linguistically diverse areas of the world, debates about language are pervasive and play out with important material and symbolic consequences for their speakers. Policies and practices that elevate one language over others – for example, through the declaration of a national language – effectively elevate the speakers of this dominant language over speakers of other minoritized languages. To understand why language is a frequent site of contested power, it is important to know how certain kinds of languages (and their speakers) are differentially situated with respect to others. Broadly speaking, there are four kinds of languages in use across the region: colonial, Indigenous, creole, and immigrant languages.

Colonial languages, including Spanish, English, Portuguese, Dutch, and French, were introduced to the region by Europeans. Historically the languages of governance and domination, with few exceptions colonial languages remain the primary language of the national elite across the region today. Wherever there is only one official language, it is almost always a colonial language. Over time, national and regional variants have developed such that even among countries where the same colonial language is spoken, dialectal variation is significant. Thus the Spanish spoken in Paraguay and that spoken in the Dominican Republic are mutually

---

[1] Not all languages are spoken; sign languages, which use manual rather than oral forms, are also full-fledged languages. Many sign languages are in use across Latin America and the Caribbean, including Nicaraguan Sign Language, which emerged as a new language very recently.

intelligible (i.e., speakers can understand one another) but have differences in vocabulary and grammar. Similarly, differences in accent make Spanish speakers from these countries audibly recognizable as Paraguayan or Dominican.

Indigenous languages are the languages that have been spoken in the region since before European invasion. Sometimes referred to as *lenguas originarias* to emphasize their origination in the region, these languages include Nahuatl, Zapoteco, Mixteco, and Mayan languages (in Mexico and Guatemala); Garifuna (in Honduras); Miskito (in Nicaragua); Kuna (in Panama); Quechua and Aymara (in the Andes); Mapudungun (in Chile and Argentina); Guaraní (in Paraguay); and Wayuunaiki (in the Amazon). As a result of early genocides and ongoing discrimination of Indigenous peoples, many Indigenous languages have been lost, are dormant (i.e., have no living speakers), or are in decline (i.e., are losing speakers). Yet there are still hundreds of remaining Indigenous languages in use today. Indigenous languages are often viewed as relics of the past, inapt for the contemporary world. As a result, some of the most innovative efforts at Indigenous language revitalization emerge not from governmental agencies but from grassroots groups that focus on revalorization and on increasing the use of Indigenous languages in ever-expanding contexts, showing that Indigenous languages can be vibrant, useful, and appropriate for any setting. Indigenous scholars, activists, and artists do much of this work through innovative projects in film, music, radio, print, and social media.

Creole languages are used across the Caribbean and in coastal areas of Central and South America. They are a direct result of the historical dynamics of the transatlantic slave trade and plantation societies. Early plantations were characterized by extreme linguistic diversity, as enslaved African and Indigenous peoples who spoke many different languages sought ways to communicate under situations of great duress. The creole languages that emerged from these circumstances have several common features. The vocabulary of a creole language is largely derived from the colonial language that was in use by local enslavers and colonial authorities. The grammar of creole languages is typically derived from the many languages that were spoken by the enslaved people who created the new language. Thus these grammars are characterized by features from West African languages including Akan, Igbo, Twi, Wolof, and Yoruba and from Indigenous language families including Taíno and Arawak. They also contain features from languages such as Irish and Hindi that were spoken by immigrants and indentured servants in the community. Today, some dominant *language ideologies* – beliefs and attitudes about language and language speakers – erroneously view creole languages as corrupted versions of colonial languages. To combat this stigma, some nations, like Haiti, have officially designated their creole, Haitian Kreyòl, as a national language and promote its use in official settings.

Linguistic diversity in Latin America and the Caribbean has been augmented by arriving immigrants over many centuries. In some countries, the Southern Cone in particular, expenditures were made by the governments of newly independent nations to attract European settlers (see Chapter 3). In some cases, the descendants of these early settlers, for example German-Chileans in southern Chile, continue to use their heritage languages. More recently, sociopolitical and migratory shifts due to the upheavals of World War II, the Cold War, and processes of accelerated globalization have created new waves of in-migration to the region, bringing speakers of many more world languages. These include Arabic speakers and speakers of East Asian languages including Mandarin, Japanese, and Korean. As a result, differing sets of **immigrant languages** are now spoken in virtually all nations of the region.

Chapters in this section illustrate some of the most pressing matters of language in society. In Chapter 13, Cru documents a grassroots arts initiative to revalorize Yucatec Maya and expand its use into new domains by supporting up-and-coming rural hip-hop artists in the Yucatán. In Chapter 14, Past provides a portrait of Haitian-Cuban poet Hilario Batista Félix, who uses Haitian Kreyòl as a medium to celebrate Blackness and narrate the experiences of diasporic Haitians both within and beyond Cuba. And in Chapter 15, Wiel explores the ways that, despite restrictive educational policies that insist on the use of Dutch in Aruban and Curaçaoan school settings, students continue to use the full scope of their linguistic repertoires with one another and their teachers.

KEY CONCEPTS

- **colonial languages**: The languages that were brought to Latin America and the Caribbean by European colonization: Spanish, English, Portuguese, Dutch, and French. With few exceptions, colonial languages remain the primary language of the national elites across the region today.
- **creole languages**: Languages used across the Caribbean and in coastal areas of Central and South America that were originally created by enslaved people under the duress of the transatlantic slave trade and plantation society.
- **immigrant languages**: Languages from other parts of the world that are now spoken in Latin America and the Caribbean by immigrants and the descendants of immigrants to the region.
- **Indigenous languages**: Languages that have been spoken in Latin America and the Caribbean since before the era of European colonization.

EXPLORE FURTHER

- To learn more about activism surrounding Indigenous languages, read **Chapter 7**.
- Aguilar, Yásnaya, Gloria Anzaldúa, and Ruperta Bautista. 2020. *Lo Lingüístico es Político*, 3ra edición. Valencia, Chiapas: Ediciones OnA.
- Contreras, Ernesto, dir. 2017. *Sueño en Otro Idioma (I Dream in Another Language)*. [Mexico]
- García, Ofelia, Dina López, and Carmina Makar. 2010. "Latin America." In *Handbook of Language and Ethnic Identity*, 2nd ed., edited by Joshua Fishman and Ofelia García. Oxford: Oxford University Press.
- Shulist, Sarah. 2018. *Transforming Indigeneity: Urbanization and Language Revitalization in the Brazilian Amazon*. Toronto: University of Toronto Press.

CHAPTER THIRTEEN

Rap *Originario* and Language Revitalization in Southern Mexico: The ADN Maya Collective

Josep Cru

In 2012 I saw a message posted on the Facebook page of Maya linguist and activist Fidencio Briceño that read: *Ma' su'utsil a t'anik maayai'. Su'utsil ma' a t'anik* (It is not shameful to speak Maya. It is shameful not to speak it), a punchy motto that neatly encapsulated negative ideologies associated with speaking an Indigenous language and the need for action. That year a couple of young budding rappers in their late teens, Pat Boy and El Cima, produced the video clip *Sangre Maya* (Mayan blood), singing in the chorus:

Sangre maya u k'i'ik'el máasewal
Be'elake' kin taasik teech u jaajile' ak ch'i'ibal
Sangre maya ma' saajako'on meyaj
Chíinpoltik lela', bobo'chi' maaya k'aay

Mayan blood, Indigenous blood
Today I'm bringing to you the true culture
Mayan blood they (Indigenous people) are not afraid of work
Listen to this rap in Maya

Witnessing these expressions by young people in support of the Yucatec Maya language, I became interested in researching what has become an ever-increasing trend of using social media and music as powerful tools to reclaim oppressed languages and cultures.

While doing ethnographic fieldwork in the Yucatán Peninsula of Mexico between 2008 and 2014, I had the opportunity to meet a good number of activists who were working toward the promotion of the Yucatec Maya language. The main goal of my research was to understand the ideological underpinnings driving the process of **language revitalization** of Yucatec

Figure 13.1. Pat Boy, Maya rapper and founder of the ADN collective. Photo by Josep Cru.

Maya, which was losing ground to Spanish. I wanted to understand the circulating discourses on language revalorization, the term activists preferred to use, and the effectiveness of official language policies aimed at recovering that language. It wasn't until the last phase of my fieldwork, though, that I realized the importance of emerging grassroots activism among young Indigenous people in reclaiming the use of Yucatec Maya. In one of my later field trips, I met the rapper Pat Boy (Figure 13.1) and I have followed his work ever since. In this chapter, after providing some background on language policy and planning in Mexico and its impact on Indigenous languages, I look at the work of ADN Maya, a collective of young Maya artists who have become a driving force in Indigenous language and cultural revitalization in the Yucatán Peninsula.

LANGUAGE POLICY AND PLANNING IN MEXICO

Mexico stands out as one of the most linguistically and culturally diverse countries in the Americas. In the last two decades an increasing recognition of this diversity has been central to constitutional reforms and drafting of a specific law of language rights. The Mexican Constitution, for instance, was amended in 2001 to acknowledge the Indigenous contribution to the multicultural composition of the nation. Also, in 2003 the General Law on the Linguistic Rights of Indigenous Peoples was passed, recognizing Mexican Indigenous languages as "national languages" and paving the way for the subsequent creation in 2006 of the National Institute of Indigenous Languages (INALI). One of INALI's foremost tasks was the compilation of a Catalogue of National Indigenous Languages describing the highly complex linguistic diversity of Mexico, establishing 11 language families, 68 language groups, and 365 language varieties.

On an international level, in 2019 UNESCO and the member-states collaborated for the development of the International Year of Indigenous Languages, which closed in February 2020 in Mexico with the high-level event "Building a Decade of Actions for Indigenous Languages." During this event the Declaration of Los Pinos (Chapoltepek) was presented, ushering in a strategic roadmap for the Decade of Indigenous Languages (2022–2032). This international focus on Indigenous languages stems from a growing concern about the loss of linguistic diversity worldwide. Indigenous peoples are abandoning their traditional languages at an unprecedented rate because of wide-ranging homogenizing policies carried out by nation-states. These policies are often underpinned by the ideology of "one nation – one people – one language" and actively promote monolingualism while discouraging or even repressing bilingual and multilingual practices. Discrimination, racism, and marginalization also result in internalized negative beliefs among Indigenous speakers about their languages, which are labeled as backward, underdeveloped, useless in modern advanced societies, and so on. This widespread contempt engenders a process of language stigmatization that plays a key role in pushing Indigenous peoples to shift to a majority language.

In Mexico, despite the increased visibility of Indigenous languages and rising awareness about their fragile situation, top-down language policies with an emphasis on legislative reforms and poorly implemented bilingual education have proved insufficient to halt, let alone reverse, this relentless shift to Spanish. Against this background, grassroots strategies become a fundamental approach to revitalize endangered languages and cultures. These efforts are often not only part of a broader struggle for social, economic, and political justice, but also essential in many cases to reclaim an identity that has been long minoritized – subordinated by the dominant political and social groups. The creation and performance of rap in Indigenous languages, the focus of this chapter, is an example of such a bottom-up approach, which is showing positive effects on cultural and linguistic reaffirmation.

THE SOCIOLINGUISTIC CONTEXT IN THE YUCATÁN PENINSULA

The use of Yucatec Maya (locally referred to simply as Maya) is still widespread, particularly in the interior of the peninsula. However, official censuses conducted every 10 years have consistently shown a trend toward people abandoning the use of Maya in favor of Spanish. Even though censuses should be interpreted cautiously due to their limitations and ideological biases (Khubchandani 2001), it is beyond question that both the absolute number of speakers of

Maya and its percentage within the total population are gradually decreasing in the three states of the peninsula. In the last two decades, percentages of Maya speakers have sharply dropped, from 33 to 22 per cent in Yucatán state, 19 to 9 per cent in Quintana Roo, and 13 to 7 per cent in Campeche (INEGI 2020). Although some institutional support has been given to Maya language planning, focusing especially on standardization and dissemination of written norms, neither federal agencies such as INALI and the National Institute for Indigenous People (INPI) nor regional ones, for instance INDEMAYA (Institute for the Development of Maya Culture) in Yucatán state, have developed any significant projects aiming at tackling the causes of Maya language loss in the region.

Despite this reduction in numbers of Maya speakers, over 760,000 people still use Maya. Rates of bilingualism and high vitality are common in a contiguous inland area of the peninsula bordering the states of Yucatán and Quintana Roo. Moreover, levels of Maya language retention and self-ascription to the status of Indigenous person are prominent in this central area, where the people I interviewed live (Bracamonte and Lizama 2008). While the expression of social identity and labels for self-identification are complex in this region (Rhodes and Bloechl 2020), a process of ethnogenesis seems to be emerging. That means that the word *Maya* as a marker of social and ethnic identity is increasingly being used and appropriated by activists working toward cultural and linguistic revitalization (Guerrettaz 2020). Indeed, as in many other contexts of ongoing language shift to Spanish or to other dominant languages, the sense of urgency to act upon language loss has spurred a significant number of grassroots, but unconnected, initiatives and cultural mobilization in the Yucatán. Apart from a continuous creation of literature in Maya with a rich tradition in the region, bottom-up efforts, often led by committed individuals, have expanded the use of Maya in new domains, such as audiovisual productions, online newspapers, radio stations, and the dissemination of materials for Maya language learning on social media.

In the following sections I present and analyze the language practices and ideologies of some young rappers in the region who form part of the ADN Maya collective. This is a **community of practice** of bilingual young adults from Yucatán and Quintana Roo states who are singing both in Maya and Spanish, showcasing the importance of the activism of young people in grassroots cultural and language revitalization efforts through the arts.

RAP *ORIGINARIO* AND ADN MAYA

The production of different modern musical genres such as rock, reggae, and rap in Indigenous languages, or **lenguas originarias**, a widely used term in Latin America, has been flourishing and expanding throughout the continent in recent years. In Mexico a fertile musical field has emerged strongly with an increasing number of rappers who include Indigenous languages in their performances as a form of sociopolitical activism and cultural recognition. In the Yucatán Peninsula hip-hop has become a particularly salient cultural movement. There is now an established network of some 25 rappers that has grown out of the foundation of ADN Maya in 2015 around the town of Felipe Carrillo Puerto in Quintana Roo. This initiative has given rise to other local groups in that area such as Tihorappers Crew and Zona Maya Jo'otsúuk, both based in Tihosuco. While all these rappers live in rural locations, they are not geographically isolated because traveling to cities, such as Mérida or Cancún, is part of the daily life of many Yucatecans living in small villages. Their situation, however, stands in sharp contrast with other geographical settings in Latin America where, due to migration, young Indigenous rappers have settled in the peripheries of big cities.

If we think of hip-hop as a primarily urban music genre, it may seem remarkable that in the Yucatán this movement has emerged most strongly in small towns and villages of the center of the peninsula, but this is precisely the area where the Maya language enjoys relatively high vitality, despite an ongoing shift to Spanish, and where it is still present in the family and community spheres.

ADN Maya as a Community of Practice

After intermittent fieldwork in the Yucatán since 2008, I have recently been in touch with young Maya activists to follow their artistic work and their commitment to revitalize their Indigenous languages. The following excerpts are part of recent online interviews carried out with some of them during the spring of 2021. Pat Boy, a pioneer who started rapping in Maya in 2009 at the age of 18, is the founder of ADN Maya and one of the driving forces in the promotion of cultural production in Maya in the peninsula. As he recounts, "The idea of the collective is to work with artists for a year, to help them create songs, make an album, record a video in a professional way, go to festivals, events, share workshops on body expression, rhythm and rhyme structures and all of that." The collective has produced dozens of video clips that are then disseminated through social media. Their YouTube channel, ADN Maya Films, has over 8,600 subscribers and 1.7 million views as of June 2022. Conceived as a seedbed for new artists who may later become professional artists, since 2015 the collective has produced the work of over 20 Maya rappers. One such example is Balaam Ich, a rapper in his late twenties who is now a member of Zona Maya Jo'otsúuk. As he recalls,

> The name Balaam Ich was given to me when I joined the ADN collective. It was a very good experience. I was looking for invitations to events, when I saw someone go on stage, I thought it would be nice to express what I felt and that's why I joined that collective and gained experience and composed five songs.

Pat Boy and Balaam Ich's reflections attest to the power of the arts as a means to express Maya youth's feelings and to the value of the collective as a productive space for empowerment and potential professionalization. Some other young rappers, such as Dino Chan, El Chepe, or Yaalen K'uj, have also uploaded videos on YouTube, which have gathered over hundreds of thousands of views. For example, the song *Ki'imak in wool – Estoy contento* by Tihorappers had over half a million views on YouTube by the end of 2021. Notably, these videos receive overwhelmingly favorable comments. Expressions of admiration and praise are common and include phrases such as "*está chingón, está padrísimo, se me erizó la piel, está genial*" (it's awesome, it's amazing, it gave me goosebumps, it's great). These comments point to the positive impact these songs can generate, including changing negative attitudes toward Indigenous languages not only within Maya communities but also among the mainstream population (Cru 2018).

As for the content of the rappers' songs, romantic themes are frequent. A prominent example is "*In watech' tu lakal – decirte todo*," a song performed by four of the collective's rappers that has over 140,000 views on YouTube. Also salient is the presence of themes in their songs that appeal to roots, origin, territory, and the importance of nature – in other words, to the daily life in a Mayan village. These themes underpin a process of strengthening ethnic identity in which the revitalization of the Maya language plays a key part. For example, the chorus of the Maya song "*Este es mi pueblo Kantemo, Yuc*" (This is my village Kantemo, Yuc) by Dino Chan says:

Here is our village, and here is where we were born
Here is our village, and here is where we grew up
Here is our village and here we try to make a living
We go to work in the forest at the break of day

This call to the birthplace, the home village, and nature is unsurprising if we consider these artistic creations against the backdrop of migration (to urban centers in the peninsula, other parts of Mexico, and the United States) as a common phenomenon affecting Maya people.

Language wise, the appropriation of rap by these young men, with its emphasis on verbal fluency, rhythm, and rhyme can help a process of reacquisition and overcome the linguistic insecurity that is often common among speakers of **minoritized languages**. As Pat Boy points out, "Yaalen K'uj, an artist who has excelled a lot, when he entered ADN Maya he did not speak much Maya, mainly only Spanish, and with the workshops, with the rehearsals, he began to learn Maya and now he flows well, and he even greets you in Maya. He has had an interest in learning more Maya thanks to rap." Joining the collective, therefore, has a positive impact not only on the linguistic proficiency in Maya of some rappers, but also on their attitudes toward speaking the language.

Moreover, the ubiquitous use of digital technologies creates networks that facilitate knowledge and collaboration between artists and the dissemination of their work to the public through well-known and easily accessible global platforms such as YouTube, Facebook, or Spotify. Collaboration is growing among Maya rappers, as well as between artists who speak different Mexican Indigenous languages, for instance the recent video clip "*Nxetunta – Festejamos*" by Pat Boy (Maya) and Mixe Represent (Ayuujk) released in 2021.

ADN Maya has also participated in fruitful projects of cultural revitalization with Mexican academic institutions and anthropologists. One recent example is the undertaking of setting to music riddles, tongue twisters, and traditional stories in Maya (e.g., *Trabalenguas y consejas en lengua maya – K'ak'alt'aano'ob yéetel tsolxikino'ob ich maaya t'aan*). This is a commendable effort of cultural rescue through rap, which has also been a productive linguistic exercise for the rappers, by practicing pronunciation and learning new vocabulary in Maya. Pat Boy elaborates again on the rappers' different language proficiency in Maya and on how language learning becomes a collaborative process based on scaffolding:

> With time the boys are learning more Maya and it flows better, for example those who mainly speak Maya, like Dino Chan. When he started rapping, he could not converse much in Spanish, his village is very isolated and the Maya essence there is still preserved and when the boys do not know a word, some have 40 or 50 per cent of Maya, they ask each other, sometimes there are different words between Yucatán and Quintana Roo and with these workshops we learn a lot besides creating a network of good friends.

In contrast with the case of Yaalen K'uj, who was not very comfortable speaking Maya, Pat Boy stresses here the role of Dino Chan in the collective as an informal "teacher" of Maya thanks to his strong competence in the language. Similarly, in this context the linguistic proficiency of Maya elders becomes a valuable resource, and it is not uncommon for these young rappers to reconnect with their grandparents to reactivate, in some cases, a process of learning Maya that was interrupted in childhood.

As Dino Chan's song above illustrates, using a sort of **strategic essentialism**, rap celebrates ethnic pride and underpins local and regional identity, a task further achieved by a conscious branding of the project by the collective, obvious in the name *ADN* Maya (DNA Maya) or *Sangre* Maya (Mayan blood) and by rapping exclusively in Maya or by creating bilingual songs in which both Spanish and the Indigenous language are used side by side (Cru 2017). In this way, choosing to sing in Maya gives this Indigenous language a strongly symbolic and counterhegemonic role that contests entrenched ideologies favoring monolingualism in Spanish.

Furthermore, these examples show that verbal fluency and creativity in rap fits smoothly with Indigenous cultures in which orality is generally favored as a form of cultural expression. Spontaneity, informality, creativeness, and self-expression are crucial aspects in these practices, in contrast to an overemphasis of top-down official policies on the standardization of languages and on literacy as the central axis of formal Indigenous education.

Maya Rappers' Interventions in Language Pedagogy

The playful and educational possibilities of rap have led some artists to develop educational initiatives to encourage interest in Indigenous languages and to promote their learning. This includes a workshop supported by the Mexican Secretary of Culture program *Alas y Raíces* (Wings and Roots) in which children are encouraged to engage with Maya through rap. Pat Boy explains the workshop:

> In the village where we gave the workshop, Itzincab, the 20 or so children who signed up, unlike their parents, couldn't speak or understand Maya, but with our workshop they were really engaged and became interested in learning some phrases and saying some things in Maya. The children told me that when they got home, they would ask their parents: "How do you say this?" and when we saw the parents they said, "You know what? My child started to learn Maya." And the parents were already calling me *maestro* (teacher). Also, we taught them about our traditions and culture. They saw how you can be an artist and sing in Maya and leave the community and travel as I have done.

Pat Boy's quote illustrates how Itzincab, located on the outskirts of Mérida, exemplifies a community in which the shift to Spanish has progressed to such an extent that parents are not passing on the Maya language to their children.

Two important related topics in this quote are worth highlighting. First, the workshop triggered children's interest in learning Maya, even if in a tokenistic way. Second, it presented a positive example of what a young Maya person is capable of, counteracting widespread negative stereotypes associated with Maya speakers, such as "being backward," "having a rural occupation," or "being stuck in the community." As a result of the workshop, a video clip summarizing the project called "*Mi Pueblo* (My Village) Itzincab Yucatán, Featuring Dj Rakalku & Pat Boy" was created and is available on YouTube. Due to the COVID-19 pandemic, in 2020 the children's workshop project by Pat Boy, now entitled *Rap Ich Máaya* (Rap in Maya), moved online and began to be delivered using WhatsApp. The ways in which hip-hop can support critical and alternative pedagogies and decolonial approaches to education has been explored by scholars who recognize the limitations and shortcomings of top-down educational policies for the promotion of Indigenous languages and cultures in Mexico and beyond (Llanque Zonta and Tejerina Vargas 2017).

Rap and Political Mobilization

Although social claims may appear in some of the ADN collective songs, these efforts have not translated into active political mobilization in the Yucatán, despite the distinctive cultural character of the peninsula and a conflictive regional history of integration within Mexico, especially during the nineteenth century. Political demands are rare among these young people, even if constant environmental threats derived from tourism and the pressures it exerts on the territory in southern Mexico are multiplying (see the case of the so-called Maya train project, a proposed 1,525-kilometer intercity railway that would traverse the Yucatán

Peninsula). In other words, the Maya rap movement in Yucatán is integrated within the framework of the nation-state without questioning the consequences of Mexican nationalism for the rights of Indigenous peoples. This approach stands in stark contrast to other contexts in Latin America, where hip-hop has become both a platform for the expression of marginalized voices and a tool for political vindication. For some highly politicized rappers in other places, hip-hop is a key component in a broader social struggle, going beyond the search for linguistic and cultural recognition by incorporating demands for autonomy and self-determination (c.f. Sancho and Rossi 2020, Mapuche rappers in Chile; Nascimento 2018, Guaraní rappers in Brazil).

CONCLUSION

The political nature of rap with a focus on fighting racism and discrimination has inspired Indigenous youth who see these phenomena reflected in their own communities. Considering the example of ADN Maya, the local appropriation and re-creation of hip-hop as a global, popular, and attractive movement for young people can help to counteract the discriminatory and unjustified association of Indigenous languages with cultural backwardness and supposed inability to express modernity. The expansion and adaptation of minoritized languages to new spheres of life, which in this case stem from a fruitful interweaving of digital technologies and the choice of a "cool" musical form, is a fundamental aspect in any revitalization process. The goal of rapping in Maya is, in brief, to use rap proactively as a strategy to destigmatize languages that have been historically marginalized and devalued by homogenizing national language policies. My ethnographic research with ADN Maya indicates that rap, together with other musical genres, will continue to blossom throughout the Americas among Indigenous youth as a tool for artistic expression and creativity, as well as resistance and protest to the widespread oppression and racism that Indigenous peoples continue to suffer.

REFLECTION AND DISCUSSION QUESTIONS

- What are the possibilities and limitations of expanding the use of Latin American Indigenous languages through new media and technology for revitalization purposes? What are two examples from this chapter that demonstrate these strengths and weaknesses?
- What are the issues surrounding the use of strategic essentialism in contexts of widespread linguistic and cultural hybridity and mixing (*mestizaje*)?
- What are some other examples of ways in which music has played a key role in struggles for social justice and human rights?

KEY CONCEPTS

- **community of practice**: Groups of people who share a concern or a passion for something they do and learn how to do it better as they regularly interact with one another.
- **language revitalization**: An intentional process aimed at giving new life and vigor to a language that has been decreasing in use (or has ceased to be used altogether). Efforts often concentrate on bringing the language into new contexts of use and creating new speakers. Other closely related terms include *reversing language shift*, *language reclamation*, and *language revival*.
- *lengua originaria* **(Native/Indigenous language)**: The term *originaria* in Spanish emphasizes that these languages are originary, a descriptor that avoids the negative connotations that are often associated with the terms *Indigenous* and *indigeneity* in general. As a result, this term is often favored by speakers of Indigenous languages themselves.
- **minoritized language**: The term *minoritized* instead of *minority* underlines how inequities in social and political power create dominant and subordinate relations among speakers of different languages.
- **strategic essentialism**: A political strategy in which minoritized groups, nationalities, or ethnic communities mobilize, based on shared gender, cultural, or political identity, to bring forward their group identity in a unified way to achieve certain goals, such as equal rights.

EXPLORE FURTHER

- To learn more about activism surrounding language and Indigenous ethnic identity, read **Chapter 7**.
- To learn more about the ways in which music can express a community's values, read **Chapter 27**.
- To learn more about the significance of material culture such as literature, art, film, and theater for marginalized communities in Latin America and the Caribbean, read **Chapters 14, 20, 21, 24**, and **36**.
- ADN Maya Films YouTube Channel. https://tinyurl.com/ADN-Maya-Films.
- Estación Jaylli. *Cantos y Voces Plurales* (podcast). https://tinyurl.com/Estacion-Jaylli.
- Olko, Justyna, and Julia Sallabank, eds. 2021. *Revitalizing Endangered Languages: A Practical Guide*. Cambridge: Cambridge University Press.
- Terkourafi, Marina, ed. 2010. *The Languages of Global Hip Hop*. London: Bloomsbury-Continuum.
- Wyman, Leisy T., Teresa L. McCarty, and Sheila E. Nicholas, eds. 2014. *Indigenous Youth and Multilingualism: Language Identity, Ideology, and Practice in Dynamic Cultural Worlds*. New York: Routledge.

ABOUT THE AUTHOR

Josep Cru is a senior lecturer in the Department of Spanish, Portuguese, and Latin American Studies of Newcastle University. His research interests cover language policy and planning in the Hispanic world, particularly in Mexico, Chile, and Spain, more specifically looking at language revitalization efforts from the grassroots that involve music, new technologies, and linguistic activism among youth. He is also a member of Linguapax, an international NGO based in Barcelona that promotes language diversity worldwide (www.linguapax.org).

REFERENCES

Bracamonte, Pedro, and Jesús Lizama. 2008. *Tocando Fondo. Resultados Preliminares de la Encuesta sobre Marginalidad, Pobreza e Identidad del Pueblo Maya de Yucatán*. Mérida: Ciesas.

Cru, Josep. 2017. "Bilingual Rapping in Yucatán, Mexico: Strategic Choices for Maya Language Legitimation and Revitalisation." *International Journal of Bilingual Education and Bilingualism* 20 (5): 481–96. https://doi.org/10.1080/13670050.2015.1051945.

———. 2018. "Micro-Level Language Planning and YouTube Comments: Destigmatising Indigenous Languages through Rap Music." *Current Issues in Language Planning* 19 (4): 434–52. https://doi.org/10.1080/14664208.2018.1468960.

Guerrettaz, Anne M. 2020. "'We Are the *Mayas*': Indigenous Language Revitalization, Identification, and Postcolonialism in the Yucatán, Mexico." *Linguistics and Education* 58 (3): 1–16. https://doi.org/10.1016/j.linged.2019.100765.

INEGI (Instituto Nacional de Estadística y Geografía). 2020. "Censo Nacional de 2020." https://www.inegi.org.mx/temas/lengua.

Khubchandani, Lachman. 2001. "Linguistic Census." In *Language in the Media. Representations, Identities, Ideologies Concise Encyclopedia of Sociolinguistics*, edited by Rajend Mesthrie, 648–50. Amsterdam: Elsevier Science.

Llanque Zonta, Víctor E., and Verónica S. Tejerina Vargas. 2017. "The Contributions of Hip-Hop Artists to Non-Formal Intercultural Education in Bolivia." In *Indigenous Education Policy, Equity, and Intercultural Understanding in Latin America*, edited by Regina Cortina, 103–19. New York: Palgrave Macmillan.

Nascimento, André M. 2018. "Counter-Hegemonic Linguistic Ideologies and Practices in Brazilian Indigenous Rap." In *The Sociolinguistics of Hip-Hop as Critical Conscience*, edited by Andrew S. Ross and Damian J. Rivers, 213–35. New York: Palgrave Macmillan.

Rhodes, Catherine R., and Christopher Bloechl. 2020. "Speaking Maya, Being Maya: Ideological and Institutional Mediations of Language in Contemporary Yucatan." In *Handbook of the Changing World Language Map*, edited by Stanley D. Brunn and Roland Kehrein, 861–83. Switzerland: Spinger Nature.

Sancho, Naomi, and Alejandro Rossi. 2020. *Los Nietos de Lautaro Tomando el Micrófono: Sonoridad y Rap Mapuche*. Chile: Puño y Letra.

CHAPTER FOURTEEN

Kreyòl in Cuba: Writing Resistance, Affirming Haitian Heritage

Mariana F. Past

In June 2018, while participating in the Caribbean Studies Association conference in Havana, Cuba, as a scholar of Caribbean literature, I had the opportunity to attend an unforgettable panel in **Kreyòl** (Haitian Creole) and Spanish.[1] A tall man who introduced himself as Hilario Batista Félix extended the audience a warm welcome in Kreyòl. He wore a straw hat typical of Cuban *guajiros* (farmers), along with a crisp white guayabera shirt traditionally worn by Cuban men. In a voice as soft-spoken as it was dynamic, Batista read selections from his 2017 bilingual collection *Nostalji san pwen ni vigil: pwezi kreyòl nan peyi Kiba / Nostalgia sin puntos ni comas: poesía criolla en Cuba* (*Unbroken Nostalgia: Kreyòl Poetry in Cuba*; translation mine; Batista 2017; Figure 14.1). Afterwards, Batista's daughter Nathalie Batista Puente sang a captivating rendition of the popular song "*Viejo*" while accompanying herself on guitar, wearing a white dress with a red sash (commonly worn in Cuba and associated with the Revolution). The song evoked Jacques Roumain's (1944) novel *Gouverneurs de la rosée* (*Masters of the Dew*) about the impact of Haitian emigration to Cuba. In any case, the large audience was visibly moved by both performances, as was I. Batista concluded with some remarks about Kreyòl and the Haitian-Cuban community, and he invited everyone to attend a cultural event later that week. As Batista distributed flyers to those departing, announcing a robust schedule of Kreyòl programming on Radio Havana, I became determined to learn more about him, his work, and Cuba's Haitian community, which I had briefly encountered during a research trip to Cuba's eastern region and during the 2015 Festival del Caribe in Santiago de Cuba.

---

1 Standardized in 1979, Kreyòl was not recognized as an official language (alongside French) in Haiti until 1987. Some scholars (Jonassaint 2021) prefer the terms *Haitian language* or *Haitian* over Kreyòl; in their opinion, the latter reduces the status of the Haitian tongue, delegitimizing it.

Figure 14.1. Haitian-Cuban poet Hilario Batista Félix, shown on the cover of his collection *Nostalji san pwen ni vigil / Nostalgia sin puntos ni comas* (*Unbroken Nostalgia*; English translation mine). Photo by Joe O'Neil.

Since the 2018 conference Batista and I have interacted regularly; we are currently collaborating on several scholarly projects. He extended me an invitation to a Haitian cultural festival in Cuba in 2020, which was unfortunately canceled due to the COVID-19 pandemic. Since circumstances precluded in-person encounters, our communications continued via WhatsApp video and email, with Batista using Wi-Fi hotspots in a park near his home in Havana. Students in my senior seminar (at Dickinson College in Carlisle, Pennsylvania) read his book *Nostalji* (*Nostalgia*) in Spanish translation. They happily purchased the book directly from its author, who had 20 copies mailed to me from Port-au-Prince in a neat, hand-lettered package wrapped in white paper, sporting 60 colorful postage stamps. As we explored the themes in *Nostalji,* and Batista thoughtfully responded (via email) to the students' questions, I saw first-hand how he offers valuable insights into Latin American and Caribbean culture and history. Batista embodies Cuba's cultural and linguistic diversity by claiming and celebrating the heritage, identity, and presence of many fellow Haitians in Cuba. This chapter reflects an early stage of my engagement with Batista, his writing, and his linguistic and cultural activism.

HAITIANS IN CUBA

Given its proximity to Haiti, Cuba is a major site of the Haitian **diaspora**.[2] The green Sierra Maestra mountains of *Oriente* (the eastern region) lie 30 miles from Haiti. Today there are more flights between Santiago de Cuba (the island's second largest city) in Oriente and Port-au-Prince, the capital of Haiti, than to Havana, Cuba's capital. Haiti's substantial influence on Oriente dates back centuries. During the Haitian Revolution, French colonists fled to Santiago de Cuba with their enslaved human property (many of whom knew specialized crafts), leaving lasting traces in Santiago in the form of coffee plantations and French-named streets. Migration intensified from the late 1870s through the 1950s, when US political, military, and economic power played a central role in Caribbean affairs and the United Fruit Company brought thousands of Haitians to Cuba to harvest sugar cane. Other laborers were recruited to work on railways. Matthew Casey (2017) notes that by 1940 "approximately 200,000 Haitians migrated seasonally and permanently to eastern Cuba" (3). Casey's project outlines the migratory patterns that emerged, along with the fears and racial prejudices against Haitian migrants that set in. Over time, Haitians' presence in Oriente became permanent, and tight-knit communities developed where Kreyòl was spoken and Vodou, Haiti's popular religion, practices were maintained (see Chapter 6).

In Cuba, Havana dominates as a center of political authority and cultural production. Oriente – where the early stages of Cuba's 1959 Revolution were led by Fidel Castro and Che Guevara – is widely considered a remote and distinctly different region. Cuban and foreign scholars have explored the complexities of the island's culture and society using Cuban anthropologist Fernando Ortiz's (1940) metaphor of an *ajiaco* (stew) of contrasting cultures, languages, and ethnicities. The ingredients of this "stew" have drawn unequal levels of attention. Historians, sociologists, anthropologists, and musicologists have studied Cuba's African, Chinese, pan-Caribbean, and Indigenous heritages, including spiritual and folkloric dance

---

2 The global Haitian diaspora comprises over 2 million people today. While Haitians have emigrated in search of better labor and living conditions for well over a century, the largest exodus to date occurred during the father/son dictatorships of François and Jean-Claude Duvalier (1957–1986), when a great number of Haitians from all backgrounds fled to the United States, Canada, and France, as well as to other Caribbean nations including the Bahamas and Cuba (Zéphir 2004).

practices shaping ideas of nationhood, race, citizenship, and belonging (Bodenheimer 2015). But questions of regionalism and racism are less frequently addressed.

Yanique Hume (2011) observes:

> Paradoxically, whereas Santiago and the eastern region of Cuba is often acknowledged as being the cultural home and cradle of the Cuban nation, the administrative center of Havana and the west becomes the face of the nation, the Cuba the world sees and knows. Furthermore, in Cuba's plural society the rural hinterlands are marked as racially, ethnically, and culturally Other ... As a direct consequence of this, the descendants of Afro-Caribbean immigrants, although born and reared in Cuba, are often not recognized as being a constitutive element of the nation. (75)

For many Cubans, the Oriente – where political revolutions have tended to emerge – connotes poverty, backwardness, radicalism, and unrest. Oriente is also associated with Africa, Blackness, and waves of Haitian migration, and the region has long suffered economic and social neglect (Bodenheimer 2015). Although Fidel Castro famously declared that "there is no racism in Cuba," and the first decades of Cuba's Socialist Revolution indeed ushered in positive changes to Black Cubans' lives, racism persists (see Chapter 4), and members of the Haitian community have kept low profiles to avoid discrimination and mistreatment.

Despite this social marginalization, "over 400,000 Cubans either speak [Kreyòl] fluently, understand it but speak with difficulty, or have at least some familiarity with the language, [mainly in the eastern provinces. There] are also communities in Ciego de Avila and Camaguey provinces where the population still maintains Creole, their mother tongue" (Hurlich 1998). Radio Havana today broadcasts several Kreyòl language and news programs, directed by Batista (who previously worked in the field of education). While there is scant official census information about Haitians in Cuba, Hurlich indicates that Guantánamo province has historically been the country's primary region for Haitian residents and descendants, with approximately 45,000 descendants of Haitians and 4,000 native Haitians residing there.

Batista confirmed this ambiguity (via email):

> In Cuba it is not easy to know the number of Haitians or Creole speakers in the island according to a census, but there are estimates that there are roughly 4,000 Cubans who preserve the Creole culture in different manifestations such as music, language, theater, religion, painting, cooking, etc. We estimate more than 1 million Cubans are of Haitian descent, up to four generations back. It should be noted that ... emigration began with the Haitian War of Independence, which meant that there was no control over Haitians entering Cuba from different regions of the country, and later during the following years, they changed their given, Haitian last names. There were also those who refused to give their family names and denied their roots as well.

These self-imposed customs of suppression and denial stem from patterns of **internalized racism** in Cuba, wherein people of color absorb and unconsciously perpetuate societal prejudices against themselves. These silences are what Batista's writing and linguistic activism seek to fill.

Also worth noting is that the Caribbean region has historically been taught and understood in terms of discrete, nationalistic blocks: "Anglophone," "Hispanophone," and "Francophone." Such categories reflect language distinctions rooted in colonial systems of power, as well as related gaps and silences that have effectively erased Haitians, Haiti's culture, and Kreyòl from the Caribbean intellectual map. For instance, O. Nigel Bolland's *The Birth of Caribbean Civilisation: A Century of Ideas about Culture and Identity, Nation and Society* (2004) includes no texts translated from Kreyòl – implicitly disregarding Haiti's majority language as a source of knowledge production (only 8–10 per cent of the population speaks French). Why is this problematic? The Kreyòl language and the Vodou religion were potent tools enabling masses of enslaved people within the former French colony of Saint-Domingue to carry out a revolution (1791–1804) and win independence from France, establishing the first Black republic in the Western Hemisphere. The new Republic of Haiti supported other Latin American independence movements, including efforts led by Simón Bolívar in Venezuela. Kreyòl has thus served as a language of resistance and a social force since the beginning of the colonial era, and it bears further development and recognition.

HILARIO BATISTA FÉLIX, HAITIAN-CUBAN CULTURAL ACTIVIST

Hilario Batista Félix is a Haitian-Cuban poet, journalist, and linguistic activist who currently lives in Havana. Born in 1955 in the Guantánamo province of Oriente, Batista identifies primarily – and proudly – as Haitian first, then as Cuban. He is a descendant of Haitian migrant workers from Cavaillon in Haiti's southern peninsula, who came to eastern Cuba in the mid-twentieth century as part of a large-scale migration of Caribbean laborers enticed by US-controlled sugar and coffee industries. When and if they returned to Haiti, migrant laborers were referred to as *viejos* (old timers), because they generally were absent for years at a time. Batista spent his childhood on sugar cane and coffee plantations inhabited by Haitians and their descendants in Guantánamo province. His mother tongue was not Spanish but Kreyòl, an essential language in the various homes where he lived. During his youth Batista attended various Christian churches and places of worship for the Vodou and Santería religions. Beside the other children who grew up in these *bateyes* (sugar industry–based communities), Batista actively listened to his elders share stories, testimonies, and dreams about Haiti in Kreyòl. Along with the Haitian language, their memories, cultural practices, and pieces of collective wisdom were transmitted from generation to generation but are largely absent from Cuba's official history. Over time Batista has gathered up these ideas and lived experiences to tell the story of a displaced people, foster pride in Haitian culture, and promote fluency in Kreyòl.

Batista has dedicated his life and work to advancing Haitian culture and Kreyòl as a celebration and assertion of Haitian identity and presence in Cuba. Kreyòl and Vodou have served as cohesive social forces and emblems of Haitianness since before Haiti's Revolution and War for Independence (1791–1804). French, Haiti's colonial language, has predominated in terms of power and prestige, with Kreyòl only being recognized as an official language in Haiti's 1987 Constitution. Meanwhile, Kreyòl is Cuba's second most-spoken language, and Batista stands as one of its most dynamic promoters through educational programs, news broadcasts, and writing. *Nostalji* (*Nostalgia*), his poetry collection, sheds light on the experiences of Haitian-Cuban communities and Afro-Caribbean peoples overall. By evoking Haiti's spiritual traditions and revolutionary legacy of 1804, *Nostalji* affirms Black agency while contesting enduring patterns of discrimination toward Haitians in Cuba and problems of internalized racism. Fundamentally, as we will see shortly, these poems convey a sense of longing for a shared heritage and homeland, a desire for belonging within the present, and a forceful commitment to anti-racist discourse.

BANNZIL KREYÒL KIBA: ADVANCING HAITIAN LANGUAGE AND CULTURE

Batista is the founder and president of Grupo Bannzil Kreyòl Kiba, a cultural organization formed in 1997 to help preserve, further develop, and diffuse Haitian language and foster regional integration of Haitian Cubans. He notes, "Bannzil incorporates the history of all those of us who were not only mocked for being Black descendants of Haitians, but also belittled for speaking Kreyòl in a different way, called *patois*." Batista proudly observes, "We have representation in almost all of Cuba, mainly in the east and center, from Guantánamo province to Santi Spiritus and also in the western areas of Havana and Matanzas, but we find Haitian descendants throughout Cuba." For 25 years Bannzil has held biannual festivals to celebrate and encourage the development of Kreyòl and Haitian culture in Cuba and beyond (the 2020 festival was postponed to 2022 due to the COVID-19 pandemic).

Bannzil's 2018 festival comprised a wide range of lectures, debates, theatrical and dance performances, and exhibitions featuring arts and music. Besides members of the Grupo Bannzil Kreyòl Kiba, organizers involved numerous Cuban cultural institutions (including the Dirección Municipal de Cultura and the Casa del Alba Cultural, alongside international nongovernmental organizations like UNESCO's Comisión Cubana. At other times Grupo Bannzil has collaborated with the Casa de Africa, the Casa del Alba Cultural, and Cuba's first Kreyòl library, founded in 1998 at the Fernando Aguado y Rico Polytechnic Center in Havana.

Besides hosting cultural festivals and smaller monthly gatherings, Bannzil also observes International Creole Day every October 28. Batista notes, "We organize a range of events featuring workshops, colloquia, festivals, symposia, etc." He has traveled widely to present his work (and to advance Bannzil's mission), visiting the United States, Canada, Martinique, Guadeloupe,

Curaçao, Germany, Austria, and Haiti. Notably, Batista was one of three writers highlighted on the poster for the week-long Festival Entènasyonal Literati Kreyòl (International Creole Literature Festival) in Haiti in December 2019. His main concern is to build community and establish networks: "I always meet with Haitians and make them aware of the presence of Haitian culture in Cuba. I [also] support the relations of the Haitian community in the Dominican Republic." In 2020, Haiti's government formally recognized Batista for his cultural activism within Cuba and the broader Haitian diaspora.

UNBROKEN NOSTALGIA: COLLECTIVE LONGING FOR HOMELAND

Batista's *Nostalji san pwen ni vigil: pwezi kreyòl nan peyi Kiba* (*Unbroken Nostalgia: Kreyòl Poetry in Cuba*) is the first book of Haitian verse composed in Cuba. The first edition was printed in Canada in 2016, and a second, bilingual version (*Nostalgia sin puntos ni comas: poesía criolla en Cuba*) was published in 2017 by Editions Caraïbe in Haiti, with translations by Nathalie Batista Puente, the poet's daughter. New translations are currently being prepared in German and English (the latter is my current project). Batista's writing reflects the distinct heritage of generations of Haitian Cubans, engaging themes of racial and cultural identity, language and language barriers, spiritual strength, love, and longing for the Haitian homeland. Woven throughout are the questions, traditions, and lamentations of people who rarely envisioned permanent migration to Cuba.

For example, the first poem, titled "Nostalgia," highlights the profound consequences of long-term separation but evokes a shared spiritual foundation. After hearing bad news from Haiti, the poetic voice laments:

> I want to go to the land of my ancestors
> but I don't know where to go …
> *Viejo* my parents have died
> I want to plant flowers on their graves
> before the weeds grow.

Following this admission of longing, loss, and uncertainty, a compelling secret comes out:

> my umbilical cord is buried at the foot of a mapou
> that's where I want to go back to die
> *Viejo* I'm speaking with God, Elegguá and Papa Legba
> They say we can go.

The mapou tree is a sacred tree in Haiti where the speaker was born, and his passage across the water is granted by leading spirits of both Vodou and Santería, popular religions of Haiti and Cuba, acknowledging a blended cultural and religious heritage.

Batista insists that Haiti and Cuba are "*como dos hermanos*" (like two brothers). The bilingual version of his book embodies that idea. Perhaps most importantly, in a poem called "Pichón" the poet claims the validity of his multiple subjectivities:

Algunas veces me hierve la sangre
Cuando te escucho decir que no eres haitiano
Qué tiene el otro mejor que tú
Para qué estés diciendo: yo no entiende eso
Señores es hora de que comprendan que están en un error
Negando a sus padres y a sus raíces
Escucha lo que te digo tu cabeza pasua es de haitianos
Nuestra bemba es bemba de haitianos
Y lo peor estás diciendo que tu papá es francés
Qué coño francés
Dame tus manos y abre la garganta gritemos juntos
Para que en los 4 puntos cardinales nos escuchen sí fui haitiano soy haitiano y seré haitiano (12)

Sometimes my blood boils
When I hear you say you're not Haitian
that other people are better than you
Why are you saying: *I don't understand*
Friends it's time to recognize your mistake
Negating your fathers and their roots
Listen to what I tell you
Your nappy head is Haitian
Our lips are Haitian lips
And the worst is when you say your father's French
What the hell French
Give me your hands and open your throat and let's shout together
so they hear us across the four cardinal directions
yes I was Haitian I am Haitian and I will be Haitian [*translation mine*]

The speaker in this poem confronts – head-on – a fellow Haitian who pretends not to know Kreyòl, thereby rejecting his African origins and favoring the cultural model of France, Haiti's former colonizer. Such tendencies exemplify internalized racism, which the speaker corrects by embracing his interlocutor in solidarity and proclaiming their mutual, enduring Haitian identity – though they live in Cuba – marked by the use of past, present, and future verb tenses.

Nostalji challenges conventional ideas of citizenship, belonging, and diaspora by blurring distinctions between "here" and "there," affirming a dual homeland, and emphasizing "brother" instead of "other." The collection upholds Black agency by evoking Haiti's spiritual traditions and revolutionary legacy, simultaneously contesting enduring patterns of discrimination toward Haitians in Cuba and problems of internalized racism. *Nostalji* puts forward ideas, images, and feelings that resonate with Haitians around the world, serving as a kind of spiritual and psychological anchor. Batista's writing thus creates bridges to the global Haitian community, conveying and encouraging pride in Haiti's homeland and history, aspirations for fuller recognition and inclusion, and a strong stance against racism.

Batista's title, which translates literally as "Nostalgia without periods or commas," suggests an ongoing state of longing. The images, references, and recollections in the poems defy punctuation and periodization, highlighting continuity over specific historical moments. Batista's collection points back toward Haiti's revolutionary history, but also forward, knitting together and strengthening existing networks of Haitians within and beyond Cuba. The poet is both a product of global capitalist flows and ardently resistant to them; his priority is to engender pride in Haiti and its heritage. Batista's work in many ways articulates the "other side" of a significant chapter in Caribbean history, that of the racialization and exploitation of Haitian labor in the service of global capital.

Because Haiti's poorly paid labor force has historically represented the country's main resource, Haitian migrant workers have been one of the largest groups circulating within the Caribbean and Latin America – which has often benefited US corporations (Álvarez Estévez and Guzmán Pascual 2008). Casey (2017) argues that US political, military, and economic dominance was a central theme in early twentieth-century Caribbean affairs (in particular, the 1915–1934 American Occupation of Haiti and the United Fruit Company), yet the "empire" remained uneven, and workers from varying national backgrounds were received and perceived differently according to notions of race. The introduction of Haitian migrants to Cuba

> in many cases … inflamed racist discourses that had previously been applied to Cubans of African descent. One of these [discourses] equated Haitians' and Cubans' African religious practices with savagery and cannibalism. Journalists and social scientists proclaimed the incompatibility of African religious practices with civilized society. They were also concerned that these religious rites required practitioners to sacrifice small children. (9)

Batista's *Nostalji* contests such nefarious discourses about Haiti that circulated through the nineteenth and twentieth centuries. For example, in the closing poem, "*No olvides mi nombre*" ("Don't forget my name"), the poetic voice declares: "*de Cuba salí y les juro siete veces que no vine a comer los hijos de nadie.*" (I came from Cuba / and I swear seven times over that I didn't come here to eat anyone's children.)

Other poems address specific tragedies involving Haitian migrants that Batista either witnessed or heard about from others. He shared the troubling details with me (via email):

> This is a testimony, a story, a reality of many Haitians, Cubans and many others who have left their homes, families, countries for one reason or another, and must emigrate. Many

unfortunately lost their lives, in the case of Cuba. Thousands of Haitians have perished en route from Cuba's Guantánamo to the United States, and the Bahamas as well ... Yes, this has happened in many places around here. Many Haitians seeking to leave their country have died like beasts in the water.

Beyond physical tragedy, the suppression of language is another form of violence. Confronting such violence demands restoring linguistic heritage. Throughout *Nostalji*, Batista defends and promotes the use and development of Kreyòl. At one point he chides a *compadre* who addresses him in French; this resonates with contemporary debates over education and access within Haiti, where French remains the language of power:

Compadre por favor no hable francés conmigo
Quiero que hables en Kreyòl
El verdadero Kreyòl
Te pido disculpas pero es hora que hablemos nuestro lindo Kreyòl
Compadre no te enojes conmigo
Verás que comprenderé mejor tus lindas palabras pero
Dímelas en Kreyòl (51)

Compadre please don't speak French with me
I want you to speak in Kreyòl
real Kreyòl
I beg your pardon but it's time we spoke
our beautiful Kreyòl
Compadre don't get mad at me
you'll see that I'll understand your nice words better
but speak to me in Kreyòl [*translation mine*]

Politely but powerfully, these lines reject Haiti's colonial language and assert the legitimacy of Haiti's mother tongue, which is understood by all Haitians at home and a majority in the global diaspora.

Insofar as an audience is concerned, Batista notes that *Nostalji* is not only for Haitians, but "for all those who have to leave their country for one reason or another and hope to return." He dedicates his book to "the thousands and thousands of Haitians and their living or dead descendants who wander the world." Batista subsequently wrote to me, "Once again we thank you for all the historical work you are doing to help *Nostalji* ... which is still under the thicket, in the Cane Factory, being born ... [This] widespread nostalgia, it is in the souls of many people. There is no Haitian ... on the planet who is not connected with these stories, dreams, memories, jokes. Everyone who reads these poems, like it or not, is struck with nostalgia."

CONCLUSION: KREYÒL LANGUAGE AND POETRY AS RESISTANCE

Given the persistent difficulties suffered by Haitians at home, due to economic circumstances, political challenges, and destruction wrought by climate change, Haiti's diaspora appears likely to continue growing – within the Caribbean, certainly, and in new areas of Latin America including Brazil and Chile, for example, where many Haitians fled following the devastating 2010 earthquake. The assassination of Haitian president Jovenel Moïse in July 2021 has brought additional turmoil and instability to Haiti. Amidst the global COVID-19 pandemic jobs disappeared worldwide, and thousands of Haitians within Latin America who migrated north were detained at the US–Mexico border and ultimately deported to a country they barely knew. Since Haiti's Revolution, the Americas' first Black republic has remained marginalized and misrepresented within the modern world system.

In response to the reductive, exploitative images of Haiti that circulated within the international media following the 2010 tragedy, Haitian American anthropologist Gina Athena Ulysse (2015) called for "new narratives" to be created in the language that all Haitians speak. Batista's work answers that call, amplifying and broadening the possibilities for recognition and identification within the Caribbean, Latin America, and the global Haitian diaspora. *Nostalji* offers an important counterdiscourse and a valuable teaching tool, compellingly showing how legacies of prejudice, oppression, and internalized racism can be contested through verse. Simultaneously, Bannzil shows the value of cultural and linguistic activism for strengthening Haitian communities within Cuba, the Caribbean region, and worldwide.

Haiti and Cuba hold a close relationship, and – especially in Oriente – their histories are inextricably linked. Kreyòl is a vibrant mode of creation and innovation, an effective tool to wield in the continuous process of reframing Haiti and Haitians not as "exceptional" people defying reason and understanding (Trouillot 1990), but as capable, legitimate global citizens in the face of entrenched prejudices and misunderstandings.

REFLECTION AND DISCUSSION QUESTIONS

- What aspects of Hilario Batista's life and work most surprise you? In what ways does this case study coincide with, and/or challenge, what you previously understood about Cuba? Haiti? The Caribbean?
- How does Batista depict Haitian-Cuban identity? What kind of audience(s) does Batista address in *Nostalji*? What is he writing "for" and "against"?
- Literary critics generally agree that the genre of poetry lends itself to expressing things that are difficult to convey through other means. To what degree do you think poetry such as Batista's can help disrupt negative discourses surrounding Haiti and Haitians? How might it serve as a force for social and political change?

- What similarities and differences can you identify between Haitian migration to Cuba and the experiences of immigrants coming to your home country?

KEY CONCEPTS

- **diaspora**: A dispersed population with shared origins in a particular geographic locale (e.g., the African diaspora, the Jewish diaspora).
- **internalized racism**: A phenomenon wherein people of color absorb and unconsciously perpetuate societal prejudices against themselves.
- **Kreyòl (Haitian Creole)**: The name of the majority language spoken in Haiti.
- *Nostalji* **(Nostalgia)**: A concept that references a shared history and homeland; in the context of this chapter it's the land of Haiti, which many Haitian Cubans collectively long for, but few can actually remember (if they ever traveled there at all).

EXPLORE FURTHER

- To learn more about Haitians in the Haitian diaspora and in Haiti, read **Chapters 6** and **25**.
- To learn more about the significance of material culture such as music, art, film, and theater for marginalized communities in Latin America and the Caribbean, read **Chapters 13**, **20**, **21**, **24**, **27**, and **36**.
- Apter, Andrew, and Derby, Lauren, eds. 2010. *Activating the Past: History and Memory in the Black Atlantic World*. Cambridge: Cambridge Scholars Publishing.
- Delatour, Mario, dir. 2013. *Kafé Negro*.
- Mondesir, Esery, dir. 2018. *Una Sola Sangre*.
- Moore, Carlos. 2008. *Pichón: Race and Revolution in Castro's Cuba, A Memoir*. Chicago: Chicago Review Press.

ABOUT THE AUTHOR

Mariana F. Past is an associate professor of Spanish and current chair of Latin American, Latinx, and Caribbean Studies at Dickinson College in Carlisle, Pennsylvania. Her research focuses on issues related to migration/exile, Haitian–Dominican relations, and representations of the Haitian Revolution within Caribbean literary and historical works. She co-translated (with Benjamin Hebblethwaite, UFL) Michel-Rolph Trouillot's *Ti difé boulé sou istoua Ayiti* (*Stirring the Pot of Haitian History*, 2021) from Kreyòl to English.

REFERENCES

Álvarez Estévez, Rolando, and Marta Guzmán Pascual. 2008. *Cuba en el Caribe y el Caribe en Cuba.* Habana: Fundación Fernando Ortiz.

Batista, Félix Hilario. 2017. *Nostalji san pwen ni vigil: Pwezi kreyòl nan peyi Kiba*, 2nd ed. Port-au-Prince: Éditions Caraïbe.

Bodenheimer, Rebecca. 2015. *Geographies of Cubanidad: Place, Race, and Musical Performance in Contemporary Cuba.* Jackson: University Press of Mississippi.

Casey, Matthew. 2017. *Empire's Guestworkers: Haitian Migrants in Cuba during the Age of U.S. Occupation.* Cambridge: Cambridge University Press.

Hume, Yanique. 2011. "On the Margins: The Emergence of a Haitian Diasporic Enclave in Eastern Cuba." In *Geographies of the Haitian Diaspora*, edited by Regine O. Jackson, 71–90. New York: Routledge.

Hurlich, Susan. 1998. "Creole Language and Culture: Part of Cuba's Cultural Patrimony." *AfroCubaWeb*, May 21. www.afrocubaweb.com/haiticuba.htm#creole.

Jonassaint, Jean. 2021. "For the Trouillots: An Afterword to the English Translation of *Ti difé boulé sou istoua Ayiti*." In *Stirring the Pot of Haitian History* by Michel-Rolph Trouillot, translated and edited by Mariana Past and Benjamin Hebblethwaite, 175–89. Liverpool: Liverpool University Press.

Ortiz, Fernando. 1940. *Contrapunteo Cubano del Tabaco y del Azúcar.* Cuba: Ciencias Sociales.

Trouillot, Michel-Rolph. 1990. "The Odd and the Ordinary: Haiti, the Caribbean, and the World." *Cimarrón: New Perspectives on the Caribbean* 2 (3): 3–12.

Ulysse, Gina Athena. 2015. *Why Haiti Needs New Narratives: A Post-Quake Chronicle.* Middletown, CT: Wesleyan University Press.

Zéphir, Flore. 2004. *The Haitian Americans.* Westport, CT: Greenwood Press.

CHAPTER FIFTEEN

Linguistic Bias or a Chance to Get Ahead: Linguistic Repertoires in Aruban and Curaçaoan Schools

Keisha Wiel

Multilingualism has long been a feature on the islands of Aruba and Curaçao. On a day-to-day basis this means that teachers and students continuously negotiate which languages can be used under what circumstances in school settings. This sort of negotiation was evident in one Curaçaoan high school classroom on the last day of homeroom before *proefwerkweek* (exam week). Tension filled the air as the teacher, Yufrou Tjon (Miss Tjon), greeted the students in Dutch with news that they were underperforming in their classes. Yufrou Tjon wanted to know if the teachers could help. Several students looked nervously at one another, unsure of what to say. Yufrou Tjon called on Julaika, who noted that since they hadn't received grades all semester, the students didn't know how they were doing. While trying to convey her frustration, Julaika struggled to explain herself in Dutch. She looked to a classmate, Miloushka, who took over and switched into Papiamentu (a creole language with features from Spanish, Portuguese, Dutch, English, Twi, Kimbundu, and Arawak, spoken widely in the island nations of Curaçao, Aruba, and Bonaire and the language that the students spoke most comfortably) to elaborate: "*Djis pa nos wak kon nos ta para*" (Just so we can see where we stand). Before Miloushka could finish, Yufrou Tjon firmly stated in Dutch, "*praat Nederlands*" (speak Dutch). Julaika let out a "*hesusei*" (oh my God) and struggled to continue in Dutch as she took over from Miloushka.

While Miloushka pleaded, another student, Marie, noted that although students supported each other through study sessions, certain students did not want the support. She singled out Bethaliza for not receiving help. The attention turned to Bethaliza, who nervously explained herself. Struggling to communicate in Dutch, almost tearfully, Bethaliza looked to Yufrou Tjon and asked if she could use Papiamentu. Yufrou Tjon noticed the hurt in Bethaliza's eyes and warmly assented.

In this intimate classroom dynamic, teacher and students balanced communicative efficacy and personal consideration against educational protocols. School language policies in Curaçao (and Aruba) prioritize the use of Dutch as the language of instruction in high school,

Figure 15.1. Entrance to a secondary school in Aruba. Photo by Keisha Wiel.

positioning Dutch as one of the languages of instruction in Curaçao and *the* language of instruction in Aruba, contributing to the attempted erasure of Papiamentu in the classroom. Yufrou Tjon maintained official policy by correcting students when they spoke Papiamentu. As the linguistic gatekeeper, she only allowed Bethaliza to speak Papiamentu when sharing her personal story. On the islands, although there is a general acceptance that Papiamentu has a place in educational settings for cultural identity purposes, dominant ideologies associate Dutch, not Papiamentu, with educational success. This ideology was reflected through Yufrou Tjon's opinion that students should always use Dutch in the classroom to master it.

In this post-colonial society where power structures go far beyond the teacher/student dynamic, structural inequalities are maintained in part through **linguistic gatekeeping** – the regulation of language choice, including determining which languages may be used as well as which may not in educational institutions. However, as I will show in this chapter, teachers and students are also creative social actors who exercise agency in their language practices, sometimes flouting official policies and **translanguaging** to prioritize communicative efficacy. In this chapter, I start by providing background about multilingualism on the islands before presenting evidence from several interactions at schools that show how students and teachers use their full **linguistic repertoires** – the complete set of languages and language varieties that a person speaks – in these assertive ways.

"THE FOUR LANGUAGES" AND MULTILINGUALISM IN ARUBA AND CURAÇAO

Papiamentu, English, Dutch, and Spanish are the four main languages that are spoken on the island nations of Aruba and Curaçao. Each language has its own historical significance as the flow of colonialism, immigration, and tourism has shaped the islands. Throughout the colonization period, various European countries took control of Aruba and Curaçao. In 1513, the viceroy of Hispaniola, Diego Colón, declared the islands useless and sent the resident Indigenous Caquetio (Arawakan-speaking) people to be enslaved in what is now the Dominican Republic and Haiti. After the Netherlands gained independence from Spain, the Dutch West India Company gained control of the islands in 1633 and set up a colony along Santa Anna Bay. The few Caquetio who remained on the islands herded livestock, while the Dutch trafficked enslaved people from Africa for trade, making it at one point the largest trading post for the Atlantic Slave Trade. Around the same time, Sephardic Jews fleeing Spain and Portugal during the Inquisition also settled on the islands as merchants (Rupert 2012).

This colonial dynamic contributed to the four languages that thrived on the islands. Dutch was used in an official capacity, while the emergent creole language Papiamentu was used in other parts of society, not only among enslaved people but also in Jewish and Dutch families, where children learned Papiamentu through their *yayas* (enslaved nannies) (Arion 1998). In 1914, when oil was found in Lake Maracaibo in Venezuela, Standard Oil of New Jersey (ExxonMobil) and Royal Dutch Shell used the harbors of Aruba and Curaçao to refine the crude oil. Since Exxon was an American company, they preferentially hired immigrants from the English Caribbean, leading to the quadrupling of Aruba's population, as a blend of Caribbean Englishes called San Nicolas English became a prominent language alongside Dutch and Papiamentu. Recently, as American cultural influences have become more prominent through music, television, and social media on both islands, English has gained even more prominence. Spanish has always had a presence on the islands, tracing to early Sephardic Jewish populations as well as proximity and trade with nearby Venezuela and recent patterns of migration from Venezuela, Colombia, and the Dominican Republic.

Through my position as a child of the diaspora, I went into ethnographic fieldwork with my own thoughts on how the various languages were used. I noticed how Spanish-speaking immigrants worked in hotels, small restaurants, and *truk'i pans* (food trucks). I noticed that those immigrants often spoke in *Papiañol* (a mixture of Papiamentu and Spanish) when communicating with locals. I also noticed that upper-scale stores and restaurants often required that their employees speak "The Four Languages" to interact with tourists. Teenagers often spoke to each other in American English in everyday interactions while older generations translanguaged between "The Four Languages." But I also observed how quick locals were to switch to Dutch or English with white tourists from the Netherlands or the United States.

As an ethnographer working in high school classrooms, I discovered that there was a continued emphasis on Dutch as the dominant language of education, but students were also comfortable speaking in English and Papiamentu, and teachers continued to use Papiamentu as an explanatory tool when all else failed. In this chapter, I present findings from participant observation in classrooms and interviews with students and teachers at two schools, one located in Aruba and the other in Curaçao. In addition, I gave students GoPro cameras to record their interactions during lunch time and to create vlogs (video blogs). I used this visual method to give students a chance to record their own interactions without the presence of an adult, which allowed me to examine their linguistic interactions when an authority figure was not present.

COMMUNITY THROUGH A SHARED LINGUISTIC REPERTOIRE

At Kolegio Maria Liberia in Curaçao, the students were in a transitional class. In the Dutch system, secondary school starts with *brugklas* (literally meaning bridge class), which is supposed to help transition students from primary to secondary school, equivalent to middle school in the United States. The students ranged in age from 14 to 16, and the parents of most of the students were from Curaçao. Although the linguistic backgrounds of most students were similar and they spoke Papiamentu at home, at least two students spoke Dutch at home.

This shared linguistic repertoire became a marker of an intragroup community at school. Within an educational setting, students who create this type of community do so out of solidarity and need (García-Sànchez 2014). In the high schools, there was an unspoken familiarity surrounding how language worked and could be used in different environments and peer groups. For instance, at Kolegio Maria Liberia, students formed cliques based on interests. Depending on who was part of that clique, one language or a mixture of languages was spoken. But for class assignments, there was a shared understanding that the dominant language was Dutch. This presumption was evident in the interaction between students that Sanaida and Noraly recorded one day during the lunch break. They had an exam in physics and the whole class was concerned about it. Although some students did study for the exam, there was a fear that many were not adequately prepared. Noraly nervously mentioned in English on her vlog that she did not "learn" for this exam, to which Naphtaly, her friend, laughed and said in English: "The word is 'study' NOT 'learn'!" While students were joking about Noraly's word choice, Sanaida nervously turned to the group and asked, in Papiamentu, about the exam. Rudsel, a student who spoke mostly Dutch at school, began to explain a physics problem the group was reviewing together. Excerpt 1 details the conversation starting at this point.[1]

---

1 Transcription note: Spoken English is represented by bold text. Spoken Dutch is represented by italics. All other talk is in Papiamentu. All capitalized text represents a translation of the original talk in Dutch or Papiamentu.

EXCERPT 1.

1 Rudsel: *Je dingens ... maar ze geven niet de voor afstand en midden afstand* YOUR THINGS ... BUT THEY DON'T GO THROUGH THE FRONT DISTANCE AND MIDDLE DISTANCE

2 Lucio: **yeah**

3 Sanaida: No e koi mi no kier sa. Mi kier sa kon ta asi e koi pintura ... NO, I DON'T WANT TO KNOW THAT. I WANT TO KNOW HOW TO DO THE DRAWING ...

4 Sanaida: M'a lubida. Un tin ku yega e *middel punt*? I FORGOT. DON'T YOU HAVE TO GO TO THE MIDDLE POINT?

5 Rudsel: **Ok**

6 (Shanuska motions to Sanaida)

7 Shanuska: Wak wak, esun ta bai meimei. *Dus* e ta bai mei mei di e, e punta. Pasa meimei di e *op is middel punt* ... LOOK LOOK, THIS ONE GOES IN THE MIDDLE. SO, IT GOES IN THE MIDDLE OF THE, THE POINT. PASSES THROUGH AT THE CENTER POINT ...

8 Sanaida: (shushes other students so she can hear)

9 Shanuska: Paso e di dos ta bai um *evenwijdig met de ... met de ...* e liña abou. Anto despues bai dor di e *F twee*. Despues esun ta bai for di e dos ... bai para na e liña mei mei. Despues bo lo *evenwijdig met de ...* **whatever!** Anto korda bon, kaminda bo pòtlot bai ... Bo no ta hisa bo pòtlot. Bo ta *gewoon* sigi mesora. BECAUSE THE SECOND ONE GOES UM PARALLEL TO THE ... TO THE ... THE LINE BELOW. AND AFTERWARDS IT GOES THROUGH F2. AFTERWARDS, THE OTHER ONE GOES FROM THE SECOND ... IT STANDS AT THE MIDDLE LINE. AFTERWARDS YOU WILL GO PARALLEL TO THE ... WHATEVER! AND REMEMBER. WHERE YOUR PENCIL GOES ... YOU DON'T LIFT YOUR PENCIL. YOU JUST CONTINUE RIGHT AWAY.

This interaction between several physics students reveals that language flexibility was key to student interaction and community building. The intragroup community and shared multilingual repertoire among the students made it possible for Shanuska to explain the physics problem to Sanaida, free from concerns about which languages were permitted for talking about physics. This parallels the casual translanguaging that I observed happening almost everywhere in the community outside of school.

This interaction also shows how communicative practice through several languages can sometimes be difficult when one of the languages is mainly heard in institutional spaces. While the students easily translanguaged to effectively communicate, it was also apparent how Dutch was a struggle, particularly for Shanuska. Although she understood enough of the physics problem to explain it to her classmate, she did so mostly in Papiamentu, switching to Dutch only briefly, when she needed to use technical terms they had learned in physics class: "*middel punt*" (middle point), "*F twee*" (F2), and "*evenwijdig*" (parallel). After struggling to come up with the right word to finish the Dutch phrase "*evenwijdig met de …*" (parallel with the …), she exasperatedly exclaimed "whatever!" in English before returning to Papiamentu.

Many teachers told me that enforcing Dutch as the primary language in the classroom impacted students' learning. When they taught, they would begin in Dutch. Once they realized their students were not grasping the Dutch terminology, they often switched to Papiamentu or English to explain the new terms. When they felt their students sufficiently understood, they would go back to speaking Dutch. The chemistry teacher, Yufrou Juliana, mentioned that her reasoning was to help students prepare for exams. Since their final exams came from the Netherlands, students in Aruba and Curaçao needed to be able to navigate Dutch-language exams as well as native Dutch students did to be successful in school.

Teachers like Yufrou Juliana often pull double duty compared to their counterparts in the Netherlands. They must consistently transition between languages to ensure their students achieve equivalent linguistic and content knowledge as Dutch students. Based on policies set forth by the public school board in Curaçao, students must matriculate through school knowing Dutch well enough to attend university in the Netherlands. Many students in secondary education go on to university in the Netherlands. Ironically, most Dutch universities are taught in English to attract students from other European nations.

Shanuska is forced to use Dutch because it's the language that physics is taught in. Specifically for education, the Dutch language is coded as a path to success. Yet, as has been noted in other contexts, the dominant language acts "as the barrier that keeps the very few powerful, White speakers *subiendo* (rising), while it ensures that those whose language practices are different are kept *bajando* (lowering)" (García 2017, 257). This is visible in the way that Shanuska struggles to explain the physics problem. The Dutch words that she knows are specific to physics. On the other hand, to explain her point fully she resorted to translanguaging between Papiamentu, Dutch, and English, using the full breadth of her linguistic repertoire to express her knowledge of physics.

STUDENTS AS ARBITERS OF LANGUAGE USE IN THE CLASSROOM

In a second classroom, this one at Scol Di Specialista in Aruba, students were also in a transitional class, but their ages ranged from 15 to 18 years old. Their transitional class was taught in both Papiamentu and Dutch with an emphasis on Dutch as they prepared for tertiary school. Scol was broken up into tracts or "units" that focused on specific job sectors. The class I observed was part of the "Service Unit," which focused on tourism. Students learned how to professionally cook for a hotel or restaurant and interned during the final year. Once they finished Scol they were eligible to go to the tertiary school. Tertiary school is a continuation of Scol Di Specialista, which is something between a vocational school and a college. Many of the students in this class had at least one parent that was not born on the island and spoke a language other than Papiamentu at home. Students had parents from Venezuela, Jamaica, and St. Vincent. As a result, the students had differing linguistic repertoires that encompassed several languages.

As there is a hierarchy in language use on the islands, there is also a hierarchy in who gets to impose language choices. This is often exemplified in school settings where exams determine who can get in based on how well they understand Dutch. Elite institutions often act as a mechanism of gatekeeping, constraining who can attend prestigious schools (Agha 2006, 28). In Aruban and Curaçaoan schools, Dutch itself can act as a gatekeeping tool to educational advancement. Within the classroom, teachers are usually at the top of the hierarchy and determine what language is to be spoken. But within certain classrooms in Aruba and Curaçao, students can sometimes direct language interactions, as when Bethaliza asked for permission to use Papiamentu in the classroom when she wanted to relate personal challenges.

As an ethnographer, I witnessed students at Scol di Specialista in Aruba appropriating the role of linguistic gatekeeper and expanding, rather than limiting, the number of languages that were used in the classroom when they were going over instructions for a project in their *Drink Leren* (Drink Studies) course. The teacher for the class had been replaced by Yufrou Williams, their *Kook Theorie en Practicum* (Cooking Theory and Practicum) teacher. Yufrou Williams was unsure what the previous teacher had assigned, so she asked the students.[2]

EXCERPT 2.

1. Yufrou Williams: Yufrou a bisa tur bo mester hinka den dje'le? DID THE TEACHER TELL YOU WHAT YOU HAD TO PUT IN IT?
2. Frankie: Ami'n ta korda. Dat **was like two or three weeks ago.** I DON'T REMEMBER. THAT WAS LIKE TWO OR THREE WEEKS AGO.
3. Jairzinho: No, e a bisa nos pa traha un kos. Inventa bo **drink.** NO, SHE TOLD US TO MAKE SOMETHING. INVENT YOUR DRINK.
4. Frankie: se paso … YEAH BECAUSE …
5. Yufrou Williams: **No rules, anything …**
6. Jamir: E no mester ta un kos ku bo por kumpra den **shop.** IT CANNOT BE SOMETHING THAT YOU CAN BUY IN A STORE.
7. Jamir: *Letterlijk* … LITERALLY …
8. Frankie: Se … So yuh **can't like buy the shake and mix it.** Bo mester trah'e. Yuh know blend it, mix it up. YEAH … SO YOU CANNOT BUY THE SHAKE AND MIX IT. YOU HAVE TO MAKE IT. YOU BLEND IT, MIX IT UP.
9. Yufrou Williams: **So, you have to try it out at home first?**
10. Frankie: Si … YES …
11. Jairzinho: No

---

[2] Transcription note: As before, Dutch is in italics, English is bold, and Papiamentu is written in regular font. San Nicolas English (a creole) is underlined. Translation of the talk is capitalized.

12 Frankie: <u>Yeah</u>
13 Yufrou Williams: **Uh yeah ...**
14 Yufrou Williams: Kon bo ta hasi'e? Bo ta *gewoon* skibi un reseta i despues spera ku e ta sali bon? HOW ARE YOU GOING TO DO IT? ARE YOU GOING TO JUST WRITE A RECIPE AND AFTERWARDS HOPE THAT IT COMES OUT WELL?
15 Jamir: Si! YES!
16 Yufrou Williams: **Ok ...**
17 Frankie: <u>Y'all really gon tell meh</u> ... ARE YOU ALL GOING TO TELL ME ...
18 Jamir: Ooooh, bo sa kiko, buta **spinach** ku umm ... OOOOH, YOU KNOW WHAT, PUT SPINACH WITH UMM ...
19 Yufrou Williams: I, e tin ku ta dos berdura of fruta? AND IT HAS TO HAVE TWO VEGETABLES OR FRUIT?
20 Frankie: <u>yeah, it gotta be two</u> YES, IT MUST BE TWO
21 Yufrou Williams: **two, not more than that, not less than that or ...**
22 (Chantell says something softly)
23 Yufrou Williams: *Sorry?* PARDON ME?
24 Chantell: E por ta mas IT CAN BE MORE.
25 Yufrou Williams: E por ta mas si, pero **at least two** tings. IT CAN BE MORE YES, BUT AT LEAST TWO THINGS.

Because the previous teacher didn't leave a lesson plan, Yufrou Williams trusted her students to give the correct information about this assignment. What is notable about this interaction is the way the students drove the choice of languages that were used in the discussion. It started with Frankie, who translanguaged across Papiamentu, San Nicolas English, and English in line 2. The rest of the speakers took this cue and continued to translanguage to explain the assignment using these three languages. Noticeably absent was Dutch. Compared to Kolegio, which was a college preparatory institution, Scol was a school for students looking to get an early start on a profession. Although Dutch generally wasn't spoken in their Drink Studies class, it was spoken in their general classes to prepare them for tertiary school. One common perspective at this school was expressed by Meneer Thielman (Mr. Thielman), the gym teacher, who told me that teaching in Dutch was a waste of time since the "Service Unit" at the tertiary school was taught in English to prepare students to engage with American tourists. Given this pedagogical objective, Dutch was not important in courses like Drink Studies. This practical assessment about language utility was reflected in the Scol practicum courses, where students and teachers spoke a mix of Papiamentu and English, even while Dutch was used significantly in theory and subject courses. Like Yufrou Juliana, Yufrou Williams told me that she knew the students struggled with Dutch. She was concerned that they needed to know Dutch terminology because exams came from the Netherlands. Yet, unlike the students at Kolegio who were preparing to study in the Netherlands, many of the students at Scol were planning to stay in

Aruba and become part of the American-driven tourist industry, where competence in English was more important.

CONCLUSION

As the examples in this chapter have illustrated, different agents gatekeep language use in schools. Depending on the type of interaction, teachers or students determine which languages can be used. For example, students from Kolegio created a study group where translanguaging happened to understand subject-specific ideas and procedures. The shared linguistic repertoire and translanguaging practices among peers allowed Shanuska to help Sanaida with studying for an exam. In other instances, a teacher was clearly in control of classroom language use. Yufrou Tjon's explicit gatekeeping – verbally elaborated with her directive to "Speak Dutch" – left students no room for translanguaging, and other languages were excluded. Only when the tone shifted to accommodate a student's sharing of personal experiences did Yufrou Tjon allow a codeswitch. In contrast, Yufrou Williams at Scol followed the lead of the Drink Studies students, who took the initiative in their classroom to act as linguistic gatekeepers, opening the gates for multiple language varieties. As these examples show, teachers and students negotiated contextually sensitive solutions on language use in educational spaces. However, at a national level an established language hierarchy that privileged Dutch over all other languages served as the ultimate gatekeeper, influencing students' success and advancement in education. On the islands, knowing Dutch well allowed students to thrive in school and later attend international universities, all while reinforcing social hierarchies and colonial entanglements.

The full linguistic repertoires of many Aruban and Curaçaoan students are not officially represented in the classroom. This has implications not only for their matriculation at secondary school and college, but for their identities as well. In Aruba and Curaçao, language is inextricably tied to cultural identity. Papiamentu bonds the community regardless of race, social standing, or ethnicity. As Spanish and English become increasingly predominant languages on the islands, identities are shifting to be inclusive of multiple selves. Yet school settings cater to only one of these selves, the one that is attached to the Dutch colonial legacy.

In schools, students have been socialized to understand the world through a Dutch lens. Yet Aruban and Curaçaoan students live different lives than their peers in the Netherlands. And linguistic regulation in educational settings does not align with or take advantage of their multilingual repertoires. Throughout the Caribbean, nations have long grappled with colonial educational institutions and the ways they preserve linguistic barriers (Nero 2015). As examples from this chapter show, students and teachers in Aruban and Curaçaoan schools sometimes subvert educational policies and are flexible in their language use to promote camaraderie, teach, and learn. By drawing on students' full linguistic repertoires, teachers and students circumvent, if only partially, the linguistic barriers that have been long imposed through a colonial legacy. Ultimately, changes in educational language policies will be needed to create equitable opportunities.

REFLECTION AND DISCUSSION QUESTIONS

- Describe the hierarchy of languages in Aruba and Curaçao and the ways each of "the four languages" are used in daily life, as opposed to how they are positioned in education. If there is a hierarchy of language in your country or community, how does it impact the lives of the young people you know?
- In what ways did students direct the languages that were used in the classrooms in Aruba and Curaçao?
- How does translanguaging create a community among students in Aruba and Curaçao? What ways have you experienced similar community building through language in your community?

KEY CONCEPTS

- **linguistic gatekeeping**: The regulation of language choice, including determining which languages may be used as well as which may not in a given context or situation and by whom.
- **linguistic repertoire**: The complete set of languages and language varieties that a person speaks.
- **translanguaging**: A way of using language that incorporates the multiple varieties in a speaker's linguistic repertoire and that is done without concern for maintaining normative distinctions between one language and another.

EXPLORE FURTHER

- To learn more about the relationship between colonialism, language, and identity for West Indian communities, read **Chapter 9**.
- To learn more about creole languages and diaspora, read **Chapter 14**.
- Allen, Rose Mary. 2007. "*Di Ki Manera*. A Social History of Afro-Curaçaoans, 1863–1917." *African Diaspora Archaeology Newsletter* 10 (2): Article 13. https://scholarworks.umass.edu/adan/vol10/iss2/13.
- Dijkhoff, Marta, and Joyce Pereira. 2010. "Language and Education in Aruba, Bonaire and Curaçao." In *Creoles in Education: An Appraisal of Current Programs and Projects*, edited by Bettina Migge, Isabelle Léglise, and Angela Bartens, 237–72. Philadelphia: John Benjamins Publishing Company.

- "Doing Anthropology in Curaçao: An Interview with Dr. Rose Mary Allen." An episode of the *Kultura Desaroyo Podcast*. https://tinyurl.com/Doing-Anthropology.
- "*No Hasi Ko'i Pendeu.*" (Do Not Do Stupid Things). An episode of the *Vocal Fries Podcast*. https://tinyurl.com/Vocal-Fries.
- "Speaking Papiamento." An episode of the *Speaking Tongues Podcast*. https://tinyurl.com/Speaking-Papiamento.

ABOUT THE AUTHOR

Keisha Wiel is a Ph.D. candidate in the Department of Anthropology at Temple University with a concentration in linguistic anthropology. Her research examines language socialization, multilingualism, linguistic rights, and education in a post-colonial state and how the socialization of languages in education frames the identity of students. A Black woman of Aruban and Curaçaoan descent, Wiel is committed to addressing the issues and needs of linguistically marginalized students in education.

REFERENCES

Agha, Asif. 2006. "Registers of Language." In *A Companion to Linguistic Anthropology*, edited by Alessandro Duranti, 23–45. Oxford: Blackwell Publishing.

Arion, Frank Martinus. 1998. "The Victory of the Concubines and the Nannies." In *Caribbean Creolization: Reflections on the Cultural Dynamics of Language, Literature, and Identity*, edited by Kathleen M. Balutansky and Marie-Agnès Sourieau, 110–17. Gainsville: University Press of Florida.

García, Ofelia. 2017. "Translanguaging in Schools: Subiendo y Bajando, Bajando y Subiendo as Afterward." *Journal of Language, Identity, & Education* 16 (4): 256–63. https://doi.org/10.1080/15348458.2017.1329657.

García-Sánchez, Inmaculada. 2014. *Language and Muslim Immigrant Childhoods: The Politics of Belonging*. Wiley Blackwell Studies in Discourse and Culture. Chichester, UK: Wiley-Blackwell.

Nero, Shondel. 2015. "Language, Identity, and Insider/Outsider Positionality in Caribbean Creole English Research." *Applied Linguistics Review* 6 (3): 341–68. https://doi.org/10.1515/applirev-2015-0016.

Rupert, Linda. 2012. *Creolization and Contraband: Curaçao in the Early Modern Atlantic World*. Athens: University of Georgia Press.

SECTION SIX

Politics and Power

Karleen Jones West

Contemporary politics and power in Latin America and the Caribbean are shaped by the region's legacy of authoritarian rule and its relatively recent return to democratic governance. During the Cold War (1947–1989), most Latin American and Caribbean governments were **authoritarian regimes**, where political rights and civil liberties were restricted. Some authoritarian regimes were dominated by a single political party, as in Mexico (see Chapter 16), but the majority were military regimes, controlled by a single military general or a *junta* (board) of military officials. Military regimes in Latin America and the Caribbean were funded and trained in oppressive techniques by the United States to prevent the spread of Marxist communism and to facilitate extractive capitalism. Military rule in some countries, like Argentina, Brazil, and Chile, prioritized economic development to such an extent that they were run by both the military and highly trained technological and economic experts, called **technocrats**. These specialized regimes were coined **bureaucratic-authoritarian** by Argentine political scientist Guillermo O'Donnell. As Chapters 16 and 18 in this section illustrate, the institutions and norms of governance established under the region's authoritarian regimes continue to influence politics and the allocation of power in Latin America and the Caribbean today.

With the end of the Cold War in the 1980s, military rule became unsustainable and governments slowly returned to **democracy** – a political system in which, minimally, the majority of citizens have the right to vote and select the candidates of their choice, and there is genuine competition among parties running for office. The United States shifted its foreign policy in the region to focus exclusively on extractive capitalism, in particular prioritizing access to oil and other natural resources. Using its influence in the International Monetary Fund and the World Bank, the United States enforced the **Washington Consensus**, a set of neoliberal economic policies that privileged free market capitalism over social welfare. Although neoliberal policies initially led to economic growth in some Latin American and Caribbean countries, it did little to eradicate poverty and universally exacerbated inequality (see Section 8). Neoliberalism also undermined democracy in some states, like Bolivia and Peru, where governments were pressured to adopt rapid and dramatic neoliberal reforms deemed "shock therapy" for struggling economies. For example, Peru's president Alberto Fujimori (1990–2000) carried out an *auto-golpe* (or self-coup) in which he shut down Congress, purged the judiciary, and suspended the constitution to implement extensive neoliberal reforms.

By the turn of the millennium, there was widespread popular backlash against neoliberalism. The protection of civil liberties afforded by democracy created the political conditions for citizens to mobilize around newly politicized identities, such as indigeneity and progressive ideologies. The 1990s and early 2000s witnessed a rise in **social movements**, organizations that use tactics like marches, protests, and blockades to advocate for political and social change. Among the most powerful social movements in Latin America and the Caribbean were Indigenous movements that pressured governments to recognize Indigenous rights to land and self-determination. In some countries, like Bolivia and Ecuador, Indigenous uprisings led to the ousting of presidents and revised constitutions that recognize the differentiated rights of Indigenous peoples. Yet even under these new institutional frameworks, Indigenous communities today continue the fight to protect their ancestral territories against colonial systems of domination (see Chapter 19) and extractive capitalist interests (see Chapters 29 and 30).

Much of this movement activity was also channeled into the creation of popular political parties on the *New Left*, an ideology that promoted the redistribution of wealth without requiring Marxist revolution. Leaders of the New Left, such as Bolivia's president Evo Morales (2006–2019) and Brazilian president Luis Inácio "Lula" da Silva (2003–2010), created social programs aimed at decreasing poverty within the framework of liberal democracy. The popularity of the New Left in the 2000s led to the *Pink Tide*, in which most governments in the region were moving away from the neoliberal economic model. Many New Left presidents were considered populist leaders that relied heavily on their charisma and **clientelism** – the exchange of goods and services for political support – to win elections. The populist nature of New Left leaders made them particularly vulnerable to criticism from conservatives, and today many once-beloved New Left presidents have confronted accusations of fraud, corruption, and violations of the principles of democratic governance.

The chapters in this section illustrate the variety of ways that power is gained and negotiated in contemporary democracies across Latin America and the Caribbean. In Chapter 16, West explores how legislative candidates use many different forms of clientelist exchanges to win elections. In the process, West highlights how specific clientelist tactics coupled with grassroots organizing can foster the success of opposition parties in Mexico, such as the leftist PRD. In Chapter 17, Mandache juxtaposes an urban community's disenchantment with how a nongovernmental organization has addressed the challenges facing their community, while at the same time recognizing the contributions that the organization does make. In Chapter 18, Azocar analyzes how gender ideologies and technocratic expertise determine pension policy within

Chile's influential bureaucracy. Finally, in Chapter 19, Doyle demonstrates how Indigenous communities continue the struggle for land rights despite the enormous legal gains they were granted in Bolivia's groundbreaking 2009 constitution.

KEY CONCEPTS

- **authoritarian regimes**: Governments in which political rights and civil liberties are restricted.
- **bureaucratic-authoritarian regimes**: Authoritarian regimes that were run by both the military and technocrats.
- **clientelism**: The exchange of goods and services for political support.
- **democracy**: A political system in which, minimally, the majority of citizens have the right to vote and select the candidates of their choice, and there is genuine competition among parties running for office.
- **social movements**: Organizations that use tactics like marches, protests, and blockades to advocate for political and social change.
- **technocrats**: Highly trained technological and economic experts.
- **Washington Consensus**: A set of neoliberal economic policies that privileged free market capitalism over social welfare.

EXPLORE FURTHER

- To learn more about activism and social movements, read **Chapters 7**, **10**, **11**, **13**, **23**, **24**, and **30**.
- Close, David. 2017. *Latin American Politics: An Introduction*, 2nd ed. Toronto: University of Toronto Press.
- Fuentes, Carola, and Rafael Valdeavellano, dirs. 2016. *Chicago Boys*. [Chile]
- Guzmán, Patricio. 1998. *La Batalla de Chile: La Lucha de un Pueblo Sin Armas* (*The Battle of Chile: The Struggle of an Unarmed People*).
- Isbester, Katherine. 2010. *The Paradox of Democracy in Latin America: Ten Country Studies of Division and Resilience*. Toronto: University of Toronto Press.
- Khasnabish, Alex. 2008. *Zapatismo Beyond Borders: New Imaginations of Political Possibility*. Toronto: University of Toronto Press.
- Martinez, Margarita, and Miguel Salazar, dir. 2009. *Stolen Land*. [Colombia]
- Thompson-Marquez, Wendy. 2012. *Harvest of Empire*. [United States]

CHAPTER SIXTEEN

Congressional Candidates and Political Campaigns in Clientelist Systems: Condoms and Concrete in Oaxaca, Mexico

Karleen Jones West

After driving hours across southern Mexico's desert plains, then onto a dirt road curving around rocky mountain ridges, Jefte Mendez and his campaign workers stopped their truck at the bottom of a canyon carved out by a swift creek. The road ended abruptly as it entered the canyon, disappearing under the river stones, invisible beneath the rushing water. It was clear that the truck could go no further. "The bridge was taken by the river two years ago. Now the school bus stops here, at the end of the road, and the kids from the community cross the river every morning to catch it," Mendez explained, pointing to the cluster of homes on the opposite hillside where community residents lived. The kids crossed in the same way that Mendez and his campaign team would to access their next campaign site that day – via a hefty log balanced on the canyon's cliffsides about 10 feet above the creek. Two ropes were haphazardly tied along either side of the log, stretching across the river to form makeshift handholds for the log bridge. Mendez and the two other young men that accompanied him loaded bags of rice in their arms, huge duffel bags full of T-shirts, Coca-Cola, and soccer balls on their backs and shoulders, balancing their cargo as they put one foot in front of the other to reach the village of Santo Domingo de Narro. This part of the campaign trail was literally a matter of life or death – had Mendez or his crew fallen from the log, they would have faced serious, life-threatening injury.

Jefte Mendez made this journey as part of his 2012 campaign to represent the fourth district of the state of Oaxaca in Mexico's national Congress (*Congreso de la Unión*). After crossing the river, Mendez and his team participated in a series of campaign events, first lunch with the community president, then a tour of the one-room community center, and finally a gathering with constituents in the town square. Mendez's team distributed the rice and other durable goods while the candidate addressed the small crowd. He emphasized the importance of economic development, connecting the community with a new highway, and establishing other

Figure 16.1. A crowd of PRD supporters gather to celebrate the close of Mario Rafael's campaign. Photo by Karleen Jones West.

projects that would bring opportunities to Narro. When community members asked how he planned to accomplish all of this, he gave them his card with the address of his campaign headquarters and told them to come with their ideas so they could get started making formal requests for government-funded projects. Prospective voters left the event with "Mendez" T-shirts, enough rice to sustain their families for weeks, sufficient soccer balls to entertain community members for the year – and a more personal connection with Mendez.

Ultimately, Mendez's campaign efforts were not successful. When the ballots came in on election day, Mendez came in last among the major party candidates competing in the fourth district in 2012, winning just 7 per cent of district-wide votes. Mendez had worked hard on the campaign trail, traversing the challenging desert landscape to the far reaches of his congressional district and distributing valuable goods – but he lost the election. This anecdote about Mendez's experience raises questions about the role that political campaigns play not only in Mexico, but in Latin America more broadly. Across the region, candidates compete in what political scientists call **clientelist systems** – or democracies where goods and services are exchanged for electoral support. There are many varieties of clientelism, including vote buying, when candidates try to persuade new voters to support them (Stokes 2005), and turnout buying, when campaigns use goods as an incentive for their supporters to show up at the polls (Nichter 2008). In Mexico, each election cycle candidates head out into their districts – the urban *barrios* (neighborhoods) and the rural *comunidades* (communities) – to distribute everything from food and bags of concrete to job contracts to earn votes and win office. Especially in impoverished communities, voters have come to rely on election season and its campaigns as a source of goods that they otherwise could not afford; an opportunity to access services that they normally do not have. Campaign clientelism is therefore often a necessary, but costly, electoral strategy (Muñoz 2014).

In this chapter, I explore the role that campaign clientelism plays in elections in Oaxaca, Mexico. I argue that the temporary provision of goods and services during the campaign is not enough to attract voter support. Candidates must also demonstrate their capacity to connect with voters and form lasting relationships that promise goods not only during the campaign, but also once the candidate takes office. I show that because all candidates provide clientelistic goods on the campaign trail, it takes more than just rice, T-shirts, and soccer balls to buy political support. Instead, candidates' individual experience matters, and the way they demonstrate their dedication to the communities on the campaign trail is what earns voter support. Specifically, candidates who have a history of service in the district – and roots in meaningful social movements that provide opportunities to maintain clientelistic relationships in the future – have an advantage in elections in Oaxaca.

Why is it important to understand campaign clientelism? Because political scientists have oversimplified the clientelist relationship, inaccurately assuming that clientelism universally undermines democracy. Conventional wisdom is that when political parties buy electoral support with targeted goods and services, they are under no obligation to create public policies consistent with a fixed platform and ideology (Lyne 2008). In the long term, scholars argue, this results in democracies that fail to serve their constituencies; voters hold parties accountable only for what they provide during election season, rather than for widespread reforms that have lasting impacts, particularly for the poor (Taylor-Robinson 2010). However, these arguments neglect the diversity of clientelistic tactics that candidates use, primarily because it is difficult to measure clientelism with large-scale survey research and other statistical methods. Surveys suffer from social desirability bias when respondents answer questions based on what they think is acceptable or adheres to a social norm. Because people know that clientelism is problematic, they are often dishonest about the items they have been given and the influence those items had on their vote. The ethnographic case studies in this chapter show that candidates appeal to voters using their own resources and individual experience, which has important implications for democracy, particularly in Mexico. The case studies also demonstrate the variety of tactics used by candidates in campaigns and call attention to the sophisticated logic used by low-income voters to determine their vote choice.

THE LEGACY OF PRI DOMINANCE IN OAXACA

The electoral history of the state of Oaxaca sheds light on why clientelism is so fundamental to the electoral process there. For over 70 years, all of Mexico's elections were dominated by a single political party: the Institutional Revolutionary Party, known by its Spanish acronym PRI (*Partido Revolucionario Institucional*). The PRI party won every presidential election and controlled every Congress from 1929 until 2000. Mexico was not a full democracy until the dominant PRI party finally faced genuine competition and lost the presidency to the PAN (*Partido Acción Nacional*, National Action Party) in the 2000 election.

The PRI was authoritarian in nature, willing to violate and limit democracy to remain in power. Yet unlike other authoritarian regimes around the world, the PRI never outlawed political competition and consistently held elections throughout their reign. This means that the PRI had to constantly find ways to "win" elections. The PRI used a variety of tactics to dominate elections, including preventing powerful elites from joining opposition parties, engaging in widespread electoral fraud, and occasionally resorting to violence to ensure they would control political office (Magaloni 2006). But the PRI also used state resources to secure mass voter support, manipulating economic policies to ensure that a large proportion of impoverished *campesinos* (peasant farmers) remained systematically dependent on PRI patronage for survival. For example, the PRI used direct cash transfers and targeted payments including food subsidies, credit, construction contracts, and land titles to consistently secure mass support (Magaloni 2006). The PRI was therefore fundamental to creating the clientelist system that structures Mexico's elections today.

In the state of Oaxaca, the PRI has a legacy of significant political control, only losing the state's governorship once in the last 96 years. Oaxaca is situated in Mexico's impoverished southern region, with one of the highest poverty rates (62 per cent) among Mexico's 32 states alongside its neighbors of Chiapas, Guerrero, and Puebla (CONEVAL 2020). Oaxaca and other southern states are also home to some of Mexico's largest populations of Indigenous communities. Approximately one out of every three people in Oaxaca speaks an Indigenous language, and there are 16 distinct Indigenous groups officially recognized within the state (Inmujeres 2006). With the combination of historically oppressed low-income and Indigenous voters, the PRI viewed Oaxaca and its southern neighbors as rural regions that could be bought and controlled using clientelism, electoral fraud, and violence.

The PRI began to lose control over southern Mexico starting on January 1, 1994, when a group of armed Indigenous *campesinos* calling themselves the Zapatista Army of National Liberation (*Ejército Zapatista de Liberación Nacional*, EZLN) seized towns across Chiapas to fight against neoliberalism – economic policies that privilege the market over social welfare – and the PRI's stranglehold on Mexican democracy. Following the uprising in Chiapas, in neighboring Oaxaca the PRI suffered their most precipitous decline in state elections ever. The PRI-controlled Oaxacan state legislature responded further in 1995 by reforming local elections to ensure PRI dominance (Anaya-Muñoz 2003).

Despite the 1995 electoral reform, the PRI party continued to lose control in Oaxaca. In 2004, by historically narrow margins and amid accusations of fraud, the PRI won Oaxaca's governorship with the election of Ulises Ruiz (Suverza 2006). But after Ruiz violently suppressed a teachers' strike in 2006, assassinating and disappearing – or secretly abducting and murdering – dozens of activists (García Granados 2016), the PRI's reign in Oaxaca was finally disrupted. In the following governor's election in 2010, a non-PRI candidate, Gabino Cué of the Citizen's Movement party, won Oaxaca's governorship, ending the PRI's reign in Oaxaca for the first time in 80 years. Despite the PRI's best efforts to buy votes, Oaxacan voters had finally broken the cycle of PRI's electoral dominance.

CLIENTELISM, POLITICAL MACHINES, AND CANDIDATES IN OAXACA'S ELECTIONS

By 2006, PRI dominance had been disrupted, opening a space for other political parties to represent Oaxaca in Mexico's Chamber of Deputies. Oaxaca's legislative elections are now truly competitive between the PRI, the PRD (*Partido Revolucionario Democrático*, Revolutionary Democratic Party), and other major parties, yet the legacy of the PRI remains. Congressional campaigns have always been an important site for the PRI to establish the kind of clientelist linkages that are essential to securing mass voter support (Langston and Morgenstern 2009). Campaign events provide opportunities for voters to personally connect with candidates and receive handouts of food, clothing, and other material goods. Congressional campaigns are thus important for many voters, especially those with low incomes. As a result, many voters expect the distribution of goods and services during campaigns. In Oaxaca, candidates recognize that they must use electoral clientelism to be competitive. When I interviewed Victor Leonel, council member of Oaxaca's State Electoral Institute, he summarized legislative campaigns in Oaxaca, saying "all candidates use clientelism – all of them, from every party."

Previous studies of clientelism have focused on **political machines**, or political organizations that use goods and services to secure voter support. However, by focusing on national-level political machines, studies have ignored the role that individual candidates play in determining clientelist strategies. The focus on political machines assumes that the party organization uses state resources – welfare funds, jobs, government contracts – to buy electoral support. However, for much of Mexico's history, only the PRI had access to state resources because opposition parties were excluded from political power. How were **opposition parties** (parties outside of government) ever able to win elections if constituents expected candidates to provide goods and services that candidates from opposition parties had less access to than PRI candidates did? One way for opposition parties to gain support is through individual elites providing goods on their own. The use of personal, rather than state resources, enabled the rise of opposition parties like the PRD (Hilgers 2008). National-level investigations of political machines have overlooked how individual candidates use their own skills and resources to compete with dominant political machines like the PRI. In the next section, I describe the research design that enabled me to analyze how individual candidates shape their own campaigns and influence competitive democracy in Mexico.

RESEARCH DESIGN: THE 2012 ELECTIONS IN OAXACA

In May 2012, I began my campaign research in Mexico City with a visit to the headquarters of Mexico's INE (*Instituto Nacional Electoral*, National Electoral Institute) to obtain the status of an official electoral observer. Without these credentials, I would not have been able to access the campaign process in Oaxaca. Mexico's 2012 general elections involved a heightened campaign because it was a presidential election year. The PRI was desperate to regain power after being out of the presidency for 12 years, during which the PAN controlled two consecutive administrations (Vicente Fox from 2000 to 2006 and Felipe Calderón from 2006 to 2012). In 2012, the PRI nominated Enrique Peña Nieto, the handsome former governor of the state of México (2005–2011) whose fame and popularity were magnified by his marriage to a popular Mexican *telenovela* (soap opera) star. As I reached Oaxaca to start my ethnographic research, I found Peña Nieto's smiling face everywhere in the capital city – on billboards, on city buses, on posters in *bodega* (convenience store) windows; he was by far the most widely publicized presidential candidate in the state.

There is a fixed official campaign season of about six weeks in Mexico, but it varies by state and elected office. In 2012, Oaxacan legislative candidates had a little over a month on the campaign trail. My goal was to evaluate the various campaign strategies of the three major political parties, but I had only a very short time to do so. I gained access to the campaigns of six congressional candidates in Oaxaca: two PRI, two PRD, one PAN, and one from the new PANAL party (Jefte Mendez, described in the introduction). For each of the candidates I did the following: interviewed the candidate (or in one instance, the candidate's campaign director); attended multiple campaign events; gathered campaign materials; and informally interviewed campaign workers and attendees at the events. I also interviewed a variety of scholars and other professionals and experts on the campaign process in Oaxaca to ensure that I properly understood Oaxaca's electoral context: the history, rules, and regulations of the state.

THE FAILURE OF PRI CONGRESSIONAL CAMPAIGNS IN 2012

Heading onto the campaign trail, I expected the PRI to practice the most egregious forms of clientelism, given the party's legacy in Oaxaca and their push to regain their local political dominance and the Mexican presidency. This was true. However, contrary to the expectation that the historically authoritarian PRI coordinated campaigns from the top down, I found decentralized campaigns that were directed almost entirely by the individual candidates themselves. In 2012, the PRI candidates that I observed provided ample goods and services on the campaign trail but ultimately failed to attract enough support to win their elections. I argue that the candidates failed because their political experience and relationships with voters were weaker than those of their PRD competitors, and I provide case studies of two campaigns to demonstrate the power of social networks over goods.

PRI Candidate Liz Acosta

In 2012, Liz Acosta was the PRI candidate for deputy in Oaxaca's 8th District, which encompassed the urban area of Oaxaca City, the state capital. Acosta was new to politics, earning her first and only political position just four years prior when she was elected to Oaxaca's Council of Industry and Commerce. Acosta decided to run for office because she considers herself a businesswoman with valued opinions on economic policy. Referring to herself in the third person, when I interviewed her Acosta summarized her popularity in this way: "I believe that if there's an image of Liz Acosta, it's of a woman of work, a woman of struggle, a woman who is dedicated in body and spirit to health. I believe that many people have a positive image of Liz." Acosta's public image was shaped by her fame as a televised aerobics instructor, or as her husband described, "the Jane Fonda of Mexico." Building on her notoriety, Acosta opened the largest personal fitness center in Oaxaca City, called the Calipso Gym. The gym occupied nearly an entire block in one of Oaxaca's wealthier neighborhoods, its huge windows exposing the modern exercise equipment and upper-middle-class clients doing cardio inside.

In 2012, the Calipso Gym also served as the headquarters for Acosta's congressional campaign. Acosta's "campaign workshop" was in a tent in the parking lot behind the gym. There, a small team of Indigenous women from the outskirts of the city worked into the night, screen printing Acosta's name and the PRI logo onto hundreds of different items: pencils, calendars, magnets, rulers, buttons, T-shirts, reusable bags, a variety of hats – and even condoms. Acosta also converted an RV into a mobile medical unit, providing free exams to prospective constituents in the city's low-income neighborhoods. Of all the candidates that I observed, Acosta had the largest supply and variety of goods and services to distribute during her campaign.

Despite Acosta's extravagant efforts at clientelism, the disconnect with her constituents was evident in many aspects of the campaign. Acosta considered herself a public servant, building her fitness career by holding huge rallies where thousands would gather in the streets to do aerobics with Liz. But Acosta's connection to the people was too superficial to translate to a meaningful connection in politics.

As part of her campaign, Acosta visited the barrio of Vista Hermosa, located on the outskirts of Oaxaca City. Driving there, it felt like every other part of the city – until the paved concrete ended abruptly, becoming a rutted dirt road that climbed ever higher into the desert hills that form the city's border. The houses in Vista Hermosa were constructed of scraps of plywood and sheet metal instead of brick and mortar; most did not have glass windows. Acosta's high-heeled shoes got dusty as she walked through a weedy chicken yard to reach the podium and address the small audience of 20 or so residents. There, Acosta said all the right things; she wanted to serve their community by providing basic public works, like clean water and healthcare services, which the neighborhood lacked. She condemned the PRD and PAN for their clientelistic ways: "the other parties are going to tell you … 'vote for the PRD and we'll give you a food pantry and 300 pesos.' But I believe it's time that we dignify politics and first respect the intelligence of the people. [The PRD] can't build a food pantry in two days. And 300 pesos won't do much when people lack employment, lack opportunities, lack education …" Instead, she promised to invest in the community, claiming that "I, as federal deputy, of course want to be close to all of you" and claimed that she would submit a report every three to six months outlining the investments she made in communities. She promised that, unlike all the others, she would not trick them, she would not steal from them, she would not fail them.

Although Acosta's words condemned vote buying, her campaign event reiterated that clientelism was a cornerstone of her strategy to win votes. The campaign worker that introduced Acosta and managed the questions afterward emphasized several times that Acosta's mobile medical unit would be in the neighborhood the following week. Further, during the question-and-answer session following Acosta's speech, the director of a daycare approached Acosta with a contract, asking that she promise to fix the leaky roof of the daycare should she be elected.

Ultimately, despite the enormous number of resources she invested into the campaign, Acosta's promises and goods did not win her the election. Acosta was defeated by her PRD opponent, Hugo Jarquín, who had gained notoriety and political experience during the 2006 teacher's uprising in Oaxaca. In fact, the PRD strategy in 2012 was to invest in many grassroots leaders that could build upon their experience organizing and use their local networks to defeat the PRI.

PRD Candidate Mario Rafael

The case of PRD candidate Mario Rafael exemplifies the difference between the qualities of PRI and PRD candidates in Oaxaca in 2012 and highlights the importance of individual candidate's characteristics in Mexico's legislative campaigns. In 2012, Mario Rafael was running in Oaxaca's 9th District, which encompasses the urban outskirts of Oaxaca City but is primarily a rural district that includes many Indigenous constituents. Unlike Acosta, who had only been involved in the business sector of politics, and only for four years at that, Rafael had been a grassroots leader of Oaxaca's rural communities for decades. At the time of his campaign, he was state secretary of the Independent Center of Agricultural Workers and Peasants (CIOAC, *Central Independiente de Obreros Agrícolas y Campesinos*). Prior to that, Rafael had twice been elected mayor in the rural town of Zimatlan de Álvarez, where he helped found Oaxaca's state branch of the PRD.

Rafael's campaign operation stood in stark contrast to that of Acosta's. Whereas Acosta's headquarters were in her gym, far from the constituents that needed her most, Rafael's campaign headquarters were in the CIOAC offices, in the heart of his district. Rafael's prospective constituents were in and out of his office if Rafael was there, and people were able to speak directly to the candidate. Acosta's campaign office was manned by preppy college students, and Acosta herself was rarely there. Rafael's campaign events were chaotic affairs, where the candidate walked among huge gatherings of people, shaking hands, giving hugs, and listening to people's concerns. Acosta's campaign events were tightly managed, and Acosta almost never spoke directly to individuals, away from the podium and the microphone.

The varieties of clientelism used by the two candidates were also dramatically different. Rafael was always trailed by his assistant who took detailed notes documenting people's individual concerns and requests. In addition, Rafael's campaign manager would stand by the campaign vehicle with his notebook, a line of people waiting to speak with him, one by one, about the needs of their families and communities. I stood with the campaign manager as he documented that one older man needed a bag of concrete to finish constructing his home; a younger woman was concerned about a contract for phone service that never reached her community. Rafael's campaign manager explained that phone service was a valued resource for women in many of Oaxaca's rural communities, as their husbands were off in the United States doing seasonal agricultural work and they longed to communicate with them more regularly. Rafael and his campaign team came from the rural areas of Oaxaca, understood the demographics and needs of the communities, and used their deep knowledge, experience, and networks to effectively connect with prospective constituents.

Like all other candidates that I observed in Oaxaca, Rafael distributed goods during his campaign. However, unlike Acosta, who screen-printed her name on hundreds of items, Rafael only had T-shirts with his name on them. Otherwise, his goods came in the form of food and alcohol. Rafael's campaign event in Coatecas Altas, a rural village about two hours south of Oaxaca City, coincided with a local festival. Lines of people waited for plates of roasted chicken, beans, rice, and stewed vegetables provided by Rafael and the PRD. The campaign also wheeled in giant plastic barrels full of traditional Mexican beverages; most were non-alcoholic, but some filled with *pulque*, an alcoholic drink made from the fermented sap of the maguey plant native to Oaxaca. Community members took turns dipping their arms deep into the open barrels to scoop up *horchata*, a sweet rice milk, or *pulque*. At the end of the festival, constituents left with large bags of rice that would sustain their families for weeks. On election day, Rafael earned the most votes in District 9 in a close race against his PRI and PAN competitors.

CONCLUSION: CONNECTIONS VERSUS CONDOMS IN OAXACA

Clientelism is a campaign tradition in Mexico, and an essential practice for any candidate to compete in Oaxaca. However, this chapter shows that clientelism alone does not win elections, as I witnessed with the Mendez and Acosta campaigns. Despite Acosta's largesse and impressive efforts at providing extensive goods and services to voters, the voters instead supported her PRD opponent, who was deeply involved with the teacher's movement that was so vital to Oaxacan politics in the years following the 2006 uprising. Ultimately, Acosta lacked the experience and networks essential to forming meaningful connections with Oaxacan voters. Although it is beyond the scope of this study to know precisely why voters failed to support Acosta, I suspect that Oaxacan constituents are savvy and use cues from the campaign to assess whether candidates have the will and capacity to follow through on their promises. Although Acosta was rich in terms of material resources, she had only a superficial connection with low-income communities in Oaxaca City. Further, she was new to the PRI party, and therefore could not rely on the extensive PRI networks that more deeply entrenched PRI candidates use. These findings suggest that the literature on clientelism should begin to acknowledge that voters are not simply "bought" by the highest bidder in clientelist campaigns. Citizens are more sophisticated and seek candidates with strong networks that are proven to provide goods and services into the future.

The case studies in this chapter also demonstrate that there are different forms of clientelist exchanges. Rather than clientelism being a tightly controlled system directed by a political machine, it is often designed around the skills and resources of individual candidates. This is an important observation because it helps explain how opposition parties and candidates win elections in new democracies like Mexico, where authoritarian parties have long manipulated the electoral process. If opposition parties can attract resourceful candidates that effectively use their expertise and grassroots networks to form relationships with voters, then they can successfully compete and win office. Opposition candidates cannot disregard the importance of clientelist exchanges, as the Mendez and Rafael cases illustrate. But they can use their own connections and experience to strategically employ clientelism alongside other campaign tactics to earn votes. This is good news for democratization efforts around the world; when opposition parties are allowed to participate, they may benefit from the strong social networks and grassroots efforts of their movements – even if they lack lavish clientelist goods.

REFLECTION AND DISCUSSION QUESTIONS

- What role does clientelism play in democratic elections in Mexico? What evidence does the author provide to challenge critiques that clientelism corrupts elections?
- One concern that political scientists have about clientelism is that it gives the ruling party an advantage in elections, because the party that controls the government has more resources to buy votes. Are there any elements of the electoral process in your country that give certain groups more influence than others?

- Have you ever attended a campaign event for a politician in your country? Describe the event. How was it different from the events described in this chapter? How was it similar?

KEY CONCEPTS

- **clientelist systems**: Democracies where goods and services are exchanged for electoral support.
- **opposition parties**: Political parties that are excluded from executive office or control the minority of seats in the legislature. In some authoritarian regimes, opposition parties are excluded from participating in politics altogether.
- **political machines**: Political parties, or groups of individuals organized with the sole purpose of holding political office, that use coercion, vote buying, and patronage to rig elections in their favor. The PRI is an example of a political machine.

EXPLORE FURTHER

- To learn more about clientelism and non-governmental organizations, read **Chapter 17**.
- To learn more about political abuse and violence in Oaxaca, read **Chapter 23**.
- George, Samuel, dir. 2018. *The People's Choice: Mexico, Morena, and the 2018 Election*. Available at https://tinyurl.com/Peoples-Choice.

ABOUT THE AUTHOR

Karleen Jones West is a professor of political science and international relations at the State University of New York (SUNY) at Geneseo. Her research examines campaigns, elections, Indigenous movements, and the politics of sustainability in Latin America and around the world. She is the author of two books: *Who Speaks for Nature? Indigenous Movements, Public Opinion, and the Petro-State in Ecuador* (with Todd Eisenstadt) and *Candidate Matters: A Study of Ethnic Parties, Campaigns, and Elections in Latin America*.

REFERENCES

Anaya-Muñoz, Alejandro. 2003. "La Política del Reconocimiento en Oaxaca: La Preservación de una Gobernabilidad Priísta y el Desarrollo del Proyecto de Autonomía Indígena en el Estado." *Relaciones: Estudios de Historia y Sociedad* 24 (96): 267–304.

CONEVAL (*Consejo Nacional de Evaluación de la Política de Desarrollo Social*, National Council of the Evaluation of Social Development Policy). 2020. "Información de Pobreza y Evaluación en las Entidades Federativas y Municipios." https://www.coneval.org.mx/coordinacion/entidades/Paginas/inicioent.aspx.

García Granados, Marco Antonio. 2016. "Ulises Ruiz será enjuiciado." *Milenio*. April 3. https://www.milenio.com/opinion/marco-antonio-garcia-granados/cuestion-politica/ulises-ruiz-sera-enjuiciado.

Hilgers, Tina. 2008. "Causes and Consequences of Political Clientelism: Mexico's PRD in Comparative Perspective." *Latin American Politics and Society* 50 (4): 123–53. https://doi.org/10.1111/j.1548-2456.2008.00032.x.

Inmujeres (*Instituto Nacional de las Mujeres de México*, National Women's Institute of Mexico). 2006. "La Población Indígena Mexicana." http://cedoc.inmujeres.gob.mx/documentos_download/100782.pdf.

Langston, Joy, and Scott Morgenstern. 2009. "Campaigning in an Electoral Authoritarian Regime: The Case of Mexico." *Comparative Politics* 41 (2): 165–81. https://doi.org/10.5129/001041509X12911362971954.

Lyne, Mona M. 2008. *The Voter's Dilemma and Democratic Accountability: Latin America and Beyond*. University Park, PA: Penn State University Press.

Magaloni, Beatriz. 2006. *Voting for Autocracy: Hegemonic Party Survival and Its Demise in Mexico*. Cambridge: Cambridge University Press.

Muñoz, Paula. 2014. "An Informational Theory of Campaign Clientelism: The Case of Peru." *Comparative Politics* 47 (1): 79–98. https://doi.org/10.5129/00104151481362315.

Nichter, Simeon. 2008. "Vote Buying or Turnout Buying? Machine Politics and the Secret Ballot." 102 (1): 19–31. https://doi.org/10.1017/S0003055408080106.

Stokes, Susan. 2005. "Perverse Accountability: A Formal Model of Machine Politics with Evidence from Argentina." *American Political Science Review* 99 (3): 315–25. https://doi.org/10.1017/S0003055405051683.

Suverza, Alejandro. 2006. "Las Vicisitudes de Ulises Ruiz en Oaxaca." *El Universal*. June 15. https://archivo.eluniversal.com.mx/estados/61559.html.

Taylor-Robinson, Michelle M. 2010. *Do the Poor Count? Democratic Institutions and Accountability in a Context of Poverty*. University Park, PA: Penn State University Press.

CHAPTER SEVENTEEN

NGOs as "Necessary Evils": Challenges of Doing Good in Urban Northeast Brazil

Luminiţa-Anda Mandache

In May 2020 when the COVID-19 pandemic was something we thought would end quickly I received a text message from Tayson, my Brazilian friend, asking how the situation was in the United States. I complained about the challenges of teaching online and he shared his experience learning online and the frustrations that come with being cloistered in his overcrowded home. I met Tayson, now in his early twenties, when he was a teenager finishing high school. Tayson is about to graduate from college (thanks in part to scholarship and social inclusion programs implemented by the Workers' Party between 2003 and 2016) and works as an intern in the advertising department of a bank in downtown Fortaleza. He is the first in his family to graduate high school and attend a university. He was encouraged and supported to study for the national exams and apply for college by his family and by his co-workers, other youth, and community activists at the nongovernmental organization (NGO) Vai dar Certo ("It's Going to Be Ok") in his neighborhood Lagoa Verde (Figure 17.1), where I first met him.

In 2014, I traveled to Lagoa Verde, a neighborhood in the city of Fortaleza, Brazil, to visit the NGO Vai dar Certo, applauded nationally and internationally for its alternative economy projects. Both Lagoa Verde and Vai dar Certo are fictive names that I use in this chapter to talk about places and institutions in Brazil, to protect the anonymity of my research participants. What brought me to Lagoa Verde was the incongruity between Vai dar Certo's national and international reputation and its effectiveness in ameliorating the ongoing poverty in Lagoa Verde. I wanted to understand what this contradiction can tell us about development and urban poverty. Lagoa Verde is the poorest neighborhood in Fortaleza, which in turn is among the most unequal cities in the world. After that 2014 visit, I returned to Lagoa Verde for a full year in 2015 and every year since then until 2018. Since 2018, I have been in contact with friends from Brazil periodically through WhatsApp and Facebook Messenger, platforms that allow me a certain engagement in Lagoa Verde's community life. As an anthropologist in Lagoa Verde,

Figure 17.1. A street in the Lagoa Verde neighborhood, August 2017. Photo by Luminița-Anda Mandache.

I spent most of my time teaching English to low-income teenagers, women, and schoolteachers in addition to accompanying local activists and health workers in their daily work.

In this chapter, I employ the expression "necessary evil," used by a community activist in Lagoa Verde, to discuss the tension between the local reality in Lagoa Verde and the broader international development context. On one hand, at the local level there is a general skepticism in Lagoa Verde about the Vai dar Certo's work. This skepticism mainly comes from senior activists, former employees and residents who criticize the NGO's clientelist approach to development, projects they perceive to be irrelevant, and general lack of transparency (many perceive the NGO as *fechado*, or closed to the participation of the general public). *Clientelism* is the practice of exchanging votes and political support for goods and services (Hickel 2011; see also Chapter 16). On the other hand, by calling Vai dar Certo a "necessary" evil, residents and activists also acknowledge that the NGO was able to change the image of the neighborhood, from a place of misery to a place where poor people are collectively creating strategies to overcome poverty. In this chapter, I particularly emphasize how the nature of funding might shape the type of projects meant to "do good" (Fisher 1997) that an NGO develops, and I illustrate the tensions that arise when projects do not directly speak to the needs of the population that NGOs claim to serve. While scholars of development and anthropologists have long problematized the neoliberal nature of NGO work and questioned the impacts of such "development" (Alvarez 2009), less attention has been paid to the internal dynamics and challenges of these organizations and the ways in which they shape the nature of development work.

In the first part of this chapter, I provide a historical overview of Vai dar Certo and then I illustrate the "evil" or negative perception of the NGO in Lagoa Verde through the criticism brought by other activists or residents. I then discuss the "necessary" part, by illustrating the positive local impact of Vai dar Certo – an impact that is sometimes difficult to measure by economic and development indicators. Finally, I present the perspective of one of the NGO employees, situating the organization in the national and international context and discussing the tensions that made its functioning so complex and limited in impact.

HISTORY OF VAI DAR CERTO

Vai dar Certo was created in 1998 by a former Catholic priest inspired by liberation theology and the teachings of Paulo Freire; he was also a member of the Basic Ecclesial Communities (CEBs) movement, the progressive wing of the Catholic Church. According to **liberation theology**, poverty was a political matter that had to be diminished through political interventions as opposed to charity. Most of the work of the CEBs in Lagoa Verde between the 1970s and the 1990s included creating community groups and associations of women and teenagers based on mutual aid. The overarching goal of these projects was to cultivate a transformative political consciousness that made poor Brazilians understand the causes of their poverty and identify allies in their political struggle. For this purpose, Lagoa Verde had its own radio station, a local newspaper, and a preschool, all relying on the work of local volunteers. The Catholic Church deemed these efforts unnecessary after the military regime had been replaced by a constitutional democracy in 1985; after they withdrew support, these local institutions withered away. Even though exceptional by today's standards, community organizing around the CEBs, like in Lagoa Verde, was not unique, but rather was common in Brazilian and Latin American urban peripheries around that time (Hewitt 1990).

Although earlier work conducted by Vai dar Certo was in line with liberation theology, the NGO's focus shifted in the 2000s when it started receiving government funding. From the year 2000 on, the NGO developed courses meant to equip low-income teenagers and women with marketable skills that would allow them to get jobs in the wealthier parts of the city or become entrepreneurs. Entrepreneurship was also promoted through financial literacy classes and a microfinance program that allowed residents to take small loans to support their businesses. The most famous project was the creation of a local currency that circulated in the community with the goal of supporting local production and local consumption.

Projects initiated after 2000 were in line with the Workers' Party national development model emphasizing larger access to credit, especially to Brazilians previously excluded from the formal economy. This shift in the NGO's approach is a result of the historical context in which Vai dar Certo was working, mainly the Pink Tide era. The **Pink Tide** was a period at the beginning of the twenty-first century characterized by leftist politics throughout Latin America. During this period, Brazil experienced a reduction of historical inequalities through, among other things, investment in social welfare programs that benefited historically marginalized groups (Anderson 2019). Additionally, with the state on their side, forms of progressive political action diversified (Alvarez et al. 2017). Many NGOs, including Vai dar Certo, started receiving state funding while still receiving some support through international corporate social responsibility programs. In the wake of the 2016 undemocratic takeover of power in Brazil that removed the Workers' Party president Dilma Rousseff from office, it became clear that the NGO could not rely on public funding alone. Therefore, it shifted toward partnerships with private organizations, became even more attuned to buzzwords in the field of international development, and created projects imbued with techno-optimism, or the hope that technology was part of the solution to local problems. Such projects included, for example, the creation of a coding lab for teenagers. The end of the Pink Tide era forced NGOs like Vai dar Certo to adapt once more, attracting the criticism of residents who saw their work as locally irrelevant.

HOW CAN AN NGO BE "EVIL"?

Senior community leaders of Lagoa Verde who were part of the CEBs movement had their earlier grassroots political work as a reference for evaluating the work done today by Vai dar Certo. In the eyes of one schoolteacher, Marilene, Vai dar Certo's projects around financial inclusion did not address the fundamental problems of the neighborhood. She saw such projects as less relevant than the creation of residents' political consciousness, especially in a moment when democracy was under threat in Brazil. According to Marilene, Brazil's Pink Tide came with increased access to credit and consumer goods for poor Brazilians, and Vai dar Certo developed projects to ensure that residents could take advantage of these opportunities, at the expense of investing in residents' political education.

Marilene remembered that in the past, inspired by the work of Brazilian educator Augusto Boal and Paulo Freire, theater was used as a mechanism of education and reflection around things such as economic inequality and racism. A famous play that the community leaders organized before the 1990s was "Christmas in Black and White." The play was a critique of consumerism, inequality, and racism. Today, the same theater techniques are used to promote Vai dar Certo's projects, which emphasize consumerism, by advertising the different types of credit lines that are available to low-income Brazilians from Lagoa Verde.

Also, access to post-secondary education was something that many community leaders and Catholic priests were concerned with in the past. Even though in 2000 Vai dar Certo organized courses preparing high school students for college, these projects were discontinued. Instead, the NGO created projects that embraced a techno-optimism that most residents or community leaders did not relate to. Techno-optimism is the belief that technology will solve our current problems (Miller 2017). For example, Vai dar Certo created a lab where teenagers could learn how to code, taught by instructors from other Latin American countries and a European coordinator. The lab's goal was to obtain contracts with the city or other actors, including academics, and conduct research in the community using apps that local teenagers themselves had developed. In this way, the NGO thought it could act as a gatekeeper of local knowledge. In 2016, a partnership with an Ivy League university in the United States promised to bring a 3D printer to Vai dar Certo, motivated by the conviction that "anyone could be a protagonist for change," as it was announced at a local event. To many activists like Marilene, it was not clear how the 3D printer could solve local problems such as inadequate infrastructure and hunger.

Other critiques targeted the lack of transparency around NGO funds. Many activists remember that at one point their neighborhood had around 60 NGOs, but since many were funded by politicians, they disappeared when those politicians left office. Vai dar Certo lasted longer, but competition for public funds or even support from politicians was fierce; therefore, Vai dar Certo had to make alliances with certain politicians who offered their help. This reminded locals and activists of the clientelist politics that have long threatened Brazil's democracy, a place where clientelist favors and not democratic rights prevail (Nichter 2018). Additionally, rumors were circulating that the leader of the NGO and some employees were responsible for not repaying loans borrowed from Vai dar Certo through the microfinance program. Many of these critics saw these moves as undemocratic and a continuation of the clientelist politics that they were trying to break from. In other words, even though the NGO promoted a discourse about equality and the rights of the poor, the reality within the walls of the NGO told a different story, one in which favors and ties with people in power still mattered the most.

Luiza, a younger community leader, felt that the NGO was appropriating the struggles of her community and using this symbolic capital to build legitimacy. According to Luiza, the *luta do passado* (struggle of the past), in other words past efforts for social and political change, which the leader of Vai dar Certo mentioned each time he spoke at public events, was not the work of Vai dar Certo alone. *A luta do passado* was the work of previous generations of activists, of the progressive Catholic priests who lived in their community until the 1990s, and the entirety of Lagoa Verde, not Vai dar Certo alone. Luiza felt that the leader of Vai dar Certo was speaking on their behalf to obtain social and political capital, not to benefit the community. Younger educated leaders like Luiza saw the NGO as reproducing a **hegemonic** order where white foreigners, like Mario, the European coordinator of the tech lab, were brought to Brazil to coordinate projects or teach coding and be paid salaries much higher than the salaries of most local employees. To Luiza, this was business as usual, making young activists question the difference between Vai dar Certo and a capitalist enterprise.

In the eyes of many residents who lived far away from Vai dar Certo, in parts of the neighborhood that the NGO did not reach with its programs, Vai dar Certo was nothing more than a bank where they could pay bills. Many noted that the NGO was absent from the daily struggles of most residents, such as dealing with gangs who sometimes robbed public schools, or the pervasive lack of necessities such as food, water, garbage collection, or electricity. Since the NGO could not reach all residents with their programs, many also perceived the organization as *fechada* or closed to the participation of people like them. Since the 1990s, Lagoa Verde has grown, expanding into previously uninhabited areas that lack access to water or infrastructure. NGO presence has been nonexistent in these areas, as have churches until recently. Therefore, for residents living in these places, Vai dar Certo was "a place for *gringos*," foreigners from Europe and North America who were not residing in Lagoa Verde. Yet, as I will illustrate in the next section, many residents were also able to see that the NGO had a positive impact on their community, but in ways that were less easy to assess.

HOW CAN AN NGO BE "NECESSARY"?

On the first day of my fieldwork in 2015, I took the bus from the middle-class neighborhood where I was living with a host family to Lagoa Verde. The almost one-hour bus ride required me to change buses at the bus terminal. In the bus terminal, a young woman stared incessantly at me. After a while, when we were close to arriving at Lagoa Verde, she approached me: "*Oi*! I saw you in the bus terminal and I thought … this *gringa*, isn't she going to Vai dar Certo?" Neide, the young woman, was a college student at that time and one of the middle-class volunteers from more economically developed parts of the city. One Vai dar Certo employee was designated to guide and mentor volunteers like Neide who wanted to learn from this NGO about effective civic work. Neide's remark that a *gringa* on a bus at the periphery of Fortaleza could only be going to Vai dar Certo was also telling: What else would a *gringa* be doing there? It also spoke about how common it was for Brazilians in Fortaleza to hear of *gringos* going to Vai dar Certo. In the following months I learned that it wasn't just Brazilians but also international scholars who would come and conduct short- or long-term internships or studies at Vai dar Certo.

In the following days, I met Clarissa, a university professor who was conducting a study on the local impact of Vai dar Certo in Lagoa Verde, and Andreas, her son, who, after having lived in Germany for a few years, was now an undergraduate student at a Brazilian university and doing an internship at Vai dar Certo. Both Andreas and I were commuting at that time from the more affluent parts of the city toward the political and economic margins. The movement of middle-class Brazilians from the city center to the periphery is a rather exceptional one, since this route is mainly traveled in reverse by the low-income Brazilians who work in the more developed central parts of the city. But in this case, it wasn't low-income teenagers traveling to the better-off parts of the city to interact with middle-class Brazilians in often-hierarchical power relations. Instead, Vai dar Certo was one of the few places, besides the public universities, where teenagers from Lagoa Verde and middle-class Brazilians worked side by side, a rather exceptional fact considering the racial and economic inequalities that permeate social interactions in Brazil.

Inevitably, experiences with people from outside of the community made many teenagers, like Tayson, introduced earlier in this chapter, feel proud. Thanks to the work at Vai dar Certo he not only acquired skills that allowed him to later obtain an internship in a major company in Fortaleza, but also received the material and emotional support necessary to apply and be accepted to college. Being at Vai dar Certo allowed Tayson to learn English for free (private foreign language classes remain prohibitively expensive in Fortaleza), to make friends from around the world, and to broaden his social horizons. Tayson's personal situation was even more difficult since one of his brothers was involved in the local drug trade. This often made his home an unsafe place because, at times, the threats were continuous and the fear of something bad happening almost constant. In that unstable environment it was difficult for Tayson to focus on learning and on going to college. Vai dar Certo was, to him, a safe place where he could find refuge, study, eat, interact with friends, and visit on the weekends, if needed. Tayson's home situation was known at Vai dar Certo and employees supported him by never questioning his presence there, making themselves emotionally available for him, and sometimes even financially when his family needed it.

Tayson's mother took sewing classes at Vai dar Certo, and she would sometimes mention how leaving the home on Sunday to go to church or Vai dar Certo made her everyday life nicer. Even though buying a sewing machine remains expensive for many women in Lagoa Verde, just taking the sewing classes at Vai dar Certo is something many women enjoy because it is an opportunity for them to meet other women in their situation and feel respected and supported. This is an experience that I could also testify to while teaching English classes. It soon became clear that English was the secondary reason students enrolled in my classes. Both women and teenagers needed a place, other than home and school, where they could meet others like them, joke, laugh, listen to music, watch movies, and share tips about shopping deals.

Genuine care and friendship developed between the local teenagers and the Latin American and European employees of the NGO. This care was manifested, for example, through things such as making sure that Tayson and his family were safe, but also ensuring that younger employees would not travel by bus at night, putting themselves at risk. When Tayson's brother was shot dead due to his involvement in the drug trade, employees at Vai dar Certo raised money and paid for a bus that took Tayson's brother and the entire family to the cemetery in a small town in the interior of the state. This support came without being requested and with no expectations from the NGO for repayment. Tayson's family alone could not have afforded the cost of the funeral because of their precarious situation at that time. In another example, when the grandmother of a former Vai dar Certo employee, Marta, became ill and ended up in one of the poorly equipped local hospitals where no beds were available for seniors, leaders at the Vai dar Certo were able to mobilize their personal networks of friends and families who work in hospitals to provide Marta's grandmother with much needed support.

Additionally, for people less familiar with the immediate and extended network of contacts of Vai dar Certo, the NGO was important because, as some put it, it "changed the face of the neighborhood." Marilene observed that "Vai dar Certo erased the prejudice that people have about Lagoa Verde. In the past, the stereotype was that Lagoa Verde was dangerous, because the mass media advertised the neighborhood this way. But Vai dar Certo changed this. Today many people feel proud that they come from here." When talking about the mass media portrayal of Lagoa Verde, Marilene made reference to a study on the human development index of the neighborhoods in Fortaleza that was widely circulated in the local media. The study emphasized that Lagoa Verde was the area with the lowest human development index in the city (Lazari 2014). In many of the interviews that I conducted, residents in Lagoa Verde tried to convince me that the media was wrong in calling them the poorest people in the city. Other neighborhoods were as bad and, in the end, no one knocked on their door to interview them and ask about their living conditions. The interview with me was their occasion to talk about how much their neighborhood had improved, from a place that lacked all urban necessities, including water and roads, a few decades ago to one with an internationally famous NGO and a local currency. It is examples and moments like these that made many residents and community leaders think that Vai dar Certo is also necessary, not just an evil.

HOW IS AN NGO A "NECESSARY EVIL"?

Mario, a European man in his thirties from a middle-class family, was an employee of Vai dar Certo who had been working there for eight years when I met him. Mario studied in the United States and decided to make a career out of finding solutions to complex problems such as urban poverty or inequality by working with grassroots organizations. He mobilized his social and cultural capital to create a network of partnerships for Vai dar Certo, among which there are not only important public, private, and civic organizations in Brazil and in Latin America, but also international funding institutions and prestigious American universities. From his perspective, there are many challenges for an NGO with Vai dar Certo's fame and history, and these challenges have to do with the larger national and international context in which this tiny NGO at the margins of Fortaleza is embedded. Additionally, because of its fame, there are also a lot of unreasonable expectations that the NGO alone can completely transform the entire neighborhood.

Mario believes that the Pink Tide brought a lot of positive change to places like Lagoa Verde. Luiz Inácio Lula da Silva, or simply Lula, the former Workers' Party president, put

Brazil on the international map as a country able to manage its domestic problems, such as poverty and inequality, without international interference. What Mario noticed was that Vai dar Certo became dependent on federal funding during the Pink Tide, and this dependency was ultimately a problem. In 2015, employees at Vai dar Certo had no major concerns regarding their funding coming through federal grants. However, in 2016, in the wake of the undemocratic takeover of power, their concerns were clear. The insecurity and fear that government funding might be cut, which in the end happened, led Vai dar Certo to start partnerships with private actors and develop projects imbued with techno-optimism, such as the coding lab for teenagers. The NGO's overall goal was to diversify funding and attract donors through projects that spoke to the trends in international development initiatives. These efforts came with a cost: Many leaders or residents saw these new initiatives as irrelevant. In other words, even though the federal funding received by Vai dar Certo was critical, relying on this funding alone made the NGO vulnerable, and efforts to diversify funding came with a cost.

CONCLUSION

In this chapter, I summarized the story of Vai dar Certo because its history, while unique, is also typical of what has happened to community organizations and NGOs across Latin America in recent years. What is unique about Vai dar Certo is its existence in a community with a local history of collective action, including Catholic priests and workers of all kinds who have been fighting for a dignified life. What is typical about Vai dar Certo is the way in which it is influenced like other small NGOs, by international development discourse and processes, as well as the whims of powerful political actors. Vai dar Certo also reflects the ways in which small organizations, despite all their good intentions, have to adapt to continue existing. Adapting means "dancing to the music of the donors," as one employee of Vai dar Certo once put it. Or, in other words, developing projects that respond to the demands of funding institutions, be they public or private. Doing so comes at a cost. The costs include activists and residents who see these organizations as irrelevant and ignorant of the daily problems of most residents, which in the long run can erode their legitimacy and local support.

The complex understanding that residents in Lagoa Verde have about the politics of NGOs, calling Vai dar Certo a "necessary evil," also suggests that residents are not disenchanted or cynical toward politics, as some scholars have suggested (Savell 2015). These Brazilians, on the contrary, have complex and nuanced understandings of politics: They can situate the dynamics and politics of an NGO in their community in the national and often international political context. Doing so suggests that their political subjectivities, or the ways low-income Brazilians understand their political roles as citizens, are complex and are influenced by everyday life, their understanding of politics on a local, national, and international scale, and in some cases their participation in collective action.

REFLECTION AND DISCUSSION QUESTIONS

- Why do residents in Lagoa Verde call Vai dar Certo a "necessary evil"? Can you think of organizations in your community that might be characterized in the same way? Explain.
- Why did younger community leaders like Luiza criticize Vai dar Certo for hiring employees like Mario? Do you agree with their criticism?
- What should international organizations consider when funding grassroots organizations like Vai dar Certo?
- If you were the leader of Vai dar Certo, what strategies might you pursue to secure funding for the organization and remain locally relevant?

KEY CONCEPTS

- **hegemony**: A term popularized by the Italian Marxist philosopher Antonio Gramsci to describe the dominance of a certain set of ideas and ethics in a particular time period.
- **liberation theology**: A theological direction of the Catholic Church in Latin America, prevalent in the middle of the twentieth century, that emphasized the liberation of the oppressed and a stance of solidarity with the poor. This approach called for a socioeconomic understanding of the causes of oppression and inequality and efforts to build a more just society.
- **Pink Tide**: A period of progressive (or left-leaning) governments in Latin America that started with the governance of Hugo Chavez in Venezuela in 1998 and ended in 2016 with the start of the current conservative (or Blue) wave in which Latin American politics have swung back toward conservatism.

EXPLORE FURTHER

- To learn more about life in Latin American cities, read **Chapters 5**, **10**, **24**, and **25**.
- To learn more about clientelism, read **Chapter 16**.
- Freire, Paulo. 1973. *Pedagogy of the Oppressed*. New York: Bloomsbury.
- Mandache, Luminița-Anda. 2020. "The Road Back to Serfdom: Solidarity Economies on the Periphery of Fortaleza, Brazil between 1970 and 2016." *Latin American Perspectives* 46 (233): 190–205.
- Muylaert, Anna, dir. 2015. *The Second Mother*.

ABOUT THE AUTHOR

Luminița-Anda Mandache, Ph.D., is a senior Lise-Meitner fellow at the Center for Ethics and Poverty Research at the University of Salzburg, Austria. Dr. Mandache is a political and economic anthropologist interested in social movements, democracy, and political subjectivities in Latin America (Brazil) and Eastern Europe. Originally from Romania, Dr. Mandache was a first-generation college student.

REFERENCES

Alvarez, Sonia. 2009. "Beyond NGO-ization? Reflections from Latin America." *Development* 42 (2): 175–84. https://doi.org/10.1057/dev.2009.23.

Alvarez, Sonia, Jeffrey Rubin, Millie Thayer, Gianpaolo Baiocchi, and Augustin Lao-Montes, eds. 2017. *Beyond Civil Society. Activism, Participation, and Protest in Latin America*. Durham, NC: Duke University Press.

Anderson, Perry. 2019. *Brazil Apart 1964–2019*. London: Verso Books.

Fisher, William. 1997. "DOING GOOD? The Politics and Antipolitics of NGO Practices." *Annual Review of Anthropology* 26: 439–64. https://doi.org/10.1146/annurev.anthro.26.1.439.

Hewitt, W.E. 1990. "Religion and the Consolidation of Democracy in Brazil: The Role of the Comunidades Eclesiais de Base (CEBs)." *Sociological Analysis* 50 (2): 139–52. https://doi.org/10.2307/3710811.

Hickel, Allen. 2011. "Clientelism." *Annual Review of Political Science* 14: 289–310. https://doi.org/10.1146/annurev.polisci.031908.220508.

Lazari, Mariana. 2014. "Conjunto Palmeiras é o Bairro de Fortaleza com Pior Desenvolvimento." *O Povo*, February 20. https://www20.opovo.com.br/app/fortaleza/2014/02/20/noticiafortaleza,3209850/conjunto-palmeiras-e-o-bairro-de-fortaleza-com-pior-desenvolvimento.shtml.

Miller, Sebastian. 2017. "The Dangers of Techno-Optimism." *Berkeley Political Review*, November 16.

Nichter, Simeon. 2018. *Votes for Survival: Relational Clientelism in Latin America*. Cambridge: Cambridge University Press.

Savell, Stephanie. 2015. "'I'm Not a Leader': Cynicism and Good Citizenship in a Brazilian Favela." *PoLAR* 38 (2): 300–17. https://doi.org/10.1111/plar.12112.

CHAPTER EIGHTEEN

The Role of Masculinity in Connecting Knowledge and Politics: Pension Experts in Chile

Maria J. Azocar

In October 2019, large demonstrations against economic inequities took place across Chile (Figure 18.1). At the beginning of the month, the Chilean government had announced an increase in metro fares of 30 pesos (0.037 US dollars) in Santiago, the capital city. As a sign of protest, high school students jumped the metro turnstiles and called for the public to refuse to pay for metro tickets. By mid-October, demonstrations escalated all over the country. People gathered on the streets and the slogan *"no son 30 pesos, son 30 años"* (it's not 30 pesos, it's 30 years) gained widespread popularity. For protesters, the 30 years of democratic governments that followed the dictatorship of Augusto Pinochet (1973–1990) had done little to change the pillars of Chilean neoliberal capitalism and the economic precarity that it created for most Chileans. On the contrary, during this period Chile became one of Latin America's most unequal countries (Chancel et al. 2022).

Although the metro rate hike sparked the 2019 protests, pension policy quickly emerged as a key focus of protesters' demands. According to the polls taken at that time, pensions were Chileans' most pressing concern (65 per cent), followed by healthcare (46 per cent) and education (38 per cent) (CEP 2019). This was not the first expression of dissatisfaction with the Chilean pension system. Since 2012, unions and citizens have increasingly demanded the abolition of the market-oriented pension system, which is run by private pension fund companies, known as AFPs (*Administradoras de Fondos de Pensiones*). On two occasions, the government created national expert commissions to make proposals for reforming national pension policy. In 2016, just three years before the massive October 2019 demonstrations, unions organized protests in different cities, using the slogan *"No Mas AFP"* (No More AFPs) to call for the abolition of pension fund companies, which profit handsomely from Chilean workers' obligatory retirement savings.

The puzzle, however, is that despite the massive unpopularity of the AFPs, state authorities from both progressive and conservative administrations considered it unthinkable to abolish the

Figure 18.1. Chilean protests in Puerto Montt, October 2019. Photo by Natalia Reyes Escobar (CC 4.0).

existing pension system. Their response was validated by a group of pension experts, most of them economists, who since 1990 have played a key role as advisors to governmental officials, regardless of the party that was in power. How do we explain this puzzle? How has it been possible to defend the Chilean pension system despite such strong popular discontent with the policy's results?

One possible answer to this question comes from Marxist perspectives, a theoretical approach that examines how economically powerful groups leverage wealth and influence to benefit themselves. Using this approach, some analysts have observed that in Chile, private pension fund companies, insurance companies, banks, and financial intermediaries benefit greatly from the current privatized pension system (Fundación SOL 2020). Moreover, economic business power gets translated into political power (Blackburn 2002). Following this Marxist line of reasoning, pension experts working in academia, in think-tanks, or in the government can be bought by the economic elite to keep the status quo in pension policymaking. One way of buying political power, for example, is implementing a revolving door system between the state and the pension industry. Scholars have found that several pension experts accepted executive positions in pension fund companies and insurance companies after leaving their posts in the government, making significant change in pension policy difficult to obtain (Bril-Mascarenhas and Mailet 2019).

The problem with this explanation, however, is that it falls short of showing *how* economists as pension experts in Chile have been able to maintain their authority as truth tellers in relation to pension policy over the years. The power of economists as experts is not inevitable. Local and institutional logics mediate their influence over time. Furthermore, history has shown that Chilean economists' ideas have a great amount of flexibility and adaptability based on the political opportunities that arise (Markoff and Montecinos 1993). Thus, there is nothing inherently powerful in economists' knowledge claims on pension policy as opposed to the knowledge claims of other kinds of experts. The relationship established in Chile between economic pension expertise and the privatization of pension funds was not a foregone conclusion. To the contrary, economists had to invest time and resources to make that relationship relevant and establish themselves as a source of truth in pension policymaking.

To understand how economists in Chile have been able to defend the current privatized pension system despite massive popular discontent, I focus on the organized practices that Chilean economists have deployed to assert their authority as pension experts and produce credible knowledge on pension reform. Rather than asking what is regarded as true or technical in pension expertise, I ask how these divisions operate and to what effect. My approach understands expertise as a practice, not an individual capacity. Individuals fight for their status as experts by building a network in which technologies, claims, institutions, and even emotions are enrolled to give rise to expertise (Azocar 2020). In this process of expertise formation, however, I contend that the assemblage of expertise into a network operates in a context already permeated by intersectional gender power differentials. Gender, in intersection with other vectors of power, informs experts' discursive claims – that is, the ways that they define themselves and their actions considering those understandings. My approach, then, focuses on experts' practices and deliberate collective mobilization to configure their expertise in relational ways.

In the first part of this chapter, I describe the connection between gender and expertise. I use *gender* as a verb (gendering), that is, a process by which bodies, skills, instruments, and claims are coded as masculine or feminine. In the process of **gendering expertise**, a hierarchy between masculinity and femininity is created, and in so doing some groups gain more advantage by connecting themselves to the masculine sphere of science, subordinating their competitors to the feminine sphere of non-science. In the second part of the chapter, I show how Chilean economists have fought hard to be recognized by state authorities as pension experts. For example, economists have used the distinction between masculinity and femininity to devalue sociologists' expertise as feminine. Economists have also created a hierarchy of masculinity to dismiss the expertise of actuaries (mathematicians who analyze the financial costs of potential events, helping businesses minimize the cost of risks). Thus, the power of masculinity has contributed to giving economists an advantage in persuading state authorities to implement their proposed reforms. In the third part of the chapter, I examine the effects of expertise battles over pension policy. I describe the machinery put in place by economists to create exclusive channels for allocating funds in quantitative and financial knowledge and successfully shut the knowledge of other disciplines out of the public debate. As a result, economists monopolized the production of pension knowledge in Chile, thereby reproducing citizens' deep mistrust of economists as experts.

THE CHILEAN MODEL OF PENSION PROVISION

The population aged 65 and over is growing faster than all other age groups in Chile and in many other countries of the world (UN 2019). In 1994, the World Bank framed this demographic transformation as an "old age crisis" that would cause a "collapse" in government budgets (World Bank 1994, xiii). The World Bank's framework of an old age crisis mobilized a sense of alarm around the world and conceptualized elderly people's lives as a burden for the state. At the same time, the World Bank pointed to the Chilean model of pension provision as a solution to the so-called crisis.

At the time, the Chilean pension model was unique in the world. The system was implemented in 1981 during the dictatorship of Augusto Pinochet (1973–1990) and was part of a larger plan for restructuring the Chilean economy (and society) under neoliberal terms. The 1981 social security system was novel in that pensions were financed exclusively by workers' personal savings and were not subsidized by the state. This is an example of an *austerity measure*, a policy that reduces the financial obligation of the state to its citizens by cutting public services. In Chile, workers are obliged to give a percentage of their salaries to private companies that invest workers' savings in the financial market. When Chilean workers retire, the private companies calculate individuals' pensions based on their lifelong contributions and financial profits. In other parts of the world, the social security system works differently. In the United States, for example, workers give a percentage of their salaries to the state, and then the state uses those contributions to pay retirees' pensions. It is true that in some cases US workers contribute to both the state and private companies. However, in the United States, private companies work as a complement to the social security system and do not occupy a leading role in the national policy structure as they do in Chile.

In Chile, the state does not play a significant part in administering pensions, and workers' savings are invested exclusively in the financial market. In 1994, when the World Bank celebrated Chile's privatized and financialized pension system, other countries used the Chilean model as a reference for implementing similar reforms (Orenstein 2011). Recent nationwide protests in Chile, however, have contested the assertion by the World Bank that this type of system is a good solution to the challenges of an aging population.

As I stated at the beginning of this chapter, the puzzle is that despite the massive unpopularity of the current privatized pension system, Chilean state authorities have left the current system untouched and have used arguments rooted in economic science to validate the status quo. Specific groups of economists have fought for authority as pension experts, and consequently their interventions have acquired the appearance of unassailable truth in public debates. What sort of knowledge claims, alliances, and devices made such interventions possible? During moments of critique and protests, how were pension experts able to claim this authority and convince government officials to act on their reform proposals despite widespread popular disagreement with experts' views?

To answer these questions, I traced the history of Chilean policy debates on pension reform between 1981 and 2014. To carry out my research on pension expertise, I needed to study up. **Studying up** means studying people who wield power. It is important to study the processes by which power is won and maintained to shed light on the ways people can resist authoritarian uses and abuses of power and transform them into democratic power. Following this methodology, I conducted 72 in-depth interviews with economists, sociologists, actuaries, and other policy advisors. I analyzed archival data, and I reviewed 93 videos of public hearings that were held before the 2014 *Comisión Asesora Presidencial Sobre El Sistema de Pensiones* (Presidential Advisory Commission on Pension Policy). My analysis of these data sources revealed that gender ideologies have played a key role in the construction of expertise in Chile and, as a result, led to gridlock in official debates about pension policy and stymied reform.

THE ROLE OF GENDER IN EXPERTISE CONSTRUCTION

Expertise is not simply an individual capacity or educational credential. When a person holds the title of an expert, it means that someone has attributed authority to that person. Today governments increasingly rely on science and scientists to define problems and make decisions. Experts gain trust from government officials by drawing a line between what constitutes science and non-science, positioning themselves on the side of science (Gieryn 1983). Therefore, expertise is conceptualized as a practice of doing boundary work between science and non-science.

Boundary-making practices of expertise are often expressed through **jurisdictional battles** – that is, battles to gain power in a specific field (Abbott 1988). Power, however, is not neutral. Power always involves different forms of exploitation, oppression, and institutionalized inequality. For example, Witz (1990) focused on the jurisdictional battles in the US medical field. In these battles, men used legislation to exclude women from universities and professional associations. Men also made demarcations between science and non-science, privileging male physicians' science-based expertise over female midwives' and nurses' ostensibly less scientific expertise. As this example shows, gender as a form of power matters in jurisdictional battles because specific bodies (male and female) are valued differentially as experts, though the rationale for this differentiation is coded in terms of a presumed scientific gradient.

Instruments and devices can be gendered as well. For example, the qualitative/quantitative divide in social science research methods is often linked to the masculine/feminine binary between hard/soft, rational/intuitive, intellect/feeling, and objective/subjective (Oakley 1998).

However, in the same way that men are not naturally prone to become physicians, there is nothing inherently masculine about the technology of numbers. The connection between masculinity and numbers is socially constructed. In fact, for many years the use of quantitative methods in the social sciences was considered women's work. It was defined as a repetitive and low status research skill in comparison to the theoretical and more rigorous masculine qualitative research skill (Seltzer and Haldar 2015). When quantification got increasingly coded as masculine, numerical knowledge and numerical skills became socially valued in the social sciences and a sharp hierarchy emerged between disciplines (e.g., between economics and sociology) and within disciplines (e.g., between quantitative and qualitative political science; Nelson 2010).

Another way of understanding the role of gender in jurisdictional battles over expertise is through the concept of hegemonic masculinity. The term **hegemonic masculinity** describes society's ideal male and functions to justify and naturalize male–female and male–male hierarchies (Connell & Messerschmidt 2005). The hegemonic man is the "real man" in the collective imagination, and depending on the context, the specific traits of hegemonic men can vary. In the field of law, for example, Pierce (1996) argues that an ideal (male) litigator is always angry and has a "Rambo" style of confrontation (60). Here, the hegemonic man is intimidating and aggressive and approaches cross-examination as a "mental duel" to "destroy" witnesses and "rape" them. Litigators who can't perform this ideal form of legal expertise are treated as "wimps" or "too nice" for the job.

Experts and experts' skills, then, are socially constructed, and gender plays a role in these ideological constructs because people, instruments, and emotions are coded as masculine or feminine. In jurisdictional battles over expertise, therefore, gender functions as a verb: It is a process by which someone or something comes to be associated with masculinity or femininity. In this process of gendering expertise, distinctions are often made between science and non-science, and it is often the case that the sphere of science is masculinized whereas the sphere of non-science is feminized.

JURISDICTIONAL BATTLES IN PENSION EXPERTISE IN CHILE

In Chile, over the past 30 years, economists have engaged in jurisdictional battles over pension expertise with other professions. In these battles, economists have used the technology of numbers (on which their discipline lies) to claim the superiority of their expertise. For example, in conferences and public debates as well as in the interviews I conducted, economists and high-ranking officials and policy advisors opined that numbers offered a "technical" view of pension expertise, because mathematical formulas provided "hard facts" and "objective" perspectives on pension policymaking. For example, I asked Juana, a top-ranked government official, why it had been so difficult to change the pension system in Chile. In her response, she drew a line between science and mythology: "In public policy you need a diagnosis to support your argument ... You need to run some numbers to test the system, to get results. When you don't have the hard information, it is pure mythology." When I asked the same question to Pedro, another top-ranked policy advisor, he repeated a similar argument that hard facts and numbers were important, but he also added: "Unfortunately, we didn't have professionals from other disciplines ... sociologists, philosophers, participating in the debate. The debate is too technical and needs a humanist vision, but they [humanists] weren't present in the debate. There is a lot of financial engineering here and people from the humanities don't understand it."

For these economists, then, sociologists had a "humanist point of view" that was important for the debate, but at the same time sociologists' expertise was limited because they didn't understand finance. Luciano, a male economist and highly ranked policy advisor, explained this point in the following terms: "I have worked with sociologists ... my friends, trained in Germany.... I have really enjoyed our philosophical and sociological conversations, but in this [pension policy] we need to understand the concept of causality ... and they have no idea about statistics, metrics, nothing." As these quotes illustrate, economists viewed sociologists' expertise in positive terms and as a complement to their work. Sociologists' feminine, humanistic, and philosophical skills were seen to offer a counterbalance to economists' masculine, hard-fact, mathematical expertise. Yet the expertise of sociologists did not win jurisdictional battles or persuade state authorities to implement reforms. In this way, economists subordinated their colleagues' expertise even while positively categorizing their humanist, philosophical, and qualitative skills.

Economists also engaged in jurisdictional battles with actuaries. In contrast to sociologists, actuaries managed complex financial formulas, so the boundary economists drew vis-à-vis actuaries worked differently. For example, Luciano told me that economists' expertise was superior to that of actuaries because the former were better trained to ask "the right questions" in pension policymaking. Renato, a male economist who had more than 30 years of experience as a pension policy advisor, explained the superiority of his expertise vis-à-vis actuaries in the following terms: "When I discuss the conceptual part, the harder part, I feel like the economic profession makes a contribution that they [actuaries] never make ... we give them instructions." In other words, for Renato there was nothing original in actuaries' expertise; their skills were easily replaceable. In my conversations with economists, it was common to hear about their distinctive self-confidence. For example, Daniel, a male economist and high-ranked state official, told me that "economists only talk to economists. Economists only answer to economists. We think that everyone [else] is stupid." Francisco, another high-ranked state official, echoed a similar perspective: "The profile of economists is very arrogant, very. A typical economist likes to say something a couple of times, in a sophisticated way to make you feel like an idiot."

Actuaries also tended to define themselves in opposition to economists. One male actuary used an example from soccer to explain the difference: "Actuaries are not present in the

Chilean pension policy debate, but they are starting to have a voice, and I think that is great. Actuaries should be advisors, collaborators, because we are like goalkeepers, we block the ball. If we don't do that, the system can take any direction. We don't score goals. Economists score goals … they receive awards and applause and they appear in the news, not actuaries." As another actuary and senior policy advisor put it: "They [economists] often cross the line, they are opinionated, and they do things that … I laugh because they do not know a lot of mathematics. But they give opinions about everything as if they have a position for everything. But at least they have that advantage. They have been able to impose their [opinions]." As these excerpts illustrate, actuaries recognized that economists' aggressive style had helped them secure power and influence in public debates.

Chilean economists have drawn on hegemonic masculinity to establish their supremacy over other experts, and as a group they promoted the idea of science as a neutral tool that discovers objective truths and hard facts about reality. As scholarship on the sociology of knowledge has shown, scientists do not describe an objective reality. Normative questions always guide scientists' research practices, and politics always selectively displays particular knowledge. Thus, having a "boys' club" of self-declared "arrogant" economists defining the terms of what is possible, desirable, and imaginable in pension policymaking had real consequences in Chile. "Nationally recognized experts" have been able to dismiss citizens' demands, including those voiced by sociologists and actuaries who have called for changes to improve the well-being of elders and reduce the country's levels of inequality.

THE GENDERED KNOWLEDGE REGIME IN CHILEAN PENSION EXPERTISE

Experts actively work to draw boundaries between science and non-science. Gender politics matter in this process because experts use the advantages of gender hierarchies to claim that they are on the side of science. Yet social hierarchies matter in a second sense as well. The concept of knowledge regimes refers to the organizational machineries put in place to produce and disseminate ideas (Campbell and Pedersen 2014). For example, universities, think-tanks, and state agencies in Chile produce knowledge (e.g., by conducting studies, interpreting data, writing reports) on pension policy, so they are all part of a knowledge regime on pensions. **Gendered knowledge regimes** like these subordinate women and femininity and portray maleness and masculinity as neutral and the ideal (Jones et al. 2019).

In the case of Chile, economists were the ones who gained superior expert status, and they conceptualized pension expertise in very specific terms: as expertise closely related to (masculine) mathematical abstraction and financial knowledge. To position pension expertise this way, economists invested a lot of time and effort in constructing a gendered knowledge regime on pension policy. For example, economists spent years digitizing information that was recorded on paper to produce quantitative knowledge on pension policy. Economists also created exclusive channels for allocating funds. As they told me, they acted in concert to set up meetings with other economists who worked in different areas of the government and in international organizations to obtain research funds for quantitative studies. One female economist who was very critical of her colleagues' practices shared the following anecdote: "My previous boss was a sociologist. A wonderful sociologist, incredible woman. However, when she had to talk with economists at the Central Bank, for example, they ignored her. Then I came and the problem got resolved. I'd just graduated from college, I didn't know a quarter of what she knew, but I was an economist."

Professionals from other disciplines, including sociologists and actuaries, also wanted to conduct quantitative studies. However, because economists served as the gatekeepers for research funds, sociologists and actuaries ended up with insufficient resources and, in the case of sociologists, were forced to produce less expensive (and femininized) qualitative studies. As a result, the knowledge regime on pension policy in Chile became gendered by prioritizing economists' views and subordinating the views of other professionals whose claims and skills were coded as feminine. In contrast to pro-market economists, sociologists and actuaries supported greater restrictions on the functioning of private pension fund companies and greater redistribution of the wealth that the financialization of pension funds produced. Thus, it was consequential that economists were able to withhold funding, limit knowledge production, and curtail the authority undergirding sociologists and actuaries' alternative reform proposals.

In an interview with Pedro, an economist and high-ranked state official, I mentioned economists' monopoly on pension knowledge production. He was silent for some time before answering my question, and then he explained to me that, for many years, he and the team of economists he supervised had a "clouded" judgment about pension policymaking. According to him, they conducted research closer to "Wall Street rather than *la Vega Central* [popular food market in Santiago] … we gave many opinions about the pension system, but from an exclusively financial investment point of view … We were happy, investing in foreign portfolios, obtaining high profits, but we never studied people's reality … That was a big mistake, big mistake; that's why I want to redeem myself." As this comment illustrates, Pedro was introspective and frank in our interview, sharing his many regrets about past decisions. He was also quite aware of the fact that economists were not well regarded by other professionals. After all, economists framed science using a restrictive view and leveraged the hegemony of masculinity to devalue other professionals' expertise and suppress the alternative views of social problems that came from sociological researchers and were more aligned with citizens' demands. In so doing, economists' knowledge claims were wielded to validate the privatization and financialization of pension funds, despite widespread popular discontent with the effects of the policy.

CONCLUSION

This chapter has described jurisdictional battles over pension policymaking in Chile. The analysis reveals the role of gender hierarchies in the construction of expertise and knowledge regimes. In Chile, economists used mathematical abstraction and the self-confidence of hegemonic masculinity to claim the superiority of their knowledge vis-à-vis other experts, especially sociologists and actuaries. Moreover, economists acted in concert to mobilize research funds and position specific arguments as the most scientifically credible solutions to pension policy problems. They rejected interdisciplinary collaborations and blocked potential critiques of their knowledge. As a group, economists mobilized gendered boundary-making practices to define pension policy as the exclusive domain of economic scientists who would bring an ostensibly neutral and objective approach to policymaking. In so doing, economists' judgments ignored citizens' experiential knowledge of the system, which resulted in the citizenry's increasing dissatisfaction with policy results.

Marxist scholars have made an invaluable contribution to explaining the impact of the current privatized and financialized phase of capitalism. For these scholars the privatization and financialization of the economy has created a new class of rentiers with significant influence on governments and who exploit most wage earners, deepening global class inequalities (Blackburn 2002). My research shows that financialized capitalism is not *only* a process of capital accumulation. Rather, it intersects with patriarchy as a system of power. I show how economists as pension experts enacted an attitude of male self-confidence and competitiveness to define who they were and the language and norms that established their expertise as superior. As a result, economists in Chile ended up strengthening corporate power and putting the livelihoods of elders at great risk.

The 2019 massive protests against neoliberal capitalism and the economic precarity that it created for most Chilean elders made evident a deep mistrust in pension experts. As my study shows, when a small group of arrogant economists conduct research with an "I know best" type of attitude, it is unlikely they will offer alternative solutions to the neoliberal status quo or establish relationships of trust with scientists from other disciplines, such as sociologists and actuaries, who view the social world differently than they do. The good news, however, is that when people get organized, change is always possible. For example, after the 2019 social mobilizations, the need for a structural reform in the social security system became a top priority in public debate. In fact, social movements hand in hand with independent think-tanks (see, for example, the work of Fundación SOL) mobilized funds to conduct interdisciplinary studies and made concrete proposals for a new social security system that would be truly solidary. Moreover, the 2019 massive protests pressured politicians to replace the country's existing constitution, which was written during the dictatorship. In 2022, a drafted proposal for a new constitution was presented for a vote of the Chilean electorate. The proposed constitution defined social security as a public and universal good that must provide sufficient pensions. While the proposed constitution was rejected in a popular referendum, as of this publication, work to revise the Chilean constitution is ongoing. Although it remains to be seen whether structural reforms to the social security system in Chile will be effective in the short term, the truth is that the fight for better pensions has undermined a pillar of neoliberalism and has traced a path toward a radical change in Chile where everyone would be able to live their elder years with dignity.

REFLECTION AND DISCUSSION QUESTIONS

- Why was there public outcry and protest over pension policies in Chile? Why, despite public dissatisfaction, do these policies persist?
- How is expertise gendered in Chile? How does the distinction between masculinity and femininity give certain experts more power?
- What other cases can you think of in which the authority of experts and expertise has been challenged by the public? What are the tensions you see between expertise and democracy? What are possible solutions to these tensions?

KEY CONCEPTS

- **gendered knowledge regimes**: Organizational machineries that produce and disseminate ideas to subordinate women and femininity, portraying maleness and masculinity as neutral and the ideal.
- **gendering expertise**: Process by which experts, skills, instruments, and knowledge claims are coded as masculine or feminine.
- **hegemonic masculinity**: Concept used to describe a society's ideal male; the concept functions to justify and naturalize male–female and male–male hierarchies.
- **jurisdictional battles**: Battles between and within professions to gain power in a specific field.
- **studying up**: Research that focuses on people who wield power to understand the ways ordinary citizens can resist and transform authoritarian uses and abuses of power into democratic power.

EXPLORE FURTHER

- To learn more about gender and gender ideology in Latin America and the Caribbean, read **Section 4**.
- Boddenberg, Sophi, and Mitchell Moreno, dirs. 2020. *Sentido (en) Común – Un Documental Sobre la Revuelta en Chile.*
- Fundación SOL. www.fundacionsol.cl.

- Hiner, Hillary, Ana López, and Manuela Badilla. 2021 "¿El Neoliberalismo Nace y Muere en Chile? Reflexiones Sobre el 18-O desde Perspectivas Feministas." *História Unisinos* 25 (2): 276–91.
- *Social Uprising Museum*. https://museodelestallidosocial.org.
- Vivaldi, Lieta, and Barbara Sepúlveda. 2021. "Feminist Revolution: A Fight for Recognition, Redistribution and a More Just World." *Social Identities* 27 (5): 567–78.

ABOUT THE AUTHOR

Maria J. Azocar is a sociologist and an independent researcher based in Santiago, Chile. Her research examines struggles over expertise in policymaking from a feminist intersectional point of view. She was the co-chair of the Gender and Feminist Studies section of the Latin American Studies Association. Currently she is an editorial committee member of the Law & Society Association – Chile. As a feminist and queer woman, she has worked on activist and pension activist projects in Chile and the United States.

REFERENCES

Abbott, Andrew. 1988. *The System of Professions: An Essay on the Division of Expert Labor*. Chicago: University of Chicago Press.

Azocar, Maria J. 2020. "Policy Debates on Pension Reform in Chile: Economists, Masculinity and the Mobilization of Strategic Ignorance." *Social Politics: International Studies in Gender, State & Society* 27 (4): 648–69. https://doi.org/10.1093/sp/jxaa020.

Blackburn, Robin. 2002. *Banking on Death: Or, Investing in Life: The History and Future of Pensions*. London: Verso.

Bril-Mascarenhas, Tomás, and Antoine Maillet. 2019. "How to Build and Wield Business Power: The Political Economy of Pension Regulation in Chile, 1990–2018." *Latin American Politics and Society* 61 (1): 101–25. https://doi.org/10.1017/lap.2018.61.

Campbell, John L., and Ove K. Pedersen. 2014. *The National Origins of Policy Ideas: Knowledge Regimes in the United States, France, Germany, and Denmark*. Princeton, NJ: Princeton University Press.

CEP – Centro de Estudios Públicos. 2019. "Estudio Nacional de Opinión Pública." December. https://www.cepchile.cl/cep/site/docs/20200116/20200116081636/encuestacep_diciembre2019.pdf.

Chancel, Lucas, Thomas Piketty, Emmanuel Saez, and Gabriel Zucam. 2022. *World Inequality Report 2022*. World Inequality Lab. https://wir2022.wid.world/www-site/uploads/2021/12/WorldInequalityReport2022_Full_Report.pdf.

Connell, Robert W., and James W. Messerschmidt. 2005. "Hegemonic Masculinity: Rethinking the Concept." *Gender & Society* 19 (6): 829–59. https://doi.org/10.1177/0891243205278639.

Fundación SOL. 2020. "AFP para Quien? Donde se Invierten los Fondos de Pensiones en Chile." *Estudios de la Fundación SOL*.

Gieryn, Thomas F. 1983. "Boundary-Work and the Demarcation of Science from Non-Science: Strains and Interests in Professional Ideologies of Scientists." *American Sociological Review* 48 (6): 781–95. https://doi.org/10.2307/2095325.

Jones, Sally, Angela Martinez Dy, and Natalia Vershinina. 2019. "'We Were Fighting for Our Place': Resisting Gender Knowledge Regimes Through Feminist Knowledge Network Formation." *Gender, Work & Organization* 26 (6): 789–804. https://doi.org/10.1111/gwao.12288.

Markoff, John, and Verónica Montecinos. 1993. "The Ubiquitous Rise of Economists." *Journal of Public Policy* 13 (1): 37–68. https://doi.org/10.1017/S0143814X00000933.

Nelson, Julie A. 2010. "Sociology, Economics, and Gender: Can Knowledge of the Past Contribute to a Better Future?" *American Journal of Economics and Sociology* 69 (4): 1127–54. https://doi.org/10.1111/j.1536-7150.2010.00738.x.

Oakley, Ann. 1998. "Gender, Methodology and People's Ways of Knowing: Some Problems with Feminism and the Paradigm Debate in Social Science." *Sociology* 32 (4): 707–31. https://doi.org/10.1177/0038038598032004005.

Orenstein, Mitchell A. 2011. "Pension Privatization in Crisis: Death or Rebirth of a Global Policy Trend?" *International Social Security Review* 64 (3): 65–80. https://doi.org/10.1111/j.1468-246X.2011.01403.x.

Pierce, Jennifer L. 1996. *Gender Trials: Emotional Lives in Contemporary Law Firms*. Berkeley: University of California Press.

Seltzer, Michael, and Marit Haldar. 2015. "The Other Chicago School: A Sociological Tradition Expropriated and Erased." *Nordic Social Work Research* 5 (1): 25–41. https://doi.org/10.1080/2156857X.2015.1067638.

United Nations Department of Economic and Social Affairs (UN). 2019. "2019 Revision of World Population Prospects."

Witz, Anne. 1990. "Patriarchy and Professions: The Gendered Politics of Occupational Closure." *Sociology* 24 (4): 675–90. https://doi.org/10.1177/0038038590024004007.

World Bank. 1994. *Averting the Old Age Crisis: Policies to Protect the Old and Promote Growth. Summary*.

CHAPTER NINETEEN

Indigenous Governance and Legal Pluralism: Constitutional Reform and Political Conflict in Bolivia

Matthew Doyle

Gregorio Jacinto, a Kuraj Malku (head of the traditional *ayllu* authorities) and thus highest Indigenous political leader of his community, sat on the porch of his adobe brick house on the edge of the town of Bolívar in the Bolivian altiplano (high plains). He was dressed in his traditional wool poncho and wide-brimmed, sheep-hide sombrero and held, delicately balanced between the crook of his elbow and his arm in the manner of a royal scepter, a three-foot-long wooden staff topped with a silver pommel. This was his *baston de mando*, the symbol of his authority and connection to the many leaders of the past. Six other men, dressed in near identical fashion, each holding their own *baston de mando* and carrying rope whips (*chicotes*) in the loops of their belts, sat in a rough semi-circle around Gregorio and conversed excitedly in the local Quechua language. These were his *Kuraj Tatas*, the traditional *ayllu* authorities immediately beneath him. Gregorio and the *Kuraj Tatas* had traveled earlier that morning from the provincial capital to the remote village of Piruani to adjudicate a dispute between local families over land ownership. Piruani, like other village hamlets in the region of Bolívar province, lies at 4,000 meters above sea level in an austere but beautiful mosaic landscape of barren mountains, green fields, and farming terraces cut into the sides of hills, where outlying agricultural lands are managed collectively but owned and inherited by different families.

Gregorio and the traditional leaders had returned to Bolívar to solicit the participation of other local leaders in a ceremony to resolve the differences between the disputants in Piruani. However, they had been unable to secure the participation of both Bolívar's mayor and the local police, who had refused to accompany them to Piruani. From Gregorio's house both the local municipal council building and police station were visible; both were modern multi-storey buildings built under the new Movement for Socialism government that dwarfed the one-storey thatch and corrugated-iron roofed adobe brick houses of the town. I asked Gregorio why the mayor and local police had refused to accompany him and the *Kuraj Tatas* to

Figure 19.1. Arable farmland in the Bolivian altiplano. Photo by treesftf (CC BY 2.0).

Piruani. "They're afraid," he explained to me with a look of smoldering injustice in his eyes, "not just of the violence happening in the community. They are afraid to accept our authority to judge the case."

In this chapter I describe how different forms of local authority within an Indigenous community in the highlands of Bolivia entered into conflict with each other over a legal case and what this tells us about de jure **legal pluralism**: the formal recognition within the state of multiple legal systems (Thomas 2017). This is in a country where the national *Movimiento al Socialismo* (Movement for Socialism; MAS) government, following its election in 2005, sought to radically transform Bolivian society to fully include the Indigenous peoples that make up the country's majority population. Central to this project was a constitution ratified in 2009 that established a **plurinational** state where Indigenous practices concerning the judgment and punishment of transgressions are treated as independent sources of legal authority, separate from the state law and courts. Between 2015 and 2016, I carried out fieldwork in the Quechua-speaking highland Indigenous community of Bolívar province, documenting the effects of these constitutional reforms on its internal system of government. As a result of historical interaction between Bolívar and the colonial and post-colonial Bolivian state, this consists of multiple overlapping sets of authorities: the traditional *ayllu* authorities, such as Gregorio and the traditional leaders; the province-wide municipal council, which includes a mayor and elected councilors; and the peasant union.

During my fieldwork, I observed how the peasant union and *ayllu* authorities clashed over a dispute between two sets of families in the village of Piruani over ownership of an area of arable land. "The case of Piruani," as it was commonly referred to, had resulted in physical fights between members of the different families. Claimants from each side had separately approached the *ayllu* authorities, state courts, and the peasant union, which had each separately ruled on the matter. Subsequently, this conflict among families over land became a dispute between the local *ayllu* authorities and peasant union leaders regarding the legitimacy and constitutionality of each other's actions and what represented a just resolution. Crucially, this dispute between systems of authority took place because of the de jure legal pluralism guaranteed by the new plurinational constitution and through contested interpretations of its meaning. A progressive legal measure to empower Indigenous communities thus became the basis for conflict within one.

SYSTEMS OF AUTHORITY AND JUSTICE IN BOLÍVAR

The province of Bolívar, located in the mountainous high plains of the Bolivian altiplano, is the descendant of the historic *ayllu* Kirkiawi (Mendoza, Gonzáles, and Mamani 2002). It is currently recognized as both a province and a collective *Tierra Comunitaria de Origen* (Native Community Land, or TCO). Its 7,000 inhabitants live mainly in village hamlets (*comunidades*) that typically comprise some 30 families who practice subsistence agriculture, such as cultivating tubers and pseudocereals and raising sheep and llamas. Families live in clusters of adobe huts, take their herds to pasture in the surrounding hills, and labor intensely during yearly periods of sowing and harvesting. Historically, they would acquire additional foods and goods through trade with distant valley communities and the culturally mixed *mestizo* townsfolk of the provincial capital. Today, it is common for them to travel to the cities of Oruro and Cochabamba or the tropical lowlands to buy and sell goods, engage in seasonal work, or settle permanently. This can result in people having multiple residences. While families have heritable control of plots of land, this is a right to land usage within the traditional territorial organization of the *ayllu* rather than full legal ownership. Within each *comunidad*, the management of land, the conflicts surrounding it, and the associated community rituals are the responsibility of the local traditional *ayllu* authority (*jilanku*), who alongside the local peasant union leader (*dirigente*) and monthly communal assembly, form the lowest level of government within the province.

Above the *comunidad*-level are intermediate *ayllu* and union authorities at the level of the province: the *Kuraj Malku* (head of the *ayllu*), the province-level peasant union leader, and the elected municipal government. Although the *ayllu* and peasant union have overlapping functions such as resolving communal conflicts, it is union leaders who typically solicit development funds from the municipal government and nongovernmental organizations (NGOs).

Meanwhile, *ayllu* leaders are regarded as responsible for upholding the customary practices that materially and symbolically reproduce the territorial and social organization of their community. These include administering land use, making ritual offerings to the land during the opening of new fields or to local deities, and resolving conflicts, including disputes over access to pasture, common resources, and the ownership of family plots.

Features of *ayllu* communities include a lived relationship with the collectively managed land that the people inhabit, a nonmonetary economy, and rotating leadership roles, which are all mediated by principles of complementarity, reciprocity, and duality (Albó 1977; Bastien 2003). These practices and concepts in Bolívar form part of people's notions of personhood and community membership, but not all are uniformly shared or interpreted. When local *ayllu* authorities make judgments about disputes, they do not follow precise rules but draw on these constellations of shared understandings. This means each case involves a flexible interpretation of entitlements, obligations, and infractions. This feature of Bolivian highland Indigenous societies has been described by Marcelo Fernández-Osco (2001) as *justicia de acuerdos* (justice by agreement) through which the severity of transgressions and the nature of punishments is negotiated contextually, often with participation by the community.

THE CASE OF PIRUANI

I wasn't present in Piruani at the time the events took place, but I received various accounts of how the case developed. I was first provided an account of how events unfolded by Francisco Larico, a Quechua Indigenous rights activist and paralegal, who is also Gregorio's brother in law.[1] I met Francisco at a conference on Indigenous justice in La Paz, and he later agreed to an interview in Cochabamba. Our interview took place on a sunny afternoon in a café in El Prado, just north of the city center, on a long tree-lined boulevard filled with bars and restaurants. Francisco, a man in his early thirties, was critical of the MAS but still enthusiastic about the possibility of Indigenous peoples gaining autonomy over matters of justice. He had helped Gregorio with a presentation to the constitutional court in the city of Sucre that purportedly demonstrated how the resolution of the case of Piruani represented a sound example of customary *ayllu* law.

According to Francisco, the trouble began when one of the families from Piruani appropriated lands belonging to neighboring families. The problem with the case, he claimed, began with the failure to respect the proper channels in dealing with a dispute of this nature. Instead of approaching the *jilanku* (local traditional *ayllu* authority), the families whose lands had been

---

1 I do not use pseudonyms in this chapter. The subjects I discuss, who all hold political office or leadership roles, gave consent for me to use their names.

encroached upon spoke directly with the province-level peasant union. At this point, the union leaders should have involved Gregorio (as the province-level head of the *ayllu*). Instead, the union leaders passed the matter up to their union leadership at the level of the Cochabamba department. The department level of the union thereupon issued an unexpected resolution declaring the very family who had encroached on the land as the victims, and declared the other families, who were claiming their land had been encroached upon, as the aggressors, issuing them a fine of 20,000 bolivianos (approximately US$3,000). At the same time, the protagonist of the encroaching family prosecuted the other families for alleged acts of violence in the jurisdiction of the *justicia ordinaria* (state courts) in the city of Oruro. The judge eventually threw out the case, but the protagonist now had legal documents showing that the case had been taken to court and he used these documents to intimidate the other families into not pursuing the matter further.

Gregorio became involved in the case some 15 weeks after the families had taken it to the province-level peasant union instead of the *jilanku*. According to Francisco, Gregorio and his fellow *ayllu* authorities took some time to analyze the case before raising an objection with the resolution issued by the union: "They object to this resolution, indicating that it is unconstitutional. First because it didn't go through the correct procedures, second because it infringes upon the constitutional rights of Indigenous self-government and the principles of the *usos y costumbres*" (S).[2]

According to Francisco, Gregorio, and other *ayllu* authorities, the actions of the union leaders contradicted the 2009 Bolivian constitution. Indigenous communities have the right to resolve disputes internally according to their customary law. Therefore, in making a judgment without involving *ayllu* authorities, the community's constitutional rights were violated. In Bolívar, the term *usos y costumbres* is used in a similar way to "customary law," although it has a far broader meaning by encompassing local forms of governance and customs internal to the community, including those related to the communal management of land. According to the understanding of the *usos y costumbres* favored by Gregorio and other *ayllu* authorities, the nature of the judgment carried out by the union went directly against their principles. For Gregorio, the peasant union is "infected with the mentality of the *justicia ordinaria* (state courts)." When I pressed him as to what he meant, he explained this was related to money. The peasant union, like the state courts, resolves disputes through placing fines. He claimed that Olker Nina, the province-level union leader, had demanded 2,000 bolivianos from all the parties involved as a "guarantee" to resolve it.

After Gregorio judged the case, he went to Piruani to carry out a ceremony in which the different factions symbolically resolved their differences through the exchange of livestock.

---

2 (S) indicates Spanish source language and (Q) indicates Quechua.

The solution had been witnessed by all members of the community and the local *ayllu* and peasant union leaders. For Gregorio, the form in which the dispute was resolved complied with the *usos y costumbres* and was qualitatively different to that offered by either the ordinary court or the peasant union. Instead of punishing the guilty parties for the violence they had inflicted, he carried out a reparation between the warring families. They slaughtered a sheep, prepared *kanka de oveja* and *papa wathiya*, traditional delicacies of salted mutton and potatoes baked in the ground, and then sat down together as a community to feast. Gregorio pointed out that the resolution to the conflict had been carried out without money, unlike the solutions offered by the peasant union, which involve fines and provide the opportunity for corrupt union leaders to profit. Even worse, he claimed, are the ordinary courts, which are inherently corrupt, and rule in favor of whichever party can offer a larger bribe. This emphasis on the corrupting nature of money reflects a tendency for *ayllu* authorities to idealize the traditional nonmonetary economy of the *ayllu*, based on forms of reciprocal interdependence between persons and their territory, enacted through ritualized exchanges, including labor exchange and exchanges among persons, nature deities, and the land (Bastien 2003). It also reflects a particular understanding of the nature of community embodied by such territorial and social organization.

When I spoke about the case with Olker Nina, the province-level union leader, he offered a different account. As we sat on wooden benches in the courtyard of his house, and his wife prepared us tea in the kitchen, he laid out his view of the matter. First, the judgment by the department-level peasant union had sided with the encroaching family, who Gregorio claimed to be the genuine offenders. Olker viewed the union judgment to be correct because the decision had been made in the light of violence suffered by the family. He maintained that the violence exhibited in Piruani was worrying and illustrative of problems throughout the province. The custom of multigeniture had led to the successive fractioning of family lands and the intensification of competition among families over an increasingly scarce resource. This was the case even though many village *comunidades* appeared abandoned as residents, who spent most their time in the cities or tropical lowlands, only returned periodically to cultivate their land. Being absent from the community meant that it was difficult to recognize incursions upon one's land or its precise boundaries. Moreover, the local *ayllu* authorities (*jilanku*) and union leaders (*dirigente*) responsible for adjudicating these matters often resided elsewhere themselves (in the nearby cities of Cochabamba and Oruro) and only returned for monthly community meetings and cultural events, and therefore weren't readily available to address these complaints. Olker claimed Piruani to be an exemplary case of all these factors and indicative of the problems faced by the province at a time of change, including the prevalence of rural–urban migration. Moreover, Olker stated that he did not believe Gregorio had resolved the conflict. He described the situation in the following terms:

> What is it to give a solution? If they are in a problem to do with territory … we said because before we went with the mayor, everyone. We said we're going to inspect the land and

accordingly we'll give a simple [individual] titling to everyone involved in the conflict, in equal parts. But I've heard that this one, Gregorio, hasn't done it that way. He's just placed sanctions and not given a solution. (S)

For Olker, the only way to resolve the families' conflict and to stop the violence from reoccurring was to establish clear boundaries between their lands by issuing individual title deeds. As long as the land remained communally managed, he maintained, the violence would continue. He seemed to view Gregorio's claim to have provided a resolution as irresponsible because, in his opinion, it did nothing to end the conflict. For him, the exchange of livestock and the ceremony carried out by Gregorio was merely a "sanction" for the violence and not a definitive judgment on the land dispute. This sentiment was echoed in interviews I held with various local MAS politicians in the municipal government.

JUSTICE, LAND TENANCY, AND SYSTEMS OF AUTHORITY

The differences between *ayllu* authorities and union leaders over the resolution of the case of Piruani partly concern how land should be owned and managed. In the *comunidades* of the province, access to plots of arable land depends on ongoing community membership and fulfillment of social obligations. It is the *ayllu* authorities who mainly administer this system of land tenancy and perform associated rituals. Meanwhile, the case of Piruani was frequently cited by union leaders to justify replacing this system with individual land titling. In turn, local *ayllu* authorities I spoke with claimed that the union was deliberately misleading people about the way land is managed. The point was made repeatedly that the real motivation of the union and local MAS politicians in advocating individual titling was to "disappear the *ayllu*": to abolish the *ayllu* as a form of territorial organization and the traditional *ayllu* authorities themselves.

Scholars of Bolivian Andean communities have observed that conflict over land is endemic and a seemingly unavoidable feature of traditional tenancy systems (Albó 1977). Without precise boundaries, it is inevitable that individuals will encroach upon others' plots and that local authorities will not always be able to determine who is the victim and who is the offender. Even so, the cyclical rotation of the land means that feuds often resolve automatically, as *ayonoqa* (communal plots) are never cultivated consecutively for more than a few years. Once a communal plot is left fallow, a new one must be "opened" in an official ceremony in preparation for its cultivation ahead of the rainy season. This includes the *reparto* (parceling out) of the new land among families by the *jilanku*. With the opening of the new *ayonoqa*, the feuds normally come to an end. Interestingly, in Quechua, the same word used to describe the leveling of earth to prepare it for cultivation, which follows the *reparto* of lands, is also used to mean "forgive": the verb *pampachay* (meaning "to flatten" or "to level out") is used alongside the Hispanicism *perdonay*. The term implies a notion of justice and conflict resolution focused on the restoration of balance rather than on identifying the guilty party and aggressor. This does not mean there exists no concept of blame or guilt, which was described to me with the Spanish word *culpa* or the Quechua word *juch'a*. I was given examples of justice carried out in the past in which the *jilanku* would give a beating to all the parties involved in a dispute with his *chicote* (rope whip), so they could experience shame and understand the mistakes they had made before resolving their differences.

It becomes clear here why Gregorio emphasized that his resolution to the case of Piruani – using nonmonetary reparations and without quantifying damages – represented a key difference in principle. According to Gregorio, the most important thing for a man living in the highlands is his sense of dignity, resulting from his standing in the community and the public image he projects. On the one hand, paying a monetary fine allows the offender to absolve himself of the debt he owes the victim with no loss of face. On the other hand, the exchange of livestock and the ceremonial reparation he carried out made the offender publicly admit his guilt and beg forgiveness in front of the whole community. Placing fines involves attributing responsibility to parties conceived of as discrete individuals and dissolving the relationship between them once a judgment is made. Symbolic reparation of the social and cosmological order, understood as the totality of relationships of reciprocal interdependence that constitute the territorial and social organization of the *ayllu*, involves the maintenance and strengthening of these bonds.

In the case of Piruani, the *ayllu* and union authorities express opposing views regarding how resources should be owned and distributed, how disputes should be resolved, and the nature and purpose of punishment. These correspond to the Western categories of distributive, procedural, and retributive justice. Yet these are interrelated: Viewing land as an individually owned commodity or as part of the social and territorial organization of the *ayllu* informs whether resolving conflict over it should be a matter of arbitrating the rights and responsibilities of individual parties or the restoration of ties among persons and the land. In turn, this relates to whether punishment should involve individual settlement or a process of didactic reinforcement and symbolic restoration of social bonds and values. Ultimately, these differences reflect understanding their community as either comprising individuals and individual families (the viewpoint of the peasant union) or as the totality of relationships of mutual interdependence among persons and the land they inhabit (the perspective of the *ayllu* authorities).

Because the different authorities had not only offered alternative solutions but had sided with different parties, the conflict in Piruani transformed into a dispute between the peasant union and MAS municipal government on one side and the *ayllu* authorities on the other. However, the conflict between authorities was motivated largely by the need to define the nature of justice and their respective roles as systems of authority, as the new constitution and plurinational state obliges Indigenous communities to publicly define their internal systems of governance to gain recognition and benefits. This may provoke debates over what constitutes "authentic" Indigenous leadership and identity: a phenomenon that has been studied extensively in the context of communities undergoing the legal process of converting to the self-governing "Indigenous autonomies" established by the 2009 constitution (Plata and Cameron 2017).

When the matter came up in public meetings, it was clear that both sides believed the other to be going beyond the limits of their roles, referring to an idealized structure of the different social organizations and the division of labor between them. For the *ayllu* leaders, it was illegitimate for the peasant union to resolve questions of justice, as their role is to act as the external political representatives of the community and to solicit funds for development. However, the union leaders argued that they routinely assume the responsibility for many of the problems that result from conflicts over land. It was clear that union leaders broadly followed the discourse of inclusive indigeneity supported by the MAS government, conceiving Indigenous peoples as a broad class of socially and economically marginalized persons, which justified the unions' constitutional legitimacy as judicial authorities. In response, *ayllu* leaders claimed that they were uniquely responsible for maintaining the *usos y costumbres* and that they had existed as a form of authority prior to the colonization of the Americas. In this sense, they argued, they were the true Indigenous authorities, not the peasant unions.

CONTESTED JUSTICE, LEGAL PLURALISM, AND INDIGENEITY

The case of Piruani reflects current debates surrounding the interpretation of the 2009 constitutional reforms prior to the current period, when the union and *ayllu* leadership, despite representing different sources of normativity, coexisted and were regarded as mutually complementary systems of authority. It is the constitutional reforms of the national MAS government that caused the case of Piruani to transform into a dispute over the nature of justice and the legitimacy of the *ayllu* or union as sources of judicial authority. The constitution devolves judicial power to Indigenous communities like Bolívar while tacitly regarding them as internally homogenous. Local Indigenous communities are therefore compelled to accept one source of normative authority in order for their non-state legal orders to be recognized within the framework of the constitution. Meanwhile, its ambiguous and conflicting definitions of *indigeneity* and *legal pluralism* provide different local authorities with the means to dispute which authority should be recognized as the "authentic" Indigenous judicial authority, how justice should be administered, and how community membership should be understood. *Ayllu* and union leaders therefore offer competing interpretations of how the constitution defines indigeneity and legal pluralism. I observed this not only in debates and conversations surrounding the case of Piruani, but in interactions with institutions of the new plurinational state.

In July 2015 I attended a meeting in the *comunidad* of Vilaycayma, along with representatives of the *ayllu*, peasant union, and municipal council. The meeting was chaired by a lawyer from the constitutional court in Sucre as part of a process of consulting Indigenous communities on the Environmental and Agrarian Tribunal, a part of the new Bolivian state that would adjudicate agricultural and environmental matters. Those present were asked to discuss their local practices for resolving conflict. A resident in his seventies of Vilaycayma, Don Enrique Tola, accused the present leaders of his *comunidad* of being mistaken about how justice should be carried out. They had lost their customs and instead settled things with money. He described how when he was a young man, it had been normal to make someone swear a *juramento* (declaration of intent) in the presence of neighbors to prevent further transgressions:

> If you don't do this then you will be dead right here … you would make the oath, we would place a little salt and crossed blades. And this is what you would shout. Shouting this, in making the oath you would swear, Lord in my heart, that this and that … (Q)

The person making the oath would walk over the crossed blades while shouting that they should die if they did not keep their word. If they failed to do so, then *Tata Dios* (God, the father) would strike them down. In this way, the community could be sure that offenders would never repeat their crimes and would comply with the sanctions they were obliged to make to repair the damages they had caused their neighbors and to the social contract of the community. Sabino Veizaga, a former *ayllu* leader, seconded this as an example of the sort of ancestral practices they had to recover to deal with the problems taking place in communities like Piruani.

Sabino was quietly dignified, polite, and intelligent in explaining how he believed the meeting to be very important, given that Bolívar, as an "ancestral territory," had traditionally administered its own forms of justice with no recognition or oversight by the state. With the new plurinational constitution, this sort of space provided the possibility to move toward a greater understanding between the state and their community. Yet, at the same time, it was making community members a little sad that some of the judicial purview of the traditional *ayllu* authorities was being taken away from them. Here, Sabino was referring to the **jurisdictional demarcation law** that establishes clear boundaries between Indigenous and ordinary jurisdictions. While he recognized the existence of problems in *comunidades* such as Piruani, he argued that they had to assume the responsibility themselves for resolving these issues. They needed to follow the *usos y costumbres* and to reincorporate their ancestral knowledge and practices. In the past, he claimed, time was not wasted on lawyers and written documents. Rather, problems were resolved by the traditional *ayllu* authorities in the manner described by Don Enrique: by using summary punishments. This, he stated emphatically at the conclusion of his speech, was the key to overcoming the problems they were experiencing.

The notion of recovering Indigenous practices and creating an alternative to the liberal state and its system of laws, based on the collective experience and ancestral knowledge of their community, is very much part of the understanding of legal pluralism as a project of decolonization that is shared by national *ayllu* organizations and prominent *ayllu* leaders within Bolívar province. In contrast, the jurisdictional demarcation law, which defines the boundaries between the state courts and Indigenous legal systems, very much goes against any serious idea of legal decolonization. It limits the purview of Indigenous jurisdictions to those areas that are "traditionally dealt with" by Indigenous authorities and excludes them from judging major criminal offenses and interfering with key functions of the central state. Many of the traditional *ayllu* authorities believed the jurisdictional demarcation law to be unconstitutional because it places limits on the ability of Indigenous communities to manage their own justice. They interpret the constitution to be in favor of a version of legal pluralism as part of a decolonial endeavor of re-founding Bolivia.

The jurisdictional demarcation law also restates the right of local peasant unions to be involved in matters of Indigenous justice, as recognized social organizations within "Indigenous native peasant" communities. Much of the *ayllu* leadership reject this entirely and believe the inclusion of peasant unions as a recognized Indigenous organization to be a mistake. They point to the wording of articles 2 and 30 of the constitution, which state that Indigenous communities, and by extension their authorities, are those that existed prior to the Spanish colonial invasion. This supports the view that the traditional *ayllu* authorities are the authentic Indigenous leaders as they pre-date the colonization of the Americas and are therefore uniquely responsible for defending and reconstituting their *usos y costumbres*.

In addition to claiming that the constitution advocates a strong form of legal pluralism, *ayllu* figures such as Sabino also interpret its definition of indigeneity in an exclusive sense, thereby supporting their normative understandings and justifying their role as the authentically Indigenous representatives of their community. This refers to qualities of territoriality, ancestrality, and pre-colonial practices and social institutions as key to what it means to be Indigenous. Such a conception of indigeneity supports the view that their community should be understood in terms of the complex practices imbricated within the traditional organization of their territory, which are predominantly carried out by the traditional *ayllu* authorities. It therefore affirms the *ayllu* authorities', not the peasant unions', view of community membership and the centrality of their role as Indigenous judicial authorities.

CONCLUSION

The Piruani conflict occurred in part because the 2009 constitution treats Indigenous communities as internally homogenous, and while it recognizes the legal authority of Indigenous leaders and customary law, it says little about the internal makeup of Indigenous communities and contains conflicting definitions of legal pluralism and indigeneity (Schavelzon 2013). The *ayllu* and union are therefore left to contest which set of leaders should be considered the legitimate Indigenous judicial authorities and what constitutes authentic Indigenous justice within their community. It is for this reason that the case of Piruani provoked a struggle over both local power and the definition of justice. This included contested understandings of conflict resolution, the ownership of land, and the meaning of community. In doing so, the two sides offered not only separate judgments of the case but also alternative interpretations of the constitution, through which they sought to legitimate their roles as judicial authorities and their normative understandings of their community. This illustrates both the limitations of the MAS government's constitutional reforms and of any project of de jure legal pluralism that does not engage with the internally heterogeneous and essentially contested nature of unofficial systems of law.

REFLECTION AND DISCUSSION QUESTIONS

- Why did the department-level peasant union leaders and province-level head of the *ayllu* rule differently in the case of Piruani? What beliefs and values informed each of their rulings?
- What are the challenges surrounding plurinationalism in practice? How does the case of Piruani reflect those challenges?
- What is problematic about the jurisdictional demarcation law? How does it challenge efforts at decolonizing the legal system through plurinationalism?

KEY CONCEPTS

- **ayllu**: Refers to a system of pre-colonial territorial organization of the Indigenous Aymara kingdoms and Inca state and to contemporary highland regions with their own forms of territory and government (Bastien 2003).
- **jurisdictional demarcation law**: A law that establishes clear boundaries between Indigenous and ordinary jurisdictions.
- **legal pluralism**: The existence of multiple legal systems/forms of law within one area, especially common in post-colonial societies where state law may exist alongside more traditional legal systems (customary law). De jure legal pluralism refers to state recognition of de facto legal pluralism.
- **plurinational**: A nation-state that recognizes the autonomous coexistence of distinct Indigenous groups and permits Indigenous communities to exercise their own forms of justice and law within a separate jurisdiction recognized as equal to the state courts.

EXPLORE FURTHER

- To learn more about the challenges surrounding policies aimed at integrating Indigenous communities and systems into the nation-state, read **Chapter 8**.

- To learn more about practices that recognize Indigenous systems of decision making, see **Chapter 29**.
- Canessa, Andrew. 2014. "Conflict, Claim and Contradiction in the New 'Indigenous' State of Bolivia." *Critique of Anthropology* 34: 153–67.
- Goodale, Mark. 2019. *A Revolution in Fragments: Traversing Scales of Justice, Ideology and Practice in Bolivia*. Durham, NC: Duke University Press.
- Postero, Nancy. 2016. *The Indigenous State: Race, Politics, and Performance in Plurinational Bolivia*. Berkeley: University of California Press.

ABOUT THE AUTHOR

Matthew Doyle is a social anthropologist and an associate lecturer in the Department of Anthropology at University College London. He studies processes of decolonization, state reform, and Indigenous politics in Latin America. His fieldwork within a highland Indigenous community in Bolivia investigated the local effects and experiences of reforms by the national Movement for Socialism government, which seeks to include the majority Indigenous population within the nation-state, to establish new rights and forms of citizenship, and to build alternatives to capitalist development.

REFERENCES

Albó, Xavier. 1977. *La Paradoja Aymara: Solidaridad y Faccionalismo*. La Paz: CIPCA.

Bastien, Joseph W. 2003 [1985]. *Mountain of the Condor: Metaphor and Ritual in an Andean Ayllu*. Longrove, IL: Waveland Press.

Fernández-Osco, Marcelo. 2001. "La Ley del Ayllu: Justicia de Acuerdos." *Tinkazos* 9: 11–28.

Mendoza, Fernando, Félix Patzi Gonzáles, and Félix López Mamani. 2002. *Atlas de los Ayllus Sura y Qurpa Kirkiyawi: Provincias Tapacarí, Arque y Bolívar*. Cochabamba: PRODEVAT.

Plata, W., and J. Cameron. 2017. "Quienes Dicen no a las Autonomías Indígenas y Por Qué? Pragmatismo, Hibridez y Modernidades Alternativas en la Base." *Cuestión Agraria* 3: 19–60.

Schavelzon, Salvador. 2013. *El Nacimiento del Estado Plurinacional de Bolivia: Etnografía de una Asamblea Constituyente*. Buenos Aires: IWGIA.

Thomas, Marc Simon. 2017. *The Challenge of Legal Pluralism: Local Dispute Settlement and the Indian-State Relationship in Ecuador*. Oxford: Routledge.

SECTION SEVEN

Political Violence and Its Legacies

Recent history in many Latin American and Caribbean societies has been characterized by extended periods of **political violence** – the use of violence to achieve political goals – that continues to shape lives, livelihoods, politics, and culture today. Much of the violence of the twentieth century unfolded as governments across the region were grappling with poverty, social inequality, and ideological differences within their national populations. Yet specific conflicts within individual nations were not isolated. Rather, they were monitored, influenced, funded, and shaped by powerful interests in the Global North, most notably the United States and the Soviet Union. Consequently, Latin America and the Caribbean became one of the most violent theaters of the Cold War, a global ideological contest between Marxist socialism and communism, on the one hand, and extractive capitalist democracy on the other. By the time the Cold War waned, the causes of political violence in Latin America and the Caribbean had shifted in some places due to a growing international drug trade, the rise of narco-traffic organizations, and violent efforts to combat them.

Political violence manifests in many forms. Civil conflict, including military coups d'état that deposed democratically elected leaders, violent enterprises in and of themselves, often installed authoritarian leaders who used violence to quash dissent. Some of the most notable among these regimes were Pinochet's dictatorship in Chile (1973–1990), Trujillo's dictatorship in the Dominican Republic (1930–1961), the Somoza dictatorship in Nicaragua (1936–1979), Duvalier's dictatorship in Haiti (1971–1986), the dictatorship in Brazil (1964–1985), and the Dirty War in Argentina (1976–1983). These regimes shared a terror-inducing array of tactics that included indiscriminate persecution, harassment, and **disappearance** (i.e., the clandestine detention of individuals, often followed by interrogation, torture, assassination, and disposal of human remains in undisclosed locations) of those who were suspected of resisting their authority. Today, repercussions continue to manifest both for those who lived under authoritarian rule and those growing up in communities where the **collective memory** of political violence still informs family, life, and politics.

The violence of **armed conflict** – drawn out armed confrontation between the state's armed forces and the forces of one or more armed groups – impacts not only the parties who are directly involved but all people living in an area where the conflict is happening. Many armed conflicts were between government forces (including police, military, and state-sponsored paramilitaries) and guerrilla movements for revolutionary political change, many of which purported to be fighting long-standing social inequalities. Among the most notable of these conflicts occurred in Cuba in the 1950s, El Salvador in the 1980s, Guatemala from the 1950s to the 1990s, and Colombia from the 1960s to 2016. Violence perpetrated by the parties involved in these and other armed conflicts terrorized and killed millions of people. For example, in Colombia's 52-year armed conflict between government forces and FARC guerrilla fighters, both groups threatened, killed, and disappeared people in their efforts to gain or maintain political control. Over the course of Guatemala's 40-year civil war, an estimated 245,000 people, mostly Indigenous Maya, were killed or disappeared. And some of the people who are most vulnerable to the violence of the contemporary Mexican "war on drugs" belong to Indigenous groups trying to protect their territory and communities (see Chapter 11).

The chapters in this section examine the legacies of political violence, as well as **transitional justice** – efforts aimed at holding parties responsible for violence, including government agencies, and ameliorating the effects of political violence, armed conflict, and human rights violations for victims. In Chapter 20, Guglielmucci and Rozo explore how contemporary artists use ethnographic methods to tap into the mental and emotional legacies of armed conflict in Colombia, producing art that reflects intimate engagement and collective memory. In Chapter 21, Morgan, Page, and Sosa describe how watching films portraying armed conflict in the opposite country led research participants in Argentina and Colombia to reflect on their own experiences, memories, and imaginaries of conflict. In Chapter 22, Rosen challenges the notion that peace begins with the end of armed conflict, examining the violent legacy of the Guatemalan civil war and the state's neglect of people who have been disappeared since the war ended. Finally, in Chapter 23, Renero-Hannan describes a case of political incarceration in Oaxaca state, tracing the trajectory and reflecting on the ramifications of a solidary visit to an imprisoned Indigenous Zapotec leader by his family, comrades, and the activist ethnographer.

KEY CONCEPTS

- **armed conflict**: Drawn out armed confrontation between the state's armed forces and the forces of one or more armed groups.
- **collective memory**: A group of people's memory of people, places, and events that is passed from one generation to the next.
- **disappearance**: The clandestine detention of individuals, often followed by interrogation, torture, assassination, and disposal of human remains in undisclosed locations.

- **political violence**: The use of violence to achieve political goals.
- **transitional justice**: Efforts aimed at holding parties responsible for violence, including government agencies, and ameliorating the effects of political violence, armed conflict, and human rights violations for victims.

EXPLORE FURTHER

- To learn more about political violence, read **Chapters 8** and **11**.
- Carrescia, Olivia Lucia, dir. 2009. *Sacred Soil*. [Guatemala]
- Civico, Aldo. 2015. *The Para-State: An Ethnography of Colombia's Death Squads*. Berkeley: University of California Press.
- Gould, Jeffrey, and Carlos Henriquez Consalvi, dirs. 2003. *Cicatriz de la Memoria* (*Scars of Memory*). [El Salvador]
- Granovsky-Larsen, Simon. 2019. *Dealing with Peace: The Guatemalan Campesino Movement and the Post-Conflict Neoliberal State*. Toronto: University of Toronto Press.
- Guzmán, Patricio. 2010. *Nostalgia por la Luz* (*Nostalgia for the Light*). [Chile]
- Higgins, Nick, dir. 2008. *A Massacre Foretold*. [Mexico]
- Lozano, Juan José, and Hollman Morris. 2011. *Impunity*. [Colombia]
- Rush, Peter, and Olivera Simić. 2014. *The Arts of Transitional Justice: Culture, Activism, and Memory after Atrocity*. New York: Springer.
- Wood, Andrés, dir. 2010. *Machuca*. [Chile]

CHAPTER TWENTY

Violence and the Ethnographic Turn in Contemporary Colombian Art

Ana Guglielmucci and Esteban Rozo

Juan Manuel Echavarría, a contemporary Colombian artist, has traveled the country, as he says, "learning with his feet." In November 2019 he told us about his work in Puerto Berrío, a town on the Magdalena River, where between 2006 and 2013 he photographed the tombs of "the souls of corpses buried as unidentified persons," which some locals had chosen to care for. "Choosing a soul" in this context means to put a mark on the tomb of an unidentified body, name the unknown person, care for the tomb, and ask for mutual favors from the spirit. Echavarría took more than 400 pictures of these tombs of "chosen souls." An incarcerated paramilitary commander found out about Echavarría's work and invited him to speak at La Picota prison in Bogotá. In their conversation, the commander told him that the people in Puerto Berrío adopting these souls were "heroes" because the paramilitaries had thrown the bodies into the river to make them disappear. The practice of "disappearing" people usually entails murdering someone and leaving no trace of either the crime or the body of the victim. The practice of disappearing political opponents and dissidents was widely used by the military governments in Latin America throughout the Cold War. In Colombia, this practice was used by military forces but also by other actors such as paramilitary groups and guerrillas. After this conversation, Echavarría tried to incorporate the urgency that was felt by family members searching for, finding, and burying the bodies of their kin into his artistic work. For this purpose, Echavarría developed a technique he called *lenticulars*, which would allow him to superimpose one image of the tombs over another to show how the tombs have been transformed by those who adopt the souls of unidentified corpses. This technique was used in his visual work *Requiem NN* (2010; Figure 20.1) about funerary and mortuary practices in Puerto Berrío.

Figure 20.1. *Réquiem NN* (2006–2013), Juan Manuel Echavarría. Photo by Juan Manuel Echavarría.

In this chapter we explore how recent Colombian artistic production about the armed conflict has been informed by the ethnographic turn (Foster 2001), transforming both the political role of artists and art in a context of transitional justice – an approach to systematic or massive violations of human rights that both provides redress to victims and creates or enhances opportunities for the transformation of the political systems, conflicts, and other conditions that may have been at the root of human rights violations.

Specifically, we analyze how the idea of "leaving the art studio" has shaped the contemporary work of artists such as Doris Salcedo, Juan Manuel Echavarría, and Clemencia Echeverri, as well as the **politics of aesthetic representation** about the armed conflict in Colombia. The politics of aesthetic representation refers to the visual representations of the armed conflict that have been predominant in Colombia. While mainstream media emphasize direct violence in the representations they produce about the armed conflict, contemporary Colombian artists create representations of the armed conflict through traces, metaphors, and objects. After the Colombian government signed the peace agreement with FARC (Revolutionary Armed Forces of Colombia) in 2016, the Integral System of Truth, Justice, Reparation, and Non-Repetition (SIVJRNR) gave art a new role in the process of reparation for victims. The idea of "repairing" the victims refers to how the state can compensate for some of the damages the armed conflict caused. The victims of the Colombian armed conflict are people who have been disappeared, found dead, kidnapped, or injured, as well as their families. This chapter addresses how Colombian artists define the political function of art beyond reparation and transitional justice in their work, producing new ways of seeing and representing the effects of violence. The incorporation of ethnographic fieldwork in the creative process of Echavarría, Salcedo, and Echeverri entails a close relationship between victims, artists, and places that have been deeply affected by the armed conflict.[1]

THE ARMED CONFLICT, TRANSITIONAL JUSTICE, AND ART

In Colombia, the last decades of the twentieth century were characterized by a period of violence and political instability that has been referred to as the "armed conflict." There are different interpretations of the origin, causes, and development of this conflict. Its origin is associated with the assassination of Liberal popular leader Jorge Eliécer Gaitán in 1948. His killing unleashed a 10-year period of bipartisan violence between Liberals and Conservatives known as *La Violencia* (1948–1958). The first leftist guerrillas such as FARC (Revolutionary Armed Forces of Colombia), ELN (National Liberation Army), and the EPL (Popular Liberation Army) were created in the 1960s, inspired in part by the Cuban revolution of 1959. Other guerrilla groups such as M-19 and the Indigenous guerrilla Movimiento Armado Quintín Lame were created in 1970 and 1984, respectively. During the 1980s and 1990s different paramilitary groups such as the AUC (United Self-Defenses of Colombia) also emerged. An official report entitled *Basta Ya! Colombia: Memorias de Guerra y Dignidad* (*Enough Is Enough! Colombia: Memories of War and Dignity*), published in 2013 by the Colombian National Center of Historical Memory (*Centro Nacional de Memoria Histórica*), clearly states: "It is a war that is hard to explain because of its long duration, the different motives and reasons that lie behind it, the changing participation of legal and illegal actors, its geographic extension, and the particularities it assumes in each region and in the cities, as well as for its imbrication with other forms of violence" (CNMH 2013, 19).

There have been at least 11 attempts to advance peace negotiations or agreements with different guerrilla groups since 1981. The last peace agreement was signed between the government of Juan Manuel Santos (2012–2018) and FARC on November 24, 2016. The SIVJRNR was created as part of these agreements and included three mechanisms of transitional justice: (1) Special Jurisdiction for Peace, (2) the Truth Commission, and (3) the Search Unit for Missing Persons. One of the main objectives of the SIVJRNR has been to clarify the causes and consequences of the armed conflict, judge those responsible for human rights violations, and "repair" the victims.

Some of these mechanisms of reparation have involved artists and local artistic practices as ways of registering, denouncing, and representing the damage brought on by violence. Specifically,

---

1 Issues commonly associated with the origin of the armed conflict in Colombia are limited access to land for peasants, a bipartisan political system that excludes other democratic alternatives, state-led political violence and human rights violations, among others. There have also been official attempts to understand the causes and dynamics of the armed conflict in Colombia through the creation of different expert commissions.

the Truth Commission created a set of interviews with different artists under the title *nombrar lo innombrable* (naming the unnamable), where artists are presented as witnesses to the armed conflict. These official initiatives frequently consider that art can say or express things, through metaphors and other visual tropes, that are impossible to convey through other media. In addition, these initiatives assume that artistic practice can work as a catharsis that might help to heal past traumas through symbolic elaboration of what happened during the armed conflict.[2] Nonetheless, we should not take for granted that there is a direct relationship between art and the **symbolic reparation** or healing of victims. In fact, in the case of Colombia, art and artistic practice itself has been affected by different forms of violence within the conflict. While some approaches to the relationship between art and violence ask if art can "repair" victims of political violence or not, in this chapter we follow the artistic work of three Colombian artists (Juan Manuel Echavarría, Clemencia Echeverri, and Doris Salcedo) who have engaged in producing specific ways of seeing and representing the armed conflict that involve traveling to war zones, working with victims or ex-combatants, and making public interventions with the participation of different audiences.

"LEAVING THE STUDIO": ART AND THE ETHNOGRAPHIC TURN

As part of their reflexivity regarding the role of art in contexts of prolonged armed conflict, contemporary Colombian artists have transformed the ways in which they create and make works of art, moving toward ways of producing art that are more involved with the contexts, victims, and perpetrators of political violence. Carvajal González (2018) points out that in Colombia "the artist that is politically committed does not look in the press or in images taken from the archive for the mediums to speak about his time … instead, the artist goes in search of the physical sphere, the primary source. He does fieldwork: defines a territory, becomes familiar with it, constitutes a group of persons, confronts his own prejudice with his interlocutors, interrogates reality *in situ*" – the original place where specific events occurred (1–2). This transformation in the work of the artist and the role of art can be associated with what Foster calls the **ethnographic turn** in contemporary art, where there is a movement away from making works of art only for the artistic field to creating specific projects open for public debate (Foster 2001, ix).

Artists such as Echavarría, Salcedo, and Echeverri have reconsidered how they develop their work in the studio. For instance, they have created teams who travel to places where violent

---

[2] Different scholars have explored the role of artists and art in countries such as South Africa, Argentina, Chile, or former Yugoslavia, where transitional justice mechanisms have been implemented. Rush (2015) points out the limitations of understanding political transitions as just juridical processes (v), showing the importance of considering the cultural and affective dimensions around justice and other social values that have given historical legitimacy to processes of democratic or peace transitions (Bell 2014; Garnsey 2016).

events occurred and collect information from the narratives and local practices of survivors; they also take pictures and record sounds or make art interventions in these same places, such as performances or artistic installations. These artists include local appropriation and interpellation in the making of their works of art. For instance, Echavarría invites ex-combatants to participate in the making of his works of art (e.g., paintings) about specific violent events such as massacres.

This quasi-ethnographic creative process was presented at the exposition "Rivers and Silences, Retrospective of the Work of Echavarría," organized at the Museum of Modern Art of Bogotá in 2017. In this exhibition, the artist's personal pictures and field notes were displayed in a cabinet. In the field notes there were annotations and commentaries made during his trips between 2003 and 2017 to regions such as Chocó, Puerto Berrío, Montes de María, Caquetá, and Putumayo. For instance, during his trips to Chocó, Echavarría produced the video *Bocas de Ceniza* (2003–2004) with survivors of the massacre of Bojayá that took place in May 2002, where 98 people were killed amid confrontations between FARC, the army, and paramilitary groups. This series of videos were made with songs that were composed and interpreted by some of the survivors that Echavarría met while doing his fieldwork. Regarding this change in his method of making works of art, Echavarría says: "During that coming and going I started to write travel diaries and collect stories of war survivors. After *Bocas de Ceniza* I broke with the four walls of my studio in Bogotá. I escaped that bubble ... and went out to explore other rural areas of the country that were destroyed by war" (Echavarría 2018, 5).

Echavarría would take note of the testimonies of his "informants" while he traveled to remote rural areas and confronted the ruins of the armed conflict, such as abandoned schools. These ruins and remains would later become a recurring topic in his photographic series known as *Silencios* (Silences). *Silencios* is composed of a series of photographs of more than 200 blackboards found at 100 schools that had been abandoned during the armed conflict (Figure 20.2). Regarding his work *Silencios*, Echavarría recounts how

> on March 11, 2011, I was invited to the old town of Mampuján, in the district of Los Montes de María, Bolívar, Colombia. The community commemorated the 10th anniversary of their displacement by the paramilitary group "Héroes de los Montes de María" (Heroes of Los Montes de María). In the abandoned rural school of Manpuján, which had no roof and a floor covered with vegetation, I found a blackboard in one of the classrooms, and on the wall next to it, vowels were drawn ... A few days later, while inspecting the image, I discovered that in that silent blackboard an almost invisible sentence appeared: "*lo bonito es estar vivo*" (the beautiful thing is to be alive). Those blackboards ... encouraged me to seek other schools ... other memories that could be found before fading forever ... (Echavarría 2018, 108).

This creative work *in situ* has made Echavarría reflect on his creative process and get involved with survivors of different situations of war, who participate in the elaboration of videos, paintings, and exhibitions. Echavarría has promoted the debate around the ways in which

Figure 20.2. *Silencios* **(2010), Juan Manuel Echavarría.** Photo by Juan Manuel Echavarría.

we see the imprints and traces of violence on the lives and places of those who suffer from it. In all his recent exhibitions, Echavarría invites survivors and ex-combatants who serve as guides, making the audience interact with them and bringing them closer to his work. For Echavarría, the work of art is not a finished and closed object. Rather, he sees art as open to public interpellation, bringing together victims, ex-combatants, and the audience of his work.

The practice of "leaving the art studio" has also been used by Colombian artist Clemencia Echeverri. Echeverri's work is informed by questions such as the limits of understanding or making sense of violence. These kinds of questions, according to Echeverri,

> Bring me closer to events, take me to places where things have happened and from then on I decided to move out of my studio, put together a group of people I work with and visit specific places … the gaze is all traversed by something complex and it is between what I see, how the event unfolds, and how I think the image is being constructed that … you accumulate, slowly, experiences that later you work on in the studio in different ways. You can suggest making some installations with multiple channels … and an installation with a projection on the ground or with a strong sound component that dominates the image … each circumstance has its own way of being worked out in the studio (quoted in Lema and Lozano 2018).

Figure 20.3. Voluntary Testimony (2011), Clemencia Echeverri. Photo by Clemencia Echeverri.

Echeverri traces this change in her creative process to the mid-1990s, when she felt unsatisfied with some of her previous works, such as traditional sculptures in public spaces. These public sculptures lacked "affect and vital experiences, as well as connections with things that happened in the social and political realms" (Herrera Sabo 2019).

From that moment onwards, video and sound installations have been central to Echeverri's artistic work. For instance, in the video installation *Voluntary Testimony* (2011; Figure 20.3), Echeverri addresses the difficulty in trying to communicate the truth in voluntary confessions made by former paramilitary and guerrilla members in different transitional justice scenarios.[3] Through superimposed, broken, and distorted voices of demobilized combatants, Echeverri's video installation *Voluntary Testimony* shows "an incomplete process of unmasking, these people can only partially reveal their identity, their past, and their feelings" (Echeverri 2011). The installation is a critique of the "voluntary testimonies" of paramilitaries given to the Justice and Peace tribunals in which they were supposed to tell the truth about their crimes. Partial

---

3 In 2002 the government of former President Alvaro Uribe introduced a legal framework through Law 782 in which illegal armed groups or paramilitary groups (the self-titled United Self-Defense Forces of Colombia) surrendered their weapons and were reincorporated into civil society in a process known as "demobilization." In 2003, the paramilitary groups of Colombia signed an agreement to demobilize 30,000 of their members with the government. In 2005, the government introduced Act 975, known as the Justice and Peace Law. This "new" legislative framework allowed for the prosecution and sentencing of members of illegal armed groups, which were demobilized since the year 2002, using alternative sanctions. The sanctions of demobilized paramilitary members were reduced if they contributed to the search of truth of the crimes they had previously committed.

Figure 20.4. *Duelos* (2019), Clemencia Echeverri. Photo by Clemencia Echeverri.

and incomplete, the testimonies ignored or concealed information about the location of the corpses of all the disappeared people they murdered. Through this video installation, spectators confront their own difficulties in understanding and making sense of paramilitary violence.

The critique of paramilitary violence and its close relationship with state forces is developed in Echeverri's video installation *Duelos* (Echeverri 2019; Figure 20.4). In this video installation, she addresses *Operación Orion*, which was advanced by the military and paramilitary groups in 2002 and led to the disappearance of several young people that lived in Comuna 13 (the neighborhood in Medellín where the operation took place). The corpses of murdered people were thrown in a dump known as *La Escombrera* on the outskirts of Medellín. The relatives of the victims organized themselves, demanding justice and truth regarding the location of the bodies of those who were disappeared. *Duelos* proposes to "generate a moment of public mourning" through a "video installation work of nine images in synchrony that, together with three sound levels, embrace the room and evoke an endless duel that continues to happen in Colombia due to forced disappearance" (Museo Nacional de Colombia 2019). In *Duelos*, the spectator can see rubble falling to *La Escombrera* below their feet, and listen to the voices of those that were disappeared in *Operación Orión* and never found or looked for.

Doris Salcedo is another contemporary artist who addresses the wounds, pain, and traces left by the armed conflict in different places of Colombia. Salcedo views her recent artistic work as the outcome of her immersion in Colombia's turbulent social and political reality. In her own words, "as an artist I didn't choose what to do. There is a reality, a reality that imposes itself in a brutal way. I simply, in the humblest manner, obey the violent events that mark the history of the country" (Semana 2019).

Throughout her artistic production, Salcedo has emphasized collective work that has meant not only "leaving the studio," but also opening the studio to women that have survived the armed conflict or setting up the studio in public spaces such as the Plaza de Bolívar in downtown Bogotá. Salcedo has also worked closely with organizations of victims of sexual abuse, who participate in different moments of the creative process. For instance, at the end of the 1980s, Salcedo met with survivors of massacres from the region of Urabá and with relatives of disappeared persons. Based on the testimonies of survivors and relatives of victims, Salcedo started to include personal belongings of the disappeared in her artistic work. In Urabá, Salcedo also met women who told her about the impact caused by the murder and disappearance of their husbands. Salcedo was impressed with the story of a woman who would wash and iron the clothes of her murdered husband. From that story she created her installation *Untitled* (1989–1990) more commonly known as *Las Camisas* (the shirts). In this installation, with the same care that women in Urabá have for the clothes of their beloved and absent kin, Salcedo starched shirts given to her by the widows with plaster, folded them and piled them up, one on top of the other, and crossed each of them with a metallic bar in the right shoulder. This installation symbolizes both the accumulation of disappeared bodies and the accumulation of pain that relatives of victims of the armed conflict suffer.

A similar aesthetic device was put into place in Salcedo's installation *Atrabiliarios* (1992), which was created after listening to the testimonies of relatives of disappeared persons and paying close attention to how these survivors relate to the belongings of their missing kin. Family members gave Salcedo the shoes the victims wore before they were murdered or disappeared. Those worn-out shoes – primarily women's – were later "encased in niches embedded into the gallery wall, covered by a layer of stretched and preserved animal fiber, and affixed to the wall with medical sutures" (Museum of Contemporary Art Chicago 2015). These remains of the belongings of victims symbolize the presence of those who have been disappeared and how their memory keeps haunting the lives of those that survived the armed conflict. According to Andreas Huyssen (2003), the sculptures and installations of Doris Salcedo perform a "kind of memory work that activates body, space, and temporality, matter and imagination, presence and absence in a complex relationship with their beholder" (111).

In 2016, Salcedo started organizing collective mourning actions through participatory and performative works of art in the Plaza de Bolívar. In *Sumando Ausencias* (2016; Figure 20.5), Salcedo reacted to the democratic referendum that rejected the peace agreements between FARC and the government in 2016. She used more than 7,000 meters of white fabric in which protesters and other volunteers wrote some 2,300 names in ash. Each sheet of cloth, symbolizing one victim of the armed conflict, was "carried and laid down carefully by volunteers in a gesture of respect for the absent victims, then stitched together by hand over a period of 12 hours." Once complete, *Sumando Ausencias* covered the entire Plaza (Carmichael 2022).

Figure 20.5. *Sumando Ausencias* **(2016), Doris Salcedo.** Photo by Fredy Andrés Orjuela.

Salcedo's performative works in public spaces, alongside victims' political organizations, has underlined the urgency of realizing a collective mourning for the victims of the armed conflict in Colombia in the public sphere. The artist has tried to represent the symbolic and material damage that political violence has brought for different people in the country. *Sumando Ausencias* has exposed in a public space the subjective wounds and traces left by the armed conflict, bringing together personal trauma and collective mourning. The damage caused by the armed conflict, according to Salcedo, cannot be reduced to something that happened to others that live in rural Colombia. Instead it affects us all as human beings.

THE ETHNOGRAPHIC TURN AND WAYS OF SEEING THE ARMED CONFLICT IN COLOMBIA

According to John Berger (1972), "every image embodies a way of seeing," and "our perception or appreciation of an image depends also upon our own way of seeing" (10). In this chapter, we demonstrate how the ethnographic turn introduced into Colombian contemporary art produced new ways of seeing the armed conflict. We have emphasized that the act of seeing is also political and depends on the experience of the observer and the social context in which the images are produced and circulated. The ethnographic turn in Colombian contemporary artists raises questions regarding the political role of art in contexts of transitional justice. While the SIVJRNR associates the role of art with symbolic reparation for victims, the work of the artists we discuss in this chapter shows that art does not necessarily heal the wounds left by violence. In Salcedo's own words:

> I don't believe the reproduction of an image can stop violence. I don't think that art has that capacity. Art does not redeem and I don't think there is an aesthetic redemption ... I don't think you can talk about the impact of art and not even of the social impact of art, not even of political impact ... what art can create is an affective relationship that communicates the experience of the victim. It is as if the destroyed life of the victim, that was interrupted with murder, in some way can continue in the experience of the spectator (quoted in Caleidoscopio 2013).

Echavarría says that since he abandoned the art studio, he has asked himself how to represent violence in Colombia. To answer this question, Echavarría turns to the Greek myth of Medusa and Perseus to explain his own way of seeing war and its effects upon us. In his own words: "Those who looked at Medusa [who embodied horror in the myth] in her face were petrified. Perseus, to fulfill his mission of beheading her, uses his copper shield as a mirror so we can see her obliquely and indirectly. Art, like the shield of Perseus, allows us to see horror [obliquely] without petrifying ourselves." This oblique perspective used to visualize the violence associated with the armed conflict in Colombia becomes very clear in his work *Silencios* (2010; Figure 20.2), where Echavarría and his team photographed thousands of blackboards of rural schools, in which "numbers are important because they allow us to show how education has been another *victim* of war." In these photographs, according to Echavarría, horror is documented through the traces it leaves, and not through images that emphasize direct violence.

In Clemencia Echverri's work, video installation is a device used for both narration and also for involving the spectator in the work of art. In the reception of Echeverri's work, interpretation remains open, as a chasm that reveals the fragility and instability of this world:

> Her work stays on a border, on a frontier and a limit that situates the spectator in a threshold that confronts not resolution but lays out a possibility: what could have been or can come to be ... each spectator chooses his or her tolerance level, what he or she is willing to feel, imagine, ask or think as possible solution ... and how he or she can overcome the tension is experimenting (Banco de la República 2019, 15).

Echeverri emphasizes that her artistic projects are not closed works of art, because images are composed and decomposed, places and geographies are dismembered, and you can "feel the pain" of specific places

Doris Salcedo's work also avoids showing explicit images of violence and focuses more on the aftermath of violence. Salcedo addresses violence through its traces. For instance, in her work *Untitled* (1989–1990), the clothes and personal belongings of disappeared people are remnants of how families become victims of violence. Salcedo wants her works of art to be considered actions of mourning and funeral orations. In her own words: "I think the major possibilities of art are not in showing the spectacle of violence but in hiding it, it is proximity, the latency of violence, what interests me" (quoted in Princenthal, Basualdo, and Huyssen 2000). Salcedo perceives the artist as a mediator who is faced with images of horror and perversion to rescue what is human about these experiences (Malagón-Kurka 2010). Through their work, artists try to make visible what remains concealed and make public the pain and suffering inflicted through different forms of violence. Each of Salcedo's works of art is an attempt to show the traces that violence leaves on the victims. Salcedo is interested not so much in narrating specific events, but in showing how people are marked by violence. Her work tries to show the textures of violence and inscribes her aesthetic interventions in the silences that have surrounded victims of the armed conflict.

CONCLUSION

In this chapter we analyzed how the ethnographic turn that was incorporated into the creative process of contemporary Colombian artists led to new ways of seeing the armed conflict. While the role of art in processes of transitional justice has been associated with reparation for victims, the artists analyzed in this chapter don't think that art is necessarily associated with symbolic reparations or with healing the victims. Instead, artists can produce new ways of seeing war and new ways of relating to the pain of the victims. Artists can be witnesses of the traces and pain left by the armed conflict. Leaving the art studio has changed the ways in which artists make art in a country such as Colombia with an ongoing and prolonged armed conflict. Making art in Colombia now involves local communities, victims, and human rights organizations that have influenced how contemporary Colombian artists represent the devastating effects of violence upon different places and people.

REFLECTION AND DISCUSSION QUESTIONS

- How did the ethnographic turn change the creative process of the three contemporary Colombian artists who are highlighted in this chapter?
- In what sense can making art about the armed conflict in Colombia be considered a political act?
- What role can artists play in countries such as Colombia that are undergoing the process of transitional justice?
- In your opinion, to what extent can art provide symbolic reparation for victims? What do the artists featured in this chapter think about art as a symbolic reparation for victims?

KEY CONCEPTS

- **ethnographic turn**: A wave of art practices, productions, and events (since the 1990s) that show significant similarities with anthropology and ethnographic research because they rely on fieldwork as part of the creative process.
- **politics of aesthetic representation**: The politics surrounding the different visual representations of the armed conflict in Colombia; these representations may vary from those produced in the mainstream media, which emphasize direct violence, to those produced by Colombian contemporary artists that are based more on traces, metaphors, and objects that can be associated with the armed conflict.
- **symbolic reparations**: A common juridical measure used to address human rights violations in the context of international law. Broadly distinguished from material and monetary reparations, symbolic reparations are generally defined as nonpecuniary and can take many forms. Symbolic reparations may include, for instance, official apologies, changing the name of public places, the establishment of days of commemoration, and the creation of museums and parks devoted to the memory of victims, among others.

EXPLORE FURTHER

- To learn more about the legacy of armed conflict in Colombia read **Chapters 8** and **21**.
- To learn more about the significance of material culture such as music, literature, film, art, and theater for communities in Latin America and the Caribbean, read **Chapters 13**, **14**, **21**, **24**, **27**, and **36**.
- Clemencia Echeverri Estudio. https://tinyurl.com/Echeverri-Studio.
- Doris Salcedo. *Palimpsesto*. https://tinyurl.com/Palimpsesto.
- Juan Manuel Echavarría. https://jmechavarria.com/es/#1.
- Obregón, Wills, and María Emma, eds. 2021. *Narrativas Artísticas del Conflicto Armado Colombiano: Pluralidad, Memorias e Interpelaciones*. Bogotá: Ediciones Uniandes.
- Réquiem NN. https://tinyurl.com/Requiem-NN.

ABOUT THE AUTHORS

Ana Guglielmucci is a professor of anthropology in the School of Human Sciences at Universidad del Rosario in Bogotá (Colombia) and researcher at CONICET (Argentina). Her research examines the politics of memories about armed conflict in Colombia and state terrorism in Argentina. As a Latin American woman and human rights activist, she is committed to helping resolve social and political problems in South America.

Esteban Rozo is a professor of anthropology in the School of Human Sciences at Universidad del Rosario in Bogotá (Colombia) and received his Ph.D. in Anthropology and History from University of Michigan. His research focuses on practices of Christian conversion in the Colombian Amazon among different

Indigenous groups and their relationship to processes of state formation and colonization in this region. He was born and raised in Bogotá, and as a Colombian citizen and anthropologist that studies historically marginalized Indigenous groups of the Colombian Amazon, Esteban is committed to addressing issues of social and racial inequality in Colombia.

REFERENCES

Banco de la República. 2019. *Liminal. Clemencia Echeverri*. Bogotá: Banco de la República.
Bell, Vikki. 2014. *The Art of Post-Dictatorship. Ethics and Aesthetics in Transitional Argentina*. London: Routledge.
Berger, John. 1972. *Ways of Seeing*. London: Penguin.
Caleidoscopio. 2013. "Arte, Memoria y Violencia." *Razón Pública*, March 11. https://razonpublica.com/arte-violencia-y-memoria.
Carmichael, Kelly. 2022. *Sumando Ausencias*. Institute for Public Art. https://www.instituteforpublicart.org/case-studies/sumando-ausencias.
Carvajal González, Johanna. 2018. "El Relato de Guerra: Cómo el Arte Transmite la Memoria del Conflicto en Colombia," *Amerika* 18. http://journals.openedition.org/amerika/10198.
Centro Nacional de Memoria Histórica (CNMH). 2013. *Basta Ya! Colombia: Memorias de Guerra y Dignidad*. Bogotá: CNMH.
Echavarría, Juan Manuel. 2018. *Works*. Madrid: Editorial RM.
Echeverri, Clemencia. 2011. "Versión Libre/Voluntary Testimony." Clemencia Echeverri Studio. https://www.clemenciaecheverri.com/studio/index.php/projects/version-libre-2011.
———. 2019. "Duelos/Mourning." Clemencia Echeverri Studio. https://www.clemenciaecheverri.com/studio/index.php/projects/version-libre-2011.
Foster, Hal. 2001. *El Retorno de lo Real. La Vanguardia a Finales de Siglo*. Madrid: Akal.
Garnsey, Eliza. 2016. "Rewinding and Unwinding: Art and Justice in Times of Political Transition." *International Journal of Transitional Justice* 10 (3): 471–91.
Herrera Sabo, María Margarita, dir. 2019. *Lo Que el Arte No Olvida*. Trece. https://www.youtube.com/watch?v=50492voQ-5k.
Huyssen, Andreas. 2003. *Present Pasts: Urban Palimpsests and the Politics of Memory*. Stanford, CA: Stanford University Press.
Lema, Irene, and Olga Lucía Lozano, producers. 2018. *Elegía: Clemencia Echeverri*. Arcadia. https://www.youtube.com/watch?v=eCkJFD43lFY.
Malagón-Kurka, María. 2010. *Arte Como Presencia Indéxica: La Obra de Tres Artistas Colombianos en Tiempos de Violencia: Beatriz González, Oscar Muñoz y Doris Salcedo en la Década de los Noventa*. Bogotá: Ediciones Uniandes.
Museo Nacional de Colombia. 2019. *Memorias del Conflicto en Fragmentos: Duelos de Clemencia Echeverri y Antibalas de Felipe Arturo*. https://www.museonacional.gov.co/noticias/Paginas/Fragmentos_Inauguracion.aspx.
Museum of Contemporary Art Chicago. 2015. *Atrabiliarios*. https://www3.mcachicago.org/2015/salcedo/works/atrabiliarios/index.html.
Princenthal, Nancy, Carlos Basualdo, and Andreas Huyssen. 2000. *Doris Salcedo*. London: Phaidon Press.
Rush, Peter. 2015. "Preface: After Atrocity. Foreword to Transition." In *The Arts of Transitional Justice: Culture, Activism, and Memory after Atrocity*, edited by Peter D. Rush and Olivera Simic, v-xi. New York: Springer.
Semana. 2019. "Doris Salcedo: Un Recorrido Comentado Por Su Trayectoria." *Semana*, June 5. https://www.semana.com/arte/articulo/doris-salcedo-un-recorrido-comentado-por-su-trayectoria/74322.

CHAPTER TWENTY-ONE

Film Reception and Audience Ethnography: Charting Local Imaginaries of Violence in Contemporary Argentina and Colombia

Nick Morgan, Philippa Page, and Cecilia Sosa

In August 2018, we gathered in a house not far from the sea in the Puente Nayero neighborhood of Buenaventura, Colombia, for a film screening and focus group. The audience of 10 sat in plastic chairs inside the house, but since this was an informal screening other people came and went as they pleased. We showed about 40 minutes of the Argentine documentary ¿*Quién soy yo?* (directed by Estela Bravo, 2006) and then began a discussion about what the audience had seen in the film. Jhon, a community leader in his early thirties, broke the ice by responding with his first impressions. He spoke slowly, solemnly, taking his time, pausing frequently to choose his words.

Jhon began by putting himself in the position of the children in the film whose parents had been disappeared during eight years of violence under Argentina's military dictatorship (1976–1983). He initially found himself lost for words: "It leaves you speechless." But as he began to apply the film to his own experience in Colombia, he observed that "you have to take life calmly, starting with your own," expressing a fatalism related to his own experience of loss ("I had family members who were disappeared too") and to conflict in Colombia more generally. His recognition that terrible things can and do happen at any time was related to a fundamental feeling, and he noted that watching the film "fills you with so much nostalgia." Translation becomes a problem here, as in this case the word *nostalgia* connotes a deep sense of loss, combined with the speaker's feelings of impotence in the face of forces that surpass his capacities to do anything about them. In this regard, the everyday nature of Colombia's **structural violence** and the cyclical nature of political conflict feeds a sense that violence is an unexceptional part of life, destroying families and whole communities. Jhon emphasized that the horrors that have happened both in Colombia and Argentina may be felt but they are beyond the possibility of representation. "It leaves me with no words ... to explain everything that has happened both there and here, in our country," he noted.

Figure 21.1. A group of residents watch the Argentine documentary *¿Quién soy yo?/Who Am I?* in the Espacio Humanitario in Buenaventura, Colombia (top left and right); a young woman from the southern zone of greater Buenos Aires, Argentina, fills in a questionnaire as part of a focus group that followed a screening of the Colombian documentary *Falsos Positvos/False Positives* (bottom left and right). Photos by Alejo Moguillansky and Nick Morgan.

In this chapter, we describe the results of a film reception study and audience ethnography that we conducted in Argentina and Colombia, both countries that have experienced significant periods of political violence in their recent history. We argue that showing our audiences representations of conflict from unfamiliar places presents them with an interpretive challenge that begins to reveal the imaginative mappings through which both individual participants and communities make sense of conflict.

METHODS

Between August 2018 and April 2019, we carried out a series of film screenings, followed by focus group discussions, in Argentina and Colombia. These screenings were part of a broader transnational study that seeks to map the local imaginaries of violence and post-conflict transition in Algeria, Argentina, Colombia, Indonesia, and Northern Ireland. Using film reception as part of our methods, the **audience ethnography** involved observing, recording, and transcribing the post-screening discussion for subsequent analysis. The aim of the research was to achieve empirically informed, qualitative understandings of the local social imaginaries of violence and

civil conflict, with specific focus on the memory of the 1976–1983 civic-military-ecclesiastic dictatorship in Argentina and the multifaceted, decades-long conflict in Colombia. As a concept, the **social imaginary** seeks to clarify what binds social groups together. To do this, it maps the images, tropes, stories, myths, and metaphors that make up the richly textured symbolic worlds within which human actions and interactions take on meaning. Conversely, the notion of **conflict imaginaries** explores these same elements to understand what divides a community. It conceptualizes how people imagine differences and how they make sense of them in everyday life.

While both countries are in Latin America and share aspects of colonial history, the specific typology of conflict experienced in each was very different and so, as indeed we found, were the ways in which people interpreted the traumatic events that have played such an important role in shaping everyday lives and establishing a sense of collective identity. Any understanding of political violence is incomplete without an exploration of the collective representations through which social actors make sense of conflict. The project therefore set out to describe, analyze, and compare different conflict imaginaries to grasp how such understandings both reproduce violence and potentially play a confounding role in attempts to promote peaceful coexistence. Using film as a touchstone for debate gave research participants the opportunity to give free rein to their imaginations. It not only offered a way of breaking the ice but, by showing expressions of other conflicts, it allowed participants to step back for a moment to consider their own surroundings through a different prism. Showing our audiences representations of conflict from unfamiliar places thus presented them with an interpretive challenge. Immersing participants in the language of film invited them to engage imaginatively in acts of interpretation and comparison that would allow the images, metaphors, stories, and emotions that constitute conflict imaginaries to emerge.

COLOMBIA

In this chapter we are going to concentrate on the discussion that took place during a focus group at the *Espacio Humanitario* (Humanitarian Space) in the Puente Nayero neighborhood in Buenaventura. This community made a collective decision to outlaw violence, a process that has taken place in several communities across Colombia, as in the case of the well-known Peace Community in San José de Apartadó, Urabá. In these models, whole communities reject the presence of violent actors in their territories, whether they be agents of the state, paramilitaries, or insurgents. Though this rejection can often only be symbolic, it is both an indictment of political violence and a strategy that seeks to avoid local people being caught in the crossfire between opposing groups.

The Puente Nayero is a small urban space of a few blocks, consisting mainly of self-built wood and concrete dwellings and *palafitos* (houses built on stilts). Much of the area was reclaimed from the sea by the collective efforts of the community, who struggled for years to fill in the space beneath their homes with rubble, rubbish, and anything else available that came to hand. Though peace communities reject the presence of all armed actors, the *Espacio Humanitario* has a regular police and military presence who engage in frequent patrols around the neighborhood. The roads along the waterfront are unpaved, and the houses have limited access to sanitation, power, and drinking water. Alongside the structural violence of this form of exclusion, these settlements, traditionally dedicated to fishing and other maritime activities, have had to face both the struggle between drug traffickers to control the lucrative smuggling routes in Colombia's most important Pacific port and the coordinated attempts by powerful business interests to drive out people who are seen as standing in the way of the modernization of the port area. Until recently, Buenaventura's political class has shown little interest in the needs of the city's overwhelmingly Afro-Colombian population, privileging instead the commercial interests that control the port, leading activists to describe the city as "a port without a community" – a place where the human needs of the population are simply ignored. It was in response to this historic neglect that a huge civic strike brought the city to a standstill in 2017, shaking up the local political power structures.

In the years leading up to the strike, the few blocks around the *Espacio Humanitario* had come to symbolize Buenaventura's violence through their association with the notorious *casas de pique*, buildings where people were tortured and sometimes dismembered by armed gangs, their body parts washing up on the tide as a reminder to the community of what was in store for anyone who opposed the paramilitaries. Amplified by the national and international media, these events dominated the city's image for a time, much to the anger of local activists who rejected the sensationalist treatment of these events in the media. They saw such coverage as fitting in all too easily with long-standing racist tropes. Our first visit to the area during our study's pilot phase took place against this backdrop. In subsequent visits, however, we began to recognize the complexities of life in the area, in particular the links between the local population and the rural areas from which many of them had come: in most cases Afro-Colombian communities along the Naya River, whose right to collective land title had been recognized by the Colombian state during our initial visit in 2015. These communities, too, have experienced the extreme brutality of the armed conflict. In our film discussions, it was sometimes this rural context that came to the fore, rather than the local realities of the *Espacio Humanitario* and Puente Nayero.

The film *¿Quién soy yo?* focuses on the stories of children whose parents were tortured and disappeared in the 1976 military coup and its aftermath. These children were then given to families that supported the military regime with false identities and fake birth documents. The film traces the decades-long campaign of the famous Grandmothers of the Plaza de Mayo to recover their stolen grandchildren and combines archival footage with more recent testimonies by the grandmothers, the recovered grandchildren, and their relatives. *¿Quién soy yo?* is a trenchant critique of the barbarism of the military regime and its supporters. Although our Colombian participants knew little about the events described in the film, it elicited strong responses from our focus groups.

By this point we were relatively familiar figures in a neighborhood frequently visited by researchers and film crews. We thought of the screening as a way of getting to know people, but the community was not sure what we were trying to achieve nor what was to be gained by participating in our project, and the nucleus of the focus group was therefore made up mostly of community leaders, though other community members were present.

In this first film screening, the spatial, chronological, and affective nature of the conflict imaginary is already to the fore. The examples of human cruelty depicted in the film were political, to be sure, part of a specific violent conjuncture, but they were also universal, part of human nature. Jhon's reaction to the film demonstrates how the Argentine documentary captured something of his own experience. Indeed, the personal scale is key – violence is enacted on bodies, which continue to feel the aftermath of violence years after its conclusion. Juan Felipe, another community leader, took the next turn, repeating Jhon's use of the word *nostalgia*, touching his chest to show where he feels this emotion. He spoke of losing a brother-in-law, who left behind small children who barely remember him, and of finding the place where his relative was disappeared but not his body. Once again, the documentary made him feel that the experience of losing someone to political violence was so widely shared that it was practically universal; it "repeats itself in all countries." For Juan Felipe, feelings of fatalism and impotence at the fate of the Argentine children mirrored the political impotence he felt in the face of a local political scenario resistant to change. He used the example of the *falsos positivos* to make the claim that the state itself was the principal enemy of ordinary people: "Here in Colombia most murder ... it's the government that is behind them. So how do you take them on?" If the activists in Argentina were driven by a desire to enact justice, the Colombian audience members conveyed a different stance: The very notion of a transition to peace seemed impossible in Colombia, despite the much-vaunted 2016 accords between the government and the FARC (Revolutionary Armed Forces of Colombia), a guerrilla group.

Audience member Paola Yeny was more measured, taking a distance from her own emotional response to the film and attempting to draw together a series of disparate threads in ways that showed the challenge of integrating these foreign representations into a conceptual scheme, especially when it came to comparisons. Like many participants in the focus groups, her comparison included a tendency to try and decide whether the Argentine conflict was "worse" or "better" than the Colombian one she knew all too well. "They were lucky there, because they took the children from them, but they didn't kill them ... here sometimes you never see the parents again, but the kids disappear too," she told us, referring to the use of infanticide as a weapon of political violence. Such crimes remain a reality and are rooted in the Colombian conflict imaginary, and echo the interparty violence of the 1940s and 1950s when combatants were urged "to leave not even the seed." Like her fellow organizers, Paola Yeny again blamed the state, noting that "the state becomes our main enemy," though she also noted a general lack of solidarity, as community leaders continued to be killed with impunity across Colombia. Nonetheless, she felt that the accords with the FARC offered some sense of closure at least: "Transitional justice seeks real peace, because when you find out where your family member is, and what happened to them, you can begin to talk about reconciliation." The Argentine experience documented in the film suggested that knowing what happened to one's family members was merely the start of a road that does not seek reconciliation so much as justice and reparation. In this respect, however, Paola Yeny wanted to believe in the promises of the Colombian government's agreement with the FARC.

What real justice might be, however, remained implicit in Paola Yeny's complaints about the structural violence that underlay Colombia's enduring social cleavages. The territorial nature of the local conflict came to the fore, the driving force of which she saw as "the desire for land on the part of those who occupied the territory." For her, then, conflict was related to *territory*, a key term that carries a particular importance given Colombia's ethnicized politics, as shadowy forces seek to displace Afro-Colombian and Indigenous peoples from their collectively titled lands. These cleavages, she argued, were also related to a fundamental inequality, "accumulating more and more wealth is just for a few while most of the population goes hungry," and to large-scale development. In her words, "the more land is concentrated in a few hands, and the more megaprojects a region has, the more violence it's going to experience." In the local context, that reality was all too evident. "They say half of Buenaventura is going to be port, and from there on up [she gestures to indicate the direction] is going to be for us, but when you look at the megaprojects, we aren't included in them."

Orlando Castillo provided the closing reflections of the focus group, bringing the discussion to a final focus on the harassment and murder of community leaders who supported land restitution or resisted megaprojects. "What's going on in Colombia, first, is a genocide, that's obvious. Second, it's systematic, planned, and they are trying to silence the voices that drive the radical social transformation of the country." At the time, Orlando was the local organizer for our project in Buenaventura. He was the key figure in this focus group, a local organizer with links in the Naya valley who had spent years as one of the visible faces of the *Espacio Humanitario*. In the face of frequent death threats, he has continued to be a focal point in the struggle to defend the rights of the local population, following in the footsteps of his father, Don Pompilio, a survivor of the massacre carried out against militants of the *Unión Patriótica* political party in the late 1980s and early 1990s. The role of dysfunctional states, a theme raised by the Argentine documentary, sparked a reflection among Colombian audience members on the failure of Colombian institutions to protect human rights advocates. This somber panorama, however, did not deter these community leaders, though it explains in part their fatalism. Whatever risks they faced, doing nothing was not an option.

ARGENTINA

The Argentine focus groups discussed in this chapter all took place in urban or suburban neighborhoods in the federal capital and Greater Buenos Aires. The urban and predominantly middle-class character of these focus groups very much contrasted with the location, setting, and membership of the focus group in Buenaventura, Colombia. In terms of the spatial imaginary, however, Argentina's capital was, unlike Bogotá, a locus of state-perpetrated violence during the dictatorship. The largest clandestine detention and torture centers – known officially as *Clandestine Centers of Detention, Torture and Extermination* (or CCDTyE) and key to the dictatorship's hidden and "concentrationary" (Calveiro 2013) apparatus of repression – were embedded in the urban fabric of Buenos Aires and its surrounding agglomeration. Despite the classic trope of a city that "turns its back" on the river, Buenos Aires extends out from the banks of the River Plate. The river was the destination of the so-called death flights where incapacitated (drugged) detainees were thrown from planes and disappeared, making the muddy waters of the Plate the most unsettling point of reference in the spatial imaginary of state terrorism: loss and disappearance without trace. Now Buenos Aires is home to numerous sites of memory. Commemorative *baldosas* (decorated and inscribed paving stones) mark the last known location of many of the 30,000 people who remain disappeared. The Memory Park looks out over the river and contains a long, zigzagging wall bearing the names of the disappeared, their year of disappearance and age at that time. And Argentina's largest clandestine detention center, the former ESMA (The Higher School of Mechanics of the Navy), is simultaneously an active crime scene for ongoing trials and home to the National Memory Museum and adjacent archive. Every year, on March 24, National Memory Day (also the anniversary of the 1976 coup), the city hosts the nation's largest public commemorative gathering and celebration of human rights activism.

Unlike Colombia, where the tenuous promise of post-conflict (or post-agreement) transition was much fresher in the minds of people in affected communities, Argentina's transition to democracy began in December 1983. Furthermore, this transition had begun with a truth commission (1984), followed swiftly by trials of the military junta's leaders for human rights violations (1985). In the four decades of democratic governance since then, a dynamic and creative public culture of memory has thrived intergenerationally around the interlocking tenets of "memory," "truth," and "justice." Human rights activism has been particularly powerful during those times when the official treatment of the dictatorship has been shaped by a regressive right-wing politics of "reconciliation," based on a logic of forgetting and impunity.

The members of our first two screenings and focus groups in Buenos Aires were of retirement age, ranging from 65 to 75 years old. They had all lived through the 1976–1983 military-civic-ecclesiastic dictatorship as students or young professionals. The first screening took place at the University of the Third Age (UniTE) at the Public University of Lomas de Zamora. Lomas de Zamora, located within the southern zone of the Greater Buenos Aires area, is one of the most populous *partidos* (districts) of Buenos Aires. UniTE runs free university courses across the humanities and social sciences for people over 60 years of age; more than a thousand students attend. Our focus group of 15 included 12 women and 3 men of varying professions. The second screening was held at the *Camarín Nouvelle Vague*, a small neighborhood cine club that met every Friday night. It is located two blocks from the main commercial strip in the middle-class suburb of Ramos Mejía, in the province's most populous *partido*, La Matanza. A beauty salon by day, this small family-run business transformed on Friday evenings, equipping its back room with a dozen chairs, a projector, and a large screen to watch and discuss a diverse range of films that accompanied a class on the history of cinema. The group was composed of 12 participants: nine women and three men aged between 65 and 73. The course was run by film historian Matías on a voluntary basis.

In Argentina, we screened the Colombian documentary *Falsos Positivos* (2009), directed by Simone Bruno and Dado Carrillo. The documentary depicts what was at the time more than 500 cases (now over 6,400) in Colombia of "false positives." The term refers to innocent young men who were lured by the offer of work to kidnap them, dress them up as guerrilla combatants, kill them, and plant weapons next to their bodies to claim them as "casualties" in exchange for bonuses, promotion, and leave, which were offered as incentives by the government of then-president Álvaro Uribe. The documentary follows the cases of two young men who disappeared in such circumstances, interlacing the testimonial narratives of the men's relatives with the words of experts in conflict studies, justice, and human rights who situate these particular crimes within the broader context of Colombia's protracted conflict.

For both of the Argentine focus groups, the everyday experience of living amid state-perpetrated violence had marked their youth; many had stories they were still eager to share, mainly of disappeared *compañerxs* (friends/companions) or instances in which they had inadvertently witnessed or heard detentions (or *enfrentamientos*, "confrontations," as they were defined at the time) taking place near their homes. For these participants, the resonances of state-perpetrated violence were evidently more visceral, as could be observed in the gestures captured in the video recordings of the focus group discussions. As UniTE student Mariana remarked, "we belong to a very persecuted generation." The "we" framing of this statement suggested a collective experience of victimhood that was generational.

The parallels drawn between the state-sponsored violence of the Colombian false positives and the audience's collective memory of the Argentine dictatorship were immediate. This was captured by the first reaction to the film in the UniTE group. Reacting to the scenes in the documentary where affluent citizens were seen perusing the high-end stores in Bogotá while state-sponsored violence was being perpetrated elsewhere, Ana (a retired employee in her late sixties) noted that it reminded her of 1984, "when the mass graves were found and opened up and everyone said, 'Oh no!'" Simulating a gesture of shock, she asserted that expressions of surprise at the time were a "lie … We all knew." This statement became an immediate point of contention, causing the discussion to focus on the group's own experiences rather than the scenes from Colombia. Ana's opinion was categorically contested by another attendee, María José: "I'm sorry, but it wasn't common knowledge. I was at university and it was not known." Retired agricultural engineer Elsa, also in her late sixties, offered a slightly different perspective: "I never believed it. When they told me about the little boy belonging to the guerrilla fighter, that was in '84, that was when I found out. It would never even have occurred to me to think that." Elsa was referring to the systematic theft and illegal adoption of approximately 500 babies born to mothers held in captivity (which was also the subject of the Argentine documentary that the Colombian groups watched). The slippage in her intervention suggested that the perpetration of state violence was in fact common knowledge, but that it had been impossible at the time to imagine that people could be kidnapped, detained, tortured, and disappeared in such inhumane ways. This opening exchange at the UniTE focus group brought into discussion, on the one hand, attitudes to authoritarian violence that had remained fixed and entrenched in separate categories of victims, perpetrators, and the problematic category of innocent (and unsuspecting) bystanders. On the other hand, Ana's contributions represented a growing awareness among affected citizens of what Michael Rothberg (2019) has termed the "implicated subjectivity" of these so-called bystanders and with it a collective responsibility toward truth, memory, and justice.

This was evident in the Ramos group, where participants seemed keen to signal their explicit engagement with Argentina's vibrant culture of memory and human rights movement: Attending the March 24 commemorations and owning a copy of the truth commission's *Nunca Más* (*Never Again*) report were given as examples. Their activism was also evident in the vocabulary they used to describe and interpret the Colombian documentary; in their celebration of Argentina's human rights organizations, such as the internationally recognized groups the *Madres* and *Abuelas de Plaza de Mayo*; and in their reflection – individual and collective – on the lessons they had learned. Felipe, a 70-year-old retired bank employee, noted that he no longer feared participating in activism: "I was afraid back then because I was young and had a young family. Today, I am not afraid. I'm old enough to die defending an idea." Another participant, Silvina, shared the influence that her daughters have had on her political ideas: "I have three daughters and I'm learning about feminism through them, and they are thinking about a more delicate, peaceful future, one that is for everyone." At the time of the focus groups, public discourses in Argentina on violence and dictatorship had reached a fascinating juncture. The narratives of "memory," "truth," and "justice," threatened by the specters of reconciliation and impunity under then-president Mauricio Macri (2015–2019), were intersecting with the new public voices of the influential feminist movement *Ni Una Menos* (Not One Less), which was campaigning for reproductive justice and against increasingly high rates of "femi-geno-cide," a term pointing at once to the scale of contemporary femicide and the specifically gendered aspect of historic genocide (Segato 2012).

The intersection of the memory of dictatorship and the feminist movement was a fundamental point of reference in our third focus group, which took place at Liliana's home in the Almagro neighborhood of the Capital Federal.[1] Liliana is a founding member of the *Historias Desobedientes* (Disobedient Herstories), a collective of daughters, sons, and family members of *genocidas* (the authors of the dictatorship's genocide) who, since their first outing as a collective at the *Ni Una Menos* march in 2017, have united in public condemnation of the crimes committed by their perpetrator fathers. In April 2019, Liliana invited a group of five disobedient daughters to watch *Falsos Positivos*. Like the Ramos group, the members of *Historias Desobedientes* employed a specific lexicon throughout the discussion. This lexicon is an ethical, as well as a legally and politically

---

1 The names of members of the *Historias Desobedientes* group are not anonymized. Ramos participants Felipe, Mabel, and María are not anonymized. All other names have been anonymized.

accurate, way to talk about state violence in Argentina – *terrorismo de Estado* (state terrorism) or *genocidio* (genocide) – that rejects the junta's own rhetoric of being engaged in *una guerra sucia* (a dirty war) that required a "process of national reorganization." Those participants who were versed in the accepted lexicon tended to employ the same terminology to describe the violence represented in the documentary. The language is powerful, precise, and politically charged.

As well as drawing an immediate comparison between Colombia's civil conflict and the Argentine dictatorship, the latter two focus groups also pointed to a strong resonance with the structural violence of present-day Argentina. Objecting to a comparison merely with the past, Silvina (Ramos group) stated: "I don't agree that 'this happened to us.' I believe that it is happening to us, with a different message." As she tried to find the words to explain, María interjected, referencing President Macri's emphasis on "security" and what the group saw as the disproportionate use of police brutality, particularly in the most deprived neighborhoods. When interpreted through the prism of social class, these groups perceived many links between the neighborhoods portrayed in *Falsos Positivos* and contemporary violence in Argentina's informal neighborhoods, known as *barrios populares*. "It aims to eliminate them," suggested participant Mabel as she noted that the violence in the Colombian film was inflicted on the most deprived communities.

When each group attempted to explain the roots of violent civil conflict, the discussion moved toward the human condition: "Something that is inherent to human beings is egotism and the lust for power ... with different methodologies," María (Ramos group) opined. As an exile with her mother from Nazi-occupied Italy, María's personal experience of state violence already involved two different life contexts. For her, such violence was facilitated by "the bulk of humanity who deny, who turn a blind eye, who read [a situation] differently, who recount that nothing is going on." Lorna (*Historias Desobedientes*) tried several articulations to emphasize society's "implication" (Rothberg 2019).

As the dialogue between the two contexts unfolded, hierarchies of "better" or "worse" also emerged, though differently in each group. Ana (UniTE) remarked that the use of prolonged detention and torture made the Southern Cone dictatorships particularly brutal and perverse: "[In Colombia] they were less bloody, according to what the film tells me; the victim's ordeal was a question of minutes, hours at the most." The Ramos and *Historias Desobedientes* groups perceived the opposite. They were shocked by what disobedient daughter Silvia called "the naturalization of the massacre," targeting the most vulnerable populations. Lorna agreed, describing it as "a new demonstration of violence, because they did it here, but ... to cash in on each person killed seems to me to be ..." She trailed off in an attempt to describe a form of violence that was being perpetrated for financial gain. Instead, she replaced the final word with a gesture of disbelief before later noting, "It's as if there is no judiciary." As scholar and activist Mariana Tello Weiss (2019) has suggested, the 2005 Supreme Court ruling on Argentina's Impunity Laws (enacted between 1986 and 1990) and the resumption of trials for crimes against humanity were instrumental in enabling the *Historias Desobedientes* to find their public voice of condemnation.

CONCLUSION

The audience ethnographies recounted in this chapter reveal, with rich, intimate, and affective textures, how people remember and interpret violence both individually and collectively. Where audiences sought to trace similarities between the two contexts, this was at times expressed as shared feelings of loss, sadness, or powerlessness. At other times, the interpretative challenge of trying to make sense of violence from somewhere else led to competitive hierarchies of violence. In Colombia, the embryonic stages of transition were evident as audiences made repeated reference to a conflict that was only over on paper (*una paz de papel*). To these people, violence seemed inevitable, unlike the message they were getting from the Argentine documentary. Even reconciliation seemed out of reach. In Argentina, the lively discussions between audience members revealed a long-standing collective commitment to memory, truth, and justice from which people drew strength and joy. Those engaged with the discourses of human rights activism saw gestures of reconciliation as equivalent to impunity. The ongoing trials for crimes against humanity were celebrated as a fundamental part of Argentina's four decades of democracy. The images of Colombia's conflict did, however, draw comparisons with contemporary issues of social injustice in Argentina, particularly growing levels of poverty, intersecting inequalities, and alarming levels of gender-based violence. When it came to explaining the causes of political violence, it was clear that each audience would draw on their local understandings of violence and civil conflict to interpret what they were watching on screen.

REFLECTION AND DISCUSSION QUESTIONS

- How do social imaginaries shape civil conflicts and state violence? To what extent do they determine the possibilities for the transition to democracy and peace?
- How can the combination of film reception and audience ethnography help us chart the social imaginaries that structure popular understandings of local conflicts?
- What do local communities learn from thinking about conflicts other than their own and what impact, if any, does this have on their understanding of local conflict?

KEY CONCEPTS

- **audience ethnography**: An ethnographic methodology that involves participant observation and analysis of the audience in a reception study.
- **civil conflict**: A violent confrontation between two or more groups living together within a single country.
- **conflict imaginary**: How people imagine their social existence in terms of what separates them from others, either in the same social group or community or in a different polity.

- **social imaginary**: How people imagine their social existence and relationships with others living in the same polity, particularly what binds a social group together (Taylor 2004).
- **structural violence**: An indirect, nonpersonal form of violence whereby harmful effects are produced by societal systems.

EXPLORE FURTHER

- To learn more about the legacy of armed conflict in Colombia, read **Chapters 8** and **20**.
- To learn more about the significance of material culture such as music, literature, film, art, and theater for marginalized communities in Latin America and the Caribbean, read **Chapters 13**, **14**, **20**, **24**, **27**, and **36**.
- Bravo, Estela, dir. 2006. *¿Quién Soy Yo?*
- Carrillo, Dado, and Simone Bruno, dirs. 2009. *Falsos Positivos.*
- Jelin, Elizabeth. 2008. "Victims, Relatives, and Citizens in Argentina: Whose Voice Is Legitimate Enough?" In *Humanitarianism and Suffering: The Mobilization of Empathy*, edited by Richard A. Wilson and Richard D. Brown, 177–201. Cambridge: Cambridge University Press.
- Obradovic-Wochnik, Jelena. 2020. "Hidden Politics of Power and Governmentality in Transitional Justice and Peacebuilding: The Problem of 'Bringing the Local Back In.'" *Journal of International Relations and Development* 23 (10): 117–138.

ABOUT THE AUTHORS

Nick Morgan is a senior lecturer in Latin American Studies and director of the Centre of Latin American and Caribbean Studies at Newcastle University, UK.

Philippa Page is a senior lecturer in Spanish and Film, and co-director of the Humanities Research Institute at Newcastle University, UK.

Cecilia Sosa is a senior research fellow at the Centre for the Study of Post-Conflict Societies, Nottingham University, and the National Scientific and Technical Research Council (CONICET)/Universidad Tres de Febrero, Argentina.

REFERENCES

Calveiro, Pilar. 2013. *Violencias de Estado: La Guerra Antiterrorista y la Guerra Contra el Crimen como Medios de Control Global.* Buenos Aires: Siglo XXI de Argentina Editores, S.A.

Rothberg, Michael. 2019. *The Implicated Subject: Beyond Victims and Perpetrators.* Stanford, CA: Stanford University Press.

Segato, Rita. 2012. "Femigenocidio y Feminicidio: Una Propuesta de Tipificación." *Herramienta* (Buenos Aires) 49 (March).

Taylor, Charles. 2004. *Modern Social Imaginaries.* Durham, NC: Duke University Press.

Tello Weis, Mariana. 2019. "Interview." Interview by Philippa Page and Cecilia Sosa, Ciudad de Córdoba, Argentina, August 8, unpublished transcript.

CHAPTER TWENTY-TWO

Cementerio XXX: The *Desaparecidos* of "Post-Conflict" Guatemala

Sarah Maya Rosen

"My father might be here," Izabella said. I saw that she was weeping. "My father might be here in this terrible place."

When I entered Cementerio Tres Equis ("Cemetery XXX," Figure 22.1), Guatemala City's infamous cemetery for the unidentified and unclaimed dead, I had assumed that "XXX" represented the unknown names of the deceased who were buried there. I was incorrect. In fact, I would discover during my research that I had made many incorrect assumptions about the **desaparecidos** (disappeared). Perhaps more importantly, I discovered that many assumptions others have made about Guatemala's *desaparecidos* are incorrect as well. Like much ethnographic research, the questions I should have been asking did not become apparent until I became enmeshed in the community. And I was left with a strikingly more pressing ethical concern that applies to forensic anthropologists across the world: How do our assumptions impact the lives of the people we are trying to help, and how do we begin to address those assumptions?

AN INTRODUCTION TO "POST-CONFLICT" GUATEMALA

I arrived in Guatemala in April 2017 to collect ethnographic and forensic data for my Ph.D. dissertation on forensic anthropology after political violence. My research plan was to conduct surveys, semi-structured interviews, and participant observation in forensic excavations of mass graves. To forensic anthropologists, Guatemala is an intriguing example of **humanitarian forensic action**. In this case, the humanitarian crisis took the form of a decades-long civil war that claimed the lives of an estimated 200,000 Guatemalans. Through this research, I sought a deeper understanding of the impact forensic anthropological programs have on communities of survivors, the narratives surrounding the conflict, and the forensic investigators themselves.

Figure 22.1. Cementerio Tres Equis. Photo by Sarah Maya Rosen.

It quickly became apparent that these research questions could only be addressed with an understanding of the systematic inequalities that led to the conflict and remain a fundamental part of life in Guatemala today.

After an extended colonial period, which systematically disenfranchised Guatemala's Indigenous communities, Spain relinquished its control of the region in 1821. The early post-colonial governments were defined by a series of dictators, notorious for torturing and executing political dissidents (Metz 2006). In 1946, Guatemala held its first democratic elections, and in 1951 Jacobo Arbenz was elected president and ushered in a series of measures seeking to redistribute land and assets to poor and Indigenous communities. This rankled the landowners who relied on the major agribusiness of the region to maintain their wealth, especially through exports to countries like the United States. These landowners successfully lobbied the US government into intervening in Guatemala's government (Barrett 2015).

Convinced that the Guatemalan government would side with rising communist powers, the US Central Intelligence Agency orchestrated a coup in 1954, installing a military regime that provoked decades of internal violence against political dissidents, the poor, and Indigenous communities. In the following years, guerrilla movements (militias that use bursts of fast, small-scale tactics, often against more traditional military forces) emerged to combat the growing military presence. The militarized government retaliated by instituting a scorched-earth policy targeting the families and potential allies of the guerrilla fighters, with a heavy emphasis on Indigenous communities (Girón 2007). This strategy resulted in the deaths of 150,000 Guatemalans and the forcible disappearance of 50,000 people (Garcia et al. 2009) by government-sanctioned paramilitary death squads. These death squads left the corpses of victims in mass graves, both in villages and in execution centers (CEH 1999; Clouser 2009).

As reports of this violence spread in the international community, the United Nations officially intervened. Peace agreements were reached in 1996 between the Guatemalan National Revolutionary Union and the Guatemalan government (Girón 2007). These negotiations included provisions such as the formation of the Commission for Historical Clarification (CEH), which put forward recommendations for the excavation of clandestine graves to restore the dignity of victims and to return individuals to their families for reburial (UN 1999). This was part of a larger transitional justice effort that included the gathering of testimonies by truth committees and multilateral aid to communities, which sought to transition Guatemala from a time of conflict to a time of peace.

The *Fundación de Antropología Forense de Guatemala* (Forensic Anthropology Foundation of Guatemala; FAFG) began its work shortly after the release of the CEH report and still functions as a first point of contact for those who have lost family in the civil war. Nearly all forensic excavations of clandestine, and even non-clandestine, cemeteries in Guatemala are run through the FAFG (FAFG.org 2016). As of 2009, the FAFG works in at least 22 different regions and has conducted 946 investigations of clandestine mass graves. In the same year, they began efforts to become a fully licensed DNA laboratory, which they have now achieved, funded by the US Department of State, the Netherlands, and Sweden to meet the demands for the return of skeletal remains to family members (Garcia et al. 2009).

Yet to define the political violence in Guatemala solely in terms of "conflict" and "peace time" offers an incomplete understanding of that violence. In the years following the ceasefire, violent crime increased (Girón 2007). The civil war has also appeared to intensify gender, regional, and ethnic inequalities (Chamarbagwala and Morán 2011). Guatemala now contends with a new landscape of violence (Smith and Offit 2010). Human Rights Watch (2018) describes Guatemala's judicial system as grossly incompetent and corrupt, with a 95 per cent rate of impunity for homicides in 2010. Sanford (2008) observes that if violence continues to increase at the rates observed in 2008, more people will be killed in the first 25 years of peace than in the 36-year civil war itself. The Guatemalan police have also been implicated in contemporary extrajudicial executions and arbitrary detainment of suspected gang members (Human Rights Watch 2018), and gang violence is having observable, traumatic effects on young people in urban areas (Winton 2006).

Increasing attention is being paid to the shortcomings of transitional justice efforts because they do not address the underlying causes of conflict. There is a push to adopt a **transformative justice** model, which seeks to transform those underlying causes of conflict to prevent further suffering (Gready and Robins 2014). "Post-conflict" Guatemala is a prime candidate for this shift. As Bellino (2015) explains, in Guatemala, "comparisons can create a hierarchy of suffering that renders the violent past unimportant amid contemporary violence" (58). The ceasefire agreement, while currently acting as the official end of the conflict, does not truly represent the end of the violence nor of the frameworks that created the conflict – corrupt government, exploitation, entrenched poverty, and violent deaths. Rather, the paramilitary violence has morphed into gang violence, unrestrained by an impotent justice system. This is a critical facet of the forensic anthropological endeavors currently taking place in Guatemala.

FAFG ENCOUNTERS

When I arrived in Guatemala, my research plans rapidly fell apart. My primary contact, Nicholas, a forensic anthropologist who oversaw the excavation of mass graves by students who were learning forensic techniques, had disappeared – forcibly or otherwise we did not know – leaving no indication of his whereabouts nor any means to contact him. To complicate matters, when we were arranging my fieldwork, Nicholas had claimed he was affiliated with the FAFG; however, the FAFG had not heard of me nor my project when I reached out to them with my concerns for Nicholas' welfare. They explained that they had not been connected with him for several years.

The FAFG offered to consider my project on their own terms, a process that stretched into months and culminated in a polite rejection of my application. This left me at a loose end, limited to conducting unstructured interviews with those who showed an interest in my work about their experiences during the war, rather than the forensic anthropological work I had intended. However, while in the town of San Marcos on Lake Atitlan, I met Izabella, a woman who had also encountered the FAFG, but in circumstances I had not learned of before, and her story fundamentally changed my research.

Izabella's father had gone missing in 2008. She explained that during the initial investigation into his disappearance, she felt that much of the responsibility fell to her since the Ministerio Publico – the government organization that manages contemporary missing persons cases – had encouraged her to take on much of the investigation herself. Feeling that the Ministerio Publico was not doing enough, she contacted the FAFG requesting to participate in their DNA program, which seeks to match DNA collected from human skeletal remains with that of potential surviving family members to identify the deceased person. Since her father had disappeared about 12 years after the ceasefire agreement, the FAFG said they could not help her because they would not be able to use their DNA facilities for contemporary investigations until the missing persons from the war itself were identified. They explained that this policy was a stipulation imposed by the organizations that fund their laboratory. As I knew that the FAFG's DNA laboratory was the only accredited testing facility in Central America (at least as of 2009) and that they facilitate other excavations in Mexico, Izabella's story surprised me. When I discovered the details of Izabella's search for her father, I discovered the problematic limits of forensic anthropology as transitional justice as well.

CONTEMPORARY *DESAPARECIDOS* OF GUATEMALA

Izabella's father went missing from Guatemala City after a challengingly slow "high" season at Lake Atitlan, where he owned a small business that relied on the tourist economy. He had traveled to Guatemala City to speak to his brother about helping him, as his brother had inherited money that should have been shared between them. Izabella's father has not been seen since that meeting. His family and then the police searched his house and found his personal items, such as his passport and phone, inside and untouched. This led the police to assume that he had run away, potentially to die by suicide, but Izabella disagreed and suspected her uncle had him forcibly disappeared to ensure that he could keep their inheritance. The police recommended that the family check hospitals and morgues to see if he would turn up – whether alive and injured or deceased. She explained how she went to these hospitals and morgues looking for her missing father every weekend for months and then years.

At the morgues, she was given books filled with Polaroid pictures of the deceased who had been brought in for examination. She was expected to look through these books and attempt to identify anyone who could be her father. She explained to me that in the photographs the dead were in all states of decay; there were bodies with skeletonized faces that only a forensic expert could hope to identify. She said that because the morgues fill up so quickly, the unidentified are buried with only these Polaroid pictures kept for future identification. After months of this, she appealed to the Ministerio Publico and asked them if they had any news. They responded by asking her what she and her family had done in the intervening months to try to find him themselves.

From her account, the Ministerio Publico seemed to be a formidable barrier to justice, rather than an arbiter of it. To Izabella, the only way her father would ever be found would be if she kept looking for him herself. She began reaching out to DNA laboratories that could possibly help her, and this is when she contacted the FAFG, which told her their DNA laboratory was only used for victims of state violence because the funding for the laboratory – provided by foreign powers – was given on the condition that it would be used for the identification of victims of the internal conflict. She was told to send her DNA to a private DNA laboratory that would test it for a fee of US$3,000 – a price a hotel employee in Guatemala like Izabella could never afford. Furthermore, without access to the FAFG's database of DNA samples from recovered remains, she had nothing to compare the results to anyway.

MINISTERIO PUBLICO AND TRES EQUIS

A year after I first met Izabella, we visited the imposing building that is the Ministerio Publico in Guatemala City, where we were directed to sit in a waiting area to meet the new investigator. This investigator had never met Izabella, nor had she read her father's file until that day, while we waited. To their shock and concern, there was nothing in the file whatsoever. This indicated to the new investigator that the original investigator had done no work on the case. So, she began again. She wanted Izabella to give the details of her father's disappearance again; where he was last seen, what had happened in the days leading up to his disappearance, and again the question: "What have *you* done to investigate?"

Even with a new investigator, the responsibility of finding Izabella's father would lie on the family's shoulders. Had Izabella not gone back to the Ministerio Publico, had she just continued to visit the morgue, no one would have ever known her father's file was empty, and no one would have done anything about it. The investigator did reveal new information. She informed us that the cemetery Izabella had visited before was only used by the Ministerio Publico every other month; on alternate months, they sent unidentified bodies from the morgues to Cementerio Tres Equis, the section of the larger Cementerio La Verbena designated for the unidentified and unclaimed dead.

Izabella remained collected in the room, but when we left her frustration and anger were palpable. Over the long years of her father's disappearance, she had only ever been directed to one cemetery. She explained that she had specifically told the original investigator that her father went missing the day after he had dinner with her uncle to talk about money problems, and the investigator told her he had gone to get the uncle's statement. Yet the file indicated that he had not. It occurred to me then that if the investigator had lied about taking the statement, and then had given the family false information about where to search for the body, this failed search might not be a case of negligence but potentially one of corruption. We decided to go directly to the cemetery to seek more information.

Cementerio La Verbena is dusty and hot. It sits on a hill between a residential neighborhood and a series of empty lots that lead to the main roadway. To the left of the entrance was a small doorway leading to a rundown office with a man and a woman attending the desk. Izabella explained to the woman that her father is a *desaparecido* who had been missing for years, but that she had only now been told to check there. The woman behind the desk asked for the month and year of her father's disappearance, and then pulled out three large volumes containing the burial information of the unidentified that took place during that time. Izabella and I expected to see the pictures of dead faces, like those featured in the morgue's ledger. However, the only information included was the sex of the individual and an estimated age. To make matters more difficult, the ledgers were not categorized by this meager information, but rather by the order in which the bodies were buried. No other identifying information was included. The clerk pored over the entries, searching for anything that might match. After five minutes, she stopped, insisting this search was pointless and there was nothing more they could do. During this exchange, the other clerk ignored us, taking notes on a form. Beside him stood a pile of ledgers devoted to dead children; above the ledgers was a poster that read in Spanish "World's Best Dad."

Izabella and I left the office and made our way to the section of the cemetery for the unidentified. I had assumed that the three X's of Cementerio Tres Equis represented the unknown names of the unidentified dead on the tombstones. But I discovered that the three XXX's refer to the three crosses that stand at the opening of La Verbena's section for unidentified bodies. There were no tombstones. Dusty red fields of graves stretched out, shallow depressions in the earth, accumulating garbage. Human and animal remains were strewn along the pathways. Across from the unmarked graves stood an FAFG memorial, plastered with old missing person posters encouraging those with relatives missing from the internal conflict to submit their DNA for testing. Izabella looked at the faces on the missing persons posters, knowing that such services were not accessible to her because her father did not disappear during the conflict. Even if the DNA laboratory began processing non-conflict disappearances, Guatemala's current investigative system prevents the development of a database to compare DNA samples.

As we walked further into the Tres Equis section, I saw a human talus, an ankle bone, emerging from the soil. I instinctively kneeled and began to brush the dust away before I stopped myself. I had no legal or ethical right to touch this bone, even to move it from the road. Until this point in my career, I had never felt broken by the presence of human remains. I wept as I walked away, thinking of the individuals who are unaccounted for, in graves such as the one I had found under the road. How many were there? Dozens, hundreds, thousands?

THE SOCIOPOLITICS OF THE *DESAPARECIDOS*

In the academic articles I had read on forensic anthropology in Guatemala, I had not discovered a single negative portrayal of the FAFG – indeed, they perform important work – yet here was an explicit example of an individual turned away by the FAFG. The articles appear to reflect the work the FAFG does, not the work it does *not do*. This was a vital discovery that indicated there is a demographic of *desaparecidos* that has fallen through the investigative cracks.

In this case, Sweden, the Netherlands, and the United States (who also fund the FAFG laboratory through US Agency for International Development, USAID), have allegedly exerted influence by using financial resources to determine who does and who does not have access to forensic services – granting access only to those whose loved ones went missing before the ceasefire agreement in 1996. This attitude toward the civil war does not consider the lived experiences of those in Guatemala today – many of whom were affected by the clandestine violence after the ceasefire, contemporary gang violence, or the abject poverty the guerrilla fighters were attempting to combat. Izabella's father had disappeared after his business had failed. He had traveled to Guatemala City to ask for money to save himself from destitution, and then disappeared under suspicious circumstances. It takes no stretch of the imagination to classify her father as a casualty of this long-standing conflict.

According to Izabella, the FAFG could not offer her assistance in the first instance because of the limitations imposed on the laboratory by international funding organizations. These funding bodies were also some of the most influential actors in the Guatemala ceasefire agreement. The jurisdiction of Izabella's father's case, therefore, fell to the Ministerio Publico, which imposed the burden of the investigation on the family of the missing person and failed to inform Izabella of the existence of Cementerio La Verbena and its Cementerio Tres Equis section as a potential burial place. When Izabella visited the cemetery, she discovered that no investigative work had been performed by the original investigator, that La Verbena's ledger system was dysfunctional, and that there were more bodies in La Verbena than could be accounted for at that time. Since her visit, a subsequent request for assistance from the FAFG has gained no traction.

There are many possible explanations for these dynamics in Guatemala. The local government does not prioritize these types of missing persons investigations and likely does not provide any oversight of the investigators nor funding to improve and maintain La Verbena's ledger system and the Tres Equis section of the cemetery. If the outcomes of these decisions are that fewer missing people are identified and that the number of unidentified bodies in Tres Equis is indeterminable, then we must consider who benefits from this status quo. Certainly, a government consistently accused of moral bankruptcy (Smith and Offit 2010) would benefit from an environment of judicial impunity.

It is also possible, however, that these external funding organizations may also benefit from these dynamics. Guatemala has a long history of colonialist control that disempowered local populations; it is important to consider the possibility that lingering ethnocentric attitudes, especially on the part of Western funding organizations, may impact the nature of funding agreements. There have been many instances in humanitarian aid efforts across the world where predominantly Western organizations have participated in a manner that ultimately disempowered the people they were trying to help (Anderson 1998). These policies may reflect an attitude of generalized ethnocentrism, or at least ignorance, toward the countries seeking international aid. In the case of Guatemala, where organizations such as the UNDP (United Nations Development Programme), USAID, and the government of the Netherlands have allegedly restricted the scope of the FAFG DNA projects, this question also merits further exploration. Was it simply that the funding organizations had not been reflective enough, or that they had not considered the reality for Guatemalans? It is certainly possible, but it is prudent to consider an additional, political explanation.

The countries at the forefront of FAFG's funding are the same countries that were heavily involved in brokering the ceasefire agreements in the first place. For these organizations, to acknowledge that the violence had continued – and by extension that their funding stipulations did not consider the bigger picture of Guatemalan life – they would have to admit that their ceasefire had been unsuccessful. This in turn would call into question the effectiveness of the

United Nations and of the countries themselves as international peace-brokers. They would, therefore, have a vested interest in maintaining the narrative that the civil war had truly ended in 1996 with the ceasefire agreement.

These dynamics, however, are incredibly nuanced. It is likely that the motivations behind the funding for the FAFG laboratory derive from a combination of considerations. During my research, I reached out to the organizations that provide the FAFG's funding, as well as the FAFG itself, to clarify their policies. These requests for information went unacknowledged. From an ethical standpoint, it is important to note that the FAFG might not have responded because they could not be sure that I would represent them fairly, or that I had approached them with good intentions. The forensic anthropologists at the FAFG, while scientists in the same field as I, come from (and practice within) a different cultural and political-economic reality than my own. It would be fair to argue that we should analyze the FAFG's decisions with the same cultural relativity we would offer anyone during an ethnographic project, even if our critique is regarding policy and not cultural practice. This argument is less applicable, however, to the Western funding bodies, which also did not respond to my requests for information. Without access to the individuals who make these decisions, it is impossible to come to a firm conclusion as to which of the influences on their policies are most powerful. It is reasonable to claim that such a framework of influences exists, but without additional research any further analysis is merely supposition.

It is also necessary to consider the ethical conundrum that rests at the heart of this research: Is it appropriate for an anthropologist to provide criticism of another anthropologist's work when that work is conducted in a vastly different cultural and political-economic context? It is appropriate to say that the FAFG has specific policies that restrict access to their services, which are influenced by external funding sources. It may not, however, be appropriate to argue that the FAFG should, therefore, change their policies or be answerable to forensic anthropologists working outside of Guatemala. What we can do as forensic anthropologists is ask ourselves how we can best empower those we seek to serve in our own work – whether it is through acknowledging their stories, communicating openly and directly, or prioritizing their agency in the search for their missing loved ones.

Izabella is still awaiting assistance in her search. Until there is an overhaul of the forensic system in Guatemala, it is likely she will have to wait indefinitely. Yet she maintains hope that she will find her father one day. And as she explained to me, "my father's spirit has moved on; finding him is just for me now."

REFLECTION AND DISCUSSION QUESTIONS

- Why does the author discuss the period following the 1996 ceasefire agreement as "post-conflict" with quotation marks around it? Why is this important for us to recognize?

- Based on the information presented in this chapter, what is the role of the FAFG in Guatemala's "post-conflict" context? What are the challenges surrounding this role?
- What roles did countries from the Global North play in this humanitarian crisis? Do you think that organizations such as the United Nations should become involved in humanitarian crises? If yes, how do you think they should compensate for the unintended negative consequences of their actions?
- What are the ethical concerns surrounding anthropologists' critiquing the work of anthropologists in other cultural and political-economic contexts? Should the ethnical tenet of cultural relativism be extended to anthropologists' discussion of one another's work?

KEY CONCEPTS

- ***desaparecidos***: Persons who have gone missing and have never been found, often as the result of violence perpetrated by the state, paramilitary groups, or even mercenaries acting on behalf of individuals, although some *desaparecidos* could be refugees in other countries, runaways, or abducted.
- **humanitarian forensic action**: The effort to use forensic methods to identify victims of violent conflict or other humanitarian crises (i.e., natural disasters). This often includes forensic anthropologists who are trained in excavating, identifying, and repatriating human skeletal remains.
- **transformative justice**: Programs that seek to address the underlying problems that caused conflict in the first place to prevent future conflict.

EXPLORE FURTHER

- To learn about the experiences of Guatemalan refugees of the civil war and their descendants, read **Chapter 36**.
- Green, Linda. 1999. *Fear as a Way of Life: Mayan Widows in Rural Guatemala.* New York: Columbia University Press.
- Hinton, Alexander Laban, ed. 2011. *Transitional Justice: Global Mechanisms and Local Realities after Genocide and Mass Violence.* New Brunswick, NJ: Rutgers University Press.
- Sanford, Victoria. 2003. *Buried Secrets: Truth and Human Rights in Guatemala.* New York: Palgrave MacMillan.

ABOUT THE AUTHOR

Sarah Maya Rosen is an assistant professor of anthropology at Durham University. Her interdisciplinary approach seeks to recontextualize the analysis of human skeletal remains by examining the sociopolitical frameworks in which this analysis takes place. In doing so, she argues, anthropologists can better serve communities across the world that have been impacted by acts of political violence through transformative justice.

REFERENCES

Anderson, Mary B. 1998. "'You Save My Life Today, But for What Tomorrow?' Some Moral Dilemmas of Humanitarian Aid." In *Some Moral Dilemmas of Humanitarian Aid. Hard Choices: Moral Dilemmas in Humanitarian Intervention*, edited by Jonathan Moore, 137–56. Lanham, MD: Rowman and Littlefield.

Barrett, David. 2015. "Sterilizing a 'Red' Infection: Congress, the CIA, and Guatemala, 1954." https://www.cia.gov/static/58d9d3e04dae0638c71e91ee08582bed/congress-cia-guatemala.pdf.

Bellino, Michelle J. 2015. "Civic Engagement in Extreme Times: The Remaking of Justice Among Guatemala's 'Postwar' Generation." *Education, Citizenship, and Social Justice* 10 (2): 118–32. https://doi.org/10.1177/1746197915583937.

CEH. 1999. *Guatemala Memory of Silence: Report of the Commission or the Historical Clarification, Conclusions and Recommendations*. https://www.documentcloud.org/documents/357870-guatemala-memory-of-silence-the-commission-for.html.

Chamarbagwala, Rubiana, and Hilcías E. Morán. 2011. "The Human Capital Consequences of Civil War: Evidence from Guatemala." *Journal of Development Economics* 94 (1): 41–61.

Clouser, Rebecca. 2009. "Remnants of Terror: Landscapes of Fear in Post-Conflict Guatemala." *Journal of Latin American Geography* 8 (2): 7–22. https://doi.org/10.1353/lag.0.0055.

FAFG.org. 2016. "Who We Are." http://fafg.org/about-us/.

Garcia, Marco, Luis Martinez, Mishel Stephenson, John Crews, and Fredy Peccerelli. 2009. "Analysis of Complex Kinship Cases for Human Identification of Civil War Victims in Guatemala Using M-FISys Software." *Forensic Science International: Genetics Supplement Series* 2 (1): 250–2. https://doi.org/10.1016/j.fsigss.2009.08.128.

Girón, Anna Belinda Sandoval. 2007. "Taking Matters into One's Own Hands: Lynching and Violence in Post-Civil War Guatemala." *Urban Anthropology and Studies of Cultural Systems and World Economic Development* 36 (4): 357–79.

Gready, Paul, and Simon Robins. 2014. "From Transitional to Transformative Justice: A New Agenda for Practice." In *From Transitional to Transformative Justice*, edited by Paul Gready and Simon Robins, 31–56. Cambridge: University of Cambridge Press.

Human Rights Watch. 2018. "Country Chapters." https://www.hrw.org/world-report/2018/country-chapters/guatemala.

Metz, Brent. 2006. *Ch'orti': Maya Survival in Eastern Guatemala: Indigeneity in Transition*. Albuquerque: University of New Mexico Press.

Sanford, Victoria. 2008. "From Genocide to Feminicide: Impunity and Human Rights in Twenty First Century Guatemala." *Journal of Human Rights* 7 (2): 104–22. https://doi.org/10.1080/14754830802070192.

Smith, Timothy J., and Thomas A. Offit. 2010. "Confronting Violence in Postwar Guatemala: An Introduction." *Journal of Latin American and Caribbean Anthropology* 15(1): 1–15. https://doi.org/10.1111/j.1935-4940.2010.01060.x.

United Nations. 1999. "Press Briefing by Members of Guatemalan Historical Clarification Commission." http://www.un.org/press/en/1999/19990301.guate.brf.html.

Winton, Ailsa. 2006. "Youth, Gangs and Violence: Analysing the Social and Spatial Mobility of Young People in Guatemala City." *Children's Geographies* 3 (2): 167–84. https://doi.org/10.1080/14733280500161537.

CHAPTER TWENTY-THREE

A Crack in the Wall: Ethnography as Solidarity with Indigenous Political Prisoners in Oaxaca, Mexico

Bruno Renero-Hannan

> It has not been in books written, but in those not yet written but already read for generations, that the Zapatista women, the Zapatista men have learned that if you stop scratching at the crack, it closes. The wall mends itself. That is why they have to go on relentlessly. Not only to widen the crack, but above all so that it doesn't close.
>
> *Subcomandante Galeano (2015, 201)*[1]

The first time I stepped into a prison was at Ixcotel, as the Central Penitentiary of the State of Oaxaca was commonly known.[2] It was also the first time I met Álvaro Sebastián Ramírez, an Indigenous Zapotec activist and a **political prisoner** at the time. As an act of protest against political imprisonment and an act of solidarity with Álvaro, a small group of activists visited Ixcotel Prison in October 2012 to meet face to face with the long-term prisoner. The seemingly simple act of entering the prison as a group and meeting with a political prisoner was no small feat in itself, given that the Mexican government claimed that the 54-year-old Zapotec leader was a violent insurgent and had sentenced him to more than 30 years in prison. Álvaro and the event's organizers, including two of his daughters, knew that this short visit would not get him released. Yet, for the span of a few hours, our encounter briefly subverted the boundaries that

---

1 My translation.
2 Ixcotel Prison derived its name from its location in the urban neighborhood of Santa María Ixcotel, on the outskirts of Oaxaca City. It was sandwiched between the working-class neighborhood of Ixcotel and a secluded military grounds. State officials closed the prison in October 2020 on account of "structural" safety hazards. Its remaining 900 inmates were transferred to three other state and federal prisons amidst protests from relatives who objected to having their incarcerated loved ones sent further away to more dangerous facilities, and on account of the police violence against inmates that accompanied such transfers (Miranda 2020).

Figure 23.1. Outside a maximum security prison in Oaxaca, the daughter of a Loxicha Prisoner holds up her fist in a gesture of defiance. Photo by Bruno Renero-Hannan.

kept Álvaro and us on opposite sides of the prison walls, momentarily rupturing the ordinary flow of life and time inside the prison walls.

INDIGENOUS MOVEMENTS IN MEXICO

Indigenous Zapotec peoples, together with neighboring Mixtecs, Mixes, Afro-Mexicans, Huaves, Amuzgos, and others, have resided in what is today known as the State of Oaxaca, in southern Mexico, for hundreds or thousands of years. The Loxicha region, where Álvaro is from, comprises a mountainous constellation of towns, villages, and farms in the southern Sierra Madre mountain range, about 170 kilometers south of Oaxaca City, where cold pine forests give way to pineapple and palm trees near the Pacific Ocean.

Traditionally *campesinos* (peasant farmers) who make a living cultivating family *milpas* (plots of maize, squash, and beans) and coffee for regional and foreign markets, Loxicha Zapotecs today face multiple challenges to their livelihoods and way of life. These include economic and environmental pressures that make farming increasingly difficult, forcing many to migrate to cities or across the US border. But arguably the greatest threat to Loxicha's communities are patterns of violence that have taken hold in the region because of government corruption, paramilitarism, and state repression.

Over the past 30 years, Indigenous communities and organizations across Mexico have organized to resist land dispossession and other forms of political, economic, and social injustices they experience at the hands of local and national elites and transnational corporations. The most significant of these movements in Mexico has been the Zapatista Army of National Liberation (EZLN, also known as the Zapatistas) in Chiapas. The means and ends of differing Indigenous and peasant movements vary, but broadly their efforts have focused on defending their land and traditional ways of life while combating poverty, exploitation, and marginalization (see Chapter 30). By threatening the status quo, radical Indigenous movements such as the EZLN in Chiapas or the Organization of Indigenous Zapotec Communities (OPIZ) in Oaxaca, which Álvaro co-founded, have been met with military and paramilitary violence. One of the most disruptive and common tactics used to suppress Indigenous organizing in Mexico is the incarceration of Indigenous leaders under the pretense of intervening in ostensibly "internal" conflicts or combating "crime" and "terrorism."

As an instrument of political repression, the incarceration of activists and dissidents has been a favored form of political control for the Mexican state at least since the dictatorship of Porfirio Díaz (1876–1910). When a leader is incarcerated, communities, movements, organizations, and families are obliged to drastically alter and reorganize their lives around the new reality of the prison and the legal system. In the cases of some long-term political prisoners like Álvaro, the exigencies of solidarity and advocacy became the central focus of his former organization and his family members, shaping childhoods and cultivating a new generation of activists in the crucible of Indigenous and anti-carceral struggles.

In this chapter, I introduce the stories of Álvaro and his daughter Erika, two people who became central, as *compas* (comrades; short for *compañeros/as*) and co-ethnographers, in my engaged anthropological fieldwork and study of political imprisonment and resistance in Oaxaca. I discuss some of the ways in which the pernicious effects of political abuse radiate outside of walls containing political prisoners, impacting their families and especially the women in those families as they navigate the policed boundaries of the prison in solidarity with their imprisoned loved ones. I also highlight the ways in which prisoners, their family members, and activists work in solidarity with one another, sometimes in ways as subtle as sharing a meal or listening to a story.

THE FORUM

The day before the prison visit, a modestly attended public forum "against political prisons and repression" took place in the auditorium of the local *escuela normal* (teachers' college). The forum was primarily focused on Álvaro's case; however, various speakers showcased the struggles and voices of several incarcerated Indigenous activists across Mexico. The organizers of the forum and the prisoners it extolled were all direct or indirect supporters of the Zapatistas, whose 1994 insurgency had germinated into a confederacy of autonomous revolutionary Maya communities in the neighboring state of Chiapas and generated a diffuse transnational solidarity movement around its communities and its principles – including in nearby Oaxaca. By self-identifying and organizing as *adherentes* (adherents) of the "Sixth Declaration of the Lacandón Jungle" (or simply "The Sixth," as the Zapatistas' foundational 2005 anti-capitalist manifesto is known), the coalition of activists and prisoners at the forum aligned itself with the militant wing of Mexico's Indigenous movement, as well as a transnational network of anti-capitalist and anti-state activists.

One of the speakers at the forum was Álvaro's daughter, Erika Sebastián Luis, who shared some of her experiences as a young Zapotec woman growing up in the shadow of her father's persecution and incarceration. Like Erika's, many of the voices at the forum that day assumed the form of **testimonio** (testimony), a Latin American literary genre that blends personal narratives with accounts of broader political and collective struggles, generating "personal narratives of history in progress" (see Chapter 34; cf. Stephen 2013, 13–17). The culmination of the forum was a "call-in" by Álvaro from a payphone inside Ixcotel to Erika's mobile phone, which she held up to the microphone, through which he greeted and thanked the audience before reading a short statement – a crackling voice denouncing prison from inside a prison.

In the evening, as the forum concluded with an informal roundtable discussion, the organizers invited the handful of participants who remained to join them in visiting Álvaro in Ixcotel the following day as a group – defying the prison walls by crossing them and bringing the act of solidarity directly to him.

THE LOXICHA PRISONERS

Álvaro was widely known as a "Loxicha Prisoner." Initially, the term "Loxicha Prisoners" referred to the roughly 250 Zapotec *campesinos* from San Agustín Loxicha who were arrested in droves in the late 1990s and early 2000s. These arrests took place amidst a sharp rise in state-sponsored military and paramilitary violence in the Indigenous and peasant communities of southern Mexico (Oaxaca, Chiapas, Guerrero, and elsewhere). The Loxicha Prisoners were deemed "political" (as opposed to "common") prisoners, primarily for two reasons: first, because the Mexican government persecuted and incarcerated them for allegedly belonging to the Popular Revolutionary Army (EPR), a clandestine guerrilla organization that led an uprising in 1996, even though none of the Loxicha Prisoners avowed any association with the EPR; second, because they were actually the victims of state and paramilitary violence that targeted Loxicha's own homegrown, radical Indigenous movement – the Organization of Indigenous Zapotec Communities (OPIZ), as well as local authorities, activists, community organizers, and many others who were simply caught in the dragnet.

Under the leadership of Álvaro and other Zapotec activists, the OPIZ movement grew out of a local grassroots mobilization against corruption and rural violence in Loxicha in the mid-1980s. A decade later (and just weeks before the militarization and mass arrests began in Loxicha), thousands of OPIZ supporters marched from Loxicha to Oaxaca City in September 1996, picketing and briefly shutting down the international airport, before marching on and occupying Oaxaca's touristic downtown plaza, the Zócalo, outside the governor's offices. Through this mobilization, the OPIZ revealed a stunning capacity to mobilize protestors beyond their villages, effectively embarrassing the state government and, thus, Mexico's ruling party, the Institutional Revolutionary Party (PRI), into accepting negotiations with local authorities from Loxicha. Their demands included infrastructure and services, such as roads, schools, hospitals, and aid to farmers. Following these negotiations, the governor vowed to address the protestors' demands in exchange for lifting the occupation. Weeks later, under the pretense of rooting out EPR guerrillas, the Mexican Army occupied the Loxicha region, initiating an era of mass violence there and the racialized criminalization of Indigenous Loxicha Zapotecs. To date, many of the OPIZ's original demands for basic infrastructure in Loxicha remain unmet (on documented human rights violations at the time, see CNDH 2003).

Álvaro, a respected leader in the OPIZ movement since the 1980s, was arrested in late 1997. By 2012, Álvaro was one of the last seven Loxicha Prisoners, six of whom remained incarcerated at Ixcotel Prison (and one at Etla Prison) since the late 1990s. In oral history interviews that we later conducted in Álvaro's cell at Ixcotel, I learned that he had been detained by plainclothes police in Oaxaca City and was forcibly disappeared, tortured, and interrogated for seven days before joining the ranks of the Loxicha Prisoners. Álvaro was 40 years old when he fell prisoner. He would spend the next 20 years in prison. In order to see him, his wife and his four children, too, would spend the better part of two decades in and out of prison.

ENTERING IXCOTEL

The October morning after the forum, I waited near the prison gates for Erika and the others to arrive. I was anxious they might have arrived early and perhaps gone in without me. As an outsider with a habit of asking questions (i.e., an anthropologist), I was accustomed to occasionally being met with suspicion in certain circles. As an **activist anthropologist**, I also knew that generating relationships of trust and collaboration with other activists takes time and humility, in addition to engagement (cf. Hale 2006). So, rather than visit the Loxicha Prisoners on my own sooner, I waited until I could do so from a position of explicit and consensual political alignment, in collaboration and dialogue with the prisoners and their close family.

Across the street from where I waited near the prison gate, women carrying large woven market bags walked in and out of the open facades of family homes that also operated as *misceláneas* (small convenience stores). Those nearest the prison catered primarily to guards and visitors. In addition to selling groceries and household items for visitors to pick up before getting in line, these also provided an indispensable service for visitors: For 10 pesos (roughly 50

US cents), you could entrust them with your keys, wallet, purse, and various other items that were forbidden inside the prison. I did my best to remain inconspicuous, avoiding the stern, often menacing gazes of the black-uniformed state police officers cradling long gray shotguns at the gate. From the street, I could see over the prison walls through the barbed wire fence on top of the concrete rampart: a scraggly skyline of water tanks, lines of hanging laundry, even a couple of medicinal houseplants on the roofs of the dormitories – nearly indistinguishable from those on the roofs of the surrounding houses.

Eventually the others arrived and I was glad to be in their company as I prepared to cross a threshold, for the first time, that some of them had crossed countless times before. Ten of us passed the outer gate and the guards and made our way toward the administration building and the lines of visitors waiting to go in. I admit I had doubts about whether the guards would let us through, considering that Álvaro's daughters were well known to them, and now they were arriving with a retinue of young, activist companions. Most of us were in our twenties and thirties, apart from two veteran schoolteachers in their fifties and Álvaro's youngest daughter, who was still a teenager.

Raised bilingual in Loxicha Zapotec and Spanish and politically savvy, like her father, Erika was the main force sustaining the campaign for Álvaro's freedom. She was born in Loxicha but had spent most of her life in central Oaxaca, where she, her mother, and her siblings had moved to be closer to the prison, joining dozens of other women and families protesting for the release of their wrongly incarcerated loved ones and an end to the militarization of their communities back home. In Oaxaca, Erika met Oscar, her partner, in 2006 during the massive urban rebellion of the Popular Assembly of the Peoples of Oaxaca (APPO), bonding over their shared dedication to the cause of Indigenous rights and autonomy and their admiration for the Zapatistas.[3] In addition to Erika and Oscar, the rest of the prison visit group consisted of the two veteran teachers, anarchists and prison abolitionists from Mexico City, Adherents of The Sixth from Chiapas, a Mazatec *Magonista* (Indigenous follower of the historical Mexican revolutionary and anarchist Ricardo Flores Magón) from northern Oaxaca, and me – an American-Mexican ethnographer, living between Oaxaca City and Loxicha.

Once inside the gates, those of us who were first-time visitors were required to register our personal information with the administration and answer questions about whom we were visiting and our relationship with the inmate. "He's a friend," Erika instructed us to say, this being the only permissible category of visitors outside of immediate relatives or legal counsel. In fact, "common" prisoners at Ixcotel did not have the right to visits from "friends" – this was a special privilege that the Loxicha Prisoners had fought for and won, years earlier.[4] However, Erika warned us that the administration's decisions regarding new visitors were often unpredictable and seemingly arbitrary. Fortunately, on this occasion the warden let us all through, setting the

---

3 On the APPO, social movements, and testimony, see Renero-Hannan 2018 and Stephen 2013.
4 In 2017, amid tightening security measures at Ixcotel, "friends" became inadmissible, ending my visits with Álvaro until his release later that year.

stage for me to continue visiting Álvaro (as well as four of the other Loxicha Prisoners) over the next five years – although I knew none of this then as I walked out of the administrators' offices, nervous and excited, and joined the others in the long line of visitors waiting to go through security and customs inspection.

Some of the other visitors in line for inspection with us were clearly more familiar than I was with the process of entering a prison. The activists from other states were involved in various forms of prisoner support and solidarity as part of their activism elsewhere in Mexico. Erika and her sister, Tanis, had been visiting Álvaro in Ixcotel and Etla prisons since they were children and could be described as part-time inmates themselves. They appeared particularly confident in the face of the long security lines, the guard's aggressive questions, the invasive pat-downs, and the guards' openly hostile treatment of visitors. Later I would learn that this stoicism was a survival strategy developed, in the two young women's cases, over a lifetime to defend themselves against the realities of everyday harassment and abuse by the police.

Erika and Tanis' experiences with police mistreatment were also reflected in those of the other Loxicha Prisoners' relatives, as well as those of hundreds of other visitors to Ixcotel every week, the vast majority of whom were women who assumed the role of caretaker for incarcerated kin. In this capacity, women (and sometimes men) frequently arrived carrying large market bags filled with food or household necessities (cleaning supplies, which prisoners were required to purchase for themselves), tall stacks of *tlayudas* (broad Oaxacan tortillas), bulk quantities of instant coffee and sugar, or large vats of soup, which the guards would rummage through with huge spoons or latex gloves, allegedly searching for contraband. Occasionally, the guards would reject certain items, often scolding the person who brought it, raising their voice so that everyone in line would hear, and the visitor would have to dispose of the item (often acquired or produced and transported at great personal cost) if they wanted to enter. Some guards seemed to take pleasure in haranguing and demeaning these visitors, who were mostly Indigenous and women. After the first inspection and the customs line came the metal detector and the pat-down, which took place in a small room, behind closed doors. I later learned from Erika and other women that this is where the worst abuse often happened: Behind closed doors, they were mistreated, groped, or otherwise humiliated by police, at times being made to strip and squat before the officer. For Indigenous women, like Erika and Tanis, the experiences of abuse and mistreatment of their incarcerated loved ones were replicated in the liminal space between the gates to the outside world and the interior prison walls.

After the pat-downs came another line to get past the armored turnstiles; yet another line, fingerprint scanners, another set of gates, another wait. The last stop was a room where two guards sat behind a long wooden table, registering the names of visitors a second time and confiscating their identification documents, which they exchanged for a plastic poker chip with a number written on it in sharpie. Numbered poker chips in hand, our group finally reconvened. Walking up a ramp, past a barred gate, we found ourselves – quite suddenly – inside the prison. Far from the image I had envisioned of men and women sitting passively in cages, the scene inside Ixcotel was all movement and commotion.

INSIDE THE PRISON

Those inside the prison desired nothing more than to get out. Yet here we were moving in the opposite direction, although with the luxury – and fundamental difference – that, after a few hours, we would walk out of the prison the same way we came in. Before long, this walking into prison while being able to walk out would become a cruel and crucial aspect of my ethnographic and political praxis for several years.

After the lines and the inspections, we stepped into the prison. Activist friends who had spent time in Ixcotel had tried to tell me it was like a town (*como un pueblo*), yet I was still amazed seeing it myself. What most astounded me was how vibrant and full of movement the prison was. The air was buzzing as we walked along the broad, outdoor corridor that traces a rough square along the perimeter of Ixcotel – between the tall, turreted rampart and an inner compound of buildings – with the air of a Mexican plaza on market day. Like all visitors, we were greeted by a scraggly group of young men asking for alms and offering to shine our shoes (same as you might meet on any street) before our guides shooed them away. We kept walking, now past a group of four men, huddled in the shade of the rampart, weaving baskets and stitching soccer balls, while chatting and cracking a joke (the same as you might meet in a market). Further down, a couple of men ordered *aguas frescas* (fresh fruit waters) and quesadillas and flirted with the woman taking their orders through a window to the women's block of the prison. Yet Ixcotel was nonetheless a prison – defined by its segregation of a population of captives and a much smaller population of heavily armed guards. Still, I found the degree of movement there surprising, almost as if the inside of the prison were an extension of the working-class, urban landscape surrounding it.

That there was a feeling of "townness" to this place should perhaps not have been surprising, considering that Mexican prisons are populated by people from working-class neighborhoods and Indigenous communities – people who must keep working to survive, even inside the prison. Almost everyone in Ixcotel had a job: sewing baskets, stitching soccer balls, shining shoes, working in the woodshop, preparing food, selling wares, or hustling (selling drugs and contraband). The options for making money were limited and prescribed by corporations, merchants, and the prison authorities who profited from cheap, non-union, captive labor. For all its vibrant bustle, this place was still a prison: a squalid bunker whose inhabitants were exploited for their labor and forbidden to leave.

Erika led us further along the corridor of the perimeter, around two corners to the north side, in the direction of the Sierra Juárez mountains, visible from Álvaro's cell window on the second floor of Cell 22, which the remaining Loxicha Prisoners shared. Álvaro was standing outside Cell 22 waiting for us to arrive, grinning and beaming with happiness. Some of the other Loxicha Prisoners were there too (I recognized them from photographs I had seen in old newspapers and online): Tomás, a schoolteacher and former mayor of San Agustín Loxicha, sat in the shade nearby, weaving colorful trays out of plastic yarn and wire. Nearby, Moisés, an erstwhile farmer and community organizer, was stitching soccer balls near the door of the cell where a small lime tree was growing.

The 11 of us sat in a circle, on small wooden stools, under a sheet metal roof supported by wooden beams, adjacent to the cell. The improvised roof also covered a wide, three-tiered wooden altar that the prisoners constructed for their icons of the Virgin of Guadalupe and Virgin of Juquila, festooned with aging flowers. Erika and her co-organizers presented Álvaro with a large vinyl poster that they had designed and printed for the forum, which showed a black silhouette of Álvaro's face upon a bright red and green background, in the style of Zapatista political prisoners' campaigns in Chiapas. They'd had to argue and negotiate with the guards at the entrance, but managed to convince them to let us bring the poster in. Álvaro was speechless as he unfurled the poster; then he hung it from one side of the altar, "with the ladies' permission!" he joked, gesturing toward the icons of the Virgin Mary.

As I learned from his testimony over those two days, as well as from our later conversations, Álvaro identified staunchly as an Adherent of The Sixth. Throughout our conversation and exchanges that day, he frequently returned to the subject of Zapatista principles and The Sixth. Álvaro's political activism and his imprisonment both pre-dated the publication of the Zapatista manifesto, yet as a prisoner he came to view his own struggles in light of the Zapatista principles and as part of the larger anti-capitalist and autonomist struggle that is laid out in The Sixth. He drew upon the concepts and analyses of The Sixth in his own **activist social analysis**, using these as a political lens through which to analyze his own reality, while linking his struggle to a broader Indigenous movement and its transnational network of supporters.

Álvaro's joy at having so many of us visiting him was evident. At one point, he began to cry, scrunching his face, and making a fist to hold back the tears. He had only ever cried twice in prison, he declared, as a way of both complimenting us and thanking us. He said the last time he cried was when a group of French comrades (also Adherents of The Sixth) had visited him in prison. He told us that, despite not sharing a common language, they had spoken "as if we were all brothers and sisters!"

Later, he invited us, two at a time, to follow him up to the second floor of Cell 22, to his tiny room atop a raised platform on the self-made second floor, which he constructed himself after learning carpentry in prison to create more room inside the cell. Inside his cramped, self-fashioned room was a thin cot where he slept and a wooden chair. A couple of nooks along the wall held a few items of clothing and toiletries. In another nook, above the cot, stood books on Mexican history and appeals law, the autobiography of Nelson Mandela (arguably the world's most famous political prisoner), and several notebooks brimming with loose pages, covered in handwriting that looked as if they, too, wanted to escape from their confines. On the wall by the door hung a photograph of the Zapatistas' spokesperson, Subcomandante Marcos, standing in front of a statue of Lucio Cabañas, a schoolteacher who led a guerrilla uprising in Guerrero in the late 1960s and early 1970s. Álvaro carefully hung his new poster on the back of the door, near the other images, creating an unlikely collage of revolutionary icons and aesthetics inside a prison cell.

Before parting ways, I asked Álvaro if he would be interested in sharing more of his testimony with me and collaborating on an oral history project, grounded in an activist research methodology – an ethnography of solidarity – and he agreed. Álvaro, Erika, and I would meet again many times in this space, throughout the five years of his remaining sentence (and elsewhere, after his release in 2017). Sitting on the edge of his cot, Álvaro would narrate memories, anecdotes, reflections, and jokes faster than I could write, while I sat in the chair opposite him, my notebook pressed against one leg crossed over the other, my pen racing to catch every word.

CONCLUSION

In this chapter, I shared a narrative of Álvaro Sebastián Ramírez, his family, and anti-carceral resistance, using the gates and interiors of Ixcotel Prison as a vehicle to illustrate some of the complex ways that, on the one hand, the prison walls – and the police apparatus that is in place to enforce them – exact ongoing forms of violence not only on prisoners but on their family members and political networks, exposing them to recursive forms of surveillance, control, and humiliation as they cross the borders of the prison for visits. On the other hand, in defiance of the same prison walls, prisoners and their supporters (family members and activists) creatively persist in their resistance against political violence and incarceration, inflicting cracks in the system to advance their personal and collective commitments to liberation and dignity.

The goal of solidarity in this scenario is, ultimately, the liberation of the prisoners. Yet the strategy for achieving this goal is not to bring down the prison walls all at once (an unrealistic and demoralizing proposition), but rather to create and sustain a multitude of small cracks and fissures in the walls, thus scaling down the act of unmaking the walls, while preserving ongoing ties of sociality (togetherness) that transcend the walls. As the Zapatistas put it in the epigraph to this chapter: "Not only to widen the crack, but above all so that it doesn't close."

AUTHOR'S NOTE

Álvaro Sebastián Ramírez (1958–2022) was assassinated on July 19, 2022, for daring to imagine a better world and then fighting for it. This chapter is written in memoriam for Álvaro and to honor his family's struggle for truth and justice.[5]

---

[5] In the wake of Álvaro's assassination in 2022, I have opted to use his real name, at his family's request.

REFLECTION AND DISCUSSION QUESTIONS

- What tactics has the Mexican state used in its repression of Indigenous movements, leaders, communities, and families?
- What is solidarity? What are the goals of prisoner solidarity? And what forms has it taken in the struggle against political imprisonment in Mexico?
- What do you think are the potentials and the limitations of engaged ethnography as a form of solidarity? What do you imagine might be the possible outcomes of pursuing a similar ethnographic study while maintaining a position of political neutrality?

KEY CONCEPTS

- **activist anthropology**: A methodology and ethics of ethnographic research that is designed and carried out collaboratively in the pursuit of social justice.
- **activist social analysis**: The analytical frameworks and modes of knowledge production that are generated by activists and social movements in the pursuit of political interventions.
- **political prisoner**: Someone incarcerated for their political beliefs or activities.
- **testimonio**: A genre of Latin American narrative that features eyewitness accounts of major political events from the perspective of the marginalized to provide a counter-narrative to official accounts. They make visible situations of oppression and resistance to such oppression, as well as build collective identities.

EXPLORE FURTHER

- To learn more about Indigenous activists in Mexico and the challenges they face, read **Chapters 11** and **30**.
- EZLN. 2005. "Sexta Declaración de La Selva Lacandona." https://tinyurl.com/The-Sixth.
- Gibler, John. 2009. *Mexico Unconquered: Chronicles of Power and Revolt*. San Francisco: City Lights.
- Henck, Nick, ed. 2018. *The Zapatistas' Dignified Rage: Final Public Speeches of Subcommander Marcos*. Translated by Henry Gales. Chico, CA; Edinburgh: AK Press.

ABOUT THE AUTHOR

Bruno Renero-Hannan is an assistant professor of anthropology at SUNY Geneseo. Renero-Hannan grew up bilingual and bicultural between Mexico City and Texas. His research and teaching focus on Latin American history and culture, social movements, political violence, and historical memory, including long-term advocacy with Indigenous activists and political prisoners in Oaxaca, Mexico.

REFERENCES

Comisión Nacional de Derechos Humanos (CNDH). 2003. "Informe Especial: Caso de La Región Loxicha." https://www.cndh.org.mx/sites/default/files/doc/Informes/Especiales/2003_loxicha.pdf.

Hale, Charles R. 2006. "Activist Research v. Cultural Critique: Indigenous Land Rights and the Contradictions of Politically Engaged Anthropology." *Cultural Anthropology* 21 (1): 96–120. https://doi.org/10.1525/can.2006.21.1.96.

Miranda, Fernando. 2020. "Cierran Definitivamente Prisión de Ixcotel; Trasladan a Población Penitenciaria a Penal de Tanivet." *El Universal Oaxaca*, October 26. https://oaxaca.eluniversal.com.mx/municipios/26-10-2020/cierran-definitivamente-prision-de-ixcotel-trasladan-poblacion-penitenciaria.

Renero-Hannan, Bruno. 2018. "In the Wake of Insurgency: Testimony and the Politics of Memory and Silence in Oaxaca." Ph.D. diss., Ann Arbor: University of Michigan.

Stephen, Lynn. 2013. *We Are the Face of Oaxaca: Testimony and Social Movements*. Durham, NC: Duke University Press.

Subcomandante Galeano. 2015. "El Muro y la Grieta: Primer Apunto Sobre el Método Zapatista." In *El Pensamiento Crítico Frente a la Hidra Capitalista I: Participación de la Comisión Sexta del EZLN*. Mexico.

SECTION EIGHT

Poverty, Precarity, and Resilience

While there is great affluence in every nation of Latin America and the Caribbean, the region is characterized by some of the highest rates of economic inequality in the world. Wealth is inequitably distributed, leaving a quarter of all people in the region poor and one in five people chronically poor (i.e., living in poverty throughout their lifespan; Vakis, Rigolini, and Lucchetti 2015). This chronic poverty is evidence that structural factors deprive people of the means for improving their lives. Such endemic poverty poses an enduring challenge that is shared across the region, though it manifests differently across settings.

Several theories provide competing explanations about the causes of the economic insecurity in the region. Modernization theory posits that poverty is the product of a nation-state's failure to modernize. Dependence theory contends that poverty follows from a nation's economic dependence on international aid. What these explanations fail to acknowledge is that today's poverty and social inequality result in large part from the enduring effects of colonialism and its manifestations in the post-colonial and contemporary eras. After Latin American and Caribbean nations declared their independence from European control, their economic and governmental systems were hampered by **neocolonialism** – the exercise of economic, political, and cultural pressures to control formerly colonized independent nation-states. Neocolonial processes ensured that much of the wealth and resources that were generated in the region continued to flow out of the countries of origin and into institutions and businesses situated in former colonial states, benefiting only a small Latin American/Caribbean elite.

During the last four decades, pressures to open national economies to international capital have spurred neoliberal economic reforms that prioritize privatization and reduce spending on social welfare programs in healthcare, education, housing, sanitation, and transportation. These policy measures, enacted under pressure from international economic agencies and governments in the Global North, have compromised the ability of Latin American and Caribbean nations to provide equitable education, protect public health, or prioritize sustainability and ecological protection, even as they grapple with growing populations, uneven development, and climate change.

In the 1960s, liberation theologist Johan Galtung coined the term **structural violence** to describe how political economic, legal, religious, cultural, and social structures negatively impact the ability of individuals, communities, and societies to attain their full potential and meet their human needs. This theoretical concept emphasizes that, like more direct physical forms of violence, the experiences of social inequality and injustice cause real harm to bodies and communities. In many cases, poverty and precarity are exacerbated by phenomena that are described as natural disasters. These can include devastating storms like Hurricane Maria or epidemics like COVID-19 and Zika. Ethnographers who work with communities that are facing these challenges point out that mechanisms of structural violence are what turn natural events into humanitarian emergencies, dismantling economic achievements and threatening individual, family, and community survival (see Chapter 12).

The ethnographic case studies in this section demonstrate the creative ways individuals and communities cope with poverty and precarity, demonstrating their **resilience** – perseverance, adaptability, and the ability to overcome or recover from challenges. Although these strategies do not resolve the effects of inequality and structural violence – only widespread global political economic and social change can erase the social and structural issues plaguing marginalized communities – they do demonstrate how individuals and communities tackle the challenges of poverty and inequity in the course of daily life.

In Chapter 24, Klein examines how working-class youth challenge pervasive negative discourses about race and the poverty and marginality of the São Paulo neighborhoods where they live, forwarding instead a range of projects that recast the urban periphery and its residents as cosmopolitan and open to difference. In Chapter 25, Hippert describes how low-income Dominicans, Haitians, and Haitian-Dominicans rely on an informal, trust-based system of store credit that allows people to meet their basic needs amidst a precarious job market. In Chapter 26, Nelson uses the experience of Juana, a Maya woman in Chiapas, Mexico, to examine the challenges and unexpected opportunities that emerged from the economic hardships of the COVID-19 pandemic. Finally, in Chapter 27, Cambero Scott explores how Puerto Rican music and musicians contributed to collective efforts to recover materially, mentally, and emotionally from Hurricane Maria.

KEY CONCEPTS

- **neocolonialism**: The exercise of economic, political, and cultural pressures to control formerly colonized independent nation-states.
- **resilience**: Perseverance, adaptability, and the ability to overcome or recover from challenges.
- **structural violence**: An indirect, nonpersonal form of violence whereby harmful effects are produced by societal systems.

EXPLORE FURTHER

- To learn more about poverty, precarity, and resilience, read **Chapters 6**, **12**, **33**, and **Section 9**.
- Bollaín, Icíar, dir. 2010. *También la lluvia* (*Even the Rain*). [Bolivia]
- Hernández, Maricarmen, Samuel Law, and Javier Auyero. 2022. "How Do the Urban Poor Survive? A Comparative Ethnography of Subsistence Strategies in Argentina, Ecuador, and Mexico." *Qualitative Sociology* 45: 1–29.
- Honigmann, Heddy, dir. 2009. *Oblivion*. [Peru]
- Kenny, Mary Lorena. 2007. *Hidden Heads of Households: Child Labor in Urban Northeast Brazil*. Toronto: University of Toronto Press.
- Pérez, Fernando, dir. 2003. *Suite Habana* (*Havana Suite*). [Cuba]

REFERENCE

Vakis, Renos, Jamele Rigolini, and Leonardo Lucchetti. 2015. *Left Behind: Chronic Poverty in Latin America and the Caribbean*. Washington, DC: World Bank.

CHAPTER TWENTY-FOUR

Flipping the City: Space and Subjectivity in São Paulo, Brazil's Zona Sul Periphery

Charles H. Klein

On July 31, 2014, then São Paulo Mayor Fernando Haddad signed a new Strategic Master Plan to guide the city's development for the next 16 years. According to the Haddad administration's online overview at the time, the plan's primary objective was to "humanize and re-equilibrate São Paulo, bringing together housing and jobs, and confronting socio-spatial inequalities" (Prefeitura da Cidade de São Paulo n.d.). The Strategic Master Plan's attention to using city planning mechanisms to address socioeconomic inequalities and the quality of urban life stands in stark contrast to the city's unbridled growth and expanding inequalities throughout much of the twentieth century. In historical perspective, São Paulo's Strategic Master Plan is the outgrowth of decades of political mobilization around housing and urban living conditions that accelerated during Brazil's re-democratization in the 1980s. With the 1988 Brazilian Constitution, an emerging social justice–based urban planning paradigm was solidified into law. Most importantly, Article 182 establishes the "social function of land" and the "well-being of inhabitants" as constitutional principles and requires all cities with populations over 20,000 to create strategic master plans to direct urban development.

In the fall of 2016, the likelihood of the São Paulo Strategic Master Plan helping re-equilibrate the city diminished significantly when João Doria, a business magnate representing the neoliberal-oriented Brazilian Social Democracy Party (*Partido da Social Democracia Brasileira*), defeated Haddad in the mayoral elections. Curious to see how the Doria administration would approach implementing the 2014 Strategic Master Plan, I regularly visited the city's website. In early 2017, I noticed that the passage on inequalities and the social use of land had vanished. In its place, a new overview emphasized the link between a healthy city and a pro-business environment and a desire to return to the "actual city that pre-dates that Plan" (Prefeitura de São Paulo – Urbanismo e Licenciamento n.d.).

Figure 24.1. Linn da Quebrada Mural, Downtown São Paulo, September 2019. Photo by Charles H. Klein.

This shift from centering the Strategic Master Plan on improving the quality of urban life to promoting globally directed economic development is evident in one of the Doria administration's centerpiece initiatives, the *Cidade Linda* (Beautiful City) program (Prefeitura de São Paulo 2017). Launched in 2017, the Beautiful City program supported the removal of trash from dirty streets and open spaces and authorized the painting over of street murals and tagging on public properties. In promoting the program, the mayor stated that "the city is dirty, poorly cared for and covered in spray-paint tags," and that taggers are "criminals" who "probably steal cell phones" to pay for their paint (Sims 2017). Given São Paulo's reputation as a global street art leader and graffiti's role in vitalizing a city famous for its greyness, the "Beautiful City" program can be seen as being as much about erasing the presence of (lower-income and Black) **periphery** residents (i.e., those from the sprawling, often infrastructure-poor, lower-income communities that surround the city's central areas) from São Paulo's wealthier districts than about beautifying the city.

The São Paulo Strategic Master Plan is just one example of an ongoing struggle over what life should be in Brazil's historically unequal urban spaces. In 2013, millions of previously poor urban Brazilians, including many from the so-called new middle classes, took to the streets to protest the poor quality of public transportation, housing, and education, and the high levels of corruption endemic throughout Brazilian society. About six months later, thousands of mostly Black youth from the São Paulo peripheries staged flash mobs in shopping malls in the *rolezinho* movement. Through occupying upper- and middle-class commercial recreational spaces where they often suffer multiple forms of harassment, periphery Black youth self-consciously and joyfully reclaimed their right to the city. This disruption of long-standing class- and race-based spatial divisions unsettled traditional middle-class (read white) Brazilians and the mainstream media, who typically associate Black youth with violence and an out-of-control periphery (see Chapter 5).

In this chapter, I examine some of these competing visions of what urban life in São Paulo is and might be. Rather than concentrating on the macro-level political developments or the well-documented dynamics that support the (re)production of material inequalities and social vulnerabilities in urban contexts, my analysis centers on how differently positioned social actors imagine and construct the city's peripheries as spaces of possibility. These heterogeneous visions of the periphery as a good — and perhaps better — place than "the center" work against the dominant conception of the periphery as the epitome of urbanism gone wrong, be it in terms of violence, aesthetics, or social vulnerability. And while positive periphery identities in Brazil are by no means a new phenomenon (e.g., São Paulo's still strong, periphery-based hip-hop and graffiti movements date back to the late 1980s), Luiz Inácio Lula da Silva's (Lula) election as the country's first Workers' Party (*Partido dos Trabalhadores*, PT) president in 2002 sparked a period of marked socioeconomic change that impacted public policy and the everyday lives and dreams of periphery residents. These developments included upward economic mobility for millions of poor and working-class Brazilians through rising wages and expanded credit; redistributive social programs such as the much-lauded Family Grant Program; and expanded higher education opportunities for lower-income students through federal scholarship, loans, and racial/class-based quota admissions programs.

My discussion builds on nine, four-to-eight-week long ethnographic research trips in São Paulo's Zona Sul conducted from 2014 to 2019, including a three-year project on the so-called new middle class. I begin with an overview of São Paulo's spatial landscape and "the periphery." I then explore the growth in recent years of Zona Sul–based cultural movements that assert what I call *insurgent cosmopolitan periphery subjectivities*. I argue that these organic cultural movements simultaneously — and unevenly — reinforce social segregation and support the creation of new periphery-based subjectivities and life ways.

THINKING ABOUT SÃO PAULO'S PERIPHERIES

With a population of 11.9 million, and over 20.9 million in the 39 municipalities that make up its sprawling metropolitan area, São Paulo is one of the world's largest urban areas. Unlike Rio de Janeiro, São Paulo was not an important colonial center, and only with the coffee boom in the late nineteenth century did the city assume a central role in Brazil's economy and political order. By 1930 São Paulo's population reached 1 million, and the city grew rapidly throughout the first half of the twentieth century as its metropolitan area became Brazil's industrial center. Population in the metro area skyrocketed from 2.5 million in 1950 to 12 million in 1980, largely through the internal migration of millions from Brazil's historically poor and underdeveloped northeastern region to São Paulo and other cities in the more economically developed southeast. By 2010, the metro population reached 20 million, and the region's economy was reconfigured with a decline in manufacturing and a solidification of São Paulo's current role as Brazil's financial, international business, and technology center.

São Paulo's spatial expansion has occurred in an uneven manner in which wealth has concentrated in central regions with modernist architecture, high levels of infrastructure, and mostly high-density residential areas. As in other Latin American urban landscapes, concentric rings of increasingly poorer neighborhoods surround this still-expanding center. Many of these ring communities are self-built, and to this day millions of residents have uncertain legal title to their land and homes, with nearly 1.5 million city residents living in *favelas* (slums) with poor infrastructure and social services. Yet notwithstanding higher levels of wealth in center regions and increasing social vulnerability as one moves out, São Paulo's peripheries contain significant socioeconomic heterogeneity, including millions of working- and lower-middle-class populations concentrated in the city's inner and middle periphery rings. Over time, these closer-in periphery communities have become officially designated neighborhoods with paved streets, sewer systems, and commercial districts, and more recently shopping malls and metro/train stations.

In policy and everyday life, most Paulistanos use a binary center/periphery conceptual framework to describe these socio-spatial realities. The *Centro Expandido* (the greater center) contains São Paulo's three principal business districts – the historic Centro, Avenida Paulista, and the newer Berrini region along the Rio Pinheiros – and many elite and middle-class residential neighborhoods. Surrounding the Centro Expandido are regions designated by their geographical direction in relation to the center: the *Zona Oeste* (western zone), *Zona Norte* (northern zone), *Zona Sul* (southern zone), and *Zona Leste* (eastern zone), which together constitute "*a periferia*" (the periphery). In addition to capturing physical spatial divisions, the center/periphery dyad expresses a series of oppositions that define residents by attributed social characteristics, such as rich::poor, white::Black, non-*Nordestina/o*::*Nordestina/o* (northeasterner), educated::uneducated, good citizen::marginal; modern::traditional, and cosmopolitan::non-cosmopolitan.

If the center/periphery dyad continues to play a central role in structuring how Paulistanos conceive of and experience the urban landscape, my interactions with Zona Sul residents highlight the multiple and contested meanings of the *periferia* category and the supposed attributes of its residents. For many, socioeconomic class parallels the center/periphery spatial divide. Marcos, a 40-year-old mixed-race community and environmental activist in the outer Zona Sul, provided me with this explanation as we walked through the unpaved and muddy streets of his neighborhood:

> The divide we usually talk about is the other side of the bridge. That is, the Tiête River is the dividing line that marks the division of social classes. The people on the other side of the river have a different vision of things, and they look upon those on the other side [the periphery] with distrust.

The importance of the river and bridge as dividing lines between the Zona Sul and the Center is captured in the classic rap *"Da Ponte Pra Cá"*/*"From This Side of the Bridge"* by the nationally renowned Zona Sul–based Racionais MC's. Marcos further links these differences to unequal educational opportunities and infrastructure levels: "And where do you have the manual laborers? They live in Grajaú, Parelheiros, Jardim Ângela [Zona Sul periphery neighborhoods], which all have precarious transportation, schools, and healthcare."

A few weeks later I visited a community cultural center run by a group of Black youth activists (in their late teens and early twenties) in the outer Zona Sul. In response to my same question "What is the periphery?" they expressed conflicting ideas on the physical, ideological, and social boundaries of the periphery. For these youth, access to urban space and amenities is the key element distinguishing the center from the periphery. As Jaime explains,

> I think the center begins in Grajaú, because that's where you catch the train. From here you have to go an hour and a half by bus to get to the closest train station, which is Grajaú. From there, you can go many places and connect with the yellow, blue, and green metro lines. Everything is more accessible, and it's faster to get there. From the moment you get to Grajaú, you have arrived in the Republic.

The youth in turn expressed markedly different opinions on whether such physical/infrastructure divides necessarily translate into social difference. Like Marcos, Guilherme thinks that the culture and demeanor of residents of the periphery and center are profoundly different, so much so that they constitute distinct species:

> In the center, there are museums, theater. In the periphery, we have *saraus* (open-mike poetry readings) and community events with authors. The demeanor (*jeito*) of a person from the center is different from a person from the community. The person from the community is simpler, and the people who come to the *sarau* are doormen, bricklayers, people who work in these kinds of jobs, and the people from the center are bankers, businessmen, that kind of thing. The way they speak is totally different. It is literally like they are extraterrestrials.

In reply, Vanessa countered,

> I think that it is us who put this idea forward – it's us who make this division. I don't think that they speak differently. I think that it comes from culture. I know many people there that are businesspeople and all that, and they talk the same as me. So, I don't agree with you.

And if Vanessa feels mostly comfortable in social spaces in the center, Alessandra describes how middle-class individuals from the center disrespect them because they are from the periphery:

> I think a little differently on this question of youth [from the center] and their vision [of us]. Just yesterday, at the event [a book reading in the Center] … we were talking together when another group of youth came in, and I felt a distancing, each of them moving away from us … And later we sat on a sofa, where there were backpacks, and some women came and said "excuse me," took the bags, and went to another sofa and put the bags there.

This comment generated a passionate discussion of how people from the center generally associate periphery youth, and especially those who are Afro-Brazilian, with crime and violence. Here, all the activists came together and positioned themselves as *periféricas/os* (periphery residents) in opposition to racist and classist youth from the center. This practice of flipping a commonly held perception (e.g., the periphery as dangerous) on its head is a dynamic shared by many periphery cultural political movements, which simultaneously present a positive Black, periphery cultural identity and identify economic structures, the state, racism, and sexism as key forces behind violence and inequality in São Paulo. In the case study that follows, I explore how periphery-based cultural activists have consciously mobilized positive periphery space-based identities, and in the process partially destabilized "the center" as the key reference point in the São Paulo urban landscape.

INSURGENT COSMOPOLITAN SUBJECTIVITIES IN THE ZONA SUL

> I could live in France, no, I could live in Japan.
>
> *Fabiana, six years old, Parque Regina, Zona Sul*

In early 2016 I participated in a free guitar and ukulele course for young teens in Parque Regina, a working-class neighborhood in the Zona Sul's Campo Limpo district. For six consecutive Saturday mornings I attended the class, held in the park in front of my second-storey studio apartment. On one of these mornings, three junior high–aged girls came up to me and started a conversation. After pleasantries, they explained to me, "It's important to know about the world and ask questions. Like that guy [Galileo] who got into trouble for saying the Earth goes around the Sun." Our conversation shifted to English words (the colors), whether I had been to Disneyland, and Oregon's climate – all standard topics when I talk to youth. Then one of them shifted conversational gears and asked me, "Isn't it a crime in the US to say things against gay people and Black people?" I answered yes and said that these were called "hate crimes" in English and that a person could pay a fine or even be jailed for saying aggressive and deprecating things against women, Black people, gay people, and people of different religions.

She responded, "That's a good idea – in Brazil, people will say these things right to your face." I was a bit taken aback, as I would not have expected three public school seventh graders in Campo Limpo to know about hate crime laws in the United States or directly connect them to the violence experienced by gay people and Black people in both countries.

That same day, over *feijoada* (pork and bean stew) and beer, I found out that one of the adults associated with the music class had gone on a short trip to Europe in the early 2000s as part of an intrafirm soccer tournament staged by the multinational corporation where a friend of his worked. Two weeks later, I learned that two outer Zona Sul youth activists were about to go to Berlin – a German couple had visited their organization and decided to sponsor an all-expenses paid trip for them to share their experiences and learn about community organizing in Europe. A few months later, several thousand of their Facebook friends (myself included) read about their trip, a highlight of which was a meeting with the German foreign relations minister. Later that year, a collective of Zona Sul–based Afro-feminist activists, including a member of our São Paulo new-middle-class research project team, went on a self-financed trip to Mexico and Colombia to participate in several international political organizing events. The collective shared these experiences of pan-Latin American solidarity in the 174-page "*Luta, Resistência, Memória em América Latina*" ("Struggle, Resistance, Memory in Latin America") edition of their *Fala Guerreira* (*Speak Warrior Woman*) magazine (Projeto Fala Guerreira! 2017). On the higher education front, another Afro-Brazilian member of our São Paulo research team told me that her sister had recently returned from being an exchange student in Australia. And while implementing a household survey on an unimposing street in Jardim Nakamura, the poorest of the four communities in the new-middle-class project, we discovered that a resident had visited Europe multiple times and had a son studying in Cambridge, Massachusetts.

Over the past decades, I have come across many similar stories of Zona Sul periphery residents, often Afro-Brazilians in their twenties and thirties, graduating from college or traveling to international destinations, possibilities that would have been extremely unlikely in the pre-Lula years and outside of the realm of possible for their parents. While by no means erasing structural inequities and the many forms of violence that shape the everyday lives of periphery residents, these "improbable trajectories" (Alessandra Tavares, personal communication, 2018) are shared via interconnected social media networks and contribute to the construction of what I call *cosmopolitan periphery subjectivities*. By **subjectivities**, I refer to individuals' experiences of reality and how they see themselves within society, including their understandings of their gender, race/ethnicity, sexuality, class, and regional identity. My use of the term *cosmopolitan*, in turn, follows a growing body of work on vernacular, subaltern, and everyday cosmopolitanisms. These approaches identify **cosmopolitanism**'s key defining feature as an openness to difference, rather than particular preferences, practices, or class subjectivities, such as the distinction-centered cosmopolitanism of traditional middle-class and elite Brazilians. In the case of Zona Sul periphery cosmopolitans, these subjectivities combine elements commonly associated with the periphery (e.g., language style, clothing, music, space-based identities that distinguish periphery residents from those of the "center") and active engagement with transnational cultural and political networks.

Seen in this light, cosmopolitan periphery subjectivities among young adults in the Zona Sul represent a departure from the worldviews of their parents, most of whom came to the city as migrants from other parts of Brazil and to a substantial degree re-created the small-town atmospheres of their communities of origin. At the same time, these cosmopolitan periphery subjectivities are a self-conscious assertion that "the center" does not have a monopoly on access to – or participation in – knowledge exchange, personal development, and political engagement, all of which have been greatly facilitated among lower-income Brazilians through the use of social media.

A vibrant example of Zona Sul cosmopolitan periphery subjectivities is the *Cia Humbalada de Teatro* (Humbalada Theater Company), which was located a few blocks from the last stop on the #9/Emerald train in Grajaú. Established in 2004 and in operation until 2019, the inclusive group was "a center of cultural resistance in the periphery" and consisted of "women, *bichas* (fags), monsters, *povos da mata* (savages), mothers and Black people doing theater" (Cia Humbalada de Teatro 2017). Over the years, the Cia Humbalada offered its diverse publics a safe space in Grajaú and produced original theater pieces, a carnaval *bloco*, cultural events, and parties, including *Grajaú Conta Dandaras, Grajaú Conta Zumbi*, a three-hour theatrical tour de force that presents life in Grajaú as a form of resistance paralleling the seventeenth *quilombo* (slave settlement) of Palmares, established by the fugitive slaves and existing outside of Portuguese control for nearly 100 years. I attended the show during its two-week February 2017 run at the SESC-Belenzini, a popular cultural and leisure center located in the Zona Leste periphery.

The play begins with the cast, dressed in African costumes, guiding the audience on a musical procession into the performance space. In its first half, skits address the rush hour commute on the #9/Emerald train, homo-affectivity (three macho men drinking beer at a *boteca*, two of whom end up exchanging an unexpected passionate kiss after their friend leaves), and a rap about homophobia. In the second half, the tone shifts from comedy to intense drama, and in the play's longest scene six women recount their painful stories of motherhood (e.g., being a single mother, having a child taken away by the state, abortion, the death of a child by gun violence), all told while they chop onions. After an expressionist nude dance in which the cast bathes together, the exploration of gender/sexual oppression and liberation continues with a monologue in which a trans woman shares the abuses she suffered in school and her dreams of flying away. In the penultimate scene, the show shifts gears again with an Afro-Brazilian religious ritual in which women from the audience join an ecstatic dance. The piece concludes with the cast back in African costumes singing the play's theme song.

The Cia Humbalada displayed this seamless mixing of gender/sexual, race, class, and periphery-centric politics a few weeks later in its annual carnaval *bloco* (neighborhood "block" carnival group). Here, several hundred revelers, nearly all from the Zona Sul, the majority Afro-Brazilian, perhaps half LGBTQ+ and many in drag, romped through the streets of Grajaú – the neighborhood that youth cultural activist Jaime described above as "the entrance to the

Republic." To the smiles, cheers, and occasional incredulous looks of residents along our route, we danced behind the sound truck to the *bloco*'s nontraditional Carnaval theme song. From its opening stanza, "No more silence, I am going to rub my butt in the face of the ignorant," the song shamelessly flaunts its resistance, a *pode* (we can) that will not accept the *não pode* (you can't) that structures social and political inequalities in Brazil. The rap continues in the second stanza with a critique of masculinist politics ("The dirty Fatherland, untrustworthy scrotums") and an affirmation of Black female sexuality in the third ("My body, my rules – I have sex, I have color") before intentionally invoking liquid modernity sociologist Zygmunt Bauman in a "Don't touch me" (*Não meter a mão*) call to take to the streets and get down.

As the *Grajaú Conta Dandaras, Grajaú Conta Zumbi* performances and the *bloco* strikingly demonstrate, the Zona Sul cosmopolitanism displayed here is simultaneously an assertion of a positive view of the periphery and a form of resistance to the multiple axes of oppression periphery residents face. This reinvention is situated within a cultural political landscape that includes thriving open mic poetry readings, rap, and graffiti movements (Pardue 2010; Vaz 2008). Rather than fighting for a predetermined future or using a predefined political strategy, these "citizen artists" (Vaz 2008) operate according to an insurgent logic that "destabilizes the present and renders it fragile, defamiliarizing the coherence with which it usually presents itself" (Holston 2009, 34). In the case of Afro-feminist and queer activists like the Cia Humbalada group, this destabilization includes not only a reimagining of the periphery but also an explicit rejection of the masculinist performative style and gender ideologies that typically characterize the better-known rap and graffiti movements.

A second characteristic of insurgent periphery cultural movements in Zona Sul is their complex positioning vis-à-vis the state, political parties, and long-standing social movements. On the one hand, the insurgent citizen artist networks with whom I have interacted generally characterize their political engagement as a form of resistance to experiences of intersectionalities (Moutinho, Alves, and Mateuzi 2016). In this *luta* (struggle), the state is seen as a significant source of material and symbolic violence (Carmo 2017) rather than a privileged avenue through which to redress concerns. At the same time, like many Brazilians today, most Zona Sul cultural activists and insurgent cosmopolitans I know express a profound disenchantment – and indeed disgust – with the current state of Brazilian electoral and institutional politics.

It is important to highlight that such positioning on the margins of the state and political parties does not indicate political disengagement but a critical recognition of the need for new, periphery-centric political strategies. As Jane, a Zona Sul citizen artist who has worked in several state-supported community programs and NGOs, explained to me in 2017,

> I like the chaos that is Grajaú, the cultural scene that we have today, which we didn't used to have. Today, we produce culture, and this is new. We have had a boom in the past four years across the peripheries, not just Grajaú, but the scene in M'Boi Mirim [another Zona Sul neighborhood], and the folks at Cooperifa [the most well-known *sarau* in the Zona Sul].

In this way, like other recent multi-nodal, insurgent São Paulo political movements (e.g., the 2013 street protests and the 2014 *rolezinho* movements described in the introduction), the social and political transformations that Jane works toward sometimes burst into activity, then recede into the background and reconfigure (or not) in the fluxes through which we assemble our lives.

CONCLUSION

In this chapter I have described some of the ways in which intersectional cultural activists work to reinvent São Paulo's Zona Sul peripheries and counter, if in different ways, the dominant images of the periphery as a place of violence, insufficient infrastructure, and urbanism gone wrong. In these transformations, the Zona Sul emerges as a unique physical location and ethos that is largely distinct from the "center" and its life ways. Yet, as I navigate the often-jarring contours of São Paulo's socio-spatial and political landscapes, I find myself wondering how residents of the peripheries and centers might come together – in whatever forms – to work toward transforming the city and achieving (at least some of) the goals outlined in São Paulo's Strategic Master Plan.

During the first Lula administration in the mid-2000s, it appeared that such a shared vision of the future existed, with many Brazilians of different social classes believing that the country was on a path toward greater economic and social equality. By the time I completed the original version of this chapter in 2017, such optimism seemed a relic of a bygone era. Since then the situation has become even more unsettled: A worsening economy has undone most of the economic gains that lower-income Brazilians experienced in the PT years, income inequality is rising, and in 2019 the divisive right-wing populist Jair Bolsonaro became Brazil's president. And then came the COVID-19 pandemic, which further intensified political divisions and disproportionately impacted urban periphery communities like the Zona Sul.

What do these developments suggest about the insurgent cosmopolitanism and intersectional political movements I have explored in this chapter? On the political front, like Brazil more generally, the Zona Sul is the scene of everyday tensions and disputes between those who support Bolsonaro's conservative, moral rejuvenation political project and those who defend the PT's project of economic development and expansion of individual and social rights (Klein et al. 2020). At the same time, the ongoing economic downturn and a shift to the right in São Paulo municipal- and state-level politics have challenged many intersectional-grounded cultural political collectives in the Zona Sul. A case in point is the Cia Humbalada de Teatro, which disbanded in 2019 in the face of internal disagreements and individual and organizational financial difficulties. Facing a changed economic and sociopolitical landscape, many collective-based activists have shifted their primary focus from intersectional politics to creating solidarity networks to respond to the immense material and health needs raised by the COVID-19 pandemic. This politics of care combines collecting and distributing food and medical supplies while simultaneously critiquing the state's abandonment of socioeconomically vulnerable communities (Carmo 2022).

Exactly what the future holds for São Paulo's Zona Sul remains to be seen. But rather than offer a definitive prognosis, I conclude with an excerpt from the *Grajaú Conta Dandaras, Grajaú Conta Zumbis* program (Cia Humbalada de Teatro 2017) that I think continues to capture the resilience and aspirations of many urban periphery communities in Brazil and beyond:

> Maybe this will be our last production of our 13-year trajectory of struggle, resistance, joys, abysses, and immensities. It is the drawing of a utopia, the end of a 13-year cycle. Who knows what other cycles will be born tomorrow. What we propose now is that we will rise up and fly. And one thing we know – Grajaú will go on, and it cannot bleed anymore.

REFLECTION AND DISCUSSION QUESTIONS

- What is the center/periphery divide, and in what ways do insurgent periphery cosmopolitans reproduce or unsettle this division?
- What do you see as the possibilities and limits of the Cia Humbalada do Teatro's cultural politics? Do you think they can play a role in addressing São Paulo's pronounced inequalities?
- What are some examples of insurgent periphery subjectivities in your country?

KEY CONCEPTS

- **cosmopolitanism**: An openness to difference, including the ability to negotiate diverse ideas, practices, and cultures.
- **periphery**: Sprawling, often infrastructure-poor neighborhoods that surround the central districts of most Brazilian cities such as São Paulo.
- **subjectivities**: Individuals' experiences of reality and how they see themselves within society, including constructions of gender, race/ethnicity, sexuality, class, and regional identity. Although unique to particular individuals, subjectivities are (re)produced in the everyday world of social interactions and interact continuously with macro-level forces.

EXPLORE FURTHER

- To learn more racial inequality and racism in Brazil, read **Chapters 5**, **12**, and **31**.
- To learn more about life in Latin American cities, read **Chapters 5**, **10**, and **17**.
- Caldeira, Teresa P. R. 2014. "Gender Is Still the Battleground: Youth, Cultural Production and the Remaking of Public Space in São Paulo." In *The Routledge Handbook on Cities of the Global South*, edited by Susan Parnell and Sophie Oldfield, 435–50. New York: Routledge.

- Friendly, Abigail. 2017. "Urban Policy, Social Movements, and the Right to the City in Brazil." *Latin American Perspectives* 44 (2): 132–48.

ABOUT THE AUTHOR

Charles H. Klein is an associate professor and chair of the Anthropology Department at Portland State University. An applied medical and urban anthropologist with over 25 years of research experience in Brazil and the United States, his current research focuses on developing Trans Women Connected, a sexual health promotion app for transgender women in the United States, examining intersectional cultural politics in São Paulo, Brazil, and exploring the ways in which epigenetics is transforming how we think about health, race, and equity.

REFERENCES

Carmo, Milena Mateuzi. 2022. "'Hunger Doesn't Wait': The Struggle of Women in the Peripheries of São Paulo during the COVID-19 Pandemic." *Vibrant – The Online Journal of the Association of Brazilian Anthropology* 19. https://doi.org/10.1590/1809-43412022v19e908.

———. 2017. *Margem Adentro: Políticas Sociais, Sujeitos e Resistências na Zona Sul de São Paulo*. Master's thesis, Faculdade de Filosofia, Letras e Ciências Humanas, University of São Paulo, São Paulo. www.teses.usp.br.

Cia Humalada de Teatro. 2017. *Grajaú Conta Dandaras, Grajaú Conta Zumbi*. São Paulo: Humbalada.

Holston, James. 2009. *Insurgent Citizenship: Disjunctions of Democracy and Modernity in Brazil*. Princeton, NJ: Princeton University Press.

Klein, Charles H., Alesandara Kelly Taveres, and Milena Mateuzi Carmo. 2020. "Between 'Us' and 'Them': Political Subjectivities in the Shadows of the 2018 Brazilian Election." *Revista de Antropologia* 63 (2): 1–26. https://doi.org/10.11606/2179-0892.ra.2020.171482.

Moutinho, Laura, Valéria Alves, and Milena Mateuzi. 2016. "'Quanto Mais Você Me Nega, Mais Eu Me Reafirmo': Visibilidade e Afetos na Cena Negra Periférica Paulistana." *Revista TOMO*. Accessed online; website no longer available.

Pardue, Derek. 2010. "Making Territorial Claims: Brazilian Hip Hop and the Socio-Geographical Dynamics of *Periferia*: Making Territorial Claims." *City & Society* 22 (1): 48–71. https://doi.org/10.1111/j.1548-744X.2010.01030.x.

Prefeitura da Cidade de São Paulo. n.d. http://www.prefeitura.sp.gov.br/cidade/secretarias/desenvolvimento_urbano/legislacao/plano_diretor/index.php.

Prefeitura de São Paulo. 2017. "Prefeitura Institui o Programa 'São Paulo Cidade Linda.'" Accessed online; website no longer available.

Prefeitura de São Paulo – Urbanismo e Licenciamento. n.d. *Plano Diretor Estratégico do Município de São Paulo*. Accessed online; website no longer available.

Projeto Fala Guerreira! 2017. *Luta, Resistência, Memória em América Latina* (Vol. 4). São Paulo: Projeto Fala Guerreira! Mulher e Mídia na Quebrada.

Sims, Shannon. 2017. "Paint It Grey: The Controversial Plan to, 'Beautify' São Paulo." *The Guardian*. February 23. https://www.theguardian.com/cities/2017/feb/23/sao-paulo-street-art-paint-over-joao-doria-brazil-graffiti.

Vaz, Sérgio. 2008. *Cooperifa: Antropofagia Periférica*. São Paulo: Aeroplano.

CHAPTER TWENTY-FIVE

Ties that Bind in the Dominican Republic: Buying Food on Credit in Corner Stores

Christine Hippert

Pepe, a 60-year-old Dominican man with salt and pepper cropped hair and a wide smile, owns a *colmado* (corner store, Figure 25.1) in the heart of the Callejón, a low-income neighborhood in an international tourist destination on the north shore of the Dominican Republic. Residents prefer to shop in *colmados* like Pepe's because some customers are allowed to pay for their purchases using *fiao* (in-store credit); however, not everyone is afforded *fiao*. Pepe explained: "The door is always opened for responsible people, you know, those who I know will pay me." I'd heard this phrase, "the door is always opened," often from other shopkeepers as they talked to or about their most trusted customers. Pepe continued: "I need these customers – I have debts, you know? If these responsible people don't shop here, they'll shop somewhere else. I would be ruined. I work hard to keep the door open for them."

In response, I asked Pepe, "When is the door not opened for someone? How do you know that someone will pay you back?"

"Oh yes, the door closes, that's for sure," Pepe replied. "I can't give everyone credit. If I did, I can't pay my own debts because there are lazy people here, those who don't work, and they are thieves and wouldn't pay me back."

"But what about people who only work during tourist seasons? Are they lazy? Do you allow them to buy on credit when there are no tourists?" I asked.

"Well, my friend, yes, this is a problem … For these people, they are responsible people when they are able to be. But more than anything, I'm talking about the Haitians. I can't trust them."

"So you mean like Joel? And Esther? How about Robe? It appears to me that you lend to Haitians quite a bit," I pushed him.

"Well, yeah, I do, but they're not like other Haitians."

Figure 25.1. A typical *colmado* (corner store) in the Dominican Republic. Photo by Christine Hippert.

"Like who? What do you mean?" I asked.

"Well, I suppose they [Joel, Esther, and Robe] have become responsible people, they prove that to me," was Pepe's explanation.

"Are Haitian customers the only ones who are not responsible, who fail to pay their debts? Do Dominicans do that, too, or is it just Haitians?" I asked.

"No, you're right, there are Dominicans, too," conceded Pepe. "The door is always open, Cristina, until it isn't, you know?"

In this chapter, I explain how buying food on credit is a social process, revealing a new **moral economy** – cultural norms within an economic exchange system. *Fiao* functions as a social safety net and creates ties that bind people together, especially Dominicans and Haitians, in ways that are not found in other social, cultural, and economic venues in the Dominican Republic due to widespread anti-Haitian sentiment.

LIVING AND WORKING IN CABARETE, DOMINICAN REPUBLIC

Cabarete is a small coastal community that has grown from a sleepy fishing village to an international tourist destination over the last few decades. During the 1980s, a series of government administrations made tourism the cornerstone of their economic policies, and the beautiful beaches on the Dominican coast became the focal point of financial and development investment (Moya Pons 1998). Cabarete has not been overrun by all-inclusive resorts that are found in the city of Puerto Plata nearby, or like Punta Cana on the southeastern coast. But Cabarete does consist of small- and medium-scale beachfront hotels that attract both tourists and migrant laborers from around the world. People migrate to Cabarete to work in restaurants, gift shops, and hotels as clerks, waitstaff, gardeners, cleaning staff, translators, tour guides, or to walk up and down the area beaches selling handmade candies and jewelry or braiding tourists' hair at very low prices. This region is also known for sexual tourism (Brennan 2004). Most people working in the tourist industry are employed as day-laborers as the tourist seasons ebb and flow according to the holiday calendars in the Global North and in the Dominican Republic.

My research in Cabarete focuses on two intercultural neighborhoods (places were Dominicans, Haitians, and others live side by side): Callejón de la Loma (El Callejón) and La Cienaga, where over half of Cabarete's population, working-class people who depend on the tourism economy, reside. Cabarete, and the north coast region overall, is especially vulnerable to food insecurity due to the high degree of migration, poverty, and international tourism. The rate of poverty in the region is grave, with 44.7 per cent of all homes categorized as "poor." Additionally, 45 per cent of people in this region are chronically malnourished (Oficina Nacional de Estadísticas 2016). Responding to this financial stress, gaining access to *fiao* in neighborhood *colmados* has become an increasingly pervasive economic strategy to secure household needs for both Dominicans and Haitians alike. Since March 2020, the COVID-19 pandemic and mitigation strategies such as intermittent economic shutdowns and international travel restrictions have made living and working in Cabarete even more difficult for residents of the Callejón and La Cienaga who rely on tourism income. The residents of both neighborhoods identify as Dominican (65 per cent), Haitian (30 per cent), with others identifying as international residents (mainly Europeans or Canadians who live and work there during the winter months) or Dominicans of Haitian descent.

Long-standing discrimination against Haitians has affected everyday life in the Dominican Republic. Historic and persistent ethnic and racial ideologies in the Dominican Republic construct Dominicans as people of Spanish descent (irrespective of African ancestry and phenotypic features) and Haitians or Dominicans of Haitian descent as "Black." Anti-Black ideologies, referred to as anti-Haitianism, stem not only from Spanish colonial era struggles (Keys et al. 2015) but also from resentment over the 22-year Haitian colonization of the Dominican Republic (1822–1844; García-Peña 2015) and the racist anti-Haitian rhetoric of dictator Rafael Trujillo

(1930–1961). In 2013, *La Sentencia TC 0168-13* was upheld by the Supreme Court, effectively annulling citizenship to residents who were born to non-Dominican parents who lived and worked – often for their entire lives – in the Dominican Republic (Guzmán 2019). Although the ruling doesn't explicitly target Haitians, it affects Dominicans of Haitian heritage. Consequently, access to basic needs, such as healthcare, housing, jobs, and even the ability to freely travel on public transportation within the Dominican Republic, has become more difficult for Dominicans of Haitian heritage living in the Dominican Republic.

Scholars have questioned how anti-Haitianism affects interpersonal Dominican–Haitian relations (Martínez 2003), especially within contexts like Cabarete where working-class and poor Dominicans, Dominco-Haitians, and Haitian migrants engage with one another on a regular basis. More so than in any other cultural venue in the Dominican Republic, *colmados* bring together people with different ethnic and racial identities. During my ethnographic fieldwork, I conducted participant observation in seven *colmados* owned by Dominicans, four owned by Haitians (all of whom migrated to Cabarete within the last 20 years), and one owned by a Dominico-Haitian who had migrated to Cabarete from another part of the Dominican Republic.

Often, customers shop in *colmados* without money in hand. I often heard the phrase, "*fiame/dame fiao*" or "*ban mwen kredi*" (loosely translated as "put it on my tab," in Spanish and Haitian Kreyòl, respectively) uttered by shoppers in *colmados*. However, gaining access to credit is not automatic; instead, shopkeepers and their customers negotiate and balance their needs in a process that pivots on everyone's shared similarities of being poor, rather than on the differences of being Haitian or Dominican, as one might assume considering anti-Haitian sentiment in the country. People strive to be known as *gente responsable* (responsible people), meaning people who are good to their word and pay off their debt. In a social context in which people might be suspicious of people of different ethnic/racial identities, as Pepe was in the opening story of this chapter, being *gente responsable* is an inherently intercultural process, involving finding people to count on in times of need irrespective of perceived differences.

SHOPPING IN *COLMADOS*

El Callejón and La Cienaga are home to about 30 *colmados*, small shops of no more than 15 x 30 meters, owned by both men and women and by both Dominicans and Haitians. Although in Cabarete there is a big-box grocery store, called Janet's, all residents of El Callejón and La Cienaga primarily shop in *colmados* for several reasons. First, these small *colmados* are usually within walking distance, so people don't have to travel far to reach one. Second, *colmados* carry staple foods that Dominicans, migrant Haitians, and Dominicans of Haitian descent depend on to prepare their meals, such as bulk fruits and vegetables, rice and dried or prepared stewed beans, spices, bottled water, and some *colmados* even butcher meat on the spot for their customers.

Third, unlike the big-box grocery stores, *colmados* sell items in small quantities, which is necessary both economically, especially for working-class and underemployed customers who are often short on cash, and also practically because daily cuts to electricity prevent residents from being able to store food for long periods of time, thus forcing them to shop every day to feed their families to prevent food spoilage. However, the primary reason people prefer to shop at *colmados*, especially when they are low on cash, is that shopkeepers allow certain shoppers to buy food and supplies on credit.

Residents of both neighborhoods often report that they shop almost exclusively at two different *colmados* within their neighborhood, but it is not uncommon for them to stop at a different *colmado* when they are outside of their neighborhood. Everyone expressed their dependence on *colmados*. For example, when I asked Belkis about how much and how often she shops at *colmados*, she indicated that "there is no way I could feed my kids and me if there weren't any corner stores. Really, Cristina, I maybe buy food at Janet's not even once a month. I have to buy food on credit, and I can't do that at Janet's."

Colmados' prices are fixed. There are no coupons, no sales, and no special offers in *colmados*. Everyone knows that the price of a product at one *colmado* will be the price at another. Interviewees report that they can't remember when a shopkeeper gave a sale or undercut other *colmados*' prices. In fact, if they did so, people would be angry at them for trying to undercut other *colmados* and therefore the plan to attract more customers would backfire. Echoing Rosing's (2007) findings, the moral economy of *colmados* in Cabarete is predicated upon fair, predictable pricing that avoids price gouging to attract more shoppers.

While prices are predictable, accessing store credit is not. Although buying food on credit is vital to maintaining local household food security, not all shoppers are afforded this privilege. *Fiao* is a social contract between shoppers and shopkeepers requiring people in the community to vouch for one another's character in a system of **balanced reciprocal exchanges**, or mutually beneficial transactions between customers, who want to buy food on credit, and shopkeepers, who use credit to attract shoppers to their stores. Determining eligibility for in-store credit is sort of like determining people's credit score: Shopkeepers must quickly evaluate customers for their ability to pay off their loan in a timely manner so that both shopkeepers and shoppers mutually benefit from the exchange. If shopkeepers allow too many people to buy on credit and they fail to repay their loans, the store could go out of business.

Shopkeepers always have their *cuaderno* (notebook) on hand for those customers that don't have money to cover their purchases, either in whole or in part. When a shopper asks to buy food on credit, the shopkeeper decides to allow the purchase or not, and if it's allowed, writes the person's name and the sum that is borrowed in a notebook that resembles children's school notebooks. Sometimes the person has a long column of debt in the notebook; sometimes there are sums that are scratched out, indicating that they have paid some of their debt. Debts are typically paid every 15 days, when workers are paid in the Dominican Republic. Shopkeepers anticipate this and can budget accordingly. If a borrower cannot pay the whole debt, then it is expected that they will pay part of this debt. Those people who pay down their debt, even parts of their debt, in a timely manner are considered *gente responsable*.

THE THREE TYPES OF *FIAO*

Overall, there are three types of *fiao* exchanges in *colmados* in Cabarete: (1) giving credit to someone who is well known to pay it back, (2) gift-giving to someone in need so they won't go hungry, and (3) giving credit to someone who is not known as *gente responsable*. The first, and most common, type of *fiao* exchange is one in which the shopkeeper knows and trusts the customer – a family member, neighbor, friend – to repay their debt, and therefore allows the person to buy on credit. Stronger than a close social tie is the fact that the customer is known to "have a job." This phrase was used by all shopkeepers in interviews with me and is a key factor in delineating who is *gente responsable*. However, knowing as I do that most residents in El Callejón and La Cienaga work in the unpredictable tourist industry, I questioned shopkeepers about how they knew if their customers would continue to have jobs when it was time to pay off their debts. "I don't," said Jhonny, a Dominican shopkeeper. "But I have to hope that he knows someone who could help him pay me in that situation." As Jhonny indicates, it is common practice for shopkeepers to give in-store credit to people under the assumption that if borrowers are unable to repay the loan, they will find a family member or friend to repay it for them. These friends or family members are people who they have helped repay their own loans in the past. I asked Jhonny if he had given *fiao* to people who were known to be *gente responsable* but then were not able to pay off their debt and needed to borrow from others to do so. He acknowledged that indeed this happens but doesn't concern him: As long as customers pay their debt, he doesn't care from where or whom the money comes.

Every shopkeeper discussed this circle of debt and the role that customers' debt repayment plays in the financial health of *colmados*. Shopkeepers provided me with many stories of *colmados* that had gone into financial ruin and closed because of failed debt repayment. "Not only do I have people who owe me money," reported a Dominican shopkeeper named Isayis, "but I owe the distributors money. When customers don't pay me back, I can't pay my bills, and my business suffers. The door is always open, until it isn't, you know?" Distributors also have *fiao* notebooks documenting shopkeepers' debt, just as shopkeepers must record their customers' debts. If customers fail to repay their debts, then shopkeepers can't pay their own debts. As Isayis describes, *fiao* as a system is fragile. The system can only maintain itself if people at all levels – distributors, shopkeepers, and customers – are *gente responsable*.

The second type of *fiao* exchange engages shopkeepers with people who are not considered *gente responsable*. Sometimes a resident of the community comes to a shopkeeper and asks for a gift. These residents do not work or haven't worked for some time, and they use this request as their last resort: They've burned other bridges, such as with family and friends, because they've failed to repay these loans. "Usually," said Anouse, a Haitian shopkeeper in El Callejón, "this person is hungry and needs me to help him … or their kids would go hungry." Anouse illustrates this further with a story about a woman who came to her to ask for items for herself and her infant: disposable diapers, milk, and eggs. Anouse knew in this case that she was giving a gift that would never be repaid. I asked her how often she did this, and she said that she gives these types of gifts only once to a person who asks. Often, shopkeepers refer to their beliefs as Catholics or Christians to explain their gift-giving. Anouse illustrates: "I'm a believer [in God] and this is what he wants me to do [looking up and pointing at the sky]." Rozalín, another shopkeeper, stated that "if we give too many gifts, our *colmado* would without a doubt fall [into financial ruin]."

In every case, when I first asked shopkeepers how they know who or who isn't *gente responsable*, they remarked, "people who pay their debts," with a strange look on their faces, as if I failed to understand the objective of financial transactions. However, when I pushed them further to discuss how they might be able to distinguish responsible people when they first meet someone, then they answered, as did Anouse: "Ah, when that happens, I ask for a reference, someone who I know who can vouch for them as responsible people." Anouse's response details the third type of *fiao* exchange: In cases when the shopkeeper gets a request for *fiao* from someone they don't know, it is common practice for the prospective customer to bring a person with them, a reference, to vouch for their character. The reference tells the shopkeeper two things: (1) that the person has financial income coming from somewhere and can be trusted to pay their debt, and (2) that the reference will allow the shopkeeper to put the total amount borrowed in their own *fiao* column. The function of this third type of *fiao* exchange is crucial, indebting the borrower to the reference, not the shopkeeper. If the borrower fails to pay the debt, then the reference is responsible for that debt. This, in fact, decreases the risk to the shopkeeper. Overall, when shopkeepers like Pepe say "the door is open," they refer not only to the relationship between customer and shopkeeper who are engaging in the specific transaction, but also to the networks that *fiao* creates by weaving together people who vouch for each other. The door is opened only for customers who can find *gente responsable* to vouch for them. This third category of *fiao* encourages social networking among residents who are looking for responsible people upon whom they can rely on for future help. The expected *fiao* practice of vouching for someone until a person can prove themselves responsible demonstrates the importance of social networks among customers, as well as between customers and owners of *colmados*.

THE HARD WORK OF CREATING TIES THAT BIND

The case of the exchanges made between Oscar, Ana, Jonás, and Pepe is a typical example of the ways that intercultural *fiao* exchanges are made in *colmados* in Cabarete. Oscar, a 41-year-old Dominican who has lived in La Cienaga for 12 years, regularly buys food on credit in Ana's, Jonás's, and Pepe's *colmados*. Each of these shopkeepers is of a different heritage: Ana is Haitian, Jonás is Dominico-Haitian, and Pepe is Dominican. Like most residents in the Callejón and La Cienaga, Oscar engages in multiple livelihood strategies in Cabarete. He speaks three languages to varying degrees – Spanish, German, and English – which he uses in his positions as a local tour guide and as a part-time after-school teacher in a local NGO. Additionally, every couple of months Oscar fills in and drives his cousin's motorcycle taxi (*motoconcho*), and he and his cousin split the profits Oscar makes for the days he works. Oscar's jobs as a tour guide, teacher, and *motoconcho* driver expose him to not only many tourists, but also to local residents who work in the tourism industry. Using these three income-generating strategies, Oscar is quite well known as *gente responsable* and is almost never denied *fiao* in *colmados*. And he has earned this distinction despite the gaps in his income during the ebbs and flows of the tourist economy. When I ask him if he ever shops using *fiao* in other *colmados*, he says no, he doesn't have to: "I don't need to shop elsewhere because they [Ana, Jonás, and Pepe] know I'm responsible, so they give me *fiao*," replies Oscar.

Over the course of the 12 years that Oscar has lived in Cabarete, he has vouched for more than 20 people throughout the Callejón and La Cienaga in Ana's, Jonás', and Pepe's *colmados*. He has learned to successfully provision his household by strategically and exclusively shopping at these three *colmados*, and when asked, vouching for new shoppers from different spheres of his life for Ana, Jonás, and Pepe. Oscar has vouched for shoppers who have become important *gente responsable* at each of these *colmados*. When I inquired about the criteria he uses for deciding when and with whom to extend credit, he explained:

> Cristina, this can be a mess if I don't do it right. For example, if I say yes to [vouch for] someone who I know is not working, or I know has a hard time keeping a job, then not only does the shopkeeper suffer, but I'm going to suffer too, you know? I may have three different jobs, but I need people to pay me back if I help them out. When there are no tourists, I don't work for my cousin, I barely have two jobs then. I have to say yes to the right people. Sometimes, the right people might be someone I know is a hard worker, who has a job, but they just moved to the neighborhood and they don't make much money … This is Josué. I vouched for him when he first came to Cabarete [in 2014] at Pepe's *colmado* … Pepe didn't want to do it [give him *fiao*], but Pepe trusted me. Now, Josué has his own page in Pepe's notebook. Josué works hard, both to get jobs but also to repay his debt … to me and to shopkeepers. He is like my *primo hermano* [first cousin] … he is like family. Besides, Josué has lent me money when I've needed it, too. One day, I needed gas for the motorcycle taxi and I wouldn't have been able to work that day if Josué didn't lend me cash for it.

Oscar makes it clear that he trusts Josué as he would a close family member, like a first cousin, explaining that this **fictive kinship** is based in part on the consistent loans they have given each other over the years. Oscar's vouching for Josué, a Haitian migrant, led Pepe, a Dominican, to trust him well enough to give Josué his own *fiao* notebook page. In fact, Josué is one of the Haitians to whom Pepe regularly gives in-store credit – even though he claims that "all Haitians are thieves" and that he "can't trust them."

Collecting loan repayments from people who vouch for them is what is referred to as "hard work" and is part of being *gente responsable*. For example, Belkis, a 42-year-old Dominican single mother of three children in La Cienaga, discussed the hard work involved with collecting what is owed to her from several people in the community. "I vouched for three people in September at Rozalín's *colmado* because they all moved here from [elsewhere], and I spent three months going to their houses to see when they would pay it back," she reported. In all, these three borrowers owed Belkis approximately US$9.30, an amount that exceeded her income as a housecleaner in two area hotels. Belkis admits that she vouched for these shoppers because they had come to the area with a promise of steady jobs: One borrower was hired at a local construction firm where his cousin was working, one borrower was seeking out jobs as a hairstylist at local salons, and another borrower was applying at area restaurants as a cook. Belkis recognized the potential for future balanced reciprocal exchanges with these new residents, two of whom were Dominico-Haitian, and the third who was Dominican.

Belkis reported making 10 different visits to the homes of these three borrowers over the course of three months. Sometimes her arrival was met with an invitation to eat a small snack, usually a mango or a couple of pieces of fried breadfruit, and a partial repayment of what was owed to her. "I am never repaid in full in a single visit," she told me. In one of these visits, she was given US$2 from a borrower who owed her almost US$3; Belkis exclaimed that this high repayment rate (two-thirds of the total amount owed) was rare, but she welcomed it: "That saved me that week because I needed to pay my own debt at Pepe's *colmado*." Typically, she counts on receiving about one-third of what she is owed in any individual visit – the result of the hard work in which she engages from being *gente responsable* and extending credit to others.

CONCLUSION

Conflict has come to be expected as the norm for intercultural interactions in the Dominican Republic. However, while there may be a centuries-old tension between the neighboring countries of the Dominican Republic and Haiti, we cannot and should not assume that interpersonal relations between and among Dominicans and Haitians are always similarly strained. *Colmados* are one important site where Haitian and Dominican shopkeepers and customers engage with people of diverse backgrounds, and interethnic tension is reduced due to the practicalities of everyday life for the working class. *Fiao* is a set of ties that bind together Haitians and Dominicans, facilitating intercultural networks that people need to survive, creating social networks that transcend any sort of suspicion or outright racial/ethnic discrimination. In no way do I claim that there is no interpersonal discrimination against Haitians in the Dominican Republic; Pepe's statements that Haitians are "untrustworthy" demonstrates that discrimination persists. But the case study of *fiao* in Cabarete highlights the complexity of Dominican–Haitian relations, shows that everyday life in the Dominican Republic requires intercultural engagement, and gives a more nuanced perspective on when and how discrimination is experienced in the Dominican Republic.

Yet this complexity exists within a global economy rooted in generating profits from tourism by keeping wages low and maintaining high rates of under- and unemployment. Therefore, while *fiao* can be a helpful strategy for residents to buy food and for shopkeepers to maintain their businesses, *fiao* is not a sustainable, long-term strategy to curb poverty. For all its benefits, *fiao* keeps people indebted and fails to decrease poverty in the region. Instead, a more beneficial and sustainable solution would be that residents of Cabarete earn a **living wage**, or the amount of money needed to pay for necessities – an unrealistic prospect at this point because of the parameters of international capitalism. It is hopeful to learn of practices like *fiao* that build solidarity, but it remains to be seen if this solidarity leads to any collective action calling for better working conditions for low-paid laborers.

REFLECTION AND DISCUSSION QUESTIONS

- What factors have fueled anti-Haitian sentiment in the Dominican Republic? How is this similar/dissimilar to the treatment of migrants and immigrants in your own country?
- How do shopkeepers determine who is responsible (*gente responsable*)? What kinds of hard work do *gente responsable* engage in?
- How do the three types of *fiao* encourage intercultural interaction?
- Do you use credit to buy what you need? Do you rely on other people to help you access what you need? What kinds of "ties that bind" do you create in your own life?

KEY CONCEPTS

- **balanced reciprocal exchanges**: Mutually beneficial transactions between people, such as customers, who are allowed to buy food on credit, and shopkeepers, who use *fiao* to attract shoppers to their stores.
- **fictive kinship**: Close, dependable relationships that develop between people who are not kin and often are distinguished using labels such as *brother*, *sister*, or *mother*.
- **living wage**: The amount of money workers need to earn to pay for life's necessities, such as food, housing, and healthcare.
- **moral economy**: The cultural norms that develop within an economic exchange system, such as the emergence of the three different types of *fiao* in Cabarete.

EXPLORE FURTHER

- To learn more about Haitians in the Haitian diaspora and in Haiti, read **Chapters 6** and **14**.
- To learn more about life in Latin American cities, read **Chapters 5**, **10**, **17**, and **24**.
- Bishop, Marlon. 2017. "A Border Drawn in Blood." *National Public Radio: Latino USA*. October 6. https://tinyurl.com/Border-Drawn-In-Blood.

- PBS. 2021. "Stateless." *Point of View*. Season 34, episode 3. July 20. https://www.pbs.org/pov/films/stateless.
- Regalado, Pedro A. 2016. "Bodegas and Colmados: Dominican Vernacular Space in Washington Heights." *The Gotham Center for New York City History*, May 10. https://tinyurl.com/Bodegas-and-Colmados.

ABOUT THE AUTHOR

Christine Hippert is a professor of anthropology at the University of Wisconsin – La Crosse. Her research examines people's experiences of community development, healthcare, and food security as they relate to social constructions and the cultural politics of racial, ethnic, gender, and national identities throughout Latin America and the Caribbean, primarily in the Dominican Republic, Bolivia, and Mexico. She has also conducted applied anthropological research in the United States. She is the author of *Not Even a Grain of Rice: Buying Food on Credit in the Dominican Republic* (2021, Lexington Books).

REFERENCES

Brennan, Denise. 2004. *What's Love Got to Do with It? Transnational Desire and Sex Tourism in the Dominican Republic*. Durham, NC: Duke University Press.

García-Peña, Lorgia. 2015. "Translating Blackness: Dominicans Negotiating Race and Belonging." *The Black Scholar* 45 (2): 10–20. https://doi.org/10.1080/00064246.2015.1012993.

Guzmán, Elena. 2019. "Checkpoint Nation." *NACLA*, March 22. https://nacla.org/news/2019/03/22/checkpoint-nation.

Keys, Hunter M., Bonnie N. Kaiser, Jennifer W. Foster, Rosa Y. Burgos Minaya, and Brandon A. Kohr. 2015. "Perceived Discrimination, Humiliation, and Mental Health: A Mixed-Methods Study among Haitian Migrants in the Dominican Republic." *Ethnicity and Health* 20 (3): 219–40. https://doi.org/10.1080/13557858.2014.907389.

Martínez, Samuel. 2003. "Not a Cockfight: Re-thinking Haitian-Dominican Relations." *Latin American Perspectives* 30 (3): 80–101. https://doi.org/10.1177/0094582X03030003006.

Moya Pons, Frank. 1998. *Dominican Republic: A National History*. Princeton, NJ: Markus Weiner.

Oficina Nacional de Estadísticas. 2016. "Tu Municipio en Cifras." https://www.one.gob.do/datos-y-estadisticas/.

Rosing, Howard. 2007. *La Comida Vacía: Neoliberal Restructuring and Urban Food Access in the Dominican Republic*. Unpublished diss., State University of New York, Binghamton.

CHAPTER TWENTY-SIX

"If It Wasn't for COVID, I Wouldn't Be Married": Disruption, Agency, and Making a Living in Chiapas, Mexico

Katie Nelson

After months of difficulty brought on by the COVID-19 pandemic, Juana's life shifted suddenly on December 2, 2020, just after dawn. She told me it was a cool morning. I imagine that a light wind blew over and then down the cement walls encircling her family compound, carrying with it the smell of burning firewood and cooking food from neighboring homes. Juana said she put on her hand-woven shawl and called a taxi to her house. She was carrying some of her weavings in her bag and pretended as though she was going to the market to sell them. When the taxi arrived, she got in, closed the door, and looked back at the gate to her home. Then she left. Instead of driving to the market, the taxi drove around the town for about 10 minutes and then quietly pulled up to the home of her fiancé, just a block away from her home. This event marks a moment she made an important change in her life, one that she chose and she wanted, yet one she knew would cause difficulty with her family. She accurately predicted her family would object, and the social and familial consequences would be significant. Nevertheless, it was her choice to elope. She felt empowered by the choice but also nervous about what would come of her new life with her new husband.

This story and this chapter are about Juana, a 43-year-old Tzotzil-speaking Mayan woman from a highland community in Chiapas, Mexico, and what led her to this moment. But let's start with some fuller context. The COVID-19 pandemic posed difficulties for people and nations throughout the world. The pandemic hit Mexico especially hard. To keep the economy open, the Mexican government initially downplayed the risks of the virus. This resulted in a weak federal response and an anemic testing capacity – less than 2 per cent of the population (Valle and Knaul 2021). Health officials suspect the death and infection rates were significantly undercounted. Even so, by December 2021, Mexico had the highest COVID-19 fatalities, proportional to their population, in the world. And in terms of the number of COVID-19

Figure 26.1. A woman weaving in Chiapas, Mexico. Photo by Alan de La Cruz on Unsplash.

deaths, Mexico was fourth in the world, just behind Brazil in Latin America (Johns Hopkins Center for Systems and Science Engineering 2021). Scholars are only beginning to unpack the cascading consequences of the pandemic, which include increasing social inequality and economic marginalization in many countries. Yet the disruption caused by the pandemic also provided an opportunity for agentive change. That is, it allowed some people to make a change in their current life path. As a sort of rite of passage, some people have emerged from the liminality of the pandemic and reintegrated into society with new social roles and identities. This is the case for Juana.

Juana and her family hand-weave textiles on backstrap looms and embroider them with flowers and stylized animals in vibrant colors (see Figure 26.1). They have made a living weaving and selling their textiles to tourists for over 40 years. However, the COVID-19 pandemic significantly restricted national and international tourism to her town. For the first time in memory, the family had no income. Juana adapted by reaching out to her networks for help. Her family wove masks instead of shawls, blouses, and bags, and Juana sold them to contacts in Mexico City, Guadalajara, and the United States. But this was not enough income, and the family had to rely on savings and selling some appliances and a motorbike to get by. As the peak of the pandemic was winding down, but the end was not in sight, Juana made an important recalculation for her life on that day in December. She decided to leave her family's textile weaving business to marry a local small businessman and try to have children.

Juana's decision is striking because for the 20+ years I have known her she had never planned to marry and intended to remain living with her family in their matriarchal family compound indefinitely. Interestingly, Juana sees her decision to leave her home and family business as a reflection of her strong social networks, social capital, and agency, rather than a need to be supported by a husband. The uncertainties of the pandemic, while financially difficult, provided her with an opportunity to reimagine her life and life course.

In this chapter, I will explore Juana's lived experience and the ways that global issues such as economic disruption and vulnerability became motivating factors for change. Through the lens of an ethnographic portrait of her life, I will explore these issues in the context of larger global processes and how they contributed to changes in Juana's life.

MEETING AND LEARNING FROM JUANA

I first met Juana in 2002, when we were both in our early twenties. I had just graduated from Macalester College and was conducting ethnographic research on behalf of the Science Museum of Minnesota to document changes in *huipil* textile designs. **Huipiles** (pronounced "we-peel-ayes") are a type of hand-woven blouse that Mayan women in the region weave and wear, and every town has its own distinctive style and designs. I spent time in the city of Salapo, a town of about 30,000 (in 2002) predominantly Mayan Tzotzil-speaking people. Salapo received numerous tourists each year and had regularly established bus and van routes that locals used to travel to larger regional cities to buy food and other goods. Some of the men in the town had worked in the United States, many in agricultural labor in the southwest, particularly California, and returned with money to build or improve their family homes and businesses. Other families were supported by remittances – money sent from relatives working in the United States or in other parts of Mexico. Most families relied on a combination of subsistence farming, intermittent agricultural labor, and the sale of handicrafts.

I was touring towns and villages in the region, and Juana's was the first home I visited in Salapo. We seemed to get along well. Juana was smart, relaxed, warm, and funny. I admired her savvy business and people skills. I visited her every week, and her family eventually invited me to stay with them, which I did for several months while I completed my fieldwork. I slept in a modest hand-sawn wood-frame bed Juana and her sister set up for me in the front room of the house, which also served as a tourist reception room. It had smooth, compacted mud floors, and walls composed of thick branches and thatched leaves. Textiles hung from the rafters, including rare, traditional woven bridal gowns, which they encouraged tourists to try on. The rest of the home compound was made of cement and had more typical furniture and appliances, except for a stove. Juana and her family preferred cooking on an open wood fire in the center of the compound. There was always a pot of something simmering and a low fire crackling. A sheet covered the open garage, hiding their modest pickup truck. Juana said this was so that tourists would experience a more "authentic" rural Mexican Indigenous experience.

On days they were expecting tourists I would get up before dawn and help get the space ready. Once the buses arrived, I tried to stay out of the way in one of the back rooms or the kitchen so as not to interfere with their sales or be too conspicuous. Nevertheless, I always watched them work. Occasionally, if the tourists included Americans or Canadians, Juana would encourage me to greet them. I only learned a handful of words and phrases in Tzotzil. Unless I was included in the conversation, Juana and her family primarily spoke to one another in Tzotzil, punctuated by occasional terms in Spanish. I usually was able to capture the gist of most conversations. Nevertheless, everyone, except for Juana's mother, also spoke enough Spanish to carry on regular conversations. Juana and I were both about equally fluent in Spanish and used that common language to communicate.

In 2003 I returned to the United States, went on to graduate school in California and then Guadalajara, Mexico. Eventually I moved back to Minnesota, where I had grown up, began teaching college, and had three children. Juana stayed in Salapo with her family. She helped grow her family's business but chose not to travel outside of Chiapas. We stayed in contact over the years. I would send her care packages and she would send me weavings. We both got smartphones in 2010 and later used various social networking apps to chat and exchange photos. Despite the many differences between us, including native language, an imbalance of power, weaving skill, citizenship, artistic ability, mobility, formal education, business experience, wealth, and so on, our friendship has remained important to both of us over the years.

A BRIEF HISTORY OF JUANA AND SALAPO

Salapo is located in Chiapas, the southernmost Mexican state on the Yucatán Peninsula. Chiapas has the highest population of Indigenous people in the country. It is also the poorest state in Mexico, with a poverty rate of about 76 per cent in 2020, compared to 43 per cent of Mexico as a whole (Ministry of Education 2021). Most of the Indigenous population lives in the highland region of the Sierra Madre de Chiapas mountain range, dispersed among hundreds of small villages and towns that dot the landscape. Although seven different Maya languages are spoken throughout the state, Tzotzil is the most common. Migration to larger Mexican cities and to the United States has been a strategy that many, mostly men, have taken to alleviate poverty. As a result, in 2021 the population in Chiapas had an imbalance of women and men, composed of 46 per cent men and 54 per cent women (Ministry of Education, 2021). One consequence of this imbalance is that women take on a significant role in family economies, engaging in a variety of economic strategies and activities such as selling crafts. Consequently, as Nace (2018) points out, whenever the already tenuous economic situation in Chiapas gets worse, women oftentimes become the shock absorbers to these new economic realities.

Juana was born in Salapo in 1978, the fifth of seven children. Starting in 1975, her older brother and father launched a flower cultivating business. They grew flowers and sold them in larger cities during certain holidays: orange marigolds for the Day of the Dead and white dahlias for community festivals. In 1980, one of her father's good friends became the mayor of Salapo. One day he brought two tourists from Mexico City to visit their home. The tourists were interested in how they wove their fabric. In a conversation via WhatsApp, Juana shared: "For some reason, I remember this moment very well. I was a very small child and I stood at the gate and watched them come and ask to enter … I was shy because at that time I did not speak any Spanish. I had not met many people outside my town."

At the time, Juana said that her family only wove and embroidered their own clothing. They did not sell to tourists. In fact, no one in Salapo sold to tourists at that time. However, the tourists wanted to take home samples of their weaving. Gradually more and more tourists arrived in Salapo and at Juana's house. The family, and then later many households in the town, began catering to these tourists and wove textiles specifically for sale to tourists, including bags, scarves, and shawls. After Juana's father died of cancer in 1982, the family was left with a lot of debt from his medical treatments. Juana's mother took control of the family's finances and began in earnest the family business of weaving and selling to tourists. Juana's older brother supplemented the family's income working as a wage-earning agricultural laborer for local farmers, and her older sisters wove and embroidered. Overall, the weaving business was the primary means the family made a living.

At the age of eight, Juana began learning to weave and embroider. She said it took her a long time to become good at it: "[Before] my weaving was ugly and poorly done, most of it went into the fire. It wasn't until I was 15 years old that I became good at it" (personal communication with author, September 1, 2021). She said she had little direct instruction, but modeled her work after her sisters' and mother's art and longed to be a productive part of the family. She saw weaving as both an important cultural tradition and a valuable way of making a living. By her early twenties, Juana was a competent and confident saleswoman and weaver. She regularly interacted with a range of people and had formed friendships and partnerships with tour guides, van and bus operators, retail owners, weaving cooperatives, journalists, local politicians, and researchers, among others.

Juana's personal experience closely follows what happened on a national scale in Mexico. Throughout the twentieth century, many Indigenous people in Chiapas worked in agriculture and subsistence farming, mainly in the cultivation of corn. The little surplus they harvested was sold to purchase other commercial products and foods they could not grow. In 1982, Mexico fell into a serious economic crisis after the market for its primary export, oil, collapsed and Mexico defaulted on its international loans. The debt crisis forced significant changes to family economies in Chiapas. Because of the devaluation of the peso and a spike in inflation, many Indigenous men had to leave farming and work in other sectors of the economy or emigrate.

Then, starting in 1994, the North American Free Trade Agreement (NAFTA) was implemented, which further weakened subsistence farming economies by flooding the market with cheap, heavily subsidized corn imported from the United States. There simply was no way for small farmers to compete and make a living in agriculture. This was a moment in time in which the reliance on women's labor, and weaving in particular, deepened. Nace (2018) argues that the increase in weaving production by women in Chiapas is directly related to men's decrease in earning capacity. This in turn, Nace argues, was driven by loss of land, falling wages, declining crop prices, rising costs of living, and male migration.

Because there were initially not enough tourists to fully support families whose income relied on weaving production during the 1980s and 1990s, weavers formed cooperatives to build and support a tourist market. In order for weaving to become a viable way to make a living, artists had to make the transition from local markets to sell on a globalized scale (Nace 2018). This required weavers to interact with intermediaries to market, transport, and sell their goods throughout Mexico and internationally. It also required collaborative efforts to attract more tourists and build the infrastructure to support them. Because many Indigenous women were already producing textiles and running their own businesses of scale, they became the ones who primarily interacted with these outside agents. Men often played secondary or supportive roles in this process. Indeed, in Juana's case, Juana became the primary negotiator and contact person for her family's business.

JUANA'S AGENCY

One way we can understand Juana's experiences is through the theoretical lens of agency. In anthropology, the concept of **agency** refers to the ability of a person to express their individual power. One way this power may manifest is by making a decision that may or may not conform to one's cultural or social expectations. Oftentimes, the notion of agency is used in contrast with ideas about **social structure** or culture. Social structure can be defined as a patterned web of social forces and institutions that powerfully shape the way people think and act and even their life course. Yet as influential as structure is, the outcomes of people's lives are not entirely determined by it. Individuals (and groups) can interpret cultural rules in different ways or take actions that contradict or resist social structures.

It's important to note that while social structure and agency might appear to be in polar opposition to each other, they are actually mutually reinforcing forces that are forever changing one another. This relationship is known as a **dialectic**. In other words, while the lives of individuals are shaped by the existing social structure, individuals also have the ability – *the agency* – to make decisions and express them in behavior and actions. These actions can either reinforce existing elements of the social structure or change them. Either way, they are a feedback loop, incrementally moving and shaping social structure and individuals in complex ways.

For Juana, that day in December in the taxi represents a clear example of her agentive action. Yet it certainly did not happen in a vacuum. In fact, it cannot be fully understood outside of the context of the disruption to social structure the COVID-19 pandemic caused. Five years before that short taxi drive, Juana planned to marry a different person. I remember her telling me she had someone in her life, but that I had to strictly keep it a secret and not tell anyone in her family. She was so secretive that I began to wonder if this person represented an entirely unexpected social category, such as a woman or a non-Indigenous person. When I didn't hear anything more about it, I figured she had changed her mind or the relationship had ended. I didn't pry. Later Juana disclosed that a man had asked her family to marry her. However, her family, and in particular her mother, said no. Juana thinks they rejected the partnership because he was much younger than her, they didn't think he would be in a good position financially, and they feared he might take advantage of her. She nonetheless felt frustrated. At the time she was in her late thirties. All her sisters, including her youngest sister, were married with children. She felt powerless in this dimension of her life.

Things changed dramatically when COVID-19 quarantines began in Chiapas. Even before the first nationwide quarantine in the spring of 2020, tourism to Chiapas had begun to slow. Mexico restricted international travel, and people were encouraged to stay home. By June, tourism had completely dried up, for the first time in memory. For months, Juana's family had no income whatsoever. The little savings they had were quickly exhausted. Fearing they would run out of food, Juana's younger sister suffered repeated panic attacks and stopped eating for several weeks. Juana and her sisters sold an old refrigerator and cell phone to buy five chickens and a rooster, to ensure a supply of eggs and meat. Her sister improved. Never had Juana felt so economically vulnerable in her life.

Yet Juana acknowledges they were in a better position than many families. Juana had national and international connections outside Salapo from the years of her business work in tourism, and she developed a strategy to use these connections to improve their home economy. They stopped producing the standard tourist textiles and began to make masks embroidered with beautiful brightly colored flowers and animals. She planned to sell these masks to contacts in Mexico City, Guadalajara, and Chicago in an effort to stay afloat. The costs of reliable shipping remained a significant barrier in making this a profitable move in the long run. Without fast internet access or computer access and knowledge, scaling up this sort of business would be nearly impossible.

The massive disruptions caused by the COVID-19 pandemic dramatically changed the economy of Salapo and made significant, albeit subtle, changes to local cultural norms as well. Many people in Salapo had to be creative in how they got through the pandemic. Some people went to live with relatives in other cities; others combined resources with neighbors and friends and extended family. Still others sold things they never would have imagined selling to get by, such as jewelry, vehicles, and land. Juana said there are rumors that a few women traveled to

Tuxla Gutierrez (the capital of Chiapas) to sell sex to get by. What is clear is that many made changes to their personal lives that were not widely accepted or common before the pandemic.

Juana felt emboldened and empowered by the realization she had become the person in the family with the most powerful connections and abilities. Essentially, she was responsible for saving her family from calamity. This provided an opportunity for her to imagine a different life path. She began to question the cultural norms that dictated that her family should decide whom she would marry. She questioned why it was that she could make lots of important business decisions but not an important personal one. So, while the changes to the local economy (i.e., social structure) opened space for Juana to make personal changes, she likewise began to shape her social structure by defying cultural norms surrounding who gets to decide if and whom she married. This was not necessarily something that would have happened in the past.

DIALECTICS OF AGENCY AND SOCIAL STRUCTURE

In 2015, the Mexican Museum of Art contacted Juana's older sister Maria through a community cooperative and invited her to travel to Chicago to sell her textiles and demonstrate weaving to museum visitors. With assistance from the museum, Maria was able to get a visa to attend the Chicago event. This was remarkable, because such visas for working-class Mexicans are exceptionally difficult to obtain. I drove to Chicago and visited her. Juana was also invited, but she did not want to leave Salapo, even for a short trip. I encouraged her to go so we could visit each other in person, but she worried about feeling uncomfortable, eating new foods, and traveling further than she had before. Importantly, she was also reluctant to leave because she did not want to be seen as unusual in the eyes of people in her community. As I have discussed previously, it is not uncommon for men from Chiapas to travel, migrate, or emigrate for work. However, it is very uncommon for women to travel far, especially alone. In explaining why she didn't seek a visa, Juana told me that it was better that Maria went to Chicago because it would be seen as more acceptable by others because she was married and Juana was not. The cultural expectations that unmarried women ought to stay home and not travel alone were clear to Juana. She understood she would be viewed as a person with questionable morals and as irresponsible and disrespectful to her family.

This illustration of Juana's choice to stay home in 2015 due, in part, to social pressure is interesting in how it contrasts with her agentive decision to marry during the COVID-19 pandemic. Here we can see how the social structure (local cultural norms) affected her individually and how her (and others') individual agency has shaped social structure in Salapo. The dialectic is a clear reflection of her life. When the COVID-19 pandemic hit, the family lost money and became very vulnerable economically. However, Juana did not choose to marry to become more financially stable or to be taken care of. In fact, she said that she probably makes more money than her husband did before they were married. Instead, she chose to marry *because of* her extensive connections. She saw that throughout the pandemic she was empowered by all the connections she had developed. These connections made it clear to her that she had more power in her business life than she previously was aware of. The disruption of the pandemic made her realize that she had the ability to exercise agency in her personal life. As others in Salapo made drastic changes in their lives to adjust to the sudden economic decline, cultural norms became more flexible and malleable. People had to do things they never would have before to get by. Thus, she felt she was able to break some of the cultural gendered norms that had previously held her back. As she told me, "well, truthfully, if it wasn't for COVID, I wouldn't be married, I wouldn't have thought it was possible" (personal communication with author, October 30, 2021).

CONCLUSION

On the night that Juana eloped, members of her new husband's family walked to Juana's family's house with an offering of food and to tell them the news and explain why Juana was not coming home that night. Her family was incensed and refused the food and refused to speak with them or Juana. It took weeks of repeated attempts until her family finally agreed to meet and accept the marriage. They are now at peace with her decision. Today, Juana lives with her husband and together they run a small store. She sells quesadillas, regular and spiced beer (*Micheladas*), and a type of locally made hard liquor called *posh* in various flavors. She weaves color-coded (by flavor) bottle labels embroidered with the name "*Juana la Pochera*" or "Juana the Posh-maker" that she uses to cover each posh bottle. In her spare time, she still weaves and embroiders other items.

In Juana's absence, her sister Maria has stepped up to fill her role in the family business. Juana tells me that whenever her family needs help Juana can run the block home to attend to their needs or meet her friends and long-time contacts. She seems happy. Yet she still worries about the future. Tourism has slowly begun to return to Chiapas, but still it is not even close to the levels it was before the pandemic. As of this writing, there are no international tourists. She wonders if tourism will ever return to the levels before the pandemic. If they don't, she worries about what her family will do. She also worries about the intense competition in Salapo. So many families now weave and sell their art to tourists. How do they keep a competitive edge?

In this chapter, I used the lens of an ethnographic portrait of Juana to explore her agency in the context of larger global processes that have contributed to changes (and consistencies) in her life. The COVID-19 pandemic caused considerable disruption and vulnerability in Juana's life, which were exacerbated by underlying economic marginality and lack of national investment in highland Chiapas. Yet, paradoxically, this very disruption and vulnerability also created the opportunity for agentive action on an individual level in Juana's life. Nevertheless, the structural inequality that exists throughout Indigenous highland Chiapas may prevent Juana from being able to make further changes in her life that empower her economically and socially. Therefore, it's important to note that even though Juana has agency, structural factors may limit her agency, such as lack of national investment in communications technology and infrastructure in highland Chiapas, decreased flow of tourism to the region, and ethnic, gender, and linguistic discrimination that is present throughout Mexico and Latin America. Time will tell how the push and pull of structure and agency will play out in her life in the future.

REFLECTION AND DISCUSSION QUESTIONS

- How have larger global processes contributed to changes in Juana's life. To what extent did Juana have agency in responding to these changes?
- Out of vulnerability and disruption, Juana found agency to make changes in her life. What do you think the structural limits of this agency are? What are some limiting factors that restrain Juana's ability to further empower herself socially and economically?
- What are some ways you have exercised agency in your own life? Describe how this is connected or related to social structure.

KEY CONCEPTS

- **agency**: The degree of control an individual or group has in taking action and making decisions, which is often in tension with and limited by structural power.
- **dialectic**: A process in which two opposing concepts or powers meet in conflict and result in a new "synthesis" in which the original concepts/powers are also typically transformed as well.
- **huipiles**: A type of hand-woven blouse that Mayan women in highland Chiapas weave and wear; every town has its own distinctive style and design.
- **social structure**: The patterned web of social forces and institutions that powerfully shape the way people think and act and even their life course.

EXPLORE FURTHER

- To learn more about challenges surrounding tourism in Latin America and the Caribbean, read **Section 10** and **Chapter 4**.
- To learn more about the gendered experiences of cis women, read **Section 4** and **Chapter 35**.
- To learn more about the social and economic effects of the COVID-19 pandemic, read **Chapters 12** and **33**.

- Apreza Castro, Yolanda, Charlene Woodcock, and K'inal Antsetik, eds. 2018. *Weaving Chiapas: Maya Women's Lives in a Changing World*. Norman: University of Oklahoma Press.
- Brumfiel, Elizabeth M. 2006. "Cloth, Gender, Continuity, and Change: Fabricating Unity in Anthropology." *American Anthropologist* 108 (4): 862–77.
- Short Video of Juana Embroidering. 2020. https://tinyurl.com/Juana-Embroidering.

ABOUT THE AUTHOR

Katie Nelson, Ph.D., is an instructor of anthropology and sociology at Inver Hills Community College. Her research examines identity, citizenship, migration, and mobility in Mexico and Morocco. She is associate editor of the *Teaching and Learning Anthropology Journal*, co-author of *Doing Field Projects: Methods and Practice for Social and Anthropological Research*, and co-editor of *Gendered Lives: Global Perspectives*.

REFERENCES

Johns Hopkins Center for Systems Science and Engineering. 2021. "Mortality Analyses." https://coronavirus.jhu.edu/data/mortality.

Ministry of Education. 2021. "Chiapas." In *Data México*. https://datamexico.org/en/profile/geo/chiapas-cs.

Nace, Addison. 2018. "Weaving Authenticity: Artesanías or the Art of the Textile in Chiapas Mexico. 2018." *Textile Society of America Symposium Proceedings* 1092.

Valle, Adolfo, and Felicia Knaul. 2021. "Mexico, Facing Its Third COVID-19 Wave, Shows the Dangers of Weak Federal Coordination." *The Conversation*. August 8.

CHAPTER TWENTY-SEVEN

Music, Movements, and Maria: Narratives of Music in Post–Hurricane Maria Puerto Rico

Melissa Cambero Scott

When I first met Carlos "Xiorro" Padilla Caraballo, he was instructing a class at Taller Tambuyé, a dance studio and community cultural center in Rio Piedras, Puerto Rico, that teaches different African diasporic artforms. His class was on Kokobalé, a once endangered martial art created by enslaved Africans in Puerto Rico (PR) that is "played" or sparred during a Bomba performance – a heavily drum-based genre of music. Historically Kokobalé and Bomba served as an emotional release for enslaved people's colonial realities and formed as a way of resisting their oppressors (Duany 1984). Today they serve Puerto Ricans as they face contemporary challenges, such as the aftermath of Hurricane Maria, government neglect, and political unrest.

After answering my questions and discussing the elements of my research pertaining to Hurricane Maria, Carlos spontaneously pulled out a maraca and began performing a song he wrote titled "*Por Culpa 'e Maria*" ("Because of Maria"). As he sang the main chorus of the song, he pointed to me and the other student in the class, indicating that we should sing with him:

Because of Maria
Because of Maria
My family left
For a distant and cold land
To earn their bread

Puerto Rican genres of folk music like Bomba have a call and response musical composition. The audience sings the simple and catchy chorus together and the singer fills in the verses with lyrics spontaneously. In the case of Carlos's song, he introduced the main premise of the song, the consequences that emerged "because of Maria," and then fleshed out the song

Figure 27.1. Live music and dancing in San Juan, Puerto Rico. Photo by Güldem Üstün (CC BY 2.0).

in his solo verses. In reflecting on Carlos's rendition and our participation, it struck me that the collaborative nature of Bomba mirrors the ways in which Puerto Ricans saw recovery as a collaborative activity in the months and years following Hurricane Maria.

On September 20, 2017, Hurricane Maria made landfall in PR. It caused catastrophic damage to the small island that continues to be felt even years after the storm. The estimated death toll of the storm ranges between 1,000 and 4,645 people depending on the different methodologies used by researchers to count the mortality rate (Harris 2018). Hurricane Maria not only physically devastated PR but also brought further attention to long-term issues of neglect exercised by both the US federal government and the local Puerto Rican government. Despite Maria being the most destructive natural disaster in over a century (Coto 2018), PR received little assistance to aid in recovery. As a result of the island's colonial status as an unincorporated territory of the United States, PR did not receive sufficient resources from the federal government, a situation that was worsened by corruption at the local government level (Vinik 2018). In response to this lack of aid, Puerto Rican musicians and activists stepped in to provide support and give out supplies to underserved communities (Amatulli 2017). Like participation in a Bomba song, these musicians' aid and collaboration with their fellow Puerto Ricans living on the island exemplified the way that Puerto Ricans value collectivism as a way of defining their relationships among one another and their relationship to a Puerto Rican "nation."

Music is an important part of daily life in Puerto Rico, and in this chapter I show how it has also served as a community resource of resilience in a historical moment of great hardship. I present findings from my ethnographic fieldwork with Puerto Rican musicians, community leaders, and music fans during the period of 2019–2021 and document the role of music in their strategies for recovery and change, their symbols of solidarity, and their acts of resistance. During my fieldwork, I conducted in depth semi-structured interviews with Puerto Rican music fans, musicians, and community leaders. I also performed participant observation at concerts and performances, participating as an audience member and taking note of both the performers' and audiences' engagement with the music. In addition to fieldwork, I conducted discourse analysis on the music of popular Puerto Rican artists to examine themes of collectivism and **musical nationalism** in their lyrics. The goal of my research was to explore the ways in which music has illuminated and shaped changes within the Puerto Rican political landscape post–Hurricane Maria. In the sections that follow, first I explain Puerto Rico's status as a commonwealth of the United States. Then I discuss the role music plays in fostering a sense of musical nationalism, that considering the lack of government support after Hurricane Maria supports arguments for Puerto Rican independence. I then analyze two representative songs that illustrate significant political shifts in Puerto Rico post–Hurricane Maria, including a distancing from the United States's contemporary colonial influence.

THE CONTEMPORARY COLONY

First inhabited by the Indigenous Taíno, the Spanish colonized Puerto Rico in 1493 and it has never been a sovereign nation (Cabán 2019). The Spanish empire ruled over PR in at least some capacity for over 400 years until the United States won the Spanish-American War and gained control of the island in 1898 under the Treaty of Paris. In 1900, the US Congress passed the Foraker Act, installing a civil government in Puerto Rico but still under US federal jurisdiction. In 1917, the Jones-Shafroth Act granted US citizenship to all Puerto Ricans. The US takeover of Puerto Rico created social and cultural divides between the Spanish-speaking residents of the island and the English-speaking US officials. After the creation of the Nationalist Party of Puerto Rico (in 1922), with the goal of Puerto Rican independence, and the election of party leader Pedro Albizu Campos in 1930, violent clashes occurred between the militant party and the US-backed local government. Meanwhile, the Puerto Rican Independence Party formed in 1946, with the same goal of Puerto Rican independence but without militant tactics (Ayala and Bernabe 2009). As a result of the violent clashes, the US Federal Bureau of Investigation engaged in the unlawful surveillance of members of both parties. And vocal support for independence became taboo.

In 1952, Puerto Rico became a US commonwealth, and votes on referendums in 1967, 1993, 1998, 2012, and 2017 maintained that status; although most voters in 2012 and 2017 expressed a desire for a status change (to statehood or independence), unclear results (in 2012) and low voter turnout (in 2017) delegitimized the results. In a 2020 referendum, 52.52 per cent of the 54.72 per cent of Puerto Ricans who voted, opted for statehood (independence was listed not an option; PRSCE 2020), but the US Congress has not yet granted PR statehood. As a result of Congress's failure to act, Puerto Ricans are US citizens without congressional representation, and they are unable to vote in presidential elections (unless they move to a state). And there continue to be three factions of Puerto Rican society: those who are pro-commonwealth and want PR to keep the status quo; those who are pro-statehood, advocating for PR to become a US state; and in the minority leading up to Hurricane Maria, those who are pro-independence and advocate for PR to become a sovereign nation. These two possible "futures" for Puerto Rico – as an independent nation or as a state in the United States – are in tension with one another (one moving away from and one moving toward the United States). They offer alternative visions for what Puerto Ricans (as a collective) can and should be. Both of these "futures" for Puerto Ricans would radically change (in one way or another) the colonial status quo, and there is a lot at stake in whether one route or the other is taken.

In the aftermath of Hurricane Maria, the reality of "citizenship without representation" is something that pro-independence and pro-statehood advocates emphasize as they advocate for a change from the status quo. Some of my interviewees posited that Puerto Rico's lack of statehood and representation contributed to the federal government's delayed and minimal response to the hurricane. Furthermore, since 2020 there have been multiple instances in which local Puerto Rican officials, including governors, mayors, and municipal leaders, have been negligent in distributing hurricane recovery resources given to them by the US federal government, often leading to the expiration of much-needed essential goods in warehouses (Associated Press 2020). As these examples illustrate, Hurricane Maria's devastation was not only a product of the strength of the hurricane, which was certainly exacerbated by climate change, but was also the result of systemic damage to the island's social and material infrastructure, the results of colonialism, corruption, and capitalism (Klein 2018).

In my research, I found that Hurricane Maria was a turning point in public sentiment – with some people shifting from ideas about statehood to ideas about independence. And as I argue here, music plays an important role in fostering Puerto Rican nationalism. Although the majority of Puerto Rican music is not overtly political, it has important political overtones and implications. Thus, Puerto Rican music is not "just" about ethnicity and culture but about distinction and cultural sovereignty, especially from the United States, and the creation and representation of a collective, Puerto Rican identity.

A MUSICIAN'S PERSPECTIVE ON THE CONTEMPORARY COLONY

Puerto Ricans are very cognizant of the ways that government mismanagement and the legacy of colonialism have complicated the recovery process following the hurricane. For instance, Margarita, an activist and member of the musical group *Plena Combativa* (Combative Plena), a pro-independence, all-women project that used Plena, a Puerto Rican percussion-based music genre, to rally against injustices, explained how she felt about Puerto Rico's post–Hurricane Maria recovery process:

> A disaster this massive wasn't just the hurricane ... the massive disaster was governmental, on a political level; the truth is after everything that has happened to us, the worst was the government, which was not prepared. People that were poor became poorer and had no access to resources because they [the government] stole it.

Like Margarita, many of the Puerto Ricans I spoke with were frustrated with the government response to the hurricane and with corruption in the local government. As Puerto Ricans re-evaluate their colonial status in relation to the United States, especially in the aftermath of the hurricane, Puerto Rican genres of music with anti-racist and anti-colonial roots like Bomba and Plena, which was historically used as a storytelling device in the southern part of PR (Duany 1990), have become increasingly popular, especially since many of the influential activists on the island are also musicians.

Generally, Puerto Rican musicians like Margarita have been more likely to be pro-independence than the average Puerto Rican. Artists like Calle-13 (Esterrich 2015) and Fiel de la Vega (Anazagasty-Rodríguez 2002) have long been vocal proponents of Puerto Rican sovereignty, despite pro-independence ideologies having been relatively taboo when they released their music prior to Hurricane Maria in the 1990s and 2000s (Ayala and Bernabe 2009). However, many of my interviewees, like Carlos, believe that after Hurricane Maria people started "waking up" to systemic issues and corruption that occur due to the colonial status of the island. More specifically, there is renewed momentum surrounding the desire for cultural or political independence from the United States. The Puerto Rican music scene is a driving force behind the political energy surrounding independence, fostering collectivism and a sense of nationalism. This is reflected in the music that has been produced by Puerto Rican artists since 2017.

RHYTHM NATION

According to political scientist Benedict Anderson, a nation is "an imagined political community [that is] imagined as both inherently limited and sovereign" (Anderson 1983, 6). While in many ways Puerto Rico fits this definition, the government of the island is not sovereign. However, Duany (2000) explains that despite this lack of legal sovereignty, Puerto Ricans identify themselves as a nation and not as an extension of the United States. Puerto Ricans, regardless of whether they live on the mainland or on the island, have an ancestrally shared language, territory, and history that differentiates their heritage from other communities in the United States. Therefore, Duany suggests a conceptualization of Puerto Rico as culturally sovereign.

This framing of Puerto Rico as a culturally sovereign nation allows a conceptualization of pro-independence movements as nation-building projects. And as historians have noted, since the

United States acquired Puerto Rico, there have been several Puerto Rican nationalist movements that have emerged, always in response to the issues of social inequality and injustice resulting from PR's colonial status (Ayala and Bernabe 2009). Therefore, as nation-building projects, Puerto Rico's cultural contributions to the world, including its music, is a way of continuously asserting independence to itself and to the world. In this section I explore how Puerto Rican musicians view their art as an expression of nationalism – pride in their nation – by returning to Carlos.

As I spoke with Carlos during my Kokobalé lesson, he shared with me that when he would speak with African diasporic martial artists from other countries, they thought he was being arrogant because he spoke so highly about PR. Carlos explained to me that he intentionally evokes nationalism as a form of resistance against PR's current colonial status and to celebrate the aspects of Puerto Rican culture that pre-date US colonialism. This is considering early twentieth-century efforts by the United States to try to enforce US American cultural ideals on Puerto Ricans, even going so far as banning the Puerto Rican flag in 1948 in an attempt to squash independence movements (Ayala and Bernabe 2009). In this way, even the US government acknowledged the relationship between material culture, nationalism, and independence.

Juan, one of the organizers of Defend Puerto Rico, a project that works with Puerto Rican artists to create and share art while also meeting the needs of locals in times of crisis, explained:

> How do you colonize a people? You take their culture away, you take their beliefs away, so your god doesn't exist, pray to white Jesus you know, don't eat your rice and beans and plantains – eat McDonald's and listen to American pop songs – don't listen to **jíbaro** music. Don't listen to bomba. Don't listen to plena. Don't be who you are. Be American. But to this day we are *Puertorriqueño* (Puerto Rican) and so yes, existing in that way is a political act and it's so beautiful. We were just in Caguas to see the *jíbaro* music to keep our traditions and customs alive through music, to keep language to uplift who we are … I think that's why we hold our musicians and our music so close to us because it means so much to us.

For Juan, like for Carlos, Puerto Rican nationalism is not only a demonstration of pride in Puerto Rico, but a statement of cultural and political sovereignty.

As Juan revealed, one of the most prominent ways Puerto Ricans express pride in their culture is through musical nationalism. This term refers to the rhythms, symbols, and harmonies that become associated with a specific nation, culture, or ethnicity (Toye 1918). In the case of Puerto Rico, there are multiple examples of musical genres attributed to the island, which has led to it having a disproportionately large footprint in the global music scene (Duany 2000). Having cultural representatives on the global music scene helps to assert, to an international audience, that PR is distinct from the United States. Puerto Rican genres of music like reggaeton and salsa dominate the Latin American music industry, and artists from PR are also often highly ranked in their respective genres. Therefore, it is not surprising that when there are periods of transformation in Puerto Rico, they are often soundtracked by the music of Puerto Ricans living on the island and in its diaspora. Through their music, these musicians speak to the realities of life and the political landscape of PR. In what follows, I explore specific examples of music that speaks to Puerto Rican collectivism, musical nationalism, and the attempt to find sovereignty through it.

SOMOS LOS HIJOS DEL CAÑAVERAL (WE ARE THE CHILDREN OF THE SUGAR CANE)

On a trip to Puerto Rico in 2021, I participated in several activities involving Bomba. During my last night in the college district of Rio Piedras, I went to a *"bombazo"* (Bomba performance) featuring the group Tambuyé. There was no stage for the performance, but rather the band faced the audience with space for dancers to perform in front of them. Bomba performances involve an unspoken conversation between musicians and dancers. When a dancer is compelled by the music to dance, they enter the center of the performance, bow as a sign of respect to the band, and then begin to move in sync with the percussion. If a percussionist begins to bang their drums faster, the dancer will move their feet faster. If the dancer adds a flourish to their dance, the musician will emulate the move with their instrument. Bomba and *bombazos* are collaborative and involve many members of the community. Beyond the dancers, the audience is encouraged to sing the chorus with the band. In these ways, people can simultaneously be spectators and performers.

Once, when I called a *bombazo* a "concert," I was quickly corrected by a dancer. *Bombazos* are instead called community events, during which people express themselves emotionally and politically. Even if there is an official band leading the performance, the event is a community effort. In this way, Puerto Rican music reflects collectivist values, where the cohesion in the group is prioritized over an individual's desires (Schwartz 1990). This manifests not only in music but also in talk, for example in a preference for collective pronouns like "we" over "I" in conversations. Even on a larger scale, such as with global popular musicians like reggaeton artists Bad Bunny and Residente, artists write lyrics with collectivist themes. For instance, the two most popular songs that participants cited in interviews with me were "*Estamos Bien*" ("We're Good") by Bad Bunny (2018) and "*Hijos del Cañaveral*" ("Children of Sugarcane") by Residente (2017).

Puerto Rican artist Benito Antonio Martínez Ocasio, better known as Bad Bunny, has skyrocketed in popularity, becoming one of the most famous artists in the world and ranking as one of the most streamed artists globally in 2020 (Gonzales 2020). Part of his appeal is his supposed authenticity and his eccentricities (Del Valle Schorske 2020). The artist's rap style, lyrics, and even his samples are fully submerged in Puerto Rican language practices, a key component of Puerto Rican culture. His 2018 song collaboration "*Te Bote*" ("I Kick You Out"), which includes several contemporary Puerto Rican artists, demonstrates these practices. In his verse, Bad Bunny raps the line:

Arranca pal' carajo (¡Wuh!), mi cuerpo no te necesita (No)
Lo que pide e' un perreo sucio en La Placita

In this short bar of lyrics, the artist says he wants to have a short fling with a girl. In Spanish he has shortened the words "*para el*" to "*pa'l*" and "*es*" to "*e.*" In the line "*perreo sucio en La Placita*" (dirty dancing in La Placita), he refers to the style of dance performed to reggaeton music and La Placita, a location in San Juan with a lot of nightlife. Verses like these are dense with cultural and linguistic cues that signal to Puerto Ricans that Bad Bunny is and continues to be an everyday Puerto Rican (Del Valle Schorske 2020).

Lyrically, Bad Bunny's song "*Estamos Bien*" is not overtly political nor is it directly speaking about Hurricane Maria. Rather the song mainly boasts about being "good" or secure. Nonetheless, the lyrics do mention issues with infrastructure in Puerto Rico that were caused by the hurricane. For example, lyrics such as "*La Mercedes en PR cogiendo boquete*" (The Mercedes in PR taking a gap) refers to the eroded, potholed pavement of the street. There is also the lyric "*pa' casa no ha llega'o la luz*" (the electricity hasn't come back at home), which speaks to the realities of trying to live in Puerto Rico post–Hurricane Maria. Puerto Ricans I met were attracted to Bad Bunny as a representative of everyday Puerto Ricans and to his recognition of the struggles after the hurricane. For instance, Juan explained:

> I love his story of coming from bagging groceries at a store to becoming maybe the most popular Latin music artist in the world. I love his fluidity, I love the generation he represents and in a time when "*Estamos Bien*" [was released] like we needed it – we know that everything wasn't okay around us but we knew we were going to be alright it was definitely a soundtrack – it felt good to hear that when he did the TV show and he had the slide show of what we were going through on the island at the moment.

The performance that Juan referred to was Bad Bunny's television debut as a musical guest on the *The Tonight Show Starring Jimmy Fallon* in September 2018. It had been a year since Hurricane Maria and, prior to beginning the song, a screen appeared reading "On September 20th, 2017, Puerto Rico was exposed to the full force of Nature's Ferocity" (Esposito 2018), followed by clips of damage that occurred during the hurricane. After the clips, Bad Bunny made the statement, "After one year of the hurricane, there are still people without electricity in their homes, more than 3,000 people have died, and Trump is still in denial. But you know what? *Estamos Bien*," before he sang the song. At that moment Bad Bunny represented Puerto Ricans on an international stage, even as people outside of PR had begun to forget about the storm. His song demonstrated Puerto Rican feelings of togetherness in the face of adversity, while also reminding the outside world of the troubles that people on the island continued to face.

"*Hijos del Cañaveral*" by Residente was another song that people mentioned when I asked about the aftermath of Hurricane Maria. René Pérez Joglar, a.k.a Residente, has had a long career of being a politically engaged, pro-independence musician. He has always been very vocal about his positions, and this has sometimes led to him getting in trouble for vocalizing his beliefs. For instance, when he was a part of the rap group Calle 13, he was banned from performing at the Roberto Clemente Coliseum in 2009 for speaking out against the governor of Puerto Rico at the time, Luis G. Fortuño (Rosario 2017). Although Residente is a popular artist within the music academy, winning the most Latin Grammys in the history of the award, opinions of him among Puerto Ricans are more divisive (Garsd 2014).

Despite some of the negative opinions of Residente, his prophetic song "*Hijos del Cañaveral*," written prior to Hurricane Maria, has become an unofficial soundtrack to hurricane recovery. The song is about solidarity among Puerto Ricans and uses the imagery of sugarcane, a historically prominent crop on the island, to call on all Puerto Ricans' ancestral roots. *Jíbaros* are historical, rural farming workers and are often used in political imagery both by people who want Puerto Rico to stay a commonwealth but also by pro-independence advocates who use *jíbaro* as a symbol of anti-US colonialism. The term *jíbaro* is sometimes considered derogatory because it insinuates being poor and uneducated. However, within the recent political and cultural shifts there is more of an affinity with *jíbaros* because they represent self-sufficiency and being closer to the land (Franqui-Rivera 2015). In fact, the pro-commonwealth movement uses an image of a *jíbaro* man as their mascot. Residente has a long history of hearkening to *jíbaro* culture in his artistic expression, and in some of the promotional images for his 2018 concert in Puerto Rico he is even pictured with a traditional *jíbaro* hat held to his chest. His use of the *jíbaro* image is a way of acknowledging Puerto Rican's colonial past.

Structurally, his song "*Hijos del Cañaveral*" speaks to Puerto Ricans collectively through the use of the word "us":

> The hurricane comes and we pray to the cross
> And we play brisca when the power goes out
> The heat warms our beer
> And we bathe in the lake …
> What is ours no one takes them away from us
> Because no matter how much snow they throw, here the snow melts
> Although they plant the roots as they please
> Soursop branches don't give apples

In both "*Hijos del Cañaveral*" and "*Estamos Bien*" the artists sing from a place of unity using the pronoun "we" instead of "I." By speaking in the collective "we," "*Hijos del Cañaveral*" remarks on the specificity of living in Puerto Rico, especially in times of peril. Hurricanes are a common occurrence in PR and they usually knock out the power on the island, leaving people to cope with the heat of the tropics. The lyrics also speak to cultural perseverance against US colonialism, which is represented by the snow and apples, things that are common in the US mainland but are foreign to PR. Residente's argument, made via his lyrics, is that regardless of any colonial powers that might want to take over PR, Puerto Rican culture and its people will endure.

In addition to representing Puerto Ricans on a global stage through their music, since Hurricane Maria artists such as Bad Bunny and Residente have become more overtly political. For example, in 2019, after messages by Governor Ricardo Rossello (whose hurricane response was already under scrutiny) mocking his female co-workers and people who died due to Hurricane Maria were leaked (Chavez 2019), hundreds of thousands of Puerto Ricans rallied to oust him. During the protest, Residente, Bad Bunny, and Puerto Rican pop singer Ricky Martin were present and vocal during the demonstrations. Their music, as well as that of Bomba and Plena artists, was employed to garner attention and support (Chavez 2019). Their support and their music encouraged Puerto Ricans to rally behind a common cause so that they were able to exert the power needed to create changes in the political landscape, and in this case led to Rossello's resignation.

CONCLUSION

Music is an inextricable component of Puerto Rican cultural and, more specifically, musical nationalism. Despite being a colony since 1493 and the traumatic events of recent history, most importantly Hurricane Maria, Puerto Ricans continue to define and defend themselves through their music. Puerto Rico is a contemporary colony, one of the last of its kind, and its colonial status adds complexity to understandings of nations and nationalism. One of the most notable ways in which nationalism manifests in PR is through musical nationalism (Amrani 2018). Puerto Ricans' pride in their music as a key aspect of their national identity contributed to the salience of music for the island's post–Hurricane Maria recovery process, as well as for changes to its political landscape, including the movement for independence. In particular, the ways in which Puerto Rican music references a collective sense of self, a unity among Puerto Ricans (both on the island and in the diaspora) helped Puerto Ricans cope with the long-term aftermath of the hurricane. It also created solidarity among people who might have political differences – such as differing opinions on statehood versus independence – to combat injustices facing all Puerto Ricans.

REFLECTION AND DISCUSSION QUESTIONS

- What role does music play in the formation of a Puerto Rican national identity? How does this differ from the notion that nations must have political sovereignty?
- What role did Puerto Rican music and musicians play in Puerto Ricans' recovery from Hurricane Maria?
- How do the lyrics presented in this chapter reflect Puerto Ricans' values surrounding collectivism? What are the ways the music you listen to reflects your community's values?

KEY CONCEPTS

- ***jíbaro***: Historically, a rural farm worker; presently used in political imagery both by people who want Puerto Rico to stay a commonwealth and also by pro-independents who use the figure of the *jíbaro* as a symbol of anti-US colonialism (Franqui-Rivera 2015).
- **musical nationalism**: Rhythms, symbols, and harmonies that become associated with a specific nation, culture, or ethnicity (Toye 1918).

EXPLORE FURTHER

- For another ethnographic case study on the power of music, read **Chapter 13**.
- To learn more about other contemporary forms of US imperialism, read **Chapter 9**.
- Dávila, Arlene M. 1997. *Sponsored Identities: Cultural Politics in Puerto Rico*. Philadelphia, PA: Temple University Press.
- Quiñones Rivera, Diana, dir. 2020. *Resistimos*.
- Rivera-Rideau, Petra R. 2015. *Remixing Reggaetón: The Cultural Politics of Race in Puerto Rico*. Durham, NC: Duke University Press.

ABOUT THE AUTHOR

Melissa Cambero Scott is a Ph.D. candidate and an adjunct professor in global and sociocultural studies at Florida International University. As a biracial, Afro-Latina Dominican American who lived in Puerto Rico for four years, Melissa's identity was constructed through imperialism, and this has led her to study and illuminate colonialism and post-colonial acts of resistance.

REFERENCES

Amatulli, Jenna. 2017. "'We Were Destroyed': Ricky Martin Goes on 'Ellen' to Ask for Help for Puerto Rico." *Huffington Post*. September 28. https://www.huffingtonpost.com/entry/ricky-martin-goes-on-ellen-to-ask-for-help-for-puerto-rico_us_59ccfab5e4b0210dfdfc6d84.

Amrani, Iman. 2018. "'We Grow Up Breathing Music': How Puerto Rico Became a Pop Superpower." *The Guardian*. July 12. https://www.theguardian.com/music/2018/jul/12/grow-up-breathing-music-puerto-rico-pop-superpower-despacito.

Anazagasty-Rodríguez, José. 2002. "Colonial Capitalism, Hegemony, and Youth Praxis in Puerto Rico: Fiel a La Vega's Rock en Español." *Latin American Music Review / Revista de Música Latinoamericana* 23 (1): 79–105. https://doi.org/10.1353/lat.2002.0001.

Anderson, Benedict. 1983. *Imagined Communities: Reflections on the Origin and Spread of Nationalism*. New York: Verso.

Associated Press. 2020. "Puerto Rico Residents Outraged after Discovering Unused Aid from Hurricane Maria." *NBC News*. https://www.nbcnews.com/news/latino/puerto-rico-residents-outraged-after-discovering-warehouse-full-unused-aid-n1118501.

Ayala, César J., and Rafael Bernabe. 2009. *Puerto Rico in the American Century: A History since 1898.* Chapel Hill: University of North Carolina Press.

Cabán, Pedro. 2019. "Hurricane Maria's Aftermath: Redefining Puerto Rico's Colonial Status?" *Current History* 118 (805): 43–9. https://doi.org/10.1525/curh.2019.118.805.43.

Chavez, Nicole. 2019. "Private Leaked Texts Massive Protests and a Governor's Downfall: A Timeline of Puerto Rico's Political Unrest." *CNN.* https://www.cnn.com/2019/07/27/us/puerto-rico-governor-scandal-timeline/index.html.

Coto, Danica. 2018. "6 Months after Hurricane Maria, Puerto Rico Pleads for Help." *AP News.*

Del Valle Shorske, C. 2020. "The World According to Bad Bunny." *New York Times.* https://www.nytimes.com/interactive/2020/10/07/magazine/bad-bunny.html.

Duany, Jorge. 1984. "Popular Music in Puerto Rico: Toward an Anthropology of 'Salsa.'" *Latin American Music Review / Revista de Música Latinoamericana* 5 (2): 186–216. https://doi.org/10.2307/780072.

———. 1990. "Review: 'Salsa,' 'Plena,' and 'Danza': Recent Materials on Puerto Rican Popular Music." *Latin American Music Review / Revista de Música Latinoamericana* 11 (2): 286–96. https://doi.org/10.2307/780128.

———. 2000. "Nation on the Move: The Construction of Cultural Identities in Puerto Rico and the Diaspora." *American Ethnologist* 27 (1): 5–30. https://doi.org/10.1525/ae.2000.27.1.5.

Esposito, Suzy. 2018. "Bad Bunny Makes Powerful TV Debut on 'Fallon.'" *Rolling Stone.* https://www.rollingstone.com/music/music-latin/bad-bunny-fallon-estamos-bien-hurricane-maria-729857.

Esterrich, Carmelo. 2015. "Dream Nation: Puerto Rican Culture and the Fictions of Independence." *CENTRO: Journal of the Center for Puerto Rican Studies* 27 (1): 260–3.

Franqui-Rivera, Harry. 2015. "'So a New Day Has Dawned for Porto Rico's Jíbaro': Military Service, Manhood and Self-Government during World War I." *Latino Studies* 13 (2): 185–206. https://doi.org/10.1057/lst.2015.9.

Garsd, Jasmine. 2014. "Calle 13, On Being Loved and Hated in Latin America" *NPR.* https://www.npr.org/2014/04/05/299180900/calle-13-on-being-loved-and-hated-in-latin-america.

Gonzales, Erica. 2020. "Bad Bunny Is Spotify's Top Artist of 2020, with More Than Eight Billion Streams." *Harper's BAZAAR.* December 2. https://www.harpersbazaar.com/culture/art-books-music/a34846472/spotify-most-streamed-artist-2020-bad-bunny.

Harris, Richard. 2018. "Study Puts Puerto Rico Death Toll from Hurricane Maria Near 5,000." *National Public Radio.* May 29. https://www.npr.org/sections/health-shots/2018/05/29/615120123/study-puts-puerto-rico-death-toll-at-5-000-from-hurricane-maria-in-2017.

Klein, Naomi. 2018. *The Battle for Paradise: Puerto Rico Takes on the Disaster Capitalists.* Chicago, IL: Haymarket Books.

Puerto Rico State Commission on Elections (PRSCE). 2020. "2020 Puerto Rican Status Referendum." https://elecciones2020.ceepur.org/Escrutinio_General_93/index.html#en/default/PLEBISCITO_Resumen.xml.

Rosario, R. 2017 "'Residente' Deconstructs the Rapper's Ancestral DNA, Explains Why Puerto Rico Should Be Independent." *Vibe.* https://www.vibe.com/features/viva/residente-dna-puerto-rico-514130.

Schwartz, Shalom H. "Individualism-Collectivism: Critique and Proposed Refinements." *Journal of Cross-Cultural Psychology* 21 (2): 139–57. https://doi.org/10.1177/0022022190212001.

Toye, Francis. 1918. "A Case for Musical Nationalism." *The Musical Quarterly* 4 (1): 12–22. https://doi.org/10.1093/mq/IV.1.12.

Vinik, Danny. 2018. "How Trump Favored Texas over Puerto Rico." *POLITICO.* March 27. https://politi.co/2unqfsD.

SECTION NINE

Development and Sustainability

A major dilemma for many Latin American and Caribbean nations in their efforts to address and adapt to climate change is that one of the main drivers of economic growth in the region has historically been precisely the sorts of extractive industries that cause climate change and ecological degradation. These industries (including fossil fuel and ore mining, monoculture agriculture, timber forestry, commercial fishing, and cattle farming) and the infrastructure projects that enable them (including transportation and communication/internet systems, hydroelectric dams, and electrical grids) pollute local water and soil with toxic chemicals, emit greenhouse gases, and disrupt and displace human communities where they are located.

Today, in light of these harms, many communities of the region are involved in high-stakes struggles for the future. These struggles manifest as contests over specific projects and often involve confrontations in which the state is allied with business interests and against citizen groups. Proponents of extractive industries argue that these projects are beneficial because they generate jobs and tax revenue. Opponents argue that these limited benefits fail to outweigh the harms of these same projects, and profits from these enterprises accrue not to the communities or nations that host them but to the corporations that own them. These groups call for alternative visions of economic development that will prioritize sustainability, environmental preservation, and social justice.

Some background about *development* can be helpful for understanding these debates. The idea that some nations are developed, others are developing, and still others are plagued by underdevelopment stems from presumptions about economic governance that emerged in the mid-twentieth century, when alliances and trade relations among nation-states were being realigned in the context of the Cold War. Liberal capitalism, which held sway in Western democracies, was predicated on the ideal of economic growth. The underlying assumption of the development model was that increases in supply – including raw materials and manufactured goods – would foster job creation and increase demand, generating greater economic prosperity overall. The drawbacks of this model were largely ignored, and development was promoted as something that Latin America and the Caribbean nations could access if their governments would commit to industrialization, deregulation, and the reduction of barriers to international capital and trade.

Many scholars argue that development policies and interventions, including neoliberal structural adjustment policies that restrict spending on social welfare to channel capital for growth, are a particularly pernicious form of neocolonialism (see the introduction to Section 8) that enables transnational corporations and foreign interests to exploit countries in the Global South for natural resources and labor. Among the predominant ways that development has been promoted in Latin America and the Caribbean are **extractivism** (projects that extract natural resources to sell on the global market), infrastructure (e.g., roads, telephone/internet systems, power grids), and anti-poverty initiatives. **Sustainability** is one measure that has emerged as a way to evaluate whether a program or project can last or what its long-term impacts might be. Questions arise as to the sustainability, for example, of communities living in areas that will be increasingly susceptible to severe weather events as climate change accelerates. Many Indigenous communities and organizations point out that Indigenous systems of knowledge and traditions of land stewardship offer promising models of sustainability that avoid the exploitation of the natural world.

The chapters in this section all address ways that communities in different parts of the region are experiencing, resisting, and negotiating the challenges associated with development projects, sustainability, and climate change in their communities. In Chapter 28, Gorenstein Rivera examines competing discourses about flooding risk and perceptions about government efforts to resettle residents from a riverside community. In Chapter 29, Banks explores how extractivist industries drive Indigenous communities from their ancestral territories, focusing on one community's efforts at directing the resettlement process to mitigate the negative impacts of leaving their land. And in Chapter 30, Morosin discusses the ways that Indigenous groups critique extractivism as antithetical to Indigenous understandings of the land.

KEY CONCEPTS

- **extractivism**: Projects that extract natural resources to sell on the global market.
- **sustainability**: An approach that prioritizes meeting the needs of current multi-species populations without compromising the well-being of future populations. This approach balances concerns about the environment and economic stability.

EXPLORE FURTHER

- Crewe, Emma, and Richard Axelby. 2013. *Anthropology and Development: Culture, Morality and Politics in a Globalised World.* Cambridge: Cambridge University Press.

- Eisenstadt, Todd A., and Karleen Jones West. 2019. *Who Speaks for Nature? Indigenous Movements, Public Opinion, and the Petro-State in Ecuador*. New York: Oxford University Press.
- Escobar, Arturo. 2011. *Encountering Development: The Making and Unmaking of the Third World*. Princeton, NJ: Princeton University Press.
- Henighan, Stephen, and Candace Johnson. 2018. *Human and Environmental Justice in Guatemala*. Toronto: University of Toronto Press.
- Vincent, Susan. 2012. *Dimensions of Development: History, Community, and Change in Allpachico, Peru*. Toronto: University of Toronto Press.

CHAPTER TWENTY-EIGHT

Conceptions of Risk and Resettlement in Belenino River Communities in Peru

Sharon Gorenstein Rivera

When he was 21 years old, Sergio left the *chacra* (farm) and moved to Pueblo Libre, a small Peruvian village located alongside the Itaya River and on the outskirts of the city of Iquitos in the district of Belén. Now 76, Sergio lives with his wife, Sara, his two daughters, and his son-in-law in a spacious, two-level wood stilt house common among Beleninos (residents of Belén). The houses in Belén have wood and palm frond roofs, which result in a woody almost moldy smell when mixed with hot air. While rustic, these households usually have electric and water systems. For many months of the year, wood board bridges function as aerial sidewalks through the neighborhoods. Canoes transit under the houses, children play in the polluted water, and turkey buzzards fly in circles overhead (Figure 28.1). As a result of the many drains that flow into the Itaya River, the waste in the water includes syringes from the medical center and fecal matter. Although there hasn't been an epidemiological study in Belén, studies in similar river-side communities have highlighted the degree to which this kind of contamination impacts health (Nkwocha and Pat-Mbano 2010; Medeiros et al. 2007).

Belén exists on the outskirts of the isolated city of Iquitos, an exclusively fluvial city, which means that the only way to get there is by plane or river. The main features of this city are the fast-flowing rivers of the Amazon basin, tropical humid weather, and poor soil for agriculture and livestock. Over time, subtle changes in the river's water levels and its path of flow threaten the stability of the land (Nebel, Dragsted, and Vega 2001). Rainfall also shapes the social and urban structure of Belén. While the dry season (*bajial*) between July and August is characterized by less precipitation (200 mL/m^2), during the *tahuampa* between January and March, the rainfall can exceed 1,000 mL/m^2, varying the level of the rivers by 25 meters and flooding the riverbanks for hundreds of kilometers (Nebel, Dragsted, and Vega 2001). While fluctuations between heavy rains, flooding, and drought have been common in Peru since the nineteenth century due to the El Niño Southern Oscillation (ENSO) effect, climate change has increased

Figure 28.1. *La Vida en Creciente en Belén* **(Growing Life in Belén).** Photo by Juanjo Fernández.

"the number and recurrence of extreme flood events" in Belén (Chávez Esalva 2021, 154). However, rainfall variation also creates a diversity of geographic spaces and a regenerative cycle for flora and fauna that, and from the Beleninos' perspective, is not "flooding" but the natural ebb and flow of the river. And in fact, my research participants never raised climate change, or increased flooding, as an issue themselves.

During the rainy season, Beleninos add levels to their homes to escape rising water. In this way, people are changing the physical configurations of their housing systems to adapt to the variations in the river levels and flooding. To avoid flooding on the first floor, Sergio and his family live on the second floor of their house. In adaptation to the mixed environment of streets and water, the main means of transportation that Beleninos use are *peque peques* (canoes) and *motocars* (motorcycles with extra seats in the back).

While walking me through his home, Sergio tells me how proud he is because he built it himself and can provide shelter for his family. He ruminates about the time when he first arrived in Belén, when the district was almost empty, and he tells me how he started to organize with other neighbors to build a community. Sergio reiterates that he likes living in Belén, even though he recognizes that there are problems with urban violence and pollution. Making up part of the urban area of Iquitos, the district of Belén has 68,806 inhabitants (INEI 2008) distributed over 56 *caseríos* (small villages) and 19 neighborhoods. The port of Belén is the principal site for trade in Iquitos; it is also the area with the highest rate of crime in the region. In these ways, Belén is the most extreme example of the region's poor standing in terms of health, education, and violence (ENDES 2013).

Sergio has two jobs: During the summer months he works in agriculture, while during the period of higher rainfall between January and March he works as a fisherman. He is proud of his jobs because they have allowed him and Sara to raise their children. He believes that living in Belén allows him to survive because there is always work available. When we talk about the government project to resettle residents of Belén further away from the river to dry land as a strategy to ostensibly save them from flooding, he passionately asks me, "How am I going to survive in Varillalito? You cannot harvest that land. You cannot fish. How am I going to live in a house that looks like a tiny drawer? That house is for a couple, not for a family. Here we can have a concrete house."

Sergio and other Beleninos have structured their lives around the river, with its ebbs and flows; the flooding of the river has become a part of their daily lives. However, Peruvian government officials argue that the river is a threat and that they have a responsibility to resettle the residents of Belén in areas where there is less risk of flooding. **Conceptions of risk** are ideas and beliefs about exposure to danger and what makes something dangerous. Conceptions of risk are not always rational or quantifiable because risk constitutes a feeling or a belief that is embedded in daily routines and the processes that structure people's thinking. Importantly, risk manifests as social constructs with real effects; it is based on systems of meaning that emerge from culture, developed through social interactions, and produced through claims-making activities.

Resettlement involves a movement of a large group of people from one region to another and is often a form of obligatory migration that is imposed by state policy or international authority. Often the affected population is transferred by force to a distant region, perhaps not suited to their way of life, causing them substantial harm. This transfer may be motivated by a more powerful party's desire to make other uses of the land in question or, less often, by disastrous environmental or economic conditions that require relocation. In the case of Belén, the government's resettlement project used notions of sustainable development – efforts to transform and improve populations for the greater good – as a risk reduction strategy to not only create new perceptions of risk regarding the river but also to enable a new way of life to come into being by rejecting and stigmatizing the old one, labeling it as undeveloped and risky.

In this chapter I examine these competing conceptions of risk and explore the ways Beleninos challenge government discourses of risk and plans for resettling their community. First, I describe my research methods and experience with conducting participant observation in Belén. Then I discuss the ways that divergent conceptions of risk between members of the Belenino river communities and government officials conflicted with one another and informed Beleninos' perspectives on the resettlement project.

THE EXPERIENCE OF HANGING OUT IN BELÉN

This chapter is based on 10 months of ethnographic fieldwork in the subdistrict of Bajo Belén (referred to simply as "Belén" throughout the chapter), specifically in the communities immediately adjacent to the port and the market. These were precisely the neighborhoods included in the resettlement project. The Beleninos that shared their lives with me were generally poor, had received no more than primary school education, and were native Spanish speakers.

The experience of hanging out in Belén – what ethnographers refer to as *participant observation* – was indispensable to my research. Washing clothes and dishes and bathing (partially clothed) in the Itaya River with the women of the community, I saw multiple variations of the daily activities that occurred in all the households. I also experienced first-hand how these activities varied seasonally in relation to the volume of rainfall. The familiarity and bonding created by my participation in the everyday lives of the inhabitants of Belén and ex-Beleninos allowed me to get close in a minimally intrusive way to observe and understand their lives. During my fieldwork, in addition to countless informal conversations, I conducted 54 formal, in-depth interviews in Spanish with residents of Belén, former residents of Belén that now live in the resettlement area, public employees working at institutions related to the resettlement project, and scholars from Iquitos that study the resettlement project.

SUSTAINABLE BELÉN AND THE RESETTLEMENT PLAN

In June 2013, the Ministry of Housing, Construction, and Sanitation (MVCS) and the District Municipality of Belén started a project titled "*Belén Sostenible*" ("Sustainable Belén"). The project sought to improve the quality of life for Belén's population. The stated goals were to respect the local cultural practices and maintain an environmental, ecological, and human balance (MVCS 2013). The plan to enact these goals included trying to maintain the riverine lifestyle of community members and their connection with the river, the market, and the *chacra*, as well as helping to build and maintain the aerial sidewalks and pillars that supported the houses. The use of the term *sustainable* in the project title reflected the program's goal of valuing local resources and knowledge, including the use of wood, palm leaves, and bamboo in architectural design; urban design elements that included renewable energies, such as recycling organic materials; and through the development of activities aimed at economic growth that were compatible with the climate, like fishing. Government officials also promised to install water pipes and a sewage system to prevent the river's pollution and address public health concerns related to its pollution.

However, the ideals and aims of Sustainable Belén were almost immediately counteracted in November 2014, when the government of Peru enacted a law (N°30291) declaring the communities of Belén "at risk" due to repeated flooding and ordering the emergency resettlement of Beleninos. According to the law, seasonal flooding made the Lower Belén Flood

Zone nearly uninhabitable (Chávez Esalva 2021; El Peruano 2014). Following this decree, in 2015, the MVCS financed the New City Belén project, an initial resettlement initiative aimed at giving the inhabitants of Belén safer living conditions in the neighborhood of Varillalito, where they would have potable water, sewage systems, electricity, and resources including a medical center, market, parks, police station, elementary schools, and high schools. When the relocation project started, 197 families signed the "giving-up document," surrendering their houses in Belén to obtain property titles in Varillalito. The relocation plan was framed as a strategy to "save" Beleninos from flooding. However, participation in the program was ultimately costly for families. The resettlement area was located at kilometer 12.6 of the Iquitos-Nauta Highway, one to two hours by bus from Belén.[1] The round-trip bus fare cost four soles (US$1.25), which was a significant amount of money for the average Belenino, who made around 20 soles per day and traveled with at least two children. Furthermore, according to Beleninos I interviewed, the methods employed to encourage participation in the program were sometimes coercive.

COMPETING PERSPECTIVES ON RESETTLEMENT, RISK, AND RISK PRODUCTION

In this case study of resettlement, Beleninos' and the government's understandings of risk and development often conflicted with one another. The narratives of both groups demonstrate a view of how risk management is perceived differently by different social groups. According to government officials, public servants, and development experts, a flooding hazard in Belén constituted the main problem and required a risk assessment policy. According to this perspective, the fluctuations of the river and the rain were variables that complicated the government's ability to give Beleninos the benefits of development initiatives like the Sustainable Belén project.

Thus, the relevant governmental agencies approached nature and the river with **governmental rationality**, also referred to as *governmentality*, which is a form of power in which those who govern regulate how people live their lives under the guise of improving the wealth, health, and well-being of populations, irrespective of the viewpoints of the populations themselves (Gordon 1991). For instance, in Peru, public servants argue that Belén is uninhabitable because seasonal flooding prevents the government from building concrete structures and installing drains and lighting. In their view, resettlement was a preferable risk reduction strategy than trying to improve the existing infrastructure of Belén to make it safer year round, even if Beleninos disagreed.

For many Beleninos, the river constituted a necessary resource for survival. For them, the changes in the river level were part of their everyday reality, their community and family

---

1 The resettlement project has been at a standstill since the end of 2019.

habits, their shared knowledge of living with and on the river, and their history. From their perspective, official perceptions of flooding misinterpreted the natural river fluctuations. These Beleninos recognized that the ecology of the Amazon region naturally cohabitates with water, and they viewed themselves as part of that ecology. Thus, the water was not only considered an inevitable part of Belén, it was viewed as a critical resource that was necessary to Beleninos' cultural practices and their survival. They relied on the river for washing clothes and dishes, cooking, fishing, and bathing.

The importance of the river was apparent to me when I interviewed Marta and Eduardo, two siblings in their fifties, on the boat they use to go fishing early in the morning to sell their catch in the market. Having lived in Belén their whole lives, this sister and brother had grown up with the fluctuations in the river. To them, living on the river did not constitute a risk. Marta explained:

> They enacted a law based on a study conducted by the Navy of Peru that says that this area will disappear; we have another report that says the contrary. Every year, there is flooding, but that is natural; that does not mean that we are in danger or at risk. The government should improve the quality of life of the population here, instead of wanting to get us out.

Eduardo agreed with Marta, stating "because of the *huaycos* [mudslides/landslides], that's why they have started talking about flooding. Here we have the *creciente* and *vaciante* [higher and lower precipitation of the rain, respectively]. Here there is no risk; the only thing we have to do is be careful." Marta and Eduardo did not trust the Navy's 2015 technical report (Dirección Nacional de Hidrografía y Navegación 2015). They knew that river fluctuations were difficult to predict but did not view high water levels as flooding. They argued that the ideas about the river that were codified in the 2015 report and in resettlement policies were those of outsiders who were unfamiliar with the river and the riverine way of life. Marta and Eduardo's assertions were confirmed by a naval authority who I interviewed in 2017. The official showed me the results of the second Navy study that the siblings had mentioned, which contradicted the account in the first report, which had been used in support of the emergency law for resettlement. This interviewee assured me that the official who signed the earlier report was probably confused about how the river worked. And he confirmed that while changes of the river course were not calculable, they were very gentle and did not have the characteristics of flooding.

While many Beleninos resisted resettlement, there were also local people who agreed with the resettlement project. For example, Edwin, who moved to Belén from the *chacra* when he was an adult to be close to his girlfriend's family, recognized both the government's and Beleninos' perspectives on the river and on the sustainability of Belén. He compared life in Belén to life outside of it. Edwin explained: "Don´t get me wrong, I am happy here, but I get the idea of the resettlement project. I can also sell food in Varillalito, but my in-laws want to stay here. I think it could be a good opportunity [moving to Varillalito]. I have never lived in a dry area, so maybe it is better. They [public servants] say it is better; they must know better, right?" Edwin had attended various talks about the benefits of moving to Varillalito and was convinced by the information provided during these sessions. His testimony illustrates his trust in the experts and his buy-in to the idea that the resettlement project would help secure the well-being of Beleninos (Gordon 1991, 38–9). Similarly, Pablo, a public servant who lived in Belén until adolescence, acknowledged both government and local perspectives:

> I get it, *Belén Sostenible* was not sustainable, but it doesn't mean that it is not possible. It was a political opportunity to think about new cities. The technical part of the project was very idealistic because the maintenance is too expensive. It is similar to the Varillalito project, it is not ok; it is not even finished … Ollanta [former Peruvian president] promised something to the Beleninos that he couldn't accomplish. But again, it is not true that you can't build houses on the water. There are many cities – look at Venice – that is why people call Belén the Peruvian Venice.

Pablo exemplified a case in which a public servant questioned the rationale of the resettlement project. Unlike other public servants, he justified the resettlement project in a different way. For him, the Beleninos' views of the river were not the problem, but rather the unaffordability of the Sustainable Belén project was the issue. This situation brought about a political opportunity to "give something" to the Beleninos that would accomplish a political promise that was unmet by Sustainable Belén. For Pablo, even though the Varillalito project was not a good solution, the idea and the rhetoric surrounding it were an understandable response to a real problem.

RESISTING RESETTLEMENT

Among all the people I spent time with, Sergio and his family were among the most committed to staying in Belén and resisting resettlement. One day while I was visiting the family, Sergio stood up from his chair and showed me the outboard motors for his boat, asking rhetorically, "[If I move] where am I going to keep my motors, and all my material for work? How much am I going to pay for someone to keep it for me, just to be able to go fishing?" He told me that many people who had been resettled in Varillalito already wanted to come back, but the Beleninos and the authorities had an agreement to not let any "traitors" return to Belén. Sergio reasoned: "They have betrayed their people, like a soldier can betray his homeland." With a mischievous look, he told me that he knew four neighbors who moved to the resettlement area but now wanted to come back because there are no work opportunities in Varillalito, and they did not like the atmosphere. Now animated, he exclaimed that in Belén, people needed only to grab their canoes and go to the market to earn 10 soles (US$3.15) and be able to eat. Touching on housing, Sergio insisted that in Varillalito, the houses for resettled families were poorly built, "Imagine with the rainfall! Those houses are going to cave in. They are built with sand, not with earth; those houses are going to fall!"

Sergio was convinced that the authorities in Iquitos wanted residents out of Belén because they wanted to develop the space for businesses, particularly for the tourism industry. He explained that Beleninos protested resettlement in part because the arguments for resettlement were full of inaccuracies: "People in the government say that this place is uninhabitable because of the flooding, and that it is not possible to build concrete structures. But here we have houses, churches, and high schools built with it [concrete]." He elaborated that while there were some communities that flooded, theirs did not. Furthermore, he argued, Beleninos had a plan for when rainfall levels changed. He concluded: "They [government officials] do not know the geography like we do." Sergio claims that the government tried to coerce Beleninos to resettle and that, in his perspective, they actually had a hidden agenda to take advantage of their space in Belén and develop it for tourism: "They [the government] want to build a *malecón* (pier) with shops and restaurants, all owned by them [government officials]. They think that Belén looks ugly, therefore they want to get rid of our houses to build something nicer for tourists."

In addition to their doubts about work and living conditions in the resettlement area and about the motives for the resettlement plan, Sergio and Sara conceived of risk differently from how it was being officially defined. Whereas Sergio and Sara saw the fluctuations in the river as a resource, the Peruvian government saw flooding as a risk for the safety and security of the inhabitants of Belén. The Peruvian government proposed ideas about risk that delegitimized the Beleninos' views of their riverine home. According to Sergio, the government not only failed to inform residents about the real purposes of the resettlement project, but also used intimidation strategies to influence their decision making surrounding resettlement. For instance, some of the public servants in charge of the resettlement project in Belén purportedly threatened and intimidated Beleninos by telling them that "a navy truck was going to come to destroy their houses if they didn't want to leave." The justification for such tactics was that resettlement would save Beleninos from flooding. As this example illustrates, however, by applying a particular interpretation of "risk," the government's strategy to reduce risk manifested as an exercise of state power that aimed at regulating the lives of Beleninos. Following on the perceived failure of the Sustainable Belén project to improve the living conditions of Beleninos, government agencies designed the relocation project as a risk reduction policy. Simultaneously, the resettlement plan aimed to generate and maintain a sense of legitimacy for the relevant political actors in the eyes of the public (Marlor 2010). All of this was predicated on the assumption that Beleninos "didn't know how to live." Instead of leveraging local knowledge about living in this riverine environment as the basis for public policies, the resettlement policies delegitimized Beleninos worldview of the river and reframed it as a risk rather than a resource.

When I asked how the community had responded to pressures to relocate, Sergio recounted how "one day, the head of the Ministry of Housing, Construction, and Sanitation came, and we all took out our whistles and started to make noise. All the neighbors went outside their houses, and we saw that the MVCS wanted to have a meeting to advertise Varillalito. We closed off their path, and we prevented the meeting. The police came and told them that it was not a good idea to come into the district unannounced, that Beleninos have an internal law, and that they need to talk with the community leader in advance." Rosa interjected, adding that Beleninos were very peaceful, but they had their limits, and that the people would rise up against the MVCS because Belén was their home. Sergio elaborated: "I am committed to this town; it is painful to see people leave. I will fight until death. I owe this community, and they owe me as well. I will fight for my people, and I will only leave this place if I am dead. There are laws here that we can use to defend ourselves, I have studied those. I sowed the land here and I am still here; all my kids grew up here. I will defend myself and all the people who want to fight for this town." With no more to say and tears in his eyes, he gazed out at his surroundings – stilt homes with palm frond roofs, children playing while women washed their family's clothes in the river, people coming and going to the market using the aerial sidewalks through the neighborhood, and canoes navigating the waterways.

CONCLUSION

Peruvian government officials' justification for the resettlement project has centered on Beleninos' inability to live on the river, which Beleninos argue isn't the case – they depend on the river to live. Thus, government officials and Beleninos have different notions of development and of risk. Government agents see Belén as an underdeveloped, polluted, and dangerous place without access to potable water and drains, which are public health concerns. Beleninos agree that these are areas of concern; from their perspective, some of the features of their surroundings, like water pollution, are indeed risky. However, they argue that the government should be responsible for improving the conditions that they deem "underdeveloped" rather than resettle community members. The government's approach to development, however, prioritizes experts' perceptions of what is best for the health and wealth of Beleninos, disregarding the ways in which Beleninos see fishing, the local market, farming, social networks, and rainfall as resources. For Beleninos, projects that propose to help them make the most of their local knowledge and these resources, like the defunct Sustainable Belén initiative, were a more sustainable form of development than resettlement initiatives.

In this case, the resettlement project is a product of governmental rationality that exerted power to regulate how Beleninos live their lives, including breaking down enduring ways of life and attempting to construct new ones in the resettlement area. For government officials, the fluctuations of the river and the rainfall are variables that present an obstacle to the government's ability to develop the region. In their view, as a risk reduction and development strategy, resettlement is easier than investing in the existing community. In making decisions surrounding resettlement, the government officials forwarded conceptions of risk that framed river fluctuations as "flooding," delegitimizing Beleninos' differing conceptions of risk. The majority of Beleninos considered living on the river to be an essential resource for their socioeconomic welfare. For them, the nature that surrounded them, as well as the market, were crucial to their survival.

Resettlement as a risk reduction and development strategy was confusing to Beleninos. The Sustainable Belén project featured ideas for development that supported the local and cultural context of Beleninos and engaged with local resources and local knowledge, which Beleninos saw as a sustainable approach. This project considered the variation in the intensity of rainfall as a natural outcome of the El Niño effect, which had impacted the region for generations. Then suddenly, when government officials realized that the project was not economically feasible, it changed its narrative and reframed Belén as a site that was as "undeveloped," (Li 1999), "at risk," and in need of governmental intervention. They advocated for resettlement rather than investment in meeting the needs of the community in Belén. This abrupt change in their policy demonstrates how the constructions of risk are not neutral. Rather, they emerge within a power structure that does not equally consider competing meanings of risk among those who are positioned as experts and those who are framed as nonexperts. Perceptions of expertise also played a role in some Beleninos' decisions to resettle in Varillalito under the assumption that the government "knows better" (Scott 1998). However, other Beleninos continued to defend their view of the river, notions of their socioeconomic welfare, sense of Belenino identity, and trust in local knowledge. In their view, the river was a resource for their survival and the government's perspective was that of an uninformed outsider.

This chapter illustrates the importance of risk as a concept that is constructed reflexively, in constant tension across diverse worldviews and cultures. However, it also underscores the variable of power that gives or takes away the legitimacy of differing definitions of risk. This approach to risk explains why after the failure of the Sustainable Belén project, most public servants, and even some Beleninos themselves, accepted the government's changing ideas about the river and conceptions of what would be best for Beleninos. They believed in the legitimacy of the government's new discourse about the risks of living on the river. Looking at risk as inherently political enriches our understanding of environmental management regarding climate change and disasters and the role power plays in deciding who is at risk and what should be done to manage that risk.

REFLECTION AND DISCUSSION QUESTIONS

- How do Beleninos' and state representatives' understandings of the river and risk differ? How do these differences affect the resettlement project?
- Why is it relevant to investigate the complexity surrounding the government's and Beleninos' notions of risk?
- Why do some public servants consider river communities to be "undeveloped"?

KEY CONCEPTS

- **conceptions of risk**: Ideas and beliefs about exposure to danger and what makes something dangerous.
- **governmental rationality/governmentality**: A form of power that aims to regulate how people live their lives under the guise of increasing their wealth, health, and well-being.
- **resettlement**: The movement of a large group of people from one region to another, often a form of forced migration imposed by state policy or international authority.

EXPLORE FURTHER

- To learn more about alternative approaches to resettlement, read **Chapter 29**.
- To learn about another community living in the Amazon region, read **Chapter 32**.
- Gorenstein, Sharon. 2021. "Lessons Learned from River Communities in Peru." *Contexts* 20 (2): 54–9.

ABOUT THE AUTHOR

Sharon Gorenstein Rivera is an adjunct professor in the Department of Social and Political Sciences at the Universidad del Pacífico in Lima, Peru. Her research focuses on marginality and deviance, gender and sexuality, political ethnography, and institutional and interpersonal violence in Latin America. As a cisgender Peruvian Latina Jewish woman, she is committed to using standpoint theory and intersectionality to address gender, class, and race inequity in her personal life and through both research and teaching.

REFERENCES

Chávez Eslava, Angel Wilson. 2021. "Resistance and Resilience of the Community of Belén, Iquitos, Peru, to Resettlement." In *Rethinking Urban Risk and Resettlement in the Global South*, edited by Cassidy Johnson, Garima Jain, and Allan Lavell, 154–68. London: UCL Press.

Dirección Nacional de Hidrografía y Navegación. 2015. *Informe Técnico: Variación Del Rio Amazonas en relación al Río Itaya*. Loreto.

El Peruano. 2014. "Ley que Modifica la Ley 30291." https://busquedas.elperuano.pe/normaslegales/ley-que-modifica-la-ley-30291-ley-que-declara-en-emergencia-ley-no-31232-1965811-3.

ENDES (Instituto Nacional de Estadística e Informática). 2013. "Perú, Encuesta Demográfica y de Salud Familiar." https://proyectos.inei.gob.pe/endes/2012/Libro.pdf.

Gordon, Colin. 1991. "Governmental Rationality: An Introduction." In *The Foucault Effect: Studies in Governmentality*, edited by Graham Burchell, Colin Gordon, and Peter Miller, 1–52. Chicago: University of Chicago Press.

INEI (Instituto Nacional de Estadística e Informática). 2008. "Censos Nacionales 2007? XI de Población y VI de Vivienda." https://www.inei.gob.pe/media/MenuRecursivo/publicaciones_digitales/Est/Lib1136/libro.pdf.

Li, Tania Murray. 1999. "Compromising Power: Development, Culture, and Rule in Indonesia." *Cultural Anthropology* 14 (3): 295–322. https://doi.org/10.1525/can.1999.14.3.295.

Marlor, Chantelle. 2010. "Bureaucracy, Democracy and Exclusion: Why Indigenous Knowledge Holders Have a Hard Time Being Taken Seriously." *Qualitative Sociology* 33: 513–31. https://doi.org/10.1007/s11133-010-9168-7.

Medeiros, Jansen Fernandes, Victor Py-Daniel, Ulysses Carvalho Barbosa, and Emanuelle De Sousa Farias. 2007. "Epidemiological Studies of Mansonella Ozzardi (Nematoda, Onchocercidae) in Indigenous communities of Pauini Municipality, Amazonas, Brazil." *Acta Amazonica* 37: 241–6. https://doi.org/10.1590/S0044-59672007000200010.

MVCS (Ministerio de Vivienda, Construcción y Saneamiento). 2013. "¿Qué hacemos?" https://www.gob.pe/institucion/vivienda/institucional.

Nebel, Gustav, Jens Dragsted, and Angel Salazar Vega. 2001. "Litter Fall, Biomass and Net Primary Production in Flood Plain Forests in the Peruvian Amazon." *Forest Ecology and Management* 150 (1–2), 93–102. https://doi.org/10.1016/S0378-1127(00)00683-6.

Nkwocha, Edmund, and Edith Chinwe Pat-Mbano. 2010. "Effect of Gas Flaring on Buildings in the Oil Producing Rural Communities of River State, Nigeria." *African Research Review* 4 (2). https://doi.org/10.4314/afrrev.v4i2.58293.

Scott, James C. 1998. *Seeing Like a State.* New Haven, CT: Yale University Press.

CHAPTER TWENTY-NINE

Forced Displacement and Indigenous Resettlement Planning in Colombia's Coal Region

Emma Banks

The first time I traveled to Tamaquito II, I watched as the Toyota's driver carefully forded two rivers and navigated bumpy dirt roads. I arrived with a group of activists supporting Latin American communities impacted by multinational mining companies. When we arrived at the rural settlement, I heard bird calls from the forest and bleating from the goats grazing in the fields. I also observed the community's proximity to the fences surrounding the Cerrejón open-pit coal mine where daily explosions and the sound of heavy machinery interrupted the peaceful atmosphere.

We met 25 Indigenous families living in a rural settlement. They told us that after years of internal debate, they had decided to leave their ancestral home and rebuild elsewhere. Community elders described the sense of freedom they had before the mine arrived; they hunted in the foothills, fished in the river, and grazed their animals in the pasture lands. Now they had lost their hunting lands to deforestation, the river was contaminated, and their animals disappeared behind the mine's fences. The elder generation knew they had to move to give their grandchildren a better life but felt uncertain about the future. Would future generations know how to grow their own food or hunt? Would they learn the Wayuunaiki language?

At the end of the meeting, the community treated us to a performance. A group of girls danced barefoot in an arena, donning brightly colored gowns. Men accompanied them on percussion and woodwind instruments. Women brought out woven bags to sell. As we left the community, I thought of the elders' worries that future generations would no longer learn these traditions because the community would no longer be connected to their **territory**. For Indigenous peoples, territory signifies an ancestral attachment to the land, which connects them to their history and culture. Being displaced from their territory would sever the connection Tamaquito II had to their spiritual and cultural sites.

Figure 29.1. Jairo Fuentes, leader of Tamaquito II, prepares boys from the community to take part in the Wayúu version of *lucha libre* during the community's Wayúu games in 2017. Photo by Emma Banks.

Tamaquito II is an Indigenous community in the Guajira region of Colombia. From 1945 to 2013, the community lay in a valley with access to forests, rivers, and farmland that provided subsistence livelihoods. In the 1990s, the tranquility that Tamaquito II residents enjoyed in their territory was threatened as coal-mining companies moved into the same zone. After decades of living next to an open-pit coal mine, the community opted to resettle in 2013. This chapter focuses on how Tamaquito II indigenized their resettlement process. **Indigenization** is the process by which Indigenous groups transform dominant models of development into programs that complement their culture, traditions, and organizations. Resettlement entails a community having to leave their ancestral land and rebuild in a new site (see also Chapter 28). The Cerrejón Coal Company was responsible for Tamaquito II's displacement from their old site, so it funded the construction of the resettlement site and the programs to help the community transition to a new life. In most resettlement negotiations, trained experts make top-down plans and communities have little say in the resettlement planning process. By indigenizing the process, Tamaquito II created a community definition of sustainable development and a community-led resettlement plan.

I began working with Tamaquito II residents in 2013 as a graduate student and solidarity activist. Between 2013 and 2022, I conducted 21 months of ethnographic fieldwork with communities in the Guajira region, interviewing residents, participating in community events, and traveling with activists. I attended weekly resettlement negotiations between Tamaquito II and the coal company as an international observer. Over the last nine years, I have observed the many challenges they have endured to rebuild their community in a new place.

The United Nations estimates some 70 million people are displaced by conflict, climate, disaster, and development every year (UNHCR 2019). Displacement caused by extractive development projects receives little attention compared to other forms of displacement, but it is a major driver of social inequalities in Latin America. Extractive development projects create **sacrifice zones**: ecologically damaged areas where vulnerable people are forced to give up their way of life for others to profit (Lerner 2012). Foreign-owned corporations forced Tamaquito II to sacrifice their territory so they could make millions from coal. The impacts of climate change make sacrifice zones more precarious. Over the last few decades, climate change has led to extreme droughts in La Guajira, which have made rural livelihoods harder to sustain and threaten to cause future displacements from rural areas (Unidad de Planeación Minero Energética 2015). Communities like Tamaquito II are made vulnerable both by coal mining and the climate change caused by coal, yet they do not see the revenues from coal mining, nor do they consume coal power. All La Guajira's coal is shipped to foreign markets, mostly in Europe and North America. Coal-fired power plants account for 40 per cent of global carbon dioxide emissions (Jakob et al. 2020, 704).

This chapter narrates Tamaquito II's displacement and resettlement process. First, I offer a brief introduction to the Wayúu people. Next, I explore the history of coal mining in the region and use interviews to show why Tamaquito II chose to resettle. Next, I will discuss Tamaquito II's use of Indigenous consultation methods that allowed residents to turn a top-down process into a community-first approach. I then show how the community implemented a plan to reclaim their culture, traditions, and territory. I conclude by reflecting on community-defined sustainable development.

DISPLACEMENT AND RESETTLEMENT

Tamaquito II is one of hundreds of Wayúu communities that occupy the Guajira region, the most northeastern part of Colombia (see Chapter 8). Wayúu people have long prided themselves on their autonomy, referring to themselves as an "unconquered" Indigenous group. By selectively adapting European tools of war, mainly guns and horses, the Wayúu maintained economic and political power during the colonial era (Polo Acuña 2005). Unlike most Indigenous peoples who faced the erasure of their culture and genocide at the hands of the Spanish military, the Wayúu remained the dominant ethnic group in La Guajira throughout Spain's reign.

In the 1920s, land conflict, drought, and poor economic conditions drove Wayúu clans from the northern peninsula to the fertile valleys of the southern Guajira (De la Pedraja 1981). Tamaquito II was founded in 1945, at the peak of this land conflict and environmental degradation. In the fertile valleys, people in Tamaquito II sustained themselves through hunting, fishing, agriculture, and herding. Residents' lives dramatically changed when coal mines began to encroach on their territory and displace their neighbors in the 1990s.

ARRIVAL OF COAL-MINING COMPANIES

Coal-mining companies began prospecting in La Guajira in the late 1970s and started operating the Cerrejón concession in 1984 as a joint operation between the Colombian state and Exxon (Carbones de Cerrejón Ltd. 2010). This collaboration reflected mid-twentieth-century policies in which the Colombian government maintained partial control over oil, gas, and mining projects to guarantee state profits. Between 2000 and 2001, the multinational mining companies BHP Billiton, Glencore, and Anglo American acquired the Cerrejón concession. The privatization of the concession was part of neoliberal reforms in the 1990s and 2000s that decreased state control and regulation of industry. Today, Cerrejón is one of the biggest open-pit coal mines in the world and the largest of its kind in Colombia, occupying 69,000 hectares of land and exporting over 30 million metric tons of coal per year (Carbones de Cerrejón Ltd. 2018). As of 2022, Glencore is the sole shareholder.

Prior to resettlement, Tamaquito II's territory was located near a river, their main water source, and nestled in the foothills of the Serranía de Perijá mountain range, which provided residents with land at different elevations to grow crops such as citrus, bananas, coffee, tubers, corn, and beans. Residents also relied on their ancestral knowledge to gather wild plants, including *guáimaro*, a highly nutritious fruit. They also used the communal land to graze their sheep and goat herds. When the coal mine expanded in the late 1990s, the residents of Tamaquito II lost access to forest resources and grazing lands.

Residents of Tamaquito II were keen observers of the natural world because their livelihoods, spirituality, and culture were all connected to their territory. At one community gathering, I learned about the importance of diverse animal species. As elders called out names, a young man from the community was diligently writing a list of the animals the community had lost because of their displacement: iguana, rabbit, jaguar, *guara* (maned wolf), monkey, fox, puma, *tigrillo* (a wild cat like a puma), and capybara. I was seated beside Doña Rosita, one of the community elders. As I was copying down the list, she whispered in Wayuunaiki (of which

I only ever learned a few basic words) the names of some of the missing animals, then she tried to explain to me what they were in Spanish so that I would understand. In Tamaquito II's original location, people hunted animals for food and to keep them away from their livestock. The presence of those animals was also an important indicator of the health of their ecosystem; when animal populations began to decline, the community knew there was an ecological threat in their territory.

In an interview, Jairo Fuentes Epiayu, the young leader of Tamaquito II, described how observing his community's changing way of life led him to activism. He joined the community's council as a teenager and became the *cabildo* (the elected leader of the council) in his early twenties. He described how in 2001 the people of Tamaquito II were shocked when the mining company violently displaced Tabaco, a neighboring Afro-descendant community:

> When the displacement of the community of Tabaco happened, that was one of the biggest impacts on the community. We sold things to the town, we exchanged products, and there was a lot of commerce and an abundance of food. At that time, we were rich. We had pure water and lots of other resources.

People from Tamaquito II relied on Tabaco for access to public works: the school, the health center, and the post office. Tamaquito II had no school or health center of its own, and without Tabaco, families there were left cut off from these essential services. Families also lost income from trading and from laboring on Tabaco's large farms. Additionally, community members used to cross the Venezuelan border to find work on farms there, a common practice because Wayúu people are considered dual citizens and at the time Venezuela had a more robust economy. In the early 2000s, this became more dangerous due to the presence of both left-wing guerrillas and right-wing paramilitaries engaged in a turf war to control the smuggling of cheap consumer goods and subsidized gas from Venezuela. Jairo told me the story of a group of men who traveled to work on a farm just across the border but never came back. Despite their families filing multiple claims with the district attorney, their deaths were never investigated. Men stopped crossing the border for work, fearing they could be killed too. Without income, services, or land access, life in the community was hard. Not only were they living in a sacrifice zone, but they also faced violence from armed groups near their territory. Residents began to ask whether they should leave their territory and rebuild elsewhere.

AUTONOMOUS CONSULTATION

Tamaquito II families collectively made the decision to resettle through **autonomous consultation**, a process that empowers communities to make corporations and governments consult with them on their own terms. Autonomous consultation is an example of how Latin American communities have indigenized international laws. For decades, Indigenous groups across Latin America fought for the right to control development projects in their territories. In 1989, the International Labor Organization passed The Indigenous and Tribal People's Convention (ILO 169) in response to Indigenous activism. On the rights to consultation, Article 6.1.A. of the convention states that governments must "consult the peoples concerned, through appropriate procedures and in particular through their representative institutions, whenever consideration is being given to legislative or administrative measures which may affect them directly" (International Labor Organization 1989). Starting in the 1990s, the governments of Latin American countries began adopting consultation measures into their legal frameworks.

Consultation laws represented a compromise between Indigenous peoples' desires for autonomous control over their lands and governments' desires to attract foreign investment in natural resource extraction. While the latter position often dominated, these laws created a space for Indigenous communities to define consultation within their traditional organizations and decision-making methods. Rachel Sieder (2006) observed how Indigenous Guatemalans developed their own ways of carrying out consultations, determining that communities should have the autonomy to make decisions without the interference of governments or corporations. During autonomous consultation, the entire Indigenous community comes together to discuss their options and to look for consensus on all plans (Guariyú et al. 2015).

Through training with Yanama, a Wayúu-run organization that focuses on popular education by and for Indigenous people, the people of the Tamaquito II were introduced to autonomous consultation. In their use of this model, each adult in the community voted on every plan or decision. Sara Pushaina, a leader and educator from Tamaquito II, described autonomous consultation to me in an interview we conducted on her patio. She was dressed in a colorful hand-embroidered dress, beaded bracelets, and carrying a woven purse, all items she made using the handicraft skills she learned from her grandmother. She led a community artisans cooperative through which women in Tamaquito II sold bags, dresses, and jewelry. Sara had recently returned from earning a master's degree in ethnoeducation, a model that incorporates Indigenous language and culture into school curriculum. She described how autonomous consultation complements the Wayúu tradition of community dialogue:

> Whenever a difficulty or failure comes up, we hold an assembly with the community, in which each person gives their opinion, and they say if it's good or bad. It is autonomous, so they decide whether to accept it or not. Because if the company says no, then the community will not sign an agreement. There are no meetings with the company to vote because the community decides.

As Sara explained, while the community's relationship with the company was highly unequal, Tamaquito II was able to control their resettlement agreement by using autonomous consultation and refusing to allow the company to make all the decisions.

To bring these plans to fruition, Tamaquito II had to indigenize established law. Residents worked with a lawyer from the NGO Indepaz named Leonardo González. Leonardo helped the community frame their plans to align with the International Finance Corporation's (IFC) involuntary resettlement standards and Colombian constitutional law. Cerrejón shareholding companies had all adopted IFC standards into their policies, which meant the company had to comply with them. By working with Leonardo, community members created a bottom-up form of consultation while aligning their demands with the top-down IFC guidelines.

RESETTLEMENT COMPENSATION SCHEMES

IFC resettlement standards are built around the collective relocation of the community and individual compensation and indemnities for each nuclear family. The company carrying out the resettlement typically hires consultants who survey the community's land, housing, and income. From these surveys, they create an impact matrix: a calculation scheme that incorporates social, economic, and other harms of resettlement. They use the impact matrix to determine how to compensate each family's economic losses and to design infrastructure and livelihood replacements. This model is top down because resettlement experts determine impacts and compensation.

Rather than rely on a team of experts to decide what impacts the community would suffer and how to compensate residents, the people of Tamaquito II indigenized the impact matrix. In 2016, I attended a series of meetings between the community and Cerrejón officials in which the Tamaquito II negotiated the funding and design for a cooperative agricultural project. In one meeting, a young Wayúu man drew an impact matrix based on community input. He divided the matrix into four categories of losses: employment, hunting and fishing, agriculture, and *guáimaro* fruit trees. With input from the community, he calculated each loss to come up with a compensation sum to use as start-up funding for the macro project. These categories exceeded the simple "livelihood" and "income" categories of a typical impact matrix by accounting for complex losses they felt from leaving their territory, including the loss of spiritual sites, hunting grounds, fruit trees, and water sources.

By designing their impact matrix, they proved their right to collective rural resettlement that would honor their traditional livelihoods and culture. The other resettlements built by Cerrejón are located directly outside the town of Barrancas. Those communities have little access to land, and most residents now rely on outside income in the mine or in services that support the mine and its workers. For development planners, this outcome is considered a success because families have increased their access to wage work, but many residents lament the loss of rural livelihoods and their sense of community. Tamaquito II fought for their right to define their own development goals and to rebuild their territory.

THE STRUGGLE TO REBUILD TERRITORY

During autonomous consultation, Tamaquito II created a system for determining compensation that included both tangible and intangible harms done to the community, everything from loss of agricultural lands to loss of spiritual connection to the earth. Wayúu people develop an attachment to their territory over generations, which makes their land a cultural and spiritual place. In practice, making the resettlement site into a territory was challenging.

One day when I visited Doña Rosita to look at her handwoven bags and hammocks to purchase as Christmas gifts for friends and family back home, we chatted over cups of steaming sweet coffee. She showed me the hammock she and her husband shared in their bedroom. She explained that the hammock was cooler than a bed and it allowed her to connect to the earth, which helped her dream. But since resettling, she had trouble dreaming because she could not connect to her territory. Wayúu parents bury their babies' umbilical cords in the ground to connect them to that place. When a Wayúu person dies, they become an ancestor, so community cemeteries are important sites. Umbilical cords and cemeteries connect Wayúu people to the territory and allow them to dream. They interpret their dreams to provide spiritual guidance (Romero 2010).

The day I interviewed Eduardo Fuentes Epiayu (Jairo's brother), he was returning from a trip to the original Tamaquito II. He got up early and rode his motorcycle for two hours to get to the old site. He told me it was worth it to feel "at home again." I asked Eduardo about the difference in how he felt in the old territory versus the new. He replied: "We were in our place of origin, but we had to move, that's resettlement. It's hard for anyone. I've been here almost three years and it's been hard to adapt. It hasn't been easy, maybe it's easier for kids who are born here and can adapt to Mother Earth, but as an adult, it's difficult." I then asked how he felt when he went back, and he replied: "When I get there, I feel different because it's my territory, where my umbilical cord is buried. That territory is part of us because we visit it and take care of it." Eduardo reminded me that although Tamaquito II indigenized its resettlement plan, the community lost its sense of place by moving.

To make the new Tamaquito II feel like a territory the community began incorporating Wayúu teachings into the school. Cerrejón helped fund this program as part of the compensation agreement. The school implemented an ethnoeducation program to incorporate the Wayuunaiki language. When I interviewed Sara, she described the problem of Wayuunaiki disappearing, which had prompted her to study ethnoeducation:

> Of course, it's important because this generation must know at least a little about the culture, and so that they become leaders in this land. Sure, they must learn Spanish. [Ethnoeducation] helps them strengthen what they learn at home, in the community. Our language is our primordial base.

Sara pointed out that for Tamaquito II to retain its Indigenous identity in the long term, children had to be invested in the culture. Without this connection, Tamaquito II would just be a town, not a territory. As part of implementing a cultural education, Tamaquito II began hosting an annual Wayúu dance and games festival. The last time I attended the festival in 2018, I drank sweetened corn *chicha* (a traditional beverage) and enjoyed a plate of goat meat with yucca. The community had built three separate outdoor spaces. In the largest, girls performed their dances in their brightly colored gowns. In the other rings, boys and men competed in their version of *lucha libre* (wrestling) and rock tosses.

As part of their 2013 resettlement agreement, Tamaquito II created an impact and compensation category for spiritual payments. The community constructed a new cemetery and held a ceremony to bring spirits to the new site. In Wayúu tradition, families bury their dead twice. In the first burial, they bury the entire body. In the second ceremony held years later, the matriarch of the family unearths and cleans the bones to rebury them as part of returning the deceased to the territory. During the second funeral, extended family attends to reinforce clan relationships (Nájera Nájera and Lozano Santos 2010). Families in Tamaquito II all selected one loved one to be buried in a community ceremony in the new cemetery.

On the day of the ceremony, a cool breeze and clouds rolled over the mountains, promising afternoon rain. After four years of drought (exasperated by climate change), 2016 was a more promising year for rain. Residents were preparing to plant yucca, squash, beans, plantains, and melons. There was a renewed sense of hope as the spring rains quenched the parched earth, making the surrounding mountains green once again.

At the cemetery, each clan had exhumed the bones of one ancestor to reinter. Each matriarch of the family had a small casket or vessel with the bones in front of them. The women were dressed in white dresses; white symbolizes the movement of the deceased to the spirit world. They gathered around the coffins, crying as they remembered the loss of their loved ones as part of ritual mourning. In a matter of minutes, the sunny afternoon turned dark and storm clouds rolled in. We quickly took down our hammocks and gathered our bags as we were drenched by a torrential downpour. As we ran for cover, Eduardo commented that the weather was a blessing for the new cemetery: a sign of approval from the ancestors and *Wounmainkat* (Mother Earth).

CONCLUSION: BEYOND TAMAQUITO II

In December 2016, the community held an event to commemorate the closing of their resettlement agreement with the Cerrejón Coal Company. Gathered in the community pavilion, Jairo Fuentes stood up front dressed in a white cotton shirt with the name and symbols of eight Wayúu clans embroidered down each side. He opened the ceremony by first addressing his community in Wayuunaiki and then welcoming the guests in Spanish. He then offered advice to other communities:

> The most important thing for us has been unity, the one voice we have, the participation of everyone: wise elders, youth, women, and children who must all be part of our future to bring development and sustainability to the community in the long term. As a community, we defend our rights and the company defends its interests, we know that. The company has its politics, we have our autonomous politics.
>
> We have our rules: The principle of dialogue is the most important one. We must sit down and look at our principles and values to find agreement. Today we are closing the resettlement agreement so that we can be autonomous. This is my message for the other communities who are in the process: Before sitting down to negotiate you should establish principles of respect. I don't want you to think of Tamaquito as the only model, but instead, use us as an example of good dialogue.

Jairo was addressing other communities facing resettlement in the Cerrejón impact zone, but his words offer advice for communities across Latin America confronting displacement because of climate change and extractive development projects about how to define sustainable development on their terms. Governments and corporations are displacing vulnerable communities to make way for roads, dams, mines, and large-scale agriculture. This form of development creates sacrifice zones that force already vulnerable populations into precarious conditions.

Tamaquito II refused a top-down resettlement agreement that would have forced the residents to take up urban jobs, work for the mining company, or migrate to nearby cities for opportunities. Residents defined sustainable development as a collective endeavor that honors their desire to remain rural producers and to rebuild a territory with cultural meaning. The community still faces many challenges today, including the increased droughts brought on by climate change that threaten their rural livelihoods. Nonetheless, the community continues to adapt to climate challenges by consulting with NGOs and state programs to shift their agricultural production to drought-resistant crops. They recently launched a pilot program to grow traditional medicinal plants and are exploring ecotourism opportunities to guarantee their economic base. Their form of development strengthens the community's economy without overconsuming; although they are impacted by climate change, their low-carbon lifestyle contributes little to it.

Tamaquito II's success demonstrates that communities can indigenize international resettlement guidelines to define their own impact, compensation, and development goals. All communities slated for resettlement should be given the chance to design their own plans without pressure or scare tactics from companies or governments. Autonomous consultation is one path communities can take to achieve a more equitable outcome.

REFLECTION AND DISCUSSION QUESTIONS

- Why is territory important for Indigenous communities such as the Wayúu? How does resettlement threaten the relationship between Indigenous communities and their territory?
- What future challenges do you think Tamaquito II might face in building a sustainable community? How may climate change be an obstacle?
- Can you think of other cases where communities are struggling against a powerful corporation? How can autonomous consultation help them gain power?

KEY CONCEPTS

- **autonomous consultation**: A process through which Indigenous communities make decisions about their future on their own terms.
- **indigenization**: The process by which Indigenous groups transform dominant models of development into programs that complement their culture, traditions, and organizations.
- **sacrifice zones**: Areas with permanently damaged environments that harm local populations for the benefit of business interests.
- **territory**: Collective lands traditionally held by Indigenous peoples that have a cultural, social, and spiritual value.

EXPLORE FURTHER

- To learn more about challenges facing Wayúu communities in La Guajira, Colombia, because of armed conflict, read **Chapter 8**.
- To learn about Indigenous activism against mining, read **Chapter 30**.
- For an ethnographic case study on government rather than community-led resettlement, read **Chapter 28**.
- Banks, Emma. 2016. "'We Are Victims Too': Incorporating Communities Displaced by Natural Resource Extraction in Colombia's Post-Conflict Agenda." *NACLA*. August 31.
- Chomsky, Aviva, Garry M. Leech, and Steve Striffler. 2007. *The People Behind Colombian Coal: Mining, Multinationals and Human Rights*. Bogotá: Casa Editorial Pisando Callos.
- Oliver-Smith, Anthony. 2009. *Development & Dispossession: The Crisis of Forced Displacement and Resettlement*. Santa Fe, NM: School for Advanced Research Press.
- Schanze, Jens, dir. 2015. *La Buena Vida*.

ABOUT THE AUTHOR

Emma Banks is an assistant professor of international relations at Bucknell University. Her research focuses on how marginalized communities reinvent themselves to accommodate extractive capitalism. She is part of a network of solidarity activists that support Colombian movements for a just post-coal future.

REFERENCES

Carbones de Cerrejón Ltd. 2010. "Historia." *Cerrejón: Nuestra Empresa* (blog). http://www.cerrejon.com/site/nuestra-empresa/historia.aspx.

———.2018. "Carbón, Nuestro Producto." *Cerrejón: Nuestra Empresa* (blog). https://www.cerrejon.com/index.php/nuestra-operacion/nuestro-producto/.

De la Pedraja, René. 1981. "La Guajira en el Siglo XIX: Indígenas, Contrabando y Carbón." *Desarrollo y Sociedad* 6: 329–59. https://doi.org/10.13043/dys.6.5.

Guariyú, Luis Emiro, Martha Cecilia García Velandia, Mauricio Archila Neira, Sergio Coronado, Tatiana Cuenca, and Zohany Arboleda Mutis. 2015. *"Hasta Cuando Soñemos": Extractivismo e Interculturalidad en el Sur de La Guajira*. Bogotá: Centro de Investigación y Educación Popular.

International Labor Organization. 1989. *Convention C169 – Indigenous and Tribal Peoples Convention* (No. 169).

Jakob, Michael, Jan Christoph Steckel, Frank Jotzo, Benjamin K. Sovacool, Laura Cornelsen, Rohit Chandra, Ottmar Edenhofer, et al. 2020. "The Future of Coal in a Carbon-Constrained Climate." *Nature Climate Change* 10 (8): 704–7. https://doi.org/10.1038/s41558-020-0866-1.

Lerner, Steve. 2012. *Sacrifice Zones: The Front Lines of Toxic Chemical Exposure in the United States*. Cambridge, MA: MIT Press.

Nájera Nájera, Mildred, and Juanita Lozano Santos. 2010. "Curar la Carne para Conjurar la Muerte. Exhumación, Segundo Velorio y Segundo Entierro Entre los Wayúu: Rituales y Prácticas Sociales." *Boletín de Antropología* 23 (40): 11–31.

Polo Acuña, José. 2005. *Etnicidad, Conflicto Social y Cultura Fronteriza en La Guajira: 1700–1850*. Bogotá: Universidad de los Andes, Facultad de Ciencias Sociales-Ceso.

Romero, Fanny Longa. 2010. "Ajapüjawa (Dream Spirit) in the Wayúu Death and Vengeance Rituals." *Espaço Ameríndio* 4 (2): 117–46. https://doi.org/10.22456/1982-6524.17108.

Sieder, Rachel. 2006. "El Derecho Indígena y La Globalización Legal en la Posguerra Guatemalteca." *Alteridades* 16 (31): 23–37.

UNHCR. 2019. "Global Trends – Forced Displacement in 2018." *UNHCR Global Trends 2018*. https://www.unhcr.org/globaltrends2018/.

Unidad de Planeación Minero Energética (UPME). 2015. *Integración de las Energías Renovables no Convencionales en Colombia*. Bogotá: Unidad de Planeación Minero Energética.

CHAPTER THIRTY

"No a La Mina": Indigenous Organizations' Rejection of Toxic Mega-Mining in Mexico's Isthmus of Tehuantepec

Alessandro Morosin

In late October 2016, about 50 locals held a meeting in the ethnic *Ikoots* fishing community of San Francisco del Mar (*Pueblo Viejo*). The town with a population of 885 lies on an inlet between the Superior Lagoon and the Gulf of Tehuantepec on the coast of Oaxaca, Mexico. The audience wanted to be informed about mining and other projects in the region that would affect them and their children. Manuel Antonio Ruiz, coordinator of an Indigenous community school in nearby San Francisco Ixhuatán, had invited me to observe the meeting. We arrived at this remote town from Ixhuatán after riding for an hour in the back of a pickup truck. The meeting took place outdoors on the edge of a lagoon, under the shade of the fishing cooperative's concrete roof. Fishermen and their children (students of Manuel's) sat in blue plastic chairs facing the speakers. As hot winds blew loudly, Manuel convened the gathering with these words: "We live in difficult times. Defenders of their rivers and lands have been killed throughout our nation. The government is planning a Special Economic Zone on our lands. This will directly impact our lives, mostly in Indigenous areas."

At the same meeting, Marcelino Nolasco[1] spoke as a representative of Centro de Derecho Humanos-Tepeyac (Tepeyac Human Rights Center), a progressive nongovernmental organization based in Tehuantepec:

> National capitalists want to liberalize the Port of Salina Cruz for export, and international capitalists want the region's raw materials. Power companies are paying families 8 pesos per square meter of land to install power transmission lines. The number of wind turbines will

---

1 Marcelino died of COVID-19 on January 25, 2021. He was actively and passionately involved in Indigenous education, ecclesiastical base work, and the defense of territory in the Isthmus. For an homage, see EDUCA (2021).

Figure 30.1. Alejandro García Velázquez, a leading member of the Grupo Ecologista Zanatepec, holds up his organization's banner in the town plaza of Santo Domingo Zanatepec, Oaxaca at the *¡No a la minería, sí a la vida!* **(No to Mining, Yes to Life!) march of 3,000 people in Zanatepec on the anniversary of the Mexican Revolution (November 20, 2016).** Photo by Alessandro Morosin.

double. Then there's mining, the most damaging project of all. The local Ostuta River is in danger, since a dam is being proposed there in order to generate hydroelectricity for the mine in the highlands of Zanatepec, which would contaminate the people downstream.

Marcelino's sweeping analysis exposed some disturbing effects of megaprojects in the Isthmus and how new mining activity endangers communities in this region of Oaxaca. This chapter presents the results of ethnographic research with land defenders in Mexico's Isthmus of Tehuantepec, in the state of Oaxaca. This state is home to some of Mexico's greatest ethnic and linguistic diversity, as well as some of the nation's most impoverished municipalities (MPPN 2019). This region of southern Mexico is the site of what's now being called the Interoceanic Corridor, a megaproject that purports to attract more international capital and industries in the coming years. While some believe this massive government plan will bring development and progress, the Special Economic Zone is controversial in the Isthmus. Canadian mining corporations are attempting to exploit gold and silver near the lands where my research participants reside. Those who are in a position to reap the largest profits from gold mining are national and international owners of financial capital (Bárcenas and Galicia 2011).

The land defender organizations I discuss in this chapter oppose open-pit mining for social and ecological reasons. Around the world and in Mexico, gold mining has contaminated drinking water, land, and air with cyanide and mercury, making it one of the most environmentally damaging industries. The expansion of open-pit mining is one of the many trends today that threatens to disconnect Indigenous peoples from their traditional territories and fundamentally alter their ways of life. It depends on vast quantities of water being diverted from local sources. The industry also reinforces the racist, neocolonial ways in which the political elites of Latin America have excluded poor, rural, and Indigenous people from consideration. In this chapter, I discuss this problem in terms of Oaxaca's existing rural and Indigenous activism, while highlighting what Isthmus activists are doing to prevent mining and protect Indigenous ways of life. Just as the global climate emergency disproportionately endangers the more impoverished sections of societies in the Global South, many of the Indigenous/*campesino* (peasant) activists I interview are aware of how climate change has already been impacting their lives, particularly through rising temperatures and drought that threaten to desertify Oaxaca's most productive lands. In this way, the open-pit mining industry's links to crop failures and deforestation will make Oaxaca even more vulnerable to climate change.

Various scholars view extractivism (*extractivismo*) as an economic development model pushed by wealthy imperialist nations that exploits Latin America's raw materials, including resources like minerals and oil (e.g., Gudynas 2009). Many social movement activists in Oaxaca see Indigenous cosmovisions as a more sustainable alternative to extractivism. The term **Indigenous cosmovisions** represents the worldviews and values of pre-Hispanic peoples in Latin America and their understanding of their place within the universe. One of these worldviews, referred to in contemporary years as *comunalidad*, is an ethnic Zapotec idea based on mutual aid, territorial sovereignty, and respect for the natural environment. *Comunalidad* has been called an "Indigenous analytical theory" and a "neo-indigenist current" (Acosta 2014, 15). According to this perspective, communities are bonded by their awareness of a common language, territory, and collective identity (Martínez Luna 2010). *Comunalidad* and other Indigenous cosmovisions promote renovation and conservation of natural resources. By contrast, the short-term, growth-oriented, individualistic worldview and relations of capitalism tend to treat "nature" as something external and separate from human societies, to be used and exploited with little restraint.

In the years since the 1994 Zapatista (EZLN) uprising, various Zapotec intellectuals of the Tehuantepec Isthmus have adopted Indigenous cosmovisions to frame their environmental justice movements (e.g., Manzo 2011). Anti-mine networks see themselves as fighting for the defense of Life (*la vida*) in reciprocal unity with other communities and peoples in Latin America. To illustrate this, I center the voices of several groups who have been organizing against mining in three of the towns where I carried out ethnographic fieldwork in 2016 and 2017.

OVERVIEW: MEXICO'S MINING SECTOR AND INDIGENOUS RESISTANCE

The lives, health, and cultures of many rural and Indigenous communities who reside near mines are being threatened in the name of development and modernization. To Mexican scholar Nemer Narchi, these mining projects exemplify a form of **environmental violence**: They threaten people's livelihoods and cultures by "appropriating, transforming, and destroying natural resources" (Narchi 2015, 9). Environmental violence may result from negligence and poor planning, but it may also take the form of conscious aggression against people who challenge extractive policies and industries. In Mexico, environmental activism is particularly deadly: Mexico's environmentalists and land defenders are killed at the highest rate in Latin America, with an increase of 67 per cent from 2019 to 2020 (Global Witness 2021).

Despite such daunting risks and challenges, collective struggles in the name of life, livelihoods, and nature continue to proliferate throughout Mexico. The renowned Mexican ethnoecologist Victor Toledo has been calling attention to the ecological destruction of Mexico's natural resources by corporations, while championing Indigenous communities and social movements who are engaged in what he sees as "a final battle for Mother Earth" (see, e.g., Toledo et al. 2015). Another important writer, Darcy Tetreault, exposes the extent to which Canadian imperialism and large Canadian gold-mining companies dominate Mexico's mining sector (Tetreault 2016). These academic concepts have real meaning in the lives of people impacted by mining and other megaprojects. My research participants in Oaxaca name their situation as a **socio-environmental conflict**. This term refers to a dispute among social groups that combines *ecological issues* with concerns for the *material livelihoods* of marginalized people.

The arrival of large-scale mining projects throughout Mexico has brought many hardships, such as corruption, armed violence, and rivers contaminated with arsenic. At the same time, it has divided various communities between those who favor the mining industry and those who do not. Community members or local officials receive monetary bribes to allow mining companies access to the lands, while those who continue to publicly protest and oppose the mining companies must take measures to protect themselves from threats, intimidation, violence, kidnapping, and even murder. For example, upon beginning my work in the Isthmus of Tehuantepec, I was aware of how leaders of anti-mine movements in Oaxaca's Central Valley region had been killed and injured in paramilitary attacks (Matias 2016). The legality and legitimacy of these mining projects remains in dispute throughout swaths of Mexico (Bárcenas 2017).

Indigenous Peoples: Systematically Excluded, but Never Passive

Naturally, there are many class, political, and social differences among Indigenous Oaxacans. Nevertheless, whether they identify with Zapotec, Mixtec, Mixe, Zoque, or other ethnic groups, they do not wish to have their histories or their contemporary ways of life erased, either by the national government or by multinational corporations. The activism described in this chapter is overcoming divisions between ethnic groups as more of these diverse communities begin to perceive their common interests and concerns. In the Isthmus of Tehuantepec, anti-mine activists are organized into loose collaborative networks that include Catholic liberation theologists, human rights groups, environmental civil society organizations, small ranchers, Indigenous feminists, volunteer community radio operators, farmers, students, and teachers.

The people of the Isthmus of Tehuantepec have drawn on their own culture to create new sophisticated forms of environmental defense in response to mining companies. To a large degree, today's movements for "defense of land, life, and territory" in the Tehuantepec Isthmus are based on a history of mobilization against outside domination. Since the 1970s, the Zapotecs in this region have challenged inequality and fought for self-determination. In 1981, through the COCEI movement/party, the district of Juchitán was the first in Mexico to elect their own leaders to oppose what was then a dictatorship by the PRI (Institutional Revolutionary Party; Campbell 1993). More recently, the Isthmus became ground zero for an intense movement against massive wind energy parks that privatized the lands of Zapotec *campesinos* through various irregularities (e.g., Ávila-Calero 2017). Once they discovered that mining companies had been granted permits to explore for gold (Chaca 2018a), several communities were already prepared to mount a countercampaign. Because community members already belonged to activist networks who had experienced socio-environmental conflicts and were well informed about the problems of gold mining in Latin America, these communities were better placed to respond to mining corporations in their own backyard. These emerging collaborations between Indigenous groups attracted media attention while making "*No a Las Minas*" (No to Mines) a central platform (Chaca 2018b). Nevertheless, this work has been long and complex.

Indigenous cosmovisions have become increasingly focused and channeled in opposition to global capitalism as well as neoliberal Mexican government policies. Land defenders challenge the links between financial institutions, transnational companies, and Mexico's political authorities. In their strategies, demands, and forms of interrelating, these groups develop their own worldviews on how humans should relate sustainably with nature.

Data and Methods

The data for this chapter came from ethnographic fieldwork, principally in the towns of Ciudad Ixtepec, San Francisco Ixhuatán, and Santo Domingo Zanatepec. Between September 2016 and March 2017 I conducted 43 digitally recorded, semi-structured interviews in Spanish with a sample of 53 consenting adult participants in Oaxaca's anti-mine movements (32 men, 21 women). I selected this site and located these participants out of a desire to document their activism and explore how Indigenous values shape anti-mine mobilizations. The respondents requested to be named rather than remain anonymous. Therefore, I use the real names of places, people, and organizations instead of pseudonyms.

TESTIMONIES AND NARRATIVES FROM ANTI-MINE ACTIVISTS

Mines and anti-mine movements have become more prominent throughout Mexico, but large-scale metal mining is still a new proposal in the Isthmus of Tehuantepec. Here, Canadian-based mining corporations seem to be "playing a long game" to gain permission to mine for gold and other precious metals. Indigenous activists have been coordinating to prevent toxic open-pit mining before it can get started.

Santo Domingo Zanatepec is one of several mango-producing municipalities on the eastern side of the Isthmus. Roberto Gamboa is a local mango farmer with extensive experience in anti-mining and human rights work who has advised and shaped the local movement since its inception. Originally from Mexico City, he works within a national movement called REMA (the National Network of Mexicans Affected by Mining) that is connected to other anti-mine movements in Latin America. As we sat around his kitchen table in Zanatepec, Gamboa described mining as a threat to the lands of *campesinos*:

> Look, the minerals belong to the nation. They're administered by the government, which gives the mining companies a permit, right? But the mineral is underneath the ground. The owners of the territory are *comuneros* and *ejidatarios*. To extract this mineral, the companies need legal permission, so the government gives a contract so that the nation's property [the minerals] can be extracted. But the land is not property of the nation; it's property of *los pueblos* (rural/Indigenous communities). The government's goal is that social property in land gets privatized little by little …

Comuneros and *ejidatarios* in this municipality are farmers whose lands are part of the traditional Indigenous system of land tenure. According to the Mexican Constitution, these are *social* properties, which means they cannot be sold to foreigners.

While Gamboa's analysis centers more on agrarian issues and less on cultural/ethnic identities, other participants view the mining question as an ecological threat to all inhabitants of the region. Alejandro García Velázquez is a native of Zanatepec. He is a founder and director of the Grupo Ecologista Zanatepec, a local environmental group involved in anti-mine advocacy. He is known in the community as *Pescador* (fisherman). Alejandro shares his memories of how his nickname is tied to his childhood memories of the local Ostuta River:

> I was born on a ranch. Our origin is 100 per cent *campesino*, and we have a sentimental relation with nature. The river would flow 20 meters from the ranch. Every day, we would live off of nature. We would eat from the fields and the river. We created a dependency, a spiritual relation with nature. And later, with the passing of time, this made me observe that form of life and that nature, which I wasn't conscious of during my childhood. We learned that nature was being disturbed. It wasn't being looked after. My family was large. Every

day we depended on the land and the river. I personally feel a profound sense of veneration for the river because it fed me and my siblings. My nickname is *Pescador*. For me this is an honor because it suggests my contribution to the household. I would catch fish from the river and bring them home, daily, so that we could all eat. And when there was some left over, I would put it on a plate and sell whatever could be sold to the neighborhood. And so even when I later left the *pueblo* to study in Mexico City, I brought with me this sense that things in nature are being harmed.

When introducing me to the Grupo Ecologista Zanatepec, Alejandro described how the Ostuta River supported his family's livelihood. He joined the student movement in Mexico City in the early 1970s but returned to his *pueblo* of Zanatepec years later. Here, he carries on that same environmentalist ethic while being a publicly recognizable voice against the mining industry.

Ruben Valencia of Ciudad Ixtepec is a younger generation activist and an active participant of a coalition known as Comité Ixtepecano Vida Territorio. At a meeting in the lagoon communities of San Francisco del Mar, he tells the fishermen why he organizes against mine companies in his hometown:

> The ancient Zapotecs of Ixtepec always knew that gold existed in Ixtepec: 1.2 million ounces, according to a Mexican newspaper. Like cancer, it's best to attack this problem early, before mining can get underway. The company needs 26 permits, and only two of those require direct permission from community members. Strong winds would bring cyanide dust not only to Ixtepec but to other *pueblos*, so you should organize for your own good, not just to help us.

Ruben described the activism in Ixtepec he has participated in and framed mining as an issue of Indigenous sovereignty:

> Since February, we've done 35 film projections and gotten 5,000 signatures against the mine. When we in the Comité Ixtepecano located a landmark in the mountains that marked the mining company's property, we led a march of 100 people up there to destroy the landmark (*la mojonera*), and it was mainly the women who destroyed it. People don't recognize that we're Indigenous and we have rights. The national criteria for being Indigenous is not just language, it's also the food, the cultural elements, the communal assemblies of a people …

This illustrates how the town of Ixtepec (directly impacted by mining exploration) still maintains Indigenous customs – despite having become more urbanized and even though most residents no longer speak Zapotec. Ruben's example shows the extent to which a community can be mobilized to challenge a powerful mining corporation before the mine officially installs itself.

The fishermen at the meeting responded with many supportive comments and questions. A young man asked whether there would be any community benefit to working with the mining companies. Ruben was firm in reiterating that sustainable mining is an impossibility:

> The idea of sustainable development is exactly the kind of argument the companies use to gain support. Even if they could clean up the arsenic and cyanide, they would have to cut down all the forest just to open the mine. There has never been any experience of [sustainable development based on mining] in this country. Look at the Sonora River: The mining company never paid their fines for polluting the Sonora River with arsenic. We shouldn't fall for lies.

Ruben's sophisticated answer to the question is in line with environmental reality, since there are no examples of ethical large-scale gold mining. His concrete example was also important for inoculating the local population against corporate propaganda that is nowadays saturated with shallow "sustainability" rhetoric.

Subsequently, I attended a series of meetings convened by the Comité Ixtepecano in Ciudad Ixtepec in mid-November 2016. The city of Ixtepec (with a population of 10,000 inhabitants) is 12 miles north of Juchitán. One meeting engaged residents who depend on agriculture (e.g., corn, sorghum, sesame) and small-scale cattle ranching where lands are owned communally. About 40 adults congregated that evening into the offices of the COCEI's women's committee (*Ni Runni Binni*, in Zapotec). I took note of the assertive and enthusiastic participation of women in the discussion. As the Comité Ixtepecano screened documentary footage about a small community in Oaxaca's Central Valley region who stood up to Canadian subsidiary Plata Real who wanted the town's gold, the audience seemed to share in the inspiration and indignation. The Comité revealed that this same mining company had been trying to gain access to Ixtepec's land and minerals. Speakers pointed to how mining companies might further contribute to militarization throughout the Istmo.[2]

Another meeting in Ixtepec took place at the local *Sociedad Agricola* (Agrarian Society), which democratically regulates irrigation for Ixtepec's fields and ranches. The crowd of about 70 people, overwhelmingly older adults and about evenly split between men and women, listened to activists from Ixtepec speak about the proposed Lote Niza mining project, but also heard men from Salina Cruz, Tehuantepec, Juchitán, La Hollaga, and Zanatepec talk about mining projects and free trade projects. This meeting was an example of a regional movement being built, with solidarity between different localities. Charismatic speakers from across the

---

2 For a significant and critical assessment of the roots of "organized crime" and drug-related violence in contemporary Mexico, see Osuna (2021).

Isthmus recounted how the arrival of dams, illicit forestry, and oil refining over the past several decades have brought wealth to a relative few while impoverishing the natural resource base of the Isthmus (Lucio 2016). The consensus was that open-pit mining by Canadian transnationals would bring much worse consequences.

After the president of the Association of Ranchers (*Asociación Ganadera*) spoke, an elderly man gave his talk purely in Zapotec, then repeated it in Spanish. This man said he was a fisherman who worked in Salina Cruz years before the major PEMEX refinery had been built there:

> The government said that the oil refinery wouldn't affect us. But yes, it did – all the beaches in Salina Cruz are now poor and polluted.[3] It will be the same with the mine. It will affect you, *compañeros*! In Juchitán, for some fucking money, the people became divided and the wind parks came in. Our children will suffer this. It will affect you!

A coordinator of neighborhood committees (*coordinador de colonias*) from Salina Cruz then spoke about how the city he grew up in is now unrecognizable, but still impoverished. He ridiculed the government's notion that the jobs and investment from the refinery would turn Salina Cruz into a first world city:

> Just go to *la colonia petrolera* (the oil quarter) where the people live. They say that we are against progress. But where is the progress? What the refinery *did* do was kill the fishing industry and take the water. I know many communities nearby that still don't have electricity.

Marcelino of Centro de Derechos Humanos-Tepeyac noted, "The history of the Istmo is a history of dispossession, of failed infrastructure. But it's also a history of resistance." Activists' statements contrasted how infrastructure projects promised a better life but tended to leave the oppressive social relations and corrupt political structures intact – while environmental problems mounted. Activists who promoted "resistance" to protect land and territory want to recapture the cultural and political traditions of Indigenous peoples. At meetings like this one, they are beginning to envision a more democratic and anti-capitalist future for the Istmo, and even for Mexico as a whole.

Current Mexican president Lopez Obrador has been moving ahead on an ambitious agenda for Mexico's south and southeast. The main difference with previous neoliberal capitalist proposals for the Isthmus and Lopez Obrador's proposal is his insistence that this time the development will be *by and for* the region's Indigenous peoples. For this reason, community activists who oppose mining and the Interoceanic Corridor face an even more complicated task of reframing development on their own terms.

---

3 In fact, it was reported on October 24, 2022, that another oil spill by PEMEX (the national Mexican oil company) had polluted four beaches in Salina Cruz, which led to a suspension of fishing activity. For more, see Manzo (2022).

At the meeting, an Ixtepec man who identified with a local branch of the COCEI, Heriberto, stated that "Ixtepec is an Indigenous and *campesino* community. We have native corn. We will fight so that these companies don't pollute it." Isabel Nuñez, an older woman representing the Comité Ixtepecano, said that the only development she wanted is "one that's in accord with our lives and cultures." Over the course of my fieldwork, I would ask participants the question: "You're against the mines, but what kind of alternative is your movement *for*?" Respondents commonly answered, "We're for life itself" (*La vida*), by which they mean a specific set of social relations and interaction with nature that they can collectively decide. This answer, and the fervent oratory I would hear at meetings, exemplifies the *comunalidad* worldview that Istmo organizations are acting on as they enter into conflict with multiple forms of extractivism.

CONCLUSION: FUTURE IMPLICATIONS

Since many of the Istmo's people still viscerally identify with values of reciprocity, *comunalidad* has become part of a strategy that coheres various regions, social strata, ethnic groups, and types of activists into motion. These articulations of land defenders are advancing their vision for an Isthmus with diversity, autonomy, and dignity (Manzo 2021). Anti-mine actors in the towns of Ixtepec, Ixhuatán, and Zanatepec connect with civil society groups like REMA and the Tepeyac Human Rights Center to educate the population about the social and environmental implications of open-pit mining.

This example shows how Indigenous organizations resist mining companies, and how they refute the sustainability rhetoric from corporate *and* government forces that paints the mining industry as a net-benefit. While many other groups and community members tend to be co-opted into accepting bribes in exchange for inviting companies to use their land, genuine sustainable development declines to accept neoliberalism as an economic model and works for its abolition. The *comunalidad* idea, applied to socio-ecological movements, necessarily involves the direct participation of land defenders. It explicitly valorizes activist knowledge about the nation's laws and territory. Finally, it aims to form coalitions of trust and other forms of working relationships. It entails building unity within and among the impacted communities/towns, along with coalitions among national and international social movement organizations who play crucial roles in developing a community's capacity to declare itself "free of mining."

The same can be said for the kind of movement that is needed to prevent climate change from destroying life on the planet and nature as we know it: We need to rupture out of long-discredited but stubborn assumptions about the inevitability of profit-driven development – a way of life that exacerbates violence against people and nature. In its place, we must build global coalitions and organizations with the ability to defend rights and territory, while also planning and coordinating at multiple levels. In broad strokes, this approach has the potential to completely transform production, agriculture, transportation, and industry while decisively halting fossil fuel emissions. The movements described in this chapter can be viewed as initial, potential representatives of that very process of significant social change.

As of 2017, the Comité Ixtepecano was able to cancel the mining concession in the municipality of Ixtepec spanning 8,150 hectares in size. And Zanatepec is now officially a *Pueblo Libre de Minería* (Mining-Free Community) because multiple local administrations have publicly pledged to prevent any mining activity in the territory. But the problem is regional and structural. Zanatepec borders the mountainous municipality of San Miguel Chimalapa. There, the Canadian company Minaurum Gold is still exploring for gold in hopes of initiating gold mining in the 6,409 hectares of territory where it holds a concession until the year 2058. *Campesinos* and activists in Zanatepec, San Miguel, and other nearby communities are continuing to work to protect the rivers and land from exploitation, but there is still a long road ahead to protect the Isthmus. Indigenous organizations point out that such megaprojects are being justified as "solutions" to problems that the global capitalist system has created in the first place.

REFLECTION AND DISCUSSION QUESTIONS

- Why are Indigenous and rural communities in Mexico more likely to become sites for exploitative, extractive development?
- In your view, are there ways in which a non-Western worldview like *comunalidad* could be applied or adapted beyond the immediate context of Oaxaca, such as in urban areas or other countries?
- Look deeper into the role of mining corporations, especially in the lesser-developed nations of the Global South. Which additional key problems do you find? Which steps should be taken to plan economic development that benefits society as a whole while also respecting the health and autonomy of historically marginalized communities?

KEY CONCEPTS

- **comunalidad**: An Indigenous way of life among ethnic Zapotec groups in the Sierra Norte of Oaxaca, Mexico, that emphasizes reciprocity with nature and communal decision making by local assemblies.
- **environmental violence**: Any treatment of nature and landscapes that intentionally or unintentionally undermines the biophysical processes that provide humans or entire ecosystems with life support.
- **Indigenous cosmovisions**: Traditional worldviews by which Indigenous peoples conceptualize their place in the universe and their relations with nature.
- **socio-environmental conflicts**: Disputes and clashes over both the natural environment as well as the material livelihoods of people that depend directly on the natural

environment. Similar to the North American idea of *environmental justice*. Distinct from middle-class forms of environmentalism that de-emphasize poverty, such as conservation of natural resources for purely aesthetic reasons.

EXPLORE FURTHER

- To learn more about the effects of coal mining on Indigenous communities, read **Chapter 29**.
- To learn more about Indigenous activists in Mexico and the challenges they face, read **Chapters 11** and **23**.
- Comité Ixtepecano Vida y Territorio (Ixtepecan Life and Territory Committee). https://tinyurl.com/Comite-Ixtepecano.
- Mines and Communities (MAC). http://www.minesandcommunities.org.
- Red Mexicana de Afectados por la Minería (Mexican Network of People Affected by Mining, REMA). http://www.remamx.org.
- TeleSUR English. 2015. *Inside the Americas – Mining Company Ousted by Zapotec Community*. https://tinyurl.com/Inside-the-Americas.

ABOUT THE AUTHOR

Alessandro Morosin is a sociologist interested in global inequality, revolutionary change, environmental justice, and criminalization of social movements. He is an assistant professor of sociology and criminology at the University of La Verne. He is very grateful to the many contacts and friends in the Isthmus of Tehuantepec, and Mexico in general, who have shared their life experiences and political struggles with him.

REFERENCES

Acosta, Richards Alberto Monroy Acosta. 2014. "Wejën Kajën: La Comunalidad, Una Vision Contemporanea de Resistencia a Partir de los Modos de Vida de los Pueblos Indigenas." Master's thesis, National Autonomous University of Mexico.

Ávila-Calero, Sofia. 2017. "Contesting Energy Transitions: Wind Power and Conflicts in the Isthmus of Tehuantepec." *Journal of Political Ecology* 24 (1): 992–1012. https://doi.org/10.2458/v24i1.20979.

Bárcenas, Francisco L. 2017. *La Vida o el Mineral: Los Cuatro Ciclos del Despojo Minero en México*. Madrid: Akal Publishers.

Bárcenas, Francisco L., and Mayra M.E. Galicia. 2011. *El Mineral o la Vida: La Legislación Minera en México*. Mexico: Centro de Orientación y Asesoría a Pueblos Indígenas.

Campbell, Howard B., ed. 1993. *Zapotec Struggles: Histories, Politics, and Representations from Juchitán, Oaxaca*. Washington DC: Smithsonian Institution Press.

Chaca, Roselia. 2018a. "Mineras Siguen Scechando al Istmo; Sabitantes de la Sona se Sponen a su Ingreso." *El Universal Oaxaca*. https://oaxaca.eluniversal.com.mx/especiales/26-12-2018/mineras-siguen-acechando-al-istmo-habitantes-de-la-zona-se-oponen-su-ingreso.

———. 2018b. "En San Miguel Chimalapa Dicen No a Minera Canadiense." *El Universal Oaxaca*.
EDUCA. 2021. "Fallece Marcelino Nolasco Defensor del Territorio y Coordinador del CDH Tepeyac." https://www.educaoaxaca.org/fallece-marcelino-nolasco-defensor-del-territorio-y-coordinador-del-cdh-tepeyac.
Global Witness. 2021. "Last Line of Defense: The Industries Causing the Climate Crisis and Attacks against Land and Environmental Defenders." https://www.globalwitness.org/en/campaigns/environmental-activists/last-line-defence.
Gudynas, Eduardo. 2009. "Diez Tesis Urgentes Sobre el Nuevo Extractivismo." *Extractivismo, Política y Sociedad:* 187.
Lucio, Carlos. 2016. *Conflictos Socioambientales, Derechos Humanos y Movimiento Indígena en el Istmo de Tehuantepec*. Zacatecas: Universidad Autonoma de Zacatecas Press.
Maldonado Alvarado, Benjamin. 2010. "Comunidad, Comunalidad y Colonialismo en Oaxaca, México: La Nueva Educación Comunitaria y su Contexto." Ph.D. diss. Leiden, Netherlands: Leiden University.
Manzo, Carlos. 2011. Comunalidad, Resistencia Indígena y Neocolonialismo en el Istmo de Tehuantepec, Siglos XVI-XXI. Ce-Acatl.
Manzo, Diana. 2021. "'El Istmo que Queremos y Defendemos, No es para Megaproyectos' Recalcaron Pueblos y Colectivos Oaxaqueños." Istmo Press.
Manzo, Diana. 2022. "Pemex Contamina Playas del Istmo Oaxaqueños por Derrame de Combustible." EDUCA.
Martínez Luna, J. 2010. *Eso que Llaman Comunalidad*. Culturas Populares, CONACULTA, Secretaría de la Cultura-Gobierno de Oaxaca & Fundación Alfredo Harp Helú Oaxaca AC.
Matias, Pedro. 2016. "'Toman' Minera en San José del Progreso, Oaxaca: Exigen Salida de Empresa Canadiense." Proceso. https://www.proceso.com.mx/nacional/estados/2016/5/6/toman-minera-en-san-jose-del-progreso-oaxaca-exigen-salida-de-empresa-canadiense-163917.html.
MPPN (Multidimensional Poverty Peer Network). 2019. "How Has Poverty Reduction Been Achieved in Oaxaca, Mexico?" https://mppn.org/interview-oaxaca-mexico.
Narchi, Nemer E. 2015. "Environmental Violence in Mexico: A Conceptual Introduction." *Latin American Perspectives* 42 (5): 5–18. https://doi.org/10.1177/0094582X15579909.
Osuna, Steven. 2021. "Securing Manifest Destiny." *Journal of World-Systems Research* 27 (1): 12–34. https://doi.org/10.5195/jwsr.2021.1023.
Tetreault, Darcy. 2016. "Free-Market Mining in Mexico." *Critical Sociology* 42 (4–5): 643–59. https://doi.org/10.1177/0896920514540188.
Toledo, Víctor M., David Garrido, and Narciso Barrera-Bassols. 2015. "The Struggle for Life: Socio Environmental Conflicts in Mexico." *Latin American Perspectives* 42 (5): 133–47. https://doi.org/10.1177/0094582X15588104.

SECTION TEN

Tourism and Its Effects

Tourism plays a significant and sometimes critical role in sustaining economies of all scales in Latin America and the Caribbean. Among the nations with the largest tourism industries are Mexico and Costa Rica in North and Central America, Argentina and Brazil in South America, and the Dominican Republic, Cuba, Jamaica, the Bahamas, Aruba, and Barbados in the Caribbean. Because the nature of tourism is predicated on a financial exchange where local resources are commodified for the consumption of outsiders, research on tourism provides important insights about how globalization and intercultural encounters shape contemporary life, work, health, and leisure.

Tourism can vary widely and may cater to international, intraregional, or domestic visitors. Activities and settings also vary, ranging from beach vacations at massive corporate resorts to adventure or backpacker tourism, where travelers seek experiences that take them away from touristic centers in an effort to intimately engage with places and people. Ironically, these latter tourists often interact more with one another than with the residents of the places they visit. Yet even where there is little interpersonal connection made, tourism invariably impacts people and communities. Ethnographers point out that, wherever it emerges, tourism shapes work and subsistence, social relations, aesthetic judgments, health, and cultural reproduction.

The benefits, risks, and costs of tourism are often unequally distributed across groups that have a stake in the industry, and those with greater power and influence typically stand to gain more when competing interests are in tension. For example, while tourism can lead to job growth in hosting communities, the types of employment, working conditions, pay grades, and precarity of employment opportunities that fluctuate with tourism seasons dampen the positive economic impact tourism can have (see Chapter 25). These factors also vary depending on the type of tourism that is prevalent in a given place.

Some of the predominant forms of tourism in Latin America and the Caribbean include sex tourism, cultural ethnotourism, and ecotourism. **Sex tourism** is the term used to describe travel with the intent of engaging in sexual activity – often involving transactions of money or material resources. In these cases, ethical, public health, and human rights issues can emerge when these exchanges happen between individuals who have greater relative wealth and power and people who are poor, have few other outlets for making a living, or are otherwise marginalized, as well as when satisfaction of demand is met by means that violate the human rights of participants in the industry (e.g., sex trafficking or the exploitation of children).

Cultural **ethnotourism** – tourism focused on a society's material culture (e.g., music, dance, art, and religious/spiritual traditions) – can exacerbate the appropriation and commodification of cultural practices and beliefs, as well as people. For example, global interest in Amazonian shamanism, and in particular the use of hallucinogenic *ayahuasca* in shamanic rituals, has led to the emergence of neoshamans who promise tourists authentic ritual experiences, capitalizing on Indigenous traditions for personal economic gain.

Ecotourism – travel to areas of natural beauty or significance – runs the risk of environmental damage, as well as displacing people from their land as the tourism infrastructure of hotels, restaurants, roads, and travel agencies expands. Some argue that extending the conception of ecotourism to include conservation, environmental education, and ensuring benefits to local communities can help mitigate negative effects.

The chapters in this section explore ways that tourism industries impact health, Indigenous community well-being and self-determination, and cultural reproduction. In Chapter 31, Medeiros and Henriksen examine how occupational segregation in Brazil's ecotourism industry prevents Afro-descendant Brazilians from accessing the full socioeconomic benefits of ecotourism in their communities. In Chapter 32, Renkert explores the use of food traditions in an Amazonian community in Ecuador that engages in cultural ethnotourism as a means of Indigenous autonomy and cultural resilience. In Chapter 33, Krumrine compares the development of children living in a community where adults have transitioned from small-scale agriculture to paid work in the tourist industry versus those in a neighboring community that is not involved in tourism. Her results speak to the complex effects of the tourism economy on children's health, growth, and development.

KEY CONCEPTS

- **ecotourism**: Travel to areas of natural beauty or significance.
- **ethnotourism**: Tourism focused on a society's material culture (e.g., music, dance, art, and religious/spiritual traditions).
- **sex tourism**: Travel with the intent of engaging in sexual activity – often involving transactions of money or material resources.

EXPLORE FURTHER

- To learn more about challenges surrounding tourism in Latin America and the Caribbean, read **Chapters 4** and **25**.
- Cabezas, Amalia L. 2009. *Economies of Desire: Sex and Tourism in Cuba and the Dominican Republic*. Philadelphia: Temple University Press.
- Davidov, Veronica M. 2013. *Ecotourism and Cultural Production: An Anthropology of Indigenous Spaces in Ecuador*. New York: Palgrave Macmillan.
- Guelke, Karoline. 2021. *The Living Inca Town: Tourist Encounters in the Peruvian Andes*. Toronto: University of Toronto Press.

CHAPTER THIRTY-ONE

Structural Racism and Occupational Segregation in the Ecotourism Industry of Northeast Brazil

Melanie A. Medeiros and Tiffany Henriksen

The town of Brogodó, situated in the interior of Bahia State in Northeast Brazil, is located just outside a national park that draws thousands of visitors annually. Throughout the tourist season, local Afro-descendant guides sit on the steps of Brogodó's open-air bus station in the misty dawn hours every day, waiting for the early bus from Salvador de Bahia to arrive. Irrespective of the hour, these guides create an energetic, unofficial welcome committee, and as tourists disembark from their red-eye bus ride, the guides offer to take them to an inn to rest or to schedule a guided tour of the national park. Most mornings there are not enough ecotourists to employ all the guides at the station. Men like 23-year-old David explained to us that he would return to the bus station twice more each day, hoping that his efforts would result in a commission from an inn or a gig as a guide. For people like David, the elusiveness of income in the ecotourism industry and the persistence of employment instability raised doubts about the presumed socioeconomic benefits of ecotourism for rural communities in Brazil (Moura-Fé 2015). Despite Brogodó's flourishing ecotourism industry, social disparities at the intersections of race, class, and geography persist, and locally born Afro-descendant residents of Brogodó continue to suffer as a result of structural inequities and social inequality.

Ecotourism focuses on providing tourists with experiences in the natural world, for example with guided hiking, backpacking, caving, and swimming trips. In theory the industry promotes both environmental preservation and socioeconomic growth. Although ecotourists often appreciate cultural activities that complement their excursions in natural sites, these activities are not the primary focus of their itineraries. Thus, the ecotourism industry in the interior of Bahia differs substantially from tourism in Brazilian coastal cities such as Salvador, where the Afro-Brazilian cultural products of music, dance, art, religion, and *capoeira* are the focal points of tourism, affording Afro-descendants income opportunities – albeit still limited ones – as local purveyors of culture (Williams 2013). Ecotourism in the interior of Bahia also contrasts

Figure 31.1. The touristic historical center of Brogodó. Photo by Melanie A. Medeiros.

with ecotourism in other parts of Brazil, for example the Amazon, where tourists often prefer Indigenous Brazilian guides, who they perceive to be authentic brokers of the natural world. In the absence of an analogous mythology connecting Afro-descendant Brazilians to the land where they and their ancestors have lived for well over a century, local Afro-descendant people in Brogodó are not valued by the ecotourism industry as cultural or ecological guides, and subsequently are subjected to **occupational segregation** (Harrison and Lloyd 2013). In our ethnographic research in Brogodó, we found that structural racism severely limited the ability of locally born Brazilians of African descent to participate fully in the local ecotourism industry. In this chapter, we draw on evidence from this research to investigate the relationship between structural racism and employment in the ecotourism industry.

THE TOURISTSCAPE OF BROGODÓ, BAHIA, BRAZIL

Brogodó is nestled amid green mountains that strikingly contrast with the surrounding landscape of the semiarid Sertão subregion of Northeast Brazil. After 1985, Brogodó experienced a shift in its socioeconomic structure from small-scale diamond mining and subsistence farming to ecotourism when the national park adjacent to the town was created. The park has become a popular ecotourism destination for domestic and international travelers, who visit to explore the park's rivers, waterfalls, mountains, and caves. As a gateway to the park, Brogodó boasts the area's largest tourist infrastructure, containing inns, hotels, tour agencies, shops, and restaurants. The **touristscape** of Brogodó encompasses the many sites within the town where tourism is the focus, as well as the people who inhabit, engage with, or move through these sites daily (Williams 2013). We use the term *touristscape* to highlight the ways in which global hierarchies of inequality along the lines of race, ethnicity, gender, class, and citizenship manifest within local tourism industries, contributing to social inequality and unequal access to opportunities (Brennan 2004).

Locally born residents of Brogodó are of African descent and use the term *nativo* to identify themselves. Being *nativo* indicates a person's long-standing connection to the region, rooted in its mining history. The mid-nineteenth-century diamond-mining boom in the area depended on the labor of exploited free laborers and enslaved people before slavery was abolished in 1888. When the mining boom ended in the late nineteenth century, miners of African descent who had little social and geographic mobility remained in the region, most of them living in abject poverty as they searched for any remaining diamonds and farmed for subsistence. The identity label *nativo* encompasses a shared regional history linked to economic stratification based on (primarily) African ancestry and is a way of distinguishing locally born residents from people who have moved into the region – *pessoas da fora* (people from the outside), whom we refer to as non-*nativos* and most of whom Brazilians would categorize as "white." Because *nativos* did not differentiate between Brazilians and foreign-born residents when describing their relationships and interactions with "outsiders," we discuss the two groups together.

As a result of the success of the ecotourism industry, Brogodó became a prosperous town. However, according to the 2010 census, 80 per cent of private households had a household income of less than or equal to minimum wage – R$510 per month (US$170), and 7 per cent of households did not have an income at all (IBGE 2011). These statistics indicate that although there had been income gains since the 2003 Brazilian demographic study of poverty and inequality, in which the incidence of relative poverty in Brogodó was 47.12 per cent, most individuals and households in Brogodó were still living off an average nominal monthly per capita income of only R$375, or US$120. These economic circumstances were partially the result of an exceedingly high unemployment rate of 38 per cent (IBGE 2011).

In our conversations with them, *nativos* attributed income and unemployment rates to exclusionary employment practices in the ecotourism industry. They explained that non-*nativos* who moved to Brogodó following the creation of the park owned the most prosperous ecotourism businesses, and those business owners preferred to hire non-*nativos* to work in higher-paying positions while *nativos* were relegated to lower-paying positions. In a town as small as Brogodó, socioeconomic inequalities were apparent in the quality of housing and consumption patterns, and as a result, *nativos* often expressed discontent with their social position and, at times, resentment toward the more affluent non-*nativos*. Most of Brogodó's *nativos* lived in coated brickwork

Figure 31.2. A hilltop *nativo* neighborhood in Brogodó. Photo by Melanie A. Medeiros.

houses (IBGE 2011) – small, two- to three-room structures – on the deeply eroded unpaved roads that sloped steeply uphill from the town's center (Figure 31.2), whereas business owners and other non-*nativos* lived in renovated homes in the center of town or in large, newly built houses on its outskirts. The under-resourced residential neighborhoods that were inhabited by *nativos* starkly contrasted with the small and lively town center, where restaurants, tourism agencies, and shops lined quaint cobblestone streets and the town's two main squares.

STRUCTURAL RACISM IN BRAZIL

Brazil is characterized by one of the most racially diverse populations in Latin America, but dominant ideas about racial mixing (*mestiçagem*) have contributed to an imagination of Brazil as a racial democracy. This myth of racial democracy has resulted in what has been called the "social lynching" of Black people: the misrecognition of racial discrimination and racial inequities as class differences (Smith 2016, 8). The myth disregards that Black Brazilians make up the majority of people living below the poverty line (Lebon 2007) and 75 per cent of the poorest tenth of the Brazilian population, whereas white Brazilians make up 83 per cent of the richest 1 per cent of the population (Pagano 2014). Research on disparities has found that a startlingly high 12 per cent of income inequality in Brazil aligns with differences in skin color (compared to 2.4 per cent in the United States; World Bank 2004). These persistent racial and class hierarchies in Brazil are the result of and contribute to the minoritization and marginalization of working-class Black Brazilians, including the experience of occupational discrimination (Santos and Inocêncio 2006).

Black people in Brazil suffer from many forms of structural racism – including unequal access to social resources such as healthcare, quality education, and adequate housing and sanitation (Paixão 2013). And although racial identities in Brazil are complex and fluid (see the introduction to Section 2), Afro-descendant Brazilians, such as *nativos* in Brogodó, face significant obstacles to upward mobility and the achievement of middle- or upper-class status and prestige. Although Brazilian census categories do not represent the multitude of racial identification terms in Brazil, it bears mentioning for this discussion that 76 per cent of residents of Brogodó identified as *preta* (Black) or *parda* (Brown; IBGE 2011).

OCCUPATIONAL SEGREGATION IN BROGODÓ'S TOURISTSCAPE

Among employers in the ecotourism industry, discourse surrounding the employability of *nativos* focused on perceived shortcomings in their education, language, and communication skills – in other words, lamenting *nativos*' lack of **cultural capital** (formal education and other skills that reflect that education). For employers, *nativos*' lack of cultural capital justified occupational segregation in which they routinely employed *nativos* in lower-paying, behind-the-scenes positions (e.g., cooking and janitorial work) and non-*nativos* in higher-paying, public-facing positions (e.g., tour guides, receptionists, restaurant servers, managers) that required employees to interact with tourists daily. In this section, we explore employers' and employees' perspectives on the relationship between cultural capital and employment, and we examine the structural inequities that undermined *nativos*' access to the kinds of cultural capital that were perceived as necessary for the better jobs in ecotourism.

Both Brazilian and foreign-born employers deemed *nativos* to be less qualified for public-facing positions, asserting that they lacked language and communication skills to interact with domestic and international tourists. For example, 35-year-old Nathan, the European owner of an inexpensive hostel, explained his preference for non-*nativo* employees for certain positions: "I hire people from everywhere and people from Brogodó … It could be difficult to find them [employees] from Brogodó. The *nativo* … maybe doesn't know what tourists want … how to receive them, what they prefer, what they like. I want someone who tries to speak with the tourist."[1]

---

1 Several of our interviews were conducted in English, and when employing direct quotes, we do not correct the English-language grammatical errors of our participants.

Nathan believed that *nativos* lacked the cultural capital and **habitus** – an embodied way of being in the world, including one's disposition, speech, and bodily presentation – necessary to effectively engage with tourists. He continued, explaining that for cleaning the hostel, "it is good to go with people from here [Brogodó] during the day because there's not a lot of people [in the hostel], so it is the moment to have someone [working] who doesn't speak English but wants to work."

Although we do not have data on the preferences of domestic and international tourists themselves, Nathan's explanation illustrates how employers in Brogodó felt strongly that their businesses were better served by having non-*nativos* in public-facing positions. When employers hired *nativos*, it was typically in maintenance, cleaning, gardening, cooking, or laundry – jobs that did not require interaction with tourists. This pattern in Brogodó differs significantly from other sites in Brazil where Black or Indigenous Brazilians are key figures in tourism, partially due to the preferences of international tourists.

As a result of their lack of cultural capital, as reflected in their habitus, *nativos* were largely limited to positions that paid minimum wage or less. In Brogodó, the average value of the nominal total monthly income for those identifying as Black was R$548; as Brown, R$557; and as white, R$1,248 (IBGE 2011). *Nativos* were also more likely to be offered employment on a temporary, day-to-day basis. Therefore, not only were *nativos* earning less income, the contingency of their work also contributed to their structural vulnerability (see Chapter 12).

The common belief that *nativos* were not qualified for public-facing employment was often expressed alongside perceptions that individuals from outside of Brogodó were qualified for these roles. Tour agencies that organized everything from car-based day trips to multiple-day backpacking trips were more likely to hire educated, English-speaking guides who were originally from outside of Brogodó. These agency-contracted guides were paid a competitive salary, protected by the agency's insurance coverage, and supported by the agency's vehicles and office. In comparison, *nativos* were more likely to work as freelance guides, offering their services at a lower price and without office-based support for organizing transportation and other tour logistics. Non-*nativo* guides' cultural capital helped ensure them a steady income as contracted guides, whereas freelance guides struggled to work consistently enough to achieve financial security.

Marco, a 33-year-old *nativo* tour guide explained why non-*nativos* were considered more desirable employees for public-facing work: "He [the non-*nativo*] has a good formal education so he knows how to communicate better. He comes with the hustling attitude of big cities. He is much more articulate than we are here." Marco referred not only to the non-*nativos*' education level but also the ways an urban lifestyle and communication style prepared individuals to interact with other similarly socialized tourists from both within and outside of Brazil. These non-*nativos*' cultural capital and upbringing outside of rural Bahia were embodied in their habitus, contributing to the perception that they were better suited for public-facing positions and helping them secure desirable employment positions in the ecotourism industry. Non-*nativos*' suitability for certain positions was evaluated not only based on their English-language skills but also on their verbal proficiency in the variety of Portuguese that is spoken among the urban Brazilian middle and upper classes (Roth-Gordon 2017). Thus, employers sought employees with communication skills in English and in a variety of Brazilian Portuguese that differed from that of Brogodó's *nativos*. They justified their employment decisions by rationalizing that *nativos* lacked the requisite abilities for communicating with tourists.

STRUCTURAL INEQUITIES AND EDUCATION

Nativos' lack of access to formal education was largely due to structural racism, including a deprioritization of investment in Northeast Brazil, where most residents are Black (Hasenbalg and Silva 1992). Since the early twentieth century, Brazil's educational system has been decentralized and unequal, and by the 1990s Brazil's education system was considered one of the worst in Latin America (Borges 2008). While efforts have been made to improve the public education system, the state of Bahia continues to suffer from substandard public education (INEP 2003; Borges 2008). Middle- and upper-class Brazilians are able to circumvent the inadequate public education system by enrolling their children in private schools, where students receive a superior education and adequate preparation to pass Brazil's university entrance exam. By contrast, most working-class students in the northeast, most of whom are Black, are reliant on the inadequate public educational system and, as a result, are unable to pass the entrance exams that determine access to public universities (Mikulak 2011).[2]

Nativos were aware that the education available to them was inadequate; they described a pervasive lack of resources and blamed this on the misuse of education funds by the local government in Brogodó. They believed that funds allocated for improvements in education infrastructure, including clean water, desks, and books, or for hiring teachers and increasing the number of classes, were not actually reaching the schools. Their concerns indexed a general distrust and dissatisfaction that *nativos* felt toward the local and regional government and educational institutions. Public school students in Brogodó attended school for only four hours a day, and *nativo* parents complained that teachers, most of whom were not from Brogodó, canceled classes regularly to extend their own vacations. Residents of Brogodó who had greater disposable income – mostly non-*nativos* – paid for their children to attend a private school in town, further cementing the social inequalities in the community.

In 2010, a striking 63 per cent of Brogodó residents had not completed elementary school, 10.6 per cent had completed only elementary school, 22.3 per cent were high school graduates, and 3.7 per cent were college graduates (IBGE 2011). These statistics illustrate the results

---

2 In an attempt to resolve this issue, in 2012 President Rousseff signed the Law of Social Quotas, requiring that all public universities enroll students from public schools at a rate of 50 per cent and enroll students who mirror the racial composition of the state's population (Hordge-Freeman 2015).

of limited educational opportunities for rural, working-class *nativos*. School completion statistics for Brogodó also show racial disparities in education. Sixty-five per cent of individuals identifying as Black or Brown had no schooling or had not completed elementary or middle school, in comparison to 51 per cent of those identifying as white (IBGE 2011). Among individuals over 15 years of age, the illiteracy rate was 18.7 per cent, with an illiteracy rate of 24 per cent among individuals identifying as Black, 17.3 per cent identifying as Brown, and 15.5 per cent identifying as white. These statistics reveal disparities in cultural capital resulting from class, geographic, and racial dynamics. *Nativos*' dearth of cultural capital was reflected in the habitus of *nativos* across generations, which employers naturalized and used as a justification for excluding *nativos* from public-facing employment in the ecotourism industry.

BARRIERS TO TECHNICAL TRAINING THAT WOULD FILL THE EDUCATION GAP

In anticipation of increases in tourism due to the 2014 World Cup and 2016 Olympics in Rio de Janeiro, the federal government established a vocational and technical school in Brogodó – *Serviço Nacional de Aprendizagem Comercial* (National Commercial Apprenticeship Service, SENAC). SENAC offered courses in tourism, including hotel reception, guiding, and cooking, which were targeted to the local ecotourism industry. In theory, this new adult education program could have provided a way for *nativos* to gain relevant skills for work in the local ecotourism industry. However, several economic, cultural, and social obstacles prevented *nativos*' participation in the courses. Several of the courses required a high school diploma, and only 26.4 per cent of *nativos* had completed high school (IBGE 2011). Other obstacles to enrolling in SENAC courses included the time commitment that courses required and conflicts with people's existing family and work responsibilities. Silvana, a non-*nativo* manager of a tour agency who completed SENAC's year-long professional guide course told us "for one year we study every night. It's free but … the problem is time. But it is a choice. To be a professional guide to earn this money, they have to stop [working] to study." Silvana implied that people had to weigh the benefits of taking the guide course against the cons of losing income while they were studying, but for many *nativos* this trade-off was financially impossible. Unlike middle- and upper-class non-*nativos*, *nativos* were unlikely to have the savings that they would need to survive with a reduced income for the duration of a professionalization course.

For some *nativos*, the prospect of taking a SENAC course was unfamiliar and intimidating. Gabriela, a 25-year-old *nativa* who worked at an inn, considered why *nativos* were less likely to enroll: "Maybe because we are not accustomed to it … To have a course, it's new … in Brogodó … When you grow up … maybe the people [who are] younger will have a new vision. When you are 25 and you've never seen or done it [school or training] before it's difficult to start." Marco also explained: "Education is not our background ... Just because we don't have the habit ... For us it is difficult because of this." For *nativos* who did not have the practice of going to school, sitting in class for several hours every night was thought to be challenging and deterred some people from participating in courses. This aspect of *nativos*' habitus both reflected their lack of cultural capital and complicated their ability to acquire it, another deleterious effect of structural inequities.

Hierarchical social relations and power structures also influenced *nativos*' desire and ability to participate in the SENAC courses. Because of the complex local social relations, *nativos* and non-*nativos* did not interact as peers, and geographic spaces and places in Brogodó, such as town squares, were divided between the two groups. Owing to the cultural capital they already had, non-*nativos* were comfortable navigating educational institutions and, as a result, actively enrolled in SENAC courses from the start. Soon the SENAC classroom became a primarily non-*nativo* space, and the program, which could have played a role in addressing inequities, actually reproduced the privilege of non-*nativos*. More research is needed to understand how institutional policies and non-*nativos*' attitudes and behavior toward *nativos* within these courses may have led to the feelings of exclusion and non-belonging that *nativos* expressed in relation to the SENAC program.

In Brogodó's touristscape, the dominant discourse surrounding *nativos*' employability indicates that occupational segregation in this setting was the product of structural inequities and historical processes that restricted access for rural, working-class northeast Brazilians to cultural capital, and in turn shaped their habitus. This discourse justified exclusionary employment practices by constructing *nativos* as unsuited, and non-*nativos* as suited, to performing the tasks associated with public-facing employment. Our findings reveal that this is one way that structural inequities contribute to and reproduce social and economic inequality in Brogodó. At the same time and at a broader scale, it is evident that these local structural inequities were rooted in the Brazilian government's failure to invest in a region where most residents are Black, pointing to structural racism as an underlying cause of inequality.

CONCLUSION

In Brazil, structural racism limits rural, Black Brazilians' access to cultural capital, which alongside a history of oppression, discrimination, and social and economic inequality is reflected in their habitus. Discourse among the dominant group of middle- and upper-class Brazilians, including employers, naturalizes this habitus and critiques it as unsuited for certain forms of employment, thus justifying occupational segregation. Elsewhere (Medeiros and Henriksen 2019) we explore how one's habitus is also a key component of the construction of race in Brazil, in such a way that someone with African phenotypic traits who also embodies the habitus of an uneducated, rural, working-class person is more likely to be racialized as Black, and someone with an educated, middle- or upper-class, and urban habitus as white or whiter. The category of "white" subsumes and assumes cultural capital, which then affords opportunities, including employment opportunities, to individuals who exhibit whiteness. In Brogodó, the criteria of whiteness was largely unrecognized by employers, who justified their employment decisions in terms of education and skills, rather than a conscious or subconscious preference for white employees.

The study of structural racism and occupational segregation within the geography, structures, institutions, and social relations of a touristscape highlights the ways in which the ecotourism industry conforms to globalized social hierarchies based in race and class, and also perpetuates social and economic inequality through the unequal distribution of power and opportunities (Brennan 2004). *Nativos'* experiences in the ecotourism industry in Brogodó are indicative of the ways in which, through discourse and practice, structural racism contributes to and naturalizes broader-level social inequality in Brazil and throughout Latin America and the Caribbean.

Brazilian studies show that for ecotourism to fulfill its potential socioeconomic benefits for rural (Oliveira et al. 2010) and Afro-Brazilian communities (Cruz and Valente 2005), state and federal government investment is needed to develop social infrastructure and an inclusive ecotourism industry. Without a concerted effort on the part of the state and stakeholders in the ecotourism industry, the full socioeconomic benefits of ecotourism for underserved and often neglected communities will not be realized. However, while these suggestions address issues surrounding education, skills, and small enterprise development at a local level, they overlook the ways in which racial ideology influences employment practices (Medeiros and Henriksen 2019). We suggest that the elimination of occupational segregation requires systematic change, including popular support for policies that acknowledge and address structural racism, racial ideology, and racist employment practices.

REFLECTION AND DISCUSSION QUESTIONS

- Describe Brogodó's touristscape. Who are the various actors and what roles do they play in the ecotourism industry?
- How do evaluations of *nativos'* cultural capital impact their employment opportunities in the ecotourism industry? What is the relationship between cultural capital, habitus, and employment opportunities?
- How is occupational segregation a product of structural racism? How does it perpetuate social inequality in communities such as Brogodó?
- What efforts could be made to address occupational segregation and reduce social inequalities in the tourism industry?

KEY CONCEPTS

- **cultural capital**: Formal education and other skills that reflect that education.
- **habitus**: An embodied way of being in the world, including one's disposition, speech, bodily presentation, and taste; often influenced by a person's cultural capital.
- **occupational segregation**: Exclusion from certain forms of employment.
- **touristscape**: The many sites within a town or city where tourism is the focus, as well as the people who inhabit, engage with, or move through these sites daily (Williams 2013).

EXPLORE FURTHER

- To learn more about the relationship between racism and tourism, read **Chapter 4**.
- To learn more about racial inequality and racism in Brazil, read **Chapters 5**, **12**, and **24**.
- Carrier-Moisan, Marie-Eve. 2020. *Gringo Love: Stories of Sex Tourism in Brazil*. Toronto: University of Toronto Press.
- Medeiros, M. A. 2018. *Marriage, Divorce, and Distress in Northeast Brazil: Black Women's Perspectives on Love, Respect, and Kinship*. New Brunswick, NJ: Rutgers University Press.

ABOUT THE AUTHORS

Melanie A. Medeiros is an associate professor of anthropology at SUNY Geneseo, author of *Marriage, Divorce, and Distress in Northeast Brazil: Black Women's Perspectives on Love, Respect, and Kinship* (2018), and co-editor of *Black Women in Latin America and the Caribbean: Critical Research and Perspectives* (2023).

Tiffany Henriksen is a SUNY Geneseo alum and graduate student in elementary education at Lesley University.

REFERENCES

Borges, André. 2008. "State Government, Political Competition and Education Reform: Comparative Lessons from Brazil." *Bulletin of Latin American Research* 27 (2): 235–54. https://doi.org/10.1111/j.1470-9856.2008.00265.x.

Brennan, Denise. 2004. *What's Love Got to Do with It? Transnational Desires and Sex Tourism in the Dominican Republic*. Durham, NC: Duke University Press.

Cruz, Kelma C. Melo dos Santos, and Ana Lúcia E. Farah Valente. 2005. "A Cachoeira do Poço Encantado: Empreendimento Familiar e Presença Kalunga na Cadeia do Ecoturismo em Teresina de Goiás." *RER, Rio de Janeiro* 43 (4): 779–804. https://doi.org/10.1590/S0103-20032005000400008.

Harrison, Jill L., and Sarah E. Lloyd. 2013. "New Jobs, New Workers, and New Inequalities: Explaining Employers' Roles in Occupational Segregation by Nativity and Race." *Social Problems* 60 (3): 281–301. https://doi.org/10.1525/sp.2013.60.3.281.

Hasenbalg, Carlos A., and Nelson do Valle Silva. 1992. "Raça e Oportunidades Educacionais no Brasil." In *Relações Raciais no Brasil Contemporâneo*, edited by Nelson do Valle Silva and Carlos Hasenbalg, 79–100. Rio de Janeiro: Rio Fundo Editora.

Hordge-Freeman, Elizabeth. 2015. *The Color of Love: Racial Features, Stigma, and Socialization in Black Brazilian Families*. Austin: University of Texas Press.

IBGE (Instituto Brasileiro de Geografia e Estatística). 2011. *Censo Demográfico 2010: Características da População e dos Domicílios*. Rio de Janeiro: IBGE. http://www.ibge.gov.br.

INEP (Instituto Nacional de Estudos e Pesquisas Educacionais Anísio Teixeira). 2003. *A Educação no Brasil na Década de 90*. Brasília, Brazil: INEP.

Lebon, Nathalie. 2007. "Beyond Confronting the Myth of Racial Democracy: The Role of Afro-Brazilian Women Scholars and Activists." *Latin American Perspectives* 34: 52–76. https://doi.org/10.1177/0094582X07308263.

Medeiros, Melanie A., and Tiffany Henriksen. 2019. "Race and Employment Practices in Northeast Brazil's Ecotourism Industry: An Analysis of Cultural Capital, Symbolic Capital and Symbolic Power." *Latin American Research Review* 54 (2): 366–80. https://doi.org/10.25222/larr.573.

Mikulak, Marcia. L. 2011. "The Symbolic Power of Color: Constructions of Race, Skin-Color, and Identity in Brazil." *Humanity and Society* 35: 62–99. https://doi.org/10.1177/016059761103500104.

Moura-Fé, Marcelo Martins. 2015. "Geoturismo: Uma Proposta de Turismo Sustentável e Conservacionista para a Região Nordeste do Brasil." *Sociedade & Natureza, Uberlândia* 27 (1): 53–66. https://doi.org/10.1590/1982-451320150104.

Oliveira, Fagno Taveras de, Ivan Crespo Silva, Jackson Fernando Rego Matos, and Francisco Adilson dos Santos Hara. 2010. "Ecoturismo no Rio Puraquequara: Suporte para Inclusão Social e Proteção Ambiental." *Sociedade & Natureza, Uberlândia* 22 (2): 283–95. https://doi.org/10.1590/S1982-45132010000200005.

Pagano, Anna. 2014. "Everyday Narratives on Race and Health in Brazil." *Medical Anthropology Quarterly* 28 (2): 221–41.

Paixão, Marcelo. 2013. *500 Anos de Solidão: Estudos sobre Sesigualdades Raciais no Brasil*. Curitiba, Brazil: Editora Appris.

Roth-Gordon, Jennifer. 2017. *Race and the Brazilian Body: Blackness, Whiteness, and Everyday Language in Rio de Janeiro*. Berkeley: University of California Press.

Santos, Sales Augusto dos, and Nelson Olokofá Inocêncio. 2006. "Brazilian Indifference to Racial Inequality in the Labor Market." *Latin American Perspectives* 33 (4): 13–29. https://doi.org/10.1177/0094582X06289873.

Smith, Christen A. 2016. *Afro-Paradise: Blackness, Violence, and Performance in Brazil*. Urbana: University of Illinois Press.

Williams, Erica Lorraine. 2013. *Sex Tourism in Bahia: Ambiguous Entanglements*. Urbana: University of Illinois Press.

World Bank. 2004. *Inequality and Economic Development in Brazil*. Washington, DC: The World Bank.

CHAPTER THIRTY-TWO

Between the Edible and the Inedible: Cultural Tourism and Culinary Meaning in the Ecuadorian Amazon

Sarah Rachelle Renkert

A week before I left the Kichwa Añangu Community during my first fieldwork visit to Ecuador, Jacobo, the manager of the Napo Cultural Center, approached me as I was grinding cacao with a family of French tourists. With his hands cupped behind his back, he said, "Sarita, I have a gift for you." The sly smirk on his face told me that I was not going to love this "gift." He opened his hands, revealing a squirming *chontacuro* (palm weevil grub, Figure 32.1). The tourists cringed, while Jacobo and the other Kichwa employees broke into laughter. As I stared at the wriggling, chubby grub, I knew that he was expecting me to eat it.

Jacobo had been around tourists long enough to know that few outsiders would be willing to eat a live grub. Instead, the lodge presents tourists with fried *chontacuros* served on a dessert platter. But I was "The Anthropologist," the person who was supposed to be immersing myself in Kichwa culture. Despite every inch of my body begging me to resist, I could not say no. I grabbed the grub by the head, and it exploded in my mouth as I bit down. To my unaccustomed palate, the taste was repugnant. I could only swallow it by chugging the steaming coffee I had poured just minutes earlier. Amidst my anguish, the room burst into a chorus of collective laughter.

The foods we eat tell meaningful stories about who we are. They act as **symbolically coded edibles**, communicating our lived experiences to ourselves and others (Abrahams 1984, 20). No matter how extravagant or mundane the eating occasion, consumed foods allow us to begin decoding the eater's sense of cultural belonging and identity, lived experiences, social interactions, and the subtleties of individual taste and preferences. Likewise, the foods we avoid, those foods that are considered unpalatable, inedible, or even taboo, also communicate our sense of group belonging, social boundaries, and cultural norms (Long 2004). Ultimately, the meaning conveyed by a symbolically coded edible is often dynamic and flexible. The encoded symbolism of any given food item will have different interpretive meanings across time and space, while also changing based on the life experiences and cultural interactions of both the eater and the decoders.

Figure 32.1. *Chontacuros* **ready to be cooked in bijao leaves (left); a tour guide in the Kichwa Añangu Community holding a bowl of** *chicha* **(right).** Photos by Sarah Rachelle Renkert.

In taking on the task of decoding symbolically coded edibles, this chapter turns to the Ecuadorian Amazon to explore the complex meanings of two traditional comestibles commonly consumed in the Kichwa Añangu Community: *chontacuros*, a type of palm weevil grub, and *chicha*, a fermented beverage made from *yuca* (cassava or manioc). Members of the Kichwa Añangu Community own and operate two tourism lodges, which are visited by other Ecuadorian nationals and foreign tourists, largely from the United States and Europe. Central to the tourists' experience in Añangu is the consumption of symbolically coded edibles. These culinary exposures present an ideal setting for considering the multiple meanings emerging from symbolically coded edibles as the Añangu share their history, traditions, and culture through their cuisine, while tourists embark on a journey of culinary exploration.

In taking on the task of decoding *chontacuros* and *chicha* as symbolically coded edibles, this chapter is going to draw on what the anthropologist Sidney Mintz has called food's "**inside meaning**" and "**outside meaning**" (Mintz 1985, 167; Mintz 1996, 20). The foods Añangu community members present to tourists may be understood as being traditional, normal, or even sacred (inside meaning for the hosts). However, for tourists, these same food items may be seen as new, strange, potentially unappealing, and even grotesque (inside meaning for the tourists). Meanwhile, outside meaning, which Mintz has also called **structural power** (Mintz 1996, 22), involves the exterior conditions that change a food's inside meaning over time. These are the broader structures, such as globalization, cultural imperialism, or shifting economic or ecological conditions, which come to change how foods are locally understood and their role in everyday life (Mintz 1996, 22). The influence of these structures may normalize or introduce foods that were once strange, while making strange foods that were once celebrated and traditional. In the case of cultural tourism, a food's inside meaning may be influenced by outside meaning through persistent cultural encounters and clashes.

In this chapter, I begin by introducing the Añangu community and its tourism project. I then consider the implications and cultural dynamics of contrasting inside meanings (tourists versus host) through the consumption of a *chontacuro*, before turning to *chicha* to examine how outside meaning can influence inside meaning. Here, I will also consider how inside meaning can defy the influence of outside meaning as Añangu Community members attempt to maintain agency and control over the local meaning of *chicha* as a symbolically coded edible.

THE KICHWA AÑANGU COMMUNITY

The Kichwa Añangu Community is located on 21,400 hectares in Ecuador's famously biodiverse Yasuní National Park (Torres 2013). At the time of my fieldwork (2015–2016), approximately 188 Kichwa people were living in the community. Añangu community members identify as being an "organized community." They prioritize democratic decision making, communal work sessions (*mingas*), and the enforcement of strict rules to maintain their organization and protect their environment. For example, attendance at *mingas* and monthly meetings are required, and families must each maintain a *chacra* (garden or small farm) where they cultivate traditional foods. Additionally, because of the environmental pressures confronting the Amazon, the community members engage in limited tree felling, while hunting, livestock, and large-scale agriculture are prohibited. They have also resisted any attempt to extract petroleum from their oil-rich land.

Añangu's community members have collectively decided to dedicate their livelihood to community-owned tourism, specializing in ecotourism and cultural tourism. Currently, they own and operate the Napo Wildlife Center and the Napo Cultural Center. In 2010, the community also started the Kuri Muyu Women's Organization. The Kuri Muyu is a cultural interpretation center, run by Añangu's mothers, who are known locally as *Mamakunas*. While visiting the Kuri Muyu, tourists from both lodges visit two traditional architectural structures (the *huagra wasi* and the *maloca*), practice a Kichwa dance, learn about Kichwa ancestral practices, drink *chicha*, and purchase artisanal crafts made by the *Mamakunas*. In Añangu, decisions about tourism operations are made by all adult community members, who also collectively decide how profits from the tourism project will be invested in local initiatives, such as improving the school, the water supply system, or investing in sustainable energy sources (Renkert 2019).

Tourism has presented challenges for community members in Añangu, including shifting market demand, growing competition, and the impact of large-scale events, such as flooding from the climate crises, an up-river petroleum spill, and the global COVID-19 pandemic. However, ownership over their tourism project has allowed community members to use tourism as a vehicle for combating challenges faced by many Indigenous communities throughout the Amazon. Notably, while many communities have been forced to turn to commodity agriculture (e.g., soy, palm production), ranching, and the extractive industries (e.g., petroleum extraction, logging, mining), ecotourism allows the community to focus on protecting their environment. Tourism also creates local jobs for Añangu's youth, incentivizing them to stay in the community, rather than move to urban centers or seek employment with other tourism operators or the extractive industries.

Furthermore, due to the ongoing legacy of the colonial encounter, the economic pressures of capitalism, and the dominance of Western cultural practices, Amazonian Indigenous communities have had to fight to maintain their local identities and cultural practices for centuries. This is an ongoing concern for parents in Añangu, who fear that their children are learning to prefer "Western culture" to "Kichwa culture" through exposure to television, social media, trips to urban centers, imported foods, and even visiting tourists. For example, in reflecting on the fear that imported foods are replacing symbolically coded edibles, Tómas, a community leader, explains: "Today, our children do not know how to catch an animal or get their own food, and many of them ... no longer want to drink *chicha*. They only want sugar, Tang, coffee, or Quaker [oatmeal]."

However, for community members in Añangu, cultural tourism has become a way to publicly celebrate Kichwa culture while infusing traditional practices into everyday community life. In the words of Lidia, a *Mamakuna*, the community pursues tourism "to not lose our culture, to show guests what it looks like, and also for our children, so that they do not forget our customs ... They are forgetting how to drink *chicha*, how to speak our language, they are forgetting. So that's why we have the organization." While Añangu community members are not trying to replicate their ancestral past, they do want to maintain a sense of pride in their Kichwa identity and have autonomy over defining what it means to be Kichwa today.

One means by which tourists engage in Kichwa culture is through the consumption of traditional Kichwa symbolically coded edibles. When tourists first arrive, they are greeted with a cold glass of sweetened *guayusa* tea (a caffeinated holly species native to the Amazon) and a plate of *patacones* (mashed and fried plantains). Over the next two or three days, they will also consume *maito de pescado* (fish cooked in bijao leaves), *ceviche de palmito* (palm heart ceviche), *patasmuyo* (white cacao seeds), *chicha*, and of course, fried *chontacuros*. On their final morning, they have the option to attend a *guayusada*, where before dawn they visit a *maloca* (a round structure that was ancestrally used as a Kichwa home), where they are served warm, unsweetened *guayusa* while a *Rukumama* (grandmother) offers to interpret their dreams. Through the daily presentation of these comestibles to tourists, the Añangu also prioritize these foods and drinks in their own diets, with the goal of continuously normalizing them for younger generations.

THE GRUB AND THE CRUX OF THE CULTURAL DIVIDE: CONFLICTING INSIDE MEANINGS

On the day Jacobo presented me with the live *chontacuro* in front of the French tourists, the distinct symbolic readings of its material form as a symbolically coded [in]edible reified the social boundaries of those people present in the room (Kalčhik 1984, 54). Although the group distinctions of native/foreigner, Indigenous/white, worker/consumer were already palpable, the *chontacuro* added an affective component in distinguishing group membership. For the Kichwa men in the room, the *chontacuro*'s inside meaning was one of culture, convenience, nutrition, medicine, and even entertainment. The *chontacuro* is a traditional Kichwa food, a convenient energy-dense snack foraged while hunting, a medicine for combating colds, and an entertaining means for watching tourists decide whether they can stomach the divide between the edible and the inedible. Meanwhile, the French tourists and I became visibly uncomfortable as we realized that Jacobo was offering me the wriggling grub as food. For the foreigners in the room, the *chontacuro*'s inside meaning was marked by a sense of inedibility and even repulsion. Its mere presence and appearance made us physically cringe.

This revulsion toward the inedible is a disgust that is often mapped onto the bodies and perceived identity of the unknown, strange, or detested **Other** who consumes the inedible (Weismantel 2001). As Long (2004) explains, the "eater of the 'not edible' is perceived as strange, perhaps dangerous, definitely not one of us" (33). However, in the space of cultural tourism, where the tourist has chosen to meet the Other, there may be a greater "willingness of humans to experience the cultural worlds of other people, as the result of curiosity about other experiences and other ways of life" (Long 2004, 45). At times, this "willingness" also comes with an expectation to experience the strange as tourists hope to witness the exotic or primitive Indigenous Other (Bunten 2010). While meeting the demands of tourists is often necessary, in community-owned tourism hosts have greater **agency** in controlling how culture is experienced. They can also challenge the exoticized stereotypes held by tourists by contextualizing inside meanings or even limiting which inside meanings are publicly shared.

One way or another, in purchasing the opportunity to engage in cultural tourism, the normalcy of a tourist's everyday life is temporarily suspended (Turner 2017, 95) as they immerse themselves in the cultural lives of their hosts (no matter how curated these experiences may be). A tourist's routines, cultural practices, and of course the foods they eat are to varying degrees set aside as they temporarily destabilize their inside meanings to explore the new, the curious, and even the seemingly exotic and strange. Perceptions of the edible and inedible, the palatable and unpalatable, and the familiar and exotic become temporarily ambiguous as the tourist leaves behind the comforts of their culinary normalcy to willingly transgress the boundaries of culinary comfort (Long 2004, 33–4).

During any culinary cross-cultural encounter, a willingness to eat new foods creates a possibility for reaching across social boundaries, ultimately challenging ethnocentricity, or the feeling that one's cultural practices are superior to others. Meanwhile, an active aversion to foods can reify differences and socially constructed boundaries (Kalčhik 1984). For me, eating the *chontacuro* was a method for communicating respect and a willingness to engage with and learn the inside meanings of my Kichwa hosts (in addition to giving a few friends a good laugh). While the brevity of the cultural tourism experience is unlikely to change the inside meaning of foods for many tourists, the exposure, no matter how brief, creates an opportunity for a tourist's inside meaning to be destabilized as they are encouraged to question the perceived normality of their own diet and interpretation of symbolically coded edibles.

CHICHA AND THE FERMENTATION OF "KICHWANESS": TENSIONS BETWEEN INSIDE MEANING AND OUTSIDE MEANING

When a tourist visits the Kuri Muyu, they are taken into a *maloca*, a replica of an ancestral Kichwa residence. They sit on benches along the periphery of the round structure while a *Mamakuna* recounts how their ancestors lived, hunted, and cultivated agriculture. She tells the visiting tourists that in Kichwa homes, a cooking fire always had three rocks, representing the mother, the father, and the children. She brings out weapons that Kichwa people historically used to hunt and defend their land. Finally, she introduces them to one of the Kichwa's most important symbolically coded edibles, *chicha*, or "*asua*" as it is called in Kichwa (Figure 32.1).

Chicha is a term commonly used to describe fermented beverages produced throughout Latin America. It is made from a variety of ingredients including maize, quinoa, peanuts, and fruits. In the Amazon, yuca is the dominant ingredient used for brewing *chicha*, which gives it a white, milky appearance. For thousands of years, *chicha* made throughout the Andes and the Amazon has traditionally been fermented using the saliva of the brewers (Logan, Hastorf, and Pearsall 2012). The saliva adds microbial components to the beer (Freire et al. 2016) and helps convert sugar into starches (Cutler and Cardenas 1947), supporting fermentation.

While in the *maloca*, the *Mamakuna* explains that traditionally, Kichwa people would drink *chicha* throughout the day, substituting the high-energy drink for solid foods as they worked. The women would take *chicha* to their *chacras* (farms), while the men would carry dried gourds full of *chicha* while hunting. She adds that *chicha* is a convivial drink, shared among people. If a tourist ever visits her home, as they enter, she will offer them a giant bowl of *chicha*. The *Mamakuna* then explains how yuca is cultivated and, using props, demonstrates the basic steps for making *chicha*.

While grating yuca, the *Mamakuna* explains that traditionally, *chicha* is made with the saliva of the brewer ("*chicha masticada*" or "chewed *chicha*"). There is always an audible reaction from the uncomfortable crowd, who generally find even the idea of drinking a beverage fermented with saliva almost unbearable. With a smile on her face, the *Mamakuna* will ask the tourists if they would like to try *chicha*. They usually hesitate for a moment, until she assures them that they no longer make *chicha masticada*. Rather, the *chicha* is fermented with grated sweet potato. Although the *chicha* presented to the tourists is the "*chicha dulce*" given to children (sweet *chicha* that has only fermented for a day or two), some guests excitedly down the *chicha*, having learned that it is the "natural beer" of the Amazon. Others will cautiously smell the sweet, fermented beverage, barely sipping from the communal bowl.

As the tourists pass around *chicha*, the *Mamakuna* will usually talk about *chicha*'s health benefits, mentioning that studies have found that *chicha* is "high in vitamin B" while repeatedly reassuring tourists that they have learned that using saliva to make *chicha* "is not sanitary" because "saliva can spread disease." This need to publicly explain that they are aware that *chicha masticada* is unsanitary is an indicator of how outside meaning has come to shape the inside meaning of *chicha* in the Kichwa Añangu Community. The *Mamakunas* know that most non-Indigenous tourists believe that "such methods of fermentation are unhygienic and reflect a 'savage' or 'barbaric' custom" (Uzendoski 2005, 135).

This association between *chicha masticada* and "savagery" dates to the Spanish colonization of South America. Just before the arrival of the Spanish, *chicha* had been a revered beverage in Tahuantinsuyu (the Inca empire) (Krögel 2011). The Spanish chronicler and priest Father Bernabé Cobo explained that the *aqllakuna* or the Inca's "chosen women" prepared *chicha* for sacred meals as offerings to the gods (Krögel 2011, 46; Cobo 1893, 47). However, according to the famed Andean chronicler and Quechua noble Felipe Guamán Poma de Ayala, "The Indians should not drink chicha chewed within the mouth ... because it is a dirty, filthy thing, instead they should drink a chicha from sprouted maize ... so that the Christians drink it" (Krögel 2011, 91; Guamán Poma 1980, 827). Despite being a sacred beverage, just decades after the arrival of the Spanish and Christianity, Guamán Poma, a Quechua noble, was advocating for the removal of saliva from *chicha* production because it was "dirty" and "filthy."

How can we explain this shift, from *chicha masticada* being a drink worthy of the gods, to one that is now considered unsanitary, filthy, and disease-ridden? Mintz explains that inside meanings are found in the "daily life conditions of consumption" (Mintz 1996, 20), or how groups internally understand the significance of their practices, beliefs, and traditions around food and foodways (Mintz 1985, 151; Mintz 1996, 23). However, this inside meaning is always entangled with the pressures of outside meaning, which are the "environing economic, social, and political (even military) conditions" (Mintz 1996, 20). In the case of *chicha*, we can see how the imposition of a Spanish colonial ideology and the ongoing dominance of Western food standards have reshaped culture over generations, eroding traditional practices and beliefs. Even in Añangu, most *chicha* today is fermented with sweet potato.

However, at times, Añangu's "behind the scenes" cultural practices defy the image presented to tourists, as members of Añangu resist the pressures of outside meaning, maintaining agency over their Kichwa identity. For example, one afternoon I wandered into the worker's kitchen at the Napo Cultural Center where I found Queta, a *Mamakuna*, and her teenage daughter making *chicha* for the staff. They had just finished boiling the yuca and were preparing to mash it in a wooden basin. Queta invited me to join them, handing me a long, wooden masher.

As we worked, Queta talked about the cultural importance of *chicha* for Kichwa people. In describing why mothers use saliva for fermentation, she did not mention *chicha masticada*'s bacterial diversity, the benefits of lactic fermentation, or its potential for preventing coliform bacterial growth common in unclean water (Bussalleu et al. 2020; Freire et al. 2016). Rather, she explained that the mother's saliva in the *chicha* is critical for holding the family together, keeping family members connected and unified.

When I asked her which *chicha* tasted better, she laughed, answering "of course, *masticada* is better." Shen then smiled and asked, "Do you want to try it?" Before I said a word, Queta set aside the sweet potato she had begun grating, grabbing a handful of mashed yuca, which she put into her mouth. After sucking on the yuca for a few moments, she spit it back into the wooden basin and then encouraged me to try. Minutes later, several *Mamakunas* joined us in the kitchen, bursting into laughter when they saw me with a mouth full of yuca. The staff soon got word that we had made *chicha masticada* and were elated. As we drank the *chicha* over the next few weeks, there was something both beautiful and rebellious about consuming this forbidden beverage, as we defied the pressures of outside meaning.

Mintz (1996) has equated outside meaning to Eric Wolf's concept of structural power (22). According to Wolf (1990), "structural power shapes the field of action so as to render some kinds of behavior possible, while making others less possible or impossible" (587). The structures that construct the "field of action" are the environing factors, such as colonialism, capitalism, patriarchy, or racism, that create or limit our potential for agency. In the consumption of *chicha masticada*, the structural power of dominant cultures and classes have sought to Otherize, exotify, and label as "savage" the consumption of *chicha* made with saliva.

In Añangu, the *Mamakunas* strategically recognize how the consumption of *chicha masticada* appears to their crowds, leading them to publicly present an inside meaning that is comfortable for visiting tourists. However, behind the curtains of the tourist stage, the inside meaning of *chicha masticada* is more complex. While the *Mamakunas* largely use sweet potato for fermenting *chicha*, demonstrating that their inside meaning has shifted, at times they will still defy the pressures of outside meaning by making *chicha masticada*. This act preserves *chicha masticada*'s ancestral value for keeping Kichwa families and communities connected, while reclaiming a cultural practice that reproduces their sense of "Kichwaness."

For the Añangu, tourism presents a means for defining the inside meaning of symbolically coded edibles such as the *chontacuros* and *chicha*. Señora Queta once told me that the *Mamakuna*'s started the Kuri Muyu "to not forget our customs, how to speak [Kichwa], drink *chicha*. No young people want to drink *chicha*." Here, Queta underscores the lived reality of how external forces can shape cultural erasure, but also emphasizes the Añangu community members' agency by demonstrating how they maintain the presence of cultural practices in their community.

CONCLUSION

Indigenous communities throughout the Amazon are facing critical challenges as they seek to protect their environment while maintaining control over their cultural identity. Centuries of ongoing colonialism and the imposition of Western ideals and lifestyles have attempted to erase the cultures of Indigenous peoples throughout the Amazon (Davidov 2013). Meanwhile, capitalism has commodified Indigenous land and resources while increasing local dependence on the market economy.

For the Añangu, community-owned tourism has become a means of creating local jobs while avoiding petroleum extraction, commodity agriculture, and the further destruction of their environment (including the palm trees that give life to the *chontacuros*!). It also allows them to center Kichwa ideals and practices in their everyday lives. While tourism presents challenges, it is also a means by which Kichwa culture is normalized and celebrated within the community. In the case of Kichwa comestibles, the everyday consumption of symbolically coded edibles is a way to proudly mark "Kichwaness."

Ultimately, inside meaning and outside meaning are always entangled as they push, pull, and gradually reshape one another. While change is inevitable, by actively defining the inside meaning of everyday practices, such as symbolically coded edibles, the Añangu aim to be agents in controlling, to the degree possible, how outside meaning shapes their community. The practice of tourism alone cannot compete with the forces of structural power such as the climate crisis, extractive industries, or the dominance of capitalism and Western cultural practices. Nonetheless, the tourism project in Añangu is one of many Indigenous movements that strives to create a different type of world, built not on selfishness or monetary wealth but on lifeways that center communal good, environmental care, and the valorization of traditional practices, a way of living that in Kichwa is known as "*Sumak Kawsay*," or the "good life."

REFLECTION AND DISCUSSION QUESTIONS

- What was the inside meaning of the *chontacuro* for the Kichwa Añangu Community members? How was this different from the inside meaning of the *chontacuro* for the foreigners? In your opinion, what are the factors that shape these distinct inside meanings?
- What is the inside meaning of *chicha* for the Kichwa Añangu Community members? How has this inside meaning been influenced by outside meanings? How are Kichwa Añangu Community members resisting the pressure of outside meanings?
- Think of a food in your life that functions as a symbolically coded edible. What does this food mean to you? What does this food communicate about you to the world?
- Think of a food that is commonly consumed within your cultural group whose meaning has changed over time (e.g., a food that was once considered unhealthy and is now seen as healthy). What were the outside factors (outside meaning) that caused the inside meaning of this food to change?

KEY CONCEPTS

- **agency**: The degree of control an individual or group has in taking action and making decisions, which is often in tension with and limited by structural power.
- **inside meaning**: How groups internally understand the significance of their material culture, practices, beliefs, and traditions.
- **outside meaning/structural power**: The external forces (e.g., globalization, capitalism, racism, climate change) that shape our lives, influencing and changing an individual or group's material culture, practices, beliefs, and traditions over time while facilitating

or limiting the degree of control an individual or group has in taking action and making decisions.
- **Other**: The "Other" is a person or group that seems unfamiliar, different, or potentially strange when compared to our biased perceptions of normality. "To Otherize" or "Otherization" is to see oneself as normal while treating someone from an unfamiliar group as abnormal, strange, or exotic.
- **symbolically coded edibles**: The foods we eat (or avoid) communicate meaningful details about an eater's sense of cultural belonging and identity, lived experiences, social interactions, economic situation, ecological setting, and individual preferences, among other factors.

EXPLORE FURTHER

- To learn about another community living in the Amazon region, read **Chapter 28**.
- Añangu Community's website. https://www.comunidadanangu.org/en.
- May, Ali. 2010. *Chicha*. https://tinyurl.com/Chicha-Ecuador.
- Napo Cultural Center. https://www.napoculturalcenter.com.
- Napo Wildlife Center. https://napowildlifecenter.com.

ABOUT THE AUTHOR

Sarah Rachelle Renkert is an assistant professor of practice in applied anthropology at Purdue University. Her primary research projects are on the politics of food aid in Huaycán, Lima, Peru, and community-owned tourism in the Ecuadorian Amazon. She has also completed applied research projects in the US southwest, focused on food security, diaper need, and Indigenous land protection and representation.

REFERENCES

Abrahams, Roger. 1984. "Equal Opportunity Eating: A Structural Excursus on Things of the Mouth." In *Ethnic and Regional Foodways in the United States: The Performance of Group Identity*, edited by Linda Keller Brown and Kay Mussell, 19–36. Knoxville: University of Tennessee Press.

Bunten, Alexis Celeste. 2010. "Indigenous Tourism: The Paradox of Gaze and Resistance." *La Ricerca Folklorica* 61: 51–9.

Bussalleu, Alejandra, Aldo Di-Liberto, Cesar Carcamo, Gabriel Carrasco-Escobar, Carol Zavaleta-Cortijo, Matthew King, Lea Berrang-Ford, Dora Maurtua, and Alejandro Llanos-Cuentas. 2020. "Cultural Values and the Coliform Bacterial Load of 'Masato,' an Amazon Indigenous Beverage." *EcoHealth* 17 (3): 370–80. https://doi.org/10.1007/s10393-020-01498-5.

Cobo, Bernabé. 1893. *Historia del Nuevo Mundo*. Vol. 4. Sevilla: Sociedad de Bibliofilos Andaluces.

Cutler, Hugh C., and Martin Cardenas. 1947. "Chicha, A Native South American Beer." *Botanical Museum Leaflets (Harvard University)* 13 (3): 33–60. https://doi.org/10.5962/p.295173.

Davidov, Veronica M. 2013. *Ecotourism and Cultural Production: An Anthropology of Indigenous Spaces in Ecuador*. New York: Palgrave Macmillan.

Freire, Ana L., Sonia Zapata, Juan Mosquera, Maria Lorena Mejia, and Gabriel Trueba. 2016. "Bacteria Associated with Human Saliva Are Major Microbial Components of Ecuadorian Indigenous Beers (Chicha)." *PeerJ* (4): e1962–e1962. https://doi.org/10.7717/peerj.1962.

Guamán Poma de Ayala, Felipe. 1980. *El Primer Nueva Corónica y Buen Gobierno: Colección América Nuestra*. Vol. 2. México, DF: Siglo Veintiuno.

Kalčhik, Susan. 1984. "Ethnic Foodways in America: Symbol and the Performance of Identity." In *Ethnic Regional Foodways United States: Performance of Group Identity*, edited by Linda Keller Brown and Kay Mussell, 37–65. Knoxville: University of Tennessee Press.

Krögel, Alison. 2011. *Food, Power, and Resistance in the Andes: Exploring Quechua Verbal and Visual Narratives*. Lanham, MD: Lexington Books.

Logan, Amanda L., Christine A. Hastorf, and Deborah M. Pearsall. 2012. "'Let's Drink Together': Early Ceremonial Use of Maize in the Titicaca Basin." *Latin American Antiquity* 23 (3): 235–58. https://doi.org/10.7183/1045-6635.23.3.235.

Long, Lucy M. 2004. "Culinary Tourism: A Folkloristic Perspective of Eating and Otherness." In *Culinary Tourism*, edited by Lucy M. Long, 20–50. Lexington: University Press of Kentucky.

Mintz, Sidney W. 1985. *Sweetness and Power: The Place of Sugar in Modern History*. New York: Viking.

———. 1996. *Tasting Food, Tasting Freedom: Excursions into Eating, Culture, and the Past*. Boston: Beacon Press.

Renkert, Sarah Rachelle. 2019. "Community-Owned Tourism and Degrowth: A Case Study in the Kichwa Añangu Community." *Journal of Sustainable Tourism* 27 (12): 1893–908. https://doi.org/10.1080/09669582.2019.1660669.

Torres, Stephany. 2013. *Historia de la Comunidad Kichwa Añangu: Nacionalidad Kichwas Amazónica – Parque Nacional Yasuní*. Ecuador: Proyecto Biocomercio GEF-CAF.

Turner, Victor W. 2017. *The Ritual Process: Structure and Anti-Structure*. Somerset, UK: Routledge.

Uzendoski, Michael. 2005. *The Napo Runa of Amazonian Ecuador: Interpretations of Culture in the New Millennium*. Urbana: University of Illinois Press.

Weismantel, Mary J. 2001. *Cholas and Pishtacos: Stories of Race and Sex in the Andes*. Chicago: University of Chicago Press.

Wolf, Eric R. 1990. "Distinguished Lecture: Facing Power – Old Insights, New Questions." *American Anthropologist* 92 (3): 586–96. https://doi.org/10.1525/aa.1990.92.3.02a00020.

CHAPTER THIRTY-THREE

Of Cash and Candy: The Complex Effects of Tourism on the Growth of Maya Children from Yucatán, Mexico

Kristi J. Krumrine

Sitting in the village park in Cobá in the early afternoon is peaceful. It is January, and while western New York is dealing with cold and snow, the temperature in Cobá is a lovely 80 degrees. The sun is warm on my shoulders and there is a cacophony of sounds from various tropical bird species. My favorite, which I still haven't managed to identify after six years of fieldwork, makes a "bling bling" sound. It's a great time to catch up on fieldnotes and simply feel present in a place with thousands of years of history. Situated in the tropical forest of the Yucatán Peninsula in Mexico, Cobá today is a bustling village of over 1,200 people. In contrast, from 600 to 900 CE, it was the site of a Late Classic Maya city-state that ruled over a population in the hundreds of thousands. The temples and ballcourts of the city center, visited each year by thousands of tourists, still stand along the outskirts of the village (Figure 33.1), but I can also see evidence of the everyday structures that once housed the people who cultivated the food for that vast city-state. From the village park, ancient house mounds, now collapsed rubble, are visible beneath the newer houses and yards of current residents. Just up the road, past the primary school and kindergarten that sit opposite the park, are remnants of a *sacbe*, an ancient road that once connected Cobá to villages and cities to the west. By mid-afternoon the solitude of the park changes as children of various ages leave school and head to a store, which is not much more than a counter in front of a small house, to buy candy, sodas, and chips.

I came to Cobá for the first time in 2008, while on vacation with my husband. Our colleague, Dr. Ellen Kintz, had worked in Cobá since the mid-1970s and was conducting development work in the village. We decided that we should see this place, about which we had, over the years, heard so much. I was instantly enamored with the village and, especially, with the children. In her book, titled *Under the Tropical Canopy: Tradition and Change among the Yucatec Maya*, Kintz (1990) described the children as "perhaps the most precious commodity that the Maya hold" and her first entry into the social world of this community of tight-knit

Figure 33.1. The ancient Mayan Cobá pyramid (Nohoch Mul) is the tallest pyramid in the Yucatán and a major tourist attraction that impacts the village of Cobá. Photo by dronepicr (CC BY 2.0).

families. This was true of my experience as well. The children are welcoming and playful, and I was immediately interested in their well-being. In many ways they have an idyllic childhood, living in family compounds where cousins are their playmates and best friends, surrounded by grandparents, aunts, and uncles. They readily help adult family members with household tasks, but also have much time to run around and play. It was also clear, however, that life could be hard. Kintz documented shortages of food, difficulties with having adequate shelter and healthcare, and inequalities in the village where some families benefited more than others from the influx of cash associated with tourism. Specifically, I wanted to know how this transition to tourism and a cash economy affected the health and growth of Cobá children.

TRADITIONAL SUBSISTENCE AND COLONIALISM

Prior to Spanish colonization, the traditional Maya subsistence system was built around **milpa** farming, where corn, beans, squash, and other foods comprising the bulk of dietary **macronutrients** were grown. Because of the poor nutritional content of the tropical soil, fields were burned prior to cultivation and shifted every few years. These early Maya also planted fruit trees, which continued to produce long after the fields had been abandoned. Deer and turkeys, which provided an important source of protein, were hunted from the milpas. Women and children planted and tended **kitchen gardens**, where tomatoes, chiles, cilantro, and other vegetables and herbs were grown, providing important **micronutrients** and flavor to the diet (Kintz 1990). Ramon trees grew everywhere and provided a nut that is a powerhouse of nutrients, including iron, which is a common deficiency in populations where corn is a staple food. Doña Maria, matriarch of a large family, told me that these versatile nuts, which can be harvested in January and stored throughout the year (Puleston 1982), were used by her mother to make tortillas when corn was scarce. Chaya bushes grew in the yards and provided a rare leafy green vegetable rich in vitamins K and C, protein, fiber, calcium, potassium, and iron. Sons provided essential labor in the milpas and extended family support was crucial for young families whose children were still too young to contribute (Kintz 1990).

When the Spanish colonized the Yucatán beginning in the sixteenth century, they built cities, such as Valladolid and Merida, and imposed their religion and culture on the Maya; however, the Yucatán was not seen as an important area for economic growth and the Maya were largely able to maintain their traditional subsistence practices. The extended kinship system continued, even while under pressure from colonial powers to abolish family compounds and for couples to live in neolocal households. Additionally, to strengthen economic security, "the Maya rapidly adopted the Hispanic *compadrazgo* (godparenthood) system to recreate an extended kinship of economic, social, and spiritual security" (Kintz 1990, 61). This system allowed the Maya to establish social ties lost to disease and famine that resulted from colonial rule. Although many Yucatec Maya were forced to work on henequen plantations, where the raw material used to make twine was produced during the last half of the nineteenth century, their traditional subsistence system survived this and was well established into the late twentieth century.

TOURISM AND CULTURAL CHANGE: A TALE OF TWO VILLAGES

When I first turn off the main road connecting Tulum to Valladolid and head toward Cobá, it is tempting to question my GPS directions, wondering if I've made a mistake. There isn't very much around. Once I see the Cobá sign on the side of the road, however, I begin to see more buildings and signs of a village. A few years after commencing fieldwork in Cobá, I was startled to see a Starbucks sign on a newly built hotel just outside of town. It's incredible how much changes from year to year. Once I pass the perpetually unmanned checkpoint at the entrance to the village, there are houses, mostly cinderblock, and a pole-and-thatch structure that functions as a souvenir shop for a family that also farms a milpa. In addition to this main road, which runs north–south, there is also a west–east road that runs along a beautiful lake and culminates in the entrance to the Zona Archaeologica, the archeological site that employs many men in the village. If I drive slowly, or better yet walk along the wooden sidewalk, I might be lucky enough to catch a glimpse of a *cocodrilo* (alligator) in the water. They certainly make the zipline that runs across the lake look more ominous! From there, the road follows along the lake before turning again into the south side of Cobá with additional residences, stores, and the medical clinic. During the day, both main streets are busy with cars, bikes, motorcycles, tour buses, and vans. They are lined with little stores, churches, and restaurants. If I sit on the large porch of the Restaurante Chile Picante, I can watch this activity while sipping a cold Coke from a bottle and munching on their excellent salsa and chips. The incredibly hard-working, friendly, and professional waitstaff likely drown out those ubiquitous noises, but for me, they always signal that I am finally back in Cobá.

This scene could not have been more different back in 1975 when Ellen Kintz first came to Cobá – people couldn't even fly into Cancun because the airport was still under construction. The roads were unpaved and, if someone were driving at night, there were no streetlights to guide the way. In fact, there was no electricity in the village at all. During a brief power outage in 2017, I was able to experience what Cobá was like before electricity and to see the bright Yucatán night sky as the Maya priests would have viewed it. Cold drinks did not come to Cobá until the first small store bought a generator (Kintz 1990). Until the 1980s, most of the houses in the village were traditional Maya pole-and-thatch constructions. These are superior during the hot summer months, since they allow breezes to run through; however, on chilly nights during the colder winter months, and especially during hurricanes and other inclement weather, having a cinder block house next door is preferred. Yards with animals such as chickens and kitchen gardens were also common. At the end of the day, men and boys would return from the milpas, possibly with a deer draped over their shoulders (Kintz 1990).

Bringing paved roads and electricity to Cobá were part of the Mexican government's plan to develop the Yucatán coast, what is referred to today as the "Riviera Maya." They developed Cancun from a small fishing village into a busy city with resorts, restaurants, hotels, and an international airport. In Cobá, the changes were more subtle, but they began with a plan to develop the adjacent archeological site into a tourist attraction. The site opened in the early 1980s and began drawing thousands of tourists each year. Most of these tourists were staying in Cancun or along the coast, visiting just for the day, but as the village opened a few small hotels, some would stay for a night or two.

Although only 20 miles away, Sahcab Mucuy can seem like a world away from the Cobá of today and much more like the Cobá from 35 years ago. It was important for my research to add a comparison village with few tourists, and I literally stumbled upon Sahcab Mucuy (SM) when I got lost in 2015 while exploring the area. Until recently, the road conditions were akin to driving on a moonscape, with giant holes enveloping both lanes. As I drove along during my first excursion, nervous that I would pop a tire, it became clear that tourist buses could never navigate these roads, even if there were an archeological site or some other tourist draw nearby. Entering SM for the first time, the differences with Cobá were immediately apparent.

Just the presence of my car in the village was cause for interest, and several women approached me to sell traditional dresses, called *huiples*, embroidered handkerchiefs, and jewelry when I stopped to ask about the location of the school. Watching children play in the primary school courtyard, it was obvious that they were smaller than children from Cobá and, listening closely, I could clearly make out Maya words being exchanged among them. There were only two small stores and both sold little in the way of food. I could see buckets of corn sitting in front of a few of the houses, likely stored from the previous season's harvest. Also, in stark contrast to Cobá, many of the yards had chickens and pigs and fewer house lots had cinder block houses. I met a traditional beekeeper, sampled different kinds of honey by reaching my hand into boxes full of stingless Yucatán bees, and toured his impressive garden. He said that he built his small museum to accommodate tourists who, sadly, never come.

EFFECTS OF DIET ON THE HEALTH AND GROWTH OF CHILDREN

The Nutrition Transition

The shift from diets largely comprising fresh fruits and vegetables, lean protein, and complex carbohydrates, coupled with high activity levels, to diets where processed, high-fat, and high-sugar foods and low activity levels predominate has occurred all over the world because of colonialism and globalization. This **nutrition transition** is associated with a more Westernized diet and, as other Western cultural practices and ideas have spread across the world, so too have dietary practices. In the Yucatán, this process has been referred to as "coca-colonization" to imply that it is largely driven by US interests and commodities (Leatherman and Goodman 2005). This dietary pattern has become the norm in the United States, where access to inexpensive, processed food with high fat, sugar, and sodium content is abundant. The reference to the Coca-Cola product both exemplifies the economic power and cultural influence of such a multinational company as well as the copious amounts of empty calories consumed through such products in the United States and elsewhere. The success of the Coca-Cola company's goal to put Coke "an arm's length from desire" (Pendergrast 2000, as quoted in Leatherman and Goodman 2005, 839) is readily apparent in Cobá, where it can be purchased on practically every block (Krumrine 2017).

The effects of diet and health on growth during childhood have been well established for over a century. Franz Boas (1912), known as the father of American anthropology, wrote a seminal book in 1912 that documented changes in height among the children and grandchildren of nineteenth-century immigrants to America. He was able to demonstrate that, when provided with better food and living conditions, the descendants of these immigrants were taller than their parents and grandparents. His paper was built upon decades of earlier work by other scholars and public health figures who demonstrated the connection between poverty, malnutrition, and chronic illness to growth in children. These biocultural studies also helped to disprove the idea of genetic determinism, as espoused by eugenicists, which claimed that characteristics such as height were completely under genetic control, a pseudoscientific argument that was used to justify anti-immigration legislation.

When we think about malnutrition, or an inadequate amount of nutrients, we tend to picture children who are very thin and emaciated. It will not come as a surprise that many of these children live in parts of the world today that experience chronic poverty, as had large numbers of children in the United States and other Western countries during the nineteenth and early twentieth centuries. For example, it is not uncommon to see marasmus, where a child is devoid of protein and energy nutrients, listed as a cause of death in historic cemetery records in western New York. Tragically, in global periphery countries, children still suffer from marasmus as well as an even bigger killer called kwashiorkor, where there are abundant carbohydrates in the diet but little to no protein. Malnutrition has an insidious relationship with chronic infectious disease; due to causing a compromised immune system, as happens with a vitamin A deficiency, malnourished children are more likely to suffer from infections, which in turn increase the severity of nutrient deficiencies through loss of appetite, vomiting, and diarrhea. For example, in many parts of the world where vaccines are unavailable, children who are malnourished have much higher mortality rates from measles (Dettwyler 1994). Both malnutrition and infectious disease, in turn, will delay skeletal growth and brain development in these children.

Sometimes, however, malnutrition looks very different. A child can have a micronutrient (vitamin and mineral) deficiency that can inhibit growth while taking in an adequate amount or even an overabundance of fat and calories. This situation is more likely to be seen in places where a nutrition transition to a more Westernized diet has occurred. This kind of malnutrition can also have negative health consequences.

Methods

I used several different methods to answer my research question, "How has the economic transition to tourism and a cash economy affected the health and growth of Maya children in Cobá?" The most important and obvious method is to take various physical measurements, what is referred to as **anthropometry**. The measurements used in this study were overall height, sitting height, knee height, weight, triceps and subscapular skinfolds, upper arm circumference, and elbow breadth. Knee height, in particular, is an important indicator of growth problems, because the lower leg is most susceptible to environmental stressors such as malnutrition. Skinfold measurements taken with calipers, though not a perfect method, give a good indication of body fat composition. When triceps skinfold is taken, together with arm circumference, it allows for determining the relative amount of muscle and fat in the arm. Comparisons can then be made to other groups, such as those in other Maya villages and children in the United States. I first measured the children when they were students in the preschool/kindergarten, ages 3–5, and then every year until they reached ages 7–9.

While these biological indicators are of primary importance for assessing growth, a study incorporating only these methods would not fully answer the research question. It would only tell us how the kids are growing while omitting the sociocultural and political-economic context explaining that growth. To assess how tourism and a cash economy has affected growth, it was important that I add an ethnographic component. This type of study is biocultural in nature, meaning that I am looking at how biological and cultural factors interact with each other. The most important ethnographic method that I used was semi-structured interviews with the mothers and other caretakers of the children who were measured. I asked mothers information about family size and structure, whether families owned conveniences such as refrigerators, phones, TVs, and cars, the kinds of foods that were grown and purchased from stores, occupations for parents, household income, education level of both parents, typical foods fed to kids for different meals, birthweight, duration of breastfeeding, and childhood illnesses. All these factors could potentially impact growth. For example, children born with low birthweights, those who are weaned from breastmilk early, and those who experience frequent illnesses such as diarrhea and respiratory infections are also likely to exhibit poor growth (Sharpe 2012). And most directly, children's nutrition is impacted by the kinds of foods that are eaten and, if they are store bought, how much money the family can put toward food purchases. In Cobá, mothers decide what foods to buy and feed to children. Additionally, children have agency in their food choices, meaning they can decide what they eat or don't eat. One mother, for example, said that while she often serves nutrient-dense chaya to her family, her son, who was included in the study, did not like it and refused to eat it.

Finally, to answer the research question about the connection between tourism and growth, I added a comparison village, different from Cobá in the importance of tourism to the family economy. I chose Sahcab Mucuy (SM), described earlier, because, unlike Cobá, it does not have a tourist site located close by. Therefore, I hypothesized that cash would be less important to the family economy and that more traditional subsistence practices, such as growing food in milpas and kitchen gardens and keeping livestock, would be more common. With fewer store-bought foods, including junk foods, and a higher amount of freshly grown and less processed foods eaten, I hypothesized that SM children would be taller, weigh less, and have less body fat than the Cobá children.

GROWTH AND ETHNOGRAPHIC FINDINGS

After five years of taking measurements and doing over 90 interviews, it is clear that children in Cobá are, indeed, heavier overall and have higher body fat values as compared to children in SM. The families in SM do grow more food, depend less on cash, and eat less junk food. However, both groups of children are short for their ages and, despite the inclusion of freshly grown foods in the diet, the SM kids are shorter than the kids from Cobá. It is likely that children in both villages are deficient in iron. In addition to lower consumption of iron-rich foods, due to higher costs, corn-based diets result in less bioavailability of iron because phytates in the corn bind to iron and reduce absorption. Children in both villages are also likely to be deficient in protein, vitamin K, and zinc. Deficiencies in vitamins A and C, which were documented in Cobá and other Maya villages in the past, are unlikely to be a problem in either village. Mothers in both SM and Cobá mention carrots, mangoes, limes, and other fruits and vegetables as common foods they give to their children.

There are several factors that can explain these growth differences between children in SM and Cobá. First, families in SM are larger in size, as compared with those in Cobá. Reduction in family size is a common phenomenon in societies that transition away from agriculture to a cash economy. Traditionally, the Maya had large families where children were an important source of labor in the milpas and kitchen gardens. In a cash economy in which children do not significantly contribute to household income, they become expensive to support. However, in SM, larger families mean fewer resources for each individual. Also, the occurrence of eating meat such as chicken and pork was much higher in Cobá than in SM, despite the fact that a few SM families kept chickens and pigs while no Cobá families had them. It is likely that the SM families had a more difficult time providing meat for children because they had less cash to buy food and were much less likely to own a refrigerator. It was also more difficult for SM families to seek medical care and medicines due to having a lower income. This puts children more at risk for growth problems resulting from chronic infections.

Many cultural changes have emerged with the rise of tourism in Cobá that have resulted in significant differences with SM. For example, views in Cobá have changed with respect to milpa farming. Even back in the 1990s, young Maya men in developed areas of the Yucatán referred to milpa farming as "*trabajo rudo*" (rough work) and expressed a desire to work in tourism instead (Leatherman and Goodman 2005, 835). The lack of participation in farming among young men in Cobá is even starker today. While it is difficult for men to maintain a milpa and work in tourism, the drop in kitchen gardening in Cobá was surprising since women spend most of their time in the home. Some of the mothers said that they could not grow a garden because they did not own the land surrounding their house; they did, however, express regret and said that they would like to garden if they had space to do so. The foods available in local Cobá stores, unfortunately, are limited to unhealthier varieties with higher sugar and lower fiber content. To purchase a wider variety of fresh fruits and vegetables and healthier packaged foods, one would have to drive to Valladolid or Tulum, both about 45 minutes away. Only a small number of Cobá families interviewed own cars.

IS TOURISM GOOD OR BAD?

The question asking whether tourism has a positive versus negative impact on growth and health does not have a straightforward answer and, certainly, is not as clear as I expected when I started the project. The fact that kids are taller in Cobá as compared with those in SM likely reflects the greater protein and iron content of the diets, as reported by Cobá mothers, including store-bought meat, milk, and eggs. Having more cash to buy higher-quality foods and refrigerators in which to store these perishable items is an important positive effect of the transition to work in tourism. However, having more cash to spend on easily accessible purchases of sodas and candy at the many small stores located in Cobá likely contributes to higher weight and body fat values in the Cobá children. Although milpa farming did not correlate with greater height values, as I had originally predicted, it did correlate with lower weight and body fat values. This is likely due to the higher fiber, complex carbohydrate, and micronutrient content of unprocessed foods and fewer sweets in the diets of SM children. The larger family sizes in SM could also explain the children's lower weight and body fat values, since there would be less cash to spend on store-bought, higher sugar and fat content foods and treats.

In addition to improved nutrition through buying and storing higher-quality foods, cash income from tourism can also contribute to better health outcomes and improve the likelihood that children will reach healthy height benchmarks. For example, for families in both Cobá and SM, obtaining healthcare for their children is difficult. According to mothers in both villages, respiratory infections are the most common childhood illnesses; however, to receive medical care, mothers often feel the necessity to take children to Valladolid or Tulum to see a private doctor, which is expensive. Most mothers expressed the view that the village health clinics were only helpful for administering parasite treatments and vaccinations. Both the clinic hours and their medicine stocks are limited. While a mother could take her child to the doctor at the clinic, she would have to drive at least 30 minutes to get to a pharmacy to fill a prescription. Without a car, this is prohibitively expensive. Children in Merida, which is the largest city in the Yucatán, have healthier average height values compared with those in Cobá and SM (Azcorra et al. 2013), which could be partially attributable to having easier and less expensive access to healthcare and medicine.

CONCLUSION: WHAT DOES THE FUTURE HOLD?

Growing food in the Yucatán has always been somewhat precarious as has the reliance on tourism for income. Climate change is negatively impacting conditions for growing food, and communities like Cobá have already moved away from milpa farming, which leads not only to dietary changes but also a reduction in knowledge that will make it hard to return. The loss of Indigenous varieties of corn and other plants will also make it difficult for people to go back to farming, even if they wish to. However, as the COVID-19 pandemic has demonstrated, it is dangerous to rely solely on tourism for income. The archeological site that employs many men in the village and provides cash income that supports other businesses and jobs was completely shut down from April through August of 2020 (Instituto Nacional de Antropología e Historia

2021). Friends in Cobá sent me videos and pictures of empty streets and restaurants. Since the archeological site reopened in September 2020, the number of tourists has remained well below pre-COVID numbers. As a result, people in Cobá have struggled to buy food and medicine, which were hardships even before COVID travel restrictions and shutdowns. Zika, swine flu, political violence, and natural disasters all reduced tourism before COVID. It is unrealistic to expect that tourism will always provide a stable income for Cobá residents.

Even for months when tourist numbers are high, it can be a struggle for many families in Cobá to afford food and medicine. For example, men who show up at the site each day are not guaranteed work, and wages are well below the federal minimum wage. A tourism-led economy, as Leatherman and Goodman (2005) point out, leads to "environmental, social and health costs for many Mayan households" and, because of economic inequalities built into the system, leave the Maya "a peripheral element in their own homeland" (844). Most of the Cobá families have access to the trappings of the wider Mexican material culture, through television and the internet, but struggle economically to participate. The most insidious example of this inequality is with access to healthcare. Because the public healthcare system in Mexico is poorly funded, the Maya must go to private clinics for major health issues, where treatment is conditional on the ability to pay. It is a terrible thing for a parent to know that there is a treatment that can save their child's life, but it is inaccessible to them because of cost. There is no amount of available tourism work that could possibly cover those kinds of expenses.

Tourism has other effects in addition to the health and growth of children. The loss of language and religious beliefs has lasting effects on the community. The irony of recent Maya acculturation after centuries of resistance to colonial rule, which Kintz first pointed out in 1990, is still true today. Families in Cobá may find it difficult to recover aspects of their agricultural, dietary, and material culture once they are lost. However, it seems that pursuing a tourism economy and preserving Maya culture are not necessarily mutually exclusive endeavors. By creating avenues for making money by showcasing traditional crafts, language, and subsistence practices, Cobá families could benefit more from tourism while keeping those traditional aspects of Maya culture alive (see Chapter 32). However, without structural reforms to healthcare and wages, Cobá families will continue to struggle to keep their children healthy.

REFLECTION AND DISCUSSION QUESTIONS

- How has tourism impacted culture in the Yucatán, and more specifically in Cobá? In what ways has cultural change in Cobá contributed to dietary changes?
- How have dietary changes affected the growth and health of children in Cobá?
- What are the benefits and drawbacks of an economy that relies heavily on tourism, such as in Cobá?
- What larger structural factors contribute to health inequalities in the Yucatán?

KEY CONCEPTS

- **anthropometry**: The study of the measurements and proportions of the human body.
- **kitchen garden**: Cultivated plot near the house where vegetables, fruits, and herbs are grown.
- **macronutrients**: The main bulk of nutrients required for energy and running body systems, including carbohydrates, fat, and protein.
- **micronutrients**: Nutrients needed in smaller amounts, including vitamins and minerals, that are critical to the healthy functioning of the human body.
- **milpa**: The field in which beans, corn, squash, and other vegetables are grown. The term is also used as a descriptor for this type of agriculture.
- **nutrition transition**: The shift from diets largely comprising fresh fruits and vegetables, lean protein, and complex carbohydrates, coupled with high activity levels, to diets where processed, high-fat, and high-sugar foods and low activity levels predominate.

EXPLORE FURTHER

- To learn more about the role tourism plays in Maya communities in Mexico, read **Chapter 26**.
- To learn more about the social and economic effects of the COVID-19 pandemic, read **Chapters 12** and **26**.
- Azcorra, Hugo, and Frederico Dickinson, eds. 2020. *Culture, Health and Environment in the Yucatan Peninsula: A Human Ecology Perspective*. New York: Springer.
- Bogin, Barry, and Ryan Keep. 1999. "Eight Thousand Years of Economic and Political History in Latin America Revealed by Anthropometry." *Annals of Human Biology* 26 (4): 333–51.
- Dammen, Siri. 2005. "Nutritional Vulnerability in Indigenous Children of the Americas: A Human Rights Issue." In *Indigenous Peoples and Poverty: An International Perspective*, edited by Robyn Eversole, John-Andrew McNeish, and Alberto D. Cimadamore, 69–94. London: Zed Books.
- Litka, Stephanie. 2013. "The Maya of Cobá: Managing Tourism in a Local Ejido." *Annals of Tourism Research* 43: 350–69.

ABOUT THE AUTHOR

Kristi J. Krumrine is a lecturer in the Department of Anthropology at the State University of New York at Geneseo. Her research interests include nutrition, growth, and health of children in contemporary and bioarcheological populations, and the history of disease and medicine.

REFERENCES

Azcorra, Hugh, Maria Ines Varela-Silva, Luis Rodriguez, Barry Bogin, and Frederico Dickinson. 2013. "Nutritional Status of Maya Children, Their Mothers, and Their Grandmothers Residing in the City of Merida, Mexico: Revisiting the Leg-Length Hypothesis." *American Journal of Human Biology* 25: 659–65. https://doi.org/10.1002/ajhb.22427.

Boas, Franz. 1912. *Changes in Bodily Form of Descendants of Immigrants*. New York: Colombia University Press.

Dettwyler, Katherine. 1994. *Dancing Skeletons: Life and Death in West Africa*. Long Grove, IL: Waveland Press.

Instituto Nacional de Antropología e Historia. 2021. March 6. Sistema Institucional Estdistica de Visitantes. https://www.estadisticas.inah.gob.mx.

Kintz, Ellen. 1990. *Under the Tropical Canopy: Tradition and Change among the Yucatec Maya*. Fort Worth, TX: Holt, Rinehart and Winston.

Krumrine, Kristi. 2017. "Effects of Diet and Culture Change on Growth, Development and Nutrition among Yucatec Maya Children." Ph.D. diss., SUNY Buffalo.

Leatherman, Thomas, and Alan Goodman. 2005. "Coca-Colonization of Diets in the Yucatan." *Social Science & Medicine* 61: 833–46. https://doi.org/10.1016/j.socscimed.2004.08.047.

Pendergrast, Mark. 2000. *For God, Country, and Coca-Cola: The Unauthorized History of the Great American Soft Drink and the Company That Makes It*. New York: Charles Scribner's Sons.

Puleston, Dennis. 1982. "The Role of Ramon in Maya Subsistence." In *Maya Subsistence: Studies in Memory of Dennis E. Puleston*, edited by Kent Flannery, 353–66. New York: Academic Press.

Sharpe, Pamela. 2012. "Explaining the Short Stature of the Poor: Chronic Childhood Disease and Growth in Nineteenth-Century England." *Economic History Review* 65 (4): 1475–94. https://doi.org/10.1111/j.1468-0289.2011.00629.x.

SECTION ELEVEN

Migration and Kinship

While migration is often viewed as a modern phenomenon, and sometimes cast as a modern problem, it is, in fact, a central part of human history and has been a characteristic behavior of our species for at least 100,000 years. One of the last regions on earth to be populated by humans, Latin America and the Caribbean has been characterized by ongoing processes of migration for a very long time. Archaeological evidence suggests that people arrived and spread across continental Latin America between 20,000 and 30,000 years ago, and the earliest people to reside in the islands of the Caribbean may have arrived there as early as 8,000 years before the present (see Chapter 2).

Today, people's motivations for and experiences with migration vary greatly, but certain patterns are consistent across much of the region. These include a range of common **push factors** driving people to migrate away from their homes: political instability, violence, climate change and natural disasters, under-resourced healthcare systems, a dearth of economic opportunities, and other obstacles that compromise people's ability to survive and thrive. Presently, Honduras has one of the highest outmigration rates in the region, the result of widespread violence that has become commonplace and is perpetrated by both state and nonstate actors. This violence, and the associated humanitarian crisis it has created, is suffered disproportionately by LGBTQ+ people, people with disabilities, journalists, activists, and women, as well as children and youth who resist recruitment into gangs. In 2017 alone, more than 75,000 Hondurans formally sought asylum in another country due to well-warranted fear for their lives (Human Rights Watch 2021).

In weighing decisions about migration, people and communities are also influenced by **pull factors** – variables that encourage migration to a certain place – including perceptions of safety in a receiving community, presence of family members, access to education and healthcare, and job opportunities. For example, financial opportunities in Belize's tourism industry *pull* Guatemalan women to migrate to Belize, where they can more readily sell their handicrafts than at home.

Internal migration is the movement of people from one place to another within the confines of a nation-state. In Latin America and the Caribbean, this most often takes the form of rural to urban migration, as people seek employment, safety, or social opportunities in cities. For example, in Jamaica, a dearth of economic opportunities and declining subsistence systems in rural areas contribute to individual and household decisions to relocate to Kingston and other cities. Internal migrants often face challenges that exacerbate their precarity, even as they move in pursuit of security. Barriers include competitive job markets, lack of social connections, and scarcity of safe and secure housing.

International migration involves crossing nation-state boundaries and is often complicated by xenophobic and nativist discourses and policies that illegalize migration and stigmatize migrants. While the international migration of citizens from Latin American and Caribbean nations to the United States and other countries of the Global North garners considerable attention, there are also dynamic patterns of migration happening within Latin America and the Caribbean. Political and economic turmoil in Venezuela since the turn of the millennium, for example, has triggered waves of outmigration by Venezuelans to other parts of South America. Since Colombia reopened its border with Venezuela in 2016, the number of Venezuelans living in Colombia alone has risen to an estimated 1.7 million (World Bank 2021).

Transnational migrants – international migrants who maintain active ties with their home communities – often sustain family members or prepare for their own eventual return by sending **remittances**. These funds help families subsidize household expenses and education, and sometimes enable investments in land, farming, home construction, or business ventures. Transnational ties are facilitated by advances in communication technologies, which allow people to maintain connections over long distances and periods of separation. Nevertheless, migration ultimately impacts **kinship** (i.e., social relationships between people who are connected genealogically, by marriage, or through other salient means, including *comadrazgo* (godmother) and *compadrazgo* (godfather) relations) in consequential ways. For example, in Nicaragua many older women take on the responsibilities of raising grandchildren when their own children emigrate, serving as the center of transnational families.

The chapters in this section explore the effects of international migration on individuals and kinship networks. In Chapter 34, Fouratt examines transnational relationships of Nicaraguan migrants in Costa Rica, focusing on their communication with those who remain in Nicaragua facing government repression. In Chapter 35, Haenn explores the dynamics between women whose sons have emigrated to the United States and their daughters-in-law, focusing on the impacts remittances have on gender norms and kinship bonds. In Chapter 36, Gembus explores how young Guatemalan-Mexicans reconcile their grandparents' refugee narratives about fleeing Guatemala with their parents' experiences of emigrating to the United States, and what both sets of migration stories mean for them.

KEY CONCEPTS

- **internal migration**: The movement of people from one place to another within the confines of a nation-state.
- **international migration**: The movement of people across nation-state boundaries, often complicated by xenophobic and nativist discourses and policies that illegalize migration and stigmatize migrants.
- **kinship**: Social relationships between people who are connected genealogically, by marriage, or through other salient means, including *comadrazgo* (godmother) and *compadrazgo* (godfather) relations.
- **pull factors**: Variables that encourage migration to a certain place – including perceptions of safety in a receiving community, presence of family members, access to education and healthcare, and job opportunities.
- **push factors**: Variables that drive people to migrate away from their homes: political instability, violence, climate change and natural disasters, under-resourced healthcare systems, a dearth of economic opportunities, and other obstacles that compromise people's ability to survive and thrive.
- **remittances**: Money sent from one person to another, including money sent by migrants to people back home.
- **transnational migrants**: International migrants who maintain active ties with their home communities, often through sending remittances.

EXPLORE FURTHER

- To learn more about the push factors contributing to people's decisions to migrate, read the chapters in **Sections 7**, **8**, and **9** and watch *Harvest of Empire* (directed by Peter Getzels and Eduardo López, 2012).
- Yarris, Kristin E. 2017. *Care Across Generations: Solidarity and Sacrifice in Transnational Families.* Redwood City, CA: Stanford University Press.

REFERENCES

Human Rights Watch. 2021. "Honduras: Events of 2020." https://www.hrw.org/world-report/2021/country-chapters/honduras#.

World Bank. 2021. "Supporting Colombian Host Communities and Venezuelan Migrants during the COVID-19 Pandemic." https://www.worldbank.org/en/results/2021/10/31/supporting-colombian-host-communities-and-venezuelan-migrants-during-the-covid-19-pandemic.

CHAPTER THIRTY-FOUR

Digital Solidarities, Transnational Families, and the Nicaraguan Refugee Crisis in Costa Rica

Caitlin E. Fouratt

On April 19, 2018, I woke up in southern California to dozens of WhatsApp and Facebook messages from Nicaraguan friends and colleagues sharing stories of police attacking student protestors on the streets of Managua, Masaya, and other Nicaraguan cities. One friend, Andrea, forwarded videos from her nephew who had been chased inside a church by Sandinista youth, the militant youth arm of the Sandinista party: "Caty, he wrote his ID number on his arm, in case they come in and kill them all. Please, spread this so the world knows what's happening in Nicaragua."

Andrea, like many Nicaraguans trying to make sense of the massive civil protests and violent repression of 2018 (Figure 34.1), was living in Costa Rica at the time as a migrant domestic worker. As protests spread and the Nicaraguan government censored or suspended news media, Nicaraguan migrants in Costa Rica found themselves viewing the conflict through social media and messages from family and friends back home. Many expressed a sense of helplessness and frustration at being simultaneously connected to loved ones and too far to help as their children, elderly parents, and extended families faced violence and uncertainty.

In this chapter, I explore how the transnational connections Nicaraguan families have developed over the last 20 years in Costa Rica have contributed to new solidarities in the face of government repression in Nicaragua. I draw on more than two years of participant observation and interviews with migrant and non-migrant family members. I focus on families' use of messaging apps and other information and communications technologies (ICTs) to examine how transnational families both enact virtual co-presence and attempt to build broader solidarities in the face of a nation in crisis.

Figure 34.1. "Masaya Will Bloom" – July 2018 march in Masaya, Nicaragua, in honor of victims killed in April during protests. Photo by Jorge Mejía Peralta (CC BY 2.0).

METHODS: TRACING TRANSNATIONAL MIGRATION

I began working with Nicaraguan migrants in Costa Rica in 2005 as a Fulbright scholar and have continued researching, observing, and participating in the work of recognizing migrants' rights in Costa Rica since then. Between 2009 and 2012, I conducted 24 months of multi-sited fieldwork with Nicaraguans in Costa Rica and their family members in Nicaragua. Since then, I have returned often to both Costa Rica and Nicaragua to interview and observe family and migration dynamics. In 2016, I began working with asylum seekers living in Costa Rica. This long-term engagement with migrant communities has allowed me to observe changing family connections over time as well as dramatic shifts in migration dynamics in the region.

In 2018, my work with Nicaraguan migrant families and my newer project with refugees collided when almost 100,000 Nicaraguans fled to Costa Rica in the face of government repression. I arrived in Costa Rica in June 2018 to conduct participant observation in the asylum office of the Costa Rican government's migration directorate. There, I met newly arrived Nicaraguan students, activists, and people who had been targeted by paramilitary groups for offering aid to protestors. Many already had family or friends in Costa Rica.

Like many scholars of migration, I conducted multi-sited ethnographic fieldwork by following migrants' routes between countries, communities, and households to trace their social and family connections. This participant observation and interviews in both host and home communities, with migrants and non-migrants, provided insight into the multiple spatial and temporal realities of migrants' and transnational family members' lives (Berg 2017; Fitzgerald 2006; Marcus 1995). The multi-sited and mobile methods employed in migration research have changed over time, in parallel with changes in transnational family communication. Smartphones and messaging apps have increased the possibilities for immediate connection among members of transnational families. They have also reshaped how migration scholars do fieldwork and connect with their interlocutors.

The ubiquity of WhatsApp and other messaging apps means that researchers with long-term connections to interlocutors never really "leave" the field, even when miles or continents away. Such instantaneous digital connection has shifted the expectations and the relationship between researchers and interlocutors. Research participants are more easily accessible for follow up. Indeed, I have been able to trace asylum seekers' progress through the immigration system from afar. However, such connection brings with it new ethical obligations and tensions as ethnographers become imbricated in networks of solidarity and witnessing, especially in moments of crisis. What were my responsibilities to research participants who faced choices between violence and food scarcity in Nicaragua or migrating without visas to Costa Rica? How could I, from my office in California, support their fight to tell the world about what was happening in Nicaragua?

SOUTH–SOUTH MIGRATION AND NICARAGUAN MIGRATION TO COSTA RICA

Although roughly half of all migrants globally migrate within the Global South, we know relatively little about so-called South–South migration (De Lombaerde, Guo, and Neto 2014; Ratha and Shaw 2007). **South–South migration** refers to migration among countries in the Global South and includes not only migration among low-income countries, but also middle-income countries, like Costa Rica or Argentina, which serve as centers of attraction within Latin America (Khan and Hossain 2017; Kofman and Raghuram 2009). Research on Central American migration has largely focused on migration to the United States and the legacy of political conflict, economic crisis, and US intervention in Guatemala, El Salvador, and Honduras (Abrego 2017; Coutin 2007; Heidbrink 2014; Menjivar 2006; Schmalzbauer 2004). However, there has been much less attention given to the diversity of migration pathways within Central America and the importance of intraregional migration. While in sheer size Central American migration to the United States dwarfs migration to Costa Rica, Costa Rica has the highest percentage of foreign-born population of any Latin American country (Cerrutti and Parrado 2015).

Costa Rica has become a major migrant destination within Central America because of uneven processes of regional economic development and political conflict since the colonial era. Current Nicaraguan migration is a direct result of chronic economic crisis and political conflict since the 1970s. During the Sandinista Revolution in the 1980s, Costa Rica received more than 30,000 Nicaraguans fleeing the Contra War who established strong networks that have encouraged continued migration. Since the end of the Sandinista Revolution in 1990, migration has been prompted primarily by economic factors: unemployment, low wages, the dismantling of the social safety net in Nicaragua, and a relatively thriving export-oriented economy in Costa Rica. By the early 2000s, about 10 per cent of Nicaragua's population lived outside its borders (Baumeister 2006), and remittances, the money and gifts migrants send back home, represented the largest source of national income (Martínez Franzoni and Voorend 2011). In contrast, Costa Rica's export-oriented development has generated a high demand for low-wage migrant labor. Nicaraguans make up almost 7 per cent of the Costa Rican population and play a key role in the construction, agriculture, and service sectors (INEC 2011; Morales and Castro 2006). Since the 1990s, this economic migration has also shifted from the temporary migration of male migrant laborers to more permanent settlement and the migration of more women and families (Mahler 2000).

In terms of family life, migration within Central America entails different expectations for family relationships, remittance sending, and return visits than migration to more distant destinations like the United States. For example, during annual Easter and Christmas holidays, some 70,000 migrants in Costa Rica return to Nicaragua to visit family (Solano 2013). Relatively short and inexpensive travel between the two countries also facilitates movement, and until recently lax border enforcement has made undocumented migration relatively low risk. However, the past 15 years have witnessed the tightening of Costa Rican immigration restrictions, which have made gaining legal status more difficult and limited the flexibility of Nicaraguan transnational family configurations. While on paper Costa Rican immigration law provides for family reunification, in practice legal status is hard to attain. These contradictions have generated a situation in which there is a high level of cross-border mobility as well as high levels of settlement in Costa Rica, creating enduring transnational dynamics.

FAMILY SOLIDARITIES AND VIRTUAL CO-PRESENCE

Transnational families, that is, families in which members live in two or more countries, are fraught with tensions over separation and distance (Abrego 2009; Boehm 2012; Dreby 2010). In my research, the most common form that transnational families take is of a migrant parent or parents in Costa Rica and children and grandmother caregivers in Nicaragua (Yarris 2017). Many also have younger children born in Costa Rica. For these families, migration represents a gamble: Migrants hope that by leaving they will be able to better provide for their families, but the costs of absence may outweigh the economic stability migration can bring (Boehm 2019; Dreby 2010; Pribilsky 2007).

Transnational family dynamics are tied to ideas and norms about gender and family roles. For example, scholars have noted that migrant mothers' absences are especially hard on children left behind (Abrego 2009; Parreñas 2005; Yarris 2017). Others have found that men are often less involved in long-distance parenting (Akesson 2009; Carling, Menjívar, and Schmalzbauer 2012; Parreñas 2005; Schmalzbauer 2004). Migrants' economic opportunities and legal status, as well as possibilities for travel and communication also impact transnational family life. Migrants employ a variety of techniques to maintain family and community ties, including phone calls, text messages, and other forms of communication, travel, and sending money and gifts (Baldassar 2008). Indeed, through cross-border communication, migrants and non-migrant family members enact care for one another (Arnold 2021). However, migrants' and non-migrants' interpretations of migration are multifaceted and change over time depending on geography, generation, and gender (McKenzie and Menjívar 2011). Indeed, families back home often experience great ambivalence over migrant parents' absences and the remittances they send back (Yarris 2017).

Since 2011, the increasing availability of prepaid cell phones in Costa Rica has reshaped possibilities for sustaining transnational ties between Costa Rica and Nicaragua. When I first traveled to Costa Rica as an undergraduate studying abroad in 2003, I, like many migrant women I would later work with, had to purchase an international calling card and use a public payphone to call my parents every two weeks. Cell phones were nearly impossible for noncitizens to access, and international calls within Latin America were especially expensive. Juana, a Nicaraguan woman I met in 2011 who had been in Costa Rica for more than 10 years at the time, complained about the high prices of phone calls through "el ICE," the *Instituto Costarricense de Electricidad*, the Costa Rican electricity and communications agency: "If you think about it, even ICE is cruel to us [migrants] because it's cheaper to call the United States than to call Nicaragua. That doesn't make any sense. It's so expensive!"

Back in Nicaragua, few homes had landlines, and families would visit internet cafés or pay to use the landline at a wealthier neighbor's house. This allowed transnational families regular, though infrequent and expensive, communication. In 2009, I visited the sending community of Achuapa, a small town in northern Nicaragua where local officials estimate that up to 30 per cent of the population has emigrated. There, many family members discussed the disconnect between migrants in Costa Rica, Europe, or Panama and families in the small town. At the time, there was just one internet café and only a few families had cell phones. Physical distance between transnational family members was exacerbated by temporal disconnection and reinforced by such piecemeal communications. In communities of origin, children's lives revolved around school, extended family, and the rhythms of life in Nicaragua, while migrant parents' lives revolved around work and often their lack of legal status in Costa Rica (cf. Dreby 2010).

Starting in 2011, though, the liberalization of the telecommunications sector in Costa Rica resulted in the proliferation of prepaid cell-phone services that do not require consumers to have legal status or citizenship. During this time, many families in Nicaragua prioritized using remittances to purchase smartphones or internet access in their homes, facilitating transnational communication. Now, instead of occasional and "awkward" phone calls, as one of my teenage interviewees in Nicaragua put it, family members can be in daily contact through WhatsApp, Facebook, and other messaging platforms. They not only text but also share voice messages, inspiring poems, funny memes, and popular songs. These forms of **virtual co-presence** bridge the geographic and temporal distances to create and sustain connections between family members (Baldassar 2008; Arnold 2021).

Take Lisseth, a teenager from Managua whose mother, Dulce, had been in Costa Rica for more than 10 years. In 2011, her mother sent her a computer and started paying for internet access at home. Lisseth explained: "Well, last December, she brought us that computer. She has her Facebook; I have my Facebook. And we can chat there. I tell her things and we chat. Or if we don't have time to chat on Facebook, she calls us, and we call to stay in contact too." The ability to contact her mother whenever she wants to tell her something has changed their relationship. When she was a child, Lisseth had trouble understanding why her mother had left: "Before, I used to say that my mom couldn't be here because she didn't love me. That's what I thought as a child. But now I know that she left to seek a better life for my brother and me." Lisseth not only gained a new perspective on her mother's migration but also developed a stronger relationship with her thanks to their virtual connection. She said that growing up, she would go to an aunt or her grandmother with problems, but that she always felt like she was missing her mother's insight and advice. With the new computer, that changed:

> And so now, whenever I need to tell her something we call her or my aunts call her and we talk. And now, thanks to the computer I chat with her more frequently. I used to only call her once a month or every two weeks. Now we talk almost daily; we chat daily.

A few months later, Dulce sent money so Lisseth could have her own cell phone, and she would proudly text me from it. Today, she and her mom tag each other in photos on Facebook and leave WhatsApp voice messages throughout the day, sharing not only major events and problems but everyday thoughts and cares.

Lisseth's experience shows how forms of virtual co-presence do not necessarily replace a migrant parent's absence, but they do help to bridge the emotional divide by giving migrant parents insight into children's and caregivers' daily lives. They also give those back home insight into the struggles migrant relatives face in Costa Rica. Such instantaneous connection can be critical in moments of family crisis – managing illness or unforeseen events. These close connections would become critical in 2018, as Nicaraguan families faced a national crisis of state repression and violence.

THE 2018 PROTESTS: A CRISIS IN THE COMMUNITY OF CARE

In April 2018, ongoing protests over the mishandling of a wildfire in the Nicaraguan Indio Maiz biosphere reserve were joined by public outcry over pension reforms. The combined protests gained momentum as students joined pensioners and human rights and environmental activists in protests that quickly expanded to encompass calls for President Daniel Ortega's resignation.

Protestors were met with riot police firing live ammunition. In the days that followed, students barricaded themselves in universities and churches. Paramilitary and police groups circulated through Managua, Masaya, Leon, and other cities, conducting extrajudicial detentions and beating protestors and their supporters. So far, the conflict has resulted in more than 300 people dead, thousands wounded, and an unknown number still missing or held as political prisoners (Cruz-Feliciano 2021).

While Daniel Ortega first came to power during the Sandinista Revolution of the 1980s, his current administration bears little resemblance to the radical dreams of social and economic transformation of that revolution. Although Ortega's motto – "Nicaragua: Socialist, Christian, and in Solidarity" – echoes revolutionary values, Ortega has consolidated power in his office and his person, strengthened clientelistic relationships at all levels, and ridiculed dissent and protest. As anthropologist Julienne Weegels (2018) has noted, "Ortega governs from a position beyond the law."

The April 2018 protests gave voice to more than a decade of frustration with the Ortega regime and a crisis in the community of care of the nation. The **community of care**, a term I borrow from Ellen Moodie (2011), implies the promises of democracy in post-war Central America to fulfill desires for belonging and equality. In Nicaragua, the community of care encompasses not just desires for democracy but for solidarity, a key value of the Sandinista Revolution of the 1980s that has been revitalized under the current Ortega regime. As Gioconda Belli (1982), the Nicaraguan revolutionary and poet wrote, "solidarity is the tenderness of the people," that is, it encompasses both an affective dimension and a moral call to action on behalf of the oppressed. Yet Ortega's authoritarian politics, increasing militarization of the state, and criminalization of opposition have exposed cracks in these official notions of solidarity. Indeed, most transnational families I worked with expressed deep dissatisfaction with Ortega's regime, even if they identified with the Sandinista Party. After all, many emigrated because they could not find work, afford healthcare, or create economic stability for their families at home in Nicaragua.

DIGITAL SOLIDARITIES IN A MOMENT OF CRISIS

For both migrants already living in Costa Rica and their families back home, the forms of virtual co-presence they had developed over years of transnational family life became key to navigating this crisis of the community of care by mitigating immediate threats and creating networks of solidarity. In the immediate aftermath of the protests, migrants in Costa Rica relied on cell phones to ascertain the safety of loved ones and, like Andrea, to make sense of and circulate information about what was going on in Nicaragua. Andrea's nephew eventually made it out of the cathedral, where a group of students had been cornered by Sandinista youth and police. As Ortega shut down or censored major television stations and expelled several foreign journalists, most of the migrants I worked with in Costa Rica learned about what was happening from loved ones who were either participating in or trying to avoid contact with the protests. When I received Andrea's message about her nephew, I reached out to Lisseth, who at the time was a student at one of the universities that had been closed. She replied via Facebook messenger almost immediately: "Things have gotten out of hand, but our family, everyone's good, *gracias a Dios*." Her mother, in Costa Rica, warned her to stay off the streets and away from campus until things had calmed down.

In the weeks that followed, transnational networks would be mobilized to organize the movement of tens of thousands of Nicaraguans fleeing to Costa Rica, providing information to protestors about safe routes through and out of the country. Newly arrived asylum seekers in Costa Rica talked about the importance of Facebook posts in knowing where government forces might be; in connecting protestors to food, water, and supplies; and to keeping opposition members informed as the Ortega administration began to limit coverage of the conflict and crack down on the opposition press. Digital networks functioned to ease the risks of travel as folks leaving attempted to circumvent paramilitary and police forces, blockades set up by the protestors, and Costa Rican border police. What had for decades been a relatively porous and open border suddenly presented significant challenges for those fleeing violence. Andrea used her contacts with activists in the northern region of Costa Rica to coordinate safe transit for her nephew and his father. Such solidarity building incorporated not just transnational family members, but also immigrant advocates, researchers, and others into expansive transnational networks of solidarity and care, in direct opposition to Nicaraguan state violence. I found myself asking migration police for advice about acquaintances who were attempting to cross "*por monte*," that is, through the forests and hills that characterize the border region. Over several separate message chains, I was advised of various "safe" routes across unpatrolled sections of the border by migration police, asylum officers, and colleagues at local NGOs.

Those same digital networks would be used to warn asylum seekers of Ortega supporters' infiltration of Costa Rica. Carolina, a young woman from Muy Muy, Matagalpa, where some of the most violent confrontations between police and protestors occurred, recounted nearly bumping into a police officer from her Nicaraguan hometown in Costa Rica. She had been meeting with a cousin and some friends in the Parque de la Merced, a park in downtown San José that is a key place where Nicaraguan migrants gather, socialize, and network. The cliché is that if you go to la Merced any Sunday, you're sure to find someone from your hometown. In Carolina's case, this was true but terrifying, when the man she recognized across the plaza was an Orteguista officer who had beaten protestors at the blockades in Muy Muy. She worried that if he saw her, he would report back to authorities in her hometown and her elderly father would suffer. When

I passed these concerns on to a colleague at a Costa Rican NGO, she replied, "Oh of course, we've seen a lot of infiltration like that" and asked if Carolina had taken a picture with her phone. Soon, the police officer's face was making its rounds among NGO staff, networks of asylum seekers, and had been passed along to government asylum officers. Lists of names and pictures of other Ortega-linked agents circulated widely, alerting Costa Rican officials and NGO staff to the "infiltration" of supposedly safe spaces by individuals who could pose a danger to asylum seekers.

DIGITAL SOLIDARITY AND WITNESSING

Nicaraguan transnational families not only employed digital connections to enact practical forms of solidarity for those fleeing the violence in Nicaragua; they also engaged in broader forms of solidarity and witnessing that challenged official discourses that minimized and criminalized opposition. As the Ortega administration featured its own countermarches on state-controlled media, and Vice-President/First Lady Rosario Murillo called protestors vampires, vandals, criminals, and terrorists, the circulation of students' cell-phone videos, barricaded in university labs or local churches, documented state-sanctioned violence.

This on-the-ground, first-hand witnessing of state-sanctioned violence contested official narratives that position Ortega and his wife and vice-president as the only legitimate voices of "*el pueblo*," the people. Ortega and Murillo spent more than a decade systematically demobilizing social movements in Nicaragua, even those that emerged as part of the original Sandinista Revolution. But they could not control the circulation of first-hand accounts or social media posts. As these accounts moved beyond personal family and social networks to circulate throughout the Nicaraguan diaspora and beyond, they took on the quality of the quintessentially Latin American form of **testimonio** (testimony). Through personal narratives of history in progress, *testimonios* contribute to the creation of social memory – the collective memories and shared history that shape people's perceptions of their identities as part of a group. In this case, these *testimonios* recalled earlier memories of collective revolutionary struggle during the Sandinista Revolution. The circulation and dissemination of *testimonios* serve to create experiences of "a passionate politics" of collective struggle among those who listen, share, and recycle the stories of individual activists (Stephen 2017, 99).

Sharing and commenting on videos served to incorporate migrants into this work of dismantling official discourses and forming broader solidarities. Social media provided a sense of shared temporality not just within families but among the larger transnational nation as those in Nicaragua, Costa Rica, and beyond participated in sense-making and meaning-making around the events despite their physical distance. Videos, tweets, and photos that made comparisons to the fall of the Somoza dictatorship in 1979 situated the conflict within narratives of generations of revolutionary struggle in Nicaragua. While Ortega's regime has long co-opted narratives of solidarity and popular struggle, the opposition explicitly used Sandinista revolutionary symbols to challenge these narratives and reframe Ortega as the dictator. It was an opportunity to draw on the strength of transnational connections developed over years and multiple migrations to build broader solidarity around a community of care under threat. Transnational family members saw both the protests and their own migration decisions as the results of decades of frustration with the failure of the original Sandinista Revolution, the poverty they experienced under subsequent regimes focused on neoliberal reforms and foreign investment, and their disappointment in the unfulfilled promises of Ortega's return to power.

CONCLUSION

For Nicaraguan transnational families who participated virtually in making sense of the protests and ensuing violence or in helping asylum seekers cross the border to Costa Rica, ICTs served to bridge temporal separations. Such separations, though commonplace within transnational families, were heightened by the conflict. Despite state discourses of solidarity and revolution, working-class Nicaraguans found their already precarious family lives more uncertain in the wake of protests and state violence. In this context, the transnational intimacies and virtual co-presence strengthened by families represented key resources for resolving fears and providing safe routes to Costa Rica.

At the same time, these transnational networks served to develop broader political identities by situating both migrants and non-migrants within national narratives of solidarity and revolution. While digital transnational connections play key roles in the rapid reorganization of care activities during family crises, the Nicaraguan refugee "crisis" demonstrates their importance when the wider nation or community of care is in crisis. By circulating videos and pleas of family members, Nicaraguans worked to incorporate migrants, advocates, researchers, and others into expansive transnational networks of solidarity and care, in direct opposition to Nicaraguan state violence. As the repression persists more than three years later and tens of thousands of Nicaraguans seek refuge abroad, Andrea's call to share what is happening in Nicaragua continues to challenge us to find effective avenues of solidarity from afar.

REFLECTION AND DISCUSSION QUESTIONS

- What are some differences you see between migration within Central America and Central American migration to the United States? How might these differences affect transnational families separated by borders?
- How have increasing access to technology – specifically cell phones, social media, and messaging apps – changed the ways transnational families maintain relationships across borders?

- How have digital technologies like messaging apps changed your relationship to your family and loved ones? How have they affected your political engagement with broader social issues?
- Some critics of online political engagement see the circulation of information, memes, and protests as a kind of passive participation that ultimately has limited impact in social, political, and economic transformation. Do you agree? Why or why not?

KEY CONCEPTS

- **community of care**: A term used by anthropologist Ellen Moodie (2011) that refers to a responsive democracy committed to equality and justice and inspiring a sense of belonging. Moodie refers to the community of care as part of the promise of the transition to peace from civil war in Central American countries at the end of the 1980s.
- **South–South migration**: Migration within the Global South among low- and middle-income countries. Much of this migration takes place within regions, though there is also South–South migration across regions, as in the case of African migration to Latin America, for example.
- *testimonio*: A genre of Latin American narrative that features eyewitness accounts of major political events from the perspective of the marginalized to provide a counter-narrative to official accounts. They make visible situations of oppression and resistance to such oppression as well as build collective identities.
- **transnational families**: Families in which members live in different countries and participate in family life across borders. Understandings of separation and expectations for connection within families vary among members, often by age, gender, and location.
- **virtual co-presence**: The ways in which members of transnational families employ different technologies to "be with" family members even when physically separated across borders. Virtual co-presence can be created through video and phone calls, text messages, gifts, and more.

EXPLORE FURTHER

- To learn more about the effects of political violence, read **Chapters 8** and **11** and the chapters in **Section 7**.
- To learn more about transnational families, read **Chapters 35** and **36**.
- Boehm, Deborah A. 2012. *Intimate Migrations: Gender, Family, and Illegality Among Transnational Mexicans*. New York: NYU Press.
- Chamorro, Luciana. 2019. "The April Civic Uprising and Its Sandinista Roots." Hot Spots. *Fieldsights, Society for Cultural Anthropology*, January 23. https://tinyurl.com/Fieldsights.

- Nikunen, Kaarina. 2019. *Media Solidarities: Emotions, Power and Justice in the Digital Age.* Los Angeles: Sage.
- *(No) Soy (In)Visible.* A podcast project by *La Red de Jóvenes sin Fronteras* (Costa Rica) and California State University – Long Beach students of International Studies. https://tinyurl.com/No-Soy-Invisible.

ABOUT THE AUTHOR

Caitlin E. Fouratt is an associate professor of international studies at California State University Long Beach. Her research examines experiences of migrants, refugees, and transnational families in Latin America. As a cisgender white woman with US and Costa Rican citizenship, Caitlin is committed to addressing xenophobia and repressive immigration policies in the United States, Central America, and beyond through her research and teaching. She is the author of *Flexible Families: Nicaraguan Transnational Families in Costa Rica* (2022, Vanderbilt University Press).

REFERENCES

Abrego, Leisy. 2009. "Economic Well-Being in Salvadoran Transnational Families: How Gender Affects Remittance Practices." *Journal of Marriage and Families* 71: 1070–85. https://doi.org/10.1111/j.1741-3737.2009.00653.x.

———. 2017. "On Silences: Salvadoran Refugees Then and Now." *Latino Studies* 15 (1): 73–85. https://doi.org/10.1057/s41276-017-0044-4.

Akesson, Lisa. 2009. "Remittances and Inequality in Cape Verde: The Impact of Changing Family Organization." *Global Networks* 9 (3): 381–98. https://doi.org/10.1111/j.1471-0374.2009.00259.x.

Arnold, Lynnette. 2021. "Communication as Care across Borders: Forging and Co-Opting Relationships of Obligation in Transnational Salvadoran Families." *American Anthropologist* 123 (1): 137–49. https://doi.org/10.1111/aman.13517.

Baldassar, Loretta. 2008. "Missing Kin and Longing to Be Together: Emotions and the Construction of Co-Presence in Transnational Relationships." *Journal of Intercultural Studies* 29 (3): 247–66. https://doi.org/10.1080/07256860802169196.

Baumeister, Eduardo. 2006. "Migración Internacional y Desarrollo En Nicaragua." *Serie Poblacion y Desarrollo.* Santiago, Chile: CEPAL.

Belli, Gioconda. 1982. "La Ternura de los Pueblos." In *Truenos y Arco Iris*, edited by Belli Gioconda, 19. Managua, Nicaragua: Editorial Nueva Nicaragua.

Berg, Ulla D. 2017. *Mobile Selves: Race, Migration, and Belonging in Peru and the U.S.* New York: NYU Press.

Boehm, Deborah A. 2012. *Intimate Migrations: Gender, Family, and Illegality among Transnational Mexican.* New York: NYU Press.

———. 2019. "Un/Making Family: Relatedness, Migration, and Displacement in a Global Age." In *The Cambridge Handbook of Kinship*, edited by Sandra C. Bamford, 432–50. Cambridge: Cambridge University Press.

Carling, Jørgen, Cecilia Menjívar, and Leah Schmalzbauer. 2012. "Central Themes in the Study of Transnational Parenthood." *Journal of Ethnic & Migration Studies* 38 (2): 191–217. https://doi.org/10.1080/1369183X.2012.646417.

Cerrutti, Marcela, and Emilio Parrado. 2015. "Intraregional Migration in South America: Trends and a Research Agenda." *Annual Review of Sociology* 41: 399–421. https://doi.org/10.1146/annurev-soc-073014-112249.

Coutin, Susan Bibler. 2007. *Nations of Emigrants: Shifting Boundaries of Citizenship in El Salvador and the United States.* Ithaca, NY: Cornell University Press.

Cruz-Feliciano, Héctor M. 2021. "Whither Nicaragua Three Years On?" *Latin American Perspectives* 48 (6): 9–20. https://doi.org/10.1177/0094582X211041065.

De Lombaerde, Philippe, Fei Guo, and Helion Póvoa Neto. 2014. "Introduction to the Special Collection." *International Migration Review* 48 (1): 103–12. https://doi.org/10.1111/imre.12083.

Dreby, Joanna. 2010. *Divided by Borders: Mexican Migrants and Their Children.* Berkeley: University of California Press.

Fitzgerald, David. 2006. "Towards a Theoretical Ethnography of Migration." *Qualitative Sociology* 29 (1): 1–24. https://doi.org/10.1007/s11133-005-9005-6.

Heidbrink, Lauren. 2014. *Migrant Youth, Transnational Families, and the State: Care and Contested Interests.* Philadelphia: University of Pennsylvania Press.

INEC, Instituto Nacional de Estadísticas y Censos. 2011. *X Censo Nacional de Población y VI de Vivienda 2011 Resultados Generales.* San José: INEC.

Khan, M. Adil, and Munshi Israil Hossain. 2017. "The Emerging Phenomenon of Post-Globalized, South-South Migration: In Search of a Theoretical Framework." In *South-South Migration: Emerging Patterns, Opportunities and Risks,* edited by Patricia Short, Moazzem Hossain, and M. Adil Khan, 11–33. London: Routledge.

Kofman, Eleonore, and Parvati Raghuram. 2009. "The Implications of Migration for Gender and Care Regimes in the South." In *Social Policy and Development Programme Papers.* Geneva: United Nations Research Institute for Social Development.

Mahler, Sarah J. 2000. *Migration and Transnational Issues: Recent Trends and Prospects for 2020.* CA 2020: Working Paper. Hamburg: Institut für Iberoamerika-Kunde.

Marcus, George. 1995. "Ethnography in/of the World System: The Emergence of Multi-Sited Ethnography." *Annual Review of Anthropology* 24: 95–117. https://doi.org/10.1146/annurev.an.24.100195.000523.

Martínez Franzoni, Juliana, and Koen Voorend. 2011. "Who Cares in Nicaragua? A Care Regime in an Exclusionary Social Policy Context." *Development and Change* 42 (4): 995–1022. https://doi.org/10.1111/j.1467-7660.2011.01719.x.

McKenzie, Sean, and Cecilia Menjívar. 2011. "The Meanings of Migration, Remittances and Gifts: Views of Honduran Women Who Stay." *Global Networks* 11 (1): 63–81. https://doi.org/10.1111/j.1471-0374.2011.00307.x.

Menjivar, Cecilia. 2006. "Liminal Legality: Salvadoran and Guatemalan Immigrants' Lives in the United States." *American Journal of Sociology* 111: 999–1037. https://doi.org/10.1086/499509.

Moodie, Ellen. 2011. *El Salvador in the Aftermath of Peace: Crime, Uncertainty, and the Transition to Democracy.* Philadelphia: University of Pennsylvania Press.

Morales, Abelardo, and Carlos Castro. 2006. *Migración, Empleo y Pobreza.* San José, Costa Rica: FLACSO.

Parreñas, Rhacel Salazar. 2005. *Children of Global Migration: Transnational Families and Gendered Woes.* Stanford, CA: Stanford University Press.

Pribilsky, Jason. 2007. *La Chulla Vida: Gender, Migration, and the Family in Andean Ecuador and New York City.* Syracuse, NY: Syracuse University Press.

Ratha, Dilip, and William Shaw. 2007. "South-South Migration and Remittances." Working Paper No. 109. Washington, DC: World Bank.

Schmalzbauer, Leah. 2004. "Searching for Wages and Mothering from Afar: The Case of Honduran Transnational Families." *Journal of Marriage and Family* 66 (5): 1317–31. https://doi.org/10.1111/j.0022-2445.2004.00095.x.

Solano, Hugo. 2013. "Más de 70.000 Cruzarán La Frontera de Peñas Blancas Para Semana Santa." *La Nación*, March 19. http://www.nacion.com/archivo/mas-de-70-000-cruzaran-la-frontera-de-penas-blancas-para-semana-santa/IR3DA2P7ZVERRMJ734PEWESBYY/story.

Stephen, Lynn. 2017. "Bearing Witness: Testimony in Latin American Anthropology and Related Fields." *Journal of Latin American and Caribbean Anthropology* 22 (1): 85–109. https://doi.org/10.1111/jlca.12262.

Weegels, Julienne. 2018. "Inside Out: Confinement, Revolt and Repression in Nicaragua." *Association for Political and Legal Anthropology* (blog). October 3. https://politicalandlegalanthro.org/2018/10/03/inside-out-confinement-revolt-and-repression-in-nicaragua.

Yarris, Kristin E. 2017. *Care Across Generations: Solidarity and Sacrifice in Transnational Families*. Stanford, CA: Stanford University Press.

CHAPTER THIRTY-FIVE

Love, Money, and a Secret Divorce: Patriarchy and Senior Women's Caregiving in Mexican Migration

Nora Haenn

There was something in her neighbor's voice that caught Carmen's attention. "Does Octavio send money to Dolores?" the neighbor had asked. At the time, Carmen's son, Octavio, had been living in the United States for a few years. Every month, he sent $1,000 in remittances to his wife, Dolores.

Carmen had crossed paths with her neighbor while walking down the street of her hometown of Aserradero, a community of 1,000 people nestled in the forests of southern Mexico. By the turn of the new millennium, a series of Mexican and US policies (including NAFTA, Gálvez 2018) had shrunk rural Mexicans' economic options (and continue to do so), encouraging Aserraderans to travel to the United States. The travelers were mostly men, and their absence sent women on migration-related journeys of their own.

In Aserradero, $1,000 a month was a significant income. At the time, 6 per cent of Mexican households (or 26.5 million households) received remittances from family living abroad. On average, people received $200 per month (Ordaz Díaz 2009). Dolores not only received five times that amount, she did so in a county, Calakmul, where more than half the residents worked as semi-subsistence farmers. Cropping five to ten acres of land and with multiple people working odd jobs, a family might net $400 per month (Schmook and Radel 2008). Even police officers and government secretaries earned only half the sum Dolores received.

Unsurprisingly, when Calakmul county residents (or *Calakmuleños*) were able to access US jobs, many emigrated. By 2003, 7 per cent of the county's population over the age of 17 resided in the United States (Schmook and Radel 2008). Some 90 per cent of sojourners were young men traveling as undocumented migrants.

For Carmen, her neighbor's question was not entirely unexpected. *Calakmuleños* gossiped about couples undergoing a man's migration with an intensity that indicated the depth

Figure 35.1. A Mexican woman. Photo by Justin McWilliams (CC BY-ND 2.0).

of social pressures migration brought about, especially when it came to gender (Dreby 2009; Skolnik et al. 2012). Although *Calakmuleños* recognized and acknowledged queer members of their community, when it came to migration, their gaze focused forcefully on heteronormative couples.

Still, Carmen found a strangeness in her neighbor's tone. It seemed to go beyond the usual stirring of the rumor mill. Why did her neighbor ask about Dolores and the money? Carmen wondered.

Dolores lived just two doors from Carmen's own home, and Carmen kept an eye on the comings and goings at her daughter-in-law's house. Recently, Carmen had noticed one young man visiting with some frequency. At the time of the neighbor's question, Carmen suspected Dolores was having an affair. International migration often creates separations that leave spouses vulnerable to infidelity (Hirsch et al. 2009). As a result, research shows Mexico's migrant couples are at greater risk of divorce (Frank and Wildsmith 2005).

Carmen, however, could not approach Dolores on the matter. The two women barely spoke. Tensions between a mother-in-law and a daughter-in-law were common in this part of Mexico, and a man's migration could exacerbate the strain. When husbands traveled, their wives found themselves under surveillance (see also Rodman 2006). Mothers-in-law scrutinized their daughters-in-law's actions, probing for signs of wasteful spending and adultery. Mothers-in-law reported on their daughters-in-law's actions to stateside sons, who then demanded their wives account for their behavior.

I watched these dynamics jeopardize many marriages. To young wives, their mothers-in-law's accusations seemed out of proportion, leaving daughters-in-law to hurl an allegation of their own: Their in-laws were out to grab the remittances. One young wife, Dolores's neighbor, found herself accused of infidelity by her stateside husband after he received photos purportedly depicting her with another man. "I don't even have his address," she tearfully said of her husband. "I don't know where he is." The husband refused to name her accusers. Stunned, she could only imagine her in-laws had produced the photos. Why would they go to such lengths? "Well," the woman explained, "supposedly when husbands leave they send a lot of money. Then, it's almost always his family that starts to gossip. It's easy for them to say, 'You know, your wife is going out with this guy,' because they think if he leaves his wife, he'll send money to the person who invented the lie."

Indeed, Carmen's relationship with her son remained strong, and the two spoke regularly. Nothing in these conversations suggested anything amiss in his marriage. But Carmen harbored doubts about her daughter-in-law. And as she delved into that question – "Does Octavio send money to Dolores?" – she concluded that, sometimes, the mothers-in-law were rightfully concerned. From Carmen's perspective, mothering a migrant man sometimes meant carrying out emotional work on behalf of an absent son by disciplining his wife.

Sitting down to write this chapter, I asked Google why people migrate to the United States. Number two on the list of results summed things up this way: better job opportunities, better living conditions, to be with their spouses/families, to escape violence, to get the best education. If Google reflects popular thinking, the list is revealing. It assumes migrants are people whose ethnicity, skin color, age, family position, and gender do not matter much. Yet in Calakmul and elsewhere, depending on how a person occupies these social categories, their experiences of emigration differ markedly whether they themselves travel or not (Mahler and Pessar 2006). The list also assumes people who migrate do so permanently. Yet *Calakmuleños* always said an emigrant's sojourn was temporary, fearing permanent migration meant never seeing a loved one again (Haenn 2019). Perhaps most importantly, the list overlooks the reason *Calakmuleños* gave for traveling: to meet family goals *in Mexico*. Travel to the United States was a means to an end, and the end was always located in Calakmul.

This disconnect between popular US understandings and the emotionally complicated events transpiring in places like Calakmul arises in part from an approach to migration that focuses on migrants themselves. To address this lopsidedness, researchers call for studies that consider an array of actors who participate in migration. These actors might include state authorities who write economic policies, employers of immigrant workers, and migrants' extended families (Krissman 2005). This larger set includes two groups, those who migrate and those who do not. The combination is purposeful, because for some people to be mobile others must be immobile. The interdependence of travelers and stayers raises key questions: Who travels? Who doesn't? Why are people travelers at some points in their life and stayers at others? What do people expect of travelers versus stayers?

Recognizing the interdependence of movers and stayers, researchers ask us to consider "regimes of (im)mobility" (Glick Schiller and Salazar 2013). **Regimes of (im)mobility** entail the multiple pressures shaping migratory settings, making movers of some people and stayers of others. In Calakmul, this regime included the US job market and economic policies such as NAFTA. The regime also included gender ideals that marked women as non-travelers, although globally women and men are equally likely to travel for work (Sharpe 2002). Calakmul is home to a patriarchal society, meaning men's power both at home and in public was typically greater than women's. Thus, the regime marked men as travelers who would continue to hold a place of privileged authority in the family even while abroad.

Regimes of (im)mobility do not entirely determine people's migration-related decisions. Instead, regimes constrain people's options, nudging individuals in one direction or another. Regimes offer men, women, and people of different age groups access to different choices. In this sense, migration is a gendered and generational activity (Lutz 2010).

Importantly, regimes of (im)mobility include emotional dimensions that are also gendered and generational (Faier 2011). At first glance, emotions appear to be individualized. Certainly, people bring to migration their unique, personal experiences. However, given the way regimes of (im)mobility repeatedly place individuals in particular situations, such regimes *also* shape patterned feelings (Boehm 2013). For example, the emotions of government authorities who draft policies understandably differ from those of *Calakmuleña* mothers watching their sons risk a life-threatening journey to the United States.

Sometimes these emotions arise from migration's inherent qualities. Migration demands family separation and, thus, emotional loss. At the same time, in some regimes of (im)mobility, people *expect* individuals to display certain feelings regardless of whether people actually have those emotions (Brettell 2017). In the following, we watch Carmen occupy multiple positions in Calakmul's regime of (im)mobility, sometimes displaying culturally appropriate emotions and sometimes not.

The case of Carmen and Dolores brings into view a range of emotional work women undertake in migratory settings, especially older women. Research on older women's roles in migration tends to focus on their care for grandchildren whose parents live abroad (Yarris 2017). For Carmen and Dolores, it was the intermingling of love, money, and family authority that made for potent feelings. In the name of caring for her absent son, Carmen responded to disagreements with her daughter-in-law by imposing patriarchal family rules on Dolores. These same rules had disadvantaged Carmen as a young wife, led to her own migration, and were rapidly undergoing migration-related change.

A MOTHER-IN-LAW'S MIGRATION

To explain the story of Dolores and the money, Carmen first told me about her own marriage. Women of Carmen's generation were expected to suffer as wives. They had little hope for escape from a bad marriage, as *Calakmuleños* stigmatized divorce. Thus, in the 1980s, as a 26-year-old mother of four, Carmen was relieved when her husband announced his plans to travel to the United States. "Look," Carmen recalled, "we couldn't put up with each other anymore. Because he used to come home very drunk and insult me and hit me."

Carmen's husband was one of the first international migrants from Calakmul, and Carmen was unusual in another way. She was one of the few women to travel to the United States: "I didn't feel much when he left. I was tranquil. But after a few months went by, I began to miss him."

Carmen weighed the decision to emigrate in consultation with her husband's parents. Women of Carmen's generation were raised to accept their in-laws as authority figures, a belief rooted in a practice called **patrilocal residence**. Under patrilocal residence, newlyweds live with or near the husband's parents. In some patriarchal societies, patrilocal residence is crucial for acculturating young women into submissiveness. The combination of patrilocal residence and **patriarchy** is so common across the globe, migration researchers have called for reconsidering its taken-for-granted quality in migration studies (Mahler and Pessar 2006).

Carmen needed her in-laws' support for another reason. They could care for her children while she was away. Then, two events convinced Carmen she needed to emigrate to save her marriage. A neighbor whose husband was also in the United States found herself abandoned when her husband remarried and stopped sending financial support. Carmen's husband signaled he might do the same: "My husband was saying he wasn't coming back, so I thought, 'Something is going on.'"

Carmen joined her husband in Colorado where the two worked in a restaurant and shared a house with seven other workers. Whether it was the time apart, the living with strangers, or something else, Carmen remembers her husband seemed like a different person. He stopped drinking and became an affectionate spouse. On their days off, Carmen and her husband toured nearby towns. Years later, Carmen surmised her husband emigrated because he wanted a fresh start. In Aserradero, he felt trapped in friendships that encouraged his drinking.

While in Colorado, Carmen knew nothing of the family's finances. Her husband had always handled the family's money, and he cashed her paycheck. Still, she knew enough about the cost of living that when the couple considered bringing their children to join them, the finances gave her pause. Carmen would have to continue working and place her children in childcare. "When would I see my children?" she wondered. "My children would be all locked up." Instead, Carmen urged a return to Mexico: "And I don't know how much money we brought [with us], but he bought the children clothes and toys. And then he started to drink again. I said to him, 'You said you wouldn't drink. Why are you drinking now?' And we began to have problems again." This time when he was drunk, Carmen's husband blamed her for the family's poverty. He thought about returning to the United States, but Carmen resisted. Crucially, Carmen's mother-in-law agreed with her: "My mother-in-law always said 'no' to the idea. She said, 'What's going to happen with these children?'"

PATRIARCHY AND PATRILOCAL FAMILIES

When I spoke with Carmen, she was nearing 60 years of age, had been widowed for three years, and was running a taco stand to earn money. Her marriage had never improved. The poverty and subordination Carmen lived as a wife were common for her generation. In contrast, women typically held more authority over their children, in whom they invested emotionally. These dynamics were rooted in the patrilocal family systems described above and influenced the emotional dimensions of Calakmul's regime of (im)mobility. Patrilocal life often places mothers-in-law in opposition to daughters-in-law while encouraging women to internalize their own subordination. Patrilocal residence creates these tensions by restricting women's access to cash and emotional support, forcing them to wait years before acquiring authority. Here we take a closer look at patrilocal life, because it helps explain why when migration made money and pleasure available to young wives, senior women reacted with anger and disbelief (Mathews and Manago 2019). Patrilocal residence is common in places like Calakmul where people marry in their teens with few resources to set up their own house. For brides, entering patrilocal residence effectively means going to work for their mothers-in-law. The stories have mostly been told from the perspective of daughters-in-law. In her research on Mexico, Julia Pauli (2008) writes that many daughters-in-law viewed "themselves as prisoners while living within their mother-in-law's house. They say they are *encerrada* (locked away)" (176).

Rural Mexicans prohibited public dating until recently, which meant mothers-in-law and daughters-in-law had little opportunity to interact before the marriage. In Pauli's words, many women joined their husband's families as strangers "without money, social standing, or a voice of their own" (Pauli, 2008, 176). Their mothers-in-law often insisted on the behavior demanded of them when they first married, expecting younger women to throw themselves silently into housework (see also McClusky 2001).

Patrilocal residence and patriarchal values also affected a woman's feelings for her children (Mathews and Manago 2019). As daughters-in-law, women might experience intense isolation, a loneliness alleviated when they had children of their own (Pauli 2008). Mothers then relied on their children for emotional support. Children could also bring a disadvantaged wife status, especially if a woman gave birth to a son. Aware of how their society prized men, women often gave special considerations to their sons.

In Carmen's case, after describing her marital suffering, she talked about her investments in Octavio, especially her efforts to assure he finished high school. Octavio was 13 years old when

Carmen returned from the United States. His relationship with Dolores started at roughly the same time. When Octavio dropped out of high school, Carmen blamed the relationship:

> Octavio decided he wouldn't study anymore, and my husband scolded him. My husband told him, "Well, if you aren't going to study, go get a job." And I blamed the girlfriend. I said to him that because he was busy being a boyfriend, he wasn't concentrating on his studies.

Sent to work in his grandfather's cornfield, Octavio decided he did not want a life of manual labor. He turned to his mother, and the two conspired to convince Octavio's father to allow him to resume his schooling. Carmen laughed recounting her successful, behind-the-scenes maneuvers: "So they say we mothers are the conciliators (*alcahuetas*), and it's true."

If patrilocal residence norms had been in full force, Carmen might next expect a boost in status when Octavio married Dolores and brought a daughter-in-law into the home. For older women, power over a daughter-in-law was one of the few arenas where their authority consistently superseded a man's. As we see below, this next step did not happen in Carmen's life. Nonetheless, the emotional resonance of patrilocal life remained.

Given patrilocal residence, a woman might display deference to her husband while drawing power from her bond with her son. Carmen's own marriage never offered more than a fleeting satisfaction. But for how long could she rely on her son? This question weighed on many Calakmul mothers because it had no clear answer. Individual families varied in how much a wife could depend on her husband and the extent she needed or wanted a son's support. Also, a son's relationship to his mother naturally changed with time, as children and married life demanded more of his attention. Money easily became part of these dynamics. The sharing of money signals intimacy and offers a concrete measure of care (Zelizer 2000). And, in the financial arena as well as the emotional, a woman might find her son, rather than her husband, the more reliable caregiver.

MONEY AS CARE, MONEY AS PLEASURE

To understand why older women might rely financially on their sons, and why younger women's access to money stirred potent emotions, we need to return to married life as Carmen's generation knew it. Recall that Carmen's husband handled the family finances. For Carmen's generation, marital rules did not require husbands to share money with their wives. Men could not only keep money to themselves, patriarchal rules allowed men to spend it on their personal pleasures. As Carmen knew first-hand, drinking was one pleasure men might indulge in. For *Calakmuleños*, marital infidelity was another.

The lack of financial sharing began during patrilocal residence. As a young husband, a man might route his earnings to his mother. The man's mother served as household manager, providing food and other necessities for the couple. Once the pair acquired a house of their own, a mother's claims to her son's earnings decreased. For the wife, however, the couple's independent living might not change her situation. With the pattern of withholding established, additional gender rules made it easy for a man to refuse to share. For example, chores that required spending, such as food shopping, were men's jobs. Individual couples adapted this framework to their particular situation, and families exhibited an array of financial arrangements. Nonetheless, across Calakmul many wives felt they could not ask their husbands for money. These wives were forced to manage their households as best they could.

A woman's access to money changed once her son was old enough to work, with family rules pressuring young men to support their mothers. After years of receiving their mothers' doting attentions, sons absorbed the message that they should be grateful. It was a debt sons could never repay. Instead, sons described the payments as "a small help." But as a son's responsibilities to his own wife and children grew, the new demands risked leaving a mother penniless, again. One assessment of mothers-in-law's mistreatment of their daughters-in-law points to this insecurity. Fearing poverty, a mother might pressure her son to care for her by pitting her son against his wife. In effect, mothers asked their sons to choose between the two women (McClusky 2001).

Financial worries and their traditional role as manager of a son's earnings gave mothers-in-law a keen interest in how daughters-in-law handled remittances. At the same time, *Calakmuleños* held another compelling notion when it came to money, a value that heightened the way remittances can serve as "a testing ground for the traditional belief that the husband and his family own the money" (Singh 2019, 197). When *Calakmuleño* men shared money, they signaled care and affection. Taken further, money was an integral part of Calakmul's "sexual economy." In a **sexual economy**, one partner financially supports the other "in exchange for their sexual, reproductive and caring attentions" (Cole 2010, 73). Prior to international migration, *Calakmuleños* assumed a husband with extra income was susceptible to adultery. He could easily find a woman whose poverty attracted her to a man with an income.

Calakmuleños frowned upon men's infidelity. Nonetheless, Carmen and her peers were expected to suffer a husband's dalliances. *Calakmuleños* also discouraged the bare exchange of money for romance. Instead, they viewed men's spending on affairs as giving life to an underlying emotional bond. Love could grow from a man's spending. In some cases, a man might even use money to acquire a second wife.

By the time Octavio and Dolores married, the bargain husbands and wives struck around money and pleasure was changing. Although men retained authority, women of Dolores's generation expected marriage to bring emotional satisfaction. Migratory wealth led young women to believe they had a right to money and its associated indulgences. With migration, a new word entered *Calakmuleños*' vocabulary, the *gastada* or "allowance" women received from their husbands. While the word communicated wives' continued subordination, the very idea that women held a named claim to money was an important innovation.

These changes could baffle mothers-in-law raised to believe daughters-in-law should live as mute servants. With their sons abroad and young wives receiving remittances, the confusion sometimes turned to fury. Senior women took offense at their daughters-in-law's shopping trips. They saw infidelity in young wives' conversations with men. Notably, mothers expressed only disappointment at a son's adultery (if it came to light). In contrast, reporting on their daughters-in-law, mothers telephoned their sons urging them to stop remitting to their wives. The common refrain accompanying these requests? "You're only supporting her boyfriend."

Carmen's story interested me because I mostly heard about the emotional demands of Calakmul's regime of (im)mobility from daughters-in-law. In fact, *Calakmuleños* were noticeably quiet on senior women's interests in remittances, as if the idea that motherly love might carry more complicated emotions had to be "mystified, denied, or reinterpreted" (Constable 2009, 55). Meanwhile, daughters-in-law tearfully recounted intense family pressures and marriages on the brink (McEvoy et al. 2012).

In Carmen's telling, the difficulties in Dolores and Octavio's relationship began long before he emigrated. On one occasion, Carmen complained to her son that Dolores held too much power: "It seems to me you're not the one wearing the pants. Why can't you control your wife?" While abroad, Octavio wanted Dolores to enter patrilocal residence. Dolores lived with her own mother at the time and had other ideas. In Carmen's words, "Octavio wanted me to build a house here in the backyard. We readied the terrain, talked with a carpenter, and bought the timber. Then I heard rumors that Dolores was saying I wanted to coop her up, like a hen in a hen house." Carmen suggested Octavio find a house elsewhere.

Repeatedly and unsuccessfully, Carmen sought to make a submissive daughter-in-law of Dolores. Then Carmen's neighbor asked, "Does Octavio send money to Dolores?" In response, Carmen posed questions of her own. She returned to the neighbor, who worked in the civil registry. Civil registries are government offices that keep records of vital events, such as births and deaths. In Calakmul, engaged couples were married by the registrar who then issued their wedding certificate. Calakmul had too few people to merit a divorce court. In order to divorce, *Calakmuleños* traveled to a regional court located two hours from Aserradero. Once the court had finalized a divorce, it sent a record of the proceeding to Calakmul's registry.

In this way, Carmen learned Dolores had secretly divorced Octavio. The news came as a shock. Not only was Carmen unaware a divorce was in the works, her son was equally in the dark. Carmen quickly connected the secrecy to Dolores's male visitor. A divorce would allow Dolores to marry her new beau, but a divorce would also end those remittances. By surreptitiously divorcing Octavio, Dolores could keep both the money and her new man.

Outraged, Carmen traveled to the divorce court. There she learned Dolores had presented witnesses who falsely testified that Octavio no longer spoke with her and no longer sent money. *Calakmuleños* equated the lack of remittances with the end of a marriage, and the judge agreed to this premise.

Carmen had watched powerlessly while Dolores lived independently, even enjoyably, in Octavio's absence. The divorce gave Carmen an opening to act. Given the egregiousness of Dolores's actions, it was hard to separate to what extent Carmen was motivated by caring for Octavio and to what extent she sought to force upon Dolores long-standing patriarchal rules. Whatever the case, Carmen would set things right.

Carmen relitigated the divorce. She had Octavio mail her remittance receipts to prove he never stopped sending money and requested the court reopen the case considering this evidence. The judge agreed and ultimately issued a new divorce decree. As Carmen noted with satisfaction, this second ending was not as financially advantageous to Dolores. The new decree stipulated Dolores receive alimony in an amount standard for the region, about $35 per month.

CONCLUSION

Migration is an emotionally complex process. As Carmen and Dolores show, these emotions often center on love, money, and family authority. Not all participants in the migratory endeavor feel the same way about these matters, and feelings change with time. Regimes of (im)mobility influence people's emotions, especially by making movers of some people and stayers of others. What's more, such regimes can demand different emotional labor from different identity groups. *Calakmuleños* called the wives of emigrants "Black Widows," suggesting a model wife mourned her husband's absence. *Calakmuleños*, however, had no moniker for mothers who saw their job as protecting a son's interests, including assuring his wife's behavior and sentiments conformed to ideals.

In this way, Calakmul's regime of (im)mobility operated through powerful patriarchal norms. Carmen adhered to these norms despite knowing first-hand the conflicting emotions young wives experienced. Meanwhile, the slim authority Calakmul's patriarchy assigned older women could create no-win situations for migratory families. When I spoke with Carmen, Octavio was still in the United States. Although Carmen had defended her son's interests, his divorce left Octavio little to come home to. Octavio's marriage had been particularly troubled, but many emigrant men watched their marriages dissolve under the weight of a mother's scrutiny. All in all, the longer these men stayed in the United States, the less likely they were to return to Mexico.

REFLECTION AND DISCUSSION QUESTIONS

- What emotions did Calakmul's regime of (im)mobility expect of women? How were these expectations partly rooted in patriarchal ideals?
- What roles did *Calakmuleños* ascribe to money in marriage?
- How did Dolores's actions build upon older marital power dynamics? How did her actions change those dynamics?

KEY CONCEPTS

- **patriarchy**: Power structures that subordinate women to men's authority and in which women may internalize and support men's authority.
- **patrilocal residence**: A family system in which newlyweds live with or near the husband's parents.
- **regime of (im)mobility**: The pressures shaping migratory settings, making movers of some people and stayers of others.
- **sexual economy**: An arrangement between intimate partners in which one person financially supports the other in exchange for sexual attention and other care.

EXPLORE FURTHER

- To learn more about the gendered experiences of cis women, read **Section 4** and **Chapter 26**.
- To learn more about transnational families, read **Chapters 34** and **36**.
- Allen, Judy Levy. 2018. "Episode 26: Psychological Distress among Undocumented Immigrants (Guest: Luz Garcini)." *Mexico Centered Podcast*. https://tinyurl.com/MexicoCentered.
- Boehm, Deborah A. 2008. "'Now I Am a Man *and* a Woman!': Gendered Moves and Migrations in a Transnational Mexican Community." *Latin American Perspectives* 35(1): 16–30.
- Hirsch, J., 2003. *A Courtship after Marriage: Sexuality and Love in Mexican Transnational Families*. Berkeley: University of California Press.
- Khazan, Olga. 2017. "We Expect Too Much from Our Romantic Partners: An Interview with Eli Finkel, author of *The All or Nothing Marriage*." *The Atlantic*, September 29.

ABOUT THE AUTHOR

Nora Haenn is a professor of anthropology and international studies at North Carolina State University. Her research examines the culture of international migration, environmental management, and economic development. She is the author of *Marriage after Migration: An Ethnography of Money, Romance, and Gender in Globalizing Mexico*.

REFERENCES

Boehm, Deborah A. 2013. *Intimate Migrations: Gender, Family, and Illegality among Mexican Transnational Families*. New York: New York University Press.

Brettell, Caroline. 2017. "Marriage and Migration." *Annual Review of Anthropology* 46: 81–97. https://doi.org/10.1146/annurev-anthro-102116-041237.

Cole, Jennifer. 2010. *Sex and Salvation: Imagining the Future in Madagascar*. Chicago: University of Chicago Press.

Constable, Nicole. 2009. "The Commodification of Intimacy: Marriage, Sex, and Reproductive Labor." *Annual Review of Anthropology* 38: 49–64. https://doi.org/10.1146/annurev.anthro.37.081407.085133.

Dreby, Joanna. 2009. "Gender and Transnational Gossip." *Qualitative Sociology* 32 (1): 33–52. https://doi.org/10.1007/s11133-008-9117-x.

Faier, Lieba. 2011. "Theorizing the Intimacies of Migration: Commentary on the Emotional Formations of Transnational Worlds." *International Migration* 49 (6): 107–12. https://doi.org/10.1111/j.1468-2435.2011.00708.x.

Frank, Reanne, and Elizabeth Wildsmith. 2005. "The Grass Widows of Mexico: Migration and Union Dissolution in a Binational Context." *Social Forces* 83 (3): 919–47. https://doi.org/10.1353/sof.2005.0031.

Gálvez, Alyshia. 2018. *Eating NAFTA: Trade, Food Policies, and the Destruction of Mexico*. Berkeley: University of California Press.

Glick Schiller, Nina, and Noel B. Salazar, 2013. "Regimes of Mobility across the Globe." *Journal of Ethnic and Migration Studies* 39 (2): 183–200. https://doi.org/10.1080/1369183X.2013.723253.

Haenn, Nora. 2019. *Marriage after Migration: An Ethnography of Money, Romance, and Gender in Globalizing Mexico*. New York: Oxford University Press.

Hirsch, Jennifer S., Holly Wardlow, Daniel Jordan Smith, Harriett M. Phinney, Shanti Parikh, and Constance A Nathanson. 2009. *The Secret: Love, Marriage, and HIV*. Nashville: Vanderbilt University Press.

Krissman, Fred. 2005. "'*Sin Coyote ni Patrón*': Why the 'Migrant Network' Fails to Explain International Migration." *International Migration Review* 1 (39): 4–44. https://doi.org/10.1111/j.1747-7379.2005.tb00254.x.

Lutz, Helma. 2010. "Gender in the Migratory Process." *Journal of Ethnic and Migration Studies* 36 (10): 1647–63. https://doi.org/10.1080/1369183X.2010.489373.

Mahler, Sarah J., and Patricia R. Pessar. 2006. "Gender Matters: Ethnographers Bring Gender from the Periphery toward the Core of Migration Studies." *International Migration Review* 40 (1): 27–63. https://doi.org/10.1111/j.1747-7379.2006.00002.x.

Mathews, Holly F., and Adriana M. Manago. 2019. "Introduction: Understanding Women's Psychological Responses to Various Forms of Patriarchy." In *The Psychology of Women Under Patriarchy*, edited by Holly F. Mathews and Adriana M. Manago, 1–30. Santa Fe, NM: School for Advanced Research.

McClusky, Laura. 2001. *"Here, Our Culture Is Hard": Stories of Domestic Violence from a Mayan Community in Belize*. Austin: University of Texas Press.

McEvoy, Jamie, Peggy Petrzelka, Claudia Radel, and Birgit Schmook. 2012. "Gendered Mobility and Morality in a Southeastern Mexican Community: Impacts of Male Labour Migration on the Women Left Behind." *Mobilities* 7 (3): 369–88. https://doi.org/10.1080/17450101.2012.655977.

Ordaz Díaz, Juan Luis. 2009. *Migration Observatory*. BBVA: Mexico City. https://www.bbvaresearch.com/wp-content/uploads/mult/090727_ObsMigraMexico_2_eng_tcm348-198646.pdf.

Pauli, Julia. 2008. "A House of One's Own: Gender, Migration, and Residence in Rural Mexico." *American Ethnologist* 35 (1): 171–87. https://doi.org/10.1111/j.1548-1425.2008.00012.x.

Rodman, Debra H. 2006. *Gender, Migration, and Transnational Identities: Maya and Ladino Relations in Eastern Guatemala*. Ph.D. diss., University of Florida.

Schmook, Birgit, and Claudia Radel. 2008. "International Labor Migration from a Tropical Development Frontier: Globalizing Households and an Incipient Forest Transition." *Human Ecology* 36 (6): 891–908. https://doi.org/10.1007/s10745-008-9207-0.

Sharpe, Pamela, ed. 2002. *Women, Gender and Labour Migration: Historical and Cultural Perspectives*. London: Routledge.

Singh, Supriya. 2019. "The Daughter-in-Law Questions Remittances: Changes in the Gender of Remittances among Indian Migrants to Australia." *Global Networks* 19 (2): 197–217. https://doi.org/10.1111/glob.12215.

Skolnik, Jocelyn, Sandra Lazo de la Vega, and Timothy Steigenga. 2012. "Chisme across Borders: The Impact of Gossip in a Guatemalan Transnational Community." *Migraciones Internacionales* 6 (3): 9–38.

Yarris, Kristin E. 2017. *Care across Generations: Solidarity and Sacrifice in Transnational Families*. Stanford, CA: Stanford University Press.

Zelizer, Viviana A. 2000. "The Purchase of Intimacy." *Law & Social Inquiry* 25 (3): 817–48. https://doi.org/10.1111/j.1747-4469.2000.tb00162.x.

CHAPTER THIRTY-SIX

"I Am Going without Knowing the History of My People": Young People's Engagement with the Past, Present, and Future in the Guatemalan Diaspora in Southern Mexico

Malte Gembus

On a hot summer morning, 16-year-old Yeni and 17-year-old Ivan stepped onto the stage of La Gloria's *salon municipal* (municipal hall), a space in the town center for public events. The theater-in-the-round featured a center stage encircled by wooden chairs and metal benches (Figure 36.1). The hall was decorated with prints of old photos that the young performers had retrieved from family archives. Yeni and Ivan were part of a youth group, Jocox, tasked with performing the town's origin story on the thirty-fourth anniversary of La Gloria's June 5 founding.

The local schools had suspended their classes to attend the event and to celebrate La Gloria's past. The audience consisted of both younger and older residents – the actors' fellow students and family members and neighbors – all of them patiently watching the two young people enter the stage. There was a certain expectation about what would happen in the performance; the town's history is retold every year during the patron-saint festivities in September. A group of older audience members told me that they were curious to see how the young people would represent "our history."

On stage, Yeni was carrying a ball with her. She put the ball on the ground and started passing it back and forth to Ivan. The crowd seemed surprised by this unexpected beginning to the story. "What have you been up to my friend?" Yeni asked, and Ivan responded that he had just finished high school and was getting prepared to leave town. "Where are you going?" Yeni asked. Ivan said, "Up there *pa'l Norte* (to the North), you know how it is." Yeni nodded, and they kept on passing the ball. "I am leaving with a huge doubt though," Ivan said suddenly. "I am leaving without knowing the history of my people." Yeni looked at him with astonishment and replied that she had heard from her granddad that it was the water that told these stories of

Figure 36.1. The Jocox group performing their play in August 2018. Photo by Malte Gembus.

the past, but only if one listened. Ivan laughed and said that it sounded like her granddad was a bit *loco* (crazy). He looked at Yeni more seriously and added, "But hey why not, go on then, tell me this story."

The two teenagers left the stage and the other 10 young actors entered, beginning the part of the performance where the Jocox youth group told the origin story of La Gloria, the small town on the Mexican-Guatemalan border in which they all grew up. The young actors portrayed the persecution that their parents and grandparents suffered during the Guatemalan Civil War and the plight of their first years in Chiapas, Mexico, in the 1980s when they lived as refugees in camps. The play ended with the founding of their hometown, La Gloria. At the end of the performance Yeni and Ivan appeared again on stage to say goodbye to one another. Yeni said to Ivan, "Here, take a bottle of water with you, and also good luck. You'll need it; these journeys are full of danger." The two gave each other a hug and music indicated the end of the play. The other actors joined the two on stage and the complete Jocox group formed a circle and yelled "*Muchas, muchas gracias*" while the crowd applauded.

This chapter examines second-generation Guatemalan-Mexican youth identities within a community where members continue to reflect on their recent past of civil-war-inflicted emigration from Guatemala in the 1980s and where new generations embark on journeys to the United States to work. The town of La Gloria emerges as a safe haven linking these two migratory patterns and temporalities; it is a transient place shaped by events that often seem to happen in distant localities and times: Guatemala in the 1980s and the United States in the present.

La Gloria was founded by Akateko-speaking Guatemalan refugees who, after fleeing Guatemala, were housed in camps in Chiapas, Mexico. After the town's formation in 1984 people continued to refer to La Gloria as a "camp" and with that label came certain symbolic implications related to ephemerality. However, far from transient, La Gloria has since become an established town where generations of the Guatemalan **diaspora** are born and raised and where local meanings of Akateko identity, indigeneity, and diaspora are being negotiated and produced.

La Gloria is an important town for the Guatemalan diaspora in southern Mexico. It is the largest settlement where Akateko is still widely spoken and where the annual traditions and customs are practiced, most importantly the celebration of the patron saint San Miguel (or Mekel in Akateko). La Gloria's young residents occupy a central role in the social and symbolic making of this dynamic town. Unlike their parents and grandparents who arrived as refugees, the 15- to 18-year-old participants in my ethnographic study were born in La Gloria, and unlike many of their older siblings, friends, and neighbors (at the time of my research), these young people had not yet moved away from La Gloria. Today teenagers and children (together with the elderly) make up the majority of La Gloria's residents. Many adults of working age were physically absent, however they contributed economically by sending remittances from the United States to sustain young and old family members. For this and other reasons, migration is often invoked as a fragmenting force creating economic and social rupture in rural sending communities (Green 2011) such as La Gloria. Ruíz-Lagier (2013) states that in La Gloria "new conflicts surged among the new generations because of sociocultural changes deriving from the phenomena of migration" (189). In such fluid environments, maintaining a sense of cultural continuity and collective belonging seems complicated. This chapter examines the role collective remembrance of the past plays in processes of identity making in La Gloria. It looks at how narratives of the past interact with young people's aspirations for the future, including their consideration of US-bound migration.

The past and the ways it is remembered play a major role in the lives of people in La Gloria. This chapter does not focus on the Guatemalan Civil War, *el refugio* (the refuge), or the foundation of La Gloria as historical events, but rather explores the ways in which these events are imagined, mediated, and performed by young people. I argue that the young people's mediated performances create important intergenerational links between the refugees' experience of fleeing Guatemala in the 1980s and the experience of contemporary migration toward the United States, therefore associating migration with ancestral and intergenerational continuity rather than rupture.

ETHNOGRAPHIC FIELDWORK IN LA GLORIA AND THE SOUTHERN UNITED STATES

The 1980s are known in Guatemala as the decade of *la violencia* (the violence; see Chapter 22). La Gloria was founded by Guatemalan refugees escaping the escalating violence of the Guatemalan Civil War (1960–1996), which was fought between insurgent groups and several *juntas* (military dictatorships) embedded in Cold War dynamics. At the same time in Chiapas (on the Mexican side of the border), this period is remembered as *el refugio* (the refuge), stressing the fact that between 150,000 and 250,000 people – mostly speakers of Indigenous languages from the Guatemalan highlands – crossed the border and settled in Mexico. In April 1984, one of the United Nations High Commissioner for Refugees (UNHCR)-administrated refugee camps called *el Chupadero* was attacked by the Guatemalan military. As a result, a large group of Akateko-speaking refugees who originated from the Guatemalan region of San Miguel Acatán abandoned the camps and formed a town of their own. The refugees' trajectory took many different forms in the late 1980s and early 1990s: Some migrated further into the Mexican north and subsequently to the United States, some returned to Guatemala, and others settled permanently in southern Mexico.

La Gloria is now a town of about 2,300 inhabitants (Ruíz-Lagier 2013, 113) located in the Chiapan border region between Guatemala and Mexico. US-bound migration quickly became a common pattern in the decade following La Gloria's founding. Remittances from the United States or money being sent from other parts of Mexico, especially from the tourist destinations of the Riviera Maya in Quintana Roo, now make up the subsistence of most families in La Gloria.

My ethnographic engagement with La Gloria and its residents spans from 2017 until the present day. I initially started volunteering as a substitute English teacher at the local high school and offered creative youth activities in the students' free time. A youth group emerged out of these initial activities, consisting of young men and women between the ages of 15 and 18. We would meet up once or twice a week to explore topics around La Gloria's "Past, Present, and Future" in creative ways. All but one of the 15 long-term Jocox group members were born and raised in La Gloria and were the children and grandchildren of refugees.

Together with local community leaders, we organized a sociocultural event in June 2018 where the young people presented a theater piece and photography exhibition. The play portrayed La Gloria's origin story as it is told annually during the patron-saint celebration. However, the young actors decided to include additional scenes dealing with contemporary issues in La Gloria such as migration and local social divisions, which I discuss later in this chapter. After June 2018, the youth group continued its activities through regular meetups, and the creative productions were presented later that year in different communities around Chiapas, as well as in two different locations in Guatemala as part of an international festival on Indigenous rights called *FicMayab*. I also conducted fieldwork visits to the southeast of the United States (Alabama, Tennessee, Georgia, North Carolina) in 2018 and 2021 to meet up with some of the initial Jocox group members who had migrated to this region.

STORYTELLING BETWEEN PAST AND FUTURE

"It really is the same, isn't it?" Ivan said to me on a hot June afternoon from the passenger seat of my rental car as we were taking a left turn toward the interstate that would take us from Tennessee to Alabama. A couple of weeks earlier I had come to the southeast of the United States to visit him and other founding members of La Gloria's Jocox youth group. By 2021, three years after the youth group disbanded, most of its former members were living in Tennessee, Georgia, and Alabama. Some planned to return to La Gloria eventually and others planned to stay in the United States. "What do you mean by it's the same?" I asked Ivan, who had just been telling me about his experiences crossing the US–Mexico border. He elaborated: "Well you know the dogs and *la migra* (US Border Patrol and Immigration and Customs Enforcement officers) in their uniforms, and us on the other side hiding behind bushes so they can't see us. It really is like what we showed in the play. It's like what our grandparents went through when they came to Mexico. Just back then it wasn't *la migra* they were hiding from, it was the *Ejército de Guatemala* (Guatemalan Military). They [grandparents] also had to leave their homes behind out of necessity, walk for days, always in hiding, not knowing if they would make it to the other side."

By sharing his stories with me, Ivan established a direct link between the two domains, temporalities, and generations of migration in between which he grew up. A seemingly banal act, storytelling gains depth when thinking about it in the context of emerging identities.

Jackson (2002, 250) argues "stories are redemptive … not because they preserve or represent the truth of any individual life but because they offer the perennial possibility that one sees oneself as, and discovers oneself through, another, despite the barriers of space, time and difference." Jackson highlights the intersubjective qualities of storytelling and outlines the implications storytelling has for collective and individual being and belonging. While telling me about his own experience of crossing the border, Ivan was reminded both of the theater performance in which he played a central part and of the inherited stories of his grandparents' experience as refugees in the 1980s. Through intergenerational transmission of stories and theater performances, Ivan had experienced his life in La Gloria as interrelated and connected to the experiences and stories from the *generación del refugio* (refugee generation). Now finding himself in the **double diaspora** of the United States, he continued to see his life in frames of continuity. By connecting these stories Ivan invoked a type of ancestral continuity where his experiences were framed within the experiences of generations that came before him. And his perspective gives evidence for the idea that "stories are thus like ancestors … so too in time do stories become ancestral, abstracted from our individual preoccupations so that they may articulate, as myths, a vision of a shared humanity" (Jackson 2002, 250). Ivan recognized that the act of border crossing was one undertaken by both his ancestors and him. Thus, border crossing was a central part of what it meant to be Akateko living in the diaspora. The process of migrating out of necessity to ensure survival, of crossing borders, and of constantly avoiding being detected by uniformed state authorities had become symbols, experiences, and stories that were central to being Akateko in the diaspora. These experiences described and connected the lived reality of multiple generations.

THEATRICAL PERFORMANCES AS STORYTELLING AND OPPORTUNITIES FOR REFLECTION

From the Perspective of the Younger Generation

Jocox's play about La Gloria's founding story demonstrates how young people's performances of the past were framed by their imaginations of contemporary migration to the United States. Their performances point us toward the ways in which the remembrance of refugee pasts and the aspirations toward migrant futures interact, fuse, and mesh when the young participants tell the story of their community. When working on the play in 2017 and 2018, migration was one of the topics most frequently discussed by the young people, since it impacted their town and their future prospects. It was the young actors who decided to begin and end the play with the "side story" about youths' reckoning with the possibilities and dangers of migrating to the United States. The origin story, dealing with migration in the 1980s, appeared within the frames of contemporary considerations and struggles. By framing the telling of the town's past with the contemporary considerations around migration, the young people managed to combine two domains that affected virtually all community members.

Ivan explicitly mentioned these links during our conversation in the car when he reflected on his participation in the play and his subsequent journey to the United States. The play itself had already moved the two domains in immediate proximity to one another, as connected parts of the staged drama. In the play it was in the moment of migrating that Ivan (in his stage role) started to reflect about the past and "the history of my people." Offstage and three years later, Ivan looked back at his own border crossing experience and re-established the same connections, now from his perspective as a member of a double diaspora. The young actors in the play appealed to issues that were of shared collective concern, therefore skillfully crafting their performances to speak to La Gloria's wider public. Both older and younger residents were concerned with the contemporary issues of migration as they were aware of and engaged in the stories of the "refugee generation." In this way, the young actors reiterated their active participation in the social making of their hometown and of localized forms of identification that connect La Gloria's residents. Actively linking collective pasts, presents, and futures can be viewed as one the core aspects that forge collective identities, especially under the ever-changing conditions of double diaspora. Young people in La Gloria established ancestral connections through performance; in return, the performances themselves became memories and stories that are being retold and reflected upon as their lives unfold. Ivan used his memories of the play to make sense of his own recent border crossing journey and his situation as a migrant in the United States.

From the Perspective of the Older Generation

In 2018, after the Jocox theater performance ended, Don Alex, one of La Gloria's community leaders, helped me tidy the hall. Alex and his family fled to Chiapas in the 1980s when he was 18 years old and a medical student. Even though he was unable to finish his degree during the tumultuous years as a refugee, Alex dedicated himself to the development and running of La Gloria's clinic. He was a well-connected and well-known person in La Gloria and served as the town's municipal representative for a term. Alex was involved in matters that concerned La Gloria as a whole, which meant that he was invested and supported in any public events that brought the community together, such as the young people's theater performance. While moving chairs around in the municipal hall after the performance, he stopped for a second and looked at the old photos decorating the walls. He said to me: "You know, the performance today really made me think of this saying that I heard somewhere a long time ago, 'A people that doesn't know its past is doomed to lose out on its future.' This is how it is here in La Gloria; we should actually write that in large letters on the wall right here for everyone to see and remember." A couple of weeks later I was back in La Gloria and passed by Don Alex's house. He waved and told me to come in for a cold drink and a chat about the event with the young people. "I was very impressed," Alex said. "Some people have come to me and told me they had never seen young people working so hard, because most of them [young people] are just out there smoking and drinking or doing nothing, but here they were putting in hard work and showed that they care about our past."

Alex's reaction to the young people's performance highlights some aspects of intergenerational relations in La Gloria, which are intertwined with migration. The young people's performance made Alex think about the role memory plays for La Gloria as a community, and he highlighted the importance remembrance had for its future development. It was after seeing the Jocox group portraying both domains and temporalities of migration through their play that Alex started reflecting on the intergenerational continuities of remembrance and how they hold La Gloria together as a community. Alex equally reflected on another aspect of intergenerational relationships in La Gloria when he invoked stereotypes that older community members held about younger residents. The most common stereotypes included apathy, laziness, and deviance but also young people's lack of knowledge about and valuing of La Gloria's history and origins. These tropes were repeated to me multiple times during my fieldwork by older residents and highlight the intergenerational dimension of remembrance in La Gloria.

STORYTELLING AND COLLECTIVE IDENTITY IN LA GLORIA

Migration is always present in La Gloria. Stories of the Guatemalan Civil War and the plight of the refugee generation slide into everyday conversations just as often as more recent anecdotes and accounts from and about those that have left to the United States. The young people witness two-storey houses being built with money sent from abroad. Motorbikes, large and expensive *trocas* (pickup trucks), and all kinds of technological gadgets (cell phones, speakers, headphones, etc.) bought with money sent via remittances are paraded around town by young people who themselves aspire to migrate one day. The same young people engage with their families' refugee past by participating in the collective retelling of the "La Gloria story" during the annual patron-saint celebration, in quotidian acts of anecdotal storytelling about the past, or in the creative projects about past, present, and future that formed part of my engaged fieldwork. It is the young people's unique perspective situated in between domains that allows them to create links and bridge chronological and geographic distances between the refugee experience of the 1980s and the plight of contemporary US-bound migrants. Storytelling emerged here as one of the principal activities through which these links were established and expressed.

In acts of storytelling, migration was often framed as a "necessity" to counteract poverty and improve the life of one's family. Like in my conversation with Ivan during our drive, the narratives around migration that community members shared with me revolved around necessity. The meaning of *necessity* can differ from one generation to the next: Whereas the flight from

Guatemala in the 1980s was often referred to as a necessity to ensure survival during the years of persecution and *la violencia*, economic deprivation in rural southern Mexico made migration for work a necessity. At other times migration was referred to as a danger: Stories of the persecution by the Guatemalan military in the 1980s and the dangerous border crossings to the United States were retold as reminders of the lethal threats inherent in migration. Thus, the tropes of necessity and danger were present in stories about both the refugee generation from the 1980s as well as in the narratives about migration to the United States.

Youth were crucial in the telling of these stories. As one of La Gloria's largest group of residents, young people's creative engagement with the past and future of their community highlighted the ways in which they actively participated in the social making of their town. They were active makers in processes where meanings of remembrance and future aspirations were negotiated in narrative interaction, which in turn produced localized forms of identification.

Youth's active participation was a response to the marginalization young Guatemalans experience in the diaspora. The racialized hierarchies inherent in the Mexican nation-state (Hernández-Castillo 2001; Ruíz-Lagier 2013) place these young people on its symbolic and material margins as speakers of an Indigenous language and offspring of refugees from the Guatemalan highlands. Within their own community, young people were marginalized in intergenerational hierarchies; older residents such as Don Alex associated youth with deviance and the loss of the community's Indigenous roots and traditions. The young participants' strategies for counteracting these exclusions consisted of actively linking past and present forms and experiences of migration. Young people maintained a sense of belonging despite these multiple exclusions and by playing an active role in the social making of La Gloria–specific forms of remembrance and identification.

Identification with a group can be established by tracing continuities between its members from past to present (and into the future). Through the play, the young actors publicly reminded Don Alex and the rest of the audience about La Gloria's shared past and linked it to contemporary and aspirational aspects of life for La Gloria's young people, therefore contributing to defining what being part of *Ja'eb a Gloria* (Us from La Gloria) looks like. The young people counteracted multiple registers of exclusion that they as Indigenous diasporic young people face both internally and externally. By actively engaging and participating in performing and representing their town's past, present, and future, the young actors managed to maintain a sense of belonging and renegotiate their position in local hierarchies as well as the ways in which their town was represented externally.

Migration is often invoked to explain local divisions in La Gloria and in other sending communities like it (Green 2011; Ruíz-Lagier 2013). However, I argue that in the seemingly fragmented and dynamic circumstances common in rural sending communities, collective remembrance and collective anticipation of migration emerge as part of the "social glue" that holds La Gloria's moral community together. In La Gloria, remembrance of the refugee years happens collectively during the San Miguel celebrations and stand as a reminder of a shared past full of atrocities and hardship, but equally rich in cooperation and *jelq'ab* (literally meaning "the joining of hands" and translating to "mutual help"; see Gonzalez 2010, vi). The storytelling about contemporary migration also addresses hardship collectively and tells of solidarity in the diaspora of *el Norte*.

The experience of migrating and the subsequent sharing of anecdotes and stories about the hardship and conviviality of migration emerges as a collective endeavor that forges links among La Gloria's population. Neither of these two acts of storytelling rely on first-hand experience but rather belong to a collective "pool" (or register) of narratives that are shared among friends, neighbors, family members, and acquaintances without the necessity of the protagonist being physically present. It is in the act of storytelling that the seemingly distant domains of refugee pasts and migrant futures fuse, mesh, and become visible as expressions of collective remembrance. This remembrance has retrospective features as well as features of **anticipatory memory**. The members of the youth group equally remembered pasts they didn't live as they anticipated futures that were yet to come; thus they participated in acts of storytelling that enabled forms of collective identification through a shared past, present, and future.

CONCLUSION

In his performance in the play, Ivan made a sad face when he said that he was planning to migrate "without knowing the history of my people," and Don Alex stressed the importance for his people to remember the past to avoid "losing out on their future." Both appeals were directed toward a collectivity that emerged in the overlaps between remembrances of the past and aspirations for the future. Several years later Ivan himself migrated (not as a fictional character on stage anymore) to the United States and continued to establish the links between his experience and the experience of Akateko generations before him. Far from being purely symbolic connections, these links had practical implications and informed important life decisions for Ivan and others in La Gloria.

Migration fragments the cultural belonging, social reproduction, and intergenerational transmission in sending communities, however, as I hope to have shown throughout this chapter, new identity formations emerge through various forms of mobility and storytelling. As Stuart Hall (1997) points out, "diaspora identities are those which are constantly producing and reproducing themselves anew, through transformation and difference" (235). In La Gloria, mobility itself has become part of these diasporic identities in the flux of constant remaking through storytelling. Young people in La Gloria were crucial agents in linking these two temporalities of migration through narrative investment and concrete practices. Ivan and other young people in La Gloria engaged in storytelling that centered on border crossing and "being on the move" in both the past and the present, thus negotiating collective and intergenerational identities – not despite the fragmentations of migration, but rather through them.

REFLECTION AND DISCUSSION QUESTIONS

- What connections do young Guatemalan-Mexicans draw between their parents' and grandparents' refugee experience, the US migration experience of adult residents of their community, and their own future/present migration experience? Through what means do they draw those connections?
- What role does memory and storytelling play in diasporic settings, and how can it impact intergenerational relations and formations of "collective identities"? What memories circulate intergenerationally within your family? How do these memories shape your sense of being and belonging?
- How do youth understandings shape the Guatemalan diaspora? What specific expectations are directed toward young people in the diaspora, and how do they impact young people's aspirations for the future?

KEY CONCEPTS

- **anticipatory memory**: A concept that describes how memory can work in an anticipatory way; based on the idea that "imagining the future is just another form of memory" (Beck 2017).
- **diaspora**: A dispersed population with shared origins in a particular locale (e.g., the African diaspora, the Jewish diaspora). See also Chapter 14.
- **double diaspora**: A group of people that has gone through two consecutive diasporas.

EXPLORE FURTHER

- To learn about the legacy of the civil war in Guatemala, read **Chapter 22**.
- To learn more about transnational families, read **Chapters 34** and **35**.
- To learn more about the significance of material culture such as music, literature, film, art, and theater for marginalized communities in Latin America and the Caribbean, read **Chapters 13**, **14**, **20**, **21**, **24**, and **27**.

ABOUT THE AUTHOR

Malte Gembus (Ph.D., Goldsmiths, University of London) is a research fellow at Coventry University (UK) and a youth and community worker. His research explores processes of memory, being, and belonging among young people in diasporic contexts in Central America and arrival among newcomers in East London. He is committed to exploring the overlaps between participatory youth and community work and ethnographic inquiry.

REFERENCES

Beck, Julie. 2017. "Imagining the Future Is Just Another Form of Memory." *The Atlantic*. https://www.theatlantic.com/science/archive/2017/10/imagining-the-future-is-just-another-form-of-memory/542832.

González, Gaspar Pedro. 2010. *13 B'aktun: Mayan Visions of 2012 and Beyond*. Berkeley, CA: North Atlantic Books.

Green, Linda. 2011. "The Nobodies: Neoliberalism, Violence, and Migration." *Medical Anthropology* 30 (4): 366–85. https://doi.org/10.1080/01459740.2011.576726.

Hall, Stuart. 1997. "Cultural Identity and Diaspora." In *Undoing Place?* edited by Linda McDowell, 231–42. Abingdon, UK: Routledge.

Hernández-Castillo, Aida. 2001. *Histories and Stories from Chiapas: Border Identities in Southern Mexico*. Austin: University of Texas Press.

Jackson, Michael. 2002. *The Politics of Storytelling: Violence, Transgression and Intersubjectivity*. Chicago: University of Chicago Press.

Ruíz-Lagier, Verónica. 2013. *Ser Mexicano en Chiapas: Identidad y Ciudadanización entre los Refugiados Guatemaltecos en La Trinitaria*. Mexico City: Instituto Nacional de Antropología e Historia (INAH).

Conclusion

The Intergovernmental Panel on Climate Change (IPCC), the world's leading authority on the subject, indicates that to avoid catastrophic environmental, economic, and social consequences, global warming must be limited to no more than 2°C above preindustrial temperatures. Even if sweeping changes are made to reach this goal, Latin American and Caribbean nations will continue to grapple with the repercussions of irreversible climate change that are already impacting communities of every kind across the region. This region, perhaps more than any other, is characterized by ongoing encounters between peoples of incredibly diverse ethnic, racial, and religious backgrounds, languages, values, histories, and ways of being. And, as the ethnographic case studies in this volume attest, these diverse communities are already meeting contemporary challenges with resilience and creativity. The sorts of problems they face – including poverty, extreme weather events, racism, epidemics, state violence, displacement, and discrimination – are, in fact, global phenomena. Learning how people in Latin America and the Caribbean are drawing on legacies of knowledge from earlier generations, building new alliances, applying artistic approaches, and innovating to survive, thrive, and solve these problems is critical to addressing them elsewhere and at a global scale. We hope that this book has served as an introduction to the knowledge and diversity of experience in Latin America and the Caribbean and that it will inspire readers to learn more and to work in solidarity with people from the region toward a more just, equitable, and sustainable world.

Text Credits

Chapter 4: Reprinted with permission from *Cultural Anthropology* 28 (3): 396–419. Abridged and revised by Melanie Medeiros and the author.

Chapter 8: Reprinted with permission from the *Journal of Latin American and Caribbean Anthropology* 16 (2): 335–53. Abridged and revised by Melanie Medeiros and Jennifer Guzmán with the author's approval.

Chapter 11: Translated by Alejandro Reyes. Reprinted with permission from the *Journal of Latin American and Caribbean Anthropology* 24 (3): 635–52. Abridged and revised by Melanie Medeiros and Jennifer Guzmán with the author's approval.

Chapter 19: Reprinted from *Political and Legal Anthropology Review* 44 (1): 60–74. (CC BY 4.0). Abridged and revised by Melanie Medeiros and the author.

Chapter 24: Reprinted with permission from *City and Society* 31 (2): 142–63. Abridged and revised by the author.

Chapter 25: Reprinted with permission from the author's 2021 book *Not Even a Grain of Rice: Buying Food on Credit in the Dominican Republic*. Lanham, MD: Lexington Books. Abridged and revised by the author.

Chapter 30: Reprinted with permission from the *Journal of Political Ecology* 27: 917–38. Abridged and revised by the author.

Chapter 31: Reprinted from the *Latin American Research Review* 54(2): 366–80. (CC BY 4.0). Abridged and revised by Melanie Medeiros and Jennifer Guzmán.

Index

Page numbers in italics refer to illustrations.

Abraço a Microcefalia (I Embrace Microcephaly), 176–7, 178, 179
accent, in languages, 186
Achuapa town (Nicaragua), 473
Acosta, José de, 30
Acosta, Liz, as PRI candidate, 235–6, 237, 238
activist anthropology, 324, 330
activist social analysis, 330
actuaries
 description, 254
 and pension expertise, 258–9, 260
AD ("Anno Domini"), for dates, 27
adaptive strategies, 32, 38
ADN Maya collective, 190, 192, 193–5
ADN Maya Films, 193
AFPs (*Administradoras de Fondos de Pensiones*), 252–4, 255
African ancestry, in Cuba, 72
Afro-descendants
 in ecotourism in Brogodó, 428, 429, 430, 431–2
 in labor and mining in Brazil, 431, 433
 and race, 58, 67, 433
 See also *nativo*

agency
 concept, 365, 369, 449
 and social structure, 365, 367–9
"Age of Discovery" narrative, 47–8
agriculture, as concept, 38
Akateko people, 498, 501
Akateko-speaking Guatemalan refugees, 498, 499
Alas y Raíces (Wings and Roots) program (Mexico), 196
Alexander, Jacqui, 103
Allende, Salvador, 57
altiplano (high plains) of Peru
 description, 113
 multilingualism and Indigenous identity, 113–15
América Invertida [*America Inverted*], 45, *46*
American Anthropological Association, ethical guidelines of, 20
Añangu. *See* Kichwa Añangu Community
Anderson, Benedict, 375
animals, domestication of, 32
anonymity of the research participants, 21, 24
anthropologists

 assumptions of, 309
 colonial fieldwork approaches, 18
anthropometry, 457, 462
anti-Black state violence, 89, 93
anticipatory memory, 505, 506
anti-democratic authoritarianism, 55
anti-Haitianism, 351–2
anxious ethnic subjects, 131, 132
Arana, Marie, 46–7
Arbenz, Jacobo, 310
archaeological regions, description and map, 28, *29*
archaeological site in Cobá (Mexico), 454–5, 460–1
archaeology
 on arrival of people, 30–1, 465
 complexity in, 30
 dates and terminology, 27–8
 glossary (online), 28
 names of areas, 28
 naming in, 33
 and pre-European states, 35–6
 prehistoric lifeways, 31–2
 views of the past, 36–7
Argentina
 disappeared people, 60, 303, 304
 feminist movements, 305

Argentine dictatorship (1976–1983)
  description and transition from, 303
  film reception study, 298, 299, 302, 303–6
armed conflict, 280
  See also Colombia armed conflict
art
  and Colombia armed conflict, 283–6
  and ethnographic turn, 286–92
  as issue, 12
  in reparation for victims, 285–6
  in situ and "leaving the art studio" work, 287–92
  and transitional justice, 285–6, 286n2, 293
  and violence, 293–4
Artibonite River (Haiti), *96*, 97, 98
Aruba
  four languages in history, 215
  language repertoire and interaction by students, 218–22
  multilingualism, 213, 215–16
Aserradero community (Mexico)
  description, 483
  remittances to, 483–5
Associations of Traditional Authorities in Colombia, 128–9
Atrabiliarios (installation), 291
audience ethnography, 298, 307
austerity measure, definition and example, 255
authoritarian regimes
  anti-democratic types, 55
  concept and description, 225, 227
  examples, 55, 279
  influence today, 225
Autodefensas Unidas de Colombia (United Self-Defense Forces of Colombia), 125–6
autoethnography, 18, 24, 143
autonomous consultation
  concept, 403, 409
  description and as right, 403–4
  and Tamaquito II, 403, 404–5, 408

ayllu authorities in Bolívar province
  in the case of Piruani, 265, 267, 269–70, 271, 272–3
  description, 265, 276
  in land management, 271
  other responsibilities, 267–8
  overview, 265, 266–8
  in systems of authority, 266–8, 272–3, 274–6
ayllu communities, features of, 268
Aymara Indigenous nation (Peru)
  as identity, 116
  linguistic knowledge and self-identification, 112, 117, 118–21
  number of, 117
Aymara language
  authenticity and purity, 115–16
  in Puno region, 113–15
  in radio advertisements, 117, 118–20
Aztecs, 35, 36–7

Bad Bunny (rapper), 377–8, 380
Bajo Belén. *See* Belén
Balaam Ich (rapper), 193
balanced reciprocal exchanges, 353, 358
bands, definition and description, 33
Bannzil Kreyòl Kiba, 205, 210
Basic Ecclesial Communities (CEBs) movement, projects of, 243, 244
Basta ya! Colombia (report, 2013), 285
Batista Félix, Hilario, 200–2, *201*, 203–9
Batista Puente, Nathalie, 200, 206
BC and BCE ("Before Christ" and "Before Common Era"), for dates, 27
Belén (Peru)
  "*Belén Sostenible*" ("Sustainable Belén") project, 390–1, 393, 395, 396
  description and life in, 388–9
  features and rainfall, 387–8
  houses in, 387, 388, *388*

  and law of national government, 390–1
  research description, 390
Belén (Peru) – resettlement plan
  description, 389, 391
  resistance to, 393–5
  and risk, 391–2, 393, 395–6
  views on, 389, 392–3, 394–5
Bellino, Michelle J., 312
belonging
  as issue, 11
  racialized belonging, 11, 71, 73, 77, 78, 79, 81
  for West Indian descendants in Panama, 138–40, 142–3
Bilbao, Francisco, 49–50
biological "race," 73
"Black Atlantic," 99
Black Legend, 48–50, 51
Black Lives Matter, in Brazil, 90
Blackness and Black
  in Cuba, 72, 81
  demonization of, 102
  inequalities in Brazil, 176
  racism in Brazil, 90
  slavery and Vodou in Haiti, 99, 103
  and white comfort, 90–2
Boas, Franz, 456
Bocas de Ceniza (2003–2004) (video), 287
Bolívar, Simon, 54
Bolívar province
  communal plots of land, 271–2
  description and life in, 267
  justice system, 274
  land management and conflict resolution, 267–8, 271–2
  mayor and police in land dispute, 265–6
  systems of authority, 266–8, 272–6
  See also ayllu authorities; peasant union
Bolivia
  agricultural and environmental adjudication, 274
  customary law (*usos y costumbres*), 269–70, 274, 275

Indigenous peoples as legal authorities, 265–6, 267, 273–5
Indigenous sovereignty in, 108
juramento (declaration of intent), 274
legal pluralism in, 266, 267, 273–5, 276
money in justice system, 269, 270, 272
as plurinational state, 266, 274
Bolland, O. Nigel, 204
Bomba music and *bombazos*, 371–2, 375, 377
boundary-making practices, 256
BP ("Before Present"), for dates, 27
Bravo, Estela, 297
Brazil
 archaeological sites, 30
 COVID-19, 179–81
 education system, 435, 435n2
 health care services for disabled children, 178–9
 middle-class status and views, 84–5
 periferia (low-income neighborhoods), 176, 177, 179, 181
 Pink Tide, 244, 248–9
 race and racism, 68–9, 90, 91
 racial democracy myth, 432–3
 racial inequality in, 89, 91–2
 racial logics example, 84–5, 91–2
 skin color, 86, 88
 social clubs, 86, 88
 socioeconomic change, 339
 state violence, 89
 structural issues in CZS and Zika, 176, 179–80, 182
 structural racism, 432–3, 437
 urban planning paradigm, 337
 violence in, 88
 Zika outbreaks, 173, 174
Brazilian Constitution, 337
Briceño, Fidencio, 189
Brogodó (Bahia, Brazil), *430*, *432*
 Afro-descendants in ecotourism, 428, 429, 430, 431–2
 ecotourism to park nearby, 429, 430–1

educational inequities, 435–6
occupational segregation in touristscape, 433–5, 437, 438
structural racism, 430, 431–2, 433, 438
technical training, 436–7
touristscape, 430–2
Bruno, Simone, 304
Buenos Aires (Argentina)
 dictatorship, 303
 film reception study, 302, 303–6
"Building a Decade of Actions for Indigenous Languages" event, 191
bureaucracy, in state-level societies, 34
bureaucratic-authoritarian regimes, 225, 227

Cabarete (Dominican Republic), life and work in, 351–2
Calakmul county (Mexico)
 emotions in migration, 486
 financial relationships in migration, 489–92
 gastada ("allowance") to women, 490–1
 infidelity in, 485, 490, 491
 mother-in-law and daughter-in-law interactions, 483–5, 486, 488, 489, 490–2
 mother-in-law's experience of migration, 487–8
 patriarchy and patrilocal aspects, 487, 488–9, 492
 regime of (im)mobility, 486, 492
 wages in and work in US, 483–4
campaign (electoral) clientelism, 231
Campamento *ranchería*, 123, 127, 130
Campanur Tapia, Guadalupe, 161
campesinos (peasant farmers)
 rights and resistance, 232, 414, 416–17, 421
 way of life, 321
candidates (in elections), and clientelism, 233–4, 235–7, 238
capitalism, 225, 261, 383–4

Caquetio (Arawakan-speaking) people, 215
Caribbean
 First peoples, 30–1, 33
 future in, 509
 geography and environment, 28, 30
 issues and dynamic phenomena, 11–12
 map, *3*
 map of archaeological regions, *29*
 map of Indigenous and creole languages, *8–9*
 naming for archaeological cultures, 33
 as nationalistic blocks, 204
 prehistoric lifeways, 31–2
 sociopolitical organization, 33–5
 See also history 1400–present
Carrillo, Dado, 304
Casas, Bartolomé de las, 52
case of Piruani
 approaches to, 271–3
 authorities in, 265–6, 275–6
 ayllu authorities and peasant union in, 265, 267, 268–70, 271, 272–3
 dispute description, 267, 268–71
case studies. *See* ethnographic case studies
Casey, Matthew, 202, 208
cash transfer program, 128
Castillo, Orlando, 302
caudillos, 54
CE ("Common Era"), for dates, 27
cellphones, 84, 89
Cementerio La Verbena (Guatemala), 314, 315, 316
Cementerio Tres Equis. *See* Tres Equis cemetery
Central America
 intraregional migration, 471–2
 map and boundaries, *2*
 map of Indigenous and creole languages, *7*
 map of physiographic regions, *5*
Central Andes
 description, 28
 map, *29*

Central Andes (*continued*)
  pre-European states, 35, 36
Ceramic Age in Caribbean, 31
Cerrejón Coal Company
  in autonomous consultation, 404–5
  displacement of Tabaco, 403
  resettlement of Tamaquito II, 400–1, 405, 407
Cerrejón concession, 402
Cerrejón open-pit coal mine, 399, 402
Céspedes-Baéz, Lina María, 169
Chasteen, John Charles, 47
Chavín site and culture, 36
Ché Guevara, *76*
Cherán (Mexico), 161, 167
Chiapas (Mexico)
  cultural norms change, 366–7
  description and people, 363
  family economies, 364–5
  life during COVID-19, 360, 361, 366–7
  life of Juana (*see* Juana's lived experience)
  as refuge for Guatemalans, 499
  weaving and selling textiles, 361, 362, 363, 365
Chicago Boys, 57
chicha, *442*
  decoding, 442
  description and fermentation, 442, 446–8
  for tourists, 444, 446
chicha masticada (or "chewed chicha"), 446–8
chiefdoms, definition and description, 33
chieftainship, 34
children
  impact of diet on health and growth, 456–8
  in parents' migration, 487–8
  in patrilocal residence, 488–9
  See also Cobá children
Chile
  gendered knowledge regimes, 259–60
  nationalization of resources and industries, 57

new constitution, 261–2
pension fund companies, 252–4, 255
pension policy and system, 252–4
pension provision model, 255–6
protests, 252, *253*, 261
social security system, 261–2
study description, 256
Chile's pension experts
  battles over policy, 254–5, 257–9, 261
  and gender, 254, 258, 259–60, 261
  practices and operations of, 254
  as problem and influence in pension policy, 253–4, 255–6, 261
  recognition of, 254, 257–9
Chiquihuite Cave (Mexico), 30
chontacuros (palm weevil grub), *442*
  decoding, 442
  description, 442, 445
  eating by tourists and anthropologist, 441, 444, 445
  inside meaning, 444–5
"choosing a soul" and "chosen souls," 283
Christian fundamentalism, and Haitian Vodou, 100–1, 102
"chronic homework," 178–9
chronic poverty, 333
Cia Humbalada de Teatro (Humbalada Theater Company), 344–5, 346
Cidade Linda (Beautiful City) program (São Paulo), 338
citizenship, 108, 109
  See also Indigenous citizenship
civil conflict, 279, 307
civilizations
  description and characteristics, 33–4
  and race, 58
class, and race, 146, 155
clientelism
  campaign examples, 229–30, 231, 235–7
  concept, 226, 227, 242
  and democracy, 231

in elections in Mexico, 231, 237–8
measurement, 231
by NGO, 242, 245
in Oaxaca, 232, 233, 234–6, 237–8
political machines *vs.* individual candidates, 233–4
tactics and forms used, 232, 235–6, 237, 238
clientelist systems
  concept, 230–1, 239
  varieties, 231
climate change
  in Bélen, 387–8
  and extractive industries, 383, 401, 408, 413
  as issue, 11–12, 509
  solution to, 420–1
  and Wayúu people, 401, 408
Clovis hypothesis, 30
Cobá children
  description and life of, 452–3
  impact of tourism on health and growth, 453, 457–60
Cobá pyramid (Nohoch Mul), *453*
Cobá village (Mexico)
  description and road to, 452, 454–5
  development, 455–6
  farming and store access, 459
  healthcare access, 460, 461
  impact of COVID-19, 460–1
Cobo, Bernabé, 447
Coca-Cola, in Mexico, 456
"coca-colonization," 456
coding, as NGO project, 245
Cold War (1947–1989), 225, 279
collective identity, and storytelling, 503–5
collective memory, 280
colmados (corner stores) in Dominican Republic, *350*
  intercultural exchanges in, 355–6, 357
  shopping in, 352–4
  study of, 352
  use of *fiao*, 349–50, 351, 352, 357–8

Colombia
  cédula de ciudadanía (citizenship identity card), 128
  and coal-mining companies, 400, 402–3
  demobilization of paramilitary groups, 289n3
  film reception study, 297, 298, 299–302
  Indigenous citizenship, 128–9
  paramilitarismo, 125–6, 128
  peace communities, 299
  social inclusion for Indigenous peoples, 123–4, 126, 127, 131–2
  social markers of hierarchy, 123
  state control in La Guajira, 125, 126
Colombia armed conflict
  artistic production about, 283–6
  artworks discussed, 284, 287–92, 288, 289, 290, 292
  description and causes, 280, 285, 285n1
  and ethnographic turn, 286–7, 292–4
  fieldwork and field notes by artists, 286–8
  film reception study, 297, 299–302
  guerilla and paramilitary groups, 285, 289–90, 289n3
  peace agreements and reparations, 285–6
  in situ and "leaving the art studio" work by artists, 287–92
  transitional justice and art, 285–6
  unidentified bodies, 283
colonial era
  fieldwork approaches, 18
  history of Latin America, 50–3
  post-colonial history, 53–7
  views of the past, 36–7
colonialism
  and Conquest, 50–1
  impact on Latin America, 47
  and Maya, 454
  neocolonialism, 56, 333–4
  poverty and inequalities, 333

coloniality, 162–3, 169
colonial languages, 185–6, 187
colonization, as "coca-colonization," 456
"Columbian Exchange," 50
Columbus, 47–8
Commission for Historical Clarification (CEH) (Guatemala), 311
commodified forms of indigeneity, 131–2
community of care, 475, 479
community of practice
  ADN Maya collective as, 193–5
  concept, 198
compadrazgo (godparenthood) system, 454
"compulsory closeness" in Rio de Janeiro, 87–8
comunalidad, 413, 420, 421
conceptions of risk
  concept, 389, 397
  in resettlement project, 391, 395–6
confidentiality, 21
conflict imaginary
  concept, 299, 307
  in film reception study, 299, 301
congenital Zika syndrome (CZS)
  care by mothers and women, 177–8, 179–81, 182
  cases in Brazil, 175
  and COVID-19, 179–81
  description and effects, 174, 175, 177, 183
  fieldwork example, 177–9
  and structural issues in Brazil, 176, 179–80, 182
  See also Zika
Conquest, description and legacies, 50–1
conservatism, 55
conservatives and liberals, power contest since independence, 54–5
consultation laws for Indigenous peoples, 404
cosmopolitanism, 343, 347
Costa Rica

migration to, 471–2
telecommunications, 473–4
See also Nicaraguan migrants in Costa Rica
COVID-19
  cultural norms change in Chiapas, 366–7
  and CZS in Brazil, 179–81
  impact in Mexico, 360–1, 366, 460–1
  and Juana's lived experience, 360, 361–2, 366–9
creole languages, 186, 187
  maps, 7, 8–9, 10
criollos, 53, 152
critical cultural relativism, 22, 25
Cuba
  color complex in, 72–3
  Haitian language and culture, 205–6
  Haitians in, 200, 202–5, 207–9, 210
  ID checks for race, 71, 75, 81
  race and belonging, 73, 77, 78, 79, 81
  raciality in, 72–3, 74–5, 80–1
  racialized tourism, 75–80
  racism, 203, 204
  research project description, 74, 77
  scholarship on, 202–3
  skin color in, 71–3, 74, 77, 80–1
  socialism and revolution, 56–7, 74
  tourism industry, 74–5, 76–7
  tourist-only spaces, 75–6, 78–80
Cué, Gabino, 233
cultural capital
  concept, 433, 439
  employment of Afro-descendants in ecotourism, 433–5
cultural change, and tourism, 454–6
cultural ethnotourism, 426
cultural relativism, 22, 25
cultural survival, 104
cultural tourism
  food in, 441, 442
  for Kichwa Añangu Community, 443–4

Index 517

culture
  colonial approaches *vs.* today, 18
  concept, 25
Curaçao
  four languages in colonial history, 215
  language choice, 213–14
  language repertoire and interaction by students, 216–18, 221–2
  multilingualism, 213, 215–16

dates, writing of, 27
daughters-in-law, remittances to, 483, 484–5, 490–1
Decade of Indigenous Languages (2022–2032), 191
Defend Puerto Rico project, 376
democracy
  as battleground in Latin America, 56
  and clientelism, 231
  concept, 225, 227
  and politics in Latin America and Caribbean, 225–6
dependence theory, 333
dependency, 56, 63
desaparecidos (disappeared) in Guatemala
  assumptions about, 309
  cemeteries for, 314–15, 316
  concept, 318
  Izabella's father story (contemporary disappeared), 312–15, 316–17
  from military regime, 311
  sociopolitics of, 315–17
development
  concept and as model, 383–4
  forms in Latin America and Caribbean, 384
  and risk in Belén resettlement, 391, 395–6
Día de los Mártires (Martyrs' Day) (Panama), 139
dialectic
  of agency and social structure, 365, 367–8
  concept, 365, 369

dialects and dialectal variation, 185–6
diaspora
  concept, 211, 506
  double diaspora, 501, 506
  and identity, 498, 501, 505
dictatorships, 279
diet, impact on health and growth of children, 456–8
digital solidarities of migrants, 475–8
disappearance and disappeared
  in Argentina, 60, 303, 304
  art about, 290, 291
  concept, 279, 280
  as practice, 283
  See also *desaparecidos*
"disappearing people," in Colombia armed conflict, 283
discoveries
  as "Encounter(s)," 50
  in history of Latin America and Caribbean, 47–8
displacement of people, 168, 401, 403
  See also resettlement
domestication, 31–2, 38
Dominican Republic
  ethnic and racial ideologies, 351–2
  food insecurity and poverty, 351
  life and work in Cabarete, 351–2
  race in, 68
  shopping in *colmados*, 352–4
  tourism for economy, 351, 358
  use of *fiao*, 349
do no harm, 21, 25
Doria, João, and administration, 337–8
Dorsainvil, Justin Chrysostome, 101, 102
double diaspora, 501, 506
Duelos (video installation), 290, *290*
Dutch language on Curaçao and Aruba
  for education, 213–14, 216, 217–18, 220, 221
  as official language, 215

Echavarría, Juan Manuel, 283, *284*, 287, *288*, 293
Echeverri, Clemencia, 288–9, *289*, *290*, 293
economic inequality, 333
economic migration, 472
economists in Chile. *See* Chile's pension experts
economy
  and development, 383–4
  first global system, 52–3
  Marxist views, 261
  in neocolonialism, 56, 333
  in nineteenth-century Latin America, 56
  and tourism, 74–5, 351, 358, 461
ecotourism
  in Bahia, 429–30
  concept, 426
  structural racism, 430, 431–2, 433, 438
  technical training for, 436–7
  See also Brogodó (Bahia, Brazil)
education
  in Indigenous languages, 195–6
  inequities in, 435–6
  as NGO project, 244–5
El Cima (rapper), 189
emic, as concept, 17, 25
emic perspective, 17
Emmerich, Norberto, 163
empire building in Latin America and Caribbean, 50–1
engaged ethnography, 19, 25
English language, on Aruba and Curaçao, 215
enslaved Africans, 52, 99
Environmental and Agrarian Tribunal (Bolivia), 274
environmental violence, 414, 421
Erauso, Catalina de (the "Lt. Nun"), 60
"*Estamos Bien*" ("We're Good") (song), 377, 378
"*Este es mi pueblo Kantemo, Yuc*" (song), 194
ethics, in ethnography, 20–1
ethnicity (or ethnic identity)
  concept, 107, 109

downward mobilization, 123–4
in national census of Peru, 117
perceptions about, 107
and personal identity, 107–8
power as social construct, 108
and purist language ideology, 112–13
in radio advertisements in Puno, 117–20
ethnocentric view of the past, 36–7
ethnographers, changes in, 18
ethnographic case studies
description and role, 15, 22
interpretation, 15–17, 23–4
ethnographic fieldwork
by artists, 286–7
components and focus, 18
concept, 25
description and examples, 15, 17–18
methods and tools, 19–20
research objectives, 17, 18, 20
ethnographic research
as collaboration, 19
concept, 17, 25
introduction to, 17–19
methods and tools, 19–20
ethnographic style and stylistic features, 21–3
ethnographic turn
and art, 286–92
in Colombia armed conflict, 286–7, 292–4
concept, 286, 295
ethnography
concept, 25
description, 15, 21–2
ethics, 20–1
interpretation in, 22
ethnolinguistic differences, 112, 121
ethnolinguistic groups, and Indigenous citizenship, 112, 116
ethnotourism, 426
etic, as concept, 25
etic interpretation, 17
European descendants, 58
exchanges, in history, 50
expertise, 256–7

extractive capitalism, and political regimes, 225
extractive industries
and climate change, 383, 401, 408, 413
and consultation laws, 404
and displacement, 401
impact, 383, 401
extractivism, 384, 413

"false positives," 304
Falsos Positivos (documentary)
description, 304
screening and reactions, 304–6, 307
Famous 41 Scandal (1901), 61
Fanon, Frantz, 102
FARC (Revolutionary Armed Forces of Colombia), 284, 285, 301–2
favelas (shantytowns), 87
Federal Republic of Central America, 54
feminist movements and activism, 60, 146–7, 305
Fernández Ortega, Inés, 165
fiao (in-store credit)
access to for customers, 353
debt repayment, 349–50, 353–4, 356–7
description, 350, 352, 353, 357, 358
references and vouching for new borrowers, 355, 356–7
and responsible people (*gente responsable*), 349–50, 352, 354–5
types, 354–5
use in *colmados*, 349–50, 351, 352, 357–8
fictive kinship, 358
field notes, 19, 25, 287
fieldwork. *See* ethnographic fieldwork
films reception (films about/on/ with violence)
in Argentina, 298, 299, 302–6
in Colombia, 297, 298, 299–302
methods, 298–9
screening reactions, 297, 298, 300–2, 304–7
as study, 298–9

finca (farm), as social marker, 123
Firmin, Anténor, 103
First peoples
of Latin America and Caribbean, 30–1, 33
lifeways, 31–2
origin, 30
Fischer, Sybille, 101
food
in cultural tourism, 441, 442
in impact of tourism on health and growth, 458–9
inside and outside meaning, 442, 445, 447, 449
as reflection of identity and culture, 441
and tourism, 445
foraging, 32, 38
foraging bands, 34
forensic anthropology, in Guatemala, 309–10, 312, 315, 317
1492: Conquest of Paradise (movie), 47
France, and Haitian Revolution, 43, 99
Frerichs, Ralph, 98
Fuentes Epiayu, Eduardo, 406
Fuentes Epiayu, Jairo, *400*, 403, 407–8
Fujimori, Alberto, 226
Fundación de Antropología Forense de Guatemala (Forensic Anthropology Foundation of Guatemala; FAFG), description and work, 311, 312–13, 315, 316–17

Gaitán, Jorge Eliécer, 285
Galeano, Eduardo, 47
Galtung, Johan, 334
Gamboa, Roberto, 416
García, Ofelia, 218
García Velázquez, Alejandro, *412*, 416–17
Gen De Lwa ceremony, 95–7, 102–3
gender
and binary distinctions, 145, 146
concept, 147

gender (*continued*)
  in family economies of Mexico, 365
  intersectionality with race or class, 146
  as issue, 12
  in jurisdictional battles for power, 256–7, 258–9
  and migration, 486
  in qualitative/quantitative divide, 256–7, 258
  research on in Latin America, 145
  third gender, 146, 154
gender complementarity, 37, 38
gendered knowledge regimes, 259–60, 262
gender identity, and ethnicity, 107–8
gender ideologies, 145, 147
gendering (verb), and power, 254, 256–7
gendering expertise, 254, 262
gender roles and queerness, 157–8
gender violence. *See* sexual violence/violation
genetics
  and race, 67–8
  in settling of Caribbean, 30–1
González, Carvajal, 286
González, Leonardo, 405
governmental rationality/governmentality
  in Belén project, 391, 395
  concept, 391, 397
Grajaú Conta Dandaras, Grajaú Conta Zumbi (play), 344, 345, 347
Gran Colombia, 54
grassroot strategies, 191
"Great Divergence," 53
Greater Antilles, map of Indigenous and creole languages, *8*
Grupo Bannzil Kreyòl Kiba, 205, 210
Guajiro ethnic identity, 125
Guamán Poma de Ayala, Felipe, 447
Guatemala
  autonomous consultation, 404
  civil war/armed conflict, 62, 280, 311, 316–17, 499
  decade of violence, 499

excavations of cemeteries, 311
forensic anthropology, 309–10, 312, 315, 317
funding by foreign powers, 311, 313, 315, 316–17
history and "post-conflict" situation, 310–12
migration to Mexico, 498
military regime and death squads, 310–11
refugees to La Gloria (*see* La Gloria town)
violence today, 311–12, 315–17
See also *desaparecidos*
Guatemalan Civil War (1960–1996), 499

habitus, 434, 437–8, 439
Haddad, Fernando, 337
Haiti
  cholera epidemic, 97–8
  demonization and othering, 101–2
  diaspora, 202n2, 210
  historical background, 99–100
  migrant workers from, 208
  problems in, 210
  See also Kreyòl
Haitian Constitution, 205
Haitian Revolution (1791–1804), 43, 99, 202, 204
Haitians
  in Cuba, 200, 202–5, 207–9, 210
  in Dominican Republic, 349–50, 351, 356, 357
Haitian Vodou
  concept and description, 95, 104
  condemnation, 100–2
  in Cuba, 202, 205
  Gen De Lwa ceremony, 95–7, 102–3
  importance and role in Haiti, 103
  paradoxical status, 98, 102–4
  stigmatization of, 97–8
Hall, Stuart, 505
hate crimes, fines for, 342–3
Hay-Bunau-Varilla Treaty, 136
hegemonic masculinity, 257, 259, 262

hegemony, 250
Hidalgo, Miguel, 54
"*Hijos del Cañaveral*" ("Children of Sugarcane") (song), 377, 378, 379
hip-hop, on Yucatán Peninsula, 192–3
historical agency, 63
histories from below, 58
history
  interpretations, 42–5, 62–3
  and understanding of the past, 44–5
history 1400–present (of Latin America and Caribbean)
  colonial era, 50–3
  Conquest, 50–1
  and discoveries, 47–8, 50
  empire building, 50–1
  and global economy, 52–3
  interpretation and periodization, 44–5
  "Latin America" as interpretation, 45–7
  and legends of history, 48–50
  minimization through narratives, 42–3
  negotiations in, 51
  post-colonial era, 53–7
  race in, 58–9
  reinterpretation, 51–2
  and transculturation, 61–2
  women and queer events, 59–61
Holocene, 31, 38
Honduras, and outmigration, 465
Horswell, Michael, 154
horticulture, 38
huipiles, 362, 369
humanists, and quantitative studies, 258, 260
humanitarian forensic action, 309, 318
human migration. *See* migration
human occupation, and natural environment, 30
humans, classification of, 67
Hume, Yanique, 203
Hurlich, Susan, 203
Hurricane Maria in Puerto Rico

damage and recovery aid, 372
government response, 374–5, 379, 380
impact, 371–2, 374, 380
and independence or statehood attempts, 374, 375
musicians' support and collaboration, 372–3
songs about, 371–2, 378–80
Huyssen, Andreas, 291
hypodescent (the "one drop rule"), 68

identity
    in diaspora, 498, 501, 505
    and food, 441
    and gender, 107–8
    as issue, 11
    of research participants, 21
    and storytelling, 503–5
    See also ethnicity (or ethnic identity); *specific nations or groups of people*
images, in ethnographic fieldwork, 20
"Imaginary Couples" ("*Parejas Imaginarias*") project, 153
imagined communities (nationalism), 55, 63
immigrant languages, 186–7
immigrants from Europe, 58
"implicated subjectivity" of bystanders, 305
import substitution industrialization (ISI), 57
Inca, 35, 36, 37
indigenismo, 59
indigenization, 400, 409
Indigenous citizenship
    concept, 108, 109
    and ethnolinguistic groups, 112, 116
    institutionalization and its effect, 129–31
    move towards, 123
    programs in Colombia, 128–9
    resguardos and *reservas* for Wayúu, 126–8
Indigenous cosmovisions, 413, 415, 421

Indigenous Families in Action program (Colombia), 123, 126, 128–30
Indigenous languages
    description and use, 186, 187
    educational initiatives, 195–6
    global initiatives, 191
    learning, 195
    lengua originaria, 186, 198
    loss and stigmatization of, 191, 192
    map of the
    in Mexico, 190–1, 196
    multilingualism in Peru, 113–14
    and resistance, 204
    See also rap in Indigenous languages; *specific languages*
Indigenous languages – maps
    Caribbean – Greater and Lesser Antilles, 8, 9
    Central America, 7
    Mexico, 7
    South America, 10
Indigenous movements, 226, 321–2, 323
Indigenous nations, and sovereignty, 108, 116
Indigenous peoples
    anxiety in, 131, 132
    cash transfer program, 128
    in Conquest and empire, 51
    consultation laws for, 404
    decline and deaths, 51–2
    differences and divisions in, 414–15
    and diseases, 51
    incarceration of leaders, 322
    in legends of history, 48–9
    and modernity, 150, 152
    and race, 58, 59
    resistance by, 161, 166–7, 321–2, 323–4, 412–15
    and territory, 399
    and third gender, 146, 154
    See also *specific nations, groups of people, or countries; specific topics*
Indigenous women
    resistance by, 161, 166–7
    violence on, 162, 163, 164–6, 169

Indio, 68
inedible
    meaning in, 441
    revulsion toward, 445, 446–7
infectious diseases, and afterlife of epidemics, 182
informed consent, 20–1, 25
inside meaning, 442, 444–5, 447, 449
Integral System of Truth, Justice, Reparation, and Non-Repetition (SIVJRNR), 284, 285, 293
Inter-American Court of Human Rights (IACHR), 165
Intermediate Area
    description, 28
    map, 29
    states in, 35
internalized racism, 211
internal migration, 466, 467
International Finance Corporation's (IFC) resettlement standards, 405
International Labor Organization (ILO), 404
international migration
    concept, 466, 467
    couples separated by, 484–5
    impact in home country, 485
    regime of (im)mobility, 486, 492, 493
    travelers and stayers interdependence, 485–6, 492
    See also Calakmul county
Interoceanic Corridor megaproject, 412–13
interpretation
    of ethnographic case studies, 15–17, 23–4
    in ethnography, 22
    of history, 42–5, 62–3
    of maps, 45, 46
    and reinterpretation, 51–2
intersectionality, 58, 146, 147
interviews, in ethnographic fieldwork, 19–20
"*In watech' tu lakal – decirte todo*" (song), 194

Iquitos (Peru), 387, 388–9
Isthmus of Tehuantepec. *See* Tehuantepec Isthmus
Itaya River (Belén, Peru)
  contamination, 387
  flow changes and flooding, 387–8, 390–2, 393
  life and houses, 387, *388*
  and resettlement plan, 389, 391–2
Ixcotel Prison (Mexico)
  inside the prison, 326–9
  name, description, and closure, 320n2, 325, 327
  transfer of prisoners, 320n2
  visit to Ramírez, 320–1, 322, 324–6, 325n4, 327–9
Ixtepec city (Mexico), 417–20, 421

Jacinto, Gregorio, 265–6, 269–70, 271, 272
Jackson, Michael, 500–1
Jamaica, internal migration in, 466
jíbaro, 379, 381
Jocox youth group
  description, 500
  migration to US by, 500, 501–2
  play of origin story, 496, *497*, 498, 500, 501–3, 504
  storytelling between past and future, 500–3, 504–5
  See also La Gloria town
Juana's lived experience in Chiapas
  agency of, 366–9
  decision to marry, 361–2, 366, 367–8
  description and life in Salapo, 360, 362, 364
  impact of COVID-19, 360, 361–2, 366–9
  meeting of and learning from, 362–3
  offer of travel to Chicago, 367–8
  as weaver and saleswoman, 361, 362–3, 364, 365, 366–7, 368
jurisdictional battles
  concept, 256, 262
  gender in, 256–7, 258–9
  in pension expertise in Chile, 257–9, 261

jurisdictional demarcation law, 274–5, 276
justicia de acuerdos (justice by agreement), 268

key informant interviews, 19, 25
Kichwa Añangu Community (Ecuador)
  description and tourism in, 443–4, 446, 448–9
  food for tourists, 441, 442, 444, 446
  and symbolically coded edibles, 442, 444–9
  tourist industry, 442
Ki'imak in wool – Estoy contento (song), 194
kinship, 466, 467
Kintz, Ellen, 452, 453, 461
kitchen garden, 454, 462
knowledge regimes, 259
Kokobalé martial art, 371
Kolegio Maria Liberia school (Curaçao), 216–18, 221
Kreyòl (Haitian Creole)
  concept, 211
  and resistance, 204, 210
  standardization, 200n1
  usage and role, 204, 205, 209
Kreyòl (Haitian Creole) – in Cuba
  advance of language and culture, 205–6
  in performances, 200, 205
  poem in, 207
  usage and speakers of, 203, 204–5
Kuraj Tatas in Bolivia, 265, 267
Kuri Muyu Women's Organization, 443, 446, 448
kwashiorkor, 457
kwazad ("crusade") in Haitian Vodou, 100–1, 102

La Gloria town (Mexico-Guatemala border)
  collective remembrance of the past by youth, 499, 504–5
  fieldwork in US, 500–1
  founding and description, 498, 499

  generations and migration, 498–9, 504–5
  migration to US from, 499, 500, 501–2
  origin-story play, 496, *497*, 498, 500, 501–3, 504
  remittances in, 499, 503
  research description, 500
  storytelling and collective identity, 503–5
  storytelling between past and future, 500–3
  See also Jocox youth group
Lagoa Verde neighborhood (Fortaleza, Brazil), *242*
  contradiction in NGO work, 241, 242, 249
  earlier projects in, 243–4
  poverty, 241
  reputation of, 248
  research in, 241–2
La Guajira peninsula (Colombia)
  coal industry and mining, 401, 402
  description and history, 124–5
  displacement in, 401
  identity issues, 131–2
  mestizaje and shifting alliances, 123, 125–6
  paramilitarismo in, 125–6, 128
  as *resguardo*, 126–8
  state control, 125, 126
  See also Wayúu people
language
  importance, 185
  policy and planning in Mexico, 190–1
  single-language policies, 191
language ideologies, 121, 186
language revitalization
  concept, 198
  grassroot strategies, 191, 192
  of Yucatec Maya, 189–90, 192, 193–5, 197
languages
  diversity and types in Latin America and Caribbean, 185–7
  diversity in Mexico, 190–1

elevation of one over others, 185
variation in, 185–6
See also Indigenous languages
Larico, Francisco, 268–9
Latin America
    First peoples, 30
    future in, 509
    geography and environment, 28, 30
    independence, 54
    issues and dynamic phenomena, 11–12
    master narrative about, 45–7
    periods in history, 44
    pre-European states, 35–6
    prehistoric lifeways, 31–2
    sociopolitical organization, 33–5
    See also history 1400–present
Latin America – maps
    archaeological regions, *29*
    Indigenous and creole languages, *7, 10*
    physiogeographic regions, *5–6*
    political boundaries, *2, 4*
"Latin" America, as interpretation, 45–7
leaders and leadership, 34
Leftism, 56–7
legal pluralism
    in Bolivia, 266, 267, 273–5, 276
    concept, 266, 276
legends of history, 48–50
lengua(s) originaria(s) (Native/Indigenous language), 186, 198
lenticulars, as technique, 283
Leonel, Victor, 233
Lesser Antilles, map of Indigenous and creole languages, *9*
LGBTQ+, 146, 149
liberal capitalism, 383–4
liberalism, 54–5, 57, 63
liberals and conservatives, power contest since independence, 54–5
liberation theology, 57, 243, 250
life history interviews, 19, 25
Lima (Peru), queer rights, 153–4
linguistic gatekeeping, 214, 219, 220, 222

linguistic repertoire, 214, 222
Linn da Quebrada mural (São Paulo), *338*
living wage, 358
Locke, John, 52
logging in Mexico, 161, 167
Long, Lucy, 445
"Loxicha Prisoners," 323, 324, 325–6, 327–8
Loxicha region (Oaxaca, Mexico), 321–2, 323–4
Luis, Erika Sebastián, 322, 323, 324, 325–6, 327–8, 329
Lula (Luiz Inácio Lula da Silva), 339
Lunuen, Carolina, 161

machismo, 59, 145–6, 147
macronutrients, 453, 462
Madrasi people, 107
Malintzín (now Malinche), role in history, 59
malnutrition, 457
maps, up and down in, 45, *46*
maps of regions. See specific regions
marasmus, 457
"March for the Family" in Lima, 153–4
marianismo, 145–6, 147
Mariátegui, Aldo, 153
Martí, Jose, 50
Martin, Ricky, 380
Marxist perspectives, 253–4, 261
Masaya (Nicaragua), 470
masculinity, power of, 254
mass graves, 309, 311
material culture, 38
Maya
    anthropometry in, 457
    family size, 459
    pyramid of Cobá, *453*
    as state, 35–6
    traditional subsistence and colonialism, 453–4
    See also "Cobá" entries
Maya (word or language), 192
    See also Yucatec Maya language
men and males. See "gender" entries
Menchú, Rigoberta, 62
Mendez, Jefte, 229–30

Mercator's world map, 45
Mesoamerica
    description, 28
    lifeways, 32
    map, *29*
    pre-European states, 35–6
messaging platforms, for transnational migrants, 474
mestizaje (miscegenation; *mestiçagem* in Portuguese)
    concept, 68, 69, 132
    and Indigenous citizenship, 123
    in La Guajira, 123, 125–6
    meaning in twentieth century, 152
    in Mexico, 162
    as mosaic, 152
    in Peru, 151–2
    and race, 68–9
    as racial concept, 156
mestizo (also *mestiza, mestizx*), 58, 152, 159
mestizofilia, 162
metalwork and metallurgy, in archaeology, 32
Mexican–American War (1846–1848), 49
Mexican Constitution, 55, 190–1, 416
Mexico
    census on language, 191
    changes in family economies, 364–5
    clientelism in elections, 231, 237–8
    COVID-19, 360–1, 366, 460–1
    elections of 2012, 234
    electoral dominance of PRI, 232
    electoral tactics, 232
    environmental activism, 414
    forced displacement, 168
    illicit drugs and trafficking, 161–2
    incarceration of Indigenous leaders, 322
    Indigenous languages, 7, 190–1, 196
    Indigenous movements, 161, 166–7, 321–2, 323–4, 412–15
    land protection, 161

Mexico (*continued*)
  language policy and planning, 190–1
  maps, *2*, *5*, *7*
  political prisoners in, 329, 330
  political repression and prisons, 322–4, 329
  queer history, 61
  remittances from men to women, 483–5
  state in violence on Indigenous women, 165–6, 169
  travel to US for work, 483
  visits to prisoners, 325–6
  war on drugs policy and impact, 162–4, 165–6, 169
Michel, Claudine, 103
microaggression, 91
microcephaly
  in babies in Brazil, 173, 174, *174*, 175
  description, 183
  fieldwork example, 177
  lifetime pension, 180
micronutrients, 454, 462
migration
  actors in, 485–6
  children in, 487–8
  and collective identity, 504–5
  communications in, 471
  emotions in, 486, 492
  gender in, 486
  intergenerational stories, 500–3, 504–5
  as issue, 12
  and kinship, 466
  into Latin America and Caribbean, 30–1, 465
  as necessity and danger in, 503–4
  and patriarchy, 487, 488–9
  patterns and factors, 465–6
  storytelling between past and future, 500–1
military regimes, 225
milpa
  concept, 462
  description for Maya, 453–4, 459, 460
  impact on health and growth, 459, 460

mining
  corporations of Canada in Mexico, 413, 414, 416, 418, 421
  impact, 400, 401, 402–3, 414
  Indigenous resistance in Mexico, *412*, 412–21
Ministerio Publico (Guatemala), 312, 313, 314–15, 316
minoritized language, 191, 198
Mintz, Sidney, 442, 447, 448
"*Mi Pueblo* (My Village) Itzincab Yucatán" (video clip), 196
mixed-race identities (racial mixing), 59
modernity, 104
modernization theory, 333
modernization *vs.* dependency, 56
moral economy, 350, 358
mothers-in-law, and remittances, 484–5, 489–90, 491
Movimiento al Socialismo (Movement for Socialism; MAS), 266, 273
multiculturalism
  concept, 109, 126
  and ethnicity, 108
  in La Guajira/for Wayúu, 126–7, 128–9, 131–2
  programs for Indigenous peoples, 128, 131
multilingualism
  in altiplano of Peru, 113–15
  in Aruba and Curaçao, 213, 215–16
multi-sited ethnography, 18, 25
Murillo, Rosario, 477
musical nationalism
  concept, 376, 381
  in Puerto Rico, 374, 376–7, 378–9, 380
music and musicians in Puerto Rico
  aid and collaboration after Hurricane Maria, 372–3
  collectivist aspects, 376, 379, 380
  importance and impact, 373, 380
  in independence and sovereignty, 375, 376
  live music and dancing, *372*
  and nationalism, 374, 376–7, 378–9, 380

  popularity and examples, 377–8
  and recovery process from Hurricane Maria, 374–5, 379
  songs about Hurricane Maria, 371–2, 378–80
music in Indigenous languages, expansion of, 192
muxe, 107

Nace, Addison, 365
Napoleon, 54
narrative inquiry, 143
nation, definition of, 375
national belonging, in Panama, 138–9, 140, 141–2
National Institute of Indigenous Languages (INALI) (Mexico), 191
National Institute of Statistics and Information Technology (Peru) (*Instituto Nacional de Estadística e Informática* – INEI), survey on LGBTQ+, 149
nationality, and ethnicity, 107
nationalization of resources and industries, 57
nation building, 55
nativo in Brazil
  in ecotourism industry, 431–2, 438
  educational inequities, 435–6
  occupational segregation, 433–5, 437
  technical training, 436–7
  See also Afro-descendants
natural events, and structural violence, 334
"necessary evil," 242, 248–9
neocolonialism, 56, 333–4
neoliberalism
  description and influence, 57, 225, 384
  and pension model of Chile, 255, 261
  policies, 225–6
New City Belén project, 389, 391
New Left ideology, 226
new technologies, as status items, 84–5
New World, as term, 28

NGOs (nongovernmental organizations)
  clientelism in, 242, 245
  as "evil," 244–6
  as "necessary," 246–8
  as "necessary evil," 248–9
  tension raised by projects, 242–3, 249
  See also Vai dar Certo NGO
Nicaragua
  community of care, 475
  migration to Costa Rica, 471–2
  protests and repression of 2018, 469, 470, *470*, 475
  testimonios, 477
Nicaraguan migrants in Costa Rica
  digital solidarities, 475–8
  protests and repression of 2018, 469, 476–8
  research description, 470–1
  telecommunications, 473–4, 476–8
  transnational families dynamics, 472–3
Nina, Olker, 269, 270–1
Ni Una Menos (Not One Less) movement, 305
¡No a la minería, sí a la vida! (No to Mining, Yes to Life!) march, *412*
Noble Savages, 48
Nolasco, Marcelino, 411–12, 419
"*No olvides mi nombre*" (poem), 208
Noriega, Manuel Antonio, 140
nostalgia, 297, 301
"Nostalgia" (poem), 206
Nostalji (Nostalgia), 211
Nostalji san pwen ni vigil / Nostalgia sin puntos ni comas: poesía criolla en Cuba (Unbroken Nostalgia) (collection by Batista), 200, *201*, 201–2, 205, 206–9, 210
numbers (quantitative approach), and expertise, 256–7, 258, 260
Nuñez, Isabel, 420
nutrition transition, 456–7, 462

Oaxaca (Mexico)
  campaign examples, 229–30, 235–7, 238
  campaign of 2012 strategies study, 234
  clientelism in, 232, 233, 234–6, 237–8
  and climate change, 413
  description, 412
  elections of 2012, 234
  failure of PRI in 2012 campaigns, 234–7
  legacy of PRI dominance, 232–3
  support for candidates, 231
  voters' profile, 232
  See also Ixcotel Prison
Oaxaca City, clientelism example, 235–6
occupational segregation, 439
"old age crisis," 255
Olmec, as state, 35
"one drop rule" (hypodescent), 68
open-pit mining, impact of, 413
Operación Orion, 290
opposition parties, 233, 238, 239
Organization of Indigenous Zapotec Communities (OPIZ), 322, 323–4
organized crime in Mexico, 161–2
Oriente region (Cuba), 202, 203
Ortega, Daniel, and regime, 475, 476–8
Ortiz, Beto, 153
Ostuta River (Mexico), 416–17
Other, 445, 450
outside meaning (or structural power)
  and *chicha*, 446–8
  concept, 448, 449–50
  in food, 442, 449

Pachamama Radio, Quechua and Aymara languages and identity, 114–15, 117–20, 121
Panama (Republic of Panama)
  changes under Noriega, 140–1
  citizenship, 137–8
  Día de los Mártires (Martyrs' Day), 139
  discrimination and belonging, 139, 140
  Hay-Bunau-Varilla Treaty, 136
  independence, 136, 139
  national belonging, 138–9, 140, 141–2
  racism, 142
  Torrijos-Carter Treaty, 136, 140
  US imperialism in, 139, 140
  See also West Indian descent in Panama
Panama Canal, 135, 136–8
Panama Canal Zone
  and citizenship, 136–7, 138
  description and rules, 134, 136
  discrimination and exclusion in, 136–8
  ID checks, 134–5
  protest and riots of 1964, 139
  segregation system of US, 137
  use and occupation by US, 136
Papiamentu language
  on Aruba, 215
  on Curaçao, 213, 214, 215
  description, 213
  use in education, 214, 216, 218
paramilitarismo in Colombia, 125–6, 128
participant observation, 19, 26, 390
past
  understanding of, 44–5
  views of, 36–7
Pat Boy (rapper), 189, 190, *190*, 193–5, 196
patriarchal violence
  concept, 162, 170
  on Indigenous women's bodies in Mexico, 162, 163, 164–5, 169
patriarchy
  concept, 493
  and migration, 487, 488–9
patrilocal residence
  in Calakmul, 488, 492
  children in, 488–9
  concept, 487, 493
  and finances, 489–90
Pauli, Julia, 488
Paz, Octavio, 47
peasant union in Bolívar province
  in the case of Piruani, 267, 269–71, 272–3
  responsibilities, 267–8

peasant union in Bolívar province (*continued*)
  in systems of authority, 267–8, 272–3, 275–6
pension experts in Chile. *See* Chile's pension experts
periods and periodization, in history, 44
periphery
  center/periphery dyad in São Paulo, 340–1
  concept, 338, 347
  as spaces of possibility, 339, 343, 344, 346
Perón, Eva, 60
personal identity, and ethnicity, 107–8
Peru
  Civil Union Bill, 153
  gender presentation example, 157
  governmental rationality, 391, 395
  language and identity for Indigenous peoples, 111–21
  law about Belén being "at risk," 390–1
  mestizaje in, 151–2
  migration by Spanish in twenty-first century, 150
  national census demographics, 116–17
  national census with question on race, 149, 150, 154–5
  queer Indigenous peoples, 149–50, 153–8
  racialization ideologies, 150–1
  racial mobility, 151–2
  upward mobility, 156
  whiteness in job market, 150
peso, 52–3
phones, 84, 89
photovoice, 20, 26
physiogeographic regions – maps
  Central America, 5
  Mexico, 5
  South America, 6
Piarroux, Renaud, 98
"Pichón" (poem), 207
Pierre, Jemima, 98
Pink Legend, 48

Pink Tide, 226, 244, 248–9, 250
Piraquê social club (Brazil), 85–6, *86*
Piruani, as case. *See* case of Piruani
Piruani village (Bolivia)
  description, 265
  land ownership dispute adjudication, 265–6, 267
plantations, and creole languages, 186
plant use by First peoples, 31–2
plays. *See* theatrical performances
Plaza de Mayo protests, 60
Pleistocene (aka the Ice Age), 30, 31, 38
Plena Combativa (Combative Plena) group, 374–5
Plena music, 375
plurinational, as concept, 276
plurinational state, Bolivia as, 266, 274
Poiré, Alejandro, 165
political boundaries – maps
  Caribbean, *3*
  Central America, *2*
  Mexico, *2*
  South America, *4*
political economy, 12
political machines, 233–4, 239
political mobilization, and rap, 196–7
political prisoners, 329, 330
political repression/prisons in Mexico, 322–4, 329
political violence, 279–80, 281
politics in Latin America and Caribbean, 225–6
politics of aesthetic representation, 284, 295
polyvocality, 22–3, 26
populism, 55, 226
"*Por Culpa 'e Maria*" ("Because of Maria") (song), 371–2
Portuguese and Portugal, Conquest and empire, 50, 52, 54
post-colonial history, 53–7
pottery, in archaeology, 32
poverty, theories on, 333
power
  and gendering, 254, 256–7

  jurisdictional battles for, 256
  and politics in Latin America and Caribbean, 225–6
  and race, 67
  and risk, 396
  as social construct, 108
  and studying up, 256
PRD (*Partido Revolucionario Democrático,* Revolutionary Democratic Party), 233, 236–7
prehistoric lifeways, 31–2
prehistory and prehistoric, as terms, 27–8
presentist view of the past, 37
PRI (*Partido Revolucionario Institucional,* Institutional Revolutionary Party)
  candidate's campaign, 235–6, 237
  clientelism, 232, 233, 234–5
  failure in campaigns of 2012, 234–7
  legacy of dominance in Mexico, 232–3
Price-Mars, Jean, 103
Pristine Myth, 52
protests of 1960s, 56
pseudonyms, use in research, 21
Puente Nayero neighborhood (Buenaventura, Colombia)
  description, 299–300
  film reception study, 297, 300–2
Puerto Berrío (Colombia), 283
Puerto Rico
  African diasporic artforms, 371–2
  collectivism in, 373
  cultural sovereignty as nation, 375–6
  fieldwork description, 373
  Hurricane Maria (*see* Hurricane Maria)
  independence and statehood, 373–4, 375, 376, 379
  as US colony/commonwealth, 49, 372, 373–6
  See also music and musicians in Puerto Rico
pull factors, 465–6, 467
Puno region (Peru)
  festivities, *112*

Indigenous multilingualism, 113–14
linguistic knowledge and ethnic identity, 111–13, 117
linguistic knowledge and ethnic identity – devaluing of, 111, 115, 116, 120
multilingualism and Indigenous identity, 113–16, 120–1
radio advertisements, 117–20
Purépecha community/people, 161, 167
purist language ideology, 112–13, 115, 121
Pushaina, Sara, 404, 406–7
push factors, 465, 467

qualitative/quantitative divide, and gender, 256–7, 258
Quechua Indigenous nation
in census, 117, 155
gender roles, 157
as identity, 116, 155–6
linguistic knowledge and ethnic identity, 112, 117–18, 119–21
visits by Lima queer woman, 155–6, 157
yunza festivals, 156, 157
Quechua language
authenticity, 115–16
notions of justice in, 271–2
in Puno region, 113–15
in radio advertisements, 117–18
view in Lima, 155
Quechua-speaking highland Indigenous community, and legal authorities, 266–7
"queer" history, 61
queer Indigenous peoples
identity formation, 150
race and ethnicity in, 149–50, 153–8
queerness
concept, 153, 159
and gender roles, 157–8
queer rights, in Lima, 153–4
¿Quién soy yo? (documentary)
description, 300

screening and reactions, 297, 300–2, 307
quipu (knotted cords), 35, 44

race
biological "race," 73
as category, 52, 67, 68, 158
and class, 146, 155
concept, 69
creation (as social construct), 67, 68
and genetics, 67–8
and habitus, 437–8
historical overview, 58–9
intersectionality with gender, 146
and power, 67
questions in national census, 149, 150, 154–5
terminology in Cuba, 72
racial, as concept, 73, 82
racial democracy, 69, 432–3
racial hierarchies (*castas*), 58, 163
racial identities, differences in, 68
racial inequality
in Brazil, 89, 91–2
concept, 93
example and study of, 85, 91
quantification, 91
raciality
concept, 82
in Cuba, 72–3, 74–5, 80–1
racialization
concept, 69, 152, 159
for Cubans, 81
description and use, 68, 81
ideologies in Peru, 150–1
as issue, 11
in Panama Canal Zone, 137
as process, 158
and tourism in Cuba, 75–80
and violence, 162
racialized belonging
in Cuba, 73, 77, 78, 79, 81
as issue, 11, 71
racialized geographies
concept, 163, 170
and "War on Drugs" in Mexico, 162–4
racial logics

concept, 85, 93
example in Brazil, 84–5, 91–2
racial mixing (mixed-race identities), 59
racial mobility, in Peru, 151–2
racism
absence claims, 68–9
in Brazil, 68–9, 90, 91
in coloniality, 162–3
concept, 69, 91
in Cuba, 203, 204
in nineteenth century, 59
in Panama, 142
and sexual violence in Mexico, 166
structural racism, 430, 431–3, 437, 438
Rafael, Mario, as PRD candidate, 236–7
Ramírez, Álvaro Sebastián
call-in to forum, 323
death, 329
incarceration, 320–1, 324
as "Loxicha Prisoner," 323, 324
in oral history project, 329
visits to in Ixcotel Prison, 320–1, 322, 324–6, 325n4, 327–9
as Zapatista, 328
ramon trees and nuts, 454
ranchería, 123, 127, 129–30, 132
Rap Ich Máaya (Rap in Maya) workshop, 196
rap in Indigenous languages
expansion in Mexico, 192–3
grassroot efforts, 190, 191
and language revitalization, 193–5, 197
for political mobilization, 196–7
themes in, 194
Reconquista, 50
reflexivity (in writing), 23, 26
regime of (im)mobility, 486, 492, 493
Regional Coordination of Communal Authorities (CRAC) in Guerrero, 166–7
remittances
concept, 467, 472
to daughters-in-law, 483, 484–5, 490–1

remittances (*continued*)
 description, 466
 in La Gloria, 499, 503
 from Mexican men abroad to women, 483–5
 to mothers and mothers-in-law, 484–5, 489–90, 491
reparation for victims, 284, 285–6
Réquiem NN (artwork), 283, *284*
research objectives
 collaborative approach, 19
 on culture, 18
 description and example, 17, 18, 20
research participants, anonymity and identity, 21, 24
reserva, 127, 133
resettlement
 concept, 389, 397, 400
 indigenization of, 400–1, 405
 and risk, 391–2, 393, 395–6
 See also Belén (Peru) – resettlement plan; Tamaquito II rural settlement – resettlement
resguardo, 126–8, 133
Residente (rapper), 378–9, 380
resilience, 334
resistance
 and Indigenous languages, 204
 movements in Mexico, 161, 166–7, 321–2, 323–4, 412–15
 to resettlement in Belén, 393–5
revolutions and revolutionary events, 53–4, 56–7
Rio de Janeiro (Brazil)
 "compulsory closeness," 87–8
 everyday life for white middle-class families, 86–9, 91–2
 Piraquê social club, 85–6, *86*
 research on white middle-class families, 86–7
 safety on the streets, 84, 88–9, 90
 white comfort in, 90–2
risk
 conceptions of, 389, 391, 395–6, 397
 manifestations, 389
 and power, 396
 in resettlement, 391–2, 393, 395–6

"Rivers and Silences, retrospective of the work of Echavarría" (art exposition), 287
Rosendo Cantú, Valentina, 165
Rossello, Ricardo, 380
Ruiz, Manuel Antonio, 411
Ruiz, Ulises, 233
Ruíz-Lagier, Verónica, 498–9

sacrifice zones, 401, 409
Sahcab Mucuy village (Mexico)
 description, 455–6
 impact of tourism on health and growth, 458–9, 460
Saint-Marc city (Haiti), 95, 98–100
Salapo (Chiapas, Mexico)
 description and family life in, 360, 362–3
 tourism as business, 362–3, 364, 366, 368
Salcedo, Doris, 290–2, *292*, 293, 294
Salgado García, Nestora, 166–7, *168*
Salvador *periferia* (Brazil)
 CZS fieldwork, 177–81
 as marginalized community, 176
same-sex civil unions, in Peru, 153
San Agustín Loxicha (Mexico), 323
San Francisco del Mar community (Mexico), 411
Sangre Maya (Mayan blood) (rap song), 189
San Martín, José, 54
San Miguel Chimalapa (Mexico), 421
San Nicolas English, 215
Santiago de Cuba (city), Haitians in, 202
Santo Domingo de Narro village (Mexico), 229–30
São Paulo (Brazil)
 center/periphery dyad, 340–1
 cosmopolitan periphery subjectivities, 339, 343–7
 description and expansion, 339–40
 development and Strategic Master Plan, 337–9, 346
 economic development, 338, 346

Linn da Quebrada mural, *338*
 peripheries as spaces of possibility, 339, 343, 344, 346
 peripheries of, 340–2
 protests, 338–9
 socioeconomic inequalities, 337, 338–9, 340–1, 346
Scol Di Specialista school (Aruba), 218–21
Segato, Rita Laura, 162, 164
Sepúlveda, Juan Ginés de, 52
Service, Elman, 33
Serviço Nacional de Aprendizagem Comercial (National Commercial Apprenticeship Service, SENAC), 436–7
sex, and binary distinctions, 145
sex tourism, 425–6
sexual diversity in Latin America, 146
sexual economy, 490, 493
sexuality, as issue, 12
sexual violence/violation
 legal tools for, 169
 in militarized Indigenous territories, 165–6, 168–9
 as tool or language in Mexico, 161, 162, 164
"shapeshifters," 101
sign languages, 185n1
sikuri troops, 158
Silencios (Silences) (photographic series), 287, *288*, 293
silver, as currency, 52–3
"Sixth, The," of the Zapatistas, 323, 328
skin color
 in Brazil, 86, 88
 in Cuba, 71–3, 74, 77, 80–1
 See also race
slavery
 abolition, 52, 58–9
 and Blackness in Haiti, 99, 103
 in Brazil, 176
 enslaved Africans, 52, 99
 and Haitian Revolution, 43, 99
 and race, 52
social imaginary, 298–9, 308
social inclusion

concept, 133
Indigenous peoples in Colombia, 123–4, 126, 127, 131–2
socialism, 56–7, 74
social media, in language revitalization, 189, 195
social movements, 226, 227
social networks *vs.* clientelism, 235–7
social stratification, 30, 32, 38
social structure, 365, 367–9
socio-environmental conflicts, 414, 421
sociopolitical organization, 33–5
soft power of Latin America, 62
solidarity, in digital form, 475–8
Sor Juana Inés de la Cruz, 59–60
South America
  climate in, 28
  map and boundaries, *4*
  map of Indigenous and creole languages, *10*
  map of physiographic regions, *6*
South–South migration, 471, 479
Spanish–American War (1898), 49, 373
Spanish and Spain
  challenge in Latin America, 54
  Conquest and empire, 50–2, 54
  and global economy, 52–3
  in legends of history, 48–9
  and Maya, 36
  modern migration to Latin America, 150
  in Puerto Rico, 373
  and slavery, 52
Spanish language (*castellano*)
  on Aruba and Curaçao, 215
  in Puno region, 113, 114, 115
state or state-level societies, 33, 35–6
state violence, 55, 89, 93
Stoll, David, 62
storytelling
  and collective identity, 503–5
  description and use, 500–1
  between past and future, 500–3
strategic essentialism, 195, 198
structural power. *See* outside meaning

structural racism, 430, 431–3, 437, 438
structural violence, 308, 333, 334
structural vulnerability, 176, 179–80, 182, 183
studying up, 256, 262
subjectivity, as concept, 343, 347
suffrage for women, 60
Sumando Ausencias (artwork), 291, 292, *292*
sustainability, 384, 418, 420
sustainable development, and resettlement of Indigenous peoples, 408
symbolically coded edibles
  concept, 450
  decoding, 441–2
  in Kichwa Añangu Community, 442, 444–9
symbolic reparations, 295

Tabaco community, displacement of, 403
Tamaquito II rural settlement (Colombia)
  autonomous consultation, 403, 404–5, 408
  coal mining on territory, 400, 401, 402–3
  description and travel to, 399, 400, 401, 402
  rebuilding of territory, 406–7, 408
  reburial ceremony, 406–7
  study description, 401
  traditional culture education, 406–7
Tamaquito II rural settlement – resettlement
  compensation for, 405–6
  decision and agreement, 403, 404, 407–8
  indigenization of, 400–1, 405
  as/and loss, 402–3, 405, 406
  plan, 399, 400, 403
"*Te Bote*" ("I Kick You Out") (song), 377–8
technocrats, 225, 227
techno-optimism, 244, 245

Tehuantepec Isthmus (Oaxaca, Mexico)
  anti-mine activism, 413, 415–21
  fieldwork data and methods, 415
  megaprojects and mining projects, 411–13
Tello Weiss, Mariana, 306
territory, 399, 409
testimonio
  concept, 323, 330, 479
  description and use, 62, 323, 477
Tetreault, Darcy, 414
textiles, in archaeology, 32
theatrical performances (plays)
  origin story of La Gloria town, 496, *497*, 498, 500, 501–3, 504
  as storytelling, 501–3
thick description, 22, 26
third gender category, 146, 154
Tlaxcala city-state, 51
Tola, Enrique, 274
Toledo, Víctor, 414
Toral, Vásquez, 157–8
Torres García, Joaquín, 45, *46*
Torrijos, Omar (General), 136, 138, 140
Torrijos-Carter Treaty, 136, 140
tourism
  access to sites in Cuba, 71, 73
  bracelets for tourists, 78–9
  and cultural change, 454–6
  cultural tourism, 441, 442, 443–4
  and economy, 74–5, 351, 358, 461
  forms of, 425–6
  impact on health and growth of Cobá children, 453, 457–60
  industry in Cuba, 74–5, 76–7
  overview and impact, 425–6, 461
  racialized tourism in Cuba, 75–80
  styles in Brazil, 429–30
  See also ecotourism
touristscape
  in Brogodó, 430–2
  concept, 431, 439
  occupational segregation in, 433–5, 437, 438
Townsend, Camilla, 44
Traditional Authorities in Colombia, 128–9

transculturation, 61–2, 64
transformative justice, 312, 318
transitional justice
  and art, 285–6, 286n2, 293
  concept, 280, 281, 284
  in Guatemala, 311, 312
translanguaging
  concept, 222
  use in schools of Aruba and Curaçao, 214, 217, 220, 221
transnational families
  concept, 472, 479
  forms and dynamics, 472–3
  telecommunications, 469, 471, 473, 474
  See also Nicaraguan migrants in Costa Rica
transnational migrants, 466, 467
transnational migration, tracing of, 470–1
trauma, as characteristic, 62
Tres Equis cemetery ("Cemetery XXX") (Guatemala), *310*
  description and name, 309, 315
  and Ministerio Publico, 314–15, 316
tribes, definition and description, 33
Túpac Amaru II's rebellion (1780–1782), 53
turnout buying, 231

#UnionCivilYa demonstration (Peru), 153
United States
  "civilizing" interventions, 49–50
  coup in Guatemala, 310
  extractive capitalism in Latin America and Caribbean, 225
  imperialism and rule in Panama, 139, 140
  jurisdictional battles example, 256
  migration to from La Gloria, 499, 500, 501–2
  pension system, 255
  Puerto Rico as colony/commonwealth, 49, 372, 373–6
  racialization in, 68
  reasons to migrate to, 485

role in Latin America since indepedence, 55
  treaties with Panama, 136, 140
  See also Panama Canal Zone
Untitled (1989–1990) or *Las Camisas* (artwork), 291, 294
UN troops, and Haiti cholera epidemic, 98
urbanization, as issue, 12

Vai dar Certo ("It's Going to Be Ok") NGO
  contradiction in local *vs.* international work, 241, 242, 249
  as "evil," as "necessary," and as "necessary evil," 244–9
  foreigners and middle-class Brazilians at, 245–7, 248–9
  funding and funds transparency, 244, 245, 249
  history, 243–4, 249
Valencia, Ruben, 417–18
Valladolid Debate (1550–1551), 52
Varillalito (Peru), in resettlement plan of Belén, 391, 392–3
Vasconcelos, José, 152
Veizaga, Sabino, 274
Venezuela, and international migration, 466
"*Viejo*" (song), 200
views of the past, 36–7
violence
  and art, 293–4
  colonial view, 36–7
  in films (*see* films reception)
  "racializing effects," 162
  representation in film, 297, 299
  See also specific types of violence
Violencia, La (1946–1953), 285
virtual co-presence, 479
virtual worlds, as field sites, 18
Vista Hermosa barrio (Mexico), as clientelism example, 235–6
Vodou. *See* Haitian Vodou
Voluntary Testimony (video installation), *289*, 289–90
"Voodoo," demonization, 101–2
vote buying, 231
voting rights for women, 60

Wade, Peter, 152
"War on Drugs" in Mexico
  Indigenous deaths in, 164
  racialized geographies, 162–4
  and violence on Indigenous women, 165–6, 169
Washington Consensus, 225, 227
Wayúu ethnic identity, return to, 123, 126
Wayúu home, *124*
Wayúu people, *400*
  census of communities, 129–30
  connection to territory, 406
  description, 401–2
  identification as Indigenous, 128–9, 131–2
  Indigenous Families in Action program, 129
  and multiculturalism, 126–7, 128–9, 131–2
  power and wealth in, 124–5
  resguardo/reserva and citizenship, 126–8
  role in La Guajira peninsula, 125–6
  traditional culture education, 406–7
Weismantel, Mary, 154
West Indian descent in Panama
  changes under Noriega and move to US, 140–1
  citizenship, 136–8
  ID checks and rules in Canal Zone, 134–5
  integration into society, 141–2
  racism towards, 142
  sense of belonging, 138–40, 142–3
  treatment and exclusion, 139, 140
  work in Panama and on Canal, 136–8
West Indians, 135–6, 143
white comfort, 90–2, 93
white middle-class families, research on, 86–7
whiteness, 69, 150
whitening, 68, 72–3, 82, 151–2
White or Pink Legend, 48
white privilege, 69

white supremacy, 93
WHO (World Health Organization), and Zika, 175–6
witnessing, and digital solidarities, 477–8
Wolf, Eric, 448
women
    as agents and symbols, 59–60
    and feminism, 60
    independence of, 60
    Indigenous land protection, 161, 164–5
    murders of activists, 161
    in racialized geographies in Mexico, 163–4
    remittances to in Mexico, 483–5
    See also "gender" entries; Indigenous women
World Bank, on Chilean model of pension provision, 255

Yanama (organization), 404
youth, as political force, 55–6
yuca, for *chicha*, 446
Yucatán
    coastal development, 455
    nutrition transition, 456–7
Yucatán Peninsula
    hip-hop scene, 192–3
    political mobilization, 196–7
    sociolinguistic context, 191–2
Yucatec Maya language
    educational initiatives, 195–6
    grassroot strategies, 192
    in rap songs, 193–5, 197
    revitalization efforts, 189–90, 192, 193–5, 197
    use and loss, 191–2
yuma "race" in Cuba, 77–8, 80

Zapatista Army of National Liberation (*Ejército Zapatista de Liberación Nacional,* EZLN), 232, 322–3, 328
Zapotec peoples
    description and challenges, 321–2
    Indigenous cosmovisions, 413
    as "Loxicha Prisoners," 323
    mural with women, *16*
    perseverance, 320
    resistance, 322, 323–4, 415
Zika
    description and outbreaks timeline, 175–6
    emergence and impact on women and mothers, 173–4, 182
    and structural issue in Brazil, 176, 182
    virus, 173–4, 175–6, 183
    See also congenital Zika syndrome (CZS)
Zona Archaeologica (Cobá, Mexico), 454–5, 460–1